Computing Concepts

with

C++ Essentials

Computing Concepts

with

C++ Essentials

Third Edition

Cay Horstmann
San Jose State University

John Wiley & Sons, Inc.

ACQUISITIONS EDITOR	Paul Crockett
MARKETING MANAGER	Katherine Hepburn
PROJECT MANAGER	Cindy Johnson, Publishing Services
EDITORIAL ASSISTANT	Jovan Yglecias
PRODUCTION EDITOR	Ken Santor
SENIOR DESIGNER	Harry Nolan
COVER DESIGNER	Howard Grossman
COVER PHOTO	Roger Goldingay/RGIMAGES.COM
PHOTO EDITOR	Lisa Gee

This book was set in Adobe Caslon by Publishing Services and printed and bound by R. R. Donnelley/Crawfordsville. The cover was printed by Phoenix Color Corporation.

This book is printed on acid-free paper.

ISBN 0-471-16437-2

Printed in the United States of America

10 9 8 7 6 5 4 3 2 1

Preface

This book gives a traditional introduction to computer science using modern tools. As computer scientists, we have the good fortune of being able to introduce students to an activity that is accessible, satisfying, and deep rather than broad: namely, the activity of programming. Like the majority of computer scientists, I believe that programming is a central theme of computer science. Thus, this course teaches students how to program.

While this book remains traditional in outlook, it uses modern techniques in three ways.

- *The programming language is a subset of C++.* Although C++ is far from a perfect educational language, it makes pragmatic sense to use it. C++ is used extensively in the software industry. Convenient and inexpensive programming environments are available on all major platforms. C++ is sufficiently expressive to teach programming concepts. This book minimizes the use of error-prone constructs through the use of modern features of the C++ standard—such as reference parameters, the stream library, the `string` class, and the `vector<T>` template. Pointers are used primarily for polymorphism and the implementation of linked lists.

- *Early use of objects.* Objects are introduced in two stages. From Chapter 2 on, students learn to *use* objects—in particular, strings, streams, instances of the simple `Time` and `Employee` classes, and graphical shapes. Students become comfortable with the concepts of creating objects and calling member functions as the book continues along a traditional path, discussing branching and loops, functions, and procedures. Then in Chapter 6, students learn how to implement classes and member functions.

- *Optional use of graphics.* Students enjoy programming graphics. This book includes many exercises in which numbers and visual information reinforce each other. To do this, the book uses a very simple graphics library that is available on a number of popular platforms. Unlike traditional graphics libraries, this library uses objects in a very straightforward and effective way. The use of the library is also optional. In addition, Chapter 18 contains an introduction to graphical user interface programming, using an open-source toolkit that is similar to the Microsoft Foundation Class library.

The choice of programming language has a very visible impact on any book on programming. However, the purpose of this book is to teach computing concepts, not all details of the C++ language. C++ is used throughout as a tool for mastering the fundamentals of computer science.

Pedagogical Structure

The beginning of each chapter has the customary overview of chapter objectives and motivational introduction. Throughout the chapters, there are five sets of notes to help your students, namely those entitled "Common Error", "Productivity Hint", "Quality Tip", "Advanced Topic", and "Random Fact". These notes are specially marked so that they don't interrupt the flow of the main material. (See the listing of topics covered on pages xvi-xix.) I expect that most instructors cover only a few of these notes in class and assign others for home reading. Some notes are quite short; others extend over a page. I decided to give each note the space that is needed for a full and convincing explanation, rather than attempting to fit them into one-paragraph "tips".

 Common Errors describe the kinds of errors that students often make, with an explanation of why the errors occur, and what to do about them. Most students quickly discover the Common Error sections and read them on their own.

 Quality Tips explain good programming practices. Since most of them require an initial investment of effort, these notes carefully motivate the reason behind the advice and explain why the effort will be repaid later.

 Productivity Hints teach students how to use their tools more effectively. Many beginning students put little thought into their use of computers and software. They are often unfamiliar with tricks of the trade such as keyboard shortcuts, global search and replace, or automation of common tasks with scripts.

 Advanced Topics cover nonessential or more difficult material. Some of these topics introduce alternative syntactical constructions that are not necessarily technically advanced. In many cases, the book uses one particular language construct but explains alternatives as Advanced Topics. Instructors and students should feel free to use those constructs in their own programs if they prefer them. It has, however, been my experience that many students are grateful for the "keep it simple" approach, because it greatly reduces the number of gratuitous decisions they have to make.

 Random Facts provide historical and social information on computing, as required to fulfill the "historical and social context" requirements of the ACM curriculum guidelines, as well as capsule reviews of advanced computer science topics. Many students will read the Random Facts on their own while pretending to follow the lecture.

Most examples are in the form of complete, ready-to-run programs. The programs are available electronically, and you can give them to your students.

Appendix A contains a style guide for use with this book. I have found it highly beneficial to require a consistent style for all assignments. I realize that my style may be different from yours. If you have strong feelings about a particular issue, or if this style guide conflicts with local customs, feel free to modify it. The style guide is available in electronic form for this purpose.

Appendix B contains a syntax summary and documentation of all library functions and classes used in this book.

New in this Edition

In order to enable an early coverage of the implementation of classes, the chapters on control flow have been reorganized. Chapter 4 now covers the basics of both branches and loops. Chapters 5 and 6 make use of that material, which permits the construction of interesting functions and classes. Finally, Chapter 7 covers advanced control flow issues such as nested branches and alternate loop constructs.

The chapter on object-oriented design now contains an introduction to the Unified Modeling Language (UML) notation, and a new design case study.

The chapter on data structures has been enhanced to cover the containers and algorithms of the Standard Template Library (STL).

A new chapter on advanced C++ topics introduces operator overloading, templates, the "Big Three" (destructor, copy constructor, and assignment operator), nested classes, name spaces, and exception handling.

A new chapter on recursion pulls together examples that were previously located in separate chapters and gives a unified treatment of recursion.

The discussion of pointers has been consolidated into a separate chapter. The emphasis is on the use of pointers for modeling object relationships, but there is also a section on array/pointer duality for those who need to delve more deeply into implementation details.

In the second edition, several important sections in the chapters on control flow, arrays, and inheritance depended on the graphics library. That dependency has been removed. The graphics library is now entirely optional.

Finally, there is a new chapter that introduces graphical user interface programming. This chapter can be used as a capstone for the course, showing how classes and inheritance are put to work in a real-world class library.

Pathways through the Book

This book contains more material than could be covered in one semester, so you will need to make a choice of chapters to cover. The core material of the book is:

Chapter 1. Introduction
Chapter 2. Fundamental Data Types
Chapter 3. Objects
Chapter 4. Basic Control Flow
Chapter 5. Functions
Chapter 6. Classes
Chapter 7. Advanced Control Flow
Chapter 9. Vectors and Arrays

Note that the graphics library covered in Chapter 3 is optional.

For a course that covers inheritance and object-oriented design, you would include

Chapter 10. Pointers

Chapter 11. Inheritance

Chapter 12. Streams

Chapter 13. Object-Oriented Design

The following chapters are an introduction to algorithms and data structures.

Chapter 14. Recursion

Chapter 15. Sorting and Searching

Chapter 16. An Introduction to Data Structures

You may want to use either of the final chapters as a capstone for your course.

Chapter 17. Advanced C++ Topics

Chapter 18. Graphical User Interfaces

Figure 1 shows the dependencies between the chapters.

ACM Curriculum

The book covers the following knowledge units from the CC2001 curriculum guidelines.

PF1: Fundamental Programming Constructs (9 of 9 hours)

PF2: Algorithms and Problem Solving (6 of 6 hours)

PF3: Fundamental Data Structures (6 of 14 hours)

PF4: Recursion (3 of 5 hours)

PF5: Event-Driven Programming (2 of 4 hours)

AL1: Basic Algorithmic Analysis (2 of 4 hours)

AL3: Fundamental Computing Algorithms (2 of 12 hours)

PL1: Overview of Programming Languages (1 of 2 hours)

PL3: Introduction to Language Translation (1 of 2 hours)

PL5: Abstraction Mechanisms (2 of 3 hours)

PL6: Object-Oriented Programming (8 of 10 hours)

SP2: Social Context of Computing (1 of 3 hours)

SP5: Risks and Liabilities of Computer Systems (1 of 3 hours)

SE3: Software Environments and Tools (1 of 3 hours)

SE6: Software Validation (2 of 3 hours)

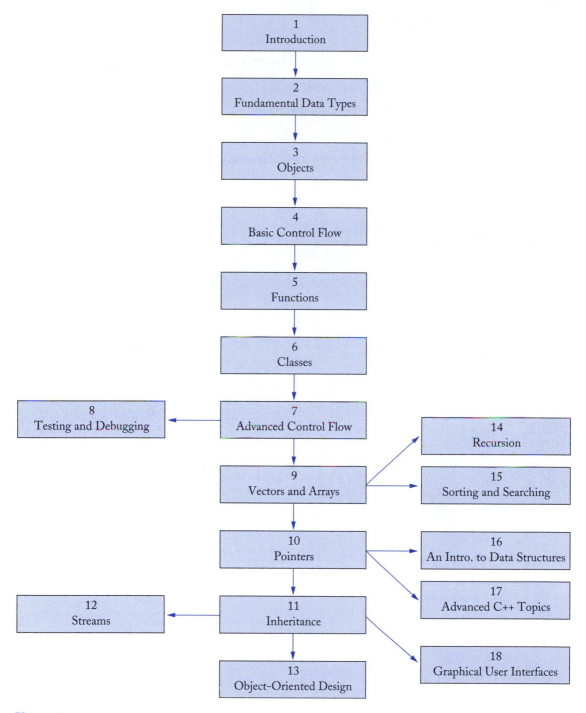

Figure 1

Chapter Dependencies

Web Resources

Additional resources for students and instructors can be found on the book's companion Web site at http://www.wiley.com/college/horstmann. These resources include:

- Source code for the Employee and Time classes and the optional graphics library
- Source code for all examples in the book
- Solutions to selected exercises (accessible to students)
- Solutions to all exercises (for instructors only)
- A laboratory manual
- A list of frequently asked questions
- Help with common compilers
- Presentation slides for lectures
- The programming style guide (Appendix A) in electronic form (for modification to suit instructor preferences)

Acknowledgments

Many thanks to Paul Crockett, Bill Zobrist, Katherine Hepburn, and Lisa Gee at John Wiley & Sons, and the team at Publishing Services for their hard work and support for this book project. This revision would not have been possible without the special efforts of Cindy Johnson of Publishing Services. She did a great job with the scheduling and production and went well beyond the call of duty to improve the consistency and quality of the manuscript.

I am very grateful to the many individuals who reviewed the manuscript, made valuable suggestions, and brought an embarrassingly large number of errors and omissions to my attention. They include:

Vladimir Akis, *CSU Los Angeles*

Ramzi Bualuan, *Notre Dame University*

Joseph DeLibero, *Arizona State University*

Jeremy Frens, *Calvin College*

Timothy Henry, *University of Rhode Island*

Robert Jarman, *Augusta State University*

Jerzy Jaromczyk, *University of Kentucky*

Vitit Kantabutra, *Idaho State University*

Brian Malloy, *Clemson University*

Jeffery Popyack, *Drexel University*

John Russo, *Wentworth Institute of Technology*

Deborah Silver, *Rutgers University*

Joel Weinstein, *New England University*

Lillian Witzke, *Milwaukee School of Engineering*

Finally, thank you to the many students and instructors who have sent me "bug reports" and suggestions for improvements.

Contents

► Syntax Boxes

▶Common Errors   ▶Quality Tips

Contents

Introduction

▶ To understand the activity of programming

▶ To learn about the architecture of computers

▶ To learn about machine languages and higher-level programming languages

▶ To become familiar with your compiler

▶ To compile and run your first C++ program

▶ To recognize syntax and logic errors

This chapter contains a brief introduction to the architecture of computers and an overview of programming languages. You will learn about the activity of programming:
how to write and run your first C++ program, how to diagnose and fix programming errors, and how to plan your programming activities.

CHAPTER CONTENTS

1.1 What Is a Computer?

You have probably used a computer for work or fun. Many people use computers for everyday tasks such as balancing a checkbook or writing a term paper. Computers are good for such tasks. They can handle repetitive chores, such as totaling up numbers or placing words on a page, without getting bored or exhausted. More importantly, the computer presents the checkbook or the term paper on the screen and lets you fix mistakes easily. Computers make good game machines because they can play sequences of sounds and pictures, involving the human user in the process.

What makes all this possible is not only the computer. The computer must be programmed to perform these tasks. One program balances checkbooks; a different program, probably designed and constructed by a different company, processes words; and a third program plays a game. The computer itself is a machine that stores data (numbers, words, pictures), interacts with devices (the monitor, the sound system, the printer), and executes programs. Programs are sequences of instructions and decisions that the computer carries out to achieve a task.

Today's computer programs are so sophisticated that it is hard to believe that they are composed of extremely primitive operations. A typical operation may be one of the following.

- Put a red dot at this screen position.

- Send the letter A to the printer.

- Get a number from this location in memory.

- Add up these two numbers.

- If this value is negative, continue the program at that instruction.

The computer user has the illusion of smooth interaction because a program contains a huge number of such operations, and because the computer can execute them at great speed.

The flexibility of a computer is quite an amazing phenomenon. The same machine can balance your checkbook, print your term paper, and play a game. In contrast, other machines carry out a much narrower range of tasks; a car drives and a toaster toasts.

Computers can carry out a wide range of tasks because they execute different programs, each of which directs the computer to work on a specific task.

1.2   What Is Programming?

A computer program tells a computer, in minute detail, the sequence of steps that are needed to fulfill a task. The act of designing and implementing these programs is called computer programming. In this book, you will learn how to program a computer—that is, how to direct the computer to execute tasks.

To use a computer you do not need to do any programming. When you write a term paper with a word processor, that program has been programmed by the manufacturer and is ready for you to use. That is only to be expected—you can drive a car without being a mechanic and toast bread without being an electrician. Most people who use computers every day never need to do any programming.

Since you are reading this introductory computer science book, it may well be your career goal to become a professional computer scientist or software engineer. Programming is not the only skill required of a computer scientist or software engineer; indeed, programming is not the only skill required to create successful computer programs. Nevertheless, the activity of programming is central to computer science. It is also a fascinating and pleasurable activity that continues to attract and motivate bright students. The discipline of computer science is particularly fortunate that it can make such an interesting activity the foundation of the learning path.

To write a computer game with motion and sound effects or a word processor that supports fancy fonts and pictures is a complex task that requires a team of many highly skilled programmers. Your first programming efforts will be more mundane. The concepts and skills you learn in this book form an important foundation, and you should not be disappointed if your first programs do not rival the sophisticated software that is familiar to you. Actually, you will find that there is an immense thrill even in simple programming tasks. It is an amazing experience to see the computer carry out a task precisely and quickly that would take you hours of drudgery, to make small changes in a program that lead to immediate improvements, and to see the computer become an extension of your mental powers.

1.3   The Anatomy of a Computer

To understand the programming process, you need to have a rudimentary understanding of the building blocks that make up a computer. We will look at a personal computer. Larger computers have faster, larger, or more powerful components, but they have fundamentally the same design.

At the heart of the computer lies the *central processing unit (CPU)* (see Figure 1). It consists of a single *chip*, or a small number of chips. A computer chip (integrated circuit) is a component with a plastic or metal housing, metal connectors, and inside wiring made principally from silicon. For a CPU chip, the inside wiring is enormously compli-

Figure 1

Central Processing Unit

cated. For example, the Pentium chip (a popular CPU for personal computers at the time of this writing) is composed of several million structural elements, called *transistors*. Figure 2 shows a magnified detail view of a CPU chip. The CPU performs program control, arithmetic, and data movement. That is, the CPU locates and executes the program instructions; it carries out arithmetic operations such as addition, subtraction, multiplication, and division; it fetches data from external memory or devices or stores data back. All data must travel through the CPU whenever it is moved from one location to another. (There are a few technical exceptions to this rule; some devices can interact directly with memory.)

The computer stores data and programs in *memory*. There are two kinds of memory. *Primary storage* is fast but expensive; it is made from memory chips (see Figure 3): so-called *random-access memory (RAM)* and *read-only memory (ROM)*. Read-only memory contains certain programs that must always be present—for example, the code needed to start the computer. Random-access memory might have been better called "read-write memory", because the CPU can read data from it and write data back to it. That makes RAM suitable to hold changing data and programs that do not have to be available permanently. RAM memory has two disadvantages. It is comparatively expensive, and it loses all its data when the power is turned off. *Secondary storage*, usually a *hard disk* (see Figure 4), provides less expensive storage that persists without electricity. A hard disk consists of rotating platters, which are coated with a magnetic material, and read/write heads, which can detect and change the magnetic flux on the platters. This is essentially the same storage process that is used in audio or video tapes. Programs and data are typically stored on the hard disk and loaded into RAM when the program starts. The program then updates the data in RAM and writes the modified data back to the hard disk.

The central processing unit, RAM memory, and the electronics controlling the hard disk and other devices are interconnected through a set of electrical lines called a *bus*.

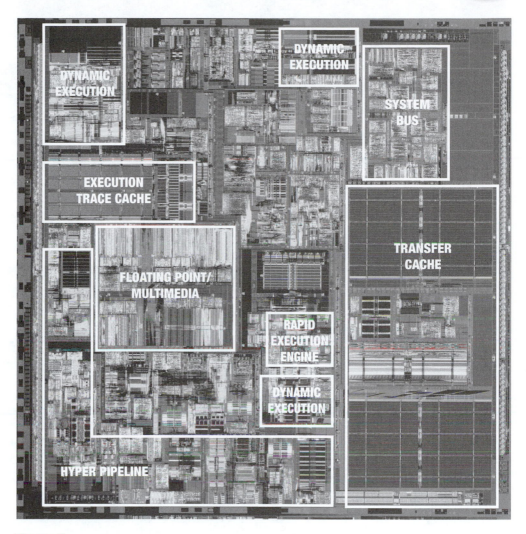

Figure 2

CPU Chip Detail

Data travels along the bus from the system memory and peripheral devices to the CPU and back. Figure 5 shows a *motherboard*, which contains the CPU, the RAM, and card slots, through which cards that control peripheral devices connect to the bus.

To interact with a human user, a computer requires peripheral devices. The computer transmits information to the user through a display screen, loudspeakers, and printers. The user can enter information and directions to the computer by using a keyboard or a pointing device such as a mouse.

Some computers are self-contained units, whereas others are interconnected through *networks*. Through the network cabling, the computer can read data and programs from central storage locations or send data to other computers. For the user of a networked

Figure 3

RAM Chips

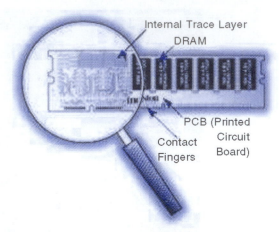

Internal Trace Layer
DRAM
PCB (Printed
Circuit
Board)
Contact
Fingers

Figure 4

A Hard Disk

computer it may not even be obvious which data reside on the computer itself and which are transmitted through the network.

Figure 6 gives a schematic overview of the architecture of a computer. Program instructions and data (such as text, numbers, audio, or video) are stored on the hard disk, on a CD-ROM, or elsewhere on the network. When a program is started, it is brought into RAM memory, from where the CPU can read it. The CPU reads the program one instruction at a time. As directed by these instructions, the CPU reads data, modifies it, and writes it back to RAM memory or the hard disk. Some program instructions will cause the CPU to place dots on the display screen or printer or to vibrate the speaker. As these actions happen many times over and at great speed, the human user will perceive images and sound. Some program instructions read user input from the keyboard or mouse. The program analyzes the nature of these inputs and then executes the next appropriate instructions.

Figure 5

A Motherboard

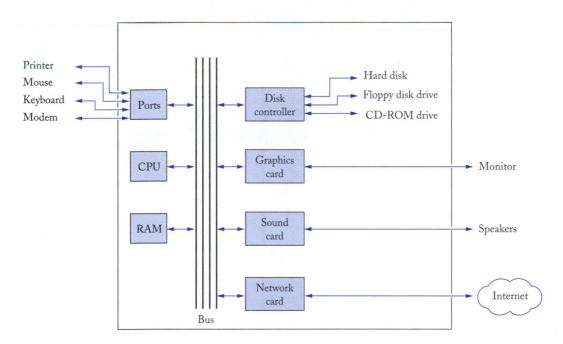

Figure 6

Schematic Design of a Personal Computer

The ENIAC and the Dawn of Computing

The ENIAC (*e*lectronic *n*umerical *i*ntegrator *a*nd *c*omputer) was the first usable electronic computer. It was designed by J. Presper Eckert and John Mauchly at the University of Pennsylvania and was completed in 1946—two years before transistors were invented. The computer was housed in a large room and consisted of many cabinets containing about 18,000 vacuum tubes (see Figure 7). Vacuum tubes burned out at the rate of several tubes per day. An attendant with a shopping cart full of tubes constantly made the rounds and replaced defective ones. The computer was programmed by connecting wires on panels. Each wiring configuration would set up the computer for a particular problem. To have the computer work on a different problem, the wires had to be replugged.

Work on the ENIAC was supported by the U.S. Navy, which was interested in computations of ballistic tables that would give the trajectory of a projectile, depending on the wind resistance, initial velocity, and atmospheric conditions. To compute the trajectories, one must find the numerical solutions of certain differential equations; hence the name "numerical integrator". Before machines like ENIAC were developed, humans did this kind of work, and until the 1950s the word "computer" referred to these people. The ENIAC was later used for peaceful purposes such as the tabulation of U.S. Census data.

Figure 7

The ENIAC

1.4   Translating Human-Readable Programs to Machine Code

On the most basic level, computer instructions are extremely primitive. The processor executes *machine instructions*. A typical sequence of machine instructions is

1. Move the contents of memory location 40000 into register eax. (A register is a storage location in the CPU.)
2. Subtract the value 100 from register eax.
3. If the result is positive, continue with the instruction that is stored in memory location 11280.

Actually, machine instructions are encoded as numbers so that they can be stored in memory. On an Intel 80386 processor, this sequence of instruction is encoded as the sequence of numbers

$$161 \ 40000 \ 45 \ 100 \ 127 \ 11280$$

On a processor from a different manufacturer, the encoding would be quite different. When this kind of processor fetches this sequence of numbers, it decodes them and executes the associated sequence of commands.

How can we communicate the command sequence to the computer? The simplest method is to place the actual numbers into the computer memory. This is, in fact, how the very earliest computers worked. However, a long program is composed of thousands of individual commands, and it is a tedious and error-prone affair to look up the numeric codes for all commands and place the codes manually into memory. As we said before, computers are really good at automating tedious and error-prone activities, and it did not take long for computer programmers to realize that the computers themselves could be harnessed to help in the programming process.

The first step was to assign short names to the commands. For example, mov denotes "move", sub "subtract", and jg "jump if greater than 0". Using these commands, the instruction sequence becomes

```
mov 40000, %eax
sub 100, %eax
jg  11280
```

That is much easier to read for humans. To get the instruction sequences accepted by the computer, though, the names must be translated into the machine codes. This is the task of another computer program: a so-called *assembler*. It takes the sequence of characters "mov %eax" and translates it into the command code 161, and carries out similar operations on the other commands. Assemblers have another feature: they can give names to *memory locations* as well as to instructions. Our program sequence might have checked that some interest rate was greater than 100 percent, and the interest rate was stored in memory location 40000. It is usually not important where a value is stored; any available memory location will do. By using symbolic names instead of memory addresses, the program gets even easier to read:

```
mov int_rate, %eax
sub 100, %eax
jg  int_error
```

It is the job of the assembler program to find suitable numeric values for the symbolic names and to put those values into the generated code sequence.

Assembler instructions were a major advance over programming with raw machine codes, but they suffer from two problems. It still takes a great many instructions to achieve even the simplest goals, and the exact instruction sequence differs from one processor to another. For example, the above sequence of assembly instructions must be rewritten for the Sun SPARC processor, which poses a real problem for people who invest a lot of time and money producing a software package. If a computer becomes obsolete, the program must be completely rewritten to run on the replacement system.

In the mid-1950s, higher-level programming languages began to appear. In these languages, the programmer expresses the idea behind the task that needs to be performed, and a special computer program, a so-called *compiler*, translates the higher-level description into machine instructions for a particular processor.

For example, in C++, the high-level programming language that we will use in this book, you might give the following instruction:

```
if (int_rate > 100) message_box("Interest rate error");
```

This means, "If the interest rate is over 100, display an error message". It is then the job of the compiler program to look at the sequence of characters "if (int_rate > 100)" and translate that into

$$161\ 40000\ 45\ 100\ 127\ 11280$$

Compilers are quite sophisticated programs. They have to translate logical statements, such as the if, into sequences of computations, tests, and jumps, and they must find memory locations for variables like int_rate. In this book, we will generally take the existence of a compiler for granted. If you become a professional computer scientist, you may well learn more about compiler-writing techniques later in your studies.

Higher-level languages are independent of the underlying hardware. For example, the instruction if (int_rate > 100) does not rely on particular machine instructions. In fact, it will compile to different code on an Intel 80386 and a Sun SPARC processor.

1.5   Programming Languages

Programming languages are independent of specific computer architecture, but they are human creations. As such, they follow certain conventions. To ease the translation process, those conventions are much stricter than they are for human languages. When you talk to another person, and you scramble or omit a word or two, your conversation partner will usually still understand what you have to say. Compilers are less forgiving. For example, if you omit the quotation mark close to the end of the instruction,

```
if (int_rate > 100) message_box("Interest rate error);
```

the C++ compiler will get quite confused and complain that it cannot translate an instruction containing this error. This is actually a good thing. If the compiler were to try to guess what you did wrong and try to fix it, it might not guess your intentions correctly.

In that case, the resulting program would do the wrong thing—quite possibly with disastrous effects, if that program controlled a device on whose functions someone's well-being depended. When a compiler reads programming instructions in a programming language, it will translate them into machine code only if the input follows the language conventions exactly.

Just as there are many human languages, there are many programming languages. Consider the instruction

```
if (int_rate > 100) message_box("Interest rate error");
```

This is how you must format the instruction in C++. C++ is a very popular programming language, and it is the one we use in this book. But in Pascal (another programming language that was common in the 1980s) the same instruction would be written as

```
if int_rate > 100 then message_box('Interest rate error');
```

In this case, the differences between the C++ and Pascal versions are slight: for other constructions, there will be far more substantial differences. Compilers are language-specific. The C++ compiler will translate only C++ code, whereas a Pascal compiler will reject anything but legal Pascal code. For example, if a C++ compiler reads the instruction `if int_rate > 100 then...`, it will complain, because the condition of the `if` statement isn't surrounded by parentheses `( )`, and the compiler doesn't expect the word `then`. The choice of the layout for a language construct such as the `if` statement is somewhat arbitrary. The designers of different languages choose different tradeoffs among readability, easy translation, and consistency with other constructs.

1.6   Programming Language Design and Evolution

There are many hundreds of programming languages in existence today. That is actually quite surprising. The idea behind a high-level programming language is to provide a medium for programming that is independent from the instruction set of a particular processor, so that one can move programs from one computer to another without rewriting them. Moving a program from one programming language to another is a difficult process, however, and it is rarely done. Thus, it seems that there would be little use for so many programming languages.

Unlike human languages, programming languages are created with specific purposes. Some programming languages make it particularly easy to express tasks from a particular problem domain. Some languages specialize in database processing; others in "artificial intelligence" programs that try to infer new facts from a given knowledge base; others in multimedia programming. The Pascal language was purposefully kept simple because it was designed as a teaching language. The C language was developed to be translated efficiently into fast machine code, with a minimum of housekeeping overhead. C++ builds on C by adding features for "object-oriented programming", a programming style that promises easier modeling of real-world objects.

Special-purpose programming languages occupy their own niches and are not used much beyond their area of specialization. It may be possible to write a multimedia program in a database language, but it is likely to be challenging. In contrast, languages like

Pascal, C, and C++ are general-purpose languages. Any task that you would like to automate can be written in these languages.

The initial version of the C language was designed about 1972, but features were added to it over the years. Because different compiler writers added different features, the language actually sprouted various dialects. Some programming instructions were understood by one compiler but rejected by another. Such divergence is a major obstacle to a programmer who wants to move code from one computer to another. An effort got underway to iron out the differences and come up with a standard version of C. The design process ended in 1989 with the completion of the ANSI (American National Standards Institute) standard. In the meantime, Bjarne Stroustrup of AT&T added features of the language Simula (an object-oriented language designed for carrying out simulations) to C. The resulting language was called C++. From 1985 until today, C++ has grown by the addition of many features, and a standardization process culminated in the publication of the international C++ standard in 1998.

C and C++ are good examples of languages that grow in an incremental fashion. As users of the language perceived shortcomings, they added features. In contrast, languages such as Pascal were designed in a more orderly fashion. One individual, or a small team, sets out to design the entire language, trying to anticipate the needs of its future users. Such planned languages have a great advantage: Because they are designed with one vision, their features tend to be logically related to each other, and separate features can be combined easily. In contrast, "grown" languages are typically a little messy; different features were designed by people with different tastes. Once a feature is a part of the language, it is difficult to remove it. Removing a feature breaks all existing programs that use it, and their authors would be very upset at the prospect of having to rewrite them. So grown languages tend to accumulate a patchwork of features that do not necessarily interact well with each other.

Planned languages are generally designed with more thought. There is more attention to readability and consistency. In contrast, a new feature in a grown language is often added in a hurry to solve a specific need, without thinking through the ramifications. You can see one trace of that phenomenon in the Pascal and C++ if statements. The Pascal version

```
if int_rate > 100 then...
```

is easier to read than the C version

```
if (int_rate > 100)...
```

because the then keyword helps the human reader along. It is actually easier to compile, too, because the then keyword tells the compiler where the condition ends and the action begins. In contrast, C++ needs the parentheses ( ) to separate the condition from the action. Why the difference? The trick with the then keyword was actually well known when Pascal and C were designed. It was used in Algol 60, a visionary language that has greatly influenced language design in the succeeding years. (Computer scientist Tony Hoare said of Algol 60: "Here is a language so far ahead of its time, that it was not only an improvement on its predecessors, but also on nearly all its successors". [1]). The designer of Pascal used if...then because it is a good solution. The designers of C were not as competent in language design. Either they did not know about the construction or they did not appreciate its benefits. Instead, they imitated the poorly designed if statement from FORTRAN, another early programming language. If they later regretted their decision, it was too late: The `if (...)` construction had been used millions of times, and nobody was willing to change existing, working code.

Languages that are designed by competent planners are generally easier to learn and use. Grown languages have the edge in the marketplace, however. Consider, for example, C++. Because C++ is simply C with some additions, any program written in C will continue to work under C++. Thus, programmers were able to reap the benefits of the new object-oriented features in C++ without having to throw away their existing C programs. That is a huge benefit. In contrast, the Modula 3 language was designed from the ground up to offer the benefits of object-oriented programming. There is no question that Modula 3 is easier to learn and use than C++, but for a programmer who already knows C the picture is different. That programmer can easily move C code to C++, whereas rewriting all the code in Modula 3 would be painful. This rewrite is difficult for two reasons. A serious program consists of many thousands or even millions of lines of code, and translating it line by line is obviously time-consuming. There is more to a programming language than just its syntax and conventions, though. The C language enjoys tremendous tool support from software packages that help programmers manage their C programs. These tools find errors, archive code, speed up programs, and help in combining useful parts of code from various sources. When a new language such as Modula 3 comes along, it has only rudimentary tool support, making it doubly hard to embrace for an ongoing project. In contrast, C tools can be easily modified to work with C++.

At this time, C++ is the premier language for general-purpose programming. For that reason, we use a subset of C++ in this book to teach you how to program. This allows you to benefit from the excellent C++ tools and to communicate easily with other programmers, many of whom use C++ every day. The drawback is that C++ is not all that easy to learn and has its share of traps and inconveniences. I don't want to give you the impression that C++ is an inferior language. It has been designed and refined by many very bright and hard-working people, and it has a tremendous application range, from hardware-oriented programs to the highest levels of abstraction. There simply are some parts of C++ that require more attention, especially by beginning students. I will point out possible pitfalls and how you can avoid them. The purpose of this book is not to teach you all of C++ but to use C++ for teaching you the art and science of writing computer programs.

Random Fact   **1.2**

Standards Organizations

Two organizations, the American National Standards Institute (ANSI) and the International Organization for Standardization (ISO), have jointly developed the definitive standard for the C++ language.

Why have standards? You encounter the benefits of standardization every day. When you buy a light bulb, you can be assured that it fits in the socket without having to measure the socket at home and the bulb in the store. In fact, you may have experienced how painful the

▼

▼

▼

lack of standards can be if you have ever purchased a flashlight with nonstandard bulbs. Replacement bulbs for such a flashlight can be difficult and expensive to obtain.

The ANSI and ISO standards organizations are associations of industry professionals who develop standards for everything from car tires and credit card shapes to programming languages. Having a standard for a programming language such as C++ means that you can take a program that you developed on one system with one manufacturer's compiler to a different system and be assured that it will continue to work.

To find out more about standards organizations, check out the following Web sites: www.ansi.org and www.iso.ch.

1.7   Becoming Familiar with Your Computer

As you use this book, you may well be doing your work on an unfamiliar computer system. You should spend some time making yourself familiar with the computer. Because computer systems vary widely, this book can only give an outline of the steps you need to follow. Using a new and unfamiliar computer system can be frustrating. Look for training courses that your campus offers, or just ask a friend to give you a brief tour.

Step 1. Log In

If you use your own home computer, you don't need to worry about logging in. Computers in a lab, however, are usually not open to everyone. Access is usually restricted to those who paid the necessary fees and who can be trusted not to mess up the configuration. You will likely need an account number and a password to gain access to the system.

Step 2. Locate the C++ Compiler

Computer systems differ greatly in this regard. Some systems let you start the compiler by selecting an icon or menu. On other systems you must use the keyboard to type a command to launch the compiler. On many personal computers there is a so-called *integrated environment* in which you can write and test your programs. On other computers you must first launch one program that functions like a word processor, in which you can enter your C++ instructions; then launch another program to translate them to machine code; and then run the resulting machine code.

Step 3. Understand Files and Folders

As a programmer, you will write C++ programs, try them out, and improve them. You will be provided a place on the computer to store them, and you need to find out where that place is. You will store your programs in *files*. A C++ file is a container of C++ instructions. Files have names, and the rules for legal names differ from one system to another. On some systems, file names cannot be longer than eight characters. Some systems allow spaces in file names; others don't. Some distinguish between upper- and lowercase letters; others don't. Most C++ compilers require that C++ files end in an *extension* .cpp or .C; for example, test.cpp.

Files are stored in *folders* or *directories*. These file containers can be nested. A folder can contain files as well as other folders, which themselves can contain more files and

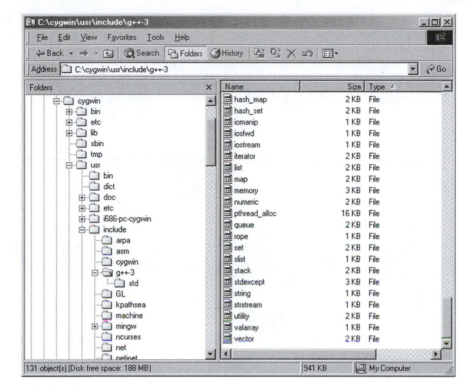

Figure 8

A Directory Hierarchy

folders (see Figure 8). This hierarchy can be quite large, especially on networked computers where some of the files may be on your local disk, others elsewhere on the network. While you need not be concerned with every branch of the hierarchy, you should familiarize yourself with your local environment. Different systems have different ways of showing files and directories. Some use a graphical display and let you move around by clicking the mouse on folder icons. In other systems, you must enter commands to visit or inspect different locations.

Step 4. Write a Simple Program

In the next section, we will introduce a very simple program. You will need to learn how to type it in, how to run it, and how to fix mistakes.

Step 5. Save Your Work

You will spend many hours typing C++ programs in and improving them. The resulting program files have some value, and you should treat them as you would other important property. A conscientious safety strategy is particularly important for computer files. They are more fragile than paper documents or other more tangible objects. It is easy to delete a file by accident, and occasionally files are lost because of a computer malfunction. Unless you keep another copy, you must retype the contents. Because you are unlikely to remember the entire file, you will likely find yourself spending almost as much time as you did to enter and improve it in the first place. This lost time may cause you to miss deadlines. It is therefore crucially important that you learn how to safeguard files and get in the habit of doing so *before* disaster strikes. You can make safety or *backup* copies of files by saving copies on a floppy or on another computer.

Productivity Hint   1.1

Backup Copies

Backing up files on floppy disks is the easiest and most convenient storage method for most people. Another increasingly popular form of backup is Internet file storage. Here are a few pointers to keep in mind.

- *Back up often.* Backing up a file takes only a few seconds, and you will hate yourself if you have to spend many hours recreating work that you could have saved easily. I recommend that you back up your work once every thirty minutes, and every time before you run a program that you wrote.

- *Rotate backups.* Use more than one floppy disk for backups, and rotate them. That is, first back up onto the first floppy disk and put it aside. Then back up onto the second floppy disk. Then use the third, and then go back to the first. That way you always have three recent backups. Even if one of the floppy disks has a defect, you can use one of the others.

- *Back up source files only.* The compiler translates the files that you write into files consisting of machine code. There is no need to back up the machine code files, since you can recreate them easily by running the compiler again. Focus your backup activity on those files that represent your effort. That way your backup disks won't fill up with files that you don't need.

- *Pay attention to the backup direction.* Backing up involves copying files from one place to another. It is important that you do this right—that is, copy from your work location to the backup location. If you do it the wrong way, you will overwrite a newer file with an older version.

- *Check your backups once in a while.* Double-check that your backups are where you think they are. There is nothing more frustrating than to find out that the backups are not there when you need them. This is particularly true if you use a backup program that stores files on an unfamiliar device (such as data tape) or in a compressed format.

- *Relax, then restore.* When you lose a file and need to restore it from backup, you are likely to be in an unhappy, nervous state. Take a deep breath and think through the recovery process before you start. It is not uncommon for an agitated computer user to wipe out the last backup when trying to restore a damaged file.

1.8   Compiling a Simple Program

You are now ready to write and run your first C++ program. The traditional choice for the very first program in a new programming language is a program that displays a simple greeting: "Hello, World!" We follow that tradition. Here is the "Hello, World!" program in C++.

File hello.cpp

```
1  #include <iostream>
2
3  using namespace std;
4
5  int main()
6  {
7     cout << "Hello, World!\n";
8     return 0;
9  }
```

You can download this program file from the companion Web site for this book. The line numbers are not part of the program. They are included so that your instructor can reference them during lectures.

We will explain this program in a minute. For now, you should make a new program file and call it `hello.cpp`. Enter the program instructions and compile and run the program, following the procedure that is appropriate for your compiler.

By the way, C++ is *case-sensitive*. You must enter upper- and lowercase letters exactly as they appear in the program listing. You cannot type `MAIN` or `Return`. On the other hand, C++ has *free-form layout*. Spaces and line breaks are not important. You can write the entire program on a single line,

```
int main(){cout<<"Hello, World!\n";return 0;}
```

or write every keyword on a separate line,

```
int
main()
{
cout
<<
"Hello, World!\n"
;
return
0;
}
```

However, good taste dictates that you lay out your programs in a readable fashion, so you should follow the layout in the program listing.

When you run the program, the message

```
Hello, World!
```

will appear on the screen. On some systems, you may need to switch to a different window to find the message.

Now that you have seen the program working, it is time to understand its makeup. The basic structure of a C++ program is shown in Syntax 1.1.

The first line,

```
#include <iostream>
```

tells the compiler to read the file iostream. That file contains the definition for the *stream input/output* package. Your program performs output onto the screen and therefore requires the services provided in iostream. You must include this file in all programs that read or write text.

By the way, you will see a slightly different syntax, #include <iostream.h>, in many C++ programs. See Advanced Topic 1.1 for more information on this issue.

The next line,

```
using namespace std;
```

tells the compiler that all names that are used in the program belong to the "standard name space". In large programs, it is quite common that different programmers will use the same names to denote different things. They can avoid name conflicts by using separate name spaces. However, for the simple programs that you will be writing in this book, separate name spaces are not necessary. You will always use the standard name space, and you can simply add the directive using namespace std; at the top of every program that you write, just below the #include directives. Name spaces are a relatively recent feature of C++, and your compiler may not yet support them. Advanced Topic 1.1 tells you how to cope with that situation.

The construction

```
int main()
{
    ...
    return 0;
}
```

Syntax 1.1 : Simple Program

header files
```
using namespace std;
int main()
{
    statements
    return 0;
}
```

Example:
```
#include <iostream>
using namespace std;
int main()
{
    cout << "Hello, World!\n";
    return 0;
}
```

Purpose: A simple program, with all program instructions in a main function.

defines a *function* called `main`. A function is a collection of programming instructions that carry out a particular task. Every C++ program must have a `main` function. Most C++ programs contain other functions besides `main`, but it will take us until Chapter 5 to discuss how to write other functions. The instructions or *statements* in the *body* of the `main` function—that is, the statements inside the curly braces {}—are executed one by one. Note that each statement ends in a semicolon.

```
cout << "Hello, World!\n";
return 0;
```

A sequence of characters enclosed in quotation marks

```
"Hello, World!\n"
```

is called a *string*. You must enclose the contents of the string inside quotation marks so that the compiler knows you literally mean `"Hello, World!\n"`. In this short program, there is actually no possible confusion. Suppose, on the other hand, you wanted to display the word *main*. By enclosing it in quotation marks, `"main"`, the compiler knows that you mean the sequence of characters m a i n, not the function named `main`. The rule is simply that you must enclose all text strings in quotation marks, so that the compiler considers them plain text and not program instructions.

The text string `"Hello, World!\n"` should not be taken *completely* literally. You do not want the odd-looking `\n` to appear on the screen. The two-character sequence `\n` actually denotes a single, nonprinting character, a so-called *newline*. When the newline character is sent to the display, the cursor is moved to the first column in the next screen row. If you don't send a newline character, then the next displayed item will simply follow the current string on the same line. In this program we only printed one item, but in general we will want to print multiple items, and it is a good habit to end all lines of output with a newline character.

The backslash `\` character is used as a so-called *escape character*. The backslash does not denote itself; instead, it is used to encode other characters that would otherwise be difficult or impossible to show in program statements. There are a few other backslash combinations that you will encounter later. Now, what do you do if you actually want to show a backslash on the display? You must enter two in a row. For example,

```
cout << "Hello\\World!\n";
```

would print

```
Hello\World!
```

Finally, how can you display a string containing quotation marks, such as

```
Hello, "World"!
```

You can't use

```
cout << "Hello, "World"!\n";
```

As soon as the compiler reads `"Hello, "`, it thinks the string is finished, and then it gets all confused about `World` followed by a second string `"!\n"`. Compilers have a one-track mind, and if a simple analysis of the input doesn't make sense to them, they just refuse to go on, and they report an error. In contrast, a human would probably realize that the second and third quotation marks were supposed to be part of the string. Well, how do we then display quotation marks on the screen? The backslash escape character again comes to the rescue. Inside a string the sequence \" denotes a literal quote, not the end of a string. The correct display statement is therefore

```
cout << "Hello, \"World\"!\n";
```

To display values on the screen, you must send them to an entity called cout. The << operator denotes the "send to" command. You can also print numerical values. For example, the statement

```
cout << 3 + 4;
```

displays the number 7.

Finally, the return statement denotes the end of the main function. When the main function ends, the program terminates. The zero value is a signal that the program ran successfully. In this small program there was nothing that could have gone wrong during the program run. In other programs there might be problems with the input or with some devices, and you would then have main return a nonzero value to indicate an error. By the way, the int in int main() indicates that main returns an integer value, not a fractional number or string.

⊗ Common Error 1.1

Omitting Semicolons

In C++ every statement must end in a semicolon. Forgetting to type a semicolon is a common error. It confuses the compiler because the compiler uses the semicolon to find where one statement ends and the next one starts. The compiler does not use line ends or closing braces to recognize the ends of statements. For example, the compiler considers

```
cout << "Hello, World!\n"
return 0;
```

a single statement, as if you had written

```
cout << "Hello, World!" return 0;
```

and then it doesn't understand that statement, because it does not expect the keyword return in the middle of an output command. The remedy is simple. Just scan every statement for a terminating semicolon, just as you would check that every English sentence ends in a period.

Advanced Topic 1.1

Compiler Differences

At some point in the near future, all compilers will be able to translate programs that conform to the C++ standard. However, at the time of this writing, most compilers fail to comply with

▼ the standard in one or more ways. If your compiler is not fully compliant, you will need to change the code that is printed in this book. Here are some common incompatibilities.

The system header files of older compilers have an extension `.h`, for example

▼
```
#include <iostream.h>
```

If your compiler requires you to use `iostream.h` instead of `iostream`, the programs in this book are still likely to work correctly. However, simply appending a `.h` does not work for all

▼ included files.

For example, in standard C++, you can include string-handling features with the directive

▼
```
#include <string>
```

However, the directive

▼
```
#include <string.h>
```

does *not* include C++ strings. Instead, it includes C-style strings, which are completely different and not as useful.

▼ Another common header file contains mathematical functions. In standard C++, you use the directive

```
#include <cmath>
```

▼ In older compilers you instead use

```
#include <math.h>
```

▼ Older compilers do not support name spaces. In that case, omit the directive `using namespace std;`

1.9   Errors

Experiment a little with the hello program. What happens if you make a typing error such as

```
cot << "Hello, World!\n";
cout << "Hello, World!\";
cout << "Hell, World!\n";
```

In the first case, the compiler will complain. It will say that it has no clue what you mean by `cot`. The exact wording of the error message is dependent on the compiler, but it might be something like "Undefined symbol cot". This is a *compile-time error* or *syntax error*. Something is wrong according to the language rules, and the compiler finds it. When the compiler finds one or more errors, it will not translate the program to machine code, and as a consequence there is no program to run. You must fix the error and compile again. In fact, the compiler is quite picky, and it is common to go through several rounds of fixing compile-time errors before compilation succeeds for the first time.

If the compiler finds an error, it will not simply stop and give up. It will try to report as many errors as it can find, so you can fix them all at once. Sometimes, however, one error throws it off track. This is likely to happen with the error in the second line. The compiler will miss the end of the string because it thinks that the \" is an embedded quote character. In such cases, it is common for the compiler to emit bogus error reports for neighboring lines. You should fix only those error messages that make sense to you and then recompile.

The error in the third line is of a different kind. The program will compile and run, but its output will be wrong. It will print

```
Hell, World!
```

This is a *run-time error* or *logic error*. The program is syntactically correct and does something, but it doesn't do what it is supposed to do. The compiler cannot find the error, and it must be flushed out when the program runs, by testing it and carefully looking at its output.

During program development, errors are unavoidable. Once a program is longer than a few lines, it requires superhuman concentration to enter it correctly without slipping up once. You will find yourself omitting semicolons or quotes more often than you would like, but the compiler will track down these problems for you.

Logic errors are more troublesome. The compiler will not find them—in fact, the compiler will cheerfully translate any program as long as its syntax is correct—but the resulting program will do something wrong. It is the responsibility of the program author to test the program and find any logic errors. Testing programs is an important topic that you will encounter many times in this book. Another important aspect of good craftsmanship is *defensive programming*: structuring programs and development processes in such a way that an error in one place in a program does not trigger a disastrous response.

The error examples that you saw so far were not difficult to diagnose or fix, but as you learn more sophisticated programming techniques, there will be much more room for error. It is an uncomfortable fact that locating all errors in a program is very difficult. Even if you can observe that a program exhibits faulty behavior, it may not be obvious what part of the program caused it and how to fix it. There are special software tools, *debuggers*, that let you trace through a program to find *bugs*—that is, logic errors. In this book you will learn how to use a debugger effectively.

Note that all these errors are different from the kind of errors that you are likely to make in calculations. If you total up a column of numbers, you may miss a minus sign or accidentally drop a carry, perhaps because you are bored or tired. Computers do not make these kinds of errors. When a computer adds up numbers, it will get the correct answer. Admittedly, computers can make overflow or roundoff errors, just as pocket calculators do, when you ask them to perform computations whose result falls outside their numeric range. An overflow error occurs if the result of a computation is very large or very small. For example, most computers and pocket calculators overflow when you try to compute 10^{1000}. A roundoff error occurs when a value cannot be represented precisely. For example, $\frac{1}{3}$ may be stored in the computer as 0.3333333, a value that is close to, but not exactly equal to $\frac{1}{3}$. If you compute $1 - 3 \times \frac{1}{3}$, you may obtain 0.0000001, not 0, as a result of the roundoff error. We will consider such errors logic errors, because the programmer should have chosen a more appropriate calculation scheme that handles overflow or roundoff correctly.

You will learn a three-part error management strategy in this book. First, you will learn about common errors and how to avoid them. Then you will learn defensive programming strategies to minimize the likelihood and impact of errors. Finally, you will learn debugging strategies to flush out those errors that remain.

⊗ Common Error 1.2

Misspelling Words

If you accidentally misspell a word, strange things may happen, and it may not always be completely obvious from the error messages what went wrong. Here is a good example of how simple spelling errors can cause trouble:

```
#include <iostream>

using namespace std;

int Main()
{
   cout << "Hello, World!\n";
   return 0;
}
```

This code defines a function called `Main`. The compiler will not consider this to be the same as the `main` function, because `Main` starts with an uppercase letter and the C++ language is *case-sensitive*. Upper- and lowercase letters are considered to be completely different from each other, and to the compiler `Main` is no better match for `main` than `rain`. The compiler will compile your `Main` function, but when the linker is ready to build the executable file, it will complain about the missing `main` function and refuse to link the program. Of course, the message "missing `main` function" should give you a clue where to look for the error.

If you get an error message that seems to indicate that the compiler is on the wrong track, it is a good idea to check for spelling and capitalization. All C++ keywords, and the names of most functions, use only lowercase letters. If you misspell the name of a symbol (for example `out` instead of `cout`), the compiler will complain about an "undefined symbol". This error message is usually a good clue that you made a spelling error.

1.10 The Compilation Process

Some C++ development environments are very convenient to use. You just enter the code in one window, click on a button or menu to compile, and click on another button or menu to run your code. Error messages show up in a second window, and the program runs in a third window. Figure 9 shows the screen layout of a popular C++ compiler with these features. With such an environment you are completely shielded from the details of the compilation process. On other systems you must carry out every step manually.

Even if you use a convenient C++ environment, it is useful to know what goes on behind the scenes, mainly because knowing the process helps you solve problems when something goes wrong.

You first enter the program statements into a text editor. The editor stores the text and gives it a name such as `hello.cpp`. If the editor window shows a name like `noname.cpp`, you should change the name. You should *save* the file to disk frequently, because otherwise the editor only stores the text in the computer's RAM memory. If something goes wrong with the computer and you need to restart it, the contents of the

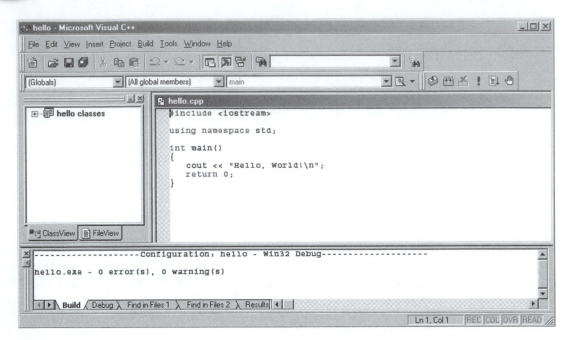

Figure 9

Screen Layout of an Integrated C++ Environment

RAM (including your program text) are lost, but anything stored on a hard disk or floppy disk is permanent even if you need to restart the computer.

When you compile your program, the compiler translates the C++ *source code* (that is, the statements that you wrote) into so-called *object code*. Object code consists of machine instructions and information on how to load the program into memory prior to execution. Object code is stored in a separate file, usually with the extension .obj or .o. For example, the object code for the hello program might be stored in hello.obj.

The object file contains only the translation of the code that you wrote. That is not enough to actually run the program. To display a string on a window, quite a bit of low-level activity is necessary. The authors of the iostream package (which defines cout and its functionality) have implemented all necessary actions and placed the required machine code into a *library*. A library is a collection of code that has been programmed and translated by someone else, ready for you to use in your program. (More complicated programs are built from more than one object file and more than one library.) A special program called the *linker* takes your object file and the necessary parts from the iostream library and builds an *executable file*. (Figure 10 gives an overview of these steps.) The executable file is usually called hello.exe or hello, depending on your computer system. It contains all machine code necessary to run the program. You can run the program by typing hello at a command prompt, or by clicking on the file icon, even after you exit the C++ environment. You can put that file on a floppy and give it to another user who doesn't have a C++ compiler or who may not know that there is such a thing as C++, and that person can run the program in the same way.

Figure 10

From Source Code to
Executable Program

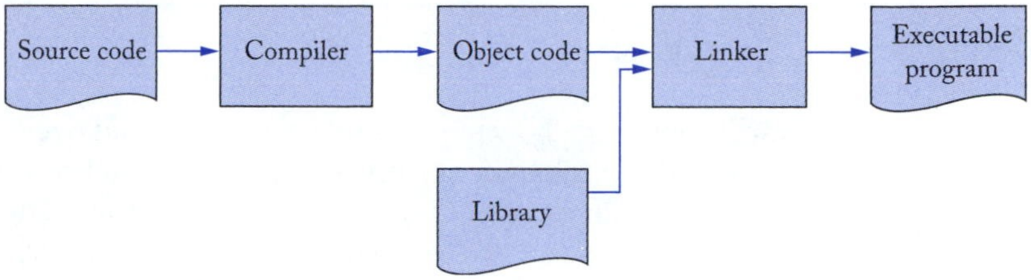

Source code → Compiler → Object code → Linker → Executable program

Library

Your programming activity centers around these files. You start in the editor, writing the source file. You compile the program and look at the error messages. You go back to the editor and fix the syntax errors. When the compiler succeeds, the linker builds the executable file. You run the executable file. If you find an error, you can run the debugger to execute it one line at a time. Once you find the cause of the error, you go back to the editor and fix it. You compile, link, and run again to see whether the error has gone away. If not, you go back to the editor. This is called the *edit-compile-debug loop* (see Figure 11). You will spend a substantial amount of time in this loop in the months and years to come.

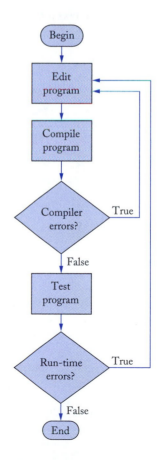

Figure 11

Edit-Compile-Debug Loop

1.11   Algorithms

You will soon learn how to program calculations and decision making in C++. But before we look at the mechanics of implementing computations in the next chapter, let us consider the planning process that precedes the implementation.

You may have run across advertisements that encourage you to pay for a computerized service that matches you up with a love partner. Let us think how this might work. You fill out a form and send it in. Others do the same. The data are processed by a computer program. Is it reasonable to assume that the computer can perform the task of finding the best match for you? Suppose your younger brother, not the computer, had all the forms on his desk. What instructions could you give him? You can't say, "Find the best-looking person of the opposite sex who likes inline skating and browsing the Internet". There is no objective standard for good looks, and your brother's opinion (or that of a computer program analyzing the digitized photo) will likely be different from yours. If you can't give written instructions for someone to solve the problem, there is no way the computer can magically solve the problem. The computer can only do what you tell it to do. It just does it faster, without getting bored or exhausted.

Now consider the following investment problem:

You put $10,000 into a bank account that earns 5 percent interest per year. How many years does it take for the account balance to be double the original?

Could you solve this problem by hand? Sure, you could. You figure out the balance as follows:

Year	Balance
0	$10,000.00
1	$10,500.00 = $10,000.00 × 1.05
2	$11,025.00 = $10,500.00 × 1.05
3	$11,576.25 = $11,025.00 × 1.05
4	$12,155.06 = $11,576.25 × 1.05

You keep going until the balance goes over $20,000. Then the last number in the year column is the answer.

Of course, carrying out this computation is intensely boring. You could tell your younger brother to do it. Seriously, the fact that a computation is boring or tedious is irrelevant to the computer. Computers are very good at carrying out repetitive calculations quickly and flawlessly. What is important to the computer (and your younger brother) is the existence of a systematic approach for finding the solution. The answer can be found by following a series of steps that involves no guesswork. Here is such a series of steps:

Step 1 Start with the table

Year	Balance
0	$10,000.00

Step 2 Repeat steps 2a–2c while the balance is less than $20,000.

Step 2a   Add a new row to the table.

Step 2b   In column 1 of the new row, put one more than the preceding year's value.

Step 2c   In column 2 of the new row, place the value of the preceding balance, multiplied by 1.05 (5 percent).

Step 3 Report the last number in the year column as the number of years required to double the investment.

Of course, these steps are not yet in a language that a computer can understand, but you will soon learn how to formulate them in C++. What is important is that the method described be

- Unambiguous
- Executable
- Terminating

The method is *unambiguous* because there are precise instructions for what to do at each step and where to go next. There is no room for guesswork or creativity. The method is *executable* because each step can be carried out in practice. Had we asked to use the actual interest rate that will be charged in years to come, and not a fixed rate of 5 percent per year, our method would not have been executable, because there is no way for anyone to know what that interest will be. Finally, the computation will eventually come to an end. With every step, the balance goes up by at least $500, so eventually it must reach $20,000.

A solution technique that is unambiguous, executable, and terminating is called an *algorithm*. We have found an algorithm to solve our investment problem, and thus we can find the solution with the computer. The existence of an algorithm is an essential prerequisite for programming a task. Sometimes finding an algorithm is very simple. At other times it requires ingenuity or planning. If you cannot find an algorithm, you cannot use the computer to solve your problem. You need to satisfy yourself that an algorithm exists, and that you understand its steps, before you start programming.

CHAPTER SUMMARY

1. Computers execute very basic operations in rapid succession. The sequence of operations is called a computer program. Different tasks (such as balancing a checkbook, printing a letter, or playing a game) require different programs. Programmers produce computer programs to make the computer solve new tasks.

2. The central processing unit (CPU) of the computer executes one operation at a time. Each operation specifies how data should be processed, how data should be brought into the CPU or out of the CPU, or what operation should be selected next.

3. Data values can be brought into the CPU for processing from storage or from input devices such as the keyboard, the mouse, or a communications link. Processed information is sent back from the CPU to storage or to output devices such as the display or a printer.

4. Storage devices include random-access memory (RAM) and secondary storage. RAM is fast, but it is expensive and loses its information when the power is turned off. Secondary storage devices use magnetic or optical technology to store information. Access time is slower, but the information is retained without the need for electrical power.

5. Computer programs are stored as machine instructions in a code that depends on the processor type. Writing instruction codes directly is difficult for human programmers. Computer scientists have found ways to make this task easier by using assembly language and higher-level programming languages. The programmer writes the programs in such a "language", and a special computer program translates it into the equivalent sequence of machine instructions. Assembly language instructions are tied to a particular processor type. Higher-level languages are independent of the processor. The same program can be translated to run on many different processor types from different manufacturers.

6. Programming languages are designed by computer scientists for a variety of purposes. Some languages are designed for specific purposes, such as database processing. In this book, we use C++, a general-purpose language that is suited for a wide range of programming tasks. C++ is popular because it is based on the C language, which is already in widespread use. To be efficient and compatible with C, the C++ language is less elegant than some newly designed languages, and C++ programmers have to live with a few unfortunate compromises. However, many excellent development tools support C++.

7. Set aside some time to become familiar with the computer system and the C++ compiler that you will use for your class work. Develop a strategy for keeping backup copies of your work before disaster strikes.

8. Every C++ program contains `#include` directives, to access necessary features such as input and output, and a function called `main`. In a simple program, `main` just displays a message on the screen and then returns with a success indicator.

9. Errors are a fact of life for the programmer. Syntax errors are faulty constructs that do not conform to the rules of the programming language. They are detected by the compiler, and no program is generated. Logic errors are constructs that can be translated into a running program, but the resulting program does not perform the action that the programmer intended. The programmer is responsible for inspecting and testing the program to guard against logic errors.

10. C++ programs are translated by a program called a compiler into machine code. In a separate step, a program called a linker combines that machine code with previously translated machine code for input/output and other services to build your program.

11. An algorithm is a description of steps to solve a problem that is unambiguous, executable, and terminating. That is, the description leaves no room for interpretation, the steps can be carried out in practice, and the result is guaranteed to be obtained after a finite amount of time. In order to solve a problem by computer, you must know an algorithm for finding the solution.

FURTHER READING

[1] C. A. R. Hoare, "Hints on Programming Language Design", *Sigact/Sigplan Symposium on Principles of Programming Languages, October 1973*. Reprinted in *Programming Languages, A Grand Tour*, ed. Ellis Horowitz, 3rd ed., Computer Science Press, 1987.

REVIEW EXERCISES

Exercise R1.1. Explain the difference between using a computer program and programming a computer.

Exercise R1.2. Name the various ways in which a computer can be programmed that were discussed in this chapter.

Exercise R1.3. Which parts of a computer can store program code? Which can store user data?

Exercise R1.4. Which parts of a computer serve to give information to the user? Which parts take user input?

Exercise R1.5. Rate the storage devices that can be part of a computer system by (*a*) speed and (*b*) cost.

Exercise R1.6. Describe the utility of the computer network in your department computer lab. To what other computers is a lab computer connected?

Exercise R1.7. Assume a computer has the following machine instructions, coded as numbers:

160 n: Move the contents of register A to memory location n.

161 n: Move the contents of memory location n to register A.

44 *n*:   Add the value *n* to register A.

45 *n*:   Subtract the value *n* from register A.

50 *n*:   Add the contents of memory location *n* to register A.

51 *n*:   Subtract the contents of memory location *n* from register A.

52 *n*:   Multiply register A with the contents of memory location *n*.

53 *n*:   Divide register A by the contents of memory location *n*.

127 *n*:   If the result of the last computation is positive, continue with the instruction that is stored in memory location *n*.

128 *n*:   If the result of the last computation is zero, continue with the instruction that is stored in memory location *n*.

Assume that each of these instructions and each value of *n* requires one memory location. Write a program in machine code to solve the investment-doubling problem.

Exercise R1.8. Design mnemonic instructions for the machine codes in the preceding exercise and write the investment-doubling program in assembler code, using your mnemonics and suitable symbolic names for variables and labels.

Exercise R1.9. Explain two benefits of higher programming languages over assembler code.

Exercise R1.10. List the programming languages mentioned in this chapter.

Exercise R1.11. Explain at least two advantages and two disadvantages of C++ over other programming languages.

Exercise R1.12. On your own computer or on your lab computer, find the exact location (folder or directory name) of

(a)   The sample file `hello.cpp`, which you wrote with the editor

(b)   The standard header file `iostream`

(c)   The header file `ccc_time.h`, needed for some of the programs in this book

Exercise R1.13. Explain the special role of the \ escape character in C++ character strings.

Exercise R1.14. Write three versions of the `hello.cpp` program that have different syntax errors. Write a version that has a logic error.

Exercise R1.15. How do you discover syntax errors? How do you discover logic errors?

Exercise R1.16. Write an algorithm to settle the following question: A bank account starts out with $10,000. Interest is compounded monthly at 6 percent per year (0.5 percent per month). Every month, $500 is withdrawn to meet college expenses. After how many years is the account depleted?

Exercise R1.17. Consider the question of the preceding exercise. Suppose the numbers ($10,000, 6 percent, $500) were user-selectable? Are there values for which the algorithm you developed would not terminate? If so, change the algorithm to make sure it always terminates.

Exercise R1.18. The value of π can be computed according to the following formula:

$$\frac{\pi}{4} = 1 - \frac{1}{3} + \frac{1}{5} - \frac{1}{7} + \frac{1}{9} - \cdots$$

Write an algorithm to compute π. Since the formula is an infinite series and an algorithm must stop after a finite number of steps, you should stop when you have the result determined up to six significant digits.

Exercise R1.19. Suppose you put your younger brother in charge of backing up your work. Write a set of detailed instructions for carrying out his task. Explain how often he should do it, and what files he needs to copy from which folder to which floppy disk. Explain how he should verify that the backup was carried out correctly.

PROGRAMMING EXERCISES

Exercise P1.1. Write a program that prints out a message "Hello, my name is Hal!" Then, on a new line, the program should print the message "What would you like me to do?" Then it is the user's turn to type in an input. You haven't yet learned how to do it—just use the following lines of code:

```
string user_input;
getline(cin, user_input);
```

Finally, the program should ignore the user input and print the message "I am sorry, I cannot do that."

This program uses the `string` data type. To access this feature, you must place the line

```
#include <string>
```

before the `main` function.

Here is a typical program run. The user input is printed in color.

```
Hello, my name is Hal!
What would you like me to do?
Clean up my room
I am sorry, I cannot do that.
```

When running the program, remember to hit the Enter key after typing the last word of the input line.

Exercise P1.2. Write a program that prints out a message "Hello, my name is Hal!" Then, on a new line, the program should print the message "What is your name?" As in Exercise P1.1, just use the following lines of code:

```
string user_name;
getline(cin, user_name);
```

Finally, the program should print the message "Hello, *user name*. I am glad to meet you!" To print the user name, simply use

```
cout << user_name;
```

As in Exercise P1.1, you must place the line

```
#include <string>
```

before the `main` function.

Here is a typical program run. The user input is printed in color.

```
Hello, my name is Hal!
What is your name?
Dave
Hello, Dave. I am glad to meet you.
```

Exercise P1.3. Write a program that computes the sum of the first ten positive integers, $1 + 2 + \cdots + 10$. *Hint*: Write a program of the form

```
int main()
{
   cout <<
   return 0;
}
```

Exercise P1.4. Write a program that computes the *product* of the first ten positive integers, $1 \times 2 \times \cdots \times 10$, and the sum of the reciprocals $1/1 + 1/2 + \cdots + 1/10$. This is harder than it sounds. First, you need to know that the $*$ symbol, not a $\times$, is used for multiplication in C++. Try writing the program, and check the results against a pocket calculator. The program's results aren't likely to be correct. Then write the numbers as *floating-point* numbers, `1.0, 2.0, . . ., 10.0`, and run the program again. Can you explain the difference in the results? We will explain this phenomenon in Chapter 2.

Exercise P1.5. Write a program that displays your name inside a box on the terminal screen, like this:

```
 -------
| Dave  |
 -------
```

Do your best to approximate lines with characters such as | - +.

Fundamental Data Types

CHAPTER GOALS

- ▶ To understand integer and floating-point numbers
- ▶ To write arithmetic expressions in C++
- ▶ To appreciate the importance of comments and good code layout
- ▶ To be able to define and initialize variables and constants
- ▶ To recognize the limitations of the `int` and `double` types and the overflow and roundoff errors that can result
- ▶ To learn how to read user input and display program output
- ▶ To be able to change the values of variables through assignment
- ▶ To use the standard C++ `string` type to define and manipulate character strings
- ▶ To be able to write simple programs that read numbers and text, process the input, and display the results

In this and the four following chapters, you will learn the basic skills needed to write programs in C++. This chapter teaches you how to manipulate numbers and character strings in C++. The goal of this chapter is to write simple programs using these basic data types.

2.1   Number Types

Consider the following simple problem. I have 8 pennies, 4 dimes, and 3 quarters in my purse. What is the total value of the coins?

Here is a C++ program that solves this problem.

File coins1.cpp

```cpp
1  #include <iostream>
2
3  using namespace std;
4
5  int main()
6  {
7     int pennies = 8;
8     int dimes = 4;
9     int quarters = 3;
10
11    double total = pennies * 0.01 + dimes * 0.10
12       + quarters * 0.25; /* total value of the coins */
13
14    cout << "Total value = " << total << "\n";
15
16    return 0;
17 }
```

This program manipulates two kinds of numbers. The coin counts (8, 4, 3) are *integers*. Integers are whole numbers without a fractional part. (Zero and negative whole numbers are integers.) The numerical values of the coins (0.01, 0.10, and 0.25) are *floating-point numbers*. Floating-point numbers can have decimal points. They are called "floating-point" because of their internal representation in the computer. The numbers 250, 2.5, 0.25, and 0.025 are all represented in a very similar way: namely, as a sequence of the significant digits—2500000—and an indication of the position of the decimal point. When the values are multiplied or divided by 10, only the position of the decimal point changes; it "floats". (Actually, internally the numbers are represented in base 2, but the principle is the same.) You have probably guessed that int is the C++ name for an integer. The name for the floating-point numbers used in this book is double; the reason is discussed in Advanced Topic 2.1.

Why have two number types? One could just use

```
double pennies = 8;
```

There are two reasons for having separate types—one philosophical and one pragmatic. By indicating that the number of pennies is an integer, we make explicit an assumption: There can only be a whole number of pennies in the purse. The program would have worked just as well with floating-point numbers to count the coins, but it is generally a good idea to choose programming solutions that document one's intentions. Pragmatically speaking, integers are more efficient than floating-point numbers. They take less storage space and they are processed faster.

In C++, multiplication is denoted by an asterisk *, not a raised dot · or a cross ×. (There are no keys for these symbols on most keyboards.) For example, $d \cdot 10$ is written as d * 10. Do not write commas or spaces in numbers in C++. For example, 10,150.75 must be entered as 10150.75. To write numbers in exponential notation in C++, use an En instead of "× 10^n". For example, 5.0×10^{-3} becomes 5.0E-3.

The output statement

```
cout << "Total value = " << total << "\n";
```

shows a useful feature: *stream* output. You can display as many items as you like (in this case, the string "Total value = ") followed by the value of total and a string containing a newline character, to move the cursor to the next line. Just separate the items that you want to print by <<. (See Syntax 2.1.) Alternatively, you could write three separate output statements

```
cout << "Total value = ";
cout << total;
cout << "\n";
```

This has exactly the same effect as displaying the three items in one statement.

Note the *comment*

```
/* total value of the coins */
```

next to the definition of total. This comment is purely for the benefit of the human reader, to explain in more detail the meaning of total. Anything enclosed between /* and */ is completely ignored by the compiler. Comments are used to explain the program to other programmers or to yourself. There is a second comment style, using the // symbol, that is very popular. See Advanced Topic 2.2 for details.

Syntax 2.1 : Output Statement

cout << *expression₁* << *expression₂* << . . . << *expression_n*;

Example: cout << pennies;
            cout << "Total value = " << total << \n";

Purpose: Print the values of one or more expressions.

The most important feature of our sample program is the introduction of *symbolic names*. We could have just programmed

```
int main()
{
   cout << "Total value = "
      << 8 * 0.01 + 4 * 0.10 + 3 * 0.25 << "\n";

   return 0;
}
```

This program computes the same answer. Compare it with the first program, though. Which one is easier to read? Which one is easier to update if we need to change the coin counts, such as by adding some nickels? By giving the symbolic names, pennies, dimes, and quarters to the counts, we made the program more readable and maintainable. This is an important consideration. You introduce symbolic names to explain what a program does, just as you use variable names such as p, d, and q in algebra.

In C++, each variable has a *type*. By defining int pennies, you proclaim that pennies can only hold integer values. If you try to put a floating-point value into the pennies variable, the fractional part will be lost.

You define a variable by first giving its type and then its name, such as int pennies. You may add an *initialization value*, such as = 8. Then you end the definition with a semicolon. See Syntax 2.2. Even though the initialization is optional, it is a good idea to always initialize variables with a specific value. See Quality Tip 2.1 for the reason.

Variable names in algebra are usually just one letter long, such as p or A, maybe with a subscript such as p_1. In C++, it is common to choose longer and more descriptive names such as price or area. You cannot type subscripts; just tag an index behind the name: price1. You can choose any variable names you like, provided you follow a few simple rules. Names must start with a letter, and the remaining characters must be

---

Syntax 2.2 : Variable Definition

type_name variable_name;
type_name variable_name = *initial_value*;

Example: double total;
            int pennies = 8;

Purpose: Define a new variable of a particular type, and optionally supply an initial value.

---

letters, numbers, or the underscore (_) character. You cannot use other symbols such as $ or %. Spaces are not permitted inside names either. Furthermore, you cannot use *reserved words* such as `double` or `return` as names, these words are reserved exclusively for their special C++ meanings. Variable names are also *case-sensitive*, that is, `Area` and `area` are *different* names. It would not be a good idea to mix the two in the same program, because it would make that program very confusing to read. To avoid any possible confusion, we will never use any uppercase letters in variable names in this book. You will find that many programmers use names like `listPrice`; however we will always choose `list_price` instead. (Because spaces are not allowed inside names, `list price` is not permissible.)

Quality Tip   2.1

Initialize Variables When You Define Them

You should always initialize a variable at the same time you define it. Let us see what happens if you define a variable but leave it uninitialized.

If you just define

```
int nickels;
```

the variable `nickels` comes into existence and memory space is found for it. However, it contains some random values since you did not initialize the variable. If you mean to initialize the variable to zero, you must do so explicitly:

```
int nickels = 0;
```

Why does an uninitialized variable contain a random value? It would seem less trouble to just put a 0 into a variable than to come up with a random value. Anyway, where does the random value come from? Does the computer roll electronic dice?

When you define a variable, sufficient space is set aside in memory to hold values of the type you specify. For example, when you declare `int nickels`, a block of memory big enough to hold integers is reserved. The compiler uses that memory whenever you inquire about the value of `nickels` or when you change it.

```
nickels =
```

When you initialize the variable, `int nickels = 0`, then a zero is placed into the newly acquired memory location.

```
nickels =        0
```

If you don't specify the initialization, the memory space is found and left as is. There is already *some* value in the memory. After all, you don't get freshly minted transistors—just an area of memory that is currently available and that you give up again when `main` ends. Its uninitialized values are just flotsam left over from prior computations. Thus, it takes no effort at all to give you a random initial value, whereas it does take a tiny effort to initialize a new memory location with zero or another value.

If you don't specify an initialization, the compiler assumes that you are not quite ready to come up with the value that you want to store in the variable. Maybe the value needs to be computed from other variables, like the `total` in our example, and you haven't defined all components yet. It is quite reasonable not to waste time initializing a variable if that initial value is never used and will be overwritten with the truly intended value momentarily.

However, suppose you have the following sequence of events:

```
int nickels; /* I'll get around to setting it presently */
int dimes = 3;
double total = nickels * 0.05 + dimes * 0.10; /* Error */
nickels = 2 * dimes;
/* Now I remember—I have twice as many nickels as dimes */
```

This is a problem. The value of `nickels` has been used before it has been set. The value for `total` is computed as follows: Take a random number and multiply it by 0.05, then add the value of the dimes. Of course, what you get is a totally unpredictable value, which is of no use at all.

There is an additional danger here. Because the value of `nickels` is random, it may be different every time you run the program. Of course, you would get tipped off pretty soon if you ran the program twice and you got two different answers. However, suppose you ran the program ten times at home or in the lab, and it always came up with one value that looked reasonable. Then you turned the program in to be graded, and it came up with a different and unreasonable answer when the grader ran it. How can this happen? Aren't computer programs supposed to be predictable and deterministic? They are—as long as you initialize all your variables. On the grader's computer, the uninitialized value for `nickels` might have been 15,054, when on your machine on that particular day it happened to have been 6.

What is the remedy? *Reorder the definitions* so that all of the variables are initialized. This is usually simple to do:

```
int dimes = 3;
int nickels = 2 * dimes;
/* I have twice as many nickels as dimes */
double total = nickels * 0.05 + dimes * 0.10; /* OK */
```

Quality Tip   2.2

Choose Descriptive Variable Names

We could have saved ourselves a lot of typing by using shorter variable names, as in

```
int main()
{
   int p = 8;
   int d = 4;
   int q = 3;

   double t = p * 0.01 + d * 0.10 + q * 0.25;
      /* total value of the coins */

   cout << "Total value = " << t << "\n";

   return 0;
}
```

Compare this program with the previous one, though. Which one is easier to read? There is no comparison. Just reading `pennies` is a lot less trouble than reading p and then *figuring out* it must mean "pennies".

In practical programming, this is particularly important when programs are written by more than one person. It may be obvious to *you* that p must stand for pennies and not percentage (or maybe pressure), but is it obvious to the person who needs to update your code years later, long after you were promoted (or laid off)? For that matter, will you remember yourself what p means when you look at the code six months from now?

Of course, you could use comments:

```cpp
int main()
{
    int p = 8; /* pennies */
    int d = 4; /* dimes */
    int q = 3; /* quarters */

    double t = p + d * 0.10 + q * 0.25;
        /* total value of the coins */

    cout << "Total value = " << t << "\n";

    return 0;
}
```

That makes the definitions pretty clear, but the computation p + d * 0.10 + q * 0.25 is still cryptic.

If you have the choice between comments and self-commenting code, choose the latter. It is better to have clear code with no comments than cryptic code with comments. There is a good reason for this. In actual practice, code is not written once and handed to a grader, to be subsequently forgotten. Programs are modified and enhanced all the time. If the code explains itself, you just have to update it to new code that explains itself. If the code requires explanation, you have to update both the code and the explanation. If you forget to update the explanation, you end up with a comment that is worse than useless because it no longer reflects what is actually going on. The next person reading it must waste time trying to understand if the code is wrong, or the comment.

Advanced Topic   2.1

Numeric Ranges and Precisions

Unfortunately, `int` and `double` values do suffer from one problem. They cannot represent arbitrary integer or floating-point numbers. On some compilers for personal computers, `int` data have a fairly restricted range, (from −32,768 to 32,767 to be exact). (This is because integers are represented using 16 bits, allowing for 216 or 65536, different values. Half of the values (from −1 to −32,768) are negative. There is one less positive value because 0 also needs to be represented.) This is insufficient for many applications. The simplest remedy is to use the `long` type. Long integers typically have a range from −2,147,483,648 to 2,147,483,647.

Floating-point numbers suffer from a different problem: *precision*. Even the double-precision floating-point numbers (`doubles`) store only about fifteen significant decimal digits.

Suppose you think that your customers might find the price of three hundred trillion dollars ($300,000,000,000,000) for your product a bit excessive, so you want to reduce it by five cents to a much more reasonable-looking $299,999,999,999,999.95. Try running the following program:

```
#include <iostream>

using namespace std;

int main()
{
   double original_price = 3E14;
   double discounted_price = original_price - 0.05;
   double discount = original_price - discounted_price;
   /* should be 0.05 */
   cout << discount << "\n"; /* prints 0.0625! */
}
```

The program prints 0.0625, not 0.05. It is off by more than a penny!

For most programs, such as those in this book, precision is not usually a problem for double numbers. However, read Common Error 2.1 for more information about a related issue: roundoff errors.

C++ has another floating-point type, called float, which has a much more limited precision—only about seven decimal digits. You should not normally use the float type in your programs. The limited precision can be a problem in some programs, and all mathematical functions return results of type double. If you try to save those results in a variable of type float, the compiler will warn about possible information loss (see Advanced Topic 2.3). To avoid these warnings, it is best to avoid float altogether.

Advanced Topic   2.2

Alternative Comment Syntax

In C++ there are two methods for writing comments. You already learned that the compiler ignores anything that you type between /* and */. The compiler also ignores any text between a // and the end of the current line (see Syntax 2.3):

```
double t = p * 0.01 + d * 0.10 + q * 0.25;
   // total value of the coins
```

This is easier to type if the comment is only a single line long. But if you have a comment that is longer than a line, then the /* . . . */ comment is simpler:

```
/*
In this program, we compute the value of a set of coins. The
user enters the count of pennies, nickels, dimes, and quarters.
The program then displays the total value.
*/
```

It would be somewhat tedious to add the // at the beginning of each line and to move them around whenever the text of the comment changes.

▼   In this book, we keep it simple and always use the /* ... */ style comments. If you like
the // style better, by all means go ahead and use it. Or you can use // for comments that will
▼   never grow beyond a single line, and /* ... */ for longer comments. The readers of your
code will be grateful for *any* comments, no matter which style you use.

Syntax 2.3 : Comment

```
/* comment text */
// comment text
```

Example: /* total value of the coins */
             // total value of the coins

Purpose: Add a comment to help a human reader understand the program.

Random Fact   2.1

The Pentium Floating-Point Bug

▼   In 1994, Intel Corporation released what was then its most powerful processor, the Pentium.
Unlike previous generations of its processors, it had a very fast floating-point unit. Intel's goal
was to compete aggressively with the makers of higher-end processors for engineering work-
▼   stations. The Pentium was an immediate huge success.

▼   In the summer of 1994, Dr. Thomas Nicely of Lynchburg College in Virginia ran an
extensive set of computations to analyze the sums of reciprocals of certain sequences of prime
numbers. The results were not always what his theory predicted, even after he took into
▼   account the inevitable roundoff errors. Then Dr. Nicely noted that the same program did
produce the correct results when running it on the slower 486 processor that preceded the
Pentium in Intel's lineup. This should not have happened. The optimal roundoff behavior of
▼   floating-point calculations has been standardized by the Institute for Electrical and Electronic Engineers (IEEE) and Intel claimed to adhere to the IEEE standard in both the 486
and the Pentium processors. Upon further checking, Dr. Nicely discovered that indeed there
▼   was a very small set of numbers for which the product of two numbers was computed differently on the two processors. For example,

$$4,195,835 - \left(\left(4,195,835/3,145,727 \right) \times 3,145,727 \right)$$

▼   is mathematically equal to 0, and it did compute as 0 on a 486 processor. On his Pentium
processor the result was 256.

▼   As it turned out, Intel had independently discovered the bug in its testing and had started
to produce chips that fixed it. The bug was caused by an error in a table that was used to
speed up the floating-point multiplication algorithm of the processor. Intel determined that
▼   the problem was exceedingly rare. They claimed that under normal use, a typical consumer

would only notice the problem once every 27,000 years. Unfortunately for Intel, Dr. Nicely had not been a normal user.

Now Intel had a real problem on its hands. It figured that the cost of replacing all Pentium processors that it had already sold would cost a great deal of money. Intel already had more orders for the chip than it could produce, and it would be particularly galling to have to give out the scarce chips as free replacements instead of selling them. Intel's management decided to punt on the issue and initially offered to replace the processors only for those customers who could prove that their work required absolute precision in mathematical calculations. Naturally, that did not go over well with the hundreds of thousands of customers who had paid retail prices of $700 and more for a Pentium chip and did not want to live with the nagging feeling that perhaps, one day, their income tax program would produce a faulty return.

Ultimately, Intel had to cave in to public demand and replaced all defective chips, at a cost of about 475 million dollars.

What do you think? Intel claims that the probability of the bug occurring in any calculation is extremely small—smaller than many chances we take every day, such as driving to work in an automobile. Indeed, many users had used their Pentium computer for many months without reporting any ill effects, and the computations that Professor Nicely was doing are hardly examples of typical user needs. As a result of its public relations blunder, Intel ended up paying a large amount of money. Undoubtedly, some of that money was added to chip prices and thus actually paid by Intel's customers. Also, a large number of processors, whose manufacture consumed energy and caused some environmental impact, were destroyed without benefitting anyone. Could Intel have been justified in wanting to replace only the processors of those users who could reasonably be expected to suffer an impact from the problem?

Suppose that, instead of stonewalling, Intel had offered you the choice of a free replacement processor or a $200 rebate. What would you have done? Would you have replaced your faulty chip, or would you have taken your chance and pocketed the money?

2.2   Input and Output

The program of the preceding section was not very useful. If I have a different collection of coins in my purse, I must change the variable initializations, recompile the program, and run it again. In particular, I must always have a C++ compiler available to adapt the program to new values. It would be more practical if the program could ask how many coins I have of each kind, and then compute the total. Here is such a program.

File coins2.cpp

```
1  #include <iostream>
2
3  using namespace std;
4
5  int main()
6  {
```

```
7      cout << "How many pennies do you have? ";
8      int pennies;
9      cin >> pennies;
10
11     cout << "How many nickels do you have? ";
12     int nickels;
13     cin >> nickels;
14
15     cout << "How many dimes do you have? ";
16     int dimes;
17     cin >> dimes;
18
19     cout << "How many quarters do you have? ";
20     int quarters;
21     cin >> quarters;
22
23     double total = pennies * 0.01 + nickels * 0.05 +
24        dimes * 0.10 + quarters * 0.25;
25           /* total value of the coins */
26
27     cout << "Total value = " << total << "\n";
28
29     return 0;
30  }
```

When this program runs, it will ask, or *prompt*, you:

```
How many pennies do you have?
```

The cursor will stay on the same line as the prompt, and you should enter a number, followed by the Enter key. Then there will be three more prompts, and finally the answer is printed and the program terminates.

Reading a number into the variable pennies is achieved by the statement

```
cin >> pennies;
```

When this statement is executed, the program waits for the user to type in a number and the Enter key. The number is then placed into the variable, and the program executes the next statement.

In this case, we did not initialize the variables that count the coins because the input statements move values into these variables. We moved the variable definitions as close as possible to the input statements to indicate where the values are set.

You can read floating-point values as well:

```
double balance;
cin >> balance;
```

When an integer is read from the keyboard, zero and negative numbers are allowed as inputs but floating-point numbers are not. For example, –10 would be allowed as an input for the number of quarters, even though it makes no sense—you can't have a negative number of coins in your purse. Fractional numbers are not accepted. If you type 10.75 when an integer input is expected, the 10 will be read and placed into the variable in the input statement. The .75 will not be skipped. It will be considered in the next input statement. (See Figure 1.) This is not intuitive and probably not what you expected.

Figure 1

Processing Input

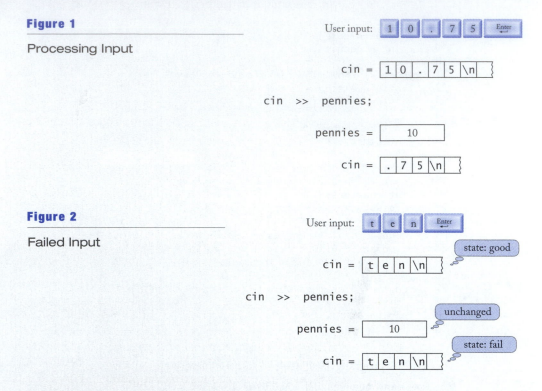

Figure 2

Failed Input

Something even worse happens if you don't enter a number at all. For example, if you type ten or help, then the input-processing routine realizes that this isn't a number, so it does not set the variable in the input statement (that is, the old value of that variable is unchanged). What's more, it sets the cin input stream to a "failed" state. This means, cin has lost confidence in the data it receives, so all subsequent input statements will be ignored. (See Figure 2.) Unfortunately, there is no warning beep or error message that alerts the user to this problem. You will learn later how to recognize and solve input problems. Of course, that is a necessary skill for building programs that can survive untrained or careless users. At this point we must just ask you to type in the right kind of responses to the input prompts.

It is possible to read more than one value at a time. For example, the input statement

```
cin >> pennies >> nickels >> dimes >> quarters;
```

reads four values from the keyboard (see Syntax 2.4). The values can be all on one line, such as

```
8 0 4 3
```

or on separate lines, such as

```
8
0
4
3
```

(See Figures 3 and 4.) All that matters is that the numbers are separated by *white space*: that is, blank spaces, tabs, or newlines. You enter a blank space by hitting the space bar, a

---

Syntax 2.4 : Input Statement

cin >> *variable*$_1$ >> *variable*$_2$ >> ... >> *variable*$_n$;

Example: `cin >> pennies;`
          `cin >> first >> middle >> last;`

Purpose: Read the value for one or more variables from the input.

---

tab by hitting the tab key (often marked with an arrow and vertical bar →|), and a new-line by the Enter key. These key strokes are used by the input reader to separate input.

Keyboard input is *buffered*. Lines of keystrokes are batched together, and the entire input line is processed when you hit the Enter key. For example, suppose the coin calculation program prompts you

    How many pennies do you have?

As a response, you enter

    8 0 4 3

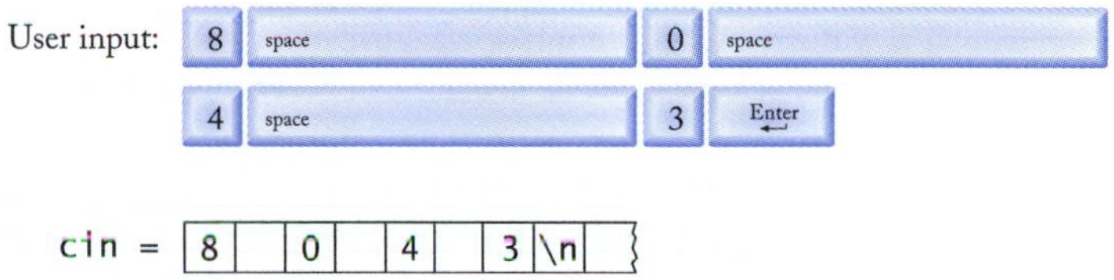

Figure 3

Separating Input
with Spaces

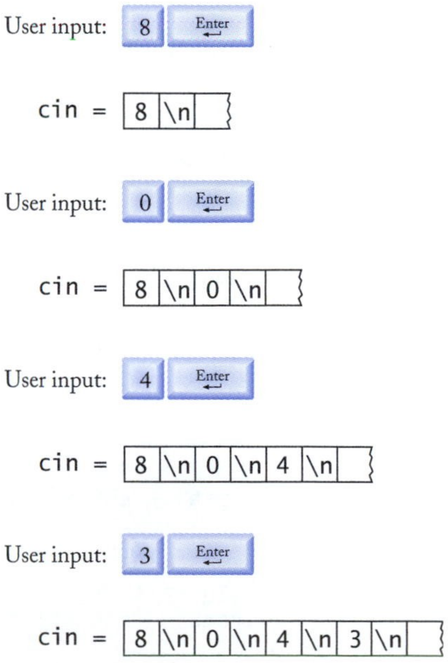

Figure 4

Separating Input with Newlines

Nothing happens until you hit the Enter key. Suppose you hit it. The line is now sent for processing by `cin`. The first input command reads the 8 and removes it from the input stream, and the other three numbers are left there for subsequent input operations. Then the prompt

```
How many nickels do you have?
```

is displayed, and the program *immediately* reads the 0 from the partially processed line. You don't get a chance to type another number. Then the other two prompts are displayed, and the other two numbers are processed.

Of course, if you know what input the program wants, this type-ahead feature can be handy, but it is surprising to most users who are used to more orderly input processing. Frankly, input from `cin` is not all that well suited for interaction with human users. It works well to read data from a file, though, and it is very simple to program.

2.3   Assignment

All but the simplest programs use variables to store values. Variables are locations in memory that can hold values of a particular type. For example, the variable `total` holds values of type `double` because we declared it as `double total`. Up to now, the variables that we used were actually not very variable. Once we stored a value in them, either by initialization or by an input command, that value never varied.

Let us compute the value of the coins in a different way, by keeping a *running total*. First, ask for the number of pennies and set the total to the value of the pennies. Then ask for the number of nickels and *add* the value of the nickels to the total. Then do the same for the dimes and quarters. Here is the program.

File coins3.cpp

```
 1  #include <iostream>
 2
 3  using namespace std;
 4
 5  int main()
 6  {
 7     cout << "How many pennies do you have? ";
 8     int count;
 9     cin >> count;
10     double total = count * 0.01;
11
12     cout << "How many nickels do you have? ";
13     cin >> count;
14     total = count * 0.05 + total;
15
16     cout << "How many dimes do you have? ";
17     cin >> count;
18     total = count * 0.10 + total;
19
```

```
20      cout << "How many quarters do you have? ";
21      cin >> count;
22      total = count * 0.25 + total;
23
24      cout << "Total value = " << total << "\n";
25
26      return 0;
27 }
```

Rather than having four variables for each coin count, there now is just one variable, count. The value of count really does vary during program execution. Each input command cin >> count puts a new value into count, wiping out the prior contents.

In this program, we only need one count variable, because we process the value right away, accumulating it into the total. Processing is done by means of *assignment statements* (see Syntax 2.5). The first processing statement, total = pennies * 0.01, is straightforward. The second statement is much more interesting:

```
total = count * 0.05 + total;
```

It means, "Compute the value of the nickel contribution (count * 0.05), add to it the value of the running total, *and place the result again into the memory location* total". (See Figure 5.)

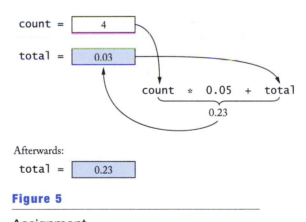

Afterwards:

total =   0.23

Figure 5

Assignment

Syntax 2.5 : Assignment

variable = expression;

Example: total = pennies * 0.01;

Purpose: Store the value of an expression in a variable.

When you make an assignment of an expression into a variable, the *types* of the variable and the expression need to match. For example, it is an error to assign

```
total = "a lot";
```

because `total` is a floating-point variable and `"a lot"` is a string. It is, however, legal, to store an integer in a floating-point variable.

```
total = count;
```

If you assign a floating-point expression to an integer, the expression will be truncated to an integer. Unfortunately, that will not necessarily be the closest integer; Common Error 2.1 contains a dramatic example. Therefore it is never a good idea to make an assignment from floating-point to integer. In fact, many compilers emit a warning if you do.

There is a subtle difference between the statements

```
double total = count * 0.01;
```

and

```
total = count * 0.05 + total;
```

The first statement is the *definition* of `total`. It is a command to create a new variable of type `double`, to give it the name `total`, and to initialize it with `count`. The second statement is an *assignment statement*: an instruction to replace the contents of the existing variable `total` with another value.

It is not possible to have multiple definitions of the same variable. The sequence of statements

```
double total = count * 0.01;
...
double total = count * 0.05 + total; /* Error */
```

is illegal. The compiler will complain about an attempt to redefine `total`, because it thinks you want to define a new variable in the second statement. On the other hand, it is perfectly legal, and indeed very common, to make multiple assignments to the same variable:

```
total = count * 0.05 + total;
...
total = count * 0.10 + total;
```

The `=` sign doesn't mean that the left-hand side *is equal* to the right-hand side but that the right-hand side value is copied into the left-hand side variable. You should not confuse this *assignment operation* with the `=` used in algebra to denote *equality*. The assignment operator is an instruction to do something, namely place a value into a variable. The mathematical equality states the fact that two values are equal. For example, in C++, it is perfectly legal to write

```
month = month + 1;
```

It means to look up the value stored in the variable `month`, to add 1 to it, and to stuff the sum back into `month`. (See Figure 6.) The net effect of executing this statement is to increment `month` by 1. Of course, in mathematics it would make no sense to write that month = month + 1; no value can equal itself plus 1.

The concepts of assignment and equality have no relationship with each other, and it is a bit unfortunate that the C++ language uses `=` to denote assignment. Other programming languages use a symbol such as `<-` or `:=`, which avoids the confusion.

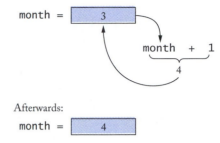

Figure 6

Incrementing a Variable

Consider once more the statement month = month + 1. This statement increments the month counter. For example, if month was 3 before execution of the statement, it is set to 4 afterwards. This increment operation is so common when writing programs that there is a special shorthand for it, namely

```
month++;
```

This statement has the exact same effect, namely to add 1 to month, but it is easier to type. As you might have guessed, there is also a decrement operator --. The statement

```
month--;
```

subtracts 1 from month.

The ++ increment operator gave the C++ programming language its name. C++ is the incremental improvement of the C language.

 Common Error 2.1

Roundoff Errors

Roundoff errors are a fact of life when calculating with floating-point numbers. You probably have encountered that phenomenon yourself with manual calculations. If you calculate 1/3 to two decimal places, you get 0.33. Multiplying again by 3, you obtain 0.99, not 1.00.

In the processor hardware, numbers are represented in the binary number system, not in decimal. You still get roundoff errors when binary digits are lost. They just may crop up at different places than you might expect. Here is an example.

```
#include <iostream>

using namespace std;

int main()
{
    double x = 4.35;
    int n = x * 100;
    cout << n << "\n"; /* prints 434! */
    return 0;
}
```

Of course, one hundred times 4.35 is 435, but the program prints 434.

Most computers represent numbers in the binary system. In the binary system, there is no exact representation for 4.35, just as there is no exact representation for 1/3 in the decimal system. The representation used by the computer is just a little less than 4.35, so 100 times that value is just a little less than 435. When a floating-point value is converted to an integer, the entire fractional part, which is almost 1, is thrown away, and the integer 434 is stored in n.

To avoid this problem, you should always add 0.5 to a positive floating-point value before converting it to an integer:

```
double y = x * 100;
int n = y + 0.5;
```

Adding 0.5 works, because it turns all values above 434.5 into values above 435.

Of course, the compiler will still issue a warning that assigning a floating-point value to an integer variable is unsafe. See Advanced Topic 2.3 on how to avoid this warning.

Advanced Topic   2.3

Casts

Occasionally, you need to store a value into a variable of a different type. Whenever there is the risk of *information loss*, the compiler issues a warning. For example, if you store a double value into an int variable, you can lose information in two ways:

- The fractional part is lost.

- The magnitude may be too large.

For example,

```
int p = 1.0E100; /* NO */
```

is not likely to work, because 10^{100} is larger than the largest representable integer.

Nevertheless, sometimes you do want to convert a floating-point value into an integer value. If you are prepared to lose the fractional part and you know that this particular floating-point number is not larger than the largest possible integer, then you can turn off the warning by using a *cast*: a conversion from one type (such as double) to another type (such as int) that is not safe in general, but that you know to be safe in a particular circumstance. You express this in C++ as follows:

```
int n = static_cast<int>(y + 0.5);
```

The static_cast notation (see Syntax 2.6) is relatively new, and not all compilers support it. If you have an older compiler, you need to use the C-style cast notation instead:

```
int n = (int)(y + 0.5);
```

Syntax 2.6 : Cast

static_cast<*type_name*>(*expression*)

Example: static_cast<int>(x + 0.5)

Purpose: Change an expression to a different type.

Productivity Hint 2.1

Avoid Unstable Layout

You should arrange program code and comments so that the program is easy to read. For example, you should not cram all statements on a single line, and you should make sure that braces {} line up.

However, you should embark on beautification efforts wisely. Some programmers like to line up the = signs in a series of assignments, like this.

```
pennies = 8;
nickels = 0;
dimes   = 4;
```

This looks very neat, but the layout is not *stable*. Suppose you add a line

```
pennies = 8;
nickels = 0;
dimes   = 4;
quarters = 3;
```

Oops, now the = signs no longer line up, and you have the extra work of lining them up *again*.

Here is another example. Many teachers recommend the following style of comments.

```
/* In this program, we compute the value of a set of coins. The
** user enters the count of pennies, nickels, dimes, and quarters.
** The program then displays the total value.
*/
```

Sure, it looks pretty, and the column of ** makes it easy to see the extent of the comment block—but whoever recommends this style never updated their comments. Suppose the program is extended to work for half-dollar coins as well. Of course, we must modify the comment to reflect that change.

```
/* In this program, we compute the value of a set of coins. The
** user enters the count of pennies, nickels, dimes, half dollars,
and quarters. ** The program then displays the total value.
*/
```

That didn't look so great. Now you, the highly paid software engineer, are supposed to rearrange the ** to tidy up the description? This scheme is a *disincentive* to keep comments up to date. Don't do it. Just block off the entire comment like this:

```
/*
In this program, we compute the value of a set of coins. The
user enters the count of pennies, nickels, dimes, and quarters.
The program then displays the total value.
*/
```

You may not care about these issues. Perhaps you plan to beautify your program just before it is finished, when you are about to turn in your homework. That is not a particularly useful approach. In practice, programs are never finished. They are continuously maintained and updated. It is better to develop the habit of laying out your programs well from the start, and keeping them legible at all times. As a consequence, you should avoid layout schemes that are hard to maintain.

Advanced Topic   2.4

Combining Assignment and Arithmetic

In C++, you can combine arithmetic and assignment. For example, the instruction

```
total += count * 0.05;
```

is a shortcut for

```
total = total + count * 0.05;
```

Similarly,

```
total -= count * 0.05;
```

means the same as

```
total = total - count * 0.05;
```

and

```
total *= 2;
```

is another way of writing

```
total = total * 2;
```

Many programmers find this a convenient shortcut. If you like it, go ahead and use it in your own code. For simplicity, we won't use it in this book, though.

2.4   Constants

We used variables such as total for two reasons. By using a name instead of a formula, we make the program easier to read. And by reserving memory space for the variable, we can change its value during program execution. It is usually a good idea to give symbolic names to constants as well, to make programs easier to read and modify.

Consider the following program:

```
int main()
{
   double bottles;
   cout << "How many bottles do you have? ";
   cin >> bottles;

   double cans;
   cout << "How many cans do you have? ";
   cin >> cans;

   double total = bottles * 2 + cans * 0.355;

   cout << "The total volume is " << total << "\n";

   return 0;
}
```

What is going on here? What is the significance of the 0.355?

This formula computes the amount of soda in a refrigerator that is filled with two-liter bottles and 12-oz. cans. (See Table 1 for conversion factors between metric and nonmetric units.) Let us make the computation clearer by using constants (see Syntax 2.7).

File volume.cpp

```
1  #include <iostream>
2
3  using namespace std;
4
5  int main()
6  {
7     double bottles;
8
9     cout << "How many bottles do you have? ";
10    cin >> bottles;
11
12    double cans;
13    cout << "How many cans do you have? ";
14    cin >> cans;
15
16    const double BOTTLE_VOLUME = 2.0;
17    const double CAN_VOLUME = 0.355;
18    double total = bottles * BOTTLE_VOLUME
19       + cans * CAN_VOLUME;
20
21    cout << "The total volume is " << total << " liter.";
22
23    return 0;
24 }
```

English	Metric
1 (fluid) ounce (oz.)	29.586 milliliter (ml)
1 gallon	3.785 liter (l)
1 ounce (oz.)	28.3495 grams (g)
1 pound (lb.)	453.6 grams
1 inch	2.54 centimeter (cm)
1 foot	30.5 centimeter
1 mile	1.609 kilometer (km)

Table 1

Conversion between Metric and Nonmetric Units

Syntax 2.7 : Constant Definition

const *type_name constant_name* = *initial_value*;

Example: `const double LITER_PER_OZ = 0.029586;`

Purpose: Define a new constant of a particular type and supply its value.

Now `CAN_VOLUME` is a named entity. Unlike `total`, it is constant. After initialization with `0.355`, it never changes.

In fact, you can do even better and explain where the value for the can volume came from.

```
const double LITER_PER_OZ = 0.029586;
const double CAN_VOLUME = 12 * LITER_PER_OZ;
    /* 12-oz. cans */
```

Sure, it is more trouble to type the constant definitions and use the constant names in the formulas. But it makes the code much more readable. It also makes the code much easier to change. Suppose the program does computations involving volumes in several different places. And suppose you need to switch from two-liter bottles to half-gallon bottles. If you simply multiply by 2 to get bottle volumes, you must now replace every 2 by 1.893 . . . well, not *every* number 2. There may have been other uses of 2 in the program that had nothing to do with bottles. You have to *look* at every number 2 and see if you need to change it. Did I mention the one formula that multiplied a case count by 36 because there were 18 bottles in every case? That number now needs to be turned into 18×1.893—hopefully we were lucky enough to find it. If, on the other hand, the constant `BOTTLE_VOLUME` is conscientiously used throughout the program, one need only update it in *one location*. Named constants are very important for program maintenance. See Quality Tip 2.3 for more information.

Constants are commonly written using capital letters to distinguish them visually from variables.

Quality Tip   2.3

Do Not Use Magic Numbers

A *magic number* is a numeric constant that appears in your code without explanation. For example,

```
if (col >= 66) . . .
```

Why 66? Maybe this program prints in a 12-point font on 8.5×11-inch paper with a 1-inch margin on the left- and right-hand sides? Indeed, then you can fit 65 characters on a line. Once you reach column 66, you are beyond the right margin and must do something special. However, these are awfully fragile assumptions. To make the program work for a different paper size, one must locate all values of 65 (and 66 and 64) and replace them, taking care not to touch those 65s (and 66s and 64s) that have nothing to do with paper size. In a program that is more than a few pages long, that is incredibly tedious and error-prone.

▼ The remedy is to use a named constant instead:

```
const int RIGHT_MARGIN = 65;
```

▼
```
if (col > RIGHT_MARGIN) . . .
```

▼ Even the most reasonable cosmic constant is going to change one day. You think there are 365 days per year? Your customers on Mars are going to be pretty unhappy about your silly prejudice. Make a constant

```
const int DAYS_PER_YEAR = 365;
```

By the way, the device
▼
```
const int THREE_HUNDRED_AND_SIXTY_FIVE = 365;
```

is counterproductive and frowned upon.

▼ You should *never* use magic numbers in your code. Any number, with the possible exceptions of 0, 1, and 2, should be declared as a named constant.

▼ **Advanced Topic**   **2.5**

Enumerated Types

▼ Sometimes a variable should only take values from a finite set of possibilities. For example, a variable describing a weekday (Monday, Tuesday, . . ., Sunday) can only have one of seven states.
In C++, we can define such *enumerated types*:

▼
```
enum Weekday { MONDAY, TUESDAY, WEDNESDAY, THURSDAY,
    FRIDAY, SATURDAY, SUNDAY };
```

▼ This makes Weekday a type, similar to int. As with any type, we can declare variables of that type.

```
Weekday homework_due_day = WEDNESDAY;
    /* homework due every Wednesday */
```

▼ Of course, you could have declared homework_due_day as an integer. Then you would need to encode the weekdays into numbers.

```
int homework_due_day = 2;
```

▼ That violates our rule against "magic numbers". You could go on and define constants

```
const int MONDAY = 0;
const int TUESDAY = 1;
const int WEDNESDAY = 2;
const int THURSDAY = 3;
const int FRIDAY = 4;
const int SATURDAY = 5;
const int SUNDAY = 6;
```

However, the Weekday enumerated type is clearer, and it is a convenience that you need not ▼ come up with the integer values yourself. It also allows the compiler to catch programming errors. For example, the following is a compile-time error:

```
Weekday homework_due_day = 10; /* compile-time error */
```

▼   In contrast, the following statement will compile without complaint and create a logical problem when the program runs:

```
int homework_due_day = 10; /* logic error */
```

▼   It is a good idea to use an enumerated type whenever a variable can have a finite set of values.

2.5   Arithmetic

You already saw how to add and multiply numbers and values stored in variables:

```
double t = p + d * 0.10 + q * 0.25;
```

All four basic arithmetic operations—addition, subtraction, multiplication, and division—are supported. You must write a * b to denote multiplication, not ab or a · b. Division is indicated with a /, not a fraction bar. For example,

$$\frac{a + b}{2}$$

becomes

```
(a + b) / 2
```

Parentheses are used just as in algebra: to indicate in which order the subexpressions should be computed. For example, in the expression (a + b) / 2, the sum a + b is computed first, and then the sum is divided by 2. In contrast, in the expression

```
a + b / 2
```

only b is divided by 2, and then the sum of a and b / 2 is formed. Just as in regular algebraic notation, multiplication and division *bind more strongly* than addition and subtraction. For example, in the expression a + b / 2, the / is carried out first, even though the + operation occurs further to the left.

Division works as you would expect, as long as at least one of the numbers involved is a floating-point number. That is,

```
7.0 / 4.0
7 / 4.0
7.0 / 4
```

all yield 1.75. However, if *both* numbers are integers, then the result of the division is always an integer, with the remainder discarded. That is,

```
7 / 4
```

evaluates to 1 because 7 divided by 4 is 1 with a remainder of 3 (which is discarded). This can be a source of subtle programming errors—see Common Error 2.2.

If you are just interested in the remainder, use the % operator:

```
7 % 4
```

is 3, the remainder of the integer division of 7 by 4. The % operator must be applied to integers only, not to floating-point values. For example, 7.0 % 4 is an error. The % symbol has no analog in algebra. It was chosen because it looks similar to /, and the remainder operation is related to division.

Here is a typical use for the integer / and % operations. Suppose we want to know the value of the coins in a purse in dollar and cents. We can compute the value as an integer, denominated in cents, and then compute the whole dollar amount and the remaining change:

File coins4.cpp

```
 1  #include <iostream>
 2
 3  using namespace std;
 4
 5  int main()
 6  {
 7     cout << "How many pennies do you have? ";
 8     int pennies;
 9     cin >> pennies;
10
11     cout << "How many nickels do you have? ";
12     int nickels;
13     cin >> nickels;
14
15     cout << "How many dimes do you have? ";
16     int dimes;
17     cin >> dimes;
18
19     cout << "How many quarters do you have? ";
20     int quarters;
21     cin >> quarters;
22
23     int value = pennies + 5 * nickels + 10 * dimes
24        + 25 * quarters;
25     int dollar = value / 100;
26     int cents = value % 100;
27
28     cout << "Total value = " << dollar << " dollars and "
29        << cents << " cents.";
30
31     return 0;
32  }
```

For example, if `value` is 243, then the output statement will display

```
Total value = 2 dollars and 43 cents.
```

To take the square root of a number, you use the `sqrt` function (see Syntax 2.8). For example, $\sqrt{x}$ is written as `sqrt(x)`. To compute x^n, you write `pow(x, n)`. However, to compute x^2, it is significantly more efficient simply to write `x * x`. To use `sqrt` and `pow`, you must place the line `#include <cmath>` at the top of your program file. The header file `cmath` is a standard C++ header that is available with all C++ systems, just like `iostream`.

As you can see, the effect of the /, `sqrt`, and `pow` operations is to flatten out mathematical terms. In algebra, you use fractions, exponents, and roots to arrange expressions

---

Syntax 2.8 : Function Call

function_name(expression$_1$, expression$_2$, ..., expression$_n$)

Example: `sqrt(x)`
         `pow(z + y, n)`

Purpose: The result of calling a function and supplying the values for the function parameters.

---

in a compact two-dimensional form. In C++, you have to write all expressions in a linear arrangement. For example, the subexpression

$$\frac{-b + \sqrt{b^2 - 4ac}}{2a}$$

of the quadratic formula becomes

```
(-b + sqrt(b * b - 4 * a * c)) / (2 * a)
```

Figure 7 shows how to analyze such an expression. With complicated expressions like these, it is not always easy to keep the parentheses matched—see Common Error 2.3.

Table 2 shows additional functions that are declared in the `cmath` header. Inputs and outputs are floating-point numbers.

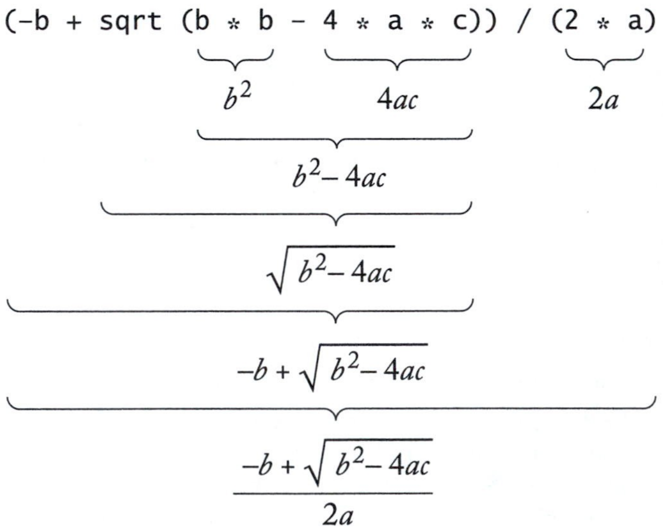

Figure 7

Analyzing an Expression

Function	Description
sin(x)	sine of x (x in radians)
cos(x)	cosine of x
tan(x)	tangent of x
asin(x)	(arc sine) $\sin^{-1} x \in [-\pi/2,\ \pi/2],\ x \in [-1,\ 1]$
acos(x)	(arc cosine) $\text{arc}^{-1} x \in [0,\ \pi],\ x \in [-1,\ 1]$
atan(x)	(arc tangent) $\tan^{-1} x \in (-\pi/2,\ \pi/2)$
atan2(y, x)	(arc tangent) $\tan^{-1}(y/x) \in [-\pi/2,\ \pi/2],\ x$ may be 0
exp(x)	e^x
log(x)	(natural log) $\ln(x),\ x > 0$
log10(x)	(decimal log) $\lg(x),\ x > 0$
sinh(x)	hyperbolic sine of x
cosh(x)	hyperbolic cosine of x
tanh(x)	hyperbolic tangent of x
ceil(x)	smallest integer $\geq x$
floor(x)	largest integer $\leq x$
fabs(x)	absolute value $|x|$

Table 2

Other Mathematical
Functions

Common Error 2.2

Integer Division

It is unfortunate that C++ uses the same symbol, namely /, for both integer and floating-point division. These are really quite different operations. It is a common error to use integer division by accident. Consider this program segment that computes the average of three integers.

```cpp
cout << "Please enter your last three test scores: ";
int s1;
int s2;
int s3;
cin >> s1 >> s2 >> s3;
double average = (s1 + s2 + s3) / 3; /* Error */
cout << "Your average score is " << average << "\n";
```

What could be wrong with that? Of course, the average of s1, s2, and s3 is

$$\frac{s1+s2+s3}{3}$$

Here, however, the / does not mean division in the mathematical sense. It denotes integer division since both s1 + s2 + s3 and 3 are integers. For example, if the scores add up to 14, the average is computed to be 4, the result of the integer division of 14 by 3. That integer 4 is then moved into the floating-point variable average. The remedy is to make the numerator or denominator into a floating-point number:

```
double total = s1 + s2 + s3;
double average = total / 3;
```

or

```
double average = (s1 + s2 + s3) / 3.0;
```

Common Error   **2.3**

Unbalanced Parentheses

Consider the expression

```
1.5 * ((-(b - sqrt(b * b - 4 * a * c)) / (2 * a))
```

What is wrong with it? Count the parentheses. There are five (and four). The parentheses are *unbalanced*. This kind of typing error is very common with complicated expressions. Now consider this expression.

```
1.5 * (sqrt(b * b - 4 * a * c))) - ((b / (2 * a))
```

This expression has five (and five), but it still is not correct. In the middle of the expression,

```
1.5 * (sqrt(b * b - 4 * a * c))) - ((b / (2 * a))
                                 ↑
```

there are only two (but three), which is an error. In the middle of an expression, the count of (must be greater or equal than the count of), and at the end of the expression the two counts must be the same.

Here is a simple trick to make the counting easier without using pencil and paper. It is difficult for the brain to keep two counts simultaneously. Keep only one count when scanning the expression. Start with 1 at the first opening parenthesis; add 1 whenever you see an opening parenthesis; and subtract one whenever you see a closing parenthesis. Say the numbers aloud as you scan the expression. If the count ever drops below zero, or is not zero at the end, the parentheses are unbalanced. For example, when scanning the previous expression, you would mutter

```
1.5 * (sqrt(b * b - 4 * a * c) ) ) - ((b / (2 * a))
       1    2                  1 0 -1
```

and you would find the error.

Common Error   **2.4**

Forgetting Header Files

Every program that you write needs at least one header file, to include facilities for input and output; that file is normally `iostream`.

If you use mathematical functions such as `sqrt`, you need to include `cmath`. If you forget to include the appropriate header file, the compiler will not know symbols such as `sqrt` or `cout`. If the compiler complains about an undefined function or symbol, check your header files.

Sometimes you may not know which header file to include. Suppose you want to compute the absolute value of an integer using the `abs` function. As it happens, `abs` is not defined in `cmath` but in `cstdlib`. How can you find the correct header file? You need to locate the documentation of the `abs` function, preferably using the online help of your editor (see Productivity Hint 2.2). Many editors have a hot key that summons help on the word under the cursor. Or you can look into the library reference manual that came with the compiler, either in printed form or online. The documentation includes a short description of the function and the name of the header file that you must include.

Some compiler documentation has not been updated to reflect the C++ standard. Here is a correspondence of all standard and old header files that are used in this book:

Standard C++ header	Old header
iostream	iostream.h
iomanip	iomanip.h
fstream	fstream.h
cmath	math.h
cstdlib	stdlib.h
string	No equivalent
vector	vector.h

Advanced Topic   **2.6**

Remainder of Negative Integers

You often compute a remainder (`a % n`) to obtain a number in the range between 0 and n - 1. However, if a is a negative number, the remainder `a % n` yields a negative number. For example, `-7 % 4` is −3. That result is inconvenient, because it does not fall into the range between 0 and 3 and because it is different from the usual mathematical definition; in mathematics, the remainder is the number that you reach by starting with a and adding or subtracting n until you reach a number between 0 and n - 1. For example, the remainder of 11 by 4 is $11 - 4 - 4 = 3$. The remainder of -7 by 4 is $-7 + 4 - 4 = 1$, which is different from -7 % 4. To compute the correct remainder for negative numbers, use the following formula:

```
int rem = n - 1 - (-a - 1) % n; /* if a is negative */
```

For example, if a is -7 and n is 4, this formula computes $3 - (7 - 1)\%4 = 3 - 2 = 1$.

Productivity Hint 2.2

Online Help

Today's integrated C++ programming environments contain sophisticated help systems. You should spend some time learning how to use the online help in your compiler. Help is available on compiler settings, keyboard shortcuts, and, most importantly, on library functions. If you are not sure how the pow function works, or cannot remember whether it was called pow or power, the online help can give you the answer quickly. Figure 8 shows a typical help screen.

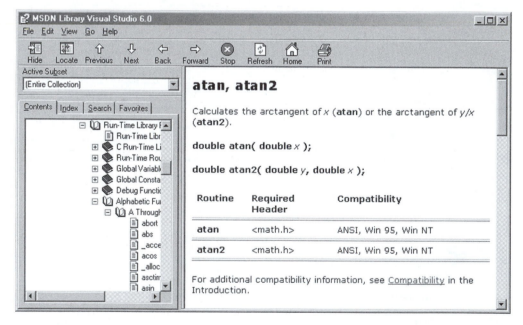

Figure 8

Online Help

Quality Tip 2.4

White Space

The compiler does not care whether you write your entire program onto a single line or place every symbol on a separate line. The human reader cares very much. You should use blank lines to group your code visually into sections. For example, you can signal to the reader that an output prompt and the corresponding input statement belong together by inserting a blank line before and after the group. You will find many examples in the source code listings in this book.

White space inside expressions is also important. It is easier to read

```
x1 = (-b + sqrt(b * b - 4 * a * c)) / (2 * a);
```

than

```
x1=(-b+sqrt(b*b-4*a*c))/(2*a);
```

Simply put spaces around all operators + - * / % =. However, don't put a space after a *unary* minus: a – used to negate a single quantity, such as -b. That way, it can be easily distinguished from a *binary* minus, as in a - b. Don't put spaces between a function name and the parentheses, but do put a space after every C++ keyword. That makes it easy to see that the sqrt in sqrt(x) is a function name, whereas the if in if (x > 0) is a keyword.

Quality Tip 2.5

Factor Out Common Code

Suppose we want to find both solutions of the quadratic equation $ax^2 + bx + c = 0$. The quadratic formula tells us that the solutions are

$$x_{1,2} = \frac{-b \pm \sqrt{b^2 - 4ac}}{2a}$$

In C++, there is no analog to the ± operation, which indicates how to obtain two solutions simultaneously. Both solutions must be computed separately.

```
x1 = (-b + sqrt(b * b - 4 * a * c)) / (2 * a);
x2 = (-b - sqrt(b * b - 4 * a * c)) / (2 * a);
```

This approach has two problems. The computation of sqrt(b * b - 4 * a * c) is carried out twice, which wastes time. Second, whenever the same code is replicated, the possibility of a typing error increases. The remedy is to *factor* out the common code:

```
double root = sqrt(b * b - 4 * a * c);
x1 = (-b + root) / (2 * a);
x2 = (-b - root) / (2 * a);
```

We could go even further and factor out the computation of 2 * a, but the gain from factoring out very simple computations is small, and the resulting code can be hard to read.

2.6   Strings

2.6.1 — String Variables

Next to numbers, *strings* are the most important data type that most programs use. A string is a sequence of characters, such as `"Hello"`. In C++, strings are enclosed in quotation marks, which are not themselves part of the string.

You can declare variables that hold strings.

```
string name = "John";
```

The `string` type is a part of the C++ standard. To use it, simply include the header file, `string`:

```
#include <string>
```

Use assignment to place a different string into the variable.

```
name = "Carl";
```

You can also read a string from the keyboard:

```
cout << "Please enter your name: ";
cin >> name;
```

When a string is read from an input stream, only one word is placed into the string variable. (Words are separated by white space.) For example, if the user types

```
Harry Hacker
```

as the response to the prompt, then only `Harry` is placed into `name`. To read the second string, another input statement must be used. This constraint makes it tricky to write an input statement that deals properly with user responses. Some users might type just their first names, others might type their first and last names, and others might even supply their middle initials.

To handle such a situation, use the `getline` command. The statement

```
getline(cin, name);
```

reads all keystrokes until the Enter key, makes a string containing all of the keystrokes, and places it into the `name` variable. With the preceding input example, `name` is set to the string `"Harry Hacker"`. This is a string containing 12 characters, one of which is a space. You should always use the `getline` function if you are not sure that the user input consists of a single word.

The number of characters in a string is called the *length* of the string. For example, the length of `"Harry Hacker"` is 12, and the length of `"Hello, World!\n"` is 14—the newline character counts as one character only. You can compute the length of a string with the `length` function. Unlike `sqrt` or `getline`, the `length` function is invoked with the *dot notation*. You write first the variable name of the string whose length you want, then a period, then the name of the function, followed by parentheses:

```
int n = name.length();
```

Many C++ functions require you to use this dot notation, and you must memorize (or look up) which do and which don't. These functions are called *member functions* (see Syntax 2.9).

Syntax 2.9 : Member Function Call

expression.function_name(expression$_1$, expression$_2$, . . . , expression$_n$)

Example: `name.length()`
`name.substr(0, n - 1)`

Purpose: The result of calling a member function and supplying the values for the function parameters.

A string of length zero, containing no characters, is called the *empty string*. It is written as "". Unlike number variables, string variables are guaranteed to be initialized; they are initialized with the empty string.

```
string response; /* initialized as "" */
```

2.6.2 — Substrings

Once you have a string, what can you do with it? You can extract substrings, and you can glue smaller strings together to form larger ones. To extract a substring, use the `substr` operation:

```
s.substr(start, length)
```

returns a string that is made up from the characters in the string `s`, starting at character `start`, and containing `length` characters. Just like `length`, `substr` uses the dot notation. Inside the parentheses, you write the parameters that describe which substring you want. Here is an example:

```
string greeting = "Hello, World!\n";
string sub = greeting.substr(0, 4);
/* sub is "Hell" */
```

The `substr` operation makes a string that consists of four characters taken from the string `greeting`. Indeed, `"Hell"` is a string of length 4 that occurs inside `greeting`. The only curious aspect of the `substr` operation is the starting position. Starting position 0 means "start at the beginning of the string". For technical reasons that used to be important but are no longer relevant, string position numbers start at 0. The first item in a sequence is labeled 0, the second one 1, and so on. For example, here are the position numbers in the `greeting` string:

H	e	l	l	o	,		W	o	r	l	d	!	\n
0	1	2	3	4	5	6	7	8	9	10	11	12	13

The position number of the last character (13) is always one less than the length of the string.

Let us figure out how to extract the substring `"World"`. Count characters starting at 0, not 1. You find that `W`, the 8th character, has position number 7. The string you want is 5 characters long. Therefore, the appropriate substring command is

```
string w = greeting.substr(7, 5);
```

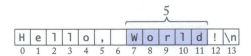

The string functions you have seen so far are summarized in Table 3.

Name	Purpose
s.length()	The length of s
s.substr(i, n)	The substring of length n of s starting at index i
getline(f, s)	Read string s from the input stream f

Table 3

String Functions

2.6.3 — Concatenation

Now that you know how to take strings apart, let us see how to put them back together. Given two strings, such as "Harry" and "Hacker", we can *concatenate* them to one long string:

```
string fname = "Harry";
string lname = "Hacker";
string name = fname + lname;
```

The + operator concatenates two strings. The resulting string is "HarryHacker". Actually, that isn't really what we are after. We'd like the first and last name separated by a space. No problem:

```
string name = fname + " " + lname;
```

Now we concatenate three strings, "Harry", " ", and "Hacker". The result is

```
"Harry Hacker"
```

You must be careful when using + for strings. One or both of the strings surrounding the + must be a string *variable*. The expression fname + " " is OK, but the expression "Harry" + " " is not. This is not a big problem; in the second case, you can just write "Harry ".

Here is a simple program that puts these concepts to work. The program asks for your full name and prints out your initials. For example, if you give your name as "Harold Joseph Hacker", the program tells you that your initials are HJH.

File initials.cpp

```
1 #include <iostream>
2 #include <string>
3
4 using namespace std;
5
6 int main()
7 {
```

Figure 9

Building the `initials` String

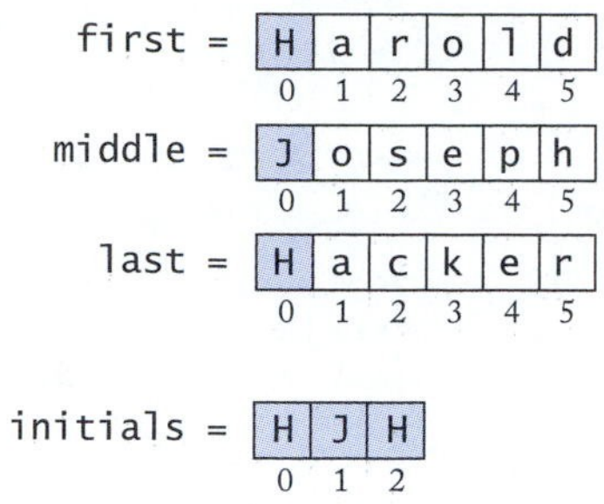

first = | H | a | r | o | l | d |
0 1 2 3 4 5

middle = | J | o | s | e | p | h |
0 1 2 3 4 5

last = | H | a | c | k | e | r |
0 1 2 3 4 5

initials = | H | J | H |
0 1 2

```
8    cout << "Enter your full name (first middle last): ";
9    string first;
10   string middle;
11   string last;
12   cin >> first >> middle >> last;
13   string initials = first.substr(0, 1)
14       + middle.substr(0, 1) + last.substr(0, 1);
15   cout << "Your initials are " << initials << "\n";
16
17   return 0;
18 }
```

The operation `first.substr(0, 1)` makes a string consisting of one character, taken from the start of `first`. The program does the same for the `middle` and `last` strings. Then it concatenates the three one-character strings to get a string of length 3, the `initials` string. (See Figure 9.)

Advanced Topic   2.7

Characters and C Strings

C++ has a data type `char` to denote individual characters. In the C language, the precursor to C++, the only way to implement strings was as sequences of individual characters. You can recognize C strings in C or C++ code by looking for types like `char*` or `char[]`. Individual characters are enclosed in single quotes. For example, `'a'` is the character *a*, whereas `"a"` is a string containing the single character *a*.

Using character sequences for strings puts a tremendous burden on the programmer to locate storage space for these sequences manually. In C, a common error is moving a string into a variable that is too small to hold all of its characters. For efficiency's sake, there is no check against this possibility, and it is all too easy for the inexperienced programmer to corrupt adjacent variables.

The standard C++ strings handle all these chores completely automatically. For most programming tasks, you do not need the data type `char` at all. Instead, just use strings of length 1 for individual characters. Chapter 9 contains a brief introduction to C strings.

2.6.4 — Formatted Output

When you display several numbers, each of them is printed with the minimum number of digits needed to show the value. This often yields ugly output. Here is an example.

```
cout << pennies << " " << pennies * 0.01 << "\n";
cout << nickels << " " << nickels * 0.05 << "\n";
cout << dimes << " " << dimes * 0.10 << "\n";
cout << quarters << " " << quarters * 0.25 << "\n";
```

A typical output might look like this.

```
1 0.01
12 0.6
4 0.4
120 30
```

What a mess! The columns don't line up, and the money values don't show dollars and cents. We need to *format* the output. Let us make each column eight characters wide, and use two digits of precision for the floating-point numbers.

You use the `setw` *manipulator* to set the width of the next output field. For example, if you want the next number to be printed in a column that is eight characters wide, you use

```
cout << setw(8);
```

This command does not produce any output; it just manipulates the stream so that it will change the output format for the next value. To use stream manipulators, you must include the `iomanip` header:

```
#include <iomanip>
```

Another manipulator, `setprecision`, is used to set the precision of the next floating-point number:

```
cout << setprecision(2);
```

You can combine manipulators with output values:

```
cout << setprecision(2) << setw(8) << x;
```

This command prints the value x in a field of width 8 and with two digits of precision, for example

```
···34.95
```

(where each · represents a space). The precision setting has no influence on integer fields.

Unfortunately, simply using `setprecision` is not sufficient for printing trailing zeroes. For example, 0.1 will still print as 0.1, not as 0.10. You have to select *fixed format*, with the command

```
cout << fixed;
```

Some older compilers do not support the `fixed` manipulator. In that case, use the more arcane command

```
cout << setiosflags(ios::fixed);
```

Combining these three manipulators finally achieves the desired result:

```
cout << fixed << setprecision(2) << setw(8) << x;
```

Mercifully, the `setprecision` and `fixed` manipulators need only to be used once; the stream remembers the formatting directives. However, `setw` must be specified anew for *every* item.

There are many more formatting commands, but these are the most commonly used ones. See, for example, reference [2] for a complete list of options.

Here is a sequence of instructions that can be used to beautify the table.

```
cout << fixed << setprecision(2);
cout << setw(8) << pennies << " "
   << setw(8) << pennies * 0.01 << "\n";
cout << setw(8) << nickels << " "
   << setw(8) << nickels * 0.05 << "\n";
cout << setw(8) << dimes << " "
   << setw(8) << dimes * 0.10 << "\n";
cout << setw(8) << quarters << " "
   << setw(8) << quarters * 0.25 << "\n";
```

Now the output is

```
  1    0.01
 12    0.60
  4    0.40
120   30.00
```

Chapter Summary

1. C++ has several data types for numbers. The most common types are `double` and `int`. Floating-point numbers can have fractional values; integers cannot. Occasionally, other numeric types are required for larger values or higher precision.

2. Numbers, strings, and other values can be stored in *variables*. A variable has a name that indicates its function to the human reader. A variable can hold different values during program execution.

3. Numbers and strings can be read from an input stream with the `>>` operator. They are written to an output stream with the `<<` operator. Output uses a general format; use stream manipulators to achieve special formats.

4. When a variable is first filled with a value, it is *initialized*. The initial value can later be replaced with another by a process called *assignment*. In C++, assignment is denoted by the `=` operator—a somewhat unfortunate choice because the C++ meaning of `=` is not the same as mathematical equality.

5. Constants are values with a symbolic name. Constants cannot be changed once they are initialized. Named constants should be used instead of numbers to make programs easier to read and maintain.

6. All common arithmetic operations are provided in C++; however, the symbols are different from mathematical notation. In particular, `*` denotes multiplication. There is no horizontal fraction bar, and `/` must be used for division. To compute a power a^b or a square root $\sqrt{a}$, the `pow` and `root` functions must be used. Other functions, such

as `sin` and `log`, are available as well. The % operator computes the remainder of an integer division.

7. Strings are sequences of characters. Strings can be *concatenated*; that is, put end to end to yield a new longer string. In C++, string concatenation is denoted by the + operator. The `substr` function extracts substrings.

FURTHER READING

[1] Franklin M. Fisher, John J. McGowan, and Joen E. Greenwood, *Folded, Spindled and Mutilated. Economic Analysis and* U.S. *vs.* IBM, MIT Press, 1983.
[2] Bjarne Stroustrup, *The C++ Programming Language*, 3rd ed., Addison-Wesley, 2000.

REVIEW EXERCISES

Exercise R2.1. Write the following mathematical expressions in C++.

$$s = s_0 + v_0 t + \frac{1}{2} g t^2$$

$$G = 4\pi^2 \frac{a^3}{p^2(m_1 + m_2)}$$

$$FV = PV \cdot \left(1 + \frac{INT}{100}\right)^{YRS}$$

$$c = \sqrt{a^2 + b^2 - 2ab\cos\gamma}$$

Exercise R2.2. Write the following C++ expressions in mathematical notation.

(a) `dm = m * (sqrt(1 + v / c) / sqrt(1 - v / c) - 1);`

(b) `volume = PI * r * r * h;`

(c) `volume = 4 * PI * pow(r, 3) / 3;`

(d) `p = atan2(z, sqrt(x * x + y * y));`

Exercise R2.3. What is wrong with this version of the quadratic formula?

```
x1 = (-b - sqrt(b * b - 4 * a * c)) / 2 * a;
x2 = (-b + sqrt(b * b - 4 * a * c)) / 2 * a;
```

Exercise R2.4. Give an example of integer overflow. Would the same example work correctly if you used floating-point? Give an example of a floating-point roundoff error. Would the same example work correctly if you used integers? When using integers, you would of course need to switch to a smaller unit, such as cents instead of dollars or milliliters instead of liters.

Exercise R2.5. Let n be an integer and x a floating-point number. Explain the difference between

```
n = x;
```

and

```
n = static_cast<int>(x + 0.5);
```

For what values of x do they give the same result? For what values of x do they give different results? What happens if x is negative?

Exercise R2.6. Find at least five *syntax* errors in the following program.

```
#include iostream

int main();
{
   cout << "Please enter two numbers:"
   cin << x, y;
   cout << "The sum of << x << "and" << y
      << "is: " x + y << "\n";
   return;
}
```

Exercise R2.7. Find at least three *logic* errors in the following program.

```
#include <iostream>

using namespace std;

int main()
{
   int total;
   int x1;
   cout << "Please enter a number:";
   cin >> x1;
   total = total + x1;
   cout << "Please enter another number:";
   int x2;
   cin >> x2;
   total = total + x1;
   float average = total / 2;
   cout << "The average of the two numbers is "
      << average << "\n"
   return 0;
}
```

Exercise R2.8. Explain the differences between 2, 2.0, "2", and "2.0".

Exercise R2.9. Explain what each of the following program segments computes:

```
x = 2;
y = x + x;
```

and

```
s = "2";
t = s + s;
```

Exercise R2.10. Uninitialized number variables can be a serious problem. Should you *always* initialize every variable with zero? Explain the advantages and disadvantages of such a strategy.

Exercise R2.11. Explain the difference between *word-oriented* and *line-oriented* input of strings. How do you achieve each in C++? When would you use each form?

Exercise R2.12. How do you get the first character of a string? The last character? How do you *remove* the first character? The last character?

Exercise R2.13. How do you get the last digit of a number? The first digit? That is, if n is 23456, how do you find out 2 and 6? *Hint:* %, log.

Exercise R2.14. This chapter contains a number of recommendations regarding variables and constants that make programs easier to read and maintain. Briefly summarize these recommendations.

Exercise R2.15. Suppose a C++ program contains the two input statements

```
cout << "Please enter your name: ";
string fname, lname;
cin >> fname >> lname;
```

and

```
cout << "Please enter your age: ";
int age;
cin >> age;
```

What is contained in the variables fname, lname, and age if the user enters the following inputs?

(a) James Carter
     56
(b) Lyndon Johnson
     49
(c) Hodding Carter 3rd
     44
(d) Richard M. Nixon
     62

Exercise R2.16. What are the values of the following expressions? In each line, assume that

```
double x = 2.5;
double y = -1.5;
int m = 18;
int n = 4;
string s = "Hello";
string t = "World";
```

(a) x + n * y - (x + n) * y
(b) m / n + m % n
(c) 5 * x - n / 5

(d) `sqrt(sqrt(n));`

(e) `static_cast<int>(x + 0.5)`

(f) `s + t;`

(g) `t + s;`

(h) `1 - (1 - (1 - (1 - (1 - n))))`

(i) `s.substr(1, 2)`

(j) `s.length() + t.length()`

PROGRAMMING EXERCISES

Exercise P2.1. Write a program that prints the values

```
1
10
100
1000
10000
100000
1000000
10000000
100000000
1000000000
10000000000
100000000000
```

as integers and as floating-point numbers. Explain the results.

Exercise P2.2. Write a program that displays the squares, cubes, and fourth powers of the numbers 1 through 5.

Exercise P2.3. Write a program that prompts the user for two integers and then prints

The sum

The difference

The product

The average

The distance (absolute value of the difference)

The maximum (the larger of the two)

The minimum (the smaller of the two)

Hint: The `max` and `min` functions are defined in the `algorithm` header.

Exercise P2.4. Write a program that prompts the user for a measurement in meters and then converts it into miles, feet, and inches.

Exercise P2.5. Write a program that prompts the user for a radius and then prints

The area and circumference of the circle with that radius

The volume and surface area of the sphere with that radius

Exercise P2.6. Write a program that asks the user for the lengths of the sides of a rectangle. Then print

The area and perimeter of the rectangle

The length of the diagonal (use the Pythagorean theorem)

Exercise P2.7. Write a program that prompts the user for

The lengths of two sides of a triangle

The size of the angle between the two sides (in degrees)

Then the program displays

The length of the third side

The sizes of the other two angles

Hint: Use the law of cosines.

Exercise P2.8. Write a program that prompts the user for

The length of a side of a triangle

The sizes of the two angles adjacent to that side (in degrees)

Then the program displays

The lengths of the other two sides

The size of the third angle

Hint: Use the law of sines.

Exercise P2.9. *Giving change.* Implement a program that directs a cashier how to give change. The program has two inputs: the amount due and the amount received from the customer. Compute the difference, and compute the dollars, quarters, dimes, nickels, and pennies that the customer should receive in return.

First transform the difference into an integer balance, denominated in pennies. Then compute the whole dollar amount. Subtract it from the balance. Compute the number of quarters needed. Repeat for dimes and nickels. Display the remaining pennies.

Exercise P2.10. Write a program that asks the user to input

The number of gallons of gas in the tank

The fuel efficiency in miles per gallon

The price of gas per gallon

Then print out how far the car can go with the gas in the tank and print the cost per 100 miles.

Exercise P2.11. *File names and extensions.* Write a program that prompts the user for the drive letter (`C`), the path (`\Windows\System`), the file name (`Readme`), and the extension (`TXT`). Then print the complete file name `C:\Windows\System\Readme.TXT`. (If you use UNIX or a Macintosh, use / or : instead to separate directories.)

Exercise P2.12. Write a program that reads a number greater than or equal to 1,000 from the user and prints it out *with a comma separating the thousands.* Here is a sample dialog; the user input is in color:

```
Please enter an integer >= 1000: 23456
23,456
```

Exercise P2.13. Write a program that reads a number between 1,000 and 999,999 from the user, where the user enters a comma in the input. Then print the number without a comma. Here is a sample dialog; the user input is in color:

```
Please enter an integer between 1,000 and 999,999: 23,456
23456
```

Hint: Read the input as a string. Measure the length of the string. Suppose it contains n characters. Then extract substrings consisting of the first $n - 4$ characters and the last three characters.

Exercise P2.14. *Printing a grid.* Write a program that prints the following grid to play tic-tac-toe.

Of course, you could simply write seven statements of the form

```
cout << "+--+--+--+";
```

You should do it the smart way, though. Define string variables to hold two kinds of patterns: a comb-shaped pattern and the bottom line. Print the comb three times and the bottom line once.

Exercise P2.15. Write a program that reads in an integer and breaks it into a sequence of individual digits. For example, the input 16384 is displayed as

```
1 6 3 8 4
```

You may assume that the input has no more than five digits and is not negative.

Exercise P2.16. The following program prints the values of sine and cosine for 0 degrees, 30 degrees, 45 degrees, 60 degrees, and 90 degrees. Rewrite the program for greater clarity by *factoring out common code.*

```
#include <iostream>

using namespace std;

const double PI = 3.141592653589793;

int main()
{
   cout << "0 degrees: " << sin(0) << " " << cos(0)
      << "\n");
   cout << "30 degrees: " << sin(30 * PI / 180) << " "
      << cos(30 * PI / 180) << "\n";
   cout << "45 degrees: " << sin(45 * PI / 180) << " "
      << cos(45 * PI / 180) << "\n";
   cout << "60 degrees: " << sin(60 * PI / 180) << " "
      << cos(60 * PI / 180) << "\n";
   cout << "90 degrees: " << sin(90 * PI / 180) << " "
      << cos(90 * PI / 180) << "\n";
   return 0;
}
```

Exercise P2.17. Rewrite the program of the preceding exercise so that the three columns of the table line up. Use formatted output.

Exercise P2.18. (Hard.) We don't yet know how to program decisions, but it turns out there is a way to fake them using substr. Write a program that asks the user to input

The number of gallons of gas in the tank

The fuel efficiency in miles per gallon

The distance the user wants to travel

Then print out

    You will make it

or

    You will not make it

The trick here is to subtract the desired distance from the number of miles the user can drive. Suppose that number is x. Suppose further we find a way of setting a value n to 1 if $x \geq 0$ and to 0 if $x < 0$. Then we can solve our problem:

```
string answer = " not "; /* note the spaces before and after not */
cout << "You will" + answer.substr(0, 5 - 4 * n) + "make it";
```

It is more fun to figure this out by yourself, but here are a few hints. First note that $x + |x|$ is $2 \cdot x$ if $x \geq 0$, 0 if $x < 0$. If you didn't have to worry about the possibility that x is zero, then you could simply look at

$$\frac{x + |x|}{x} = \begin{cases} 2 & \text{if } |x| > 0 \\ 0 & \text{if } |x| < 0 \end{cases}$$

Dividing by x doesn't work, but you can safely divide by $|x| + 1$. That gives you a fractional part, and you should use the floor and ceil functions to cope with that.

Exercise P2.19. Write a program that reads two times in military format (0900, 1730) and prints the number of hours and minutes between the two times. Here is a sample run. User input is in color.

```
Please enter the first time: 0900
Please enter the second time: 1730
8 hours 30 minutes
```

Extra credit if you can deal with the case that the first time is later than the second time:

```
Please enter the first time: 1730
Please enter the second time: 0900
15 hours 30 minutes
```

Exercise P2.20. Run the following program, and explain the output you get.

```cpp
#include <iostream>

using namespace std;

int main()
{
   int total;
   cout << "Please enter a number: ";
   double x1;
   cin >> x1;
   cout << "total = " << total << "\n";
   total = total + x1;
   cout << "total = " << total << "\n";
   cout << "Please enter a number: ";
   double x2;
   cin >> x2;
   total = total + x2;
   cout << "total = " << total << "\n";
   total = total / 2;
   cout << "total = " << total << "\n";
   cout << "The average is " << total << "\n";
   return 0;
}
```

Note the *trace messages* that are inserted to show the current contents of the total variable. Then fix up the program, run it with the trace messages in place to verify it works correctly, and remove the trace messages.

Exercise P2.21. *Writing large letters.* A large letter H can be produced like this:

```
*   *
*   *
*****
*   *
*   *
```

It can be declared as a string constant like this:

```cpp
const string LETTER_H =
   "*   *\n*   *\n*****\n*   *\n*   *\n";
```

Do the same for the letters E, L, and O. Then write the message

```
H
E
L
L
O
```

in large letters.

Exercise P2.22. Write a program that transforms numbers 1, 2, 3, . . ., 12 into the corresponding month names January, February, March, . . ., December. *Hint:* Make a very long string "January February March . . .", in which you add spaces such that each month name has *the same length*. Then use substr to extract the month you want.

Objects

CHAPTER GOALS

▶ To become familiar with objects

▶ To learn about the properties of several sample classes that were designed for this book

▶ To be able to construct objects and supply initial values

▶ To understand member functions and the dot notation

▶ To be able to modify and query the state of an object through member functions

▶ To write simple graphics programs containing points, lines, circles, and text (optional)

Y ou have learned about the basic data types of C++: numbers and strings. While it is possible to write interesting programs using only numbers and strings, most useful programs need to manipulate data items that are more complex and more closely represent entities in the real world. Examples of these data items are employee records or graphical shapes.

The C++ language is ideally suited for designing and manipulating such data items, or, as they are usually called, *objects*. It requires a certain degree of technical mastery to design new object types, but it is quite easy to manipulate object types that have been designed by others. Therefore, you will first learn how to use objects that were specifically designed for use with this textbook. In Chapter 6 you will learn how to define these and other objects. Some of the most interesting data structures that we consider are from the realm of graphics. In this chapter you will learn how to use objects that let you draw graphical shapes on the computer screen.

To keep programming simple, we introduce only a few building blocks. You will find that the ability to draw simple graphics makes programming much more fun. However, the use of the graphics library is entirely optional. The remainder of this book does not depend on graphics.

CHAPTER CONTENTS

3.1   Constructing Objects

An *object* is a value that can be created, stored, and manipulated in a programming language. In that sense, the string `"Hello"` is an object. You can create it simply by using the C++ string notation `"Hello"`. You can store it in a variable like this:

```
string greeting = "Hello";
```

You can manipulate it, for example, by computing a substring:

```
cout << greeting.substr(0, 4);
```

This particular manipulation does not affect the object. After the substring is computed, the original string is unchanged. You will see object manipulations that do change objects later in this chapter.

In C++ every object must belong to a *class*. A class is a data type, just like `int` or `double`. However, classes are *programmer-defined*, whereas `int` and `double` are defined by the designers of the C++ language. At this point, you won't yet learn how to define your own classes, so the distinction between the built-in types and programmer-defined class types is not yet important.

In this chapter you will learn to work with the class `Time`, the class `Employee`, and four classes that represent graphical shapes. These classes are not part of standard C++; they have been created for use in this book.

To use the `Time` class, you must include the file `ccc_time.h`. Unlike the `iostream` or `cmath` headers, this file is not part of the standard C++ headers. Instead, the `Time` class is supplied with this book to illustrate simple objects. Because the `ccc_time.h` file is not a system header, you do not use angle brackets `< >` in the `#include` directive; instead, you use quotation marks:

```
#include "ccc_time.h"
```

The CCC prefix is another reminder that this header file is specific to the book; CCC stands for *Computing Concepts with C++ Essentials*. The online documentation of the code library that accompanies this book gives more instructions on how to add the code for the CCC objects to your program.

Suppose you want to know how many seconds will elapse between now and midnight. This sounds like a pain to compute by hand. However, the `Time` class makes the job easy. You will see how, in this section and the next. First, you will learn how to specify an object of type `Time`. The end of the day is 11:59 P.M. and 59 seconds. Here is a `Time` object representing that time:

```
Time(23, 59, 59)
```

You specify a `Time` object by giving three values: hours, minutes, and seconds. The hours are given in "military time": between 0 and 23 hours.

When a `Time` object is specified from three integer values such as 23, 59, 59, we say that the object is *constructed* from these values, and the values used in the construction are the *construction parameters*. In general, an object value is constructed as shown in Syntax 3.1.

You should think of a time object as an entity that is very similar to a number such as 7.5 or a string such as `"Hello"`. Just as floating-point values can be stored in `double` variables, `Time` objects can be stored in `Time` variables:

```
Time day_end = Time(23, 59, 59);
```

Think of this as the analog of

```
double interest_rate = 7.5;
```

or

```
string greeting = "Hello";
```

There is a shorthand for this very common situation (See Syntax 3.2).

```
Time day_end(23, 59, 59);
```

Syntax 3.1 : Object Construction

Class_name(*construction parameters*)

Example: `Time(19, 0, 0)`

Purpose: Construct a new object for use in an expression.

Syntax 3.2 : Object Variable Definition

Class_name variable_name(construction parameters) ;

Example: `Time homework_due(19, 0, 0);`

Purpose: Define a new object variable and supply parameter values for initialization.

Figure 1

A Time Object

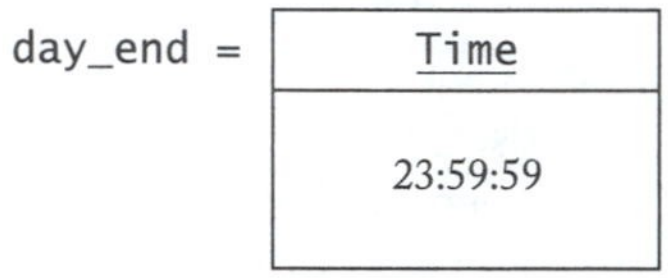

day_end =

Time
23:59:59

This defines a variable `day_end` that is initialized to the `Time` object `Time(23,59,59)`. (See Figure 1.)

Many classes have more than one construction mechanism. For example, there are two methods for constructing times: by specifying hours, minutes, and seconds, and by specifying no parameters at all. The expression

```
Time()
```

creates an object representing the current time, that is, the time when the object is constructed. Making an object with no construction parameter is called *default construction*.

Of course, you can store a default `Time` object in a variable:

```
Time now = Time();
```

The shorthand notation for using default construction is slightly inconsistent:

```
Time now; /* OK. This defines a variable and invokes the default constructor. */
```

and not

```
Time now(); /* NO! This does not define a variable */
```

For strange historical reasons, you cannot use () when defining a variable with default construction.

3.2   Using Objects

Once you have a `Time` variable, what can you do with it? Here is one useful operation. You can add a certain number of seconds to the time:

```
wake_up.add_seconds(1000);
```

Afterwards, the object in the variable `wake_up` is changed. It is no longer the time value assigned when the object was constructed, but a time object representing a time that is exactly 1,000 seconds from the time previously stored in `wake_up`. (See Figure 2.)

Whenever you apply a function (such as `add_seconds`) to an object variable (such as `wake_up`), you use the same dot notation that we already used for certain string functions:

```
int n = greeting.length();
cout << greeting.substr(0, 4);
```

Figure 2

Changing the State of an Object

wake_up =

Time
7:00:00

`wake_up.add_seconds(1000);`

Afterwards:

wake_up =

Time
7:16:40

A function that is applied to an object with the dot notation is called a *member function* in C++.

Now that you've seen how to change the state of a time object, how can you find out the current time stored in the object? You have to ask it. There are three member functions for this purpose, called

```
get_seconds()
get_minutes()
get_hours()
```

They too are applied to objects using the dot notation. (See Figure 3.)

File time1.cpp

```
 1  #include <iostream>
 2
 3  using namespace std;
 4
 5  #include "ccc_time.h"
 6
 7  int main()
 8  {
 9     Time wake_up(7, 0, 0);
10     wake_up.add_seconds(1000); /* a thousand seconds later */
11     cout << wake_up.get_hours()
12        << ":" << wake_up.get_minutes()
13        << ":" << wake_up.get_seconds() << "\n";
14
15     return 0;
16  }
```

wake_up =

Time
7:16:40

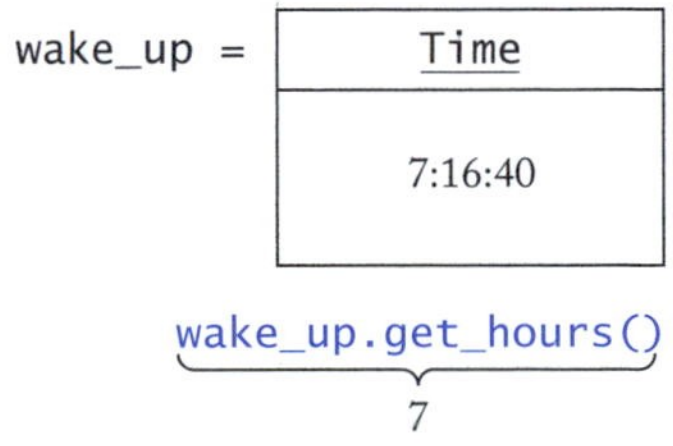

Figure 3

Querying the State of an Object

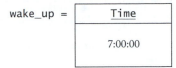

wake_up.get_hours()

7

This program displays

```
7:16:40
```

Since you can *get* the hours of a time, it seems natural to suggest that you can *set* it as well:

```
homework_due.set_hours(2); /* No! Not a supported member function */
```

Time objects do not support this member function. There is a good reason, of course. Not all hour values make sense. For example,

```
homework_due.set_hours(9999); /* Doesn't make sense */
```

Of course, one could try to come up with some meaning for such a call, but the author of the Time class decided simply not to supply these member functions. Whenever you use an object, you need to find out which member functions are supplied; other operations, however useful they may be, are simply not possible.

The Time class has only one member function that can modify Time objects: add_seconds. For example, to advance a time by one hour, you can use

```
const int SECONDS_PER_HOUR = 60 * 60;
homework_due.add_seconds(SECONDS_PER_HOUR);
```

You can move the time back by an hour:

```
homework_due.add_seconds(-SECONDS_PER_HOUR);
```

If you are entirely unhappy with the current object stored in a variable, you can overwrite it with another one:

```
homework_due = Time(23, 59, 59);
```

Figure 4 shows this replacement.

There is one final member function that a time variable can carry out: It can figure out the number of seconds between itself and another time. For example, the following

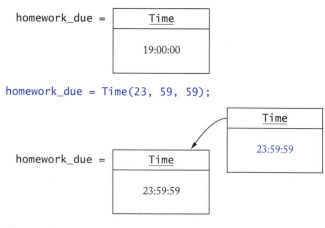

Figure 4

Replacing an Object with Another

program computes the number of seconds between the current time and the last second of the day.

File time2.cpp

```
 1 #include <iostream>
 2
 3 using namespace std;
 4
 5 #include "ccc_time.h"
 6
 7 int main()
 8 {
 9    Time now;
10    Time day_end(23, 59, 59);
11    int seconds_left = day_end.seconds_from(now);
12
13    cout << "There are "
14       << seconds_left
15       << " seconds left in this day.\n";
16
17    return 0;
18 }
```

To summarize, in C++ objects are constructed by writing the class name, followed by construction parameters in parentheses. There is a shortcut notation for initializing an object variable. Member functions are applied to objects and object variables with the dot notation. The functions of the Time class are listed in Table 1.

Name	Purpose
Time()	Constructs the current time
Time(h, m, s)	Constructs the time with hours h, minutes m, and seconds s
t.get_seconds()	Returns the seconds value of t
t.get_minutes()	Returns the minutes value of t
t.get_hours()	Returns the hours value of t
t.add_seconds(n)	Changes t to move by n seconds
t.seconds_from(t2)	Computes the number of seconds between t and t2

Table 1

Member Functions of the Time Class

Common Error   3.1

Trying to Call a Member Function without a Variable

Suppose your code contains the instruction

```
add_seconds(30); /* Error */
```

The compiler will not know which time to advance. You need to supply a variable of type Time:

```
Time liftoff(19, 0, 0);
liftoff.add_seconds(30);
```

Productivity Hint   3.1

Keyboard Shortcuts for Mouse Operations

Programmers spend a lot of time with the keyboard and the mouse. Programs and documentation are many pages long and require a lot of typing. The constant switching between the editor, compiler, and debugger takes up quite a few mouse clicks. The designers of programs such as a C++ integrated development environment have added some features to make your work easier, but it is up to you to discover them.

Just about every program has a user interface with menus and dialog boxes. Click on a menu and click on a submenu to select a task. Click on each field in a dialog box, fill in the requested answer, and click OK. These are great user interfaces for the beginner, because they are easy to master, but they are terrible user interfaces for the regular user. The constant switching between the keyboard and the mouse slows you down. You need to move a hand off the keyboard, locate the mouse, move the mouse, click the mouse, and move the hand back onto the keyboard. For that reason, most user interfaces have *keyboard shortcuts:* combinations of keystrokes that allow you to achieve the same tasks without having to switch to the mouse at all.

Many common applications use the following conventions:

- Pressing the Alt key plus the underlined key in a menu (as in "File") pulls down that menu. Inside a menu, just provide the underlined character in the submenu to activate it. For example, Alt+F O selects "File" "Open". Once your fingers know about this combination, you can open files faster than the fastest mouse artist.

- Inside dialog boxes, the Tab key is important; it moves from one option to the next. The arrow keys move within an option. The Enter key accepts all the options selected in the dialog box, and the escape key (Esc) cancels any changes.

- In a program with multiple windows, Ctrl+Tab toggles through the windows managed by that program, for example between the source and error window.

- Alt+Tab toggles between applications, letting you quickly toggle between, for example, the compiler and a folder explorer program.

- Hold down the Shift key and press the arrow keys to highlight text. Then use Ctrl+X to cut the text, Ctrl+C to copy it, and Ctrl+V to paste it. These keys are easy to remember. The V looks like an insertion mark that an editor would use to insert text. The X should remind you of crossing out text. The C is just the first letter in "Copy". (OK, so it is also the first letter in "Cut"—no mnemonic rule is perfect.) You find these reminders in the Edit menu.

Of course, the mouse has its use in text processing: to locate or select text that is on the same screen but far away from the cursor.

Take a little bit of time to learn about the keyboard shortcuts that the designers of your programs provided for you; the time investment will be repaid many times during your programming career. When you blaze through your work in the computer lab with keyboard shortcuts, you may find yourself surrounded by amazed onlookers who whisper, "I didn't know you could do *that*".

3.3   Real-Life Objects

One reason for the popularity of object-oriented programming is that it is easy to *model* entities from real life in computer programs, making programs easy to understand and modify. Consider the following program:

File employee.cpp

```
1  #include <iostream>
2
3  using namespace std;
4
5  #include "ccc_empl.h"
6
7  int main()
8  {
9     Employee harry("Hacker, Harry", 45000.00);
10
11    double new_salary = harry.get_salary() + 3000;
12    harry.set_salary(new_salary);
13
14    cout << "Name: " << harry.get_name() << "\n";
15    cout << "Salary: " << harry.get_salary() << "\n";
16
17    return 0;
18 }
```

This program creates a variable harry and initializes it with an object of type Employee. There are two construction parameters: the name of the employee and the starting salary.

We then give Harry a $3,000 raise (see Figure 5). We first find his current salary with the get_salary member function. We determine the new salary by adding $3,000. We use the set_salary member function to set the new salary.

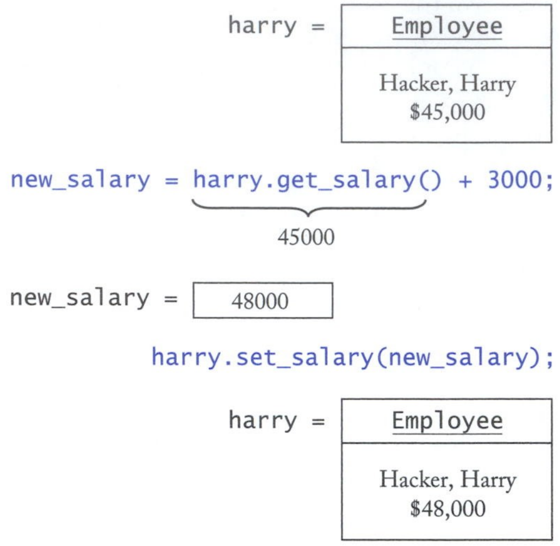

harry =

Employee
Hacker, Harry $45,000

new_salary = harry.get_salary() + 3000;

45000

new_salary = | 48000 |

harry.set_salary(new_salary);

harry =

Employee
Hacker, Harry $48,000

Figure 5

An Employee Object

Finally, we print out the name and salary number of the employee object. We use the get_name and get_salary member functions to get the name and salary.

As you can see, this program is easy to read because it carries out its computations with meaningful entities, namely employee objects.

Note that you can change the salary of an employee with the set_salary member function. However, you cannot change the name of an Employee object.

This Employee class, whose functions are listed in Table 2, is not very realistic. In real data-processing programs, employees also have ID numbers, addresses, job titles, and so on. To keep the sample programs in this book simple, this class has been stripped down to the most basic properties of employees. You need to include the header file ccc_empl.h in all programs that use the Employee class.

Name	Purpose
Employee(n, s)	Constructs an employee with name n and salary s
e.get_name()	Returns the name of e
e.get_salary()	Returns the salary of e
e.set_salary(s)	Sets salary of e to s

Table 2

Member Functions of the Employee Class

Productivity Hint   3.2

Using the Command Line Effectively

If your programming environment allows you to accomplish all routine tasks with menus and dialog boxes, you can skip this note. However, if you need to invoke the editor, the compiler, the linker, and the program manually to test, then it is well worth learning about *command line editing*.

Most operating systems (UNIX, Macintosh OS X, Windows) have a *command line interface* to interact with the computer. (In Windows, you can use the DOS command line interface by double-clicking the "Command Prompt" icon.) You launch commands at a *prompt*. The command is executed, and upon completion you get another prompt. Most professional programmers use the command line interface for repetitive tasks because it is much faster to type commands than to navigate windows and buttons.

When you develop a program, you find yourself executing the same commands over and over. Wouldn't it be nice if you didn't have to type beastly commands like

```
g++ -o myprog myprog.cpp
```

more than once? Or if you could fix a mistake rather than having to retype the command in its entirety? Many command line interfaces have an option to do just that, but they don't always make it obvious. With some versions of Windows, you need to install a program called DOSKEY. If you use UNIX, try to get the bash or tcsh shell installed for you—ask a lab assistant or system administrator to help you with the setup. With the proper setup, the up arrow key ↑ is redefined to cycle through your old commands. You can edit lines with the left and right arrow keys. You can also perform *command completion*. For example, to reissue the same gcc command, type !gcc (UNIX) or gcc and press F8 (Windows).

Random Fact   3.1

Mainframes—When Dinosaurs Ruled the Earth

When the International Business Machines Corporation, a successful manufacturer of punch-card equipment for tabulating data, first turned its attention to designing computers in the early 1950s, its planners assumed that there was a market for perhaps 50 such devices, for installation by the government, the military, and a few of the country's largest corporations. Instead, they sold about 1,500 machines of their System 650 model and went on to build and sell more powerful computers.

The so-called *mainframe* computers of the fifties, sixties, and seventies were huge. They filled up a whole room, which had to be climate-controlled to protect the delicate equipment (see Figure 6). Today, because of miniaturization technology, even mainframes are getting smaller, but they are still very expensive. (At the time of this writing, the cost for a midrange IBM 3090 is approximately 4 million dollars.)

These huge and expensive systems were an immediate success when they first appeared, because they replaced many roomfuls of even more expensive employees, who had previously performed the tasks by hand. Few of these computers do any exciting computations. They

Figure 6

A Mainframe Computer

keep mundane information, such as billing records or airline reservations; the key is that they store *lots* of information.

IBM was not the first company to build mainframe computers; that honor belongs to the Univac Corporation. However, IBM soon became the major player, partially because of technical excellence and attention to customer needs, and partially because it exploited its strengths and structured its products and services in a way that made it difficult for customers to mix IBM products with those of other vendors. In the sixties its competitors, the so-called "Seven Dwarfs"—GE, RCA, Univac, Honeywell, Burroughs, Control Data, and NCR—fell on hard times. Some went out of the computer business altogether, while others tried unsuccessfully to combine their strengths by merging their computer operations. It was generally predicted that they would all eventually fail. It was in this atmosphere that the U.S. government brought an antitrust suit against IBM in 1969. The suit went to trial in 1975 and dragged on until 1982, when the Reagan Administration abandoned it, declaring it "without merit".

Of course, by then the computing landscape had changed completely. Just as the dinosaurs gave way to smaller, nimbler creatures, three new waves of computers had appeared: the minicomputers, workstations, and microcomputers, all engineered by new companies, not the Seven Dwarfs. Today, the importance of mainframes in the marketplace has diminished, and IBM, while still a large and resourceful company, no longer dominates the computer market.

▼

▼

▼

Mainframes are still in use today for two reasons. They excel at handling large data volumes and, more importantly, the programs that control the business data have been refined over the last 20 or more years, fixing one problem at a time. Moving these programs to less expensive computers, with different languages and operating systems, is difficult and error-prone. Sun Microsystems, a leading manufacturer of workstations, was eager to prove that its mainframe system could be "downsized" to its own equipment. Sun eventually succeeded, but it took over five years—far longer than it expected.

3.4 Displaying Graphical Shapes

In the remainder of this chapter you will learn how to use a number of useful classes to render simple graphics. The graphics classes will provide a basis for interesting programming examples. This material is optional, and you can safely skip it if you are not interested in writing programs that draw graphical shapes.

There are two kinds of C++ programs that you will write in this course: *console applications* and *graphics applications*. Console applications read input from the keyboard (through `cin`) and display text output on the screen (through `cout`). Graphics programs read keystrokes and mouse clicks, and they display graphical shapes such as lines and circles, through a window object called `cwin`.

You already know how to write console programs. You include the header file `iostream` and use the `>>` and `<<` operators. To activate graphics for your programs, you must include the header file `ccc_win.h` into your program. Moreover, you need to supply the function `ccc_win_main` instead of `main` as the entry point to your program.

Unlike the `iostream` library, which is available on all C++ systems, this graphics library was created for use in this textbook. As with the `Time` and `Employee` classes, you need to add the code for the graphics objects to your programs. The online documentation for the code library describes this process.

It is slightly more complex to build a graphics program, and the `ccc_win` library does not support all computing platforms. If you prefer, you can use a text version of the graphics library that forms graphical shapes out of characters. The resulting output is not very pretty, but it is entirely sufficient for the majority of the examples in this book (see, for example, Figure 19). The online documentation of the code library describes how to select the text version of the graphics library.

To display a graphics object, you cannot just send it to `cout`:

```
Circle c;
. . .
cout << c; /* Won't display the circle */
```

The `cout` stream displays characters on the terminal, not pixels in a window. Instead, you must send the characters to a window called `cwin`:

```
cwin << c; /* The circle will appear in the graphics window */
```

In the next section you will learn how to make objects that represent graphical shapes.

3.5   Graphics Structures

Points, circles, lines, and messages are the four graphical elements that you will use to create diagrams. A *point* has an *x*- and a *y*-coordinate. For example,

```
Point(1, 3)
```

is a point with *x*-coordinate 1 and *y*-coordinate 3. What can you do with a point? You can display it in a graphics window.

File point.cpp

```
1 #include "ccc_win.h"
2
3 int ccc_win_main()
4 {
5    cwin << Point(1, 3);
6
7    return 0;
8 }
```

You frequently use points to make more complex graphical shapes.

```
Circle(Point(1, 3), 2.5);
```

This defines a circle whose center is the point with coordinates (1, 3) and whose radius is 2.5.

As always, you can store a Point object in a variable of type Point. The following code defines and initializes a Point variable and then displays the point. Then a circle with center p is created and also displayed (Figure 7).

File circle.cpp

```
1 #include "ccc_win.h"
2
3 int ccc_win_main()
4 {
5    Point p(1, 3);
6    cwin << p << Circle(p, 2.5);
7
8    return 0;
9 }
```

Figure 7

Output from circle.cpp

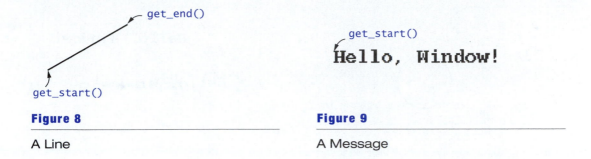

Figure 8

A Line

Figure 9

A Message

Two points can be joined by a *line* (Figure 8).

File line.cpp

```
1 #include "ccc_win.h"
2
3 int ccc_win_main()
4 {
5    Point p(1, 3);
6    Point q(4, 7);
7    Line s(p, q);
8    cwin << s;
9
10   return 0;
11 }
```

In a graphics window you can display text anywhere you like. You need to specify what you want to show and where it should appear (Figure 9).

File hellowin.cpp

```
1 #include "ccc_win.h"
2
3 int ccc_win_main()
4 {
5    Point p(1, 3);
6    Message greeting(p, "Hello, Window!");
7    cwin << greeting;
8
9    return 0;
10 }
```

The point parameter specifies the *upper left corner* of the message. The second parameter can be either a string or a number.

There is one member function that all our graphical classes implement: move. If obj is a point, circle, line, or message, then

```
obj.move(dx, dy)
```

changes the position of the object, moving the entire object by dx units in the *x*-direction

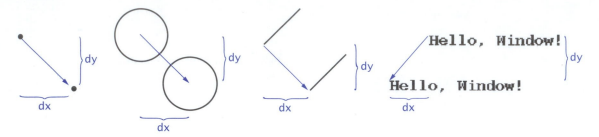

Figure 10

The move Operation

and dy units in the *y*-direction. Either or both of dx and dy can be zero or negative (see Figure 10). For example, the following code draws a square (see Figure 11).

File square.cpp

```
1  #include "ccc_win.h"
2
3  int ccc_win_main()
4  {
5     Point p(1, 3);
6     Point q = p;
7     Point r = p;
8     q.move(0, 1);
9     r.move(1, 0);
10    Line s(p, q);
11    Line t(p, r);
12    cwin << s << t;
13    s.move(1, 0);
14    t.move(0, 1);
15    cwin << s << t;
16
17    return 0;
18 }
```

After a graphical object has been constructed and perhaps moved, you sometimes want to know where it is currently located. There are two member functions for Point objects: get_x and get_y. They get the *x*- and *y*-positions of the point.

The get_center and get_radius member functions return the center and radius of a circle. The get_start and get_end member functions return the starting point and end

Figure 11

Square Drawn by square.cpp

point of a line. The `get_start` and `get_text` member functions on a `Message` object return the starting point and the message text. Since `get_center`, `get_start`, and `get_end` return `Point` objects, you may need to apply `get_x` or `get_y` to them to determine their *x*- and *y*-coordinates. For example,

```
Circle c(. . .);
. . .
double cx = c.get_center().get_x();
```

You now know how to construct graphical objects, and you have seen all member functions for manipulating and querying them (summarized in Tables 3 through 6). The design of these classes was purposefully kept simple, but as a result some common tasks require a little ingenuity (see Productivity Hint 3.3).

Table 3

Functions of the
`Point` Class

Name	Purpose
`Point(x, y)`	Constructs a point at location (x, y)
`p.get_x()`	Returns the *x*-coordinate of point p
`p.get_y()`	Returns the *y*-coordinate of point p
`p.move(dx, dy)`	Moves point p by (dx, dy)

Table 4

Functions of the
`Circle` Class

Name	Purpose
`Circle(p, r)`	Constructs a circle with center p and radius r
`c.get_center()`	Returns the center point of circle c
`c.get_radius()`	Returns the radius of circle c
`c.move(dx, dy)`	Moves circle c by (dx, dy)

Table 5

Functions of the
`Line` Class

Name	Purpose
`Line(p, q)`	Constructs a line joining points p and q
`l.get_start()`	Returns the starting point of line l
`l.get_end()`	Returns the ending point of line l
`l.move(dx, dy)`	Moves line l by (dx, dy)

Name	Purpose
Message(p, s)	Constructs a message with starting point p and text string s
Message(p, x)	Constructs a message with starting point p and a label equal to the number x
m.get_start()	Returns the starting point of message m
m.get_text()	Gets the text string of message m
m.move(dx, dy)	Moves message m by (dx, dy)

Table 6

Functions of the
Message Class

Productivity Hint 3.3

Think of Points as Objects, Not Pairs of Numbers

Suppose you want to draw a square starting with the point p as the upper left corner and with side length 1. If p has coordinates (p_x, p_y), then the upper right corner is the point with coordinates $(p_x + 1, p_y)$. Of course, you can program that:

```
Point q(p.get_x() + 1, p.get_y()); /* Cumbersome */
```

Try to think about points as objects, not pairs of numbers. Taking this point of view, there is a more elegant solution: Initialize q to be the same point as p, then move it to where it belongs:

```
Point q = p;
q.move(1, 0); /* Simple */
```

Random Fact 3.2

Computer Graphics

The generation and manipulation of visual images is one of the most exciting applications of the computer. We distinguish between different kinds of graphics.

Diagrams, such as numeric charts or maps, are artifacts that convey information to the viewer (see Figure 12). They do not directly depict anything that occurs in the natural world, but are a tool for visualizing information.

Scenes are computer-generated images that attempt to depict images of the real or an imagined world (see Figure 13). It turns out to be quite a challenge to render light and shadows accurately. Special effort must be taken so that the images do not look too neat and simple; clouds, rocks, leaves, and dust in the real world have a complex and somewhat random appearance. The degree of realism in these images is constantly improving.

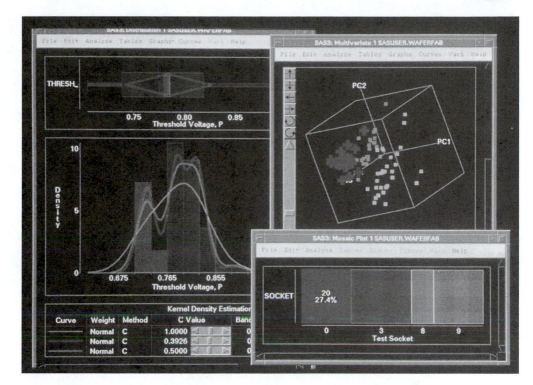

Figure 12

Diagrams

Figure 13

Scene

▼   **Figure 14**

Manipulated Image

Manipulated images are photographs or film footage of actual events that have been converted to digital form and edited by the computer (see Figure 14). For example, film sequences of the movie *Apollo 13* were produced by starting from actual images and changing the perspective, showing the launch of the rocket from a more dramatic viewpoint.

Computer graphics is one of the most challenging fields in computer science. It requires processing of massive amounts of information at very high speed. New algorithms are constantly invented for this purpose. Viewing overlapping three-dimensional objects with curved boundaries requires advanced mathematical tools. Realistic modeling of textures and biological entities requires extensive knowledge of mathematics, physics, and biology.

3.6   Choosing a Coordinate System

We need to have an agreement on the meaning of particular coordinates. For example, where is the point with *x*-coordinate 1 and *y*-coordinate 3 located? Some graphics systems use pixels, the individual dots on the display, as coordinates, but different displays have different pixel counts and densities. Using pixels makes it difficult to write programs that look pleasant on every display screen. The library supplied with this book uses a coordinate system that is independent of the display.

Figure 15 shows the default coordinate system used by this book's library. The origin is at the center of the screen, and the *x*-axis and *y*-axis are 10 units long in either direction. The axes do not actually appear (unless you create them yourself by drawing Line objects).

This default coordinate system is fine for simple test programs, but it is *useless* when dealing with real data. For example, suppose we want to show a graph plotting the average temperature (degrees Celsius) in Phoenix, Arizona, for every month of the year. The temperature ranges from 11°C in January to 33°C in July (see Table 7).

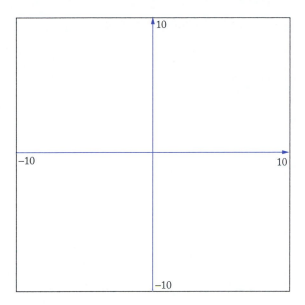

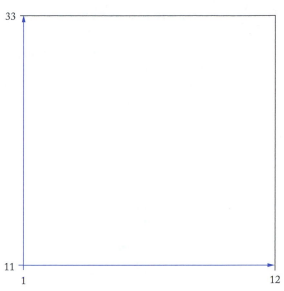

Figure 15

Default Coordinate System for
Graphics Library

Figure 16

Coordinate System for Temperature

Even the January data

```
cwin << Point(1, 11);
```

won't show up in the window at all! In this situation, we need to change from the default coordinate system to one that makes sense for our particular program. Here, the x-coordinates are the month values, ranging from 1 to 12. The y-coordinates are the temperature values, ranging from 11 to 33. Figure 16 shows the coordinate system that we need. As you can see, the top left corner is (1, 33) and the bottom right corner is (12, 11).

Table 7

Average Temperatures
in Phoenix, Arizona

Month	Average Temperature	Month	Average Temperature
January	11°C	July	33°C
February	13°C	August	32°C
March	16°C	September	29°C
April	20°C	October	23°C
May	25°C	November	16°C
June	31°C	December	12°C

To select this coordinate system, use the following instruction:

```
cwin.coord(1, 33, 12, 11);
```

Following a common convention in graphics systems, you must first specify the desired coordinates for the *top left* corner (which has *x*-coordinate 1 and *y*-coordinate 33), then the desired coordinates for the bottom right corner (*x* = 12, *y* = 11).

Here is the complete program:

File phoenix.cpp

```
1 #include "ccc_win.h"
2
3 int ccc_win_main()
4 {
5    cwin.coord(1, 33, 12, 11);
6    cwin << Point(1, 11);
7    cwin << Point(2, 13);
8    cwin << Point(3, 16);
9    cwin << Point(4, 20);
10   cwin << Point(5, 25);
11   cwin << Point(6, 31);
12   cwin << Point(7, 33);
13   cwin << Point(8, 32);
14   cwin << Point(9, 29);
15   cwin << Point(10, 23);
16   cwin << Point(11, 16);
17   cwin << Point(12, 12);
18
19   return 0;
20 }
```

Figure 17 shows the output of the program.

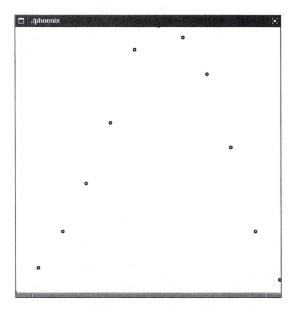

Figure 17

Average Temperatures in
Phoenix, Arizona

Productivity Hint

3.4

Choose a Convenient Coordinate System

Whenever you deal with real-world data, you should set a coordinate system that is matched to the data. Figure out which range of *x*- and *y*-coordinates is most convenient for you. For example, suppose you want to display a tic-tac-toe board (see Figure 18).

You could labor mightily and figure out where the lines are in relation to the default coordnate system, or you can simply set your own coordinate system with (0, 0) in the top left corner and (3, 3) in the bottom right corner.

```
#include "ccc_win.h"

int ccc_win_main()
{
   cwin.coord(0, 0, 3, 3);
   Line horizontal(Point(0, 1), Point(3, 1));
   cwin << horizontal;
   horizontal.move(0, 1);
   cwin << horizontal;
   Line vertical(Point(1, 0), Point(1, 3));
   cwin << vertical;
   vertical.move(1, 0);
   cwin << vertical;

   return 0;
}
```

Some people have horrible memories about coordinate transformations from their high school geometry class and have taken a vow never to think about coordinates again for the remainder of their lives. If you are among them, you should reconsider. In the CCC graphics library, coordinate systems are your friend—they do all the horrible algebra for you, so you don't have to program it by hand.

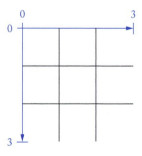

Figure 18

Coordinate System for a
Tic-Tac-Toe Board

Getting Input from the Graphics Window

Just as stream output does not work with the graphics window, you cannot use stream input either. Instead, you must ask the window to get input for you. The command is

```
string response = cwin.get_string(prompt);
```

This is how you inquire about the user name:

```
string name = cwin.get_string("Please type your name:");
```

The prompt and a field for typing the input are displayed in a special input area. Depending on your computer system, the input area is in a dialog box or at the top or bottom of the graphics window. The user can then type input. After the user hits the Enter key, the user's keystrokes are placed into the `name` string. The message prompt is then removed from the screen.

The `get_string` function always returns a string. Use `get_int` or `get_double` to read an integer or floating-point number:

```
int age = cwin.get_int("Please enter your age:");
```

The user can specify a point with the mouse. To prompt the user for mouse input, use

```
Point response = cwin.get_mouse(prompt);
```

Name	Purpose
`w.coord(x1, y1, x2, y2)`	Sets the coordinate system for subsequent drawing: (x1, y1) is the top left corner, (x2, y2) the bottom right corner
`w << x`	Displays the object x (a point, circle, line, or message) in window w
`w.clear()`	Clears window w (erases its contents)
`w.get_string(p)`	Displays prompt p in window w and returns the entered string
`w.get_int(p)`	Displays prompt p in window w and returns the entered integer
`w.get_double(p)`	Displays prompt p in window w and returns the entered floating-point value
`w.get_mouse(p)`	Displays prompt p in window w and returns the mouse click point

Table 8

Functions of the GraphicWindow Class

For example,

```
Point center = cwin.get_mouse("Click center of circle");
```

The user can move the mouse to the desired location. Once the user clicks on the mouse button, the prompt is cleared and the selected point is returned.

Here is a program that puts these functions (summarized in Table 8) to work. It asks the user to enter a name and to try to click inside a circle. Then the program displays the point that the user specified.

File click.cpp

```
1  #include "ccc_win.h"
2
3  int ccc_win_main()
4  {
5     string name = cwin.get_string("Please type your name:");
6     Circle c(Point(0, 0), 1);
7     cwin << c;
8     Point m = cwin.get_mouse("Please click inside the circle.");
9     cwin << m << Message(m, name + ", you clicked here");
10
11    return 0;
12 }
```

3.8 Comparing Visual and Numerical Information

The next example shows how one can look at the same problem both visually and numerically. You want to determine the intersection between a line and a circle. The circle is centered on the screen. The user specifies a radius of the circle and the y-intercept of a horizontal line. You then draw the circle and the line.

File intsect1.cpp

```
1  #include "ccc_win.h"
2
3  int ccc_win_main()
4  {
5     double radius = cwin.get_double("Radius: ");
6     Circle c(Point(0, 0), radius);
7
8     double b = cwin.get_double("Line position: ");
9     Line s(Point(-10, b), Point(10, b));
10
11    cwin << c << s;
12
13    return 0;
14 }
```

Figure 19 shows the output of this program.

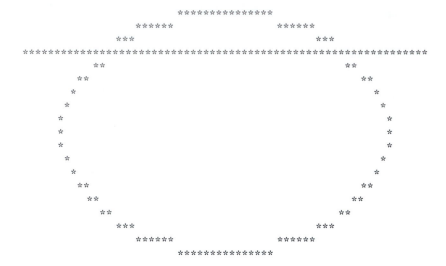

Figure 19

Intersection of a Line and a Circle
(Using the Text Version of the Graphics Library)

Now suppose you would like to know the *exact* coordinates of the intersection points. The equation of the circle is

$$x^2 + y^2 = r^2$$

where r is the radius (which was given by the user). You also know y. A horizontal line has equation $y = b$, and b is another user input. Thus x is the remaining unknown, and you can solve for it. You expect two solutions, corresponding to

$$x_{1,2} = \pm\sqrt{r^2 - b^2}$$

Plot both points and label them with the numerical values. If you do it right, these two points will show up right on top of the actual intersections in the picture. If you do it wrong, the two points will be at the wrong place.

Here is the code to compute and plot the intersection points.

File intsect2.cpp

```
1 #include "ccc_win.h"
2 #include <cmath>
3
4 using namespace std;
5
6 int ccc_win_main()
7 {
8    double radius = cwin.get_double("Radius: ");
```

```
 9      Circle c(Point(0, 0), radius);
10
11      double b = cwin.get_double("Line position: ");
12      Line s(Point(-10, b), Point(10, b));
13
14      cwin << c << s;
15
16      double root = sqrt(radius * radius - b * b);
17
18      Point p1(root, b);
19      Point p2(-root, b);
20
21      Message m1(p1, p1.get_x());
22      Message m2(p2, p2.get_x());
23
24      cwin << p1 << p2 << m1 << m2;
25
26      return 0;
27 }
```

Figure 20 shows the combined output. The results match perfectly, so you can be confident that you did everything correctly. See Quality Tip 3.1 for more information on verifying that this program works correctly.

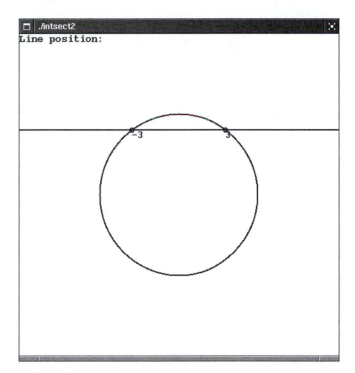

Figure 20

Computing the Intersection Points

At this point you should be careful to specify only lines that intersect the circle. If the line doesn't meet the circle, then the program will attempt to compute a square root of a negative number, and it will terminate with a math error. You do not yet know how to implement a test to protect against this situation. That will be the topic of the next chapter.

Quality Tip   3.1

Calculate Sample Data Manually

It is difficult or impossible to prove that a given program functions correctly in all cases. For gaining confidence in the correctness of a program, or for understanding why it does not function as it should, manually calculated sample data are invaluable. If the program arrives at the same results as the manual calculation, your confidence in it is strengthened. If the manual results differ from the program results, you have a starting point for the debugging process.

Surprisingly, many programmers are reluctant to perform any manual calculations as soon as a program carries out the slightest bit of algebra. Their math phobia kicks in, and they irrationally hope that they can avoid the algebra and beat the program into submission by random tinkering, such as rearranging the + and − signs. Random tinkering is always a great time sink, but it rarely leads to useful results.

It is much smarter to look for test cases that are easy to compute and representative of the problem to be solved. The example in Figure 21 shows three easy cases that can be computed by hand and then compared against program runs.

First, let the horizontal line pass through the center of the circle. Then you expect the distance between the center and the intersection point to be the same as the radius of the circle. Let the radius be 2. The y position is 0 (the center of the window). You expect

$$x_1 = \sqrt{2^2 - 0^2} = 2, \quad x_2 = -2$$

Now, that wasn't so hard.

Next, let the horizontal line touch the circle on the top. Again, fix the radius to be 2. Then the y position is also 2, and of course $x_1 = x_2 = 0$. That was pretty easy, too.

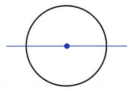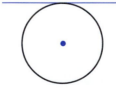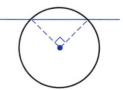

Figure 21

Three Test Cases

The first two cases were *boundary test cases* of the problem. A program may work correctly for several special cases but still fail for more typical input values. Therefore you must come up with an intermediate test case, even if it means a bit more computation. Choose a configuration where the center of the circle and the points of intersection form a right triangle. If the radius of the circle is again 2, then the height of the triangle is $\frac{1}{2}\sqrt{2}$. This looks complicated; try instead choosing the height of the triangle to be 2. Thus, the base has length 4, and the radius of the circle is $2\sqrt{2}$. Therefore, enter radius 2.828427, enter *y*-position 2, and expect $x_1 = 2, x_2 = -2$.

Running the program with these three inputs confirms the manual calculations. The computer calculations and the manual reasoning did not use the same formulas, so you can have a great deal of confidence in the validity of the program.

Random Fact   3.3

Computer Networks and the Internet

Home computers and laptops are usually self-contained units with no permanent connection to other computers. Office and lab computers, however, are usually connected with each other and with larger computers: so-called *servers*. A server can store application programs and make them available on all computers on the network. Servers can also store data, such as schedules and mail messages, that everyone can retrieve. Networks that connect the computers in one building are called *local area networks*, or LANs.

Other networks connect computers in geographically dispersed locations. Such networks are called *wide area networks* or WANs. The most prominent wide area network is the *Internet*. At the time of this writing, the Internet is in a phase of explosive growth. In 1994 the Internet connected about two million computers. Nobody knows for certain how many users have access to the Internet, but in 2002 the user population is estimated to be about half a billion. The Internet grew out of the ARPAnet, a network of computers at universities that was funded by the Advanced Research Planning Agency of the U.S. Department of Defense. The original motivation behind the creation of the network was the desire to run programs on remote computers. Using remote execution, a researcher at one institution would be able to access an underutilized computer at a different site. It quickly became apparent, though, that remote execution was not what the network was actually used for. The principal usage was *electronic mail:* the transfer of messages between computer users at different locations. To this day, electronic mail is one of the most compelling applications of the Internet.

Over time, more and more *information* became available on the Internet. The information was created by researchers and hobbyists and made freely available to anyone, either out the goodness of their hearts or for self-promotion. For example, the GNU project is producing a set of high-quality operating system utilities and program development tools that can be used freely by anyone (`ftp://prep.ai.mit.edu/pub/gnu`). Project Gutenberg makes available the text of important classic books, whose copyright has expired, in computer-readable form (`http://www.promo.net/pg`).

The first interfaces to retrieve this information were clumsy and hard to use. All that changed with the appearance of the *World Wide Web* (WWW). The World Wide Web brought two major advances to Internet information. The information could contain *graphics* and *fonts*—a great improvement over the older text-only format—and it became possible to

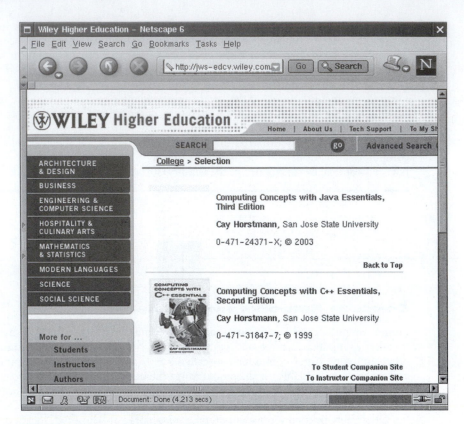

Figure 22

A Web Browser

embed *links* to other information pages. Using a *browser* such as *Netscape*, exploring the information becomes easy and fun (Figure 22).

CHAPTER SUMMARY

1. We use objects in programs when we need to manipulate data that are more complex than just numbers and strings. Every object belongs to a class. A class determines the behavior of its objects. In this chapter you became familiar with objects from a number of classes that were predefined for use with this textbook. However, you must wait until Chapter 6 to be able to define your own classes.

2. Objects are constructed with the constructor notation. Once an object is constructed, member functions can be applied to it with the dot notation.

3. This book describes a library of graphical structures that are used for interesting and entertaining examples. Points, lines, circles, and messages can be displayed in a win-

dow on the computer screen. Programs can obtain both text and mouse input from the user. When writing programs that display data sets, you should select a coordinate system that fits the data points.

FURTHER READING

[1] C. Eames and R. Eames, *A Computer Perspective*, Harvard Press, Cambridge, MA, 1973. A pictorial based on an exhibition of the history and social impact of computing. It contains many entertaining and interesting pictures of historic computing devices, their inventors, and their impact on modern life.

REVIEW EXERCISES

Exercise R3.1. Explain the difference between an object and a class.

Exercise R3.2. Give the C++ code for an *object* of class Time and for an *object variable* of class Time.

Exercise R3.3. Explain the differences between a member function and a nonmember function.

Exercise R3.4. Explain the difference between

```
Point(3, 4);
```

and

```
Point p(3, 4);
```

Exercise R3.5. What are the construction parameters for a Circle object?

Exercise R3.6. What is default construction?

Exercise R3.7. Give the C++ code to construct the following objects:
   (a)   Lunch time
   (b)   The current time
   (c)   The top right corner of the graphics window in the default coordinate system
   (d)   Your instructor as an employee (make a guess for the salary)
   (e)   A circle filling the entire graphics window in the default coordinate system
   (f)   A line representing the *x*-axis from −10 to 10.
Write the code for objects, not object variables.

Exercise R3.8. Repeat the preceding exercise, but now define variables that are initialized with the required values.

Exercise R3.9. Find the errors in the following statements:

(a) `Time now();`

(b) `Point p = (3, 4);`

(c) `p.set_x(-1);`

(d) `cout << Time`

(e) `Time due_date(2004, 4, 15);`

(f) `due_date.move(2, 12);`

(g) `seconds_from(millennium);`

(h) `Employee harry("Hacker", "Harry", 35000);`

(i) `harry.set_name("Hacker, Harriet");`

Exercise R3.10. Describe all constructors of the `Time` class. List all member functions that can be used to change a `Time` object. List all member functions that don't change the `Time` object.

Exercise R3.11. What is the value of `t` after the following operations?

```
Time t;
t = Time(20, 0, 0);
t.add_seconds(1000);
t.add_seconds(-400);
```

Exercise R3.12. If `t1` and `t2` are objects of class `Time`, is the following true or false?

`t1.add_seconds(t2.seconds_from(t1))` is the same time as `t2`

Exercise R3.13. Which five classes are used in this book for graphics programming?

Exercise R3.14. What is the value of `c.get_center` and `c.get_radius` after the following operations?

```
Circle c(Point(1, 2), 3);
c.move(4, 5);
```

Exercise R3.15. You want to plot a bar chart showing the grade distribution of all students in your class (where A = 4.0, F = 0). What coordinate system would you choose to make the plotting as simple as possible?

Exercise R3.16. Let `c` be any circle. Write C++ code to plot the circle `c` and another circle that touches `c`. *Hint:* Use move.

Exercise R3.17. Write C++ instructions to display the letters X and T in a graphics window, by plotting line segments.

Exercise R3.18. Suppose you run the program `intsect2.cpp` and give a value of 5 for the radius of the circle and 4 for the line position. Without actually running the program, determine what values you will obtain for the intersection points.

Exercise R3.19. Introduce an error in the program `intsect2.cpp`, by computing `root = sqrt(radius * radius + b * b)`. Run the program. What happens to the intersection points?

PROGRAMMING EXERCISES

Exercise P3.1. Write a program that asks for the due date of the next assignment (hour, minutes). Then print the number of minutes between the current time and the due date.

Exercise P3.2. Write a graphics program that prompts the user to click on three points. Then draw a triangle joining the three points. *Hint:* To give the user feedback about the click, it is a nice touch to draw the point after each click.

```
Point p = cwin.get_mouse("Please click on the first point");
cwin << p; /* Feedback for the user */
```

Exercise P3.3. Write a graphics program that prompts the user to click on the center of a circle, then on one of the points on the boundary of the circle. Draw the circle that the user specified. *Hint:* The radius of the circle is the distance between the two points, which is computed as

$$\sqrt{\left(a_x - b_x\right)^2 + \left(a_y - b_y\right)^2}$$

Exercise P3.4. Write a graphics program that prompts the user to click on two points. Then draw a line joining the points and write a message displaying the *slope* of the line; that is, the "rise over run" ratio. The message should be displayed at the *midpoint* of the line.

Exercise P3.5. Write a graphics program that prompts the user to click on two points. Then draw a line joining the points and write a message displaying the *length* of the line, as computed by the Pythagorean formula. The message should be displayed at the *midpoint* of the line.

Exercise P3.6. Write a graphics program that prompts the user to click on three points. Then draw a circle passing through the three points.

Exercise P3.7. Write a program that prompts the user for the first name and last name of an employee and a starting salary. Then give the employee a 5 percent raise, and print out the name and salary information stored in the employee object.

Exercise P3.8. Write a program that prompts the user for the names and salaries of three employees. Then print out the average salaries of the employees.

Exercise P3.9. Write a program to plot the following face.

Exercise P3.10. Write a program to plot the string "HELLO", using just lines and circles. Do not use the Message class, and do not use cout.

Exercise P3.11. Write a program that lets a user select two lines by prompting the user to click on both end points of the first segment, then on both end points of the second segment. Then compute the point of intersection of the lines extending through those segments, and plot it. (If the segments are parallel, then the lines don't intersect, or they are identical. In the formulas computing the intersection, this will manifest itself as a division by 0. Since you don't yet know how to write code involving decisions, your program will terminate when the division by 0 happens. Doing so is acceptable for *this* assignment.)

Here is the mathematics to compute the point of intersection. If $a = (a_x, a_y)$ and $b = (b_x, b_y)$ are the end points of the first line segment, then $ta + (1 - t)b$ runs through all points on the first line as t runs from $-\infty$ to ∞. If $c = (c_x, c_y)$ and $d = (d_x, d_y)$ are the end points of the second line segment, the second line is the collection of points $uc + (1 - u)d$. The point of intersection is the point lying on both lines. That is, it is the solution of both

$$ta + (1 - t)b = uc + (1 - u)d$$

and

$$(a - b)t + (d - c)u = d - b$$

Writing the x and y coordinates separately, we get a system of two linear equations

$$\left(a_x - b_x\right)t + \left(d_x - c_x\right)u = d_x - b_x$$
$$\left(a_y - b_y\right)t + \left(d_y - c_y\right)u = d_y - b_y$$

Find the solutions of this system. You just need the value for t. Then compute the point of intersection as $ta + (1 - t)b$.

Exercise P3.12. *Plotting a data set.* Make a bar chart to plot a data set like the following:

Name	Longest span (ft)
Golden Gate	4,200
Brooklyn	1,595
Delaware Memorial	2,150
Mackinaw	3,800

Prompt the user to type in four names and measurements. Then display a bar graph. Make the bars horizontal for easier labeling.

Golden Gate

Brooklyn

Delaware Memorial

Mackinaw

Hint: Set the window coordinates to 5,000 in the *x*-direction and 4 in the *y*-direction.

Exercise P3.13. Write a program that displays the Olympic rings. *Hint:* Construct and display the first circle, then call move four times.

Exercise P3.14. Write a graphics program that asks the user to enter the names of three employees and their salaries. Make three employee objects. Draw a stick chart showing the names and salaries of the employees.

Hacker, Harry

Cracker, Carl

Bates, Bill

Exercise P3.15. Write a graphics program that asks the user to enter four data values. Then draw a pie chart showing the data values.

Exercise P3.16. Write a graphics program that draws a clock face with the current time:

Hint: You need to determine the angles of the hour hand and the minute hand. The angle of the minute hand is easy: The minute hand travels 360 degrees in 60 minutes. The angle of the hour hand is harder; it travels 360 degrees in 12 × 60 minutes.

Exercise P3.17. Write a program that tests how fast a user can type. Get the time. Ask the user to type "The quick brown fox jumps over the lazy dog". Read a line of input. Get the current time again in another variable of type Time. Print out the seconds between the two times.

Exercise P3.18. Your boss, Juliet Jones, is getting married and decides to change her name. Complete the following program so that you can type in the new name for the boss:

```
int main()
{
    Employee boss("Jones, Juliet", 45000.00);
    /* your code goes here; leave the code above and below unchanged */

    cout << "Name: " << boss.get_name() << "\n";
    cout << "Salary: " << boss.get_salary() << "\n";

    return 0;
}
```

The problem is that there is no `set_name` member function for the `Employee` class. *Hint:* Make a new object of type `Employee` with the new name and the same salary. Then assign the new object to `boss`.

Exercise P3.19. Write a program that draws the picture of a house. It could be as simple as the figure below, or if you like, make it more elaborate (3-D, skyscraper, marble columns in the entryway, whatever).

Basic Control Flow

▶ To be able to implement decisions and loops using `if` and `while` statements

▶ To understand statement blocks

▶ To learn how to compare integers, floating-point numbers, and strings

▶ To develop strategies for processing input and handling input errors

▶ To understand the Boolean data type

▶ To avoid infinite loops and off-by-one errors

The programs you have seen to this point are able to do fast computations and render graphs, but they are very inflexible. Except for variations in the input, they work the same way with every program run. The programs you have worked with so far are further limited in that they run through a sequence of instructions once, then stop.

One of the essential features of nontrivial computer programs is their ability to make decisions and to carry out different actions, depending on the nature of the inputs. In this chapter, you will learn how to program simple and complex decisions, as well as how to implement instruction sequences that are repeated multiple times.

4.1   The if Statement

The if statement is used to implement a decision. It has two parts: a *test* and a *body* (see Syntax 4.1). If the test succeeds, the body of the statement is executed.

The body of the if statement can consist of a single statement:

```
if (area < 0)
   cout << "Error: Negative area.\n";
```

This warning message is displayed only when the area is negative (see Figure 1).

Quite often, however, the body of the if statement consists of multiple statements that must be executed in sequence whenever the test is successful. These statements must be grouped together to form a *block statement* by enclosing them in braces { } (see Syntax 4.2). For example,

```
if (area < 0)
{
   cout << "Error: Negative area.\n";
   return 1;
}
```

Syntax 4.1 : if Statement

if (*condition*) *statement*

Example: `if (x >= 0) y = sqrt(x);`

Purpose: Execute the statement if the condition is true.

Syntax 4.2 : Block Statement

```
{
    statement₁;
    statement₂;
    ...
    statementₙ;
}
```

Example:
```
{
    double length = sqrt(area);
    cout << area << "\n";
}
```

Purpose: Group several statements into a block that can be controlled by another statement.

Figure 1

A Decision

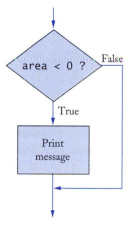

If the area is negative, then all statements inside the braces are executed: a message is printed, and the function returns an error code.

The following program puts this technique to work. This program simply prints an error message and returns an error code if the input is invalid. (It is possible to test whether a program terminated successfully or with an error, but the details are system-dependent. We simply follow the convention of having main return 0 when a program completes its task normally, a nonzero value otherwise.)

File area1.cpp

```
1 #include <iostream>
2 #include <string>
3 #include <cmath>
4
5 using namespace std;
6
7 int main()
8 {
```

```
 9    double area;
10    cout << "Please enter the area of a square: ";
11    cin >> area;
12    if (area < 0)
13    {
14       cout << "Error: Negative area.\n";
15       return 1;
16    }
17
18    /* now we know that area is >= 0 */
19
20    double length = sqrt(area);
21    cout << "The side length of the square is "
22       << length << "\n";
23
24    return 0;
25 }
```

Quality Tip   4.1

Brace Layout

The compiler doesn't care where you place braces, but we strongly recommend that you follow the simple rule of making { and } line up.

```
int main()
{
   double area;
   cin >> area;
   if (area >= 0)
   {
      double length = sqrt(area);
      ...
   }
   ...
   return 0;
}
```

This scheme makes it easy to spot matching braces. Some programmers put the opening brace on the same line as the `if`:

```
if (area >= 0) {
   double length = sqrt(area);
   ...
}
```

which makes it harder to match the braces, but it saves a line of code, allowing you to view more code on the screen without scrolling. There are passionate advocates of both styles.

It is important that you pick a layout scheme and stick with it consistently within a given programming project. Which scheme you choose may depend on your personal preference or a coding style guide that you need to follow.

Productivity Hint   4.1

Tabs

Block-structured code has the property that nested statements are indented by one or more levels:

```cpp
int main()
{
   double area;
   ...
   if (area >= 0)
   {
      double length = sqrt(area);
      ...
   }
   ...
   return 0;
}
 ↑  ↑  ↑
 0  1  2
```
Indentation level

How many spaces should you use per indentation level? Some programmers use eight spaces per level, but that isn't a good choice:

```cpp
int main()
{
        double area;
        ...
        if (area >= 0)
        {
                double length = sqrt(area);
                ...
        }
        ...
        return 0;
}
```

It crowds the code too much to the right side of the screen. As a consequence, long expressions frequently must be broken into separate lines. More common values are 2, 3, or 4 spaces per indentation level.

How do you move the cursor from the leftmost column to the appropriate indentation level? A perfectly reasonable strategy is to hit the space bar a sufficient number of times. However, many programmers use the Tab key instead. A tab moves the cursor to the next tab stop. By default, there are tab stops every 8 columns, but most editors let you change that value; you should find out how to set your editor's tab stops to, say, every 3 columns. (Note that the Tab key does not simply enter three spaces. It moves the cursor to the next tab column.)

Some editors actually help you out with an *autoindent* feature. They automatically insert as many tabs or spaces as the preceding line had, because it is quite likely that the new line is supposed to be on the same indentation level. If it isn't, you must add or remove a tab, but that is still faster than tabbing all the way from the left margin.

As nice as tabs are for data entry, they have one disadvantage: They can mess up printouts. If you send a file with tabs to a printer, the printer may either ignore the tabs altogether or set

▼

tab stops every eight columns. It is therefore best to save and print your files with spaces instead of tabs. Most editors have settings to automatically convert tabs to spaces when saving or printing. Look at the documentation of your editor to find out how to activate this useful setting.

▼

4.2   The if/else Statement

Here is a slightly different approach for ignoring negative inputs in the area program:

```
if (area >= 0)
   cout << "The side length is " << sqrt(area) << "\n";
if (area < 0)
   cout << "Error: Negative area.\n";
```

The two if statements have complementary conditions. In this situation, you can use the if/else statement (see Syntax 4.3):

```
if (area >= 0)
   cout << "The side length is " << sqrt(area) << "\n";
else
   cout << "Error: Negative area.\n";
```

The flowchart in Figure 2 gives a graphical representation of the branching behavior.

In fact, the if/else statement is a better choice than a pair of if statements with complementary conditions. If you need to modify the condition area >= 0 for some reason, you don't have to remember to update the complementary condition area < 0 as well.

Here is the area program, using an if/else statement.

File area2.cpp

```
1 #include <iostream>
2 #include <string>
3 #include <cmath>
4
5 using namespace std;
6
7 int main()
8 {
9    double area;
10   cout << "Please enter the area of a square: ";
11   cin >> area;
12
13   if (area >= 0)
14      cout << "The side length is " << sqrt(area) << "\n";
15   else
16      cout << "Error: Negative area.\n";
17
18   return 0;
19 }
```

Syntax 4.3 : if/else **Statement**

if (*condition*) *statement₁* else *statement₂*

Example: if (x >= 0) y = sqrt(x); else cout << "Bad input\n";

Purpose: Execute the first statement if the condition is true, the second statement if the
condition is false.

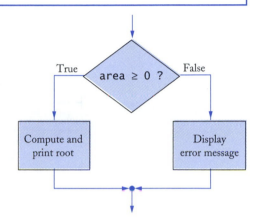

Figure 2

Flowchart for if/else Statement

Advanced Topic 4.1

The Selection Operator

C++ has a *selection operator* of the form

   test ? *value₁* : *value₂*

The value of that expression is either *value₁* if the test passes or *value₂* if it fails. For example,
we can compute the absolute value as

   y = x >= 0 ? x : -x;

which is a convenient shorthand for

   if (x >= 0) y = x;
   else y = -x;

The selection operator is similar to the if/else statement, but it works on a different syntactical level. The selection operator combines *expressions* and yields another expression. The
if/else statement combines statements and yields another statement.

   Expressions have values. For example, -b + sqrt(r) is an expression, as is x >= 0 ? x :
-x. Any expression can be made into a statement by adding a semicolon. For example, y = x
is an expression (with value x), but y = x; is a statement. Statements do not have values.
Since if/else forms a statement and does not have a value, you cannot write

   y = if (x > 0) x; else -x; /* Error */

   We don't use the selection operator in this book, but it is a convenient and legitimate construct that you will find in many C++ programs.

4.3   Relational Operators

Every if statement performs a test. In many cases, the test compares two values. For example, in the previous examples we tested area < 0 and area >= 0. The comparisons > and >= are called *relational operators*. C++ has six relational operators:

C++	Math Notation	Description
>	>	Greater than
>=	≥	Greater than or equal
<	<	Less than
<=	≤	Less than or equal
==	=	Equal
!=	≠	Not equal

As you can see, only two C++ relational operators (> and <) look as you would expect from the mathematical notation. Computer keyboards do not have keys for ≥, ≤, or ≠, but the >=, <=, and != operators are easy to remember because they look similar. The == operator is initially confusing to most newcomers to C++. In C++, = already has a meaning, namely assignment. The == operator denotes equality testing:

```
a = 5; /* assign 5 to a */
if (a == 5)  /* test whether a equals 5 */
```

You must remember to use == inside tests and to use = outside tests. (See Common Error 4.1 for more information.)

You can compare strings as well:

```
if (name == "Harry")  ...
```

In C++, letter case matters. For example, "Harry" and "HARRY" are not the same string.

If you compare strings using < <= > >=, they are compared in dictionary order. For example, the test

```
string name = "Tom";
if (name < "Dick") ...
```

fails, because in the dictionary Dick comes before Tom. Actually, the dictionary ordering used by C++ is slightly different from that of a normal dictionary. C++ is case-sensitive and sorts characters by listing numbers first, then uppercase characters, then lowercase characters. For example, 1 comes before B, which comes before a. The space character comes before all other characters. Strictly speaking, the character sort order is implementation-dependent, but the majority of systems use the so-called *ASCII code* (American Standard Code for Information Interchange), or one of its extensions, whose characters are sorted as described.

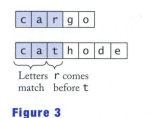

Letters   r comes
match   before t

Figure 3

Lexicographic Ordering

When comparing two strings, corresponding letters are compared until one of the strings ends or the first difference is encountered. If one of the strings ends, the longer string is considered the later one. If a character mismatch is found, compare the characters to determine which string comes later in the dictionary sequence. This process is called *lexicographic comparison*. For example, compare "car" with "cargo". The first three letters match, and we reach the end of the first string. Therefore "car" comes before "cargo" in the lexicographic ordering. Now compare "cathode" with "cargo". The first two letters match. Since t comes after r, the string "cathode" comes after "cargo" in lexicographic ordering. (See Figure 3.)

You can only compare numbers with numbers and strings with strings. The test

```
string name = "Harry";
if (name > 5)   /* Error */
```

is not valid.

You can use the relational operators only for numbers and strings. You cannot use them to compare objects of arbitrary classes. For example, if s and t are two objects of the Time class, then the comparison

```
if (s == t)   /* No! */
```

is an error.

Instead, you must test that s.get_hours() equals t.get_hours(), that s.get_minutes() equals t.get_minutes(), and that s.get_seconds() equals t.get_seconds.

 Common Error   4.1

Confusing = and ==

The rule for the correct usage of = and == is very simple: In tests, always use == and never use =. If it is so simple, why can't the compiler be helpful and flag any errors?

Actually, the C++ language allows the use of = inside tests. To understand this, we have to go back in time. For historical reasons, the expression inside an if () need not be a logical condition. Any numeric value can be used inside a condition, with the convention that 0 denotes false and any non-0 value denotes true. Furthermore, in C++ assignments are also expressions and have values. For example, the value of the expression a = 5 is 5. That can be convenient—you can capture the value of an intermediate expression in a variable:

```
x1 = (-b - (r = sqrt(b * b - 4 * a * c))) / (2 * a);
x2 = (- b + r) / (2 * a);
```

The expression r = sqrt(b * b - 4 * a * c) has a value, namely the value that is assigned to r, and thus can be nested inside the larger expression. We don't recommend this style of programming, because it is not much more trouble to set r first and then set x1 and x2, but there are situations in which the construction is useful.

These two features—namely that numbers can be used as truth values and that assignments are expressions with values—conspire to make a horrible pitfall. The test

```
if (x = y) ...
```

is legal C++, but it does not test whether x and y are equal. Instead, the code sets x to y, and if that value is not zero, the body of the if statement is executed.

Fortunately, most compilers issue a warning when they encounter such a statement. You should take such warnings seriously. (See Quality Tip 4.2 for more advice about compiler warnings.)

Some shell-shocked programmers are so nervous about using = that they use == even when they want to make an assignment:

```
x2 == (-b + r) / (2 * a);
```

Again, this is legal C++. This statement tests whether x2 equals the expression of the right-hand side. It doesn't do anything with the outcome of the test, but that is not an error. Some compilers will warn that "the code has no effect", but others will quietly accept the code.

Quality Tip   4.2

Compile with Zero Warnings

There are two kinds of messages that the compiler gives you: *errors* and *warnings*. Error messages are fatal; the compiler will not translate a program with one or more errors. Warning messages are advisory; the compiler will translate the program, but there is a good chance that the program will not do what you expect it to do.

You should make an effort to write code that emits no warnings at all. Usually, you can avoid warnings by convincing the compiler that you know what you are doing. For example, many compilers warn of a possible loss of information when you assign a floating-point expression to an integer variable:

```
int pennies = 100 * (amount_due - amount_paid);
```

Use an explicit cast (see Common Error 4.2), and the compiler will stop complaining:

```
int pennies = static_cast<int>(100 * (amount_due - amount_paid));
```

Some compilers emit warnings that can only be turned off with a great deal of skill or trouble. If you run into such a warning, confirm with your instructor that it is indeed unavoidable.

Common Error   4.2

Comparison of Floating-Point Numbers

Floating-point numbers have only a limited precision, and calculations can introduce round-off errors. For example, the following code multiplies the square root of 2 by itself. We expect to get the answer 2:

```
double r = sqrt(2);
if (r * r == 2) cout << "sqrt(2) squared is 2\n";
else cout << "sqrt(2) squared is not 2 but " << r * r << "\n".
```

Strangely enough, this program displays

```
sqrt(2) squared is not 2 but 2
```

To see what really happens, we need to see the output with higher precision. Then the answer is

```
sqrt(2) squared is not 2 but 2.0000000000000004
```

This explains why r * r didn't compare to be equal to 2. Unfortunately, roundoff errors are unavoidable. It does not make sense in most circumstances to compare floating-point numbers exactly. Instead, we should test whether they are *close* enough. That is, the magnitude of their difference should be less than some threshold. Mathematically, we would write that x and y are close enough if

$$|x - y| \le \varepsilon$$

for a very small number, ε. ε is the Greek letter epsilon, a letter commonly used to denote a very small quantity. It is common to set ε to 10^{-14} when comparing double numbers.

However, this test is often not quite good enough. Suppose x and y are rather large, say a few million each. Then one could be a roundoff error for the other even if their difference was quite a bit larger than 10^{-14}. To overcome this problem, we really need to test whether

$$\frac{x - y}{\max(|x|, |y|)} \le \varepsilon$$

This formula has one limitation. Suppose either x or y is zero. Then

$$\frac{|x - y|}{\max(|x|, |y|)}$$

has the value 1. Conceptually, there is not enough information to compare the magnitudes in this situation. In that situation, you need to set ε to a value that is appropriate for the problem domain, and check whether $|x - y| \le \varepsilon$.

Input Validation

An important application for the if statement is *input validation*. As we discussed previously, the program user must enter a sequence of digits when reading an integer from an input stream. If the user types in five when the program processes cin >> area for a number area, then the variable area is not set and the stream is set to a failed state. You can test for that failed state.

```
if (cin.fail())
{
   cout << "Error: Bad input\n";
   return 1;
}
```

For practical programs it is important to carry out a test after *every* input. Users cannot be trusted to enter data with perfect consistency, and a serious program must validate every input. To validate the area input fully, we must first test that *some* integer was read successfully and then test whether that integer was positive.

File area3.cpp

```
 1  #include <iostream>
 2  #include <string>
 3  #include <cmath>
 4
 5  using namespace std;
 6
 7  int main()
 8  {
 9     double area;
10     cout << "Please enter the area of a square: ";
11     cin >> area;
12
13     if (cin.fail())
14     {
15        cout << "Error: Bad input\n";
16        return 1;
17     }
18
19     if (area < 0)
20     {
21        cout << "Error: Negative area\n";
22        return 1;
23     }
24
25     cout << "The side length is " << sqrt(area) << "\n";
26
27     return 0;
28  }
```

The order of the `if` statements is important. Suppose we reversed the order:

```
double area;
cin >> area;

if (area < 0)
{
    cout << "Error: Negative area\n";
    return 1;
}
if (cin.fail())
{
    cout << "Error: Bad input\n";
    return 1;
}
```

If the user types an invalid input, such as `five`, then the statement `cin >> area` does not touch the value of `area`. However, `area` was never initialized, so it contains a random value. There is a 50 percent chance that the random value is negative. In that case, a confusing message `"Error: Negative area"` is displayed.

A stream variable can be the condition of an `if` statement:

```
cin >> area;

if (cin)
{
    /* the stream did not fail */
    . . .
}
else
{
    /* the stream failed */
    . . .
}
```

That is, the test `if (cin)` is exactly the opposite of the test `if (cin.fail())`. It tests whether `cin` is still in a good state. Many people find this a bit confusing, and we recommend that you explicitly query `cin.fail()`.

There is, however, one popular idiom that relies on this test. The expression `cin >> x` has a value, namely `cin`. That is what makes it possible to chain the `>>` operators: `cin >> x >> y` first executes `cin >> x`, which reads input into `x` and again yields `cin`, which is combined with `y`. The operation `cin >> y` then reads `y`.

Because the expression `cin >> x` has `cin` as its value, and you can use a stream as the condition of an `if` statement, you can use the following test:

```
if (cin >> x) . . .
```

This means "Read `x`, and if that didn't make `cin` fail, then continue". Some programmers like this style, and you should be familiar with it. We don't use it for `if` statements, because the minimal savings in keystrokes does not seem to outweigh the loss in clarity. However, as you will see later in this chapter, the idiom becomes more compelling for loops.

There are two additional functions to test the state of a stream: `good` and `eof`. However, these functions are not as useful (and are in fact used incorrectly in quite a few books). See Common Error 4.5 for more information.

Quality Tip   4.3

Avoid Conditions with Side Effects

As described in Common Error 4.1, it is legal to nest assignment statements inside test conditions:

```
if ((d = b * b - 4 * a * c) >= 0) r = sqrt(d);
```

It is also legal to read a number and then test the input stream:

```
if ((cin >> x).fail()) cout << "Error\n";
```

It is legal to use the increment or decrement operator inside other expressions:

```
if (n-- > 0) . . .
```

All these are bad programming practice, because they mix a test with another activity. The other activity (setting the variable d, reading x, decrementing n) is called a *side effect* of the test.

As you will see later in this chapter, conditions with side effects can occasionally be helpful to simplify *loops*. For if statements, they should always be avoided.

Random Fact   4.1

Minicomputers and Workstations

Within 20 years after the first computers became operational, they had become indispensable for organizing the customer and financial data of every major corporation in America. Corporate data processing required a centralized computer installation and high staffing levels to ensure the round-the-clock availability of the data. These installations were enormously

Figure 4

A Minicomputer

expensive, but they were vital to run a modern business. Major universities and large research institutions could also afford the installation of these expensive computers, but many scientific and engineering organizations and corporate divisions could not.

In the mid-1960s, when integrated circuits first became available, the cost of computers could be brought down for users who did not require as high a level of support and services (or data storage volume) as corporate data processing installations. Such users included scientists and engineers who had the expertise to operate computers. (At that time, to "operate" a computer did not just mean to turn it on. Computers came with little off-the-shelf software, and most tasks had to be programmed by the computer users.) In 1965 Digital Equipment Corporation introduced the PDP-8 *minicomputer*, housed in a single cabinet (see Figure 4) and thus small enough for departmental use. In 1978, the first 32-bit minicomputer, the VAX, was released, also by DEC. Other companies, such as Data General, brought out competing designs; the book [2] contains a fascinating description of the engineering work at Data General to bring out a machine that could compete with the VAX. Minicomputers were not just used for engineering applications, however. System integration companies would buy these machines, supply software, and resell them to smaller companies for business data processing. Minicomputers such as IBM's successful AS/400 line are still in use today, but they face stiff competition from workstations and personal computers, which are much less expensive and have increasingly powerful software.

In the early 1980s, engineering users became increasingly disenchanted with having to share computers with other users. Computers divided their attention among multiple users who were currently logged on, a process known as *time sharing*. However, graphical terminals were becoming available, and the fast processing of graphics was more than could be done in the allotted time slices. The technology again advanced to the point where an entire computer could be put into a box that would fit on a desk. A new breed of manufacturers, such as Sun Microsystems, started producing *workstations* (Figure 5). These computers are used by individuals with high computing demands—for example, electronic-circuit designers, aerospace engineers, and, more recently, cartoon artists. Workstations typically run an operating system called *UNIX*. While each workstation manufacturer has its own brand of UNIX, with slight differences in each version, it became economical for software manufacturers to produce programs that could run on several hardware platforms. This was aided by the fact that most workstation manufacturers standardized on the *X Window* system for displaying graphics.

Figure 5

A Workstation

▼   Not all workstation manufacturers were successful. The book [3] tells the story of NeXT, a company that tried to build a workstation and failed, losing over $250 million of its investors' money in the process.

▼   Nowadays workstations are used mainly for two distinct purposes: as fast graphics processors and as *servers* to store data such as electronic mail, sales information, or Web pages.

4.5   Simple Loops

Recall the investment problem from Chapter 1. You put $10,000 into a bank account that earns 5 percent interest per year. How many years does it take for the account balance to be double the original investment?

In Chapter 1 we developed an algorithm for this problem, but we didn't present enough C++ syntax to implement it. Here is the algorithm.

Step 1   Start with the table

Year	Balance
0	$10,000.00

Step 2   Repeat steps 2a . . . 2c while the balance is less than $20,000.

Step 2a   Add a new row to the table.

Step 2b   In column 1 of the new row, put one more than the preceding year's value.

Step 2c   In column 2 of the new row, place the value of the preceding balance, multiplied by 1.05 (5 percent).

Step 3   Report the last number in the year column as the answer.

You now know that each column in that table corresponds to a C++ variable, and you know how to update and print the variables. What you don't yet know is how to carry out "Repeat steps 2a . . . 2c while the balance is less than $20,000".

In C++, the while statement (see Syntax 4.4) implements such a repetition. The code

```
while (condition)
   statement
```

keeps executing the statement while the condition is true. The statement can be a block statement if you need to carry out multiple actions in the loop.

Syntax 4.4 : while Statement

while (*condition*) *statement*

Example: `while (x >= 10) x = sqrt(x);`

Purpose: Execute the statement while the condition remains true.

Here is the program that solves the investment problem:

File doublinv.cpp

```
1  #include <iostream>
2
3  using namespace std;
4
5  int main()
6  {
7     double rate = 5;
8     double initial_balance = 10000;
9     double balance = initial_balance;
10    int year = 0;
11
12    while (balance < 2 * initial_balance)
13    {
14       balance = balance * (1 + rate / 100);
15       year++;
16    }
17
18    cout << "The investment doubled after "
19       << year << " years.\n";
20
21    return 0;
22 }
```

A `while` statement is often called a *loop*. If you draw a flowchart, the control loops backwards to the test after every iteration (see Figure 6).

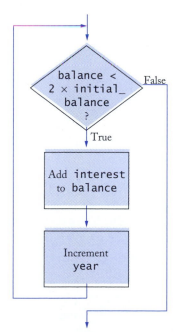

Figure 6

Flowchart of a `while` Loop

Common Error   4.3

Infinite Loops

The most annoying loop error is an infinite loop: a loop that runs forever and can be stopped only by killing the program or restarting the computer. If there are output statements in the loop, then reams and reams of output flash by on the screen. Otherwise, the program just sits there and *hangs*, seeming to do nothing. On some systems, you can kill a hanging program by hitting Ctrl + Break or Ctrl + C. On others, you can close the window in which the program runs.

A common reason for infinite loops is forgetting to update the variable that controls the loop:

```
years = 1;
while (years <= 20)
{
    interest = balance * rate / 100;
    balance = balance + interest;
}
```

Here the programmer forgot to add a years++ command in the loop. As a result, the year always stays at 1, and the loop never comes to an end.

Another common reason for an infinite loop is accidentally incrementing a counter that should be decremented (or vice versa). Consider this example:

```
years = 20;
while (years > 0)
{
    interest = balance * rate / 100;
    balance = balance + interest;
    years++;
}
```

The years variable really should have been decremented, not incremented. This is a common error because incrementing counters is so much more common than decrementing that your fingers may type the ++ on autopilot. As a consequence, years is always larger than 0, and the loop never terminates. (Actually, eventually years may exceed the largest representable positive integer and *wrap around* to a negative number. Then the loop exits—of course, with a completely wrong result.)

Common Error   4.4

Off-by-One Errors

Consider our computation of the number of years that are required to double an investment:

```
int years = 0;
while (balance < 2 * initial_balance)
{
```

```
        years++;
        double interest = balance * rate / 100;
        balance = balance + interest;
    }
    cout << "The investment doubled after "
        << years << " years.\n";
```

Should years start at 0 or at 1? Should you test for balance < 2 * initial_balance or for balance <= 2 * initial_balance? It is easy to be *off by one* in these expressions.

Some people try to solve off-by-one errors by randomly inserting +1 or –1 until the program seems to work—a terrible strategy. It can take a long time to compile and test all the various possibilities. Expending a small amount of mental effort is a real time saver.

Fortunately, off-by-one errors are easy to avoid, simply by thinking through a couple of test cases and using the information from the test cases to come up with a rationale for your decisions.

Should years start at 0 or at 1? Look at a scenario with simple values: an initial balance of $100 and an interest rate of 50 percent. After year 1, the balance is $150, and after year 2 it is $225, or over $200. So the investment doubled after 2 years. The loop executed two times, incrementing years each time. Hence years must start at 0, not at 1.

In other words, the balance variable denotes the balance after the end of the year. At the outset, the balance variable contains the balance after year 0 and not after year 1.

Next, should you use a < or <= comparison in the test? This is harder to figure out, because it is rare for the balance to be exactly twice the initial balance. There is one case when this happens, namely when the interest is 100 percent. The loop executes once. Now years is 1, and balance is exactly equal to 2 * initial_balance. Has the investment doubled after one year? It has. Therefore, the loop should not execute again. If the test condition is balance < 2 * initial_balance, the loop stops, as it should. If the test condition had been balance <= 2 * initial_balance, the loop would have executed once more.

In other words, you keep adding interest while the balance *has not yet doubled*.

Productivity Hint   4.2

Save Your Work before Every Program Run

You now have learned enough about programming that you can write programs that "hang"—that is, run forever. In some environments, you may not be able to use the keyboard or the mouse again. If you don't save your work and your program hangs, you may have to restart the development environment or even the computer and type it all again.

Therefore, you should get into the habit of *saving your work* before every program run. Some integrated environments can be configured to do this automatically, but it is not always the default behavior. You should configure your fingers to always issue a "File | Save All" command before running a program.

4.6 Processing a Sequence of Inputs

In this section, you will learn how to process a sequence of input values. You start with a sample program that reads a sequence of employee salaries and prints the average salary. Whenever you read a sequence of input values, you need to have some method of terminating the input.

Sometimes you are lucky and no input value can be zero. Then you can prompt the user to keep entering numbers, or 0 to finish that data set. If zero is allowed but negative numbers are not, you can use −1 to indicate termination. Such a value, which is not an actual input, but serves as a signal for termination, is called a *sentinel*.

File sentinel.cpp

```cpp
1  #include <iostream>
2
3  using namespace std;
4
5  int main()
6  {
7     double sum = 0;
8     int count = 0;
9     bool more = true;
10    double salary = 0;
11    while (salary != -1)
12    {
13       cout << "Enter a salary, -1 to finish: ";
14       cin >> salary;
15       if (salary != -1)
16       {
17          sum = sum + salary;
18          count++;
19       }
20    }
21    if (count > 0)
22       cout << "Average salary: " << sum / count << "\n";
23    return 0;
24 }
```

Sentinels only work if there is some restriction on the input. In many cases, though, there isn't. Suppose you want to compute the average of a data set that may contain 0 or negative values. Then you cannot use 0 or −1 to indicate the end of the input.

When reading input from the console, there is another way to indicate the end of input. You type a special character, such as Ctrl + Z on a Windows system or Ctrl + D on UNIX after you have entered all values. This closes the input stream. When you read from a closed stream, the stream enters the failed state.

The following sample program reads a set of temperature values and then prints the largest of them. To find the largest value in a sequence of values, use the following logic: Keep the maximum value of all data that you have encountered so far. Whenever a new element is read in, compare it with that tentative maximum. If the new value is larger, it becomes the new maximum; otherwise ignore it. When you have encountered the end of the input data, you know that the tentative maximum is the maximum of all inputs.

File maxtemp.cpp

```
1  #include <iostream>
2
3  using namespace std;
4
5  int main()
6  {
7     double next;
8     double highest;
9
10    cout << "Please enter the temperature values:\n";
11    if (cin >> next)
12       highest = next;
13    else
14    {
15       cout << "No data!\n";
16       return 1;
17    }
18
19    while (cin >> next)
20    {
21       if (next > highest)
22          highest = next;
23    }
24
25    cout << "The highest temperature is " << highest << "\n";
26
27    return 0;
28 }
```

Note how this program first sets the tentative maximum, `highest`, to the first input value, then it collects more inputs. At first glance, this may appear needlessly complex. Why not initialize `highest` with 0?

```
double highest = 0; /* NO! */
double next;
while (cin >> next)
{
   if (next > highest)
      highest = next;
}
```

This simpler code will appear to work fine for many input sets. However, it will fail if the input data consists of winter temperatures in Siberia, with all values negative. Then the maximum will be falsely reported as a relatively cozy zero degrees. To avoid this problem, set `highest` to the *first actual value*—not to a value that you merely hope to be smaller than all inputs.

4.7   Using Boolean Variables

Sometimes, you need to evaluate a logical condition in one part of a program and use it elsewhere. To store a condition that can be true or false, you need a *Boolean variable* of a special data type bool. Boolean variables are named after the mathematician George Boole (1815–1864), a pioneer in the study of logic.

Variables of type bool can hold exactly two values, denoted false and true. These values are not strings or integers; they are special values, just for Boolean variables.

Here is a typical use for a Boolean variable. You may decide that the combination of input and testing for success

```
while (cin >> next)
```

is rather complex. To disentangle the two, you can use a Boolean variable that controls the loop.

```
bool more = true;
while (more)
{
   cin >> next;
   if (cin.fail())
      more = false;
   else
   {
      process next
   }
}
```

By the way, it is considered gauche to write a test such as

```
while (more == true) /* don't */
```

or

```
while (more != false) /* don't */
```

Use the simpler test

```
while (more)
```

Some programmers dislike the introduction of a Boolean variable to control a loop. Advanced Topic 4.2 shows an alternative.

 Advanced Topic **4.2**

The Loop-and-a-Half Problem

Some programmers dislike loops that are controlled by a Boolean variable, such as:

```
bool more = true;
while (more)
{
   cin >> x;
   if (cin.fail())
      more = false;
   else
   {
      process x
   }
}
```

The true test for loop termination is in the middle of the loop, not at the top. This is called a *loop and a half* because one must go halfway into the loop before knowing whether one needs to terminate.

As an alternative, you can use the `break` keyword.

```
while (true)
{
   cin >> x;
   if (cin.fail()) break;
   process data
}
```

The `break` statement breaks out of the enclosing loop, independent of the loop condition.

In general, a `break` is a very poor way of exiting a loop. Misusing a `break` caused the failure of an AT&T 4ESS telephone switch on January 15, 1990. The failure propagated through the entire U.S. network, rendering it nearly unusable for about nine hours. A programmer had used a `break` to terminate an `if` statement. Unfortunately, `break` cannot be used with `if`, so the program execution broke out of the enclosing statement, skipping some variable initializations and running into chaos (see reference [1], p. 38). Using `break` statements also makes it difficult to use *correctness proof* techniques (see Advanced Topic 4.3).

In the loop-and-a-half case, break statements can be beneficial. But it is difficult to lay down clear rules as to when they are safe and when they should be avoided. We do not use the break statement in this book.

 Common Error   **4.5**

End-of-File Detection

When reading an indeterminate amount of data from a stream, you can either read until a sentinel value or read until the end of input. End of input detection is a little tricky. There is a function eof that reports the "end of file" condition, but you can call it with reliable results only *after the input stream has failed*. The following loop does not work:

```
while (more)
{
    cin >> x;
    if (cin.eof()) /* Don't! */
    {
        more = false;
    }
    else
    {
        sum = sum + x;
    }
}
```

If the stream input fails for another reason (usually because a non-number was encountered in the input), then all further input operations fail, and the end of the file is never reached. The loop then becomes an infinite loop. For example, consider the input

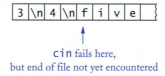

cin fails here,
but end of file not yet encountered

Instead, first test for failure and then test for eof:

```
bool more = true;
while (more)
{
    cin >> x;
    if (cin.fail())
    {
        more = false;
        if (cin.eof())
            cout << "End of data";
        else
            cout << "Bad input data";
```

```
      }
      else
      {
         sum = sum + x;
      }
   }
```

Here is another common error.

```
   while (cin)
   {
      cin >> x;
      sum = sum + x; /* Don't! */
   }
```

You must test for failure *after every input*. If the last item in the file were succeeded by white space (and it usually is followed by a newline), then that white space would mask the end of the file. Consider the following sample input:

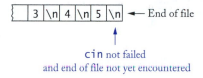

Only when another input is attempted after the last value has been read is the end of the file recognized, and input fails. Then x should not be added again to sum.

There is another function to test the stream state: good. Unfortunately, it is not a good idea to use it. If you read the very last item of a stream, then the input will succeed, but since the end of file has been encountered, the stream state will no longer be good. That is, a test

```
   while (more)
   {
      cin >> x;
      if (cin.good()) /* Don't! */
      {
         sum = sum + x;
      }
   }
```

may miss the last input. That is not good. You cannot use good to check whether the previous input succeeded. Nor can you use good to check whether the next input will succeed.

```
   if (cin.good()) /* Don't! */
   {
      cin >> x;
      sum = sum + x;
   }
```

If the next item in the input is not formatted correctly, then the input will fail, even though the stream state has been good up to now.

It appears as if this function has no good use at all. Misuse of it is a common error, perhaps because programmers prefer the cheerful cin.good() to the morose cin.fail().

Advanced Topic   4.3

Loop Invariants

Consider the task of computing a^n, where a is a floating-point number and n is a positive integer. Of course, you can multiply $a \times a \ldots \times a$, n times, but if n is large, you'll end up doing a lot of multiplications. The following loop sets r to a^n in far fewer steps:

```
double r = 1;
double b = a;
int i = n;
while (i > 0)
{
   if (i % 2 == 0) /* n is even */
   {
      b = b * b;
      i = i / 2;
   }
   else
   {
      r = r * b;
      i--;
   }
}
```

Consider the case n = 100. The function performs the following steps

i	b	r
100	a	1
50	a^2	
25	a^4	
24		a^4
12	a^8	
6	a^{16}	
3	a^{32}	
2		a^{36}
1	a^{64}	
0		a^{100}

Amazingly enough, the algorithm yields exactly a^{100}. Do you understand why? Are you convinced it will work for all values of n? Here is a clever argument to show that the function always computes the correct result. It demonstrates that whenever the program reaches the top of the while loop, it is true that

$$r \cdot b^i = a^n \qquad\qquad\qquad (I)$$

Certainly, it is true the first time around, because $b = a$ and $i = n$. Suppose that (I) holds at the beginning of the loop. The program labels the values of r, b, and i as "old" when entering the loop, and labels them as "new" when exiting the loop. Assume that upon entry

$$r_{old} \cdot b_{old}^{i_{old}} = a^n$$

In the loop you must distinguish two cases: i even and i odd. If n is even, the loop performs the following transformations:

$$r_{new} = r_{old}$$
$$b_{new} = b_{old}^2$$
$$i_{new} = i_{old}/2$$

Therefore,

$$r_{new} \cdot b_{new}^{i_{new}} = r_{old} \cdot \left(b_{old}\right)^{2 \cdot i_{old}/2}$$
$$= r_{old} \cdot b_{old}^{i_{old}}$$
$$= a^n$$

On the other hand, if i is odd, then

$$r_{new} = r_{old} \cdot b_{old}$$
$$b_{new} = b_{old}$$
$$i_{new} = i_{old} - 1$$

Therefore,

$$r_{new} \cdot b_{new}^{i_{new}} = r_{old} \cdot b_{old} \cdot b_{old}^{i_{old}-1}$$
$$= r_{old} \cdot b_{old}^{i_{old}}$$
$$= a^n$$

In either case, the new values for r, b, and i fulfill the *loop invariant* (I). So what? When the loop finally exits, (I) holds again:

$$r \cdot b^i = a^n$$

Furthermore, you know that $i = 0$ since the loop is terminating. But because $i = 0$, $r \cdot b^i = r \cdot b^0 = r$. Hence $r = a^n$, and the function really does compute the nth power of a.

This technique is quite useful because it can explain an algorithm that is not at all obvious. The condition (I) is called a loop invariant because it is true when the loop is entered, at the top of each pass, and when the loop is exited. If a loop invariant is chosen skillfully, it may be possible to deduce correctness of a computation. See [5] for another nice example.

Random Fact **4.2**

Correctness Proofs

In Advanced Topic 4.3 we introduced the technique of loop invariants. If you skipped that note, have a glance at it now. That technique can be used to prove rigorously that a function returns exactly the value that it is supposed to compute. Such a proof is far more valuable than any testing. No matter how many test cases you try, you always worry whether another case that you haven't tried yet might show a bug. A proof settles the correctness for all possible inputs.

For some time, programmers were very hopeful that proof techniques such as loop invariants would greatly reduce the need for testing. You would prove that each simple function and procedure is correct, and then put the proven components together and prove that they work together as they should. Once it is proved that main works correctly, no testing is required at all! Some researchers were so excited about these techniques that they tried to omit the programming step altogether. The designer would write down the program requirements, using the notation of formal logic. An automatic prover would prove that such a program could be written and generate the program as part of its proof.

Unfortunately, in practice these methods never worked very well. The logical notation to describe program behavior is complex. Even simple scenarios require many formulas. It is easy enough to express the idea that a function is supposed to compute a^n, but the logical formulas describing all procedures in a program controlling an airplane, for instance, would fill many pages. These formulas are created by humans, and humans make errors when they deal with difficult and tedious tasks. Experiments showed that instead of buggy programs, programmers wrote buggy logic specifications and buggy program proofs.

Van der Linden [1], p. 287, gives some examples of complicated proofs that are much harder to verify than the programs they are trying to prove.

Program proof techniques are valuable for proving the correctness of individual procedures that make computations in nonobvious ways. At this time, though, there is no hope to prove any but the most trivial programs correct in such a way that the specification and the proof can be trusted more than the program.

CHAPTER SUMMARY

1. The if statement allows a program to carry out different actions depending on the nature of the data to be processed.

2. The if statement evaluates a *condition*. Conditions can contain any value that is true or false.

3. Relational operators are used to compare numbers and strings.

4. The lexicographic or dictionary order is used to compare strings.

5. When an input stream senses an input error, it enters the failed state. You can test for failure with the fail function.

6. Loops execute a block of code repeatedly. A termination condition controls how many times the loop is executed.

7. The Boolean type `bool` has two values, `false` and `true`.

8. You can use a Boolean variable to control a loop. Set the variable to `true` before entering the loop, then set it to `false` to exit the loop.

FURTHER READING

[1] Peter van der Linden, *Expert C Programming*, Prentice-Hall, 1994.
[2] Tracy Kidder, *The Soul of a New Machine*, Little, Brown and Co., 1981.
[3] Randall E. Stross, *Steven Jobs and the NeXT Big Thing*, Atheneum, 1993.
[4] William H. Press et al., *Numerical Recipes in C*, Cambridge, 1988.
[5] Jon Bentley, *Programming Pearls*, Addison-Wesley, 1986, Chapter 4, "Writing Correct Programs."

REVIEW EXERCISES

Exercise R4.1. Find the errors in the following `if` statements.

(a) `if quarters > 0 then cout << quarters << " quarters";`

(b) `if (1 + x > pow(x, sqrt(2)) ) y = y + x;`

(c) `if (x = 1) y++; else if (x = 2) y = y + 2;`

(d) `if (x and y == 0) cwin << Point(0, 0);`

(e) `if (1 <= x <= 10) cout << "Enter y: "; cin >> y;`

(f)
```
if (s != "nick" or s != "penn"
    or s != "dime" or s != "quar")
  cout << "Input error!";
```

(g)
```
if (input == "N" or "NO")
    return 0;
```

(h) `cin >> x; if (cin.fail()) y = y + x;`

(i)
```
language = "English";
if (country == "USA")
    if (state == "PR") language = "Spanish";
else if (country = "China")
    language = "Chinese";
```

Exercise R4.2. Explain how the lexicographic ordering of strings differs from the ordering of words in a dictionary or telephone book. *Hint:* Consider strings such as IBM, `wiley.com`, Century 21, and `While-U-Wait`.

Exercise R4.3. Explain why it is more difficult to compare floating-point numbers than integers. Write C++ code to test whether an integer n equals 10 and whether a floating-point number x equals 10.

Exercise R4.4. Give an example for two floating-point numbers x and y such that fabs(x - y) is larger than 1,000, but x and y are still identical except for a roundoff error.

Exercise R4.5. Of the following pairs of strings, which comes first in lexicographic order?

- (a) "Tom", "Dick"
- (b) "Tom", "Tomato"
- (c) "church", "Churchill"
- (d) "car manufacturer", "carburetor"
- (e) "Harry", "hairy"
- (f) "C++", " Car"
- (g) "Tom", "Tom"
- (h) "Car", "Carl"
- (i) "car", "bar"

Exercise R4.6. When reading a number in, there are two possible ways for a stream to be set to the "failed" state. Give examples for both. How is the situation different when reading a string?

Exercise R4.7. What is wrong with the following program?

```
cout << "Enter the number of quarters: ";
cin >> quarters;
total = total + quarters * 0.25;
if (cin.fail()) cout << "Input error.";
```

Exercise R4.8. Reading numbers is surprisingly difficult, because a C++ input stream looks at the input one character at a time. First, white space is skipped. Then the stream consumes those input characters that can be a part of a number. Once the stream has recognized a number, it stops reading if it finds a character that cannot be a part of a number. However, if the first non-white space character is not a digit or a sign, or if the first character is a sign and the second one is not a digit, then the stream fails.

Consider a program reading an integer:

```
cout << "Enter the number of quarters: ";
int quarters;
cin >> quarters;
```

For each of the following user inputs, circle how many characters have been read and whether the stream is in the failed state or not.

- (a) 15.9
- (b) 15 9

(c) +159

(d) -15A9

(e) Fifteen

(f) -Fifteen

(g) (end of file)

(h) + 15

(i) 1.5E3

(j) +1+5

Exercise R4.9. When the stream state has been set to failed, it is possible to clear it again by calling the function `cin.clear()`. Some textbooks recommend clearing the input stream state and asking the user to try again. For example,

```
int quarters;
cin >> quarters;
if (cin.fail()) cout << "Bad input. Try again!";
cin.clear();
cin >> quarters;
if (cin.fail()) /* hopeless */
    return 1;
```

Why is this a stupid suggestion? *Hint:* What happens if the user enters `four`? Could you think of an improvement? *Hint:* `getline`.

Exercise R4.10. What is an infinite loop? On your computer, how can you terminate a program that executes an infinite loop?

Exercise R4.11. What is an "off-by-one" error? Give an example from your own programming experience.

Exercise R4.12. What is a sentinel value? Give simple rules when it is better to use a sentinel value and when it is better to use the end of the input file to denote the end of a data sequence.

Exercise R4.13. What is a "loop and a half"? Give three strategies to implement the following loop and a half:

loop
   read employee name
   if not OK, exit loop
   read employee salary
   if not OK, exit loop
   give employee 5 percent raise
   print employee data

Use a Boolean variable, a `break` statement, and a `return` statement. Which of these approaches do you find clearest?

PROGRAMMING EXERCISES

Exercise P4.1. Write a program that prints all solutions to the quadratic equation $ax^2 + bx + c = 0$. Read in a, b, c and use the quadratic formula. If the discriminant $b^2 - 4ac$ is negative, display a message stating that there are no solutions.

Exercise P4.2. Write a program that takes user input describing a playing card in the following shorthand notation:

A	Ace
2 . . . 10	Card values
J	Jack
Q	Queen
K	King
D	Diamonds
H	Hearts
S	Spades
C	Clubs

Your program should print the full description of the card. For example,

```
Enter the card notation: QS
Queen of spades
```

Exercise P4.3. According to [4], p. 184, it is not smart to use the quadratic formula to find the solutions of $ax^2 + bx + c = 0$. If a, c, or both are small, then $\sqrt{b^2 - 4ac}$ is close to b, and one of $-\left(b \pm \sqrt{b^2 - 4ac}\right)$ involves subtraction of two nearly identical quantities, which can lose several digits of precision. They recommend to compute

$$q = -\frac{1}{2}\left(b + \mathrm{sgn}(b)\sqrt{b^2 - 4ac}\right)$$

where

$$\mathrm{sgn}(b) = \begin{cases} 1 & \text{if } b \geq 0 \\ -1 & \text{if } b < 0 \end{cases}$$

Then the two solutions are

$$x_1 = q/a \text{ and } x_2 = c/q$$

Implement this algorithm and verify that it gives more accurate solutions than the quadratic formula for small a or c.

Exercise P4.4. Find the solutions to the *cubic* equation $x^3 + ax^2 + bx + c = 0$. First compute

$$q = \frac{a^2 - 3b}{9} \text{ and } r = \frac{2a^3 - 9ab + 27c}{54}$$

If $r^2 < q^3$, then there are three solutions. Compute

$$t = \cos^{-1}\left(r/\sqrt{q^3}\right)$$

The three solutions are

$$x_1 = -2\sqrt{q} \cos\left(\frac{t}{3}\right) - \frac{a}{3}$$

$$x_2 = -2\sqrt{q} \cos\left(\frac{t + 2\pi}{3}\right) - \frac{a}{3}$$

$$x_3 = -2\sqrt{q} \cos\left(\frac{t - 2\pi}{3}\right) - \frac{a}{3}$$

Otherwise, there is a single solution

$$x_1 = u + v - \frac{a}{3}$$

where

$$u = -\text{sgn}(r)\left(|r| + \sqrt{r^2 - q^3}\right)^{1/3}$$

and

$$v = \begin{cases} q/u & \text{if } u \neq 0 \\ 0 & \text{if } u = 0 \end{cases}$$

Exercise P4.5. *Intersection of lines.* As in Exercise P3.7, compute and plot the intersection of two lines, but now add error checking. If the two lines do not intersect, do not plot the point. There are two separate reasons the lines might not intersect. The lines might be parallel; in that case the determinant of the system of linear equations is zero. The point of intersection might not lie on either line; in that case, the value for t will be less than 0 or greater than 1.

Exercise P4.6. Write a program that reads in three floating-point numbers and prints the largest of the three inputs. For example:

```
Please enter three numbers: 4 9 2.5
The largest number is 9.
```

Exercise P4.7. Write a program that draws a square with corner points (0, 0) and (1, 1). Prompt the user for a mouse click. If the user clicked inside the square, then show a message "Congratulations". Otherwise, show a message "You missed".

Exercise P4.8. Write a graphics program that asks the user to specify two circles. Each circle is input by clicking on the center and typing in the radius. Draw the circles. If they intersect, then display a message "Circles intersect". Otherwise, display "Circles don't intersect". *Hint:* Compute the distance between the centers and compare it to the radii. Your program should terminate if the user enters a negative radius.

Exercise P4.9. Write a program that prints the question "Do you want to continue?" and reads a user input. If the user input is "Y", "Yes", "OK", "Sure", or "Why not?", print out "OK." If the user input is "N" or "No", then print out "Terminating". Otherwise, print "Bad input". The case of the user input should not matter; "y" or "yes" are also valid inputs.

Exercise P4.10. Write a program that translates a letter grade into a number grade. Letter grades are A, B, C, D, and F, possibly followed by + or −. Their numeric values are 4, 3, 2, 1, and 0. There is no F+ or F−. A + increases the numeric value by 0.3, a − decreases it by 0.3. However, an A+ has value 4.0.

```
Enter a letter grade: B-
The numeric value is 2.7.
```

Exercise P4.11. Write a program that translates a number between 0 and 4 into the closest letter grade. For example, the number 2.8 (which might have been the average of several grades) would be converted to B−. Break ties in favor of the better grade; for example 2.85 should be a B.

Exercise P4.12. *Roman numbers.* Write a program that converts a positive integer into the Roman number system. The Roman number system has digits

I	1
V	5
X	10
L	50
C	100
D	500
M	1,000

Numbers are formed according to the following rules. (1) Only numbers up to 3,999 are represented. (2) As in the decimal system, the thousands, hundreds, tens, and ones are expressed separately. (3) The numbers 1 to 9 are expressed as

I	1
II	2
III	3
IV	4
V	5
VI	6
VII	7
VIII	8
IX	9

As you can see, a I preceding a V or X is subtracted from the value, and you can never have more than three I's in a row. (4) Tens and hundreds are done the same way, except that the letters X, L, C and C, D, M are used instead of I, V, X, respectively.

Your program should take an input, such as 1978, and convert it to Roman numerals, MCMLXXVIII.

Exercise P4.13. Write a program that reads in three strings and sorts them lexicographically.

```
Enter three strings: Charlie Able Baker
Able
Baker
Charlie
```

Exercise P4.14. Write a program that reads in two floating-point numbers and tests whether they are the same up to two decimal places. Here are two sample runs.

```
Enter two floating-point numbers: 2.0 1.99998
They are the same up to two decimal places.
Enter two floating-point numbers: 2.0 1.98999
They are different.
```

Exercise P4.15. Write a program to simulate a bank transaction. There are two bank accounts: checking and savings. First, ask for the initial balances of the bank accounts; reject negative balances. Then ask for the transactions; options are deposit, withdrawal, and transfer. Then ask for the account; options are checking and savings. Then ask for the amount; reject transactions that overdraw an account. At the end, print the balances of both accounts.

Exercise P4.16. Write a program that reads in the name and salary of an employee object. Here the salary will denote an *hourly* wage, such as $9.25. Then ask how many hours the employee worked in the past week. Be sure to accept fractional hours. Compute the pay. Any overtime work (over 40 hours per week) is paid at 150 percent of the regular wage. Print a paycheck for the employee.

Exercise P4.17. Write a unit conversion program using the conversion factors of Table 1 in Chapter 2. Ask the users from which unit they want to convert (fl. oz, gal, oz, lb, in, ft, mi) and which unit they want to convert to (ml, l, g, kg, mm, cm, m, km). Reject incompatible conversions (such as gal → km). Ask for the value to be converted; then display the result:

```
Convert from? gal
Convert to? ml
Value? 2.5
2.5 gal = 9462.5 ml
```

Exercise P4.18. *Random walk.* Simulate the walk of a drunkard in a square street grid. Draw a grid of 10 streets horizontally and 10 streets vertically. Place a simulated inebriated person in the middle of the grid, denoted by a point. For 100 times, have the simulated person randomly pick a direction (east, west, north, south), move one block in the chosen direction, and redraw the dot. After the iterations, display the distance that the drunkard has covered. (One might expect that on average the person might not get anywhere because the moves in different directions cancel each other out in the long run, but in fact it can be shown that with probability 1 the person eventually moves outside any finite region.)

Exercise P4.19. *Projectile flight.* Suppose a cannonball is propelled straight into the air with a starting velocity v_0. Any calculus book will state that the position of the ball after t seconds is $s(t) = -\frac{1}{2}gt^2 + v_0 t$, where $g = 9.81$ m/sec^2 is the gravitational force of the earth. No calculus book ever mentions why someone would want to carry out such an obviously dangerous experiment, so we will do it in the safety of the computer.

In fact, we will confirm the theorem from calculus by a simulation. In our simulation, we will consider how the ball moves in very short time intervals Δt. In a short time interval the velocity v is nearly constant, and we can compute the distance the ball moves as $\Delta s = v\Delta t$. In our program, we will simply set

```
const double delta_t = 0.01;
```

and update the position by

```
s = s + v * delta_t;
```

The velocity changes constantly—in fact, it is reduced by the gravitational force of the earth. In a short time interval, $\Delta v = -g\Delta t$, we must keep the velocity updated as

```
v = v - g * delta_t;
```

In the next iteration the new velocity is used to update the distance.

Now run the simulation until the cannonball falls back to the earth. Get the initial velocity as an input (100 m/sec is a good value). Update the position and velocity 100 times per second, but print out the position only every full second. Also print out the values from the exact formula $s(t) = -\frac{1}{2}gt^2 + v_0 t$ for comparison.

What is the benefit of this kind of simulation when an exact formula is available? Well, the formula from the calculus book is *not* exact. Actually, the gravitational force diminishes the further the cannonball is away from the surface of the earth. This complicates the algebra sufficiently that it is not possible to give an exact formula for the actual motion, but the computer simulation can simply be extended to apply a variable gravitational force. For cannonballs, the calculus-book formula is actually good enough, but computers are necessary to compute accurate trajectories for higher-flying objects such as ballistic missiles.

Exercise P4.20. Most cannonballs are not shot upright but at an angle. If the starting velocity has magnitude v and the starting angle is α, then the velocity is actually a vector with components $v_x = v\cos\alpha$, $v_y = v\sin\alpha$. In the x-direction the velocity does not change. In the y-direction the gravitational force takes its toll. Repeat the simulation from the previous exercise, but store the position of the cannonball as a `Point` variable. Update the x- and y-positions separately, and also update the x- and y-components of the velocity separately. Every full second, plot the location of the cannonball on the graphics display. Repeat until the cannonball has reached the earth again.

This kind of problem is of historical interest. The first computers were designed to carry out just such ballistic calculations, taking into account the diminishing gravity for high-flying projectiles and wind speeds.

Exercise P4.21. *Currency conversion.* Write a program that first asks the user to type today's exchange rate between U.S. dollars and Japanese yen, then reads U.S. dollar values and converts each to yen. Use 0 or a negative input as a sentinel.

Exercise P4.22. Write a program that first asks the user to type in today's exchange rate between U.S. dollars and Japanese yen, then reads U.S. dollar values and converts each to Japanese yen. Use 0 as the sentinel value to denote the end of dollar inputs. Then the program reads a sequence of yen amounts and converts them to dollars. The second sequence is terminated by the end of the input file.

Exercise P4.23. Write a program that prints a *bar* chart from a data set. The program should be a graphics application that prompts the user first for the number of bars, then for the actual values. Assume all values are between 0 and 100. Then draw a bar chart like this.

Exercise P4.24. *Mean and standard deviation.* Write a program that reads a set of floating-point data values from the input. When the end of file is reached, print out the count of the values, the average, and the standard deviation. The average of a data set $\{x_1, \ldots, x_n\}$ is $\bar{x} = \sum x_i / n$, where $\sum x_i = x_1 + \ldots + x_n$ is the sum of the input values. The standard deviation is

$$s = \sqrt{\frac{\sum (x_i - \bar{x})^2}{n - 1}}$$

However, this formula is not suitable for the task. By the time the program has computed $\bar{x}$, the individual x_i are long gone. Until you know how to save these values, use the numerically less stable formula

$$s = \sqrt{\frac{\sum x_i^2 - \frac{1}{n}\left(\sum x_i\right)^2}{n - 1}}$$

You can compute this quantity by keeping track of the count, the sum, and the sum of squares as you process the input values.

Exercise P4.25. Write a program that plots a *regression line:* that is, the line with the best fit through a collection of points. First ask the user to specify the data points by clicking on them in the graphics window. To find the end of the input, place a small rectangle labeled "Stop" at the bottom of the screen; when the user clicks inside that rectangle, then stop gathering input. The regression line is the line with equation

$$y = \bar{y} + m(x - \bar{x}), \quad \text{where } m = \frac{\sum x_i y_i - n\bar{x}\,\bar{y}}{\sum x_i^2 - n\bar{x}^2}$$

$\bar{x}$ is the mean of the x-values and $\bar{y}$ is the mean of the y-values.

As in the preceding exercise, you need to keep track of

- the count of input values
- the sum of x, y, x^2, and xy values

To draw the regression line, compute its endpoints at the left and right edges of the screen, and draw a segment.

Chapter 5

Functions

CHAPTER GOALS

▶ To be able to program functions and procedures

▶ To become familiar with the concept of parameter passing

▶ To recognize when to use value and reference parameters

▶ To appreciate the importance of function comments

▶ To be able to determine the scope of variables

▶ To minimize the use of side effects and global variables

▶ To develop strategies for decomposing complex tasks into simpler ones

▶ To document the responsibilities of functions and their callers with preconditions

Functions are a fundamental building block of C++ programs. A function packages a computation in a form that can be easily understood and reused. In this chapter, you will learn how to design and implement your own functions, and how to break up complex tasks into sets of cooperating functions.

CHAPTER CONTENTS

5.1   Functions as Black Boxes

You have used a number of functions that were provided with the C++ system library. Examples are

sqrt   Computes the square root of a floating-point number

getline   Reads a line from a stream

You probably don't know how these functions perform their job. For example, how does sqrt compute square roots? By looking up values in a table? By repeated guessing of the answer? You will actually learn in Chapter 6 how to compute square roots using nothing more than basic arithmetic, but you don't need to know the internals of the computation to use the square root function. You can think of sqrt as a *black box*, as shown in Figure 1.

When you use sqrt(x) inside main, the *input value* or *parameter value* x is transferred, or *passed*, to the sqrt function. The execution of the main function is temporarily

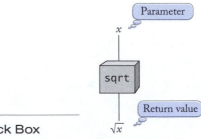

Figure 1

The sqrt Function as a Black Box

Figure 2

Execution Flow during a
Function Call

Figure 2

Execution Flow during a
Function Call

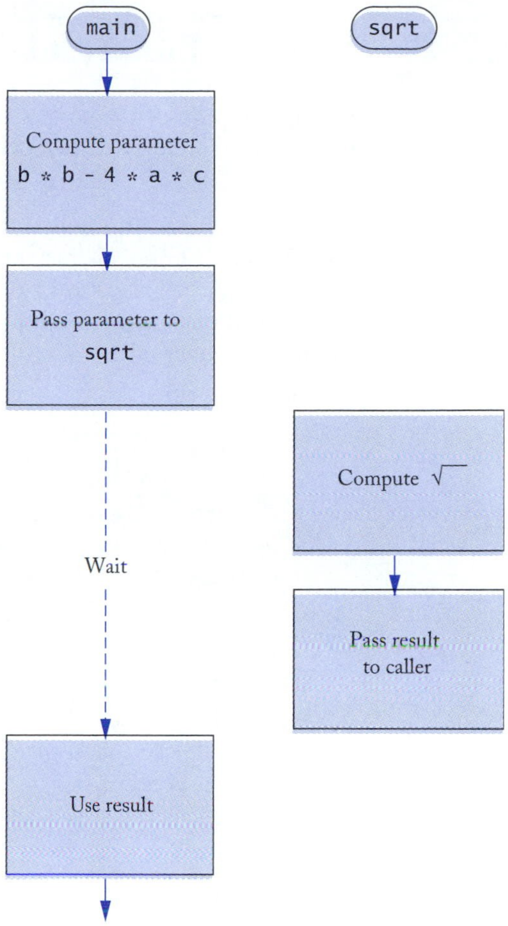

suspended. The sqrt function becomes active and computes the *output* or *return value*—the square root of the input value—using some method that (we trust) will yield the correct result. That return value is transferred back to main, which resumes the computation using the return value. The input value to a function need not be a single variable; it can be any expression, as in sqrt(b * b - 4 * a * c). Figure 2 shows the flow of execution when a function is called.

Some functions have more than one input. For example, the pow function has two parameters: pow(x, y) computes x^y. Functions can have multiple inputs, but they only have one output.

Each function takes inputs of particular types. For example, sqrt receives only numbers as parameters, whereas getline expects a stream and a string. It is an error to call sqrt with a string input.

Each function returns a value of a particular type: sqrt returns a floating-point number, substr returns a string, and main returns an integer.

5.2 Writing Functions

Let us compute the value of a savings account with an initial balance of $1,000 after 10 years. If the interest rate is p percent, then the balance after 10 years is

$$b = 1000 \times \left(1 + p/100\right)^{10}$$

For example, if the interest rate is 5 percent per year, then the initial investment of $1,000 will have grown to $1,628.94 after 10 years.

We will place this computation inside a function called `future_value`. Here is how you use the function:

```
int main()
{
   cout << "Please enter the interest rate in percent: ";
   double rate;
   cin >> rate;

   double balance = future_value(rate);
   cout << "After 10 years, the balance is "
      << balance << "\n";

   return 0;
}
```

Now write the function. The function receives a floating-point input and returns a floating-point value. You must give a *name* to the input value so you can use it in the computation. Here it is called `p`.

```
double future_value(double p)
{
   . . .
}
```

This declares a function `future_value` that returns a value of type `double` and that takes a parameter of type `double`. For the duration of the function, the parameter is stored in a *parameter variable* `p`. Just as with `main`, the body of the function is delimited by braces; see Syntax 5.1.

Syntax 5.1 : Function Definition

return_type function_name(parameter$_1$, parameter$_2$, ..., parameter$_n$)
{
    statements
}

Example:
```
double abs(double x)
{
   if (x >= 0) return x;
   else return -x;
}
```

Purpose: Define a function and supply its implementation.

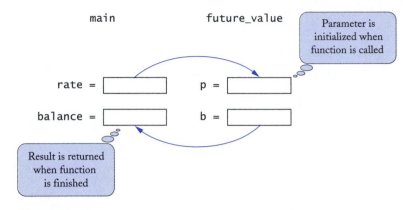

Figure 3

A Function Receiving a Parameter Value and Returning a Result

Next you need to compute the function result:

```
double future_value(double p)
{
    double b = 1000 * pow(1 + p / 100, 10);
    . . .
}
```

Finally, you need to return that result to the caller of the function:

```
double future_value(double p)
{
    double b = 1000 * pow(1 + p / 100, 10);
    return b;
}
```

This completes the definition of the future_value function. Figure 3 shows the flow of data into and out of the function.

The program is now composed of two functions: future_value and main. Both function definitions must be placed into the program file. Since main calls future_value, the future_value function must be known before the main function. The easiest way to achieve this is to place future_value first and main last in the source file. (See Advanced Topic 5.1 for an alternative.)

File futval.cpp

```
 1 #include <iostream>
 2 #include <cmath>
 3
 4 using namespace std;
 5
 6 double future_value(double p)
 7 {
 8     double b = 1000 * pow(1 + p / 100, 10);
 9     return b;
10 }
11 int main()
```

```
12  {
13     cout << "Please enter the interest rate in percent: ";
14     double rate;
15     cin >> rate;
16
17     double balance = future_value(rate);
18     cout << "After 10 years, the balance is "
19        << balance << "\n";
20
21     return 0;
22  }
```

The `future_value` function has a major blemish: The starting amount of the investment ($1,000) and the number of years (10) are *hard-wired* into the function code. It is not possible to use this function to compute the balance after 20 years. Of course, you could write a different function `future_value20`, but that would be a very clumsy solution. Instead, make the initial balance and the number of years into additional parameters:

```
double future_value(double initial_balance, double p, int n)
{
   double b = initial_balance * pow(1 + p / 100, n);
   return b;
}
```

We now need to supply those values in the function call:

```
double b = future_value(1000, rate, 10);
```

Now our function is much more valuable, because it is *reusable*. For example, we can trivially modify `main` to print the balance after 10 and 20 years.

```
double b = future_value(1000, rate, 10);
cout << "After 10 years, the balance is " << b << "\n";

b = future_value(1000, rate, 20);
cout << "After 20 years, the balance is " << b << "\n";
```

Why are we using a function in the first place? We could have made the computations directly, without a function call.

```
double b = 1000 * pow(1 + p / 100, 10);
cout << "After 10 years, the balance is " << b << "\n";

b = 1000 * pow(1 + p / 100, 20);
cout << "After 20 years, the balance is " << b << "\n";
```

If you look at these two solutions in comparison, it should be quite apparent why functions are valuable. The function allows you to abstract an *idea*—namely, the computation of compound interest. Once you understand the idea, it is clear what the change from 10 to 20 means in the two function calls. Now compare the two expressions that compute the balances directly. To understand them, you have to look closely to find that they differ only in the last number, and then you have to remember the significance of that number.

When you find yourself coding the same computation more than once, or coding a computation that is likely to be useful in other programs, you should make it into a function.

Productivity Hint   5.1

Write Functions with Reuse in Mind

Functions are fundamental building blocks of C++ programs. When properly written, they can be reused from one project to the next. As you design the interface and implementation of a function, you should keep reuse in mind.

Keep the focus of the function specific enough that it performs only one task, and solve that task completely. For example, when computing the future value of an investment, just compute the value; don't display it. Another programmer may need the computation, but might not want to display the result on the terminal.

Take the time to handle even those inputs that you may not need immediately. Now you understand the problem, and it will be easy for you to do this. If you or another programmer needs an extended version of the function later, that person must rethink the problem. This takes time, and misunderstandings can cause errors. For this reason, we turned the initial balance and interest rate into parameters of the `future_value` function.

Then you need to check for the legal range of all inputs. Does it make sense to allow negative percentages? Negative investment amounts? Fractional years? Generalizations with clear benefits should be implemented.

5.3   Function Comments

There is one final important enhancement that we need to make to the `future_value` function. We must *comment* its behavior. Comments are for human readers, not compilers, and there is no universal standard for the layout of a function comment. In this book, we will always use the following layout:

```
/**
    Computes the value of an investment with compound interest.
    @param initial_balance the initial value of the investment
    @param p the interest rate per period in percent
    @param n the number of periods the investment is held
    @return the balance after n periods
*/
double future_value(double initial_balance, double p, int n)
{
    double b = initial_balance * pow(1 + p / 100, n);
    return b;
}
```

Whoa; the comment is longer than the function! Indeed it is, but that is irrelevant. We were just lucky that this particular function was easy to compute. The comment of the function does not document the implementation but the idea—ultimately a more valuable property.

According to the documentation style used in this book, every function (except `main`) must have a comment. The first part of the comment is a brief explanation of the function. Then supply an `@param` entry for each parameter, and an `@return` entry to describe

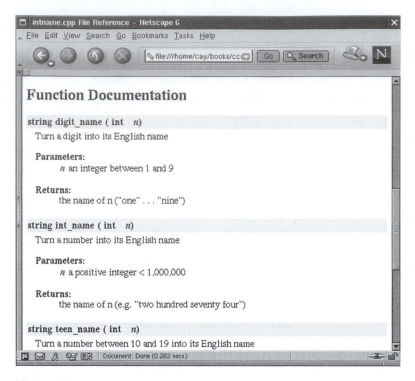

Function Documentation

string digit_name (int *n*)

Turn a digit into its English name

Parameters:
> *n* an integer between 1 and 9

Returns:
> the name of n ("one" . . . "nine")

string int_name (int *n*)

Turn a number into its English name

Parameters:
> *n* a positive integer < 1,000,000

Returns:
> the name of n (e.g. "two hundred seventy four")

string teen_name (int *n*)

Turn a number between 10 and 19 into its English name

Document: Done (0.262 secs)

Figure 4

HTML Documentation of a Function

the return value. As you will see later, some functions have no parameters or return values. For those functions, `@param` or `@return` can be omitted.

This particular documentation style is borrowed from the Java programming language—it is often called the *javadoc* style. There are a number of tools available that process C++ files and extract HTML pages containing a hyperlinked set of comments—see Figure 4. The companion Web site for this book contains instructions for downloading and using such a tool.

Occasionally, you will find that the documentation comments are silly to write. That is particularly true for general-purpose functions:

```
/**
    Computes the maximum of two integers.
    @param x an integer
    @param y another integer
    @return the larger of the two inputs
*/
int max(int x, int y)
{
   if (x > y)
      return x;
   else
      return y;
}
```

It should be pretty clear that max computes the maximum, and it is obvious that the function receives two integers x and y. Indeed, in this case, the comment is somewhat overblown. We nevertheless strongly recommend writing the comment for every function. It is easy to spend more time pondering whether the comment is too trivial to write than it takes just to write it. In practical programming, very simple functions are rare. It is harmless to have a trivial function overcommented, whereas a complicated function without any comment can cause real grief to future maintenance programmers.

Practical experience has shown that comments for individual variables are rarely useful, provided the variable names are chosen to be self-documenting. Functions make up a very important logical division of a C++ program, and a large part of the documentation effort should be concentrated on explaining their black-box behavior.

It is always a good idea to write the function comment *first*, before writing the function code. This is an excellent test to see that you firmly understand what you need to program. If you can't explain the function's inputs and outputs, you aren't ready to implement it.

Productivity Hint   5.2

Global Search and Replace

Suppose you chose an unfortunate name for a function, say fv instead of future_value, and you regret your choice. Of course, you can locate all occurrences of fv in your code and replace them manually. However, most programming editors have a command to search for all occurrences of fv automatically and replace them with future_value.

You need to specify some details for the search.

- Do you want your search to ignore case? That is, should FV be a match? In C++ you usually don't want that.

- Do you want it to match whole words only? If not, the fv in Golfville is also a match. In C++ you usually want to match whole words.

- Is this a regular expression search? No, but regular expressions can make searches even more powerful—see Productivity Hint 5.3.

- Do you want to confirm each replace or simply go ahead and replace all matches? Confirm the first three or four matches, and when you see that it works as expected, give the go-ahead to replace the rest. (By the way, a *global* replace means to replace all occurrences in the document.) Good text editors can undo a global replace that has gone awry. Find out whether or not yours will.

- Do you want the search to go from the cursor through the rest of the program file, or should it search the currently selected text? Restricting replacement to a portion of the file can be very useful, but in this example you would want to move the cursor to the top of the file and then replace until the end of the file.

Not every editor has all these options. You should investigate what your editor offers.

▼

Productivity Hint   5.3

Regular Expressions

▼

Regular expressions describe character patterns. For example, numbers have a simple form. They contain one or more digits. The regular expression describing numbers is [0-9]+. The set [0-9] denotes any digit between 0 and 9, and the + means "one or more".

▼

What good is it? A number of utility programs use regular expressions to locate matching text. Also, the search commands of some programming editors understand regular expressions. The most popular program that uses regular expressions is grep (which stands for "global regular expression print"). You can run grep from a command prompt or from inside some compilation environments. It needs a regular expression and one or more files to search. When grep runs, it displays a set of lines that match the regular expression.

▼

Suppose you want to look for all magic numbers (see Quality Tip 2.3) in a file. The command

```
grep [0-9]+ homework.cpp
```

▼

lists all lines in the file homework.cpp that contain sequences of digits. This isn't terribly useful; lines with variable names x1 will be listed. You want sequences of digits that do *not* immediately follow letters:

▼

```
grep [^A-Za-z][0-9]+ homework.cpp
```

The set [^A-Za-z] denotes any characters that are *not* between A and Z or between a and z. This works much better, and it shows only lines that contain actual numbers.

▼

There are a bewildering number of symbols (sometimes called *wildcards*) with special meanings in the regular expression syntax, and unfortunately, different programs use different styles of regular expressions. It is best to consult the program documentation for details.

▼

5.4   Return Values

When the return statement is processed, the function exits *immediately*. This is convenient for handling exceptional cases at the beginning:

```cpp
double future_value(double initial_balance, double p, int n)
{
   if (n < 0) return 0;
   if (p < 0) return 0;
   double b = initial_balance * pow(1 + p / 100, n);
   return b;
}
```

If the function is called with a negative value for p or n, then the function returns 0 and the remainder of the function is not executed. (See Figure 5.)

In the preceding example, each return statement returned a constant or a variable. Actually, the return statement can return the value of any expression, as shown in Syntax 5.2. Instead of saving the return value in a variable and returning the variable, it is often possible to eliminate the variable and return a more complex expression:

Figure 5

return Statements Exit a Function
Immediately

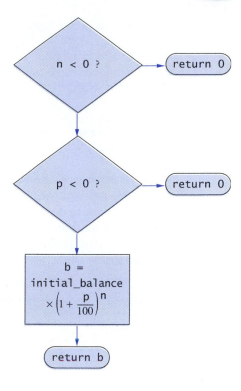

```
double future_value(double initial_balance, double p, int n)
{
    return initial_balance * pow(1 + p / 100, n);
}
```

This is commonly done for very simple functions.

It is important that every branch of a function return a value. Consider the following incorrect version of the future_value function:

```
double future_value(double initial_balance, double p, int n)
{
    if (p >= 0)
        return initial_balance * pow(1 + p / 100, n);
    /* Error */
}
```

Suppose you call future_value with a negative value for the interest rate. Of course, you aren't supposed to call that, but it might happen as the result of a coding error. Since the

---

Syntax 5.2 : return Statement

return *expression*;

Example: `return pow(1 + p / 100, n);`

Purpose: Exit a function, returning the value of the expression as the function result.

if condition is not true, the `return` statement is not executed. However, the function must return *something*. Depending on circumstances, the compiler might flag this as an error, or a random value might be returned. This is always bad news, and you must protect against this by returning some safe value.

```
double future_value(double initial_balance, double p, int n)
{
   if (p >= 0)
      return initial_balance * pow(1 + p / 100, n);
   return 0;
}
```

The last statement of every function ought to be a `return` statement. This ensures that *some* value gets returned when the function reaches the end.

A function that returns a truth value is called a *predicate*. The program at the end of this section defines an `approx_equal` function that tests whether two floating-point numbers are approximately equal. The function returns a value of type `bool`, which can be used inside a test.

```
if (approx_equal(xold, xnew)) ...
```

You have already seen another predicate function: the `fail` function to report on an input stream.

```
if (cin.fail()) cout << "Input error!\n";
```

File approx.cpp

```
 1  #include <iostream>
 2  #include <algorithm>
 3
 4  using namespace std;
 5
 6  /**
 7     Tests whether two floating-point numbers are
 8     approximately equal.
 9     @param x a floating-point number
10     @param y another floating-point number
11     @return true if x and y are approximately equal
12  */
13  bool approx_equal(double x, double y)
14  {
15     const double EPSILON = 1E-14;
16     if (x == 0) return fabs(y) <= EPSILON;
17     if (y == 0) return fabs(x) <= EPSILON;
18     return fabs(x - y) / max(fabs(x), fabs(y)) <= EPSILON;
19  }
20
21  int main()
22  {
23     double x;
24     cout << "Enter a number: ";
25     cin >> x;
26
27     double y;
28     cout << "Enter another number: ";
```

```
29     cin >> y;
30
31     if (approx_equal(x, y))
32        cout << "The numbers are approximately equal.\n";
33     else
34        cout << "The numbers are different.\n";
35
36     return 0;
37  }
```

▼ ⊗ **Common Error**   **5.1**

Missing Return Value

A function always needs to return something. If the code of the function contains several if/else branches, make sure that each one of them returns a value:

```
int sign(double x)
{
   if (x < 0) return -1;
   if (x > 0) return +1;
   /* Error: missing return value if x equals 0 */
}
```

This function computes the sign of a number: −1 for negative numbers and +1 for positive numbers. If the parameter x is zero, however, no value is returned. Most compilers will issue a warning in this situation, but if you ignore the warning and the function is ever called with a parameter value of 0, a random quantity will be returned.

5.5   Parameters

When a function starts, its *parameter variables* are initialized with the expressions in the function call. Suppose you call

```
b = future_value(total / 2, rate, year2 - year1).
```

The future_value function has three parameter variables: initial_balance, p, and n. Before the function starts, the values of the expressions total / 2 and year2 - year1 are computed. Each parameter variable is initialized with the corresponding parameter value. Thus, initial_balance becomes total / 2, p becomes rate, and n becomes year2 - year1. Figure 6 shows the parameter-passing process.

The term *parameter variable* is appropriate in C++. It is entirely legal to modify the values of the parameter variables later. Here is an example, using p as a variable:

```
double future_value(double initial_balance, double p, int n)
{
   p = 1 + p / 100;
   double b = initial_balance * pow(p, n);
   return b;
}
```

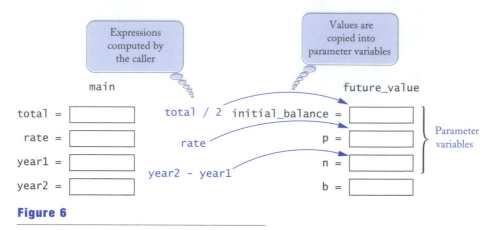

Figure 6

Parameter Passing

Actually, many programmers consider this practice bad style. It is best not to mix the concept of a parameter (input to the function) with that of a variable (local storage needed for computing the function result).

In this book we will always treat parameter variables as constants and never modify them. However, in Section 5.8 you will encounter reference parameters that refer to variables outside the function, not to local variables. Modifying a reference parameter is useful—it changes the parameter value not just inside the function, but outside it as well.

Quality Tip   5.1

Use Meaningful Names for Parameters

You can give any name you like to function parameters. Choose explicit names for parameters that have specific roles; choose simple names for those that are completely generic. The goal is to make the reader understand the purpose of the parameter without having to read the description.

`double sin(double x)` is not as good as `double sin(double radian)`. Naming the parameter radian gives additional information: namely, that the angle cannot be given in degrees.

The C++ standard library contains a function that is declared as

`double atan2(double y, double x)`

I can never remember whether it computes $\tan^{-1}(x/y)$ or $\tan^{-1}(y/x)$. I wish they had named the parameters more sensibly:

`double atan2(double numerator, double denominator)`

If a function is designed to take *any* parameter of a given type, then simple parameter names are appropriate.

`bool approx_equal(double x, double y)`

Common Error   **5.2**

Type Mismatch

The compiler takes the types of the function parameter and return value very seriously. It is an error to call a function with a value of an incompatible type. The compiler converts between integers and floating-point numbers, but it does not convert between numbers and strings or objects. For this reason, C++ is called a *strongly typed* language. This is a useful feature, because it lets the compiler find programming errors before they create havoc when the program runs.

For example, you cannot give a string to a numerical function, even if the string contains only digits:

```
string num = "1024";
double x = sqrt(num); /* Error */
```

You cannot store a numerical return value in a string variable:

```
string root = sqrt(2); /* Error */
```

Advanced Topic   **5.1**

Function Declarations

Functions need to be known before they can be used. This can be achieved easily if you first define lower-level helper functions, then the midlevel workhorse functions, and finally `main` in your program. Sometimes that ordering does not work. Suppose function `f` calls function `g`, and `g` calls `f` again. That setup is not common, but it does happen. Another situation is much more common. The function `f` may use a function such as `sqrt` that is defined in a separate file. To make `f` compile, it suffices to *declare* the functions `g` and `sqrt`. A declaration of a function lists the return value, function name, and parameters, but it contains no body:

```
int g(int n);
double sqrt(double x);
```

These are advertisements that promise that the function is implemented elsewhere, either later in the current file or in a separate file. It is easy to distinguish declarations from definitions: Declarations end in a semicolon, whereas definitions are followed by a {. . .} block (see Syntax 5.3). Declarations are also called *prototypes*.

Syntax 5.3 : Function Declaration (or Prototype)

return_type function_name(parameter$_1$, parameter$_2$, . . ., parameter$_n$) ;

Example: `double abs(double x);`

Purpose: Declare a function so that it can be called before it is defined.

The declarations of common functions such as sqrt are contained in header files. If you have a look inside cmath, you will find the declaration of sqrt and the other math functions.

Some programmers like to list all function declarations at the top of the file and then write main and then the other functions. For example, the futval.cpp file can be organized as follows:

```cpp
#include <iostream>
#include <cmath>

using namespace std;

/* declaration of future_value */
double future_value(double initial_balance, double p, int n);

int main()
{
   . . .
   /* use of future_value */
   double balance = future_value(1000, rate, 5);
   . . .
}

/* definition of future_value */
double future_value(double initial_balance, double p, int n)
{
   double b = initial_balance * pow(1 + p / 100, n);
   return b;
}
```

This arrangement has one advantage: It makes the code easier to read. You first read the top-level function main, then the helper functions such as future_value. There is, however, a drawback. Whenever you change the name of a function or one of the parameter types, you need to fix it in both places: in the declaration and in the definition.

For short programs, such as the ones in this book, this is a minor issue, and you can safely choose either approach. For longer programs, it is useful to separate declarations from definitions. Chapter 6 contains more information on how to break up larger programs into multiple files and how to place declarations into header files. As you will see in Chapter 6, member functions of classes are first declared in the class definition and then defined elsewhere.

5.6 Side Effects

Consider the future_value function, which *returns* a number. Why didn't we have the function *print* the value at the same time?

```cpp
double future_value(double initial_balance, double p, int n)
{
   double b = initial_balance * pow(1 + p / 100, n);
   cout << "The balance is now " << b << "\n";
   return b;
}
```

It is a general design principle that a function had best leave no trace of its existence except for returning a value. If a function prints out a message, it will be worthless in an environment that has no output stream, such as a graphics program or the controller of a bank teller machine.

One particularly reprehensible practice is printing error messages inside functions. You should never do that:

```
double future_value(double initial_balance, double p, int n)
{
   if (p < 0)
   {
      cout << "Bad value of p."; /* Bad style */
      return 0;
   }

   double b = initial_balance * pow(1 + p / 100, n);
   return b;
}
```

Printing an error message severely limits the reusability of the future_value function. It can be used only in programs that can print to cout, eliminating graphics programs. It can be used only in applications in which a user actually reads the output, eliminating background processing. Also, it can be used only in applications where the user can understand an error message in the English language, eliminating the majority of your potential customers. Of course, your programs must contain some messages, but you should group all the input and output activity together—for example, in main if your program is short. Let the functions do the computation, not the error report to the user.

An externally observable effect of a function is called a *side effect*. Displaying characters on the screen, updating variables outside the function, and terminating the program are examples of side effects.

In particular, a function that has no side effects can be run over and over with no surprises. Whenever it is given the same inputs, it will faithfully produce the same outputs. This is a desirable property for functions, and indeed most functions have no side effects.

5.7   Procedures

Suppose you need to print an object of type Time:

```
Time now;
cout << now.get_hours() << ":"
   << setw(2) << setfill('0') << now.get_minutes() << ":"
   << setw(2) << now.get_seconds() << setfill(' ');
```

An example printout is 9:05:30. The setw and setfill manipulators serve to supply a leading zero if the minutes or seconds are single digits.

Of course, this is a pretty common task that may well occur again:

```
cout << liftoff.get_hours() << ":"
   << setw(2) << setfill('0') << liftoff.get_minutes() << ":"
   << setw(2) << liftoff.get_seconds() << setfill(' ');
```

That is just the kind of repetition that functions are designed to handle.

File printime.cpp

```
 1 #include <iostream>
 2 #include <iomanip>
 3
 4 using namespace std;
 5
 6 #include "ccc_time.h"
 7
 8 /**
 9     Prints a time in the format h:mm:ss.
10     @param t the time to print
11 */
12 void print_time(Time t)
13 {
14    cout << t.get_hours() << ":"
15       << setw(2) << setfill('0') << t.get_minutes() << ":"
16       << setw(2) << t.get_seconds() << setfill(' ');
17 }
18
19 int main()
20 {
21    Time liftoff(7, 0, 15);
22    Time now;
23    cout << "Liftoff: ";
24    print_time(liftoff);
25    cout << "\n";
26
27    cout << "Now: ";
28    print_time(now);
29    cout << "\n";
30
31    return 0;
32 }
```

Note that this code doesn't compute any value. It performs some actions and then returns to the caller. A function without a return value is called a *procedure*. The missing return value is indicated by the keyword void. Procedures are called just as functions are, but there is no return value to use in an expression:

```
print_time(now);
```

Since a procedure does not return a value, it must have some other side effect; otherwise it would not be worth calling. This procedure has the side effect of printing the time.

Ideally, a function computes a single value and has no other observable effect. Calling the function multiple times with the same parameter returns the same value every time and leaves no other trace. Ideally, a procedure has only a side effect, such as setting variables or performing output, and returns no value.

Sometimes these ideals get muddied by the necessities of reality. Commonly, procedures return a status value. For example, a procedure print_paycheck might return a bool to indicate successful printing without a paper jam. However, computing that return value is not the principal purpose of calling the operation—you wouldn't print a check just to find out whether there is still paper in the printer. Hence, we would still call `print_paycheck` a procedure, not a function, even though it returns a value.

5.8   Reference Parameters

Let us write a procedure that raises the salary of an employee by p percent.

```
Employee harry;
. . .
raise_salary(harry, 5); /* Now Harry earns 5 percent more */
```

Here is a first attempt:

```
void raise_salary(Employee e, double by) /* Does not work */
{
    double new_salary = e.get_salary() * (1 + by / 100);
    e.set_salary(new_salary);
}
```

But this doesn't work. Let's walk through the procedure. As the procedure starts, the parameter variable e is set to the same value as harry, and by is set to 5. Then e is modified, but that modification had no effect on harry, because e is a separate variable. When the procedure exits, e is forgotten, and harry didn't get a raise.

A parameter such as e or by is called a *value parameter*, because it is a variable that is initialized with a value supplied by the caller. All parameters in the functions and procedures that we have written so far have been value parameters. In this situation, though, we don't just want e to have the same value as harry. We want e to refer to the actual variable harry (or joe or whatever employee is supplied in the call). The salary of *that* variable should be updated. There is a second type of parameter, called a *reference parameter*, with just that behavior. When we make e into a reference parameter, then e is not a new variable but a reference to an existing variable, and any change in e is actually a change in the variable to which e refers in that particular call. Figure 7 shows the difference between value and reference parameters.

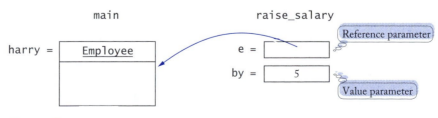

Figure 7

Reference and Value Parameters

Syntax 5.4 : Reference Parameter

type_name& parameter_name

Example: `Employee& e`
             `int& result`

Purpose: Define a parameter that is bound to a variable in the function call, to allow the
            function to modify that variable.

The syntax for a reference parameter is cryptic, as shown in Syntax 5.4.

File raisesal.cpp

```
 1  #include <iostream>
 2
 3  using namespace std;
 4
 5  #include "ccc_empl.h"
 6
 7  /**
 8      Raises an employee salary.
 9      @param e  employee receiving raise
10      @param by  the percentage of the raise
11  */
12  void raise_salary(Employee& e, double by)
13  {
14      double new_salary = e.get_salary() * (1 + by / 100);
15      e.set_salary(new_salary);
16  }
17
18  int main()
19  {
20      Employee harry("Hacker, Harry", 45000.00);
21      raise_salary(harry, 5);
22      cout << "New salary: " << harry.get_salary() << "\n";
23      return 0;
24  }
```

The & after the type name denotes a reference parameter. `Employee&` is read "employee reference" or, more briefly, "employee ref". The `raise_salary` procedure has two parameters: one of type "employee ref" and the other a floating-point number.

The `raise_salary` procedure clearly has an observable side effect: It modifies the variable supplied in the call. Apart from producing output, reference parameters are the most common mechanism for achieving a side effect.

Of course, the parameter e refers to different variables in different procedure calls. If `raise_salary` is called twice,

```
raise_salary(harry, 5 + bonus);
raise_salary(charley, 1.5);
```

then e refers to harry in the first call, raising his salary by 5 percent plus the amount bonus. In the second call, e refers to charley, raising his salary by just 1.5 percent.

Should the second parameter be a reference?

```
void raise_salary(Employee& e, double& by)
{
    double new_salary = e.get_salary() * (1 + by / 100);
    e.set_salary(new_salary);
}
```

That is not desirable. The parameter by is never modified in the procedure; hence, we gain nothing from making it a reference parameter. All we accomplish is to restrict the call pattern. A reference parameter must be bound to a *variable* in the call, whereas a value parameter can be bound to any *expression*. With by a reference parameter, the call

```
raise_salary(harry, 5 + bonus)
```

becomes illegal, because you cannot have a reference to the expression 5 + bonus. It makes no sense to change the value of an expression.

Advanced Topic   5.2

Constant References

It is not very efficient to pass variables of type Employee to a subroutine by value. An employee record contains several data items, and all of them must be copied into the parameter variable. Reference parameters are more efficient. Only the location of the variable, not its value, needs to be communicated to the function.

You can instruct the compiler to give you the efficiency of call by reference and the meaning of call by value, by using a *constant reference* as shown in Syntax 5.5. The procedure

```
void print_employee(const Employee& e)
{
    cout << "Name: " << e.get_name()
        << " Salary: " << e.get_salary() << "\n";
}
```

works exactly the same as the procedure

```
void print_employee(Employee e)
{
    cout << "Name: " << e.get_name()
        << " Salary: " << e.get_salary() << "\n";
}
```

There is just one difference: Calls to the first procedure execute faster.

Adding const& to value parameters is generally worthwhile for objects but not for numbers. Using a constant reference for an integer or floating-point number is actually slower than using a value parameter. It would be nice if the compiler could perform this optimization on its own initiative, but there are unfortunate technical reasons why it cannot.

Adding const& to speed up the passing of objects works only if the function or procedure never modifies its value parameters. While it is legal to modify a value parameter, changing a

▼

▼

constant reference is an error. In Section 5.5 it was recommended to treat value parameters as constants. If you follow that recommendation, you can apply the const& speedup.

For simplicity, const& is rarely used in this book, but you will always find it in production code.

> ### Syntax 5.5 : Constant Reference Parameter
>
> const *type_name*& *parameter_name*
>
> **Example:** const Employee& e
>
> **Purpose:** Define a parameter that is bound to a variable in the function call, to avoid the cost of copying that variable into a parameter variable.

5.9   Variable Scope and Global Variables

It sometimes happens that the same variable name is used in two functions. Consider the variable r in the following example:

```cpp
double future_value(double initial_balance, double p, int n)
{
   double r = initial_balance * pow(1 + p / 100, n);
   return r;
}

int main()
{
   cout << "Please enter the interest rate in percent: ";
   double r;
   cin >> r;

   double balance = future_value(10000, r, 10);
   cout << "After 10 years, the balance is "
      << balance << "\n";

   return 0;
}
```

Perhaps the programmer chose r to denote the *return value* in the future_value function, and independently chose r to denote the *rate* in the main function. These variables are independent of each other. You can have variables with the same name r in different functions, just as you can have different motels with the same name "Bates' Motel" in different cities.

In a program, the part within which a variable is visible is known as the *scope* of the variable. In general, the scope of a variable extends from its definition to the end of the block in which it was defined. The scopes of the variables r are indicated with color.

```
double future_value(double initial_balance, double p, int n)
{
    double r = initial_balance * pow(1 + p / 100, n);
    return r;
}

int main()
{
    cout << "Please enter the interest rate in percent: ";
    double r;
    cin >> r;

    double balance = future_value(10000, r, 10);
    cout << "After 10 years, the balance is "
        << balance << "\n";

    return 0;
}
```

C++ supports *global variables*: variables that are defined outside functions. A global variable is visible to all functions that are defined after it. Here is an example of a global variable.

File global.cpp

```
1  #include <iostream>
2  #include <cmath>
3
4  using namespace std;
5
6  double balance;
7
8  /**
9      Accumulates interest in the global variable balance.
10     @param p  the interest rate in percent
11     @param n  the number of periods the investment is held
12  */
13 void future_value(int p, int n)
14 {
15     balance = balance * pow(1 + p / 100, n);
16 }
17
18 int main()
19 {
20     balance = 10000;
21     future_value(5, 10);
22     cout << "After ten years, the balance is "
23         << balance << "\n";
24     return 0;
25 }
```

In this case, `balance` is a global variable. Note how it is set in `main` and read in `future_value`.

Of course, this is not considered a good way of transmitting data from one function to another. For example, suppose a programmer accidentally calls `future_value` before `balance` is set. Then the function computes the wrong investment result. Especially as a program gets long, these kinds of errors are extremely difficult to find. Of course, there is a simple remedy: Rewrite `future_value` and pass the initial balance as a parameter.

Sometimes global variables cannot be avoided (for example, `cin`, `cout`, and `cwin` are global variables), but you should make every effort to avoid global variables in your program.

Quality Tip   5.2

Minimize Global Variables

There are a few cases where global variables are required, but they are quite rare. If you find yourself using many global variables, you are probably writing code that will be difficult to maintain and extend. As a rule of thumb, you should have no more than two global variables for every thousand lines of code.

How can you avoid global variables? Use *parameters* and use *classes*. You can always use function parameters to transfer information from one part of a program to another. If your program manipulates many variables, that can get tedious. In this case, you need to design classes that cluster related variables together. You will learn more about this process in Chapter 6.

5.10   Stepwise Refinement

One of the most powerful strategies for problem solving is the process of *stepwise* refinement. To solve a difficult task, break it down into simpler tasks. Then keep breaking down the simpler tasks into even simpler ones, until you are left with tasks that you know how to solve.

Now apply this process to a problem of everyday life. You get up in the morning and simply must *get coffee*. How do you get coffee? You see whether you can get someone else, such as your mother or mate, to bring you some. If that fails, you must *make coffee*. How do you make coffee? If there is instant coffee available, you can *make instant coffee*. How do you make instant coffee? Simply *boil water* and mix the boiling water with the instant coffee. How do you boil water? If there is a microwave, then you fill a cup with water, place it in the microwave and heat it for three minutes. Otherwise, you fill a kettle with water and heat it on the stove until the water comes to a boil. On the other hand, if you don't have instant coffee, you must *brew coffee*. How do you brew coffee? You add water to the coffee maker, put in a filter, *grind coffee*, put the coffee in the filter, and turn the coffee maker on. How do you grind coffee? You add coffee beans to the coffee grinder and push the button for 60 seconds.

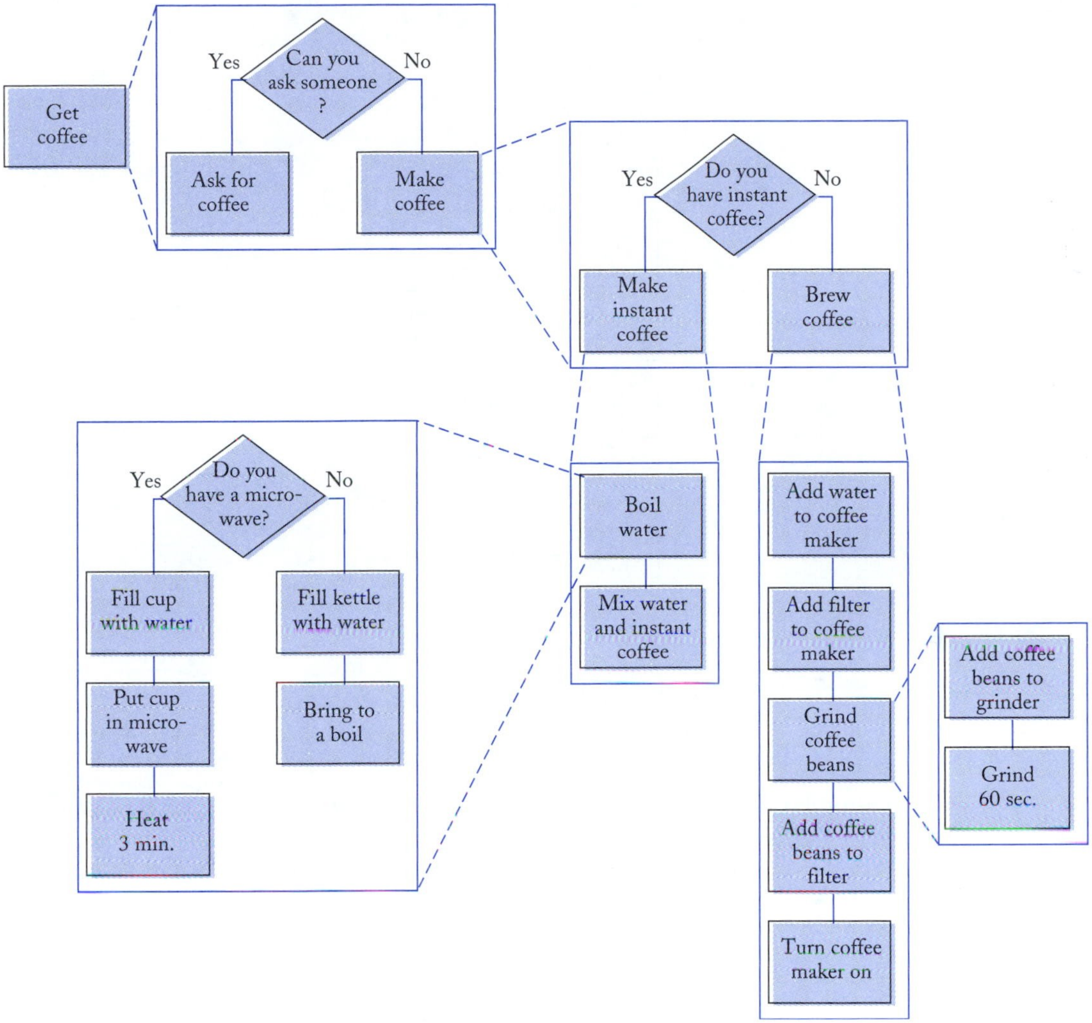

Figure 8

Flowchart of Coffee-Making Solution

The solution to the coffee problem breaks down tasks in two ways: with *decisions* and with *refinements*. We are already familiar with decisions: "If there is a microwave, use it, *else* use a kettle." *Decisions* are implemented as if/else in C++. A refinement gives a name to a composite task and later breaks that task down further: ". . . put in a filter, *grind coffee*, put the coffee in the filter. . . . To grind coffee, add coffee beans to the coffee grinder. . . ." Refinements are implemented as functions in C++. Figure 8 shows a flow-chart view of the coffee-making solution. Decisions are shown as branches, refinements

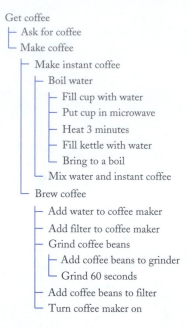

Get coffee
├─ Ask for coffee
└─ Make coffee
   ├─ Make instant coffee
   │ ├─ Boil water
   │ │ ├─ Fill cup with water
   │ │ ├─ Put cup in microwave
   │ │ ├─ Heat 3 minutes
   │ │ ├─ Fill kettle with water
   │ │ └─ Bring to a boil
   │ └─ Mix water and instant coffee
   └─ Brew coffee
      ├─ Add water to coffee maker
      ├─ Add filter to coffee maker
      ├─ Grind coffee beans
      │ ├─ Add coffee beans to grinder
      │ └─ Grind 60 seconds
      ├─ Add coffee beans to filter
      └─ Turn coffee maker on

Figure 9

Call Tree of Coffee-Making Procedure

as expanding boxes. Figure 9 shows a second view: a *call tree* of the tasks. The call tree shows which tasks are subdivided into which other tasks. It does not show decisions or loops, though. The name "call tree" is simple to explain: When you program each task as a C++ function, the call tree shows which functions call each other.

Quality Tip   5.3

Keep Functions Short

There is a certain cost for writing a function. The function needs to be documented; parameters need to be passed; the function must be tested. Some effort should be made to find whether the function can be made reusable rather than tied to a specific context. To avoid this cost, it is always tempting just to stuff more and more code in one place rather than going through the trouble of breaking up the code into separate functions. It is quite common to see inexperienced programmers produce functions that are several hundred lines long.

Ideally, each function should contain no more than one screenful of text, making it easy to read the code in the text editor. Of course, this is not always possible. As a rule of thumb, a function that is longer than 50 lines is usually suspect and should probably be broken up.

5.11   From Pseudocode to Code

When printing a check, it is customary to write the check amount both as a number ("$274.15") and as a text string ("two hundred seventy four dollars and 15 cents"). Doing so reduces the recipient's temptation to add a few digits in front of the amount (see Figure 10). For a human, this isn't particularly difficult, but how can a computer do this? There is no built-in function that turns 274 into "two hundred seventy four". We need to program this function. Here is the description of the function we want to write:

```
/**
    Turns a number into its English name.
    @param n a positive integer < 1,000,000
    @return the name of n (e.g., "two hundred seventy four")
*/
string int_name(int n)
```

Before starting the programming, we need to have a plan. Consider a simple case. If the number is between 1 and 9, we need to compute "one" . . . "nine". In fact, we need the same computation *again* for the hundreds (two hundred). Any time you need something more than once, it is a good idea to turn that into a function. Rather than writing the entire function, write only the comment:

```
/**
    Turns a digit into its English name.
    @param n an integer between 1 and 9
    @return the name of n ("one" . . . "nine")
*/
string digit_name(int n)
```

This sounds simple enough to implement, using an if/else statement with nine branches, so we will worry about the implementation later.

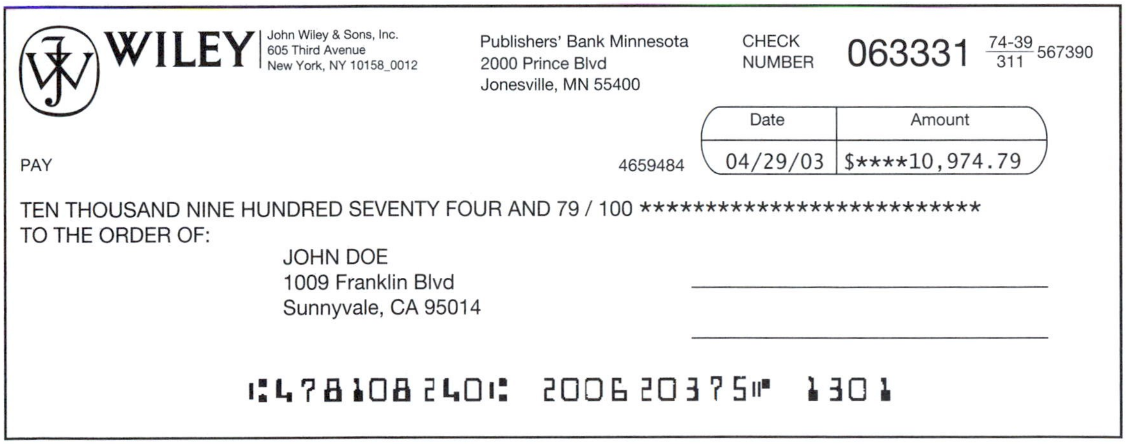

WILEY
John Wiley & Sons, Inc.
605 Third Avenue
New York, NY 10158_0012

Publishers' Bank Minnesota
2000 Prince Blvd
Jonesville, MN 55400

CHECK NUMBER   063331 $\frac{74\text{-}39}{311}$ 567390

Date	Amount
04/29/03	$****10,974.79

PAY   4659484

TEN THOUSAND NINE HUNDRED SEVENTY FOUR AND 79 / 100 ****************************
TO THE ORDER OF:
                JOHN DOE
                1009 Franklin Blvd
                Sunnyvale, CA 95014

⑆478108240⑆ 200620375⑈ 1301

Figure 10

Check Showing the Amount as Both a Number and a String

Numbers between 10 and 19 are special cases. Let us have a separate function `teen_name` that converts them into strings `"eleven"`, `"twelve"`, `"thirteen"`, and so forth:

```
/**
   Turns a number between 10 and 19 into its English name.
   @param n an integer between 10 and 19
   @return the name of n ("ten" ... "nineteen")
*/
string teen_name(int n)
```

Next, suppose that the number is between 20 and 99. Then we show the tens as `"twenty"`, `"thirty"`, ..., `"ninety"`. For simplicity and consistency, put that computation into a separate function:

```
/**
   Gives the English name of a multiple of 10.
   @param n an integer between 2 and 9
   @return the name of 10 * n ("twenty" ... "ninety")
*/
string tens_name(int n)
```

Now suppose the number is at least 20 and at most 99. If the number is evenly divisible by 10, we use `tens_name`, and we are done. Otherwise, we print the tens with `tens_name` and the ones with `digit_name`. If the number is between 100 and 999, then we show a digit, the word `"hundred"`, and the remainder as described previously.

If the number is 1,000 or larger, then we convert the multiples of a thousand, in the same format, followed by the word `"thousand"`, then the remainder. For example, to convert 23,416, we first make 23 into a string `"twenty three"`, follow that with `"thousand"`, and then convert 416.

This sounds complicated enough that it is worth turning it into *pseudocode*. Pseudocode is code that looks like C++, but the descriptions it contains are not explicit enough for the compiler to understand. Here is the pseudocode of the verbal description of the algorithm.

```
string int_name(int n)
{
   int c = n; /* the part that still needs to be converted */
   string r; /* the return value */

   if (c >= 1000)
   {
      r = name of thousands in c + "thousand";
      remove thousands from c;
   }

   if (c >= 100)
   {
      r = r + name of hundreds in c + "hundred";
      remove hundreds from c;
   }

   if (c >= 20)
   {
      r = r + name of tens in c;
      remove tens from c;
```

```
    }

    if (c >= 10)
    {
        r = r + name of c;
        c = 0;
    }

    if (c > 0)
        r = r + name of c;

    return r;
}
```

This pseudocode has a number of important improvements over the verbal description. It shows how to arrange the tests, starting with the comparisons against the larger numbers, and it shows how the smaller number is subsequently processed in further `if` statements.

On the other hand, this pseudocode is vague about the actual conversion of the pieces, just referring to "name of tens" and the like. Furthermore, we lied about spaces. As it stands, the code would produce strings with no spaces, twohundredseventyfour, for example. Compared to the complexity of the main problem, one would hope that spaces are a minor issue. It is best not to muddy the pseudocode with minor details.

Some people like to write pseudocode on paper and use it as a guide for the actual coding. Others type the pseudocode into an editor and then transform it into the final code. You may want to try out both methods and see which one works better for you.

Now turn the pseudocode into real code. The last three cases are easy, because helper functions are already developed for them:

```
if (c >= 20)
{
    r = r + " " + tens_name(c / 10);
    c = c % 10;
}

if (c >= 10)
{
    r = r + " " + teen_name(c);
    c = 0;
}

if (c > 0)
    r = r + " " + digit_name(c);
```

The case of numbers between 100 and 999 is also easy, because you know that `c / 100` is a single digit:

```
if (c >= 100)
{
    r = r + " " + digit_name(c / 100) + " hundred";
    c = c % 100;
}
```

Only the case of numbers larger than 1,000 is somewhat vexing, because the number `c / 1000` is not necessarily a digit. If `c` is 23,416, then `c / 1000` is 23, and how are we going to obtain the name of *that?* We have helper functions for the ones, teens, and tens, but not for a value like 23. However, we know that c / 1000 is less than 1,000, because we assume that c is less than one million. We also have a perfectly good function that can convert any number < 1,000 into a string—namely the function int_name itself.

```
if (c >= 1000)
{
    r = int_name(c / 1000) + " thousand";
    c = c % 1000;
}
```

Here is the function in its entirety:

```
/**
    Turns a number into its English name.
    @param n a positive integer < 1,000,000
    @return the name of n (e.g., "two hundred seventy four")
*/
string int_name(int n)
{
    int c = n; /* the part that still needs to be converted */
    string r; /* the return value */

    if (c >= 1000)
    {
        r = int_name(c / 1000) + " thousand";
        c = c % 1000;
    }

    if (c >= 100)
    {
        r = r + " " + digit_name(c / 100) + " hundred";
        c = c % 100;
    }

    if (c >= 20)
    {
        r = r + " " + tens_name(c / 10);
        c = c % 10;
    }

    if (c >= 10)
    {
        r = r + " " + teen_name(c);
        c = 0;
    }

    if (c > 0)
        r = r + " " + digit_name(c);

    return r;
}
```

You may find it odd that a function can call itself, not just other functions. This is actually not as far-fetched as it sounds at first. Here is an example from basic algebra. You probably learned in your algebra class how to compute a square of a number such as 25.4

without the benefit of a calculator. This is a handy trick if you are stuck on a desert island and need to find out how many square millimeters are in a square inch. (There are 25.4 millimeters in an inch.) Here is how you do it. You use the binomial formula

$$(a + b)^2 = a^2 + 2ab + b^2$$

with $a = 25$ and $b = 0.4$. To compute 25.4^2, you first compute the simpler squares 25^2 and 0.4^2: $25^2 = 625$ and $0.4^2 = 0.16$. Then you put everything together: $25.4^2 = 625 + 2 \times 25 \times 0.4 + 0.16 = 645.16$.

The same phenomenon happens with the `int_name` function. It receives a number like 23,456. It is stuck on the 23, so it suspends itself and calls a function to solve that task. It happens to be another copy of the same function. That function returns `"twenty three"`. The original function resumes, threads together `"twenty three thousand"`, and works on the remainder, 456.

There is one important caveat. When a function invokes itself, it must give a *simpler* assignment to the second copy of itself. For example, `int_name` couldn't just call itself with the value that it received or with 10 times that value; then the calls would never stop. That is, of course, a general truth for solving problems by a series of functions. Each function must work on a simpler part of the whole. In Chapter 14, we will examine functions that call themselves in greater detail.

Now you have seen all important building blocks for the `int_name` procedure. As mentioned previously, the helper functions must be declared or defined *before* the `int_name` function. Here is the complete program.

File intname.cpp

```
1  #include <iostream>
2  #include <string>
3
4  using namespace std;
5
6  /**
7      Turns a digit into its English name.
8      @param n  an integer between 1 and 9
9      @return the name of n ("one" ... "nine")
10 */
11 string digit_name(int n)
12 {
13     if (n == 1) return "one";
14     if (n == 2) return "two";
15     if (n == 3) return "three";
16     if (n == 4) return "four";
17     if (n == 5) return "five";
18     if (n == 6) return "six";
19     if (n == 7) return "seven";
20     if (n == 8) return "eight";
21     if (n == 9) return "nine";
22     return "";
23 }
24
25 /**
26     Turns a number between 10 and 19 into its English name.
```

```
27      @param n  an integer between 10 and 19
28      @return  the name of n  ("ten" ... "nineteen")
29   */
30   string teen_name(int n)
31   {
32      if (n == 10) return "ten";
33      if (n == 11) return "eleven";
34      if (n == 12) return "twelve";
35      if (n == 13) return "thirteen";
36      if (n == 14) return "fourteen";
37      if (n == 15) return "fifteen";
38      if (n == 16) return "sixteen";
39      if (n == 17) return "seventeen";
40      if (n == 18) return "eighteen";
41      if (n == 19) return "nineteen";
42      return "";
43   }
44
45   /**
46      Gives the English name of a multiple of 10.
47      @param n  an integer between 2 and 9
48      @return  the name of 10 * n  ("twenty" ... "ninety")
49   */
50   string tens_name(int n)
51   {
52      if (n == 2) return "twenty";
53      if (n == 3) return "thirty";
54      if (n == 4) return "forty";
55      if (n == 5) return "fifty";
56      if (n == 6) return "sixty";
57      if (n == 7) return "seventy";
58      if (n == 8) return "eighty";
59      if (n == 9) return "ninety";
60      return "";
61   }
62
63   /**
64      Turns a number into its English name.
65      @param n  a positive integer < 1,000,000
66      @return  the name of n  (e.g. "two hundred seventy four")
67   */
68   string int_name(int n)
69   {
70      int c = n; /* the part that still needs to be converted */
71      string r; /* the return value */
72
73      if (c >= 1000)
74      {
75         r = int_name(c / 1000) + " thousand";
76         c = c % 1000;
77      }
78
79      if (c >= 100)
80      {
81         r = r + " " + digit_name(c / 100) + " hundred";
82         c = c % 100;
```

```
83        }
84
85        if (c >= 20)
86        {
87           r = r + " " + tens_name(c / 10);
88           c = c % 10;
89        }
90
91        if (c >= 10)
92        {
93           r = r + " " + teen_name(c);
94           c = 0;
95        }
96
97        if (c > 0)
98           r = r + " " + digit_name(c);
99
100       return r;
101    }
102
103    int main()
104    {
105       int n;
106       cout << "Please enter a positive integer: ";
107       cin >> n;
108       cout << int_name(n);
109       return 0;
110    }
```

5.12   Walkthroughs

The int_name function is sufficiently intricate that a dry run with it is a good idea, before we entrust it to the computer. Not only is there the issue with the call to itself; there are a number of other subtleties. For example, consider

```
if (c >= 20)
{
   r = r + " " + tens_name(c);
   c = c % 10;
}

if (c >= 10)
{
   r = r + " " + teen_name(c);
   c = 0;
}
```

Why does the first branch set c = c % 10, whereas the second branch sets c = 0? Actually, when I first wrote the code, both branches set c = c % 10, and then I realized my error when testing the code in my mind with a few examples. Such a mental test is called a *walkthrough*.

A walkthrough is done with pencil and paper. Take an index card, or some other piece of paper; write down the function call that you want to study.

```
                    int_name(n = 416)
```

Then write the names of the function variables. Write them in a table, since you will update them as you walk through the code.

```
                    int_name(n = 416)

    c       r
    416     ""
```

Skip past the test c >= 1000 and enter the test c >= 100. c / 100 is 4 and c % 100 is 16. digit_name(4) is easily seen to be "four".

Write the value that you expect at the top of a separate index card.

```
                    digit_name(n = 4)

    Returns "four"?
```

Had digit_name been complicated, you would have started another index card to figure out that function call. This could get out of hand if that function calls a third function. Computers have no trouble suspending one task, working on a second one, and coming back to the first, but people lose concentration when they have to switch their mental focus too often. So, instead of walking through subordinate function calls, you can just assume that they return the correct value, as you did with digit_name.

Set this card aside and walk through it later. You may accumulate numerous cards in this way. In practice, this procedure is necessary only for complex function calls, not simple ones like digit_name.

Now you are ready to update the variables. r has changed to r + " " + digit_name(c / 100) + " hundred", that is "four hundred", and c has changed to c % 100, or 16. You can cross out the old values and write the new ones under them.

```
                        int_name(n = 416)

        c       r
       416      ""
        16      "four hundred"



```

Now you enter the branch c >= 10. teens_name(16) is sixteen, so the variables now have the values

```
                        int_name(n = 416)

        c       r
       416      ""
        16      "four hundred"
         0      "four hundred sixteen"



```

Now it becomes clear why you need to set c to 0, not to c % 10. You don't want to get into the c > 0 branch. If you did, the result would be "four hundred sixteen six". However, if c is 36, you want to produce "thirty" first and then send the leftover 6 to the c > 0 branch.

In this case the walkthrough was successful. However, you will very commonly find errors during walkthroughs. Then you fix the code and try the walkthrough again. In a team with many programmers, regular walkthroughs are a useful method of improving code quality and understanding. (See [2].)

Productivity Hint 5.4

Commenting Out a Section of Code

Sometimes you are running tests on a long program, and a part of the program is incomplete or hopelessly messed up. You may want to ignore that part for some time and focus on getting the remainder of the code to work. Of course, you can cut out that text, paste it into another file, and paste it back later, but that is a hassle. Alternatively, you could just enclose the code to be ignored in comments.

The obvious method is to place a /* at the beginning of the offending code and a */ at the end. Unfortunately, that does not work in C++, because comments do not *nest*. That is, the /* and */ do not pair up as parentheses or braces do:

```
/*

/**
    Turns a number between 10 and 19 into its English name.
    @param n an integer between 10 and 19
    @return the name of n ("ten" ... "nineteen")
*/
string teen_name(int n)
{
    if (n == 11) return "eleven";
    else . . .
}

*/
```

The */ closing delimiter after the @return comment matches up with the /* opening delimiter at the top. All remaining code is compiled, and the */ at the end of the function causes an error message. This isn't very smart, of course. Some compilers do let you nest comments, but others don't. Some people recommend that you use only // comments. If you do, you can comment out a block of code with the /* . . . */ comments—well, kind of: If you first comment out a small block and then a larger one, you run into the same problem.

There is another way of masking out a block of code: by using so-called *preprocessor directives*.

```
#if 0

/**
    Turns a number between 10 and 19 into its English name.
    @param n an integer between 10 and 19
    @return the name of n ("ten" ... "nineteen")
*/
string teen_name(int n)
{
    if (n == 11) return "eleven";
    else . . .
}

#endif
```

Preprocessing is the phase before compilation, in which #include files are included, macros are expanded, and portions of code are conditionally included or excluded. All lines starting with a # are instructions to the preprocessor. Selective inclusion of code with `#if ... #endif` is useful if you need to write a program that has slight variations to run on different platforms. Here we use the feature to exclude the code. If you want to include it temporarily, change the `#if 0` to `#if 1`. Of course, once you have completed testing, you must clean it up and remove all `#if 0` directives and any unused code. *Unlike* `/* ... */` comments, the `#if ... #endif` directives can be nested.

Productivity Hint 5.5

Empty Stubs

Some people first write all code and then start compiling and testing. Others prefer to see some results quickly. If you are among the impatient, you will like the technique of *stubs*.

A stub is a function that is completely empty and returns a trivial value. The stub can be used to test that the code compiles and to debug the logic of other parts of the program.

```
/**
    Turns a digit into its English name.
    @param n an integer between 1 and 9
    @return the name of n ("one" ... "nine")
*/
string digit_name(int n)
{
    return "mumble";
}
```

```
/**
    Turns a number between 10 and 19 into its English name.
    @param n an integer between 10 and 19
    @return the name of n ("ten" ... "nineteen")
*/
string teen_name(int n)
{
    return "mumbleteen";
}
```

```
/**
    Gives the English name of a multiple of 10.
    @param n an integer between 2 and 9
    @return the name of 10 * n ("twenty" ... "ninety")
*/
string tens_name(int n)
{
    return "mumblety";
}
```

If you combine these stubs with the `int_name` function and test it with an input of 274, you will get an output of `"mumble hundred mumblety mumble"`, which shows you that you are on the right track. You can then flesh out one stub at a time.

This method is particularly helpful if you like composing your programs directly on the computer. Of course, the initial planning requires thought, not typing, and is best done at a

▼

desk. Once you know what functions you need, however, you can enter their interface descriptions and stubs, compile, implement one function, compile and test, implement the next function, compile and test, until you are done.

5.13   Preconditions

What should a function do when it is called with inappropriate inputs? For example, how should sqrt(-1) react? What should digit_name(-1) do? There are two choices.

- A function can fail safely. For example, the digit_name function simply returns an empty string when it is called with an unexpected input.

- A function can terminate. Many of the mathematical functions do that. The documentation states what inputs are legal and what inputs are not legal. If the function is called with an illegal input, it terminates in some way.

There are different ways of terminating a function. The mathematical functions choose the most brutal one: printing a message and terminating the entire program. C++ has a very sophisticated mechanism that allows a function to terminate and send a so-called *exception*, which signals to an appropriate receiver that something has gone very wrong. As long as such a receiver is in place, it can handle the problem and avoid termination of the program. However, exception handling is complex—you will find a brief discussion in Chapter 17. For now, we will choose a simpler method, shown in Syntax 5.6: using the assert macro. (A *macro* is a special instruction to the compiler that inserts complex code into the program text.)

```
#include <cassert>
...
double future_value(double initial_balance, double p, int n)
{
    assert(p >= 0);
    assert(n >= 0);

    return initial_balance * pow(1 + p / 100, n);
}
```

Syntax 5.6 : Assertion

assert(*expression*);

Example: assert(x >= 0);

Purpose: If the expression is true, do nothing. If it is false, terminate the program, displaying the file name, line number, and expression.

If the condition inside the macro is true when the macro is encountered, then nothing happens. However, when the condition is false, the program aborts with an error message

```
assertion failure in file fincalc.cpp line 49: p >= 0
```

This is a more useful message than that issued by a failing mathematical function. Those functions just state that an error has occurred *somewhere*. The `assert` message gives the exact line number of the trouble. The error message is displayed where the tester can see it: on the terminal screen for a text program or in a dialog box for a graphics program.

More importantly, it is possible to change the behavior of `assert` when a program has been fully tested. After a certain switch has been set in the compiler, `assert` statements are simply ignored. No time-consuming test takes place, no error message is generated, and the program never aborts.

When writing a function, how should you handle bad inputs? Should you terminate or should you fail safely? Consider `sqrt`. It would be an easy matter to implement a square root function that returns 0 for negative values and the actual square root for positive values. Suppose you use that function to compute the intersection points of a circle and a line. Suppose they don't intersect, but you forgot to take that possibility into account. Now the square root of a negative number will return a wrong value, namely 0, and you will obtain two bogus intersection points. (Actually, you'll get the same point twice.) You may miss that during testing, and the faulty program may make it into production. This isn't a big deal for our graphics program, but suppose the program directs a dental drill robot. It would start drilling somewhere outside the tooth. This makes termination an attractive alternative. It is hard to overlook termination during testing, and it is better if the drill stops rather than boring through the patient's gums.

Here is what you should do when writing a function:

1. Establish clear *preconditions* for all inputs. Write in the `@param` comment what values you are not willing to handle.

2. Write `assert` statements that enforce the preconditions.

3. Be sure to supply correct results for all inputs that fulfill the precondition.

Apply this strategy to the `future_value` function:

```
/**
    Computes the value of an investment with compound interest.
    @param initial_balance the initial value of the investment
    @param p the interest rate in percent; must be ≥ 0
    @param n the number of periods the investment is held;  must be ≥ 0
    @return the balance after n periods
*/
double future_value(double initial_balance, double p, int n)
{
    assert(p >= 0);
    assert(n >= 0);

    return initial_balance * pow(1 + p / 100, n);
}
```

We advertised that `p` and `n` must be ≥ 0. Such a condition is a *precondition* of the `future_value` function. The function is responsible only for handling inputs that conform to the precondition. It is free to do *anything* if the precondition is not fulfilled. It would be perfectly legal if the function reformatted the hard disk every time it was called with a wrong input. Naturally, that isn't reasonable. Instead, we check the precondition with an assert statement. If the function is called with a bad input, the program terminates. That may not be "nice", but it is legal. Remember that the function can do anything if the precondition is not fulfilled.

Another alternative is to let the function fail safely by returning a default value when the function is called with a negative interest rate:

```
/**
    Computes the value of an investment with compound interest.
    @param initial_balance the initial value of the investment
    @param p the interest rate in percent; must be ≥ 0
    @param n the number of periods the investment is held;  must be ≥ 0
    @return   The balance after n periods
*/
double future_value(double initial_balance, double p, int n)
{
    if (p >= 0)
        return initial_balance * pow(1 + p / 100, n);
    else
        return 0;
}
```

There are advantages and disadvantages to this approach. If the program calling the future_value function has a few bugs that cause it to pass a negative interest rate as an input value, then the version with the assertion will make the bugs very obvious during testing—it is hard to ignore if the program aborts. The fail-safe version, on the other hand, will quietly return 0, and you may not notice that it performs some wrong calculations as a consequence.

Bertrand Meyer [1] compares preconditions to contracts. The function promises to compute the correct answer for all inputs that fulfill the precondition. The caller promises never to call the function with illegal inputs. If the caller fulfills its promise and gets a wrong answer, it can take the function to programmer's court. If the caller doesn't fulfill its promise and something terrible happens as a consequence, it has no recourse.

▼   **Random Fact**   5.1 ▶

The Explosive Growth of Personal Computers

In 1971, Marcian E. "Ted" Hoff, an engineer at Intel Corporation was working on a chip for a manufacturer of electronic calculators. He realized that it would be a better idea to develop a *general-purpose* chip that could be *programmed* to interface with the keys and display of a calculator, rather than to do yet another custom design. Thus, the *microprocessor* was born. At the time, its primary application was as a controller for calculators, washing machines, and the like. It took years for the computer industry to notice that a genuine central processing unit was now available as a single chip.

Hobbyists were the first to catch on. In 1974 the first computer *kit*, the Altair 8800, was available from MITS Electronics for about $350. The kit consisted of the microprocessor, a circuit board, a very small amount of memory, toggle switches, and a row of display lights. Purchasers had to solder and assemble it, then program it in machine language through the toggle switches. It was not a big hit.

The first big hit was the Apple II. It was a real computer with a keyboard, a monitor, and a floppy disk drive. When it was first released, users had a $3,000 machine that could play Space Invaders, run a primitive bookkeeping program, or let users program it in BASIC. The original Apple II did not even support lowercase letters, making it worthless for word processing. The breakthrough came in 1979, with a new *spreadsheet* program, VisiCalc. In a spreadsheet, you enter financial data and their relationships into a grid of rows and columns (see Figure 11). Then you modify some of the data and watch in real time how the others change. For example, you can see how changing the mix of widgets in a manufacturing plant might affect estimated costs and profits. Middle managers in companies, who understood computers and were fed up with having to wait for hours or days to retrieve their data runs from the computing center, snapped up VisiCalc and the computer that was needed to run it. For them, the computer was a spreadsheet machine.

The next big hit was the IBM Personal Computer, ever after known as the PC. It was the first widely available personal computer that used Intel's 16-bit processor, the 8086, whose successors are still being used in personal computers today. The success of the PC was based

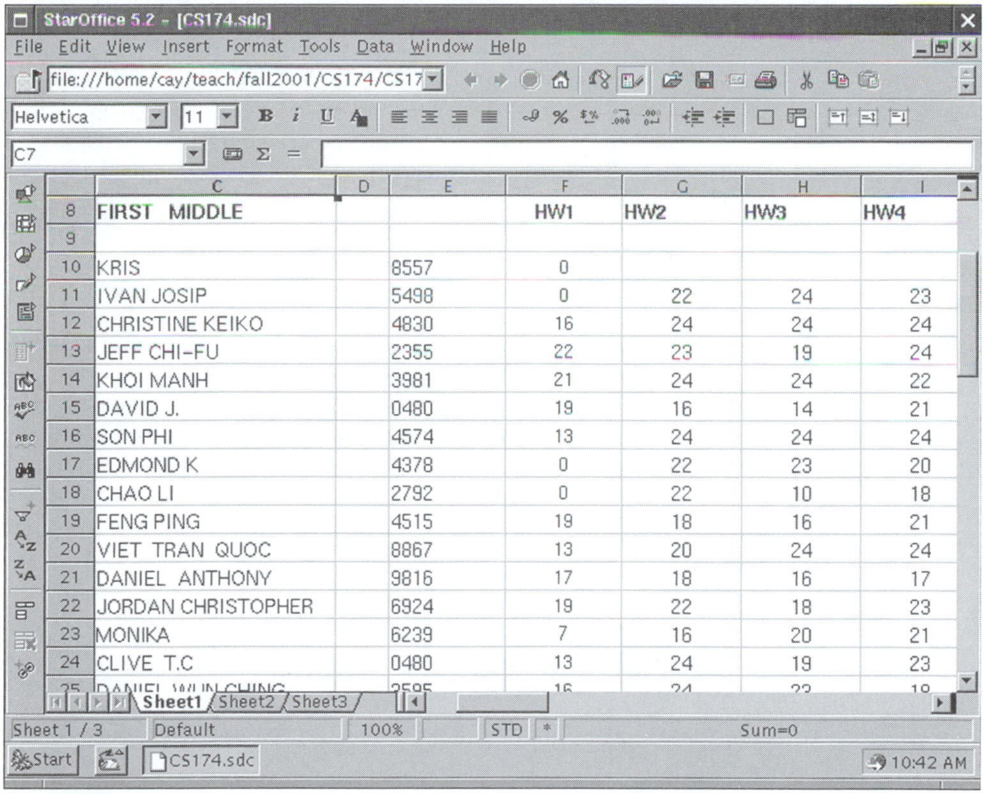

	C	D	E	F	G	H	I
8	FIRST MIDDLE			HW1	HW2	HW3	HW4
9							
10	KRIS		8557	0			
11	IVAN JOSIP		5498	0	22	24	23
12	CHRISTINE KEIKO		4830	16	24	24	24
13	JEFF CHI-FU		2355	22	23	19	24
14	KHOI MANH		3981	21	24	24	22
15	DAVID J.		0480	19	16	14	21
16	SON PHI		4574	13	24	24	24
17	EDMOND K		4378	0	22	23	20
18	CHAO LI		2792	0	22	10	18
19	FENG PING		4515	19	18	16	21
20	VIET TRAN QUOC		8867	13	20	24	24
21	DANIEL ANTHONY		9816	17	18	16	17
22	JORDAN CHRISTOPHER		6924	19	22	18	23
23	MONIKA		6239	7	16	20	21
24	CLIVE T.C		0480	13	24	19	23

Figure 11

Spreadsheet

not on any engineering breakthroughs, but on the fact that it was easy to *clone*. IBM published specifications for plug-in cards, and it went one step further. It published the exact source code of the so-called BIOS (Basic Input/Output System), which controls the keyboard, monitor, ports, and disk drives and must be installed in ROM form in every PC. This allowed third-party vendors of plug-in cards to ensure that the BIOS code, and third-party extensions of it, interacted correctly with the equipment. Of course, the code itself was the property of IBM and could not be copied legally. Perhaps IBM did not foresee that functionally equivalent versions of the BIOS nevertheless could be recreated by others. Compaq, one of the first clone vendors, had fifteen engineers, who certified that they had never seen the original IBM code, write a new version that conformed precisely to the IBM specifications. Other companies did the same, and soon there were a number of vendors selling computers that ran the same software as IBM's PC but distinguished themselves by a lower price, increased portability, or better performance. In time, IBM lost its dominant position in the PC market. It is now one of many companies producing IBM PC-compatible computers.

IBM never produced an operating system for its PCs. An operating system organizes the interaction between the user and the computer, starts application programs, and manages disk storage and other resources. Instead, IBM offered customers the option of three separate operating systems. Most customers couldn't care less about the operating system. They chose the system that was able to launch most of the few applications that existed at the time. It happened to be DOS (Disk Operating System) by Microsoft. Microsoft cheerfully licensed the same operating system to other hardware vendors and encouraged software companies to write DOS applications. A huge number of useful application programs for PC-compatible machines was the result.

PC applications were certainly useful, but they were not easy to learn. Every vendor developed a different *user interface*: the collection of keystrokes, menu options, and settings that a user needed to master to use a software package effectively. Data exchange between applications was difficult, because each program used a different data format. The Apple Macintosh changed all that in 1984. The designers of the Macintosh had the vision to supply an intuitive user interface with the computer and to force software developers to adhere to it. It took Microsoft and PC-compatible manufacturers years to catch up.

Accidental Empires [3] is highly recommended for an amusing and irreverent account of the emergence of personal computers.

At the time of this writing (2002), it is estimated that two in five U.S. households own a personal computer and one in six households with a PC is connected to the Internet. Most personal computers are used for word processing, home finance (banking, budgeting, taxes), accessing information from CD-ROM and online sources, and entertainment. Some analysts predict that the personal computer will merge with the television set and cable network into an entertainment and information appliance.

CHAPTER SUMMARY

1. A *function* receives input parameters and computes a result that depends on those inputs.

2. *Parameter values* are supplied in the function call. They are stored in the *parameter variables* of the function. The types of the parameter values and variables must match.

3. Once the function result has been computed, the `return` statement terminates the function and sends the result to the caller.

4. Function comments explain the purpose of the function and the meaning of the parameters and return value, as well as any special requirements.

5. Side effects are externally observable results caused by a function call, other than the returning of a result; for example, displaying a message. *Generally*, side effects should be avoided in functions that return values.

6. A *procedure* is a function that returns no value. Its return value usually has type `void`, and it accomplishes its purpose entirely through side effects.

7. A program consists of many functions and procedures. Just like variables, functions and procedures need to be defined before they can be used.

8. Use the process of *stepwise refinement* to decompose complex tasks into simpler ones.

9. *Preconditions* are restrictions on the function parameters. If a function is called in violation of a precondition, the function is not responsible for computing the right result. To check for conformance to preconditions, use the `assert` macro.

10. A function can call itself, but it must provide a simpler parameter to itself in successive calls.

FURTHER READING

[1] Bertrand Meyer, *Object-Oriented Software Construction*, Prentice-Hall, 1989, Chapter 7.
[2] Daniel P. Freedman and Gerald M. Weinberg, *Handbook of Walkthroughs, Inspections and Technical Reviews*, Dorset House, 1990.
[3] Robert X. Cringely, *Accidental Empires*, Addison-Wesley, 1992.

REVIEW EXERCISES

Exercise R5.1. Give realistic examples of the following:

(a) A function with a `double` parameter and a `double` return value
(b) A function with an `int` parameter and a `double` return value
(c) A function with an `int` parameter and a `string` return value
(d) A function with two `double` parameters and a `bool` return value
(e) A procedure with two `int&` parameters and no return value
(f) A function with no parameter and an `int` return value
(g) A function with a `Circle` parameter and a `double` return value
(h) A function with a `Line` parameter and a `Point` return value

Just describe what these functions do. Do not program them. For example, an answer to the first question is "sine" or "square root".

Exercise R5.2. True or false?

(a) A function has exactly one `return` statement.

(b) A function has at least one `return` statement.

(c) A function has at most one return value.

(d) A procedure (with return value `void`) never has a `return` statement.

(e) When executing a `return` statement, the function exits immediately.

(f) A function without parameters always has a side effect.

(g) A procedure (with return value `void`) always has a side effect.

(h) A function without side effects always returns the same value when called with the same parameters.

Exercise R5.3. Write detailed function comments for the following functions. Be sure to describe all conditions under which the function cannot compute its result. Just write the comments, not the functions.

(a) `double sqrt(double x)`

(b) `Point midpoint(Point a, Point b)`

(c) `double area(Circle c)`

(d) `string roman_numeral(int n)`

(e) `double slope(Line a)`

(f) `bool is_leap_year(year y)`

(g) `string weekday(int w)`

Exercise R5.4. Consider these functions:

```
double f(double x) { return g(x) + sqrt(h(x)); }
double g(double x) { return 4 * h(x); }
double h(double x) { return x * x + k(x) - 1; }
double k(double x) { return 2 * (x + 1); }
```

Without actually compiling and running a program, determine the results of the following function calls.

(a) `double x1 = f(2);`

(b) `double x2 = g(h(2));`

(c) `double x3 = k(g(2) + h(2));`

(d) `double x4 = f(0) + f(1) + f(2);`

(e) `double x5 = f(-1) + g(-1) + h(-1) + k(-1);`

Exercise R5.5. What is a predicate function? Give a definition, an example of a predicate function, and an example of how to use it.

Exercise R5.6. What is the difference between a parameter value and a return value? What is the difference between a parameter value and a parameter variable? What is the difference between a parameter value and a value parameter?

Exercise R5.7. Ideally, a function should have no side effect. Can you write a program in which no function has a side effect? Would such a program be useful?

Exercise R5.8. For the following functions and procedures, circle the parameters that must be implemented as reference parameters.

(a) `y = sin(x);`

(b) `print_paycheck(harry);`

(c) `raise_salary(harry, 5.5);`

(d) `make_uppercase(message);`

(e) `key = uppercase(input);`

(f) `change_name(harry, "Horton");`

Exercise R5.9. For each of the variables in the following program, indicate the scope. Then determine what the program prints, without actually running the program.

```
int a = 0;
int b = 0;
int f(int c)
{
   int n = 0;
   a = c;
   if (n < c)
      n = a + b;
   return n;
}

int g(int c)
{
   int n = 0;
   int a = c;
   if (n < f(c))
      n = a + b;
   return n;
}

int main()
{
   int i = 1;
   int b = g(i);
   cout << a + b + i << "\n";
   return 0;
}
```

Exercise R5.10. We have seen three kinds of variables in C++: global variables, parameter variables, and local variables. Classify the variables of the preceding exercise according to these categories.

Exercise R5.11. Use the process of stepwise refinement to describe the process of making scrambled eggs. Discuss what you do if you do not find eggs in the refrigerator. Produce a call tree.

Exercise R5.12. How many parameters does the following function have? How many return values does it have? *Hint:* The C++ notions of "parameter" and "return value" are not the same as the intuitive notions of "input" and "output".

```
void average(double& avg)
{
    cout << "Please enter two numbers: ";
    double x;
    double y;
    cin >> x >> y;
    avg = (x + y) / 2;
}
```

Exercise R5.13. What is the difference between a function and a procedure? A function and a program? The `main` procedure and a program?

Exercise R5.14. Perform a walkthrough of the `int_name` function with the following inputs:

(a) 5

(b) 12

(c) 21

(d) 321

(e) 1024

(f) 11954

(g) 0

(h) -2

Exercise R5.15. What preconditions do the following functions from the standard C++ library have?

(a) `sqrt`

(b) `tan`

(c) `log`

(d) `exp`

(e) `pow`

(f) `fabs`

Exercise R5.16. When a function is called with parameters that violate its precondition, it can terminate or fail safely. Give two examples of library functions (standard C++ or the library functions used in this book) that fail safely when called with invalid parameters, and give two examples of library functions that terminate.

Exercise R5.17. Consider the following function:

```
int f(int n)
{
    if (n <= 1) return 1;
    if (n % 2 == 0) /* n is even */
        return f(n / 2);
    else return f(3 * n + 1);
}
```

Perform walkthroughs of the computation f(1), f(2), f(3), f(4), f(5), f(6), f(7), f(8), f(9), and f(10). Can you conjecture what value this function computes for arbitrary n? Can you *prove* that the function always terminates? If so, please let the author know. At the time of this writing, this is an unsolved problem in mathematics, sometimes called the "$3n + 1$ problem" or the "Collatz problem".

Exercise R5.18. Consider the following procedure that is intended to swap the values of two integers:

```
void false_swap1(int& a, int& b)
{
   a = b;
   b = a;
}

int main()
{
   int x = 3;
   int y = 4;
   false_swap1(x, y);
   cout << x << " " << y << "\n";
   return 0;
}
```

Why doesn't the procedure swap the contents of x and y? How can you rewrite the procedure to work correctly?

Exercise R5.19. Consider the following procedure that is intended to swap the values of two integers:

```
void false_swap2(int a, int b)
{
   int temp = a;
   a = b;
   b = temp;
}

int main()
{
   int x = 3;
   int y = 4;
   false_swap2(x, y);
   cout << x << " " << y << "\n";
   return 0;
}
```

Why doesn't the procedure swap the contents of x and y? How can you rewrite the procedure to work correctly?

Exercise R5.20. Prove that the following procedure swaps two integers, without requiring a temporary variable!

```
void tricky_swap(int& a, int& b)
{
   a = a - b;
   b = a + b;
   a = b - a;
}
```

PROGRAMMING EXERCISES

Exercise P5.1. Enhance the program computing bank balances by prompting for the initial balance and the interest rate. Then print the balance after 10, 20, and 30 years.

Exercise P5.2. Write a procedure `void sort2(int& a, int& b)` that swaps the values of a and b if a is greater than b and otherwise leaves a and b unchanged. For example,

```
int u = 2;
int v = 3;
int w = 4;
int x = 1;
sort2(u, v); /* u is still 2, v is still 3 */
sort2(w, x); /* w is now 1, x is now 4 */
```

Exercise P5.3. Write a procedure `sort3(int& a, int& b, int& c)` that swaps its three inputs to arrange them in sorted order. For example,

```
int v = 3;
int w = 4;
int x = 1;
sort3(v, w, x); /* v is now 1, w is now 3, x is now 4 */
```

Hint: Use `sort2` of the preceding exercise.

Exercise P5.4. Enhance the `int_name` function so that it works correctly for values ≤ 10,000,000.

Exercise P5.5. Enhance the `int_name` function so that it works correctly for negative values and zero. *Caution:* Make sure the improved function doesn't print 20 as `"twenty zero"`.

Exercise P5.6. For some values (for example, 20), the `int_name` function returns a string with a leading space (`" twenty"`). Repair that blemish and ensure that spaces are inserted only when necessary. *Hint:* There are two ways of accomplishing this. Either ensure that leading spaces are never inserted, or remove leading spaces from the result before returning it.

Exercise P5.7. Write functions

```
double sphere_volume(double r);
double sphere_surface(double r);
double cylinder_volume(double r, double h);
double cylinder_surface(double r, double h);
double cone_volume(double r, double h);
double cone_surface(double r, double h);
```

that compute the volume and surface area of a sphere with radius r, a cylinder with a circular base with radius r and height h, and a cone with a circular base with radius r and height h. Then write a program that prompts the user for the values of r and h, calls the six functions, and prints the results.

Exercise P5.8. Write functions

```
double perimeter(Circle c);
double area(Circle c);
```

that compute the area and the perimeter of the circle c. Use these functions in a graphics program that prompts the user to specify a circle. Then display messages with the perimeter and area of the circle.

Exercise P5.9. Write a function

```
double distance(Point p, Point q)
```

that computes the distance between two points. Write a test program that asks the user to select two points. Then display the distance.

Exercise P5.10. Write a function

```
bool is_inside(Point p, Circle c)
```

that tests if a point is inside a circle. (You need to compute the distance between p and the center of the circle, and compare it to the radius.) Write a test program that asks the user to click on the center of the circle, then asks for the radius, then asks the user to click on any point on the screen. Display a message that indicates whether the user clicked inside the circle.

Exercise P5.11. Write a function

```
double get_double(string prompt)
```

that displays the prompt string, followed by a space, reads a floating-point number in, and returns it. (In other words, write a console version of cwin.get_double.) Here is a typical usage:

```
salary = get_double("Please enter your salary:");
perc_raise =
    get_double("What percentage raise would you like?");
```

If there is an input error, abort the program by calling exit(1). (You will see in Chapter 6 how to improve this behavior.)

Exercise P5.12. Write functions

```
display_H(Point p);
display_E(Point p);
display_L(Point p);
display_O(Point p);
```

that show the letters H, E, L, O on the graphics window, where the point p is the top left corner of the letter. Fit the letter in a 1 × 1 square. Then call the functions to draw the words "HELLO" and "HOLE" on the graphics display. Draw lines and circles. Do not use the Message class. Do not use cout.

Exercise P5.13. *Leap years.* Write a predicate function

```
bool leap_year(int year)
```

that tests whether a year is a leap year: that is, a year with 366 days. Leap years are necessary to keep the calendar synchronized with the sun because the earth revolves around the sun once every 365.25 days. Actually, that figure is not entirely precise, and for all dates after 1582 the *Gregorian correction* applies. Usually years that are divisible by 4 are leap years, for example 1996. However, years that are divisible by 100 (for example, 1900) are not leap years, but years that are divisible by 400 are leap years (for example, 2000).

Exercise P5.14. *Julian dates.* Suppose you would like to know how many days ago Columbus was born. It is tedious to figure this out by hand, because months have different lengths and because you have to worry about leap years. Many people, such as astronomers, who deal with dates a lot have become tired of dealing with the craziness of the calendar and instead represent days in a completely different way: the so-called Julian day number. That value is defined as the number of days that have elapsed since Jan. 1, 4713 B.C. A convenient reference point is that October 9, 1995, is Julian day 2,450,000.

Here is an algorithm to compute the Julian day number: Set `jd`, `jm`, `jy` to the day, month, and year. If the year is negative, add 1 to `jy`. (There was no year 0. Year 1 B.C. was immediately followed by year A.D. 1) If the month is larger than February, add 1 to `jm`. Otherwise, add 13 to `jm` and subtract 1 from `jy`. Then compute

```
long jul = floor(365.25 * jy) + floor(30.6001 * jm) + d
   + 1720995.0
```

We store the result in a variable of type `long`; simple integers may not have enough digits to hold the value. If the date was before October 15, 1582, return this value. Otherwise, perform the following correction:

```
int ja = 0.01 * jy;
jul = jul + 2 - ja + 0.25 * ja;
```

Now write a function

```
long julian(int year, int month, int day)
```

that converts a date into a Julian day number. Use that function in a program that prompts the user for a date in the past, then prints out how many days that is away from today's date.

Exercise P5.15. Write a procedure

```
void jul_to_date(long jul, int& year, int& month, int& day)
```

that performs the opposite conversion, from Julian day numbers to dates. Here is the algorithm. Starting with October 15, 1582 (Julian day number 2,299,161), apply the correction

```
long jalpha = ((jul - 1867216) - 0.25) / 36524.25;
jul = jul + 1 + jalpha - 0.25 * jalpha;
```

Then compute

```
long jb = jul + 1524;
long jc = 6680.0 + (jb - 2439870 - 122.1)/365.25;
long jd = 365 * jc + (0.25 * jc);
int je = (jb - jd)/30.6001;
```

The day, month, and year are computed as

```
day = jb - jd - (long)(30.6001 * je);
month = je - 1;
year = (int)(jc - 4715);
```

If the month is greater than 12, subtract 12. If the month is greater than 2, subtract one from the year. If the year is not positive, subtract 1.

Use the function to write the following program. Ask the user for a date and a number n. Then print the date that is n days away from the input date. You can use that program to find out the exact day that was 100,000 days ago. The computation is simple. First convert the input date to the Julian day number, using the function of the preceding exercise, then subtract n, and then convert back using `jul_to_date`.

Exercise P5.16. In Exercise P4.12 you were asked to write a program to convert a number to its representation in Roman numerals. At the time, you did not know how to factor out common code, and as a consequence the resulting program was rather long. Rewrite that program by implementing and using the following function:

```
string roman_digit(int n, string one, string five,
    string ten)
```

That function translates one digit, using the strings specified for the one, five, and ten values. You would call the function as follows:

```
roman_ones = roman_digit(n % 10, "I", "V", "X");
n = n / 10;
roman_tens = roman_digit(n % 10, "X", "L", "C");
 . . .
```

Exercise P5.17. Write a program that converts a Roman number such as MCMLXX-VIII to its decimal number representation. *Hint*: First write a function that yields the numeric value of each of the letters. Then convert a string as follows: Look at the first *two* characters. If the first has a larger value than the second, then simply convert the first, call the conversion function again for the substring starting with the second character, and add both values. If the first one has a smaller value than the second, compute the difference and add to it the conversion of the tail. This algorithm will convert "Pig Roman" numbers like "IC". Extra credit if you can modify it to process only genuine Roman numbers.

Exercise P5.18. Write procedures to rotate and scale a point.

```
void rotate(Point& p, double angle);
void scale(Point& p, double scale);
```

Here are the equations for the transformations. If p is the original point, α the angle of the rotation, and q the point after rotation, then

$$q_x = p_x \cos\alpha + p_y \sin\alpha$$
$$q_y = -p_x \sin\alpha + p_y \cos\alpha$$

If p is the original point, s the scale factor, and q the point after scaling, then

$$q_x = sp_x$$
$$q_y = sp_y$$

However, note that your functions need to *replace* the point with its rotated or scaled image.

Now write the following graphics program. Start out with the point (5,5). *Rotate* it five times by 10 degrees, then scale it five times by 0.95. Then start with the point (–5,–5). Repeat the following five times.

```
rotate(b, 10 * PI / 180);
scale(b, 0.95);
```

That is, interleave the rotation and scaling five times.

Exercise P5.19. *Postal bar codes*. For faster sorting of letters, the United States Postal Service encourages companies that send large volumes of mail to use a bar code denoting the zip code (see Figure 12).

The encoding scheme for a five-digit zip code is shown in Figure 13. There are full-height frame bars on each side. The five encoded digits are followed by a check digit, which is computed as follows: Add up all digits, and choose the check digit to make the sum a multiple of 10. For example, the zip code 95014 has a sum of 19, so the check digit is 1 to make the sum equal to 20.

Each digit of the zip code, and the check digit, is encoded according to the following table where 0 denotes a half bar and 1 a full bar.

	7	4	2	1	0
1	0	0	0	1	1
2	0	0	1	0	1
3	0	0	1	1	0
4	0	1	0	0	1
5	0	1	0	1	0
6	0	1	1	0	0
7	1	0	0	0	1
8	1	0	0	1	0
9	1	0	1	0	0
0	1	1	0	0	0

Note that they represent all combinations of two full and three half bars. The digit can be easily computed from the bar code using the column weights 7, 4, 2, 1, 0. For exam-

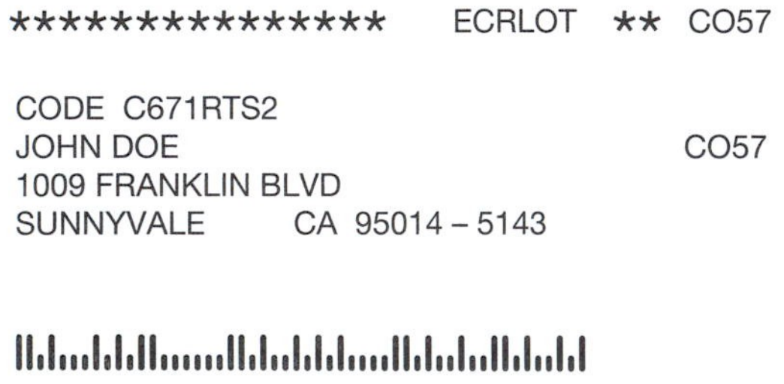
***************   ECRLOT ** CO57
CODE C671RTS2
JOHN DOE   CO57
1009 FRANKLIN BLVD
SUNNYVALE   CA 95014 – 5143

Figure 12

A Postal Bar Code

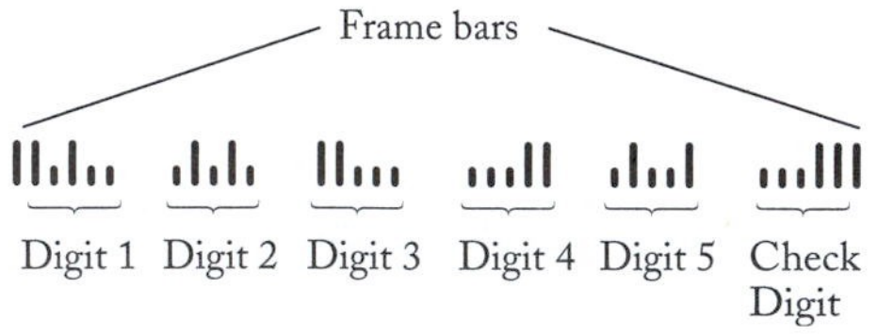
Frame bars
Digit 1
Digit 2
Digit 3
Digit 4
Digit 5
Check Digit

Figure 13

Encoding for Five-Digit Bar Codes

ple, 01100 is $0 \times 7 + 1 \times 4 + 1 \times 2 + 0 \times 1 \times 0 \times 0 = 6$. The only exception is 0, which would yield 11 according to the weight formula.

Write a program that asks the user for a zip code and prints the bar code. Use : for half bars, | for full bars. For example, 95014 becomes

```
||:|:::|:|:||:::::::||:|::|:::|||
```

Exercise P5.20. Write a program that displays the bar code, using actual bars, on your graphic screen. *Hint:* Write functions `half_bar(Point start)` and `full_bar(Point start)`.

Exercise P5.21. Write a program that reads in a bar code (with : denoting half bars and | denoting full bars) and prints out the zip code it represents. Print an error message if the bar code is not correct.

Exercise P5.22. Write a program that prints instructions to get coffee, asking the user for input whenever a decision needs to be made. Decompose each task into a procedure, for example:

```
void brew_coffee()
{
    cout << "Add water to the coffee maker.\n";
    cout << "Put a filter in the coffee maker.\n";
    grind_coffee();
    cout << "Put the coffee in the filter.\n";
    . . .
}
```

Classes

▶ To be able to implement your own classes

▶ To master the separation of interface and implementation

▶ To understand the concept of encapsulation

▶ To design and implement accessor and mutator member functions

▶ To understand object construction

▶ To learn how to distribute a program over multiple source files

In Chapter 3 you learned how to use objects from existing classes. By now, you have used employee records and graphical shapes in many programs. Recall how objects differ from numerical data types. Objects are constructed by specifying construction parameters, such as

```
Employee harry("Hacker, Harry",
   35000);
```

To use objects, either to inquire about their state or to modify them, you apply *member functions* with the *dot notation*.

```
harry.set_salary(38000);
cout << harry.get_name();
```

In this chapter you will learn how to design your own classes and member functions. As you learn the mechanics of defining classes, constructors, and member functions, you will learn how to discover useful classes that help you solve programming problems.

CHAPTER CONTENTS

6.1 Discovering Classes

If you find yourself defining a number of related variables that all refer to the same concept, stop coding and think about that concept for a while. Then define a class that abstracts the concept and contains these variables as data fields.

Suppose you read in information about computers. Each information record contains the model name, the price, and a score between 0 and 100. Here are some sample data:

```
ACMA P600
995
75
Alaris Nx686
798
57
AMAX Powerstation 600
999
75
AMS Infogold P600
795
69
AST Premmia
2080
80
Austin 600
1499
95
Blackship NX-600
695
60
Kompac 690
598
60
```

You are trying to find the "best bang for the buck": the product for which the value (score/price) is highest. The following program finds this information for you.

File bestval.cpp

```cpp
1 #include <iostream>
2 #include <string>
3
4 using namespace std;
5
6 int main()
7 {
8     string best_name = "";
9     double best_price = 1;
10    int best_score = 0;
11
12    bool more = true;
13    while (more)
14    {
15       string next_name;
16       double next_price;
17       int next_score;
18
19       cout << "Please enter the model name: ";
20       getline(cin, next_name);
21       cout << "Please enter the price: ";
22       cin >> next_price;
23       cout << "Please enter the score: ";
24       cin >> next_score;
25       string remainder; /* read remainder of line */
26       getline(cin, remainder);
27
28       if (next_score / next_price > best_score / best_price)
29       {
30          best_name = next_name;
31          best_score = next_score;
32          best_price = next_price;
33       }
34
35       cout << "More data? (y/n) ";
36       string answer;
37       getline(cin, answer);
38       if (answer != "y") more = false;
39    }
40
41    cout << "The best value is " << best_name
42       << " Price: " << best_price
43       << " Score: " << best_score << "\n";
44
45    return 0;
46 }
```

Pay special attention to the two sets of variables: best_name, best_price, best_score and next_name, next_price, next_score. The very fact that you have two sets of these variables suggests that a common concept is lurking just under the surface.

Each of these two sets of variables describes a *product*. One of them describes the best product, the other one the next product to be read in. In the following sections we will develop a Product class to simplify this program.

Common Error   6.1

Mixing >> and getline Input

It is tricky to mix >> and getline input. Consider how a product is being read in by the bestval.cpp program:

```
cout << "Please enter the model name: ";
getline(cin, next_name);
cout << "Please enter the price: ";
cin >> next_price;
cout << "Please enter the score: ";
cin >> next_score;
```

The getline function reads an entire line of input, including the newline character at the end of the line. It places all characters except for that newline character into the string next_name. The >> operator reads all white space (that is, spaces, tabs, and newlines) until it reaches a number. Then it reads only the characters in that number. It does not consume the character following the number, typically a newline. This is a problem when a call to getline immediately follows a call to >>. Then the call to getline reads only the newline, considering it as the end of an empty line.

Perhaps an example will make this clearer. Consider the first input lines of the product descriptions. Calling getline consumes the colored characters.

cin = | A | C | M | A | | P | 6 | 0 | 0 | \n | 9 | 9 | 5 | \n | 7 | 5 | \n | y | \n | }

After the call to getline, the first line has been read completely, including the newline at the end. Next, the call to cin >> next_price reads the digits.

cin = | 9 | 9 | 5 | \n | 7 | 5 | \n | y | \n | }

After the call to cin >> next_price, the digits of the number have been read, but the newline is still unread. This is not a problem for the next call to cin >> next_score. That call first skips all leading white space, including the newline, then reads the next number.

cin = | \n | 7 | 5 | \n | y | \n | }

It again leaves the newline in the input stream, because the >> operators never read any more characters than absolutely necessary. Now we have a problem. The next call to getline reads a blank line.

cin = | \n | y | \n | }

That call happens in the following context:

```
cout << "More data? (y/n) ";
string answer;
getline(cin, answer);
if (answer != "y") more = false;
```

▼   It reads only the newline and sets answer to the empty string!

$$cin = \boxed{y\ |\ \backslash n}\ \}$$

▼   The empty string is not the string "y", so more is set to false, and the loop terminates.
    This is a problem whenever an input with the >> operator is followed by a call to
getline. The intention, of course, is to skip the rest of the current line and have getline

▼   read the next line. This purpose is achieved by the following statements, which must be
inserted after the last call to the >> operator:

```
string remainder; /* read remainder of line */
```
▼
```
getline(cin, remainder);
/* now you are ready to call getline again */
```

6.2   Interfaces

To define a class, we first need to specify an *interface*. The interface of the Product class
consists of all functions that we want to apply to product objects. Looking at the program of the preceding section, we need to be able to perform the following:

- Make a new product object
- Read in a product object
- Compare two products and find out which one is better
- Print a product

The interface is specified in the *class definition*, summarized in Syntax 6.1. Here is the
C++ syntax for the interface part of the definition of the Product class:

```
class Product
{
public:
    Product();

    void read();

    bool is_better_than(Product b) const;
    void print() const;

private:
    implementation details—see Section 6.3
};
```

The interface is made up from three parts. First we list the *constructors:* the functions that
are used to initialize new objects. Constructors always have the same name as the class.
The Product class has one constructor, with no parameters. Such a constructor is called a
default constructor. It is used when you define an object without construction parameters,
like this:

```
Product best; /* uses default constructor Product() */
```

Syntax 6.1 : Class Definition

```
class Class_name
{
public:
    constructor declarations
    member function declarations
private:
    data fields
};
```

Example:
```
class Point
{
public:
    Point (double xval, double yval);
    void move(double dx, double dy);
    double get_x() const;
    double get_y() const;
private:
    double x;
    double y;
};
```

Purpose: Define the interface and data fields of a class.

As a general rule, every class should have a default constructor. All classes used in this book do.

Then we list the *mutator functions*. A mutator is an operation that modifies the object. The Product class has a single mutator: read. After you call

```
p.read();
```

the contents of p have changed.

Finally, we list the *accessor functions*. Accessors just query the object for some information without changing it. The Product class has two accessors: is_better_than and print. Applying one of these functions to a product object does not modify the object. In C++, accessor operations are tagged as const. Note the position of the const keyword: after the closing parenthesis of the parameter list, but before the semicolon that terminates the function declaration. See Common Error 6.3 for the importance of the const keyword.

Now we know *what* a Product object can do, but not *how* it does it. Of course, to use objects in our programs, we only need to use the interface. To enable any function to access the interface functions, they are placed in the public section of the class definition. As we will see in the next section, the variables used in the implementation will be placed in the private section. That makes them inaccessible to the users of the objects.

Figure 1 shows the interface of the Product class. The mutator functions are shown with arrows pointing inside the private data to indicate that they modify the data. The accessor functions are shown with arrows pointing the other way to indicate that they just read the data.

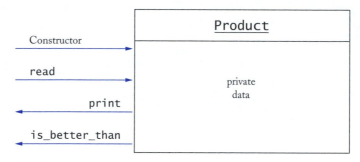

Figure 1

The Interface of the Product Class

Now that you have this interface, put it to work to simplify the program of the preceding section.

File product1.cpp

```
 1  /*
 2      This program compiles but doesn't run.
 3      See product2.cpp for the complete program.
 4  */
 5
 6  #include <iostream>
 7  #include <string>
 8
 9  using namespace std;
10
11  class Product
12  {
13  public:
14      Product();
15
16      void read();
17
18      bool is_better_than(Product b) const;
19      void print() const;
20  private:
21  };
22
23  int main()
24  {
25      Product best;
26
27      bool more = true;
28      while (more)
29      {
30          Product next;
31          next.read();
32          if (next.is_better_than(best)) best = next;
```

```
33
34        cout << "More data? (y/n) ";
35        string answer;
36        getline(cin, answer);
37        if (answer != "y") more = false;
38    }
39
40    cout << "The best value is ";
41    best.print();
42
43    return 0;
44 }
```

Wouldn't you agree that this program is much easier to read than the first version? Making Product into a class really pays off.

However, this program will not yet run. The interface definition of the class just *declares* the constructors and member functions. The actual code for these functions must be supplied separately. You will see how in Section 6.3.

 Common Error 6.2

Forgetting a Semicolon

Braces { } are common in C++ code, and usually you do not place a semicolon after the closing brace. However, class definitions always end in };. A common error is to forget that semicolon:

```
class Product
{
public:
   . . .
private:
   . . .
} /* forgot semicolon */

int main()
{
   Product best; /* many compilers report the error in this line */
   . . .
}
```

This error can be extremely confusing to many compilers. There is syntax, now obsolete but supported for compatibility with old code, to define class types and variables of that type simultaneously. Because the compiler doesn't know that you don't use that obsolete construction, it tries to analyze the code wrongly and ultimately reports an error. Unfortunately, it may report the error *several lines away* from the line in which you forgot the semicolon.

If the compiler reports bizarre errors in lines that you are sure are correct, check that each of the preceding class definitions is terminated by a semicolon.

6.3   Encapsulation

Each Product object must store the name, price, and score of the product. These data items are defined in the private section of the class definition.

```cpp
class Product
{
public:
   Product();

   void read();

   bool is_better_than(Product b) const;
   void print() const;
private:
   string name;
   double price;
   int score;
};
```

Every product object has a name field, a price field, and a score field (see Figure 2). However, there is a catch. Because these fields are defined to be private, only the constructors and member functions of the class can access them. You cannot access the fields directly:

```cpp
int main()
{
   . . .
   cout << best.name; /* Error—use print() instead */
   . . .
}
```

All data access must occur through the public interface. Thus, the data fields of an object are effectively hidden from the programmer. The act of hiding data is called *encapsulation*. While it is theoretically possible in C++ to leave data fields unencapsulated (by placing them into the public section), this is very uncommon in practice. We will always make all data fields private in this book.

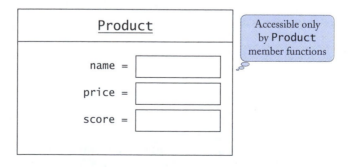

Figure 2

Encapsulation

The Product class is so simple that it is not obvious what benefit we gain from the encapsulation. The primary benefit of the encapsulation mechanism is the guarantee that the object data cannot accidentally be put in an incorrect state. To understand the benefit better, consider the Time class:

```
class Time
{
public:
   Time();
   Time(int hrs, int min, int sec);

   void add_seconds(long s);

   int get_seconds() const;
   int get_minutes() const;
   int get_hours() const;
   long seconds_from() const;
private:
   . . . /* hidden data representation */
};
```

Because the data fields are private, there are only three functions that can change these fields: the two constructors and the add_seconds mutator function. The four accessor functions cannot modify the fields, because they are declared as const.

Suppose that programmers could access data fields of the Time class directly. This would open the possibility of a type of bug, namely the creation of invalid times:

```
Time liftoff(19, 30, 0);
. . .
/* looks like the liftoff is getting delayed by another six hours */
/* won't compile, but suppose it did */
liftoff.hours = liftoff.hours + 6;
```

At first glance, there appears to be nothing wrong with this code. But if you look carefully, liftoff happens to be 19:30:00 before the hours are modified. Thus, it is 25:30:00 after the increment—an invalid time.

Fortunately, this error cannot happen with the Time class. The constructor that makes a time out of three integers checks that the construction parameters denote a valid time. If not, an error message is displayed and the program terminates. The Time() constructor sets a date object to the current time, which is always valid, and the add_seconds function knows about the length of a day and always produces a valid result. Since no other function can mess up the private data fields, we can *guarantee* that all times are always valid, thanks to the encapsulation mechanism.

6.4   Member Functions

Every member function that is advertised in the class interface must be implemented separately. Here is an example: the read function of the Product class.

```
class Product
{
```

```
public:
    Product();

    void read();

    bool is_better_than(Product b) const;
    void print() const;
private:
    string name;
    double price;
    int score;
};

void Product::read()
{
    cout << "Please enter the model name: "
    getline(cin, name);
    cout << "Please enter the price: ";
    cin >> price;
    cout << "Please enter the score: ";
    cin >> score;
    string remainder; /* read the remainder of the line */
    getline(cin, remainder);
}
```

The `Product::` prefix makes it clear that we are defining the `read` function of the `Product` class. In C++ it is perfectly legal to have `read` functions in other classes as well, and it is important to specify exactly which `read` function we are defining. See Syntax 6.2. You use the *Class_name*`::read()` syntax only when defining the function, not when calling it. When you call the `read` member function, the call has the form *object*`.read()`.

When defining an accessor member function, you must supply the keyword `const` following the closing parenthesis of the parameter list. For example, the call

---

Syntax 6.2 : Member Function Definition

return_type Class_name`::`*function_name*(*parameter*$_1$, *parameter*$_2$, . . . , *parameter*$_n$) [`const`]$_{opt}$
{
   statements
}

Example: `void Point::move(double dx, double dy)`
```
{
    x = x + dx;
    y = y + dy;
}
double Point::get_x() const
{
    return x;
}
```

Purpose: Supply the implementation of a member function.

a.is_better_than(b) only inspects the object a without modifying it. Hence is_better_than is an accessor function that should be tagged as const:

```cpp
bool Product::is_better_than(Product b) const
{
   if (b.price == 0) return false;
   if (price == 0) return true;
   return score / price > b.score / b.price;
}

void Product::print() const
{
   cout << name
      << " Price: " << price
      << " Score: " << score << "\n";
}
```

Whenever you refer to a data field, such as name or price, in a member function, it denotes that data field *of the object for which the member function was called*. For example, when called with

```cpp
best.print();
```

the Product::print() function prints best.name, best.score, and best.price. (See Figure 3.)

The code for the member function makes no mention at all of the object to which a member function is applied. It is called the *implicit parameter* of the member function. You can visualize the code of the print function like this:

```cpp
void Product::print() const
{
   cout << implicit_parameter.name
      << " Price: " << implicit_parameter.price
      << " Score: " << implicit_parameter.score << "\n";
}
```

In contrast, a parameter that is explicitly mentioned in the function definition, such as the b parameter of the is_better_than function, is called an *explicit parameter*. Every member function has exactly one implicit parameter and zero or more explicit parameters.

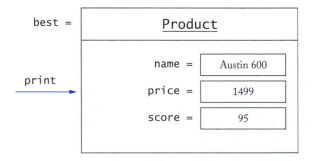

Figure 3

The Member Function Call best.print()

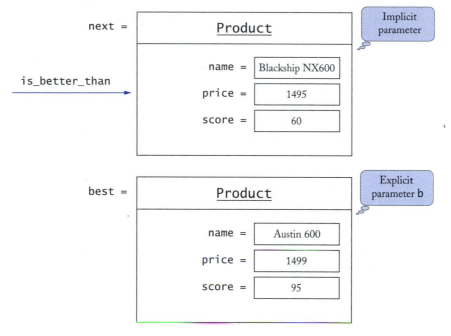

Figure 4

Implicit and Explicit Parameters of the Call `next.is_better_than(best)`

For example, the `is_better_than` function has one implicit parameter and one explicit parameter. In the call

```
if (next.is_better_than(best))
```

next is the implicit parameter and best is the explicit parameter (see Figure 4). Again, you may find it helpful to visualize the code of `Product::is_better_than` in the following way:

```
bool Product::is_better_than(Product b) const
{
    if (b.price == 0) return false;
    if (implicit_parameter.price == 0) return true;
    return implicit_parameter.score / implicit_parameter.price
        > b.score / b.price;
}
```

▼ ⊗ **Common Error**   **6.3**

const **Correctness**

▼

You should declare all accessor functions in C++ with the `const` keyword. (Recall that an accessor function is a member function that does not modify its implicit parameter.)

For example,

```
class Product
{
    . . .
    void print() const;
    . . .
};
```

If you fail to follow this rule, you build classes that other programmers cannot reuse. For example, suppose `Product::print` was not declared `const`, and another programmer used the `Product` class to build an `Order` class.

```
class Order
{
public:
    . . .
    void print() const;
private:
    string customer;
    Product article;
    . . .
};

void Order::print() const
{
    cout << customer << "\n";
    article.print(); /* Error if Product::print not const */
    . . .
}
```

The compiler refuses to compile the expression `article.print()`. Why? Because `article` is an object of class `Product`, and `Product::print` is not tagged as `const`, the compiler suspects that the call `article.print()` may modify `article`. But `article` is a data field of `Order`, and `Order::print` promises not to modify any data fields of the order. The programmer of the `Order` class uses `const` correctly and must rely on all other programmers to do the same.

If you write a program with other team members who do use `const` correctly, it is very important that you do your part as well. You should therefore get into the habit of using the `const` keyword for all member functions that do not modify their implicit parameter.

6.5 Default Constructors

There is only one remaining issue with the `Product` class. We need to define the default constructor.

The code for a constructor sets all data fields of the object. *The purpose of a constructor is to initialize the data fields of an object.*

```
Product::Product()
{
    price = 1;
    score = 0;
}
```

Syntax 6.3 : Constructor Definition

Class_name: : *Class_name(parameter₁, parameter₂, . . ., parameterₙ)*
{
    statements
}

Example: `Point::Point(double xval, double yval)`
            `{`
                `x = xval; y = yval;`
            `}`

Purpose: Supply the implementation of a constructor.

Note the curious name of the constructor function: `Product::Product`. The `Product::` indicates that we are about to define a member function of the `Product` class. The second `Product` is the name of that member function. Constructors always have the same name as their class (see Syntax 6.3).

Most default constructors set all data fields to a default value. The `Product` default constructor sets the score to 0 and the price to 1 (to avoid division by zero). The product name is automatically set to the empty string, as will be explained shortly. Not all default constructors act like that. For example, the `Time` default constructor sets the time object to the current time.

In the code for the default constructor, you need to worry about initializing only *numeric* data fields. For example, in the `Product` class you must set price and score to a value, because numeric types are not classes and have no constructors. But the name field is automatically set to the empty string by the default constructor of the `string` class. In general, all data fields of class type are automatically constructed when an object is created, but the numeric fields must be set in the class constructors.

We now have all the pieces for the version of the product comparison program that uses the `Product` class. Here is the program:

File product2.cpp

```
 1 #include <iostream>
 2 #include <string>
 3
 4 using namespace std;
 5
 6 class Product
 7 {
 8 public:
 9     /**
10         Constructs a product with score 0 and price 1.
11     */
12     Product();
13
14     /**
15         Reads in this product object.
```

```
16      */
17      void read();
18
19      /**
20          Compares two product objects.
21          @param b the object to compare with this object
22          @return true if this object is better than b
23      */
24      bool is_better_than(Product b) const;
25
26      /**
27          Prints this product object.
28      */
29      void print() const;
30  private:
31      string name;
32      double price;
33      int score;
34  };
35
36  Product::Product()
37  {
38      price = 1;
39      score = 0;
40  }
41
42  void Product::read()
43  {
44      cout << "Please enter the model name: ";
45      getline(cin, name);
46      cout << "Please enter the price: ";
47      cin >> price;
48      cout << "Please enter the score: ";
49      cin >> score;
50      string remainder; /* read remainder of line */
51      getline(cin, remainder);
52  }
53
54  bool Product::is_better_than(Product b) const
55  {
56      if (b.price == 0) return false;
57      if (price == 0) return true;
58      return score / price > b.score / b.price;
59  }
60
61  void Product::print() const
62  {
63      cout << name
64          << " Price: " << price
65          << " Score: " << score << "\n";
66  }
67
68  int main()
69  {
70      Product best;
71
```

```
72      bool more = true;
73      while (more)
74      {
75         Product next;
76         next.read();
77         if (next.is_better_than(best)) best = next;
78
79         cout << "More data? (y/n) ";
80         string answer;
81         getline(cin, answer);
82         if (answer != "y") more = false;
83      }
84
85      cout << "The best value is ";
86      best.print();
87
88      return 0;
89   }
```

Random Fact   6.1

Programmer Productivity

If you talk to your friends in this programming class, you will find that some of them consistently complete their assignments much more quickly than others. Perhaps they have more experience. Even when comparing programmers with the same education and experience, however, wide variations in competence are routinely observed and measured. It is not uncommon to have the best programmer in a team be five to ten times as productive as the worst, using any of a number of reasonable measures of productivity [1].

That is a staggering range of performance among trained professionals. In a marathon race, the best runner will not run five to ten times faster than the slowest one. Software product managers are acutely aware of these disparities. The obvious solution is, of course, to hire only the best programmers, but even in recent periods of economic slowdown, the demand for good programmers has greatly outstripped the supply.

Fortunately for all of us, joining the ranks of the best is not necessarily a question of raw intellectual power. Good judgment, experience, broad knowledge, attention to detail, and superior planning are at least as important as mental brilliance. These skills can be acquired by individuals who are genuinely interested in improving themselves.

Even the most gifted programmer can deal with only a finite number of details in a given time period. Suppose a programmer can implement and debug one procedure every two hours, or one hundred procedures per month. (This is a generous estimate. Few programmers are this productive.) If a task requires 10,000 procedures (which is typical for a medium-sized program), then a single programmer would need 100 months to complete the job. Such a project is sometimes expressed as a "100-man-month" project. But as Brooks explains in his famous book [2], the concept of "man-month" is a myth. One cannot trade months for programmers. One hundred programmers cannot finish the task in one month. In fact, 10 programmers probably couldn't finish it in 10 months. First of all, the 10 programmers need to learn about the project before they can get productive. Whenever there is a problem with a particular procedure, both the author and its users need to meet and discuss it, taking time away from all of them. A bug in one procedure may have all of its users twiddling their thumbs until it is fixed.

It is difficult to estimate these inevitable delays. They are one reason why software is often released later than originally promised. What is a manager to do when the delays mount? As Brooks points out, adding more manpower will make a late project even later, because the productive people have to stop working and train the newcomers.

You will experience these problems when you work on your first team project with other students. Be prepared for a major drop in productivity, and be sure to set ample time aside for team communications.

There is, however, no alternative to teamwork. Most important and worthwhile projects transcend the ability of one single individual. Learning to function well in a team is as important for your education as it is to be a competent programmer.

6.6   Constructors with Parameters

The Product class of the preceding section had only one constructor—the default constructor. In contrast, the Employee class has two constructors:

```
class Employee
{
public:
   Employee();
   Employee(string employee_name, double initial_salary);

   void set_salary(double new_salary);

   string get_name() const;
   double get_salary() const;
private:
   string name;
   double salary;
};
```

Both constructors have the same name as the class, Employee. But the default constructor has no parameters, whereas the second constructor has a string and a double parameter. Whenever two functions have the same name but are distinguished by their parameter types, the function name is *overloaded*. (See Advanced Topic 6.2 for more information on overloading in C++.)

Here is the implementation of the constructor that makes an employee object from a name string and a starting salary.

```
Employee::Employee(string employee_name, double initial_salary)
{
   name = employee_name;
   salary = initial_salary;
}
```

This is a straightforward situation; the constructor simply sets all data fields. Sometimes a constructor gets more complex because one of the data fields is itself an object of another class with its own constructor.

To see how to cope with this situation, suppose the `Employee` class stores the scheduled work hours of the employee:

```
class Employee
{
public:
   Employee(string employee_name, double initial_salary,
      int arrive_hour, int leave_hour);
   . . .
private:
   string name;
   double salary;
   Time arrive;
   Time leave;
};
```

This constructor must set the `name`, `salary`, `arrive`, and `leave` fields. Since the last two fields are themselves objects of a class, they must be initialized with objects:

```
Employee::Employee(string employee_name, double initial_salary,
   int arrive_hour, int leave_hour)
{
   name = employee_name;
   salary = initial_salary;
   arrive = Time(arrive_hour, 0, 0);
   leave = Time(leave_hour, 0, 0);
}
```

The `Employee` class in the library of this book does not actually store the work hours. This is just an illustration to show how to construct a data field that is itself an object of a class.

Common Error 6.4

Forgetting to Initialize All Fields in a Constructor

Just as it is a common error to forget the initialization of a variable, it is easy to forget about data fields. Every constructor needs to ensure that all data fields are set to appropriate values.

Here is a variation on the `Employee` class. The constructor receives only the name of the employee. The class user is supposed to call `set_salary` explicitly to set the salary.

```
class Employee
{
public:
   Employee(string n);
   void set_salary(double s);
   double get_salary() const;
      . . .
private:
   string name;
   double salary;
```

```
};

Employee::Employee(string n)
{
    name = n;
    /* oops—salary not initialized */
}
```

If someone calls `get_salary` before `set_salary` has been called, a random salary will be returned. The remedy is simple: Just set `salary` to 0 in the constructor.

Common Error   6.5

Trying to Reset an Object by Calling a Constructor

The constructor is invoked only when an object is first created. You cannot call the constructor to reset an object:

```
Time homework_due(19, 0, 0);
. . .
homework_due.Time(); /* Error */
```

It is true that the default constructor sets a *new* time object to the current time, but you cannot invoke a constructor on an *existing* object.

The remedy is simple: Make a new time object and overwrite the current one.

```
homework_due = Time(); /* OK */
```

Advanced Topic   6.1

Calling Constructors from Constructors

Consider again the variation of the `Employee` class with work hour fields of type `Time`. There is an unfortunate inefficiency in the constructor:

```
Employee::Employee(string employee_name, double initial_salary,
    int arrive_hour, int leave_hour)
{
    name = employee_name;
    salary = initial_salary;
    arrive = Time(arrive_hour, 0, 0);
    leave = Time(leave_hour, 0, 0);
}
```

Before the constructor code starts executing, the default constructors are automatically invoked on all data fields that are objects. In particular, the `arrive` and `leave` fields are initialized with the current time through the default constructor of the Time class. Immediately afterwards, those values are overwritten with the objects Time(arrive_hour, 0, 0) and Time(leave_hour, 0, 0).

It would be more efficient to construct the arrive and leave fields with the correct values right away. That is achieved as follows with the form described in Syntax 6.4.

```
Employee::Employee(string employee_name, double initial_salary,
    int arrive_hour, int leave_hour)
    : arrive(arrive_hour, 0, 0),
    leave(leave_hour, 0, 0)
{
    name = employee_name;
    salary = initial_salary;
}
```

Many people find this syntax confusing, and you may prefer not to use it. The price you pay is inefficient initialization, first with the default constructor, and then with the actual initial value. Note, however, that this syntax is necessary to construct objects of classes that don't have a default constructor.

Syntax 6.4 : Constructor with Field Initializer List

Class_name :: *Class_name*(*parameters*)
    : *field*₁(*expressions*), ..., *field*ₙ(*expressions*)
{
     statements
}

Example: `Point::Point(double xval, double yval)`
         `: x(xval), y(yval)`
         `{`
         `}`

Purpose: Supply the implementation of a constructor, initializing data fields before the body of the constructor.

 Advanced Topic   6.2

Overloading

When the same function name is used for more than one function, then the name is *overloaded*. In C++ you can overload function names provided the parameter types are different. For example, you can define two functions, both called print, one to print an employee record and one to print a time object:

```
void print(Employee e) /* ... */
void print(Time t) /* ... */
```

When the print function is called,

```
print(x);
```

the compiler looks at the type of x. If x is an Employee object, the first function is called. If x is a Time object, the second function is called. If x is neither, the compiler generates an error.

We have not used the overloading feature in this book. Instead, we gave each function a unique name, such as print_employee or print_time. However, we have no choice with constructors. C++ demands that the name of a constructor equal the name of the class. If a class has more than one constructor, then that name must be overloaded.

In addition to name overloading, C++ also supports *operator overloading*. You can define new meanings to the familiar C++ operators such as +, ==, and <<, provided at least one of the arguments is an object of some class. For example, we could overload the > operator to test whether one product is better than another. Then the test

```
if (next.is_better_than(best)) ...
```

could instead be written as

```
if (next > best) ...
```

To teach the compiler this new meaning of the > operator, we need to implement a function called operator> with two parameters of type Product. Simply replace is_better_than with operator>.

```
bool Product::operator>(Product b) const
{
    if (b.price == 0) return false;
    if (price == 0) return true;
    return score / price > b.score / b.price;
}
```

Operator overloading can make programs easier to read. See Chapter 17 for more information.

6.7   Accessing Data Fields

Only member functions of a class are allowed to access the private data fields of objects of that class. All other functions—that is, member functions of other classes and functions that are not member functions of any class—must go through the public interface of the class.

For example, the raise_salary function of Chapter 5 cannot read and set the salary field directly:

```
void raise_salary(Employee& e, double percent)
{
    e.salary = e.salary * (1 + percent / 100); /* Error */
}
```

Instead, it must use the get_salary and set_salary functions:

```
void raise_salary(Employee& e, double percent)
{
```

```
    double new_salary = e.get_salary()
        * (1 + percent / 100);
    e.set_salary(new_salary);
}
```

These two member functions are extremely simple:

```
double Employee::get_salary() const
{
    return salary;
}

void Employee::set_salary(double new_salary) const
{
    salary = new_salary;
}
```

In your own classes you should not automatically write accessor functions for *all* data fields. The less implementation detail you reveal, the more flexibility you have to improve the class. Consider, for example, the Product class. There was no need to supply functions such as get_score or set_price. Also, if you have a get_ function, don't feel obliged to implement a matching set_ function. For example, the Time class has a get_minutes function but not a set_minutes function.

Consider again the get_salary and set_salary functions of the Employee class. They simply get and set the value of the salary field. However, you should not assume that all functions with the prefixes get and set follow that pattern. For example, our Time class has three accessors get_hours, get_minutes, and get_seconds, but it does not use corresponding data fields hours, minutes, and seconds. Instead, there is a single data field

```
int time_in_secs;
```

The field stores the number of seconds from midnight (00:00:00). The constructor sets that value from the construction parameters:

```
Time::Time(int hour, int min, int sec)
{
    time_in_secs = 60 * 60 * hour + 60 * min + sec;
}
```

The accessors compute the hours, minutes, and seconds. For example,

```
int Time::get_minutes() const
{
    return (time_in_secs / 60) % 60;
}
```

This internal representation was chosen because it makes the add_seconds and seconds_from functions trivial to implement:

```
int Time::seconds_from(Time t) const
{
    return time_in_secs - t.time_in_secs;
}
```

Of course, the data representation is an internal implementation detail of the class that is invisible to the class user.

6.8   ## Comparing Member Functions with Nonmember Functions

Consider again the `raise_salary` function of Chapter 5.

```
void raise_salary(Employee& e, double percent)
{
   double new_salary = e.get_salary()
      * (1 + percent / 100);
   e.set_salary(new_salary);
}
```

This function is not a member function of the `Employee` class. It is not a member function of any class, in fact. Thus, the dot notation is not used when the function is called. There are two explicit arguments and no implicit argument.

```
raise_salary(harry, 7); /* raise Harry's salary by 7 percent */
```

Let us turn `raise_salary` into a member function:

```
class Employee
{
public:
   void raise_salary(double percent);
   . . .
};

void Employee::raise_salary(double percent)
{
   salary = salary * (1 + percent / 100);
}
```

Now the function must be called with the dot notation:

```
harry.raise_salary(7); /* raise Harry's salary by 7 percent */
```

Which of these two solutions is better? It depends on the *ownership* of the class. If you are designing a class, you should make useful operations into member functions. However, if you are using a class designed by someone else, then you should not add your own member functions. The author of the class that you are using may improve the class and periodically give you a new version of the code. It would be a nuisance if you had to keep adding your own modifications back into the class definition every time that happened.

Inside `main` or another nonmember function, it is easy to differentiate between member function calls and other function calls. Member functions are invoked using the dot notation; nonmember functions don't have an *"object."* preceding them. Inside member functions, however, it isn't as simple. One member function can invoke another member function on its implicit parameter. Suppose we add a member function `print` to the `Employee` class:

```
class Employee
{
public:
   void print() const;
   . . .
```

```
};

void Employee::print() const
{
   cout << "Name: " << get_name()
       << "Salary: " << get_salary()
       << "\n";
}
```

Now consider the call `harry.print()`, with implicit parameter `harry`. The call `get_name()` inside the `Employee::print` function really means `harry.get_name()`. Again, you may find it helpful to visualize the function like this:

```
void Employee::print() const
{
   cout << "Name: " << implicit_parameter.get_name()
       << "Salary: " << implicit_parameter.get_salary()
       << "\n";
}
```

In this simple situation we could equally well have accessed the `name` and `salary` data fields directly in the `Employee::print` function. In more complex situations it is very common for one member function to call another.

If you see a function call without the dot notation inside a member function, you first need to check whether that function is actually another member function of the same class. If so, it means "call this member function with the same implicit parameter".

If you compare the member and nonmember versions of `raise_salary`, you can see an important difference. The member function is allowed to modify the `salary` data field of the `Employee` object, even though it was not defined as a reference parameter.

Recall that by default, function parameters are value parameters, which the function cannot modify. You must supply an ampersand `&` to indicate that a parameter is a reference parameter, which can be modified by the function. For example, the first parameter of the nonmember version of `raise_salary` is a reference parameter (`Employee&`), because the `raise_salary` function changes the employee record.

The situation is exactly opposite for the implicit parameter of member functions. By default, the implicit parameter *can* be modified. Only if the member function is tagged as `const` must the default parameter be left unchanged.

The following table summarizes these differences.

	Explicit Parameter	Implicit Parameter
Value parameter (not changed)	Default Example: `void print(Employee)`	Use `const` Example: `void Employee::print() const`
Reference parameter (can be changed)	Use `&` Example: `void raiseSalary( Employee& e, double p)`	Default Example: `void Employee:: raiseSalary(double p)`

Quality Tip   6.1

File Layout

By now you have learned quite a few C++ features, all of which can occur in a C++ source file. Keep your source files neat and organize items in them in the following order:

- Included header files
- Constants
- Classes
- Global variables (if any)
- Functions

The member functions can come in any order. If you sort the nonmember functions so that every function is defined before it is used, then `main` comes last. If you prefer a different ordering, use function declarations (see Advanced Topic 5.1).

6.9   Separate Compilation

When you write and compile small programs, you can place all your code into a single source file. When your programs get larger or you work in a team, that situation changes. You will want to split your code into separate source files. There are two reasons why this split becomes necessary. First, it takes time to compile a file, and it seems silly to wait for the compiler to keep translating code that doesn't change. If your code is distributed over several source files, then only those files that you changed need to be recompiled. The second reason becomes apparent when you work with other programmers in a team. It would be very difficult for multiple programmers to edit a single source file simultaneously. Therefore, the program code is broken up so that each programmer is solely responsible for a separate set of files.

If your program is composed of multiple files, some of these files will define data types or functions that are needed in other files. There must be a path of communication between the files. In C++, that communication happens through the inclusion of header files.

A header file contains

- definitions of constants
- definitions of classes
- declarations of nonmember functions
- declarations of global variables

The source file contains

- definitions of member functions
- definitions of nonmember functions
- definitions of global variables

Let us consider a simple case first. We will create a set of two files, `product.h` and `product.cpp`, that contain the interface and the implementation of the `Product` class.

The header file contains the class definition. It also includes all headers that are necessary for defining the class. For example, the `Product` class is defined in terms of the `string` class. Therefore, you must include the `<string>` header as well. Anytime you include a header from the standard library, you must also include the command

```
using namespace std;
```

File product.h

```
1  #ifndef PRODUCT_H
2  #define PRODUCT_H
3
4  #include <string>
5
6  using namespace std;
7
8  class Product
9  {
10 public:
11    /**
12       Constructs a product with score 0 and price 1.
13    */
14    Product();
15
16    /**
17       Reads in this product object.
18    */
19    void read();
20
21    /**
22       Compares two product objects.
23       @param b  the object to compare with this object
24       @return  true if this object is better than b
25    */
26    bool is_better_than(Product b) const;
27
28    /**
29       Prints this product object.
30    */
31    void print() const;
32 private:
33    string name;
34    double price;
35    int score;
36 };
37
38 #endif
```

Note the curious set of preprocessor directives that bracket the file.

```
#ifndef PRODUCT_H
#define PRODUCT_H

. . .
#endif
```

These directives are a guard against multiple inclusion. Suppose a file includes product.h and another header file that itself includes product.h. Then the compiler sees the class definition twice, and it complains about two classes with the same name. (Sadly, it doesn't check whether the definitions are identical.)

The source file simply contains the definitions of the member functions. Note that the source file includes its own header file.

File product.cpp

```
1  #include <iostream>
2  #include "product.h"
3
4  using namespace std;
5
6  Product::Product()
7  {
8     price = 1;
9     score = 0;
10 }
11
12 void Product::read()
13 {
14    cout << "Please enter the model name: ";
15    getline(cin, name);
16    cout << "Please enter the price: ";
17    cin >> price;
18    cout << "Please enter the score: ";
19    cin >> score;
20    string remainder; /* read remainder of line */
21    getline(cin, remainder);
22 }
23
24 bool Product::is_better_than(Product b) const
25 {
26    if (b.price == 0) return false;
27    if (price == 0) return true;
28    return score / price > b.score / b.price;
29 }
30
31 void Product::print() const
32 {
33    cout << name
34       << " Price: " << price
35       << " Score: " << score << "\n";
36 }
```

Note that the function comments are in the header file, since they are a part of the interface, not the implementation.

The `product.cpp` file does *not* contain a `main` function. There are many potential programs that might make use of the `Product` class. Each of these programs will need to supply its own `main` function, as well as other functions and classes.

Here is a simple test program that puts the `Product` class to use. Its source file includes the `product.h` header file.

File prodtest.cpp

```
1  #include <iostream>
2  #include "product.h"
3
4  int main()
5  {
6     Product best;
7
8     bool more = true;
9     while (more)
10    {
11       Product next;
12       next.read();
13       if (next.is_better_than(best)) best = next;
14
15       cout << "More data? (y/n) ";
16       string answer;
17       getline(cin, answer);
18       if (answer != "y") more = false;
19    }
20
21    cout << "The best value is ";
22    best.print();
23
24    return 0;
25 }
```

To build the complete program, you need to compile both the `prodtest.cpp` and `product.cpp` source files. The details depend on your compiler. For example, with the Gnu compiler, you issue the commands

```
g++ -c product.cpp
g++ -c prodtest.cpp
g++ -o prodtest product.o prodtest.o
```

The first two commands translate the source files into object files that contain the machine instructions corresponding to the C++ code. The third command links together the object files, as well as all the required code from the standard library, to form an executable program.

You have just seen the simplest and most common case for designing header and source files. There are a few additional technical details that you need to know.

Place shared constants into the header file. For example,

File product.h

```
1  const int MAX_SCORE = 100;
2  . . .
```

To share a non-member function, place the definition of the function into a source file and the function prototype into the corresponding header file.

File rand.h

```
1 void rand_seed();
2 int rand_int(int a, int b);
```

File rand.cpp

```
1 #include "rand.h"
2
3 void rand_seed()
4 {
5    int seed = static_cast<int>(time(0));
6    srand(seed);
7 }
8
9 int rand_int(int a, int b)
10 {
11    return a + rand() % (b - a + 1);
12 }
```

Finally, it may occasionally be necessary to share a global variable among source files. For example, the graphics library of this book defines a global object cwin. It is declared in a header file as

```
extern GraphicWindow cwin;
```

The corresponding source file contains the definition

```
GraphicWindow cwin;
```

The extern keyword is required to distinguish the declaration from the definition.

Random Fact　6.2

Programming—Art or Science?

There has been a long discussion whether the discipline of computing is a science or not. The field is called "computer science", but that doesn't mean much. Except possibly for librarians and sociologists, few people believe that library science and social science are scientific endeavors.

A scientific discipline aims to discover certain fundamental principles dictated by the laws of nature. It operates on the *scientific method:* by posing hypotheses and testing them with experiments that are repeatable by other workers in the field. For example, a physicist may have a theory on the makeup of nuclear particles and attempt to verify or falsify that theory by running experiments in a particle collider. If an experiment cannot be verified, such as the "cold fusion" research at the University of Utah in the early 1990s, then the theory dies a quick death.

Some programmers indeed run experiments. They try out various methods of computing certain results, or of configuring computer systems, and measure the differences in performance. However, their aim is not to discover laws of nature.

▼

▼

▼

▼

▼

▼

▼

▼

Some computer scientists discover fundamental principles. One class of fundamental results, for instance, states that it is impossible to write certain kinds of computer programs, no matter how powerful the computing equipment is. For example, it is impossible to write a program that takes as its input any two C++ program files and as its output prints whether or not these two programs always compute the same results. Such a program would be very handy for grading student homework, but nobody, no matter how clever, will ever be able to write one that works for all input files. The majority of programmers write programs, however, instead of researching the limits of computation.

Some people view programming as an *art* or *craft*. A programmer who writes elegant code that is easy to understand and runs with optimum efficiency can indeed be considered a good craftsman. Calling it an art is perhaps far-fetched, because an art object requires an audience to appreciate it, whereas the program code is generally hidden from the program user.

Others call computing an *engineering discipline*. Just as mechanical engineering is based on the fundamental mathematical principles of statics, computing has certain mathematical foundations. There is more to mechanical engineering than mathematics, though, such as knowledge of materials and of project planning. The same is true for computing.

In one somewhat worrisome aspect, computing does not have the same standing as other engineering disciplines. There is little agreement as to what constitutes professional conduct in the computer field. Unlike the scientist, whose main responsibility is the search for truth, the engineer must strive for the conflicting demands of quality, safety, and economy. Engineering disciplines have professional organizations that hold their members to standards of conduct. The computer field is so new that in many cases we simply don't know the correct method for achieving certain tasks. That makes it difficult to set professional standards.

What do you think? From your limited experience, do you consider the discipline of computing an art, a craft, a science, or an engineering activity?

CHAPTER SUMMARY

1. Classes represent *concepts*, either derived from the problem that the program is supposed to solve or representing a construct that is useful for the computation.

2. Every class has a public *interface:* a collection of *member functions* through which the objects of the class can be manipulated.

3. Every class has a private *implementation:* data fields that store the state of an object. By keeping the implementation private, we protect it from being accidentally corrupted. Furthermore, the implementation can be changed easily without affecting the users of the class.

4. A *mutator* member function changes the state of the object on which it operates. An *accessor* member function does not modify the object. In C++, accessors must be tagged with `const`.

5. A *constructor* is used to initialize objects when they are created. A constructor with no parameters is called a *default* constructor.

6. The code of complex programs is distributed over multiple files. Header files contain the definitions of classes and declarations of shared constants, functions, and variables. Source files contain the function implementations.

FURTHER READING

[1] W.H. Sackmann, W.J. Erikson, and E.E. Grant, "Exploratory Experimental Studies Comparing Online and Offline Programming Performance", *Communications of the ACM*, vol. 11, no. 1 (January 1968), pp. 3–11.
[2] F. Brooks, *The Mythical Man-Month*, Addison-Wesley, 1975.

REVIEW EXERCISES

Exercise R6.1. List all classes that we have used so far in this book. Categorize them as

- Real-world entities
- Mathematical abstractions
- System services

Exercise R6.2. What is the *interface* of a class? What is the *implementation* of a class?

Exercise R6.3. What is a member function, and how does it differ from a nonmember function?

Exercise R6.4. What is a mutator function? What is an accessor function?

Exercise R6.5. What happens if you forget the const in an accessor function? What happens if you accidentally supply a const in a mutator function?

Exercise R6.6. What is an implicit parameter? How does it differ from an explicit parameter?

Exercise R6.7. How many implicit parameters can a member function have? How many implicit parameters can a nonmember function have? How many explicit parameters can a function have?

Exercise R6.8. What is a constructor?

Exercise R6.9. What is a default constructor? What is the consequence if a class does not have a default constructor?

Exercise R6.10. How many constructors can a class have? Can you have a class with no constructors? If a class has more than one constructor, which of them gets called?

Exercise R6.11. How can you define an object variable that is not initialized with a constructor?

Exercise R6.12. How are member functions declared? How are they defined?

Exercise R6.13. What is encapsulation? Why is it useful?

Exercise R6.14. Data fields are hidden in the private section of a class, but they aren't hidden very well at all. Anyone can read the private section. Explain to what extent the private keyword hides the private members of a class.

Exercise R6.15. You can read and write the salary field of the Employee class with the get_salary accessor function and the set_salary mutator function. Should every data field of a class have associated accessors and mutators? Explain why or why not.

Exercise R6.16. What changes to the Product class would be necessary if you wanted to make is_better_than into a nonmember function? (*Hint:* You would need to introduce additional accessor functions.) Write the class definition of the changed Product class, the definitions of the new member functions, and the definition of the changed is_better_than function.

Exercise R6.17. What changes to the Product class would be necessary if you wanted to make the read function into a nonmember function? (*Hint:* You would need to read in the name, price, and score and then construct a product with these properties.) Write the class definition of the changed Product class, the definition of the new constructor, and the definition of the changed read function.

Exercise R6.18. In a nonmember function, it is easy to differentiate between calls to member functions and calls to nonmember functions. How do you tell them apart? Why is it not as easy for functions that are called from a member function?

Exercise R6.19. How do you indicate whether the implicit parameter is passed by value or by reference? How do you indicate whether an explicit parameter is passed by value or by reference?

PROGRAMMING EXERCISES

Exercise P6.1. Implement all member functions of the following class:

```
class Person
{
public:
   Person();
   Person(string pname, int page);
   void get_name() const;
   void get_age() const;
private:
   string name;
   int age; /* 0 if unknown */
};
```

Exercise P6.2. Implement a class PEmployee that is just like the Employee class except that it stores an object of type Person as developed in the preceding exercise.

```
class PEmployee
{
public:
   PEmployee();
   PEmployee(string employee_name, double initial_salary);
   void set_salary(double new_salary);
   double get_salary() const;
   string get_name() const;
private:
   Person person_data;
   double salary;
};
```

Exercise P6.3. Implement a class Address. An address has a house number, a street, an optional apartment number, a city, a state, and a postal code. Supply two constructors: one with an apartment number and one without. Supply a print function that prints the address with the street on one line and the city, state, and postal code on the next line. Supply a member function comes_before that tests whether one address comes before another when the addresses are compared by postal code.

Exercise P6.4. Implement a class Account. An account has a balance, functions to add and withdraw money, and a function to query the current balance. Charge a $5 penalty if an attempt is made to withdraw more money than available in the account.

Exercise P6.5. Enhance the Account class of the preceding exercise to compute interest on the current balance. Then use the Account class to implement the problem from the beginning of the book: An account has an initial balance of $10,000, and 6 percent annual interest is compounded monthly until the investment doubles.

Exercise P6.6. Implement a class Bank. This bank has two objects, checking and savings, of the type Account that was developed in the preceding exercise. Implement four member functions:

```
deposit(double amount, string account)
withdraw(double amount, string account)
transfer(double amount, string account)
print_balances()
```

Here the account string is "S" or "C". For the deposit or withdrawal, it indicates which account is affected. For a transfer it indicates the account from which the money is taken; the money is automatically transferred to the other account.

Exercise P6.7. Implement a class Rectangle that works just like the other graphics classes such as Circle or Line. A rectangle is constructed from two corner points. The sides of the rectangle are parallel to the coordinate axes:

You do not yet know how to define a << operator to plot a rectangle. Instead, define a member function plot. Supply a function move. Pay attention to const. Then write a sample program that constructs and plots a few rectangles.

Exercise P6.8. Enhance the Rectangle class of the preceding exercise by adding member functions perimeter and area that compute the perimeter and area of the rectangle.

Exercise P6.9. Implement a class Triangle that works just like the other graphics classes such as Circle or Line. A triangle is constructed from three corner points. You do not yet know how to define a << operator to plot a triangle. Instead, define a member function plot. Supply a function move. Pay attention to const. Then write a sample program that constructs and plots a few triangles.

Exercise P6.10. Enhance the Triangle class of the preceding exercise by adding member functions perimeter and area that compute the perimeter and area of the triangle.

Exercise P6.11. Implement a class SodaCan with functions get_surface_area() and get_volume(). In the constructor, supply the height and radius of the can.

Exercise P6.12. Implement a class Car with the following properties. A car has a certain fuel efficiency (measured in miles/gallon or liters/km—pick one) and a certain amount of fuel in the gas tank. The efficiency is specified in the constructor, and the initial fuel level is 0. Supply a function drive that simulates driving the car for a certain distance, reducing the fuel level in the gas tank, and functions get_gas, returning the current fuel level, and add_gas, to tank up. Sample usage:

```
Car my_beemer(29); // 29 miles per gallon
my_beemer.add_gas(20); // tank 20 gallons
my_beemer.drive(100); // drive 100 miles
cout << my_beemer.get_gas() << "\n"; // print fuel remaining
```

Exercise P6.13. Implement a class Student. For the purpose of this exercise, a student has a name and a total quiz score. Supply an appropriate constructor and functions get_name(), add_quiz(int score), get_total_score(), and get_average_score(). To compute the latter, you also need to store the *number of quizzes* that the student took.

Exercise P6.14. Modify the Student class of the preceding exercise to compute grade point averages. Member functions are needed to add a grade, and get the current GPA. Specify grades as elements of a class Grade. Supply a constructor that constructs a grade from a string, such as "B+". You will also need a function that translates grades into their numeric values (for example, "B+" becomes 3.3).

Exercise P6.15. Define a class Country that stores the name of the country, its population, and its area. Using that class, write a program that reads in a set of countries and prints

- The country with the largest area
- The country with the largest population
- The country with the largest population density (people per square kilometer)

Exercise P6.16. Design a class House that defines a house on a street. A house has a house number and an (x, y) location, where x and y are numbers between –10 and 10. The key member function is plot, which plots the house.

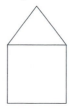

Next, design a class Street that contains a number of equally spaced houses. An object of type Street stores the first house, the last house (which can be anywhere on the screen), and the number of houses on the street. The Street::plot function needs to make the intermediate house objects on the fly, because you don't yet know how to store an arbitrary number of objects.

Use these classes in a graphics program in which the user clicks with the mouse on the locations of the first and last house, then enters the house numbers of the first and last house, and the number of houses on the street. Then the entire street is plotted.

Exercise P6.17. Design a class `Message` that models an e-mail message. A message has a recipient, a sender, and a message text. Support the following member functions:

- A constructor that takes the sender and recipient and sets the time stamp to the current time
- A member function `append` that appends a line of text to the message body
- A member function `to_string` that makes the message into one long string like this: `"From: Harry Hacker\nTo: Rudolf Reindeer\n ..."`
- A member function `print` that prints the message text. *Hint:* Use `to_string`.

Write a program that uses this class to make a message and print it.

Exercise P6.18. Design a class `Mailbox` that stores mail messages, using the `Message` class of the preceding exercise. You don't yet know how to store a collection of message objects. Instead, use the following brute force approach: The mailbox contains one very long string, which is the concatenation of all messages. You can tell where a new message starts by searching for a `From:` at the beginning of a line. This may sound like a dumb strategy, but surprisingly, many e-mail systems do just that.

Implement the following member functions:

```
void Mailbox::add_message(Message m);
Message Mailbox::get_message(int i) const;
void remove_message(int i) const;
```

What do you do if the message body happens to have a line starting with `"From: "`? Then the `to_string` function of the `Message` class should really insert a `>` in front of the `From:` so that it reads `>From:` . Again, this sounds dumb, but it is a strategy used by real e-mail systems. Extra credit if you implement this enhancement.

Exercise P6.19. Design a class `Cannonball` to model a cannonball that is fired into the air. A ball has

- An x- and a y-position
- An x- and a y-velocity

Supply the following member functions:

- A constructor with a weight and an x-position (the y-position is initially 0)
- A member function `move(double sec)` that moves the ball to the next position (First compute the distance traveled in `sec` seconds, using the current velocities, then update the x- and y-positions; then update the y-velocity by taking into account the gravitational acceleration of -9.81 m/sec²; the x-velocity is unchanged.)
- A member function `plot` that plots the current location of the cannonball
- A member function `shoot` whose parameters are the angle α and initial velocity v (Compute the x-velocity as $v \cos \alpha$ and the y-velocity as $v \sin \alpha$; then keep calling `move` with a time interval of 0.1 seconds until the x-position is 0; call `plot` after every move.)

Use this class in a program that prompts the user for the starting angle and the initial velocity. Then call `shoot`.

Chapter **7**

Advanced Control Flow

CHAPTER GOALS

▶ To recognize the correct ordering of decisions in multiple branches

▶ To program conditions using Boolean operators and variables

▶ To understand nested branches and loops

▶ To be able to program loops with the `for` and `do/while` statements

▶ To learn how to process character, word, and line input

▶ To learn how to read input from a file through redirection

▶ To implement approximations and simulations

In Chapter 4, you were introduced to branches, loops, and Boolean variables. In this chapter, you will study more complex control flow constructs such as nested branches and alternate loop types. You will learn to apply these techniques in practical programming situations, for processing text files and for implementing simulations.

7.1 Multiple Alternatives

Consider a program that asks the user to specify a coin. The user inputs "dime" or "nickel", for instance, and the program prints the value of the coin.

File coins5.cpp

```
1  #include <iostream>
2  #include <string>
3
4  using namespace std;
5
6  int main()
7  {
8     cout << "Enter coin name: ";
9     string name;
10    cin >> name;
11    double value = 0;
12
13    if (name == "penny")
14       value = 0.01;
15    else if (name == "nickel")
16       value = 0.05;
17    else if (name == "dime")
18       value = 0.10;
19    else if (name == "quarter")
20       value = 0.25;
21    else
22       cout << name << " is not a valid coin name\n";
```

```
23      cout << "Value = " << value << "\n";
24
25      return 0;
26 }
```

This code distinguishes between five cases: The name can be "penny", "nickel", "dime", or "quarter", or something else. As soon as one of the first four tests succeeds, the appropriate variable is updated, and no further tests are attempted. If none of the four cases applies, an error message is printed. Figure 1 shows the flowchart for this multiple-branch statement.

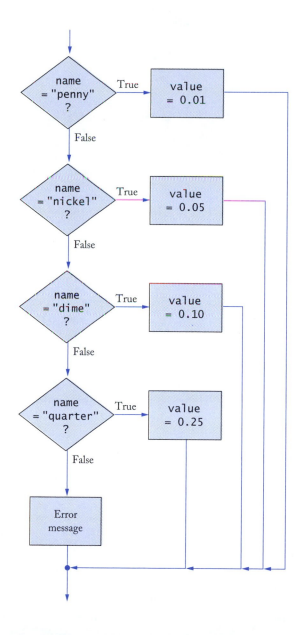

Figure 1

Multiple Alternatives

In this example the order of the tests was not important. Now consider a test where the order is important. The next program asks for a value describing the magnitude of an earthquake on the Richter scale and prints a description of the likely impact of the quake. The Richter scale is a measurement for the strength of an earthquake. Every step in the scale, for example from 6.0 to 7.0, signifies a tenfold increase in the strength of the quake. The 1989 Loma Prieta earthquake that damaged the Bay Bridge in San Francisco and destroyed many buildings in several Bay Area cities rated 7.1 on the Richter scale.

File richter.cpp

```
1  #include <iostream>
2  #include <string>
3
4  using namespace std;
5
6  int main()
7  {
8     cout << "Enter a magnitude on the Richter scale: ";
9     double richter;
10    cin >> richter;
11
12    if (richter >= 8.0)
13       cout << "Most structures fall\n";
14    else if (richter >= 7.0)
15       cout << "Many buildings destroyed\n";
16    else if (richter >= 6.0)
17       cout << "Many buildings considerably damaged, "
18          << "some collapse\n";
19    else if (richter >= 4.5)
20       cout << "Damage to poorly constructed buildings\n";
21    else if (richter >= 3.5)
22       cout << "Felt by many people, no destruction\n";
23    else if (richter >= 0)
24       cout << "Generally not felt by people\n";
25    else
26       cout << "Negative numbers are not valid\n";
27    return 0;
28 }
```

Here you must sort the conditions and test against the largest cutoff first. Suppose we reverse the order of tests:

```
if (richter >= 0) /* Tests in wrong order */
   cout << "Generally not felt by people\n";
else if (richter >= 3.5)
   cout << "Felt by many people, no destruction\n";
else if (richter >= 4.5)
   cout << "Damage to poorly constructed buildings\n";
else if (richter >= 6.0)
   cout << "Many buildings considerably damaged, "
      << "some collapse\n";
else if (richter >= 7.0)
   cout << "Many buildings destroyed\n";
else if (richter >= 8.0)
   cout << "Most structures fall\n";
```

This does not work. All positive values of `richter` fall into the first case, and the other tests will never be attempted.

In this example, it is also important that we use an `if/else/else` test, not just multiple independent `if` statements. Consider this sequence of independent tests:

```
if (richter >= 8.0) /* Didn't use else */
   cout << "Most structures fall\n";
if (richter >= 7.0)
   cout << "Many buildings destroyed\n";
if (richter >= 6.0)
   cout << "Many buildings considerably damaged, "
      << "some collapse\n";
if (richter >= 4.5)
   cout << "Damage to poorly constructed buildings\n";
if (richter >= 3.5)
   cout << "Felt by many people, no destruction\n";
if (richter >= 0)
   cout << "Generally not felt by people\n";
```

Now the alternatives are no longer exclusive. If `richter` is 5.0, then the last *three* tests all match, and three messages are printed.

Advanced Topic   7.1

The switch Statement

A sequence of `if/else/else` that compares a *single integer value* against several *constant* alternatives can be implemented as a `switch` statement. For example,

```
int digit;
...
switch(digit)
{
   case 1: digit_name = "one"; break;
   case 2: digit_name = "two"; break;
   case 3: digit_name = "three"; break;
   case 4: digit_name = "four"; break;
   case 5: digit_name = "five"; break;
   case 6: digit_name = "six"; break;
   case 7: digit_name = "seven"; break;
   case 8: digit_name = "eight"; break;
   case 9: digit_name = "nine"; break;
   default: digit_name = ""; break;
}
```

This is a shortcut for

```
int digit;
if (digit == 1) digit_name = "one";
else if (digit == 2) digit_name = "two";
else if (digit == 3) digit_name = "three";
else if (digit == 4) digit_name = "four";
else if (digit == 5) digit_name = "five";
```

```
else if (digit == 6) digit_name = "six";
else if (digit == 7) digit_name = "seven";
else if (digit == 8) digit_name = "eight";
else if (digit == 9) digit_name = "nine";
else digit_name = "";
```

Well, it isn't much of a shortcut. It has one advantage—it is obvious that all branches test the *same* value, namely digit—but the switch statement can be applied only in narrow circumstances. The test cases must be constants, and they must be integers. You cannot use

```
switch(name)
{
   case "penny": value = 0.01; break; /* Error */
   ...
}
```

There is a reason for these limitations. The compiler can generate efficient test code (using so-called jump tables or binary searches) only in the situation that is permitted in a switch statement. Of course, modern compilers will be happy to perform the same optimization for a sequence of alternatives in an if/else/else statement, so the need for the switch has largely gone away.

We forgo the switch statement in this book for a different reason. Every branch of the switch must be terminated by a break instruction. If the break is missing, execution *falls through* to the next branch, and so on, until finally a break or the end of the switch is reached. There are a few cases in which this is actually useful, but they are very rare. Peter van der Linden [1, p. 38] describes an analysis of the switch statements in the Sun C compiler front end. Of the 244 switch statements, each of which had an average of 7 cases, only 3 percent used the fall-through behavior. That is, the default—falling through to the next case unless stopped by a break—is *wrong 97 percent of the time*. Forgetting to type the break is an exceedingly common error, yielding wrong code.

We leave it to you to use the switch statement for your own code or not. At any rate, you need to have a reading knowledge of switch in case you find it in the code of other programmers.

Productivity Hint 7.1

Copy and Paste in the Editor

When you see code like

```
if (richter >= 8.0)
   cout << "Most structures fall\n";
else if (richter >= 7.0)
   cout << "Many buildings destroyed\n";
else if (richter >= 6.0)
   cout << "Many buildings considerably damaged, some collapse\n";
else if (richter >= 4.5)
   cout << "Damage to poorly constructed buildings\n";
else if (richter >= 3.5)
   cout << "Felt by many people, no destruction\n";
```

you should think "copy and paste".

▼   Make a template

```
else if (richter >= )
    cout << "";
```

▼

and copy it. This is usually done by highlighting with the mouse and then selecting Edit and then Copy from the menu bar. (If you follow Productivity Hint 3.1, you are smart and use the keyboard. Hit Shift + ↓ to highlight the entire line, then Ctrl + C to copy it. Then paste it multiple times (Ctrl + V) and fill the text into the copy. Of course, your editor may use different commands, but the concept is the same.)

▼

The ability to copy and paste is always useful when you have code from an example or another project that is similar to your current needs. To copy, paste, and modify is faster than to type everything from scratch. You are also less likely to make typing errors.

▼

▼   ⊗ **Common Error**   ▌ **7.1** ▶

The Dangling else Problem

▼

When an if statement is nested inside another if statement, the following error may occur.

▼

```
double shipping_charge = 5.00; /* $5 inside continental U.S. */

if (country == "USA")
    if (state == "HI")
        shipping_charge = 10.00; /* Hawaii is more expensive */
else /* Pitfall! */
    shipping_charge = 20.00; /* as are foreign shipments */
```

▼

The indentation level seems to suggest that the else is grouped with the test country == "USA". Unfortunately, that is not the case. The compiler ignores all indentation and follows the rule that an else always belongs to the closest if. That is, the code is actually

▼

```
double shipping_charge = 5.00; /* $5 inside continental U.S. */
if (country == "USA")
    if (state == "HI")
        shipping_charge = 10.00; /* Hawaii is more expensive */
    else /* Pitfall! */
        shipping_charge = 20.00;
```

▼

That isn't what you want. You want to group the else with the first if. For that, you must use braces.

▼

```
double shipping_charge = 5.00; /* $5 inside continental U.S. */
if (country == "USA")
{
    if (state == "HI")
        shipping_charge = 10.00; /* Hawaii is more expensive */
}
else
    shipping_charge = 20.00; /* as are foreign shipments */
```

To avoid having to think about the pairing of the else, we recommend that you *always* use a set of braces when the body of an if contains another if. In the following example, the braces are not strictly necessary but they help clarify the code:

```
double shipping_charge = 20.00; /* $20 for foreign shipments */
if (country == "USA")
{
   if (state == "HI")
      shipping_charge = 10.00; /* Hawaii is more expensive */
   else
      shipping_charge = 5.00; /* $5 inside continental U.S. */
}
```

The ambiguous else is called a *dangling* else, and it is enough of a syntactical blemish that some programming language designers developed an improved syntax that avoids it altogether. For example, Algol 68 uses the construction

if *condition* then *statement* else *statement* fi;

The else part is optional, but since the end of the if statement is clearly marked, the grouping is unambiguous if there are two if and only one else. Here are the two possible cases:

if *c1* then if *c2* then *s1* else *s2* fi fi;

if *c1* then if *c2* then *s1* fi else *s2* fi;

By the way, fi is if written backwards. Other languages use endif, which has the same purpose but is less fun.

Common Error   7.2

Forgetting to Set a Variable in Some Branches

Consider the following code:

```
double shipping_charge;

if (country == "USA")
{
   if (state == "HI")
      shipping_charge = 10.00;
   else if (state == "AK")
      shipping_charge = 8.00;
}
else
   shipping_charge = 20.00;
```

The variable shipping_charge is declared but left undefined because its value depends on several circumstances. It is then set in the various branches of the if statements. However, if the order is to be delivered inside the United States to a state other than Hawaii or Alaska, then the shipping charge is not set at all.

There are two remedies. Of course, we can check all branches of the if statements to make sure that each one of them sets the variable. In this example, we must add one case:

```
if (country == "USA")
{
   if (state == "HI")
      shipping_charge = 10.00;
   else if (state == "AK")
      shipping_charge = 8.00;
   else
      shipping_charge = 5.00; /* within continental U.S. */
}
else
   shipping_charge = 20.00;
```

The safer way is to initialize the variable with the most likely value and then have that value overwritten in the less likely situations:

```
double shipping_charge = 5.00; /* within continental U.S. */

if (country == "USA")
{
   if (state == "HI")
      shipping_charge = 10.00;
   else if (state == "AK")
      shipping_charge = 8.00;
}
else
   shipping_charge = 20.00;
```

This is slightly less efficient, but we are now assured that the variable is never left uninitialized.

7.2   Nested Branches

In the United States different tax rates are used depending on the taxpayer's marital status. There are two main tax schedules, for single and for married taxpayers. Married taxpayers add their income together and pay taxes on the total. (In fact, there are two other schedules, "head of household" and "married filing separately", which we will ignore for simplicity.) Table 1 gives the tax rate computations for each of the filing categories, using the values for the 1992 federal tax return.

Now compute the taxes due, given a filing status and an income figure. The key point is that there are two *levels* of decision making. First, you must branch on the filing status. Then, for each filing status, you must have another branch on income level.

File tax.cpp

```
1  #include <iostream>
2  #include <string>
3
4  using namespace std;
5
6  int main()
7  {
8     const double SINGLE_LEVEL1 = 21450.00;
9     const double SINGLE_LEVEL2 = 51900.00;
```

```
10
11      const double SINGLE_TAX1 = 3217.50;
12      const double SINGLE_TAX2 = 11743.50;
13
14      const double MARRIED_LEVEL1 = 35800.00;
15      const double MARRIED_LEVEL2 = 86500.00;
16
17      const double MARRIED_TAX1 = 5370.00;
18      const double MARRIED_TAX2 = 19566.00;
19
20      const double RATE1 = 0.15;
21      const double RATE2 = 0.28;
22      const double RATE3 = 0.31;
23
24      double income;
25      double tax;
26
27      cout << "Please enter your income: ";
28      cin >> income;
29
30      cout << "Please enter s for single, m for married: ";
31      string marital_status;
32      cin >> marital_status;
33
34      if (marital_status == "s")
35      {
36         if (income <= SINGLE_LEVEL1)
37            tax = RATE1 * income;
38         else if (income <= SINGLE_LEVEL2)
```

If your status is Single and if the taxable income is over	but not over	the tax is	of the amount over
$0	$21,450	15%	$0
$21,450	$51,900	$3,217.50 + 28%	$21,450
$51,900		$11,743.50 + 31%	$51,900

If your status is Married and if the taxable income is over	but not over	the tax is	of the amount over
$0	$35,800	15%	$0
$35,800	$86,500	$5,370.00 + 28%	$35,800
$86,500		$19,566.00 + 31%	$86,500

Table 1

Federal Tax Rate Schedule

```
39              tax = SINGLE_TAX1
40                  + RATE2 * (income - SINGLE_LEVEL1);
41          else
42              tax = SINGLE_TAX2
43                  + RATE3 * (income - SINGLE_LEVEL2);
44      }
45      else
46      {
47          if (income <= MARRIED_LEVEL1)
48              tax = RATE1 * income;
49          else if (income <= MARRIED_LEVEL2)
50              tax = MARRIED_TAX1
51                  + RATE2 * (income - MARRIED_LEVEL1);
52          else
53              tax = MARRIED_TAX2
54                  + RATE3 * (income - MARRIED_LEVEL2);
55      }
56      cout << "The tax is $" << tax << "\n";
57      return 0;
58 }
```

The two-level decision process is reflected in two levels of if statements. We say that the income test is *nested* inside the test for filing status. (See Figure 2 for a flowchart.) In theory, nesting can go deeper than two levels. A three-level decision process (first by state, then by status, then by income level) requires three nesting levels.

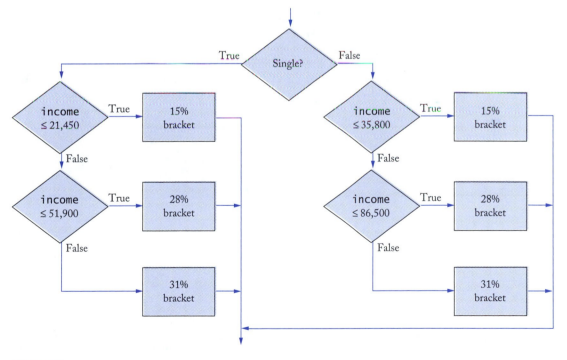

Figure 2

Income Tax Computation

Quality Tip 7.1

Prepare Test Cases Ahead of Time

Consider how to test the tax computation program. Of course, you cannot try out all possible inputs of filing status and income level. Even if you could, there would be no point in trying them all. If the program correctly computes one or two tax amounts in a given bracket, then we have a good reason to believe that all amounts will be correct. We want to aim for complete *coverage* of all cases.

There are two possibilities for the filing status and three tax brackets for each status. That makes six test cases. Then we want to test a handful of *error* conditions, such as a negative income. That makes seven test cases. For the first six you need to compute manually what answer you expect. For the remaining one, you need to know what error reports you expect. Write down the test cases and then start coding.

Should you really test seven inputs for this simple program? You certainly should. Furthermore, if you find an error in the program that wasn't covered by one of the test cases, make another test case and add it to your collection. After you fix the known mistakes, *run all test cases again*. Experience has shown that the cases that you just tried to fix are probably working now, but that errors that you fixed two or three iterations ago have a good chance of coming back! If you find that an error keeps coming back, that is usually a reliable sign that you did not fully understand some subtle interaction between features of your program.

It is always a good idea to design test cases *before* starting to code. There are two reasons for this. Working through the test cases gives you a better understanding of the algorithm that you are about to program. Furthermore, it has been noted that programmers instinctively shy away from testing fragile parts of their code. That seems hard to believe, but you will often make that observation about your own work. Watch someone else test your program. There will be times when that person enters input that makes you very nervous because you are not sure that your program can handle it, and you never dared to test it yourself. This is a well-known phenomenon, and making the test plan before writing the code offers some protection.

Productivity Hint 7.2

Make a Schedule and Make Time for Unexpected Problems

Commercial software is notorious for being delivered later than promised. For example, Microsoft originally promised that the successor to its Windows 3 operating system would be available early in 1994, then late in 1994, then in March 1995; it finally was released in August 1995. Some of the early promises might not have been realistic. It was in Microsoft's interest to let prospective customers expect the imminent availability of the product. Had customers known the actual delivery date, they might have switched to a different product in the meantime. Undeniably, though, Microsoft had not anticipated the full complexity of the tasks it had set itself to solve.

Microsoft can delay the delivery of its product, but it is likely that you cannot. As a student or a programmer, you are expected to manage your time wisely and to finish your assign-

▼

▼

▼

▼

▼

▼

▼

▼

ments on time. You can probably do simple programming exercises the night before the due date, but an assignment that looks twice as hard may well take four times as long, because more things can go wrong. You should therefore make a schedule whenever you start a programming project.

First, estimate realistically how much time it will take you to

- Design the program logic

- Develop test cases

- Type the program in and fix syntax errors

- Test and debug the program

For example, for the income tax program I might estimate 30 minutes for the design, because it is mostly done; 30 minutes for developing test cases; one hour for data entry and fixing syntax errors; and two hours for testing and debugging. That is a total of four hours. If I work two hours a day on this project, it will take me two days.

Then think of things that can go wrong. Your computer might break down. The lab might be crowded. You might be stumped by a problem with the computer system. (That is a particularly important concern for beginners. It is *very* common to lose a day over a trivial problem just because it takes time to track down a person who knows the magic command to overcome it.) As a rule of thumb, *double* the time of your estimate. That is, you should start four days, not two days, before the due date. If nothing went wrong, great; you have the program done two days early. When the inevitable problem occurs, you have a cushion of time that protects you from embarrassment and failure.

7.3   Boolean Operations

Suppose you want to test whether your homework is due right now. You need to compare the hours and minutes of two Time objects, now and homework_due. (Ignore the seconds field for simplicity.) The test passes only if both fields match. In C++ we use the && operator to combine test conditions.

File hwdue1.cpp

```
1  #include <iostream>
2
3  using namespace std;
4
5  #include "ccc_time.h"
6
7  int main()
8  {
9     cout <<
10        "Enter homework due time (hours minutes): ";
11     int hours;
12     int minutes;
13     cin >> hours >> minutes;
14     Time homework_due(hours, minutes, 0);
15     Time now;
16
```

```
17    if (now.get_hours() == homework_due.get_hours() &&
18          now.get_minutes() == homework_due.get_minutes())
19      cout << "The homework is due right now!\n";
20    else
21      cout << "The homework is not due right now!\n";
22
23    return 0;
24 }
```

The condition of the test has two parts, joined by the && operator. If the hours are equal *and* the minutes are equal, then it is due now. If either one of the fields does not match, then the test fails.

The && operator combines several tests into a new test that passes only when all conditions are true. An operator that combines test conditions is called a *logical* operator.

The || logical operator also combines two or more conditions. The resulting test succeeds if at least one of the conditions is true.

For example, in the following test we test whether an order is shipped to Alaska or Hawaii.

```
if (state == "HI" || state == "AK")
    shipping_charge = 10.00;
```

Figure 3 shows flowcharts for these examples.

You can combine both types of logical operations in one test. Here you test whether your homework has already become due. That is the case if you are already past the due hour, *or* if we are in that hour *and* past the minute.

File hwdue2.cpp

```
1 #include <iostream>
2
3 using namespace std;
4
5 #include "ccc_time.h"
6
7 int main()
8 {
9    cout <<
10       "Enter homework due time (hours minutes): ";
11    int hours;
12    int minutes;
13    cin >> hours >> minutes;
14    Time homework_due(hours, minutes, 0);
15    Time now;
16
17    if (now.get_hours() < homework_due.get_hours() ||
18          (now.get_hours() == homework_due.get_hours() &&
19          now.get_minutes() <= homework_due.get_minutes()))
20      cout << "Still time to finish the homework.\n";
21    else
22      cout << "The homework is already past due.\n";
23
24    return 0;
25 }
```

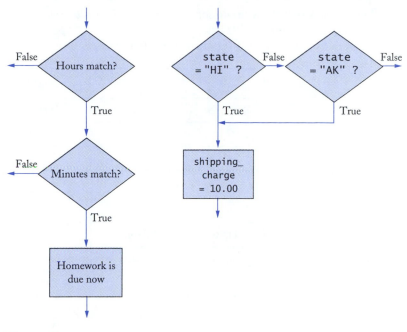

Figure 3

Flowcharts for *and* and *or* Combinations

The `&&` and `||` operators are computed using *lazy evaluation*. In other words, logical expressions are evaluated from left to right, and evaluation stops as soon as the truth value is determined. When an *or* is evaluated and the first condition is true, the second condition is not evaluated, because it does not matter what the outcome of the second test is. Here is an example:

```
double area;
cin >> area;

if (cin.fail() || area < 0) cout << "Input error.\n";
```

If the input operation fails, the test `area < 0` is not evaluated, which is just as well, because `area` is then a random value. Here is another example of the benefit of lazy evaluation:

```
if (r >= 0 && -b / 2 + sqrt(r) >= 0) ...
```

If `r` is negative, then the first condition is false, and thus the combined statement is false, no matter what the outcome of the second test is. The second test is never evaluated for negative `r`, and there is no danger of computing the square root of a negative number.

Sometimes you need to *invert* a condition with the `not` logical operator. For example, you may want to carry out a certain action only if `cin` is not in a failed state:

```
cin >> n;

if (!cin.fail()) quarters = quarters + n;
```

The ! operator takes a single condition and evaluates to true if that condition is false and to false if the condition is true.

Here is a summary of the three logical operations:

A	*B*	*A* && *B*
true	true	true
true	false	false
false	Any	false

A	*B*	*A* || *B*
true	Any	true
false	true	true
false	false	false

A	!*A*
true	false
false	true

7.3

⊗ Common Error

Multiple Relational Operators

Consider the expression

```
if (-0.5 <= x <= 0.5) /* Error */
```

This looks just like the mathematical test $-0.5 \le x \le 0.5$. Unfortunately, it is not.

Let us dissect the expression -0.5 <= x <= 0.5. The first half, -0.5 <= x, is a test with outcome true or false, depending on the value of x. The outcome of that test (true or false) is then compared against 0.5. This seems to make no sense. Can one compare truth values and floating-point numbers? Is true larger than 0.5 or not? Unfortunately, to stay compatible with the C language, C++ converts false to 0 and true to 1.

You therefore must be careful not to mix logical and arithmetic expressions in your programs. Instead, use *and* to combine two separate tests:

```
if (-0.5 <= x && x <= 0.5) ...
```

Another common error, along the same lines, is to write

```
if (x && y > 0) ... /* Error */
```

instead of

```
if (x > 0 && y > 0) ...
```

Unfortunately, the compiler will not issue an error message. Instead, it does the opposite conversion, converting x to true or false. Zero is converted to false, and any nonzero value is converted to true. If x is not zero, then it tests whether y is greater than 0, and finally it computes the and of these two truth values. Naturally, that computation makes no sense.

Common Error   7.4

Confusing && and || Conditions

It is a surprisingly common error to confuse *and* and *or* conditions. A value lies between 0 and 100 if it is at least 0 *and* at most 100. It lies outside that range if it is less than 0 *or* greater than 100. There is no golden rule; you just have to think carefully.

Often the *and* or *or* is clearly stated, and then it isn't too hard to implement it. But sometimes the wording isn't as explicit. It is quite common that the individual conditions are nicely set apart in a bulleted list, but with little indication of how they should be combined. The instructions for the 1992 tax return say that you can claim single filing status if any one of the following is true:

- You were never married.

- You were legally separated or divorced on December 31, 1992.

- You were widowed before January 1, 1992, and did not remarry in 1992.

Since the test passes if *any one* of the conditions is true, you must combine the conditions with *or*. Elsewhere, the same instructions state that you may use the more advantageous status of married filing jointly if all five of the following conditions are true:

- Your spouse died in 1990 or 1991 and you did not remarry in 1992.

- You have a child whom you can claim as dependent.

- That child lived in your home for all of 1992.

- You paid over half the cost of keeping up your home for this child.

- You filed (or could have filed) a joint return with your spouse the year he or she died.

Because *all* of the conditions must be true for the test to pass, you must combine them with an *and*.

7.4   De Morgan's Law

Suppose we want to charge a higher shipping rate if we don't ship within the continental United States.

```
if (!(country == "USA"
      && state != "AK"
      && state != "HI"))
   shipping_charge = 20.00;
```

This test is a little bit complicated, and you have to think carefully through the logic. When it is *not* true that the country is USA *and* the state is not Alaska *and* the state is not Hawaii, then charge $20.00. Huh? It is not true that some people won't be confused by this code.

The computer doesn't care, but humans generally have a hard time comprehending logical conditions with *not* operators applied to *and/or* expressions. De Morgan's Law, named after the logician Augustus De Morgan (1806–1871), can be used to simplify these Boolean expressions. De Morgan's Law has two forms: one for the negation of an *and* expression and one for the negation of an *or* expression:

$$!(A \text{ \&\& } B) \qquad \text{is the same as} \qquad !A \text{ || } !B$$
$$!(A \text{ || } B) \qquad \text{is the same as} \qquad !A \text{ \&\& } !B$$

Pay particular attention to the fact that the *and* and *or* operators are *reversed* by moving the *not* inwards. For example, the negation of "the state is Alaska *or* it is Hawaii",

```
!(state == "AK" || state == "HI")
```

is "the state is not Alaska *and* it is not Hawaii":

```
!(state == "AK") && !(state == "HI")
```

That is, of course, the same as

```
state != "AK" && state != "HI"
```

Now apply the law to our shipping charge computation:

```
!(country == "USA"
   && state != "AK"
   && state != "HI")
```

is equivalent to

```
!(country == "USA")
   || !(state != "AK")
   || !(state != "HI")
```

That yields the simpler test

```
country != "USA"
   || state == "AK"
   || state == "HI"
```

To simplify conditions with negations of *and* or *or* expressions, it is usually a good idea to apply De Morgan's Law to move the negations to the innermost level.

Random Fact 7.1

Artificial Intelligence

When one uses a sophisticated computer program such as a tax preparation package, one is bound to attribute some intelligence to the computer. The computer asks sensible questions and makes computations that we find a mental challenge. After all, if doing one's taxes were easy, we wouldn't need a computer to do it for us.

As programmers, however, we know that all this apparent intelligence is an illusion. Human programmers have carefully "coached" the software in all possible scenarios, and it simply replays the actions and decisions that were programmed into it.

Would it be possible to write computer programs that are genuinely intelligent in some sense? From the earliest days of computing, there was a sense that the human brain might be nothing but an immense computer, and that it might well be feasible to program computers to imitate some processes of human thought. Serious research into *artificial intelligence* began in the mid-1950s, and the first twenty years brought some impressive successes. Programs that play chess—surely an activity that appears to require remarkable intellectual powers—have become so good that they now routinely beat all but the best human players. In 1975 an *expert-system* program called Mycin gained fame for being better in diagnosing meningitis in patients than the average physician. *Theorem-proving* programs produced logically correct mathematical proofs. *Optical character recognition* software can read pages from a scanner, recognize the character shapes, including those that are blurred or smudged, and reconstruct the original document text, even restoring fonts and layout.

However, there were serious setbacks as well. From the very outset, one of the stated goals of the AI community was to produce software that could translate text from one language to another, for example from English to Russian. That undertaking proved to be enormously complicated. Human language appears to be much more subtle and interwoven with the human experience than had originally been thought. Even the grammar-checking tools that come with many word-processing programs today are more of a gimmick than a useful tool, and analyzing grammar is just the first step in translating sentences.

From 1982 to 1992, the Japanese government embarked on a massive research project, funded at over 40 billion Japanese yen. It was known as the *Fifth-Generation Project*. Its goal was to develop new hardware and software to improve the performance of expert system software greatly. At its outset, the project created great fear in other countries that the Japanese computer industry was about to become the undisputed leader in the field. However, the end results were disappointing and did little to bring artificial intelligence applications to market.

Successful artificial intelligence programs, such as chess-playing programs, do not actually imitate human thinking. They are just very fast in exploring many scenarios and have been tuned to recognize those cases that do not warrant further investigation. One interesting exception are *neural networks:* coarse simulations of the neuron cells in animal and human brains. Suitably interconnected cells appear to be able to "learn". For example, if a network of cells is presented with letter shapes, it can be trained to identify them. After a lengthy training period, the network can recognize letters, even if they are slanted, distorted, or smudged.

A current AI project that has created great interest is the CYC (from en*cyc*lopedia) effort by Douglas Lenat and others at MCC in Austin, Texas. That project is trying to codify the implicit assumptions that underlie human speech and writing. The team members started out analyzing news articles and asked themselves what unmentioned facts are necessary to actually understand the sentences. For example, consider the sentence "Last fall she enrolled in Michigan State". The reader automatically realizes that "fall" is not related to falling down in this context, but refers to the season. While there is a state of Michigan, here Michigan State denotes the university. A priori, a computer program has none of this knowledge. The goal of the CYC project is to extract and store the requisite facts—that is, (1) people enroll in universities; (2) Michigan is a state; (3) many states have universities named X State University, often abbreviated as X State; (4) most people enroll in a university in the fall. In 1995, the project had codified about 100,000 common-sense concepts and about a million facts of knowledge relating them. Even this massive amount of data has not proven sufficient for useful applications. It remains to be seen whether the CYC project will eventually lead to success or become another expensive AI failure.

7.5   The for Loop

Far and away the most common loop has the form

```
i = start;
while (i <= end)
{
    . . .
    i++;
}
```

Because this loop is so common, there is a special form for it (see Syntax 7.1) that amplifies the pattern:

```
for (i = start; i <= end; i++)
{
    . . .
}
```

In this case, the variable i must have been defined outside the for loop. You can also define the variable in the loop header. It then persists until the loop exits.

```
for (int i = 1; i <= 10; i++)
{
    cout << "Hello, World\n";
} // i no longer defined here
```

Syntax 7.1 : for Statement

`for (`*initialization_statement*`; ` *condition*`; ` *update_expression*`) ` *statement*

Example: `for (int i = 1; i <= 10; i++) sum = sum + i;`

Purpose: Execute the initialization statement. While the condition remains true, execute the statement and the update expression.

An important mathematical function is the *factorial*. The expression $n!$ (read n factorial) is defined to be the product $1 \times 2 \times 3 \times \ldots \times n$. Also, by convention, $0! = 1$. Factorials for negative numbers are not defined. Here are the first few values of the factorial function:

n	$n!$
0	1
1	1
2	2
3	6
4	24
5	120
6	720
7	5040
8	40320

As you can see, these values get large very quickly. The factorial function is interesting, because it describes how many ways one can scramble or *permute* n distinct objects. For example, there are $3! = 6$ rearrangements of the letters in the string "rum": namely mur, mru, umr, urm, rmu, and rum itself. There are 24 permutations of the *string* "drum".

The following program computes the factorial of an input value, using a for loop.

File forfac.cpp

```
1  #include <iostream>
2
3  using namespace std;
4
5  int main()
6  {
7     cout << "Please enter a number: ";
8     int n;
9     cin >> n;
10    int product = 1;
11    for (int i = 1; i <= n; i++)
12    {
13       product = product * i;
14    }
15    cout << n << "! = " << product << "\n";
16    return 0;
17 }
```

Figure 4

Flowchart of a for Loop

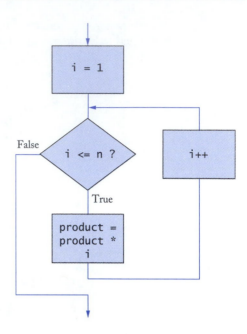

Figure 4 shows the corresponding flowchart.

The three slots in the for header can contain any three expressions. We can count down instead of up:

```
for (int n = 10; n >= 0; n--)
{
    cout << n << "\n";
}
```

The increment or decrement need not be in steps of 1:

```
for (x = -10; x <= 10; x = x + 0.5) . . .
```

It is possible—but a sign of unbelievably bad taste—to put unrelated conditions into the loop:

```
for (rate = 6; month--; cout >> balance) . . . /* bad taste */
```

We won't even begin to decipher what that might mean. You should stick with for loops that initialize, test, and update a single variable.

If the body of a loop consists of a single statement, you can omit the braces. For example, you can replace

```
for (int i = 1; i <= n; i++)
{
    product = product * i;
}
```

with

```
for (int i = 1;   i <= n; i++)
    product = product * i;
```

Quality Tip   7.2

Use for Loops for Their Intended Purpose Only

A for loop is an *idiom* for a while loop of a particular form. A counter runs from the start to the end, with the constant increment:

```
for (i = start; i < (or <=) end; i = i + increment)
{
    . . .
    /* i, start, end, increment not changed here */
}
```

If your loop doesn't match this pattern, don't use the for construction. The compiler won't prevent you from writing idiotic for loops:

```
/* bad style—unrelated header expressions */
for (cout << "Inputs: "; cin >> x; sum = sum + x)
    count++;

for (i = 0; i < s.length(); i++)
{
    /* bad style—modifies counter inside loop */
    if (s.substr(i, 1) == ".") i++;
    count++;
}
```

These loops will work, but they are plainly bad style. Use a while loop for iterations that do not fit into the for pattern.

Quality Tip   7.3

Don't Use != to Test the End of a Range

Here is a loop with a hidden danger:

```
for (i = 1; i != nyear; i++)
{
    . . .
}
```

The test i != nyear is a poor idea. What would happen if nyear happened to be negative? Of course, nyear should never be negative, because it makes no sense to have a negative number of years—but the impossible and unthinkable do happen with distressing regularity. If nyear is negative, the test i != nyear is never true, because i starts at 1 and increases with every step. The program dies in an infinite loop.

The remedy is simple. Test

```
for (i = 0; i < nyear; i++) . . .
```

For floating-point values there is another reason not to use the != operator: Because of roundoff errors, the exact termination point may never be reached.

Of course, you would never write

```
for (rate = 5; rate != 10; rate = rate + 0.3333333) . . .
```

because it looks highly unlikely that rate would match 10 exactly after 15 steps. But the same problem may happen for the harmless-looking

```
for (rate = 5; rate != 10; rate = rate + 0.1) . . .
```

The number 0.1 is exactly representable in the decimal system, but the computer represents floating-point numbers in binary. There is a slight error in any finite binary representation of 1/10, just as there is a slight error in a decimal representation 0.3333333 of 1/3. Maybe rate is exactly 10 after 50 steps; maybe it is off by a tiny amount. There is no point in taking chances. Just use < instead of !=:

```
for (rate = 5; rate < 10; rate = rate + 0.1) . . .
```

Common Error 7.5

Forgetting a Semicolon

It occasionally happens that all the work of a loop is already done in the loop header. This code looks for the position of the first period in a filename:

```
string filename; /* e.g., hello.cpp */
string name;
. . .
for (i = 0; filename.substr(i, 1) != "."; i++)
   ;

name = filename.substr(0, i); /* e.g., hello */
```

The body of the for loop is completely empty, containing just one empty statement terminated by a semicolon.

We are not advocating this strategy. This loop doesn't work correctly if filename doesn't happen to contain a period. Such an anemic loop is often a sign of poor error handling.

If you do run into a loop without a body, it is important that you really make sure the semicolon is not forgotten. If the semicolon is accidentally omitted, then the code

```
for (i = 0; filename.substr(i, 1) != "."; i++)

name = filename.substr(0, i); /* e.g., hello */
```

repeats the statement name = filename.substr(0, i) until a period is found, and then it doesn't execute it again. (If filename is "hello.cpp", the last assignment into name is "hell".)

To make the semicolon really stand out, place it on a line all by itself, as shown in the first example.

Quality Tip   7.4

Symmetric and Asymmetric Bounds

It is easy to write a loop with i going from 1 to n.

```
for (i = 1; i <= n; i++) . . .
```

The values for i are bounded by the relation $1 \le i \le n$. Because there are $\le$ on both bounds, the bounds are called *symmetric*.

When traversing the characters in a string, the bounds are *asymmetric*.

```
for (i = 0; i < s.length(); i++) . . .
```

The values for i are bounded by $0 \le i < $ s.length(), with a $\le$ to the left and a $<$ to the right. That is appropriate, because s.length() is not a valid position.

It is not a good idea to force symmetry artificially:

```
for (i = 0; i <= s.length() - 1; i++) . . .
```

That is more difficult to read and understand.

For every loop, consider which form is most natural according to the needs of the problem and use that.

Quality Tip   7.5

Count Iterations

Finding the correct lower and upper bounds for an iteration can be confusing. Should you start at 0? Should you use <= b or < b as a termination condition?

Counting the number of iterations is a very useful device for better understanding a loop. Counting is easier for loops with asymmetric bounds. The loop

```
for (i = a; i < b; i++) . . .
```

is executed b - a times. For example, the loop traversing the characters in a string,

```
for (i = 0; i < s.length(); i++) . . .
```

runs s.length() times. That makes perfect sense, since there are s.length() characters in a string.

The loop with symmetric bounds,

```
for (i = a; i <= b; i++)
```

executed b - a + 1 times. That "+1" is the source of many programming errors. For example,

```
for (x = 0; x <= 10; x++)
```

runs 11 times. Maybe that is what you want; if not, start at 1 or use < 10.

One way to visualize this "+1" error is by looking at a fence. A fence with ten sections (=) has eleven fence posts (|).

$$|=|=|=|=|=|=|=|=|=|=|$$

▼

Each section has one fence post to the left, and there is a final post on the right of the last section. Forgetting to count the last value is often called a "fence post error".

▼

If the increment is a value c other than 1, then the counts are

```
(b - a)/c       for the asymmetric loop
(b - a)/c + 1   for the symmetric loop
```

▼

For example, consider the loop

```
for (i = 10; i <= 40; i = i + 5)
```

▼

Here, a is 10, b is 40, and c is 5. Therefore, the loop executes $(40 - 10)/5 + 1 = 7$ times.

7.6   The do Loop

Sometimes you want to execute the body of a loop at least once and perform the loop test after the body was executed. The do/while loop (see Syntax 7.2) serves that purpose:

```
do
{
    statements
}
while (condition);
```

Here is an example of such a loop. The ancient Greeks were aware of a simple approximation algorithm to compute square roots. The algorithm starts by guessing a value x that might be somewhat close to the desired square root $\sqrt{a}$. The initial value doesn't have to be very close; $x = a$ is a perfectly good choice.

Now consider the quantities x and a/x. If $x < \sqrt{a}$, then $a/x > a/\sqrt{a} = \sqrt{a}$. Similarly, if $x > \sqrt{a}$, then $a/x < a/\sqrt{a} = \sqrt{a}$. That is, $\sqrt{a}$ lies between x and a/x. Make the *midpoint* of that interval your improved guess of the square root, as shown in Figure 5. You therefore set $x_{new} = (x + a/x)/2$ and repeat the procedure—that is, compute the average of x_{new} and a/x_{new}. Stop when two successive approximations differ from each other by a very small amount, using the comparison function described in Common Error 4.2.

Syntax 7.2 : do/while Statement

do *statement* while (*condition*);

Example: do x = sqrt(x); while (x >= 10);

Purpose: Execute the statement, then test the condition, and repeat the statement while the condition remains true.

Figure 5

Approximation of the Square Root

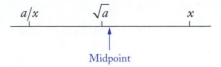

The method converges very rapidly. To compute $\sqrt{400}$, only ten steps are required:

```
400
200.5
101.24750623441396
52.599110411804922
30.101900881222353
21.695049123587058
20.06621767747577
20.000109257780434
20.000000000298428
20
```

The following function implements that algorithm:

File sqroot.cpp

```cpp
1  #include <iostream>
2  #include <cmath>
3
4  using namespace std;
5
6  int main()
7  {
8     cout << "Please enter a number: ";
9     double a;
10    cin >> a;
11
12    const double EPSILON = 1E-14;
13    double xnew = a;
14    double xold;
15
16    do
17    {
18       xold = xnew;
19       xnew = (xold + a / xold) / 2;
20    }
21    while (fabs(xnew - xold) > EPSILON);
22
23    cout << "The square root is " << xnew << "\n";
24    return 0;
25 }
```

Here the do/while loop is a good choice. You want to enter the loop at least once so that you can compute the difference between two approximations (see Figure 6).

Figure 6

Flowchart of a do Loop

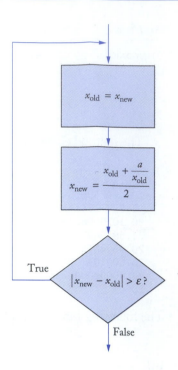

7.2

Random Fact

Spaghetti Code

In this chapter we used flowcharts to illustrate the behavior of the loop statements. It used to be common to draw flowcharts for every function, on the theory that flowcharts are easier to read and write than the actual code. Nowadays, flowcharts are no longer routinely used for program development and documentation.

Flowcharts have one fatal flaw. While it is possible to express the `while`, `for`, and `do/while` loops with flowcharts, it is also possible to draw flowcharts that cannot be programmed with loops. Consider the chart in Figure 7.

The lower half is a do/while loop:

```
do
{
    xold = xnew;
    xnew = (xold + a / xold) / 2;
}
while (fabs(xnew - xold) > EPSILON);
```

The top is an input statement and an assignment:

```
cin >> a;
xold = a / 2;
```

Figure 7

Flowchart That Cannot Be
Implemented with Loops

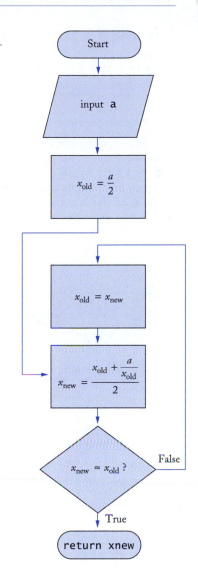

However, now we are supposed to continue in the middle of the loop, skipping the first statement.

```
cin >> a;
xold = a / 2;
goto a;

do
{
    xold = xnew;
    a: xnew = (xold + a/xold) / 2;
}
while (fabs(xnew - xold) > EPSILON);
```

In fact, why even bother with the do/while? Here is a faithful interpretation of the flowchart:

```
cin >> a;
xold = a / 2;
goto a;
b: xold = xnew;
a: xnew = (xold + a/xold) / 2;
if (fabs(xnew - xold) > EPSILON) goto b:
```

This *nonlinear* control flow turns out to be extremely hard to read and understand if you have more than one or two goto statements. Because the lines denoting the goto statements weave back and forth in complex flowcharts, the resulting code is named *spaghetti code*. The while loop was invented to untangle it.

In the 1960s the influential computer scientist Edsger Dijkstra wrote a famous note, entitled "Goto statements considered harmful" [2], in which he argued for the use of loops instead of unstructured jumps. Initially, many programmers who had been using goto for

if (c) a; else b;

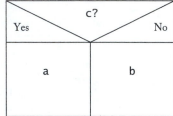

while (c) a;

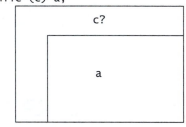

do a; while (c);

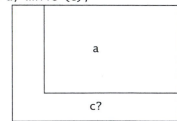

Figure 8

Structure Charts

Figure 9

Structure Chart for Square Root Loop

▼

▼

▼

years were mortally insulted and dug out examples where the use of goto does lead to clearer or faster code. Some languages started offering weaker forms of goto, such as the break statement discussed in Advanced Topic 7.1, which are less harmful. Nowadays, most computer scientists accept Dijkstra's argument and fight bigger battles than optimal loop design.

If you like to draw pictures of your code, you may consider so-called *structure charts* (see Figure 8). They avoid the problem of flow charts and are directly translatable to C++. Figure 9 shows a structure chart for the loop computing a square root.

7.7   Nested Loops

In this section you will see how to print a table that tells you the fate of a $10,000 investment under various interest rate scenarios if you keep the money for 5, 10, 15, 20, 25, and 30 years. (Note that the investment grows to almost $175,000 if you keep the money for 30 years at 10 percent interest!)

Rate	5 years	10 years	15 years	20 years	25 years	30 years
5.00	12762.82	16288.95	20789.28	26532.98	33863.55	43219.42
5.50	13069.60	17081.44	22324.76	29177.57	38133.92	49839.51
6.00	13382.26	17908.48	23965.58	32071.35	42918.71	57434.91
6.50	13700.87	18771.37	25718.41	35236.45	48276.99	66143.66
7.00	14025.52	19671.51	27590.32	38696.84	54274.33	76122.55
7.50	14356.29	20610.32	29588.77	42478.51	60983.40	87549.55
8.00	14693.28	21589.25	31721.69	46609.57	68484.75	100626.57
8.50	15036.57	22609.83	33997.43	51120.46	76867.62	115582.52
9.00	15386.24	23673.64	36424.82	56044.11	86230.81	132676.78
9.50	15742.39	24782.28	39013.22	61416.12	96683.64	152203.13
10.00	16105.10	25937.42	41772.48	67275.00	108347.06	174494.02

Of course, the basic idea is simple. Here is the pseudocode:

```
print table header
for (rate = RATE_MIN; rate <= RATE_MAX; rate = rate + RATE_INCR)
{
    print table row
}
```

How do you print a table row? You need to print values for 5, 10, . . ., 30 years. There are the dots again, so you need to program a loop.

```
for (year = YEAR_MIN; year <= YEAR_MAX; year = year + YEAR_INCR)
{
   balance = future_value(initial_balance, rate, year);
   cout << setw(10) << balance;
}
```

This loop prints a table row. It must be placed inside the preceding loop, yielding two *nested* loops.

Next, consider the table header. You could print a long string

```
"Rate   5 years   10 years   15 years   20 years   25 years   30 years"
```

However, since the header needs to change if you change the year range or increment, you should use a loop:

```
cout << "Rate ";
for (year = YEAR_MIN; year <= YEAR_MAX; year = year + YEAR_INCR)
{
   cout << setw(2) << year << " years   ";
}
```

Now you put everything together:

File table.cpp

```
 1 #include <iostream>
 2 #include <iomanip>
 3 #include <cmath>
 4
 5 using namespace std;
 6
 7 int main()
 8 {
 9    const double RATE_MIN = 5;
10    const double RATE_MAX = 10;
11    const double RATE_INCR = 0.5;
12    const int YEAR_MIN = 5;
13    const int YEAR_MAX = 30;
14    const int YEAR_INCR = 5;
15
16    /* print table header */
17
18    int year;
19    cout << "Rate ";
20    for (year = YEAR_MIN; year <= YEAR_MAX;
21          year = year + YEAR_INCR)
22    {
23       cout << setw(2) << year << " years   ";
24    }
25    cout << "\n";
26
27    cout << fixed << setprecision(2);
28
29    double rate;
30    double initial_balance = 10000;
31    for (rate = RATE_MIN; rate <= RATE_MAX;
32          rate = rate + RATE_INCR)
33    {
```

```
34          /* print table row */
35          cout << setw(5) << rate;
36          for (year = YEAR_MIN; year <= YEAR_MAX;
37             year = year + YEAR_INCR)
38          {
39             double balance =
40                initial_balance * pow(1 + rate / 100, year);
41             cout << setw(10) << balance;
42          }
43          cout << "\n";
44       }
45
46       return 0;
47    }
```

This program contains a total of three `for` loops! The first one is harmless; it just prints six columns in the table header. The other two loops are more interesting. The loop printing a single row is nested in the loop that traverses the interest rates. There are a total of 11 rates in the outer loop ($11 = (10 - 5)/0.5 + 1$, see Quality Tip 7.5). For each rate the program prints six columns of balances in the inner loop. Thus, a total of $11 \times 6 = 66$ balances are printed.

You put a loop after another loop if all iterations of the first loop need to be carried out before the first iteration of the second loop. If the first loop has m iterations and the second loop has n iterations, there are a total of $m + n$ iterations. You nest a loop inside another if all cases of the inner loop must be repeated for each iteration of the outer loop. This yields a total of $m \times n$ iterations.

Sometimes the iteration count of the inner block depends on the outer block. As an example, consider the task of printing a triangle shape such as this one:

```
[]
[][]
[][][]
[][][][]
```

The first row contains one box, the second row contains two boxes, and so on.

To print n rows, use the loop

```
for (int i = 1; i <= n; i++)
{
    print triangle row
}
```

Each row contains i boxes. That is, the following loop prints a row:

```
for (int j = 1; j <= i; j++)
    cout << "[]";
cout << "\n";
```

Putting the two loops together yields

```
for (int i = 1; i <= n; i++)
{
    for (int j = 1; j <= i; j++)
        cout << "[]";
    cout << "\n";
}
```

Note how the bounds of the inner loop depend on the outer loop.

Here is the complete program.

File triangle.cpp

```
1  #include <iostream>
2
3  using namespace std;
4
5  int main()
6  {
7     cout << "Enter number of rows: ";
8     int n;
9     cin >> n;
10
11    for (int i = 1; i <= n; i++)
12    {
13       for (int j = 1; j <= i; j++)
14          cout << "[]";
15       cout << "\n";
16    }
17
18    return 0;
19 }
```

7.8   Processing Text Input

In Chapter 4, you learned how to process input that consists of a series of numerical values. However, many useful programs process text, not numbers. In this section, you will see how to write C++ programs that read text inputs.

When processing text input, you need to make a decision. Is the input structured as a sequence of *characters*, *words*, or *lines*? Here, a *word* is any sequence of characters surrounded by white space (spaces, tabs, or newlines).

Suppose you want to write a program that counts or analyzes the words in a file. Then you use the loop

```
string word;
while (cin >> word)
{
   process word
}
```

Here you take advantage of the fact that the expression `cin >> word` has the value `cin`. You can use `cin` in a test—it is the same test as `!cin.fail()`.

For example, here is a program that counts the number of words in an input file. This program is useful if you are a writer who is paid by the word.

File words.cpp

```
1  #include <iostream>
2  #include <string>
```

```
 3
 4  using namespace std;
 5
 6  int main()
 7  {
 8      int count = 0;
 9      string word;
10      while (cin >> word)
11      {
12          count++;
13      }
14
15      cout << count << " words.\n";
16
17      return 0;
18  }
```

On the other hand, sometimes it doesn't make sense to process input a word at a time. For example, you may have a sequence of employee names

```
Hacker, Harry J.
Tester, Tony
. . .
```

You would want to process this file one line at a time, using the `getline` function.

```
string line;
while (getline(cin, line))
{
    process line
}
```

Again, this loop takes advantage of the fact that the `getline` function returns `cin`, and you can test that `cin` hasn't yet failed.

Finally, neither the word nor line boundaries may be meaningful for your processing. In that case, read the input one character at a time. Use the loop

```
char ch;
while (cin.get(ch))
{
    process ch
}
```

Here, `ch` is a variable of type `char`, the character data type. For example, the following loop counts how many sentences are contained in an input file:

```
int sentences = 0;
char ch;
while (cin.get(ch))
{
    if (ch == '.' || ch == '!' || ch == '?')
        sentences++;
}
```

Note that character constants are delimited with single quotes (such as `'!'`). We will discuss the `char` data type in greater detail in Chapter 9.

Productivity Hint   7.3

Redirection of Input and Output

Consider the word-counting program of Section 7.8. How would you use it? You would type text in, and at the end of the input the program would tell you how many words you typed. However, none of the words would be saved for posterity. That is truly dumb—you would never want to use such a program.

Such programs are not intended for keyboard input. The program makes a lot of sense if input is read from a *file*. The command line interfaces of most operating systems provide a way to link a file to the input of a program, as if all the characters in the file had actually been typed by a user. If you type

```
words < article.txt
```

the word-counting program is executed. Its input instructions no longer expect input from the keyboard. All input commands (>>, getline, get) get their input from the file article.txt.

This mechanism works for any program that reads its input from the standard input stream cin. By default, cin is tied to the keyboard, but it can be tied to any file by specifying *input redirection* on the command line.

If you have always launched your program from the integrated environment, you need to find out whether your environment supports input redirection. If it does not, you need to learn how to open a command window (often called a *shell*) and launch the program in the command window by typing its name and redirection instructions.

You can also redirect output. In this program, that is not terribly useful. If you run

```
words < article.txt > output.txt
```

the file output.txt contains a single line such as "513 words". However, redirecting output is obviously useful for programs that produce lots of output. You can print the file containing the output or edit it before you turn it in for grading.

Advanced Topic   7.2

Pipes

Output of one program can become the input of another program. Here is a simple program that writes each word of the input file onto a separate line:

```cpp
#include <iostream>
#include <string>

using namespace std;

int main()
{
   string word;
   while (cin >> word)
      cout << word << "\n";
   return 0;
}
```

▼ Let us call this program *split*. Then

```
split < article.txt
```

▼ lists the words in the file `article.txt`, one on each line. That isn't too exciting, but it becomes useful when combined with another program: *sort*. You have not yet learned how to write a program that sorts strings, but most operating systems have a sort program. A sorted list of the words in a file would be quite useful—for example, for making an index. You can save the unsorted words in a temporary file.

```
split < article.txt > temp.txt
sort < temp.txt > sorted.txt
```

▼ Now the sorted words are in the file `sorted.txt`. Because this operation is so common, there is a command line shorthand for it.

```
split < article.txt | sort > sorted.txt
```

▼ The split program runs first, reading input from `article.txt`. Its output becomes the input of the sort program. The output of sort is saved in the file `sorted.txt`. The operator instructs the operating system to construct a *pipe* linking the output of the first program to the input of the second.

The file `sorted.txt` has one blemish. It is likely to contain runs of repeated words, like

a

a

a

an

an

anteater

asia

This is easy to fix with another program that removes *adjacent* duplicates. Removing duplicates in arbitrary positions is quite hard, but adjacent duplicates are easy to handle:

```cpp
#include <iostream>
#include <string>

using namespace std;

int main()
{
   string last;
   string word;
   while (cin >> word)
   {
      if (word != last)
         cout << word << "\n";
      last = word;
   }
   return 0;
}
```

Figure 10

A Series of Pipes

Let us call this program *unique*. The sorted word list, with duplicates removed, is obtained as the series of pipes

```
split < article.txt | sort | unique > sorted.txt
```

(See Figure 10.)

Redirection and pipes make it possible to combine simple programs to do useful work. This approach was pioneered by the UNIX operating system. UNIX comes with dozens of commands that perform common tasks and are designed to be combined with each other.

Common Error   7.6

Underestimating the Size of a Data Set

It is a common programming error to underestimate the amount of input data that a user will pour into an unsuspecting program. A program that was designed to handle input lines that are at most 255 characters long will surely fail when the first user runs it with a file whose lines are 1,000 characters long. Your text editor may or may not be able to generate such long lines, but it is easy enough to write a program that produces output with very long lines. That program just won't print a newline between outputs. The output of such a program may well become the input of your program, and you should never make any assumptions that input lines are short.

Here is another common problem. In Section 7.8 we wrote a program that counted the number of words in a file. How many words might be in an input file? If you enter a test file by hand, surely no more than a few dozen. If you take another convenient file from your hard disk, say a readme.txt file from some software package, there may be a few thousand words. If you feed in the entire text of *Alice in Wonderland* or *War and Peace* (which are available on the Internet), you all of a sudden have to count a few hundred thousand words.

A famous article [4] analyzed how several UNIX programs reacted when they were fed large or random data sets. Sadly, about a quarter didn't do well at all, crashing or hanging without a reasonable error message. For example, in some versions of UNIX the tape backup program *tar* cannot handle file names that are longer than 100 characters, which is a pretty unreasonable limitation. Many of these shortcomings are caused by features of the C language that this book neatly sidesteps with the string and vector types.

7.9   Simulations

In a simulation we generate random events and evaluate their outcomes. Here is a typical problem that can be decided by running a simulation, the *Buffon needle experiment*, devised by Comte Georges-Louis Leclerc de Buffon (1707–1788), a French naturalist. A needle of length 1 inch is dropped onto paper that is ruled with lines 2 inches apart. If the needle drops onto a line, we count it as a *hit*. Buffon conjectured that the quotient *tries/hits* approximates π. (See Figure 11.)

Now, how can you run this experiment in the computer? You don't actually want to build a robot that drops needles on paper. The C++ library has a *random number generator*, which produces numbers that appear to be completely random. Calling `rand()` yields a random integer between 0 and `RAND_MAX` (which is an implementation-dependent constant, typically 32767 or 2147483647). The `rand` function is defined in the `cstdlib` header. The following program calls the `rand` function ten times.

File random.cpp

```
 1 #include <iostream>
 2 #include <cstdlib>
 3
 4 using namespace std;
 5
 6 int main()
 7 {
 8    int i;
 9    for (i = 1; i <= 10; i++)
10    {
11       int r = rand();
12       cout << r << "\n";
13    }
14    return 0;
15 }
```

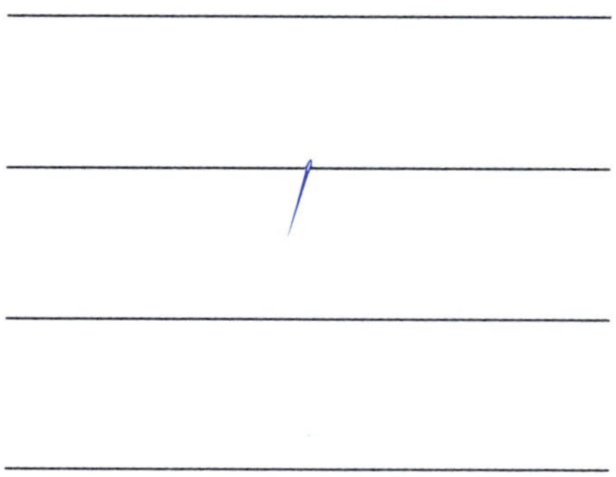

Figure 11

The Buffon Needle Experiment

Here is the program output:

```
41
18467
6334
26500
19169
15724
11478
29358
26962
24464
```

Actually, the numbers are not completely random. They are drawn from very long sequences of numbers that don't repeat for a long time. These sequences are actually computed from fairly simple formulas; they just behave like random numbers. For that reason, they are often called *pseudorandom* numbers. How to generate good sequences of numbers that behave like truly random sequences is an important and well-studied problem in computer science. We won't investigate this issue further. Just use the random numbers produced by rand.

Try running the program again. You will get the *exact same output*! This confirms that the random numbers are generated by formulas. However, when running simulations, you don't always want to get the same results. To overcome this problem, you need to specify a *seed* for the random number sequence. Every time you use a new seed, the random number generator starts generating a new sequence. The seed is set with the srand function. A simple value to use as a seed is the number of seconds that have elapsed since midnight:

```
Time now;
int seed = now.seconds_from(Time(0, 0, 0));
srand(seed);
```

In the program below, you will find a function rand_seed that carries out the same operation without requiring the Time class. (It uses the standard time function defined in the ctime header.) Simply call rand_seed() once in your program, before generating any random numbers. Then the random numbers will be different in every program run.

Of course, in actual applications, you want to generate random numbers in different ranges. For example, to simulate the throw of a die, you need random numbers between 1 and 6. The following rand_int function generates random integers between two bounds a and b as follows. As you know from Quality Tip 7.5, there are b - a + 1 values between a and b, including the bounds themselves. First compute rand() % (b - a + 1) to obtain a random value between 0 and b - a, then add that to a, yielding a random value between a and b:

```
int rand_int(int a, int b)
{
    return a + rand() % (b - a + 1);
}
```

A word of caution: Neither the rand_seed nor the rand_int function is suitable for serious applications, such as the generation of passwords. But they will work fine for our purposes. For example, here is a program that simulates the throw of a pair of dice by calling rand_int(1, 6).

File dice.cpp

```cpp
1  #include <iostream>
2  #include <string>
3  #include <cstdlib>
4  #include <ctime>
5
6  using namespace std;
7
8  /**
9     Sets the seed of the random number generator.
10 */
11 void rand_seed()
12 {
13    int seed = static_cast<int>(time(0));
14    srand(seed);
15 }
16
17 /**
18    Computes a random integer in a range.
19    @param a the bottom of the range
20    @param b the top of the range
21    @return a random integer x, a <= x and x <= b
22 */
23 int rand_int(int a, int b)
24 {
25    return a + rand() % (b - a + 1);
26 }
27
28 int main()
29 {
30    rand_seed();
31    int i;
32    for (i = 1; i <= 10; i++)
33    {
34       int d1 = rand_int(1, 6);
35       int d2 = rand_int(1, 6);
36       cout << d1 << " " << d2 << "\n";
37    }
38    cout << "\n";
39    return 0;
40 }
```

Here is a typical outcome:

```
5 1
2 1
1 2
5 1
1 2
6 4
4 4
6 1
6 3
5 2
```

Figure 12

A Hit in the Buffon Needle Experiment

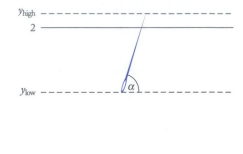

To run the Buffon needle experiment you have to work a little harder. When you throw a die, it has to come up with one of six faces. When throwing a needle, however, there are many possible outcomes.

You must generate a random *floating-point number*. To generate random floating-point values, you use a different approach.

First, note that the quantity `rand() * 1.0 / RAND_MAX` is a random floating-point value between 0 and 1. (You have to multiply by `1.0` to ensure that one of the operands of the / operator is a floating-point value. The division `rand() / RAND_MAX` would be an integer division—see Common Error 2.2.) To generate a random value in a different range, you have to make a simple transformation:

```
double rand_double(double a, double b)
{
   return a + (b - a) * rand() * (1.0 / RAND_MAX);
}
```

For the Buffon needle experiment, you must generate two random numbers: one to describe the starting position and one to describe the angle of the needle with the *x*-axis. Then you need to test whether the needle touches a grid line. Stop after 10,000 tries.

Generate the *lower* point of the needle. Its *x*-coordinate is irrelevant, and you may assume its *y*-coordinate y_{low} to be any random number between 0 and 2. The angle α between the needle and the x-axis can be any value between −90 degrees and 90 degrees. The upper end of the needle has *y*-coordinate

$$y_{high} = y_{low} + \sin \alpha$$

The needle is a hit if y_{high} is at least 2, as shown in Figure 12.

Here is the program that carries out the simulation of the needle experiment.

File buffon.cpp

```
1 #include <iostream>
2 #include <cstdlib>
3 #include <cmath>
4 #include <ctime>
5
```

```
 6 using namespace std;
 7
 8 /**
 9     Sets the seed of the random number generator.
10 */
11 void rand_seed()
12 {
13     int seed = static_cast<int>(time(0));
14     srand(seed);
15 }
16
17 /**
18     Computes a random floating-point number in a range.
19     @param a  the bottom of the range
20     @param b  the top of the range
21     @return  a random floating-point number x, a <= x and x <= b
22 */
23 double rand_double(double a, double b)
24 {
25     return a + (b - a) * rand() * (1.0 / RAND_MAX);
26 }
27
28 /**
29     Converts an angle from degrees to radians.
30     @param alpha  the angle in degrees
31     @return  the angle in radians
32 */
33 double deg2rad(double alpha)
34 {
35     const double PI = 3.141592653589793;
36     return alpha * PI / 180;
37 }
38
39 int main()
40 {
41     int NTRIES = 10000;
42     int hits = 0;
43     rand_seed();
44     for (int i = 1; i <= NTRIES; i++)
45     {
46         double ylow = rand_double(0, 2);
47         double angle = rand_double(0, 180);
48         double yhigh = ylow + sin(deg2rad(angle));
49         if (yhigh >= 2) hits++;
50     }
51     cout << "Tries / Hits = "
52         << NTRIES * (1.0 / hits) << "\n";
53     return 0;
54 }
```

On one computer I obtained the result 3.10 when running 10,000 iterations and 3.1429 when running 100,000 iterations.

The point of this program is *not* to compute π (after all, we needed the value of π in the deg2rad function). Rather, the point is to show how a physical experiment can be simulated on the computer. Buffon had to drop the needle physically thousands of times and record the results, which must have been a rather dull activity. We can have the computer execute the experiment quickly and accurately.

Simulations are very common computer applications. All simulations use essentially the same pattern as the code of this example: In a loop, a large number of sample values are generated. The values of certain observations are recorded for each sample. Finally, when the simulation is completed, the averages of the observed values are printed out.

A typical example of a simulation is the modeling of customer queues at a bank or a supermarket. Rather than observing real customers, one simulates their arrival and their transactions at the teller window or checkout stand in the computer. One can try out different staffing or building layout patterns in the computer simply by making changes in the program. In the real world, making many such changes and measuring their effect would be impossible, or at least very expensive.

CHAPTER SUMMARY

1. Multiple conditions can be combined to evaluate complex decisions. The correct arrangement depends on the logic of the problem to be solved.

2. Complex combinations of conditions can be simplified by storing intermediate condition outcomes in Boolean variables, or by applying De Morgan's Law.

3. In addition to the `while` loop, there are two specialized loop types, the `for` and `do` loops. The `for` loop is used when a value runs from a starting point to an ending point with a constant increment or decrement. The `do` loop is appropriate when the loop body must be executed at least once.

4. Branches and loops can be nested.

5. You can read text input as words, lines, or characters.

6. Use input redirection to read input from a file. Use output redirection to capture program output in a file.

7. In a simulation program, you use the computer to simulate an activity. You can introduce randomness by calling the random number generator.

FURTHER READING

[1] Peter van der Linden, *Expert C Programming*, Prentice-Hall, 1994.
[2] E. W. Dijkstra, "Goto Statements Considered Harmful", *Communications of the ACM*, vol. 11, no. 3 (March 1968), pp. 147–148.
[3] Barton P. Miller, Louis Fericksen, and Bryan So, "An Empirical Study of the Reliability of UNIX Utilities", *Communications of the ACM*, vol. 33, no. 12 (December 1990), pp. 32–44.
[4] Kai Lai Chung, *Elementary Probability Theory with Stochastic Processes*, Undergraduate Texts in Mathematics, Springer-Verlag, 1974.
[5] Rudolf Flesch, *How to Write Plain English*, Barnes & Noble Books, 1979.

Review Exercises

Exercise R7.1. Explain the difference between an if/else/else statement and nested if statements. Give an example for each.

Exercise R7.2. Give an example for an if/else/else statement where the order of the tests does not matter. Give an example where the order of the tests matters.

Exercise R7.3. Complete the following truth table by finding the truth values of the Boolean expressions for all combinations of the Boolean inputs p, q, and r.

p	q	r	p && q || !r	!(p && (q && !r))
false	false	false		
false	false	false		
false	true	false		
. . . 5 more combinations . . .				

Exercise R7.4. Before implementing any complex algorithm, it is a good idea to understand and analyze it. The purpose of this exercise is to gain a better understanding of the tax computation algorithm.

Some people object to the fact that the tax rates increase with higher incomes, claiming that certain taxpayers are then better off *not* to work hard and get a raise, since they would then have to pay a higher tax rate and actually end up with less money after taxes. Can you find such an income level? If not, why?

Another feature of the tax code is the *marriage penalty*. Under certain circumstances, a married couple pays higher taxes than the sum of what the two partners would pay if they both were single. Find examples for such income levels.

Exercise R7.5. True or false? *A* && *B* is the same as *B* && *A* for any Boolean conditions *A* and *B*.

Exercise R7.6. Explain the difference between

```
s = 0;
if (x > 0) s++;
if (y > 0) s++;
```

and

```
s = 0;
if (x > 0) s++;
else if (y > 0) s++;
```

Exercise R7.7. Use De Morgan's Law to simplify the following Boolean expressions.

(a) `!(x > 0 && y > 0)`

(b) `!(x != 0 || y != 0)`

(c) `!(country == "USA" && state != "HI" && state != "AK")`

(d) `!(x % 4 != 0 || !(x % 100 == 0 && x % 400 != 0))`

Exercise R7.8. Make up another C++ code example that shows the dangling `else` problem, using the following statement. A student with a GPA of at least 1.5, but less than 2, is on probation. With less than 1.5, the student is failing.

Exercise R7.9. Write code to test whether two objects of type `Line` look the same when displayed on the graphics screen.

```
Line a;
Line b;
if (your condition goes here)
cwin << Message(Point(0, 0), "They look the same!");
```

Hint: If p and q are points, then `Line(p, q)` and `Line(q, p)` look the same.

Exercise R7.10. How can you test whether two objects t1 and t2 of type `Time` represent the same time, without comparing the hour, minute, and second values?

Exercise R7.11. Consider the following test to see whether a point falls inside a rectangle.

```
Point p = cwin.get_mouse("Click inside the rectangle");
bool x_inside = false;
if (x1 <= p.get_x() && p.get_x() <= x2)
   x_inside = true;
bool y_inside = false;
if (y1 <= p.get_y() && p.get_y() <= y2)
   y_inside = true;
if (x_inside && y_inside)
   cwin << Message(p, "Congratulations!");
```

Rewrite this code to eliminate the explicit `true` and `false` values, by setting `x_inside` and `y_inside` to the values of Boolean expressions.

Exercise R7.12. Give a set of test cases for the tax program in Section 7.2. Manually compute the expected results.

Exercise R7.13. Which loop statements does C++ support? Give simple rules when to use each loop type.

Exercise R7.14. Is the following code legal?

```
int i;
for (i = 0; i < 10; i++)
{
   int i;
   for (i = 0; i < 10; i++)
      cout << i;
   cout << "\n";
}
```

What does it print? Is it good coding style? If not, how would you improve it?

Exercise R7.15. How often do the following loops execute? Assume that i is not changed in the loop body.

(a) `for (i = 1; i <= 10; i++) . . .`

(b) `for (i = 0; i < 10; i++) . . .`

(c) `for (i = 10; i > 0; i--) . . .`

(d) `for (i = -10; i <= 10; i++) . . .`

(e) `for (i = 10; i >= 0; i++) . . .`

(f) `for (i = -10; i <= 10; i = i + 2) . . .`

(g) `for (i = -10; i <= 10; i = i + 3) . . .`

Exercise R7.16. Rewrite the following for loop into a while loop.

```
int i;
int s = 0;
for (i = 1; i <= 10; i++) s = s + i;
```

Exercise R7.17. Rewrite the following do/while loop into a while loop.

```
int n;
cin >> n;
double x = 0;
double s;
do
{
   s = 1.0 / (1 + n * n);
   n++;
   x = x + s;
}
while (s > 0.01);
```

Exercise R7.18. There are two methods to supply input to cin. Describe both methods. Explain how the "end of file" is signaled in both cases.

Exercise R7.19. In Windows and UNIX, there is no special "end of file" character stored in a file. Verify this statement by producing a file with known character count—for example, a file consisting of the following three lines

```
Hello
cruel
world
```

Then look at the directory listing. How many characters does the file contain? Remember to count the newline characters. (In Windows, you may be surprised that the count is not what you expect. Windows text files store each newline as a two-character sequence. The input and output streams automatically translate between this carriage return/line feed sequence used by files and the "\n" character used by C++ programs, so you don't need to worry about it.) Why does this prove that there is no "end of file" character? Why do you nevertheless need to type Ctrl + Z/Ctrl + D to end console input?

Exercise R7.20. There are three kinds of text input: character-oriented, word-oriented, and line-oriented. Explain the differences between them, show how to implement each in C++, and give simple rules for when to use each kind.

Exercise R7.21. Negative numbers do not have a square root. What happens inside the square root algorithm if a is negative?

Exercise R7.22. What are the values of s and n after the following loops?

(a)
```
int s = 1;
int n = 1;
while (s < 10) s = s + n;
n++;
```

(b)
```
int s = 1;
int n;
for (n = 1; n < 5; n++) s = s + n;
```

(c)
```
int s = 1;
int n = 1;
do
{
   s = s + n;
   n++;
}
while (s < 10 * n);
```

Exercise R7.23. What do the following loops print? Work out the answer without using the computer.

(a)
```
int s = 1;
int n;
for (n = 1; n <= 5; n++)
{
   s = s + n;
   cout << s;
}
```

(b)
```
int s = 1;
int n;
for (n = 1; n <= 5; cout << s)
{
   n = n + 2;
   s = s + n;
}
```

(c)
```
int s = 1;
int n;
for (n = 1; n <= 5; n++)
{
   s = s + n;
   n++;
}
cout << s << " " << n;
```

Exercise R7.24. What do the following program segments print? Find the answers by hand, not by using the computer.

(a)
```
int i;
int n = 1;
for (i = 2; i < 5; i++) n = n + i;
cout << n;
int i;
double n = 1 / 2;
for (i = 2; i <= 5; i++) n = n + 1.0 / i;
cout << i;
```

(b)
```
double x = 1;
double y = 1;
int i = 0;
do
{
   y = y / 2;
   x = x + y;
   i++;
}
while (x < 1.8);
cout << i;
```

(c)
```
double x = 1;
double y = 1;
int i = 0;
while (y >= 1.5)
{
   x = x / 2;
   y = x + y;
   i++;
}
cout << i;
```

Exercise R7.25. Give an example of a for loop where symmetric bounds are more natural. Give an example of a for loop where asymmetric bounds are more natural.

Exercise R7.26. What are nested loops? Give an example where a nested loop is typically used.

Exercise R7.27. Suppose you didn't know about the method for computing square roots that was introduced in Section 7.6. If you had to compute square roots by hand, you would probably use a different approximation method. For example, suppose you need to compute the square root of 300. You would first find that $17^2 = 289$ is smaller than 300 and $18^2 = 324$ is larger than 300. Then you would try 17.1^2, 17.2^2, and so on. Write pseudocode for an algorithm that uses this strategy. Be precise about the progression from one step to the next and the termination criterion.

PROGRAMMING EXERCISES

Exercise P7.1. If you look at the tax tables in Section 7.2, you will note that the percentages 15%, 28%, and 31% are identical for both single and married taxpayers, but the cutoffs for the tax brackets are different. Married people get to pay 15% on their first $35,800, then pay 28% on the next $50,700, and 31% on the remainder. Single people pay 15% on their first $21,450, then pay 28% on the next $30,450, and 31% on the remainder. Write a tax program with the following logic: Set variables `cutoff15` and `cutoff28` that depend on marital status. Then have a single formula that computes the tax, depending on the incomes and the cutoffs. Verify that your results are identical to that of the `tax.cpp` program.

Exercise P7.2. A year with 366 days is called a leap year. A year is a leap year if it is divisible by four (for example, 1980), except that it is not a leap year if it is divisible by 100 (for example, 1900); however, it is a leap year if it is divisible by 400 (for example, 2000). There were no exceptions before the introduction of the Gregorian calendar on October 15, 1582 (1500 was a leap year). Write a program that asks the user for a year and computes whether that year is a leap year.

Exercise P7.3. Write a program that asks the user to enter a month (1 January, 2 February, and so on) and then prints the number of days of a month. For February, print "28 or 29 days".

```
Enter a month: 5
30 days
```

Exercise P7.4. The *Fibonacci numbers* are defined by the sequence

$$f_1 = 1$$
$$f_2 = 1$$
$$f_n = f_{n-1} + f_{n-2}$$

As in the algorithm to compute the square root of a number, reformulate that as

```
fold1 = 1;
fold2 = 1;
fnew = fold1 + fold2;
```

After that, discard `fold2`, which is no longer needed, and set `fold2` to `fold1` and `fold1` to `fnew`. Repeat `fnew` for an appropriate number of times.

Implement a program that computes the Fibonacci numbers in that way.

Exercise P7.5. The series of pipes in Advanced Topic 7.2 has one final problem: The output file contains upper- and lowercase versions of the same word, such as "The" and "the". Modify the procedure, either by changing one of the programs or, in the true spirit of piping, by writing another short program and adding it to the series.

Exercise P7.6. *Flesch Readability Index.* The following index [5] was invented by Flesch as a simple tool to gauge the legibility of a document without linguistic analysis.

1. Count all words in the file. A *word* is any sequence of characters delimited by white space, whether or not it is an actual English word.

2. Count all syllables in each word. To make this simple, use the following rules: Each *group* of adjacent vowels (a, e, i, o, u, y) counts as one syllable (for example, the "ea" in "real" contributes one syllable, but the "e . . . a" in "regal" counts as two

syllables). However, an "e" at the end of a word doesn't count as a syllable. Also each word has at least one syllable, even if the previous rules give a count of 0.

3. Count all sentences. A sentence is ended by a period, colon, semicolon, question mark, or exclamation mark.

4. The index is computed by

$$\text{Index} = 206.835 - 84.6 \times \frac{\text{Number of syllables}}{\text{Number of words}} - 1.015 \times \frac{\text{Number of words}}{\text{Number of sentences}}$$

rounded to the nearest integer.

This index is a number, usually between 0 and 100, indicating how difficult the text is to read. Some examples of random material for various publications are

Comics	95
Consumer ads	82
Sports Illustrated	65
Time	57
New York Times	39
Auto insurance policy	10
Internal Revenue Code	−6

Translated into educational levels, the indices are

91–100	5th grader
81–90	6th grader
71–80	7th grader
66–70	8th grader
61–65	9th grader
51–60	High school student
31–50	College student
0–30	College graduate
Less than 0	Law school graduate

The purpose of the index is to force authors to rewrite their text until the index is high enough. This is achieved by reducing the length of sentences and by removing long words. For example, the sentence

The following index was invented by Flesch as a simple tool to estimate the legibility of a document without linguistic analysis.

can be rewritten as

Flesch invented an index to check whether a document is easy to read. To compute the index, you need not look at the meaning of the words.

His book [5] contains delightful examples of translating government regulations into "plain English".

Your program should read in a text file, one word at a time, and compute the legibility index.

Exercise P7.7. *Factoring of integers.* Write a program that asks the user for an integer and then prints out all its factors. For example, when the user enters 150, the program should print

```
2
3
5
5
```

Exercise P7.8. *Prime numbers.* Write a program that prompts the user for an integer and then prints out all prime numbers up to that integer. For example, when the user enters 20, the program should print

```
2
3
5
7
11
13
17
19
```

Recall that a number is a prime number if it is not divisible by any number except 1 and itself.

Exercise P7.9. The best known iterative method for computing roots is *Newton-Raphson approximation.* To find the zero of a function whose derivative is also known, compute

$$x_{\text{new}} = x_{\text{old}} - f(x_{\text{old}})/f'(x_{\text{old}})$$

This method actually yields the same algorithm for finding square roots as does the classical Greek method. Finding $\sqrt{a}$ is the same as finding a zero of $f(x) = x^2 - a$. Thus,

$$x_{\text{new}} - x_{\text{old}} - \frac{f(x_{\text{old}})}{f'(x_{\text{old}})} = x_{\text{old}} - \frac{x_{\text{old}}^2 - a}{2x_{\text{old}}}$$

Clearly this method generalizes to find cube roots and nth roots. For this exercise, write a program to compute nth roots of floating-point numbers. Prompt the user for a and n, then obtain $\sqrt[n]{a}$ by computing a zero of the function $f(x) = x^n - a$.

Exercise P7.10. Write a program that reads a file from standard input and rewrites the file to standard output, replacing all tab characters \t with the *appropriate* number of spaces. Make the distance between tab columns a constant and set it to 3, the value used in this book for program code. Then expand tabs to the number of spaces necessary to move to the next tab column. *That may be less than three spaces.*

For example, the line

```
\t { \t n = 0 ; \n }
```

must be converted to

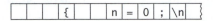

Exercise P7.11. Write a program that reads a series of floating-point numbers and prints
- The maximum value
- The minimum value
- The average value

Exercise P7.12. *The game of Nim.* This is a well-known game with a number of variants. The following variant has an interesting winning strategy. Two players alternately take marbles from a pile. In each move, a player chooses how many marbles to take. The player must take at least one but at most half of the marbles. Then the other player takes a turn. The player who takes the last marble loses.

You will write a program in which the computer plays against a human opponent. Generate a random integer between 10 and 100 to denote the initial size of the pile. Generate a random integer between 0 and 1 to decide whether the computer or the human takes the first turn. Generate a random integer between 0 and 1 to decide whether the computer plays *smart* or *stupid*. In stupid mode the computer simply takes a random legal value (between 1 and $n/2$) from the pile whenever it has a turn. In smart mode the computer takes off enough marbles to make the size of the pile a power of two minus 1—that is, 3, 7, 15, 31, or 63. That is always a legal move, except if the size of the pile is currently one less than a power of two. In that case, the computer makes a random legal move.

You will note that the computer cannot be beaten in smart mode when it has the first move, unless the pile size happens to be 15, 31, or 63. Of course, a human player who has the first turn and knows the winning strategy can win against the computer.

Exercise P7.13. The value of e^x can be computed as the power series

$$e^x = \sum_{n=1}^{\infty} \frac{x^n}{n!} = 1 + x + \frac{x^2}{2!} + \frac{x^3}{3!} + \dots$$

Write a function `exponential(x)` that computes e^x using this formula. Of course, you can't compute an infinite sum. Just keep adding values until an individual summand (term) is less than a certain threshold. At each step, you need to compute the new term and add it to the total. It would be a poor idea to compute

```
summand = pow(x, n) / factorial(n)
```

Instead, update the summand in each step:

```
summand = summand * x / n;
```

Exercise P7.14. Program the following simulation: Darts are thrown at random points onto a square with corners (1, 1) and (−1, −1). If the dart lands inside the unit circle (that is, the circle with center (0, 0) and radius 1), it is a hit. Otherwise it is a miss. Run this simulation and use it to determine an approximate value for π. Explain why this is a better method for estimating π than the Buffon needle program.

Exercise P7.15. It is easy and fun to draw graphs of curves with the C++ graphics library. Simply draw 100 line segments joining the points $(x, f(x))$ and $(x + d, f(x + d))$, where x ranges from x_{min} to x_{max} and $d = (x_{max} - x_{min})/100$. Draw the curve $f(x) = x^3/100 - x + 10$, where x ranges from -10 to 10 in this fashion.

Exercise P7.16. Draw a picture of the "four-leaved rose" whose equation in polar coordinates is $r = \cos 2\theta$, $0 \le \theta \le 2\pi$. Let θ go from 0 to 2π in 100 steps. Each time, compute r and then compute the (x, y) coordinates from the polar coordinates by using the formula

$$x = r \cos \theta$$
$$y = r \sin \theta$$

You will get extra credit if you can vary the number of petals.

Testing and Debugging

- ▶ To learn how to design test harnesses for testing components of your programs in isolation
- ▶ To understand the principles of test case selection and evaluation
- ▶ To be able to use assertions to document program assumptions
- ▶ To become familiar with the debugger
- ▶ To learn strategies for effective debugging

A complex program never works right the first time; it needs to be tested. It is easier to test a program if it has been designed with testing in mind. This is a common engineering practice: On television circuit boards or in the wiring of an automobile, you will find lights and wire connectors that serve no direct purpose for the TV or car but are put in place for the repair person in case something goes wrong. In the first part of this chapter you will learn how to instrument your programs in a similar way. It is a little more work up-front, but that work is amply repaid by shortened debugging times.

In the second part of this chapter you will learn how to run the debugger to cope with programs that don't do the right thing.

8.1   Unit Tests

The single most important testing tool is the *unit test* of a function or procedure. For this test, the procedure is compiled outside the program in which it will be used, together with a *test harness* that feeds arguments to the procedure.

The test arguments can come from one of three sources: from user input, by running through a range of values in a loop, and as random values.

Here is a test harness for the `squareroot` function of Chapter 7:

File sqrtest1.cpp

```
 1  #include <iostream>
 2  #include <cmath>
 3
 4  using namespace std;
 5
 6  /**
 7      Tests whether two floating-point numbers are
 8      approximately equal.
 9      @param x a floating-point number
10      @param y another floating-point number
11      @return true if x and y are approximately equal
12  */
13  bool approx_equal(double x, double y)
14  {
15      const double EPSILON = 1E-14;
16      if (x == 0) return fabs(y) <= EPSILON;
17      if (y == 0) return fabs(x) <= EPSILON;
18      return fabs(x - y) / max(fabs(x), fabs(y)) <= EPSILON;
19  }
20
21  /* Function to be tested */
22
23  /**
24      Computes the square root using Heron's formula.
25      @param a an integer ≥ 0
26      @return the square root of a
27  */
28  double squareroot(double a)
29  {
```

```
30      if (a == 0) return 0;
31
32      double xnew = a;
33      double xold;
34
35      do
36      {
37          xold = xnew;
38          xnew = (xold + a / xold) / 2;
39      }
40      while (!approx_equal(xnew, xold));
41
42      return xnew;
43  }
44
45  /* Test harness */
46
47  int main()
48  {
49      double x;
50      while (cin >> x)
51      {
52          double y = squareroot(x);
53          cout << "squareroot of " << x << " = " << y << "\n";
54      }
55      return 0;
56  }
```

When you run this test harness, you need to enter inputs and to force an end of input when you are done, by typing a key such as Ctrl + z or Ctrl + D (see Section 4.6). You can also store the test data in a file and use redirection:

```
sqrtest1 < test1.in
```

For each test case, the harness code calls the `squareroot` function and prints the result. You can then manually check the computations. Once you have confidence that the function works correctly, you can plug it into your program.

It is also possible to generate test cases automatically. If there are few possible inputs, it is feasible to run through a representative number of them with a loop:

File sqrtest2.cpp

```
1  #include <iostream>
2  #include <cmath>
3
4  using namespace std;
5
6  /**
7      Tests whether two floating-point numbers are
8      approximately equal.
9      @param x a floating-point number
10     @param y another floating-point number
11     @return true if x and y are approximately equal
12  */
```

```
13  bool approx_equal(double x, double y)
14  {
15      const double EPSILON = 1E-14;
16      if (x == 0) return fabs(y) <= EPSILON;
17      if (y == 0) return fabs(x) <= EPSILON;
18      return fabs(x - y) / max(fabs(x), fabs(y)) <= EPSILON;
19  }
20
21  /* Function to be tested */
22
23  /**
24      Computes the square root using Heron's formula.
25      @param a an integer ≥ 0
26      @return the square root of a
27  */
28  double squareroot(double a)
29  {
30      if (a == 0) return 0;
31
32      double xnew = a;
33      double xold;
34
35      do
36      {
37          xold = xnew;
38          xnew = (xold + a / xold) / 2;
39      }
40      while (!approx_equal(xnew, xold));
41
42      return xnew;
43  }
44
45  /* Test harness */
46
47  int main()
48  {
49      double x;
50      for (x = 0; x <= 10; x = x + 0.5)
51      {
52          double y = squareroot(x);
53          cout << "squareroot of " << x << " = " << y << "\n";
54      }
55
56      return 0;
57  }
```

Note that we purposefully test boundary cases (zero) and fractional numbers.

Unfortunately, this test is restricted to only a small subset of values. To overcome that limitation, random generation of test cases can be useful.

File sqrtest3.cpp

```
1  #include <iostream>
2  #include <cstdlib>
```

```
 3  #include <cmath>
 4  #include <ctime>
 5
 6  using namespace std;
 7
 8  /**
 9      Sets the seed of the random number generator.
10  */
11  void rand_seed()
12  {
13     int seed = static_cast<int>(time(0));
14     srand(seed);
15  }
16
17  /**
18      Computes a random floating-point number in a range.
19      @param a  the bottom of the range
20      @param b  the top of the range
21      @return a random floating-point number x,
22      a <= x and x <= b
23  */
24  double rand_double(double a, double b)
25  {
26     return a + (b - a) * rand() * (1.0 / RAND_MAX);
27  }
28
29  /**
30      Tests whether two floating-point numbers are
31      approximately equal.
32      @param x  a floating-point number
33      @param y  another floating-point number
34      @return true if x and y are approximately equal
35  */
36  bool approx_equal(double x, double y)
37  {
38     const double EPSILON = 1E-14;
39     if (x == 0) return fabs(y) <= EPSILON;
40     if (y == 0) return fabs(x) <= EPSILON;
41     return fabs(x - y) / max(fabs(x), fabs(y)) <= EPSILON;
42  }
43
44  /* Function to be tested */
45
46  /**
47      Computes the square root using Heron's formula.
48      @param a  an integer ≥ 0
49      @return the square root of a
50  */
51  double squareroot(double a)
52  {
53     if (a == 0) return 0;
54
55     double xnew = a;
56     double xold;
57
58     do
```

```
59     {
60         xold = xnew;
61         xnew = (xold + a / xold) / 2;
62     }
63     while (!approx_equal(xnew, xold));
64
65     return xnew;
66 }
67
68 /* Test harness */
69
70 int main()
71 {
72     rand_seed();
73     int i;
74     for (i = 1; i <= 100; i++)
75     {
76         double x = rand_double(0, 1E6);
77         double y = squareroot(x);
78         cout << "squareroot of " << x << " = " << y << "\n";
79     }
80
81     return 0;
82 }
```

No matter how you generate the test cases, the important point is that you test the procedure thoroughly before you put it into the program. If you ever put together a computer or fixed a car, you probably followed a similar process. Rather than simply throwing all the parts together and hoping for the best, you probably first tested each part in isolation. It takes a little longer, but it greatly reduces the possibility of complete failure once the parts are put together.

8.2   Selecting Test Cases

Selecting good test cases is an important skill for debugging programs. Of course, you want to test your program with inputs that a typical user might supply.

You should test all program features. In the program that prints English names of numbers, you should check typical test cases such as 5, 19, 29, 1093, 1728, 30000. These tests are *positive* tests. They consist of legitimate inputs, and you expect the program to handle them correctly.

Next, you should include *boundary cases*. Test what happens if the input is 0 or -1. Boundary cases are still legitimate inputs, and you expect that the program will handle them correctly, usually in some trivial way.

Finally, gather *negative* test cases. These are inputs that you expect the program to reject. Examples are inputs in the wrong format such as five.

How should you collect test cases? This is easy for programs that get all their input from standard input. Just make each test case into a file—say, test1.in, test2.in, `test3.in`. These files contain the keystrokes that you would normally type at the keyboard when the program runs. Feed the files into the program to be tested by using redirection:

```
program < test1.in > test1.out
program < test2.in > test2.out
program < test3.in > test3.out
```

Then study the outputs to determine if they are correct.

    Keeping a test case in a file is smart, because you can then use it to test every version of the program. In fact, it is a common and useful practice to make a test file whenever you find a program bug. You can use that file to verify that your bug fix really works. Don't throw it away; feed it to the next version after that and all subsequent versions. Such a collection of test cases is called a *test suite*.

    You will be surprised how often a bug that you fixed will reappear in a future version. This is a phenomenon known as *cycling*. Sometimes you don't quite understand the reason for a bug and apply a quick fix that appears to work. Later, you apply a different quick fix that solves a second problem but makes the first problem reappear. Of course, it is always best to really think through what causes a bug and fix the root cause instead of doing a sequence of "Band-Aid" solutions. If you don't succeed in doing that, however, at least you want to have an honest appraisal of how well the program works. By keeping all old test cases and testing them all against every new version, you get that feedback. The process of testing against a set of past failures is called *regression testing*.

    Testing the functionality of the program without consideration of its internal structure is called *black-box testing*. This is an important part of testing, because, after all, the users of a program do not know its internal structure. If a program works perfectly on all positive inputs and fails gracefully on all negative ones, then it does its job.

    However, it is impossible to ensure absolutely that a program will work correctly on all inputs, just by supplying a finite number of test cases. As the famous computer scientist Edsger Dijkstra pointed out, testing can only show the presence of bugs—not their absence. To gain more confidence in the correctness of a program, it is useful to consider its internal structure. Testing strategies that look inside a program are called *white-box testing*. Performing unit tests of each procedure and function is a part of white-box testing.

    You want to make sure that each part of your program is exercised at least once by one of your test cases. This is called *test coverage*. If some code is never executed by any of your test cases, you have no way of knowing whether that code would perform correctly if it ever were executed by user input. That means that you need to look at every `if/else` branch to see that each of them is reached by some test case. Many conditional branches are in the code only to take care of strange and abnormal inputs, but they still do something. It is a common phenomenon that they end up doing something incorrect but that those faults are never discovered during testing because nobody supplied the strange and abnormal inputs. Of course, these flaws become immediately apparent when the program is released and the first user types in a bad input and is incensed when the program crashes. A test suite should ensure that each part of the code is covered by some input.

    For example, in testing the `int_name` function of Chapter 5 you want to make sure that every `if` statement is entered for at least one test case and that it is skipped for another test case. For example, you might test the inputs 1234 and 1034 to see what happens if the test `if (c >= 100)` is entered and what happens if it is skipped.

It is a good idea to write the first test cases *before* the program is written completely. Designing a few test cases can give you insight into what the program should do, which is valuable for implementing it. You will also have something to throw at the program when it compiles for the first time. Of course, the initial set of test cases will be augmented as the debugging process progresses.

Modern programs can be quite challenging to test. In a program with a graphical user interface, the user can click random buttons with a mouse and supply input in random order. Programs that receive their data through a network connection need to be tested by simulating occasional network delays and failures. All this is much harder, since you cannot simply place keystrokes in a file. You need not worry about these complexities in this course, and there are tools to automate testing in these scenarios. The basic principles of regression testing (never throwing a test case away) and complete coverage (executing all code at least once) still hold.

8.3 Test Case Evaluation

In the last section, we worried about how to get test *inputs*. Now let us consider what to do with the *outputs*.

How do you know whether the output is correct? Sometimes you can verify the output by calculating the correct values by hand. For example, for a payroll program you can compute taxes manually.

Sometimes a computation does a lot of work, and it is not practical to do the computation manually. That is the case with many approximation algorithms, which may run through dozens or hundreds of iterations before they arrive at the final answer. The square root function of Section 7.6 is an example of such an approximation.

How can we test that the square root function works correctly? We can supply test inputs for which we know the answer, such as 4 and 900, and also $\frac{25}{4}$, so that we don't restrict the inputs to integers.

Alternatively, we can write a test harness program that verifies that the output values fulfill certain properties. For the square root program we can compute the square root, compute the square of the result, and verify that we obtain the original input:

File sqrtest4.cpp

```
1  #include <iostream>
2  #include <cstdlib>
3  #include <cmath>
4  #include <ctime>
5
6  using namespace std;
   ...
   /* same as sqrtest3.cpp */
   ...
68 /* Test harness */
69
```

```
70  int main()
71  {
72     int i;
73     for (i = 1; i <= 100; i++)
74     {
75        double x = rand_double(0, 1E6);
76        double y = squareroot(x);
77        if (!approx_equal(y * y, x))
78           cout << "Test failed. ";
79        else
80           cout << "Test passed. ";
81        cout << "squareroot of " << x << " = " << y << "\n";
82     }
83
84     return 0;
85  }
```

Finally, there may be a less efficient way of computing the same value that a function produces. We can then run a test harness that computes the function to be tested, together with the slower process, and compares the answers. For example, $\sqrt{x} = x^{1/2}$, so we can use the slower pow function to generate the same value. Such a slower but reliable procedure is called an *oracle*.

File sqrtest5.cpp

```
1  #include <iostream>
2  #include <cstdlib>
3  #include <cmath>
4  #include <ctime>
5
6  using namespace std;
   ...
   /* same as sqrtest3.cpp */
   ...
68  /* Test harness */
69
70  int main()
71  {
72     rand_seed();
73     int i;
74     for (i = 1; i <= 100; i++)
75     {
76        double x = rand_double(0, 1E6);
77        double y = squareroot(x);
78        if (!approx_equal(y, pow(x, 0.5)))
79           cout << "Test failed. ";
80        else
81           cout << "Test passed. ";
82        cout << "squareroot of " << x << " = " << y << "\n";
83     }
84
85     return 0;
86  }
```

Productivity Hint   8.1

Batch Files and Shell Scripts

If you need to perform the same tasks repeatedly on the command line, then it is worth learning about the automation features offered by your operating system.

Under DOS, you use *batch files* to execute a number of commands automatically. For example, suppose you need to test a program with three inputs:

```
program < test1.in
program < test2.in
program < test3.in
```

Then you find a bug, fix it, and run the tests again. Now you need to type the three commands once more. There has to be a better way. Under DOS, put the commands in a text file and call it `test.bat`. Then you just type

```
test
```

and the three commands in the batch file execute automatically.

It is easy to make the batch file more useful. If you are done with program and start working on program2, you can of course write a batch file `test2.bat`, but you can do better than that. Give the test batch file a *parameter*. That is, call it with

```
test program
```

or

```
test program2
```

You need to change the batch file to make this work. In a batch file, `%1` denotes the first string that you type after the name of the batch file, `%2` the second string, and so on:

File test.bat

```
1  %1 < test1.in
2  %1 < test2.in
3  %1 < test3.in
```

What if you have more than three test files? DOS batch files have a very primitive `for` loop:

File test2.bat

```
1  for %%f in (test*.in) do %1 < %%f
```

If you work in a computer lab, you will want a batch file that copies all your files onto a floppy disk when you are ready to go home. Put the following lines in a file `gohome.bat`:

File gohome.bat

```
1  copy *.cpp a:
2  copy *.h a:
3  copy *.txt a:
4  copy *.in a:
```

▼

There are lots of uses for batch files, and it is well worth it to learn more about them.

Batch files are a feature of the DOS operating system, not of C++. On a UNIX system, *shell scripts* are used for the same purpose.

▼

8.4   Assertions

We covered assertions previously in Section 5.13, but this is a good place to remind you of their power again.

Programs often contain implicit assumptions. For example, denominators need to be nonzero; salaries should not be negative. Sometimes the iron force of logic ensures that these conditions are satisfied. If you divide by 1 + x * x, then that value will never be zero, and you need not worry. Negative salaries, however, are not necessarily ruled out by logic but merely by convention. Surely nobody would ever work for a negative salary, but such a value might creep into a program due to an input or processing error. In practice the "impossible" happens with distressing regularity.

Assertions provide a valuable sanity check.

```
void raise_salary(Employee& e, double by)
{
    assert(e.get_salary() >= 0);
    assert(by >= -100);
    double new_salary = e.get_salary() * (1 + by / 100);
    e.set_salary(new_salary);
}
```

If an assertion is not satisfied, the program terminates with a useful error message showing the line number and the code of the failed assertion:

```
assertion failure in file fincalc.cpp line 61: by >= -100
```

That is a powerful signal that something went wrong elsewhere and that the program needs further testing.

8.5   Program Traces

Sometimes you run a program and you are not sure where it spends its time. To get a printout of the program flow, you can insert trace messages into the beginning and end of every procedure:

```
string digit_name(int n)
{
    cout << "Entering digit_name\n";
    . . .
    cout << "Exiting digit_name\n";
}
```

It is also useful to print the input parameters when a procedure is entered and to print return values when a function is exited:

```
string digit_name(int n)
{
    cout << "Entering digit_name. n = " << n << "\n";
    . . .
    cout << "Exiting digit_name. Return value = "
        << s << "\n";
    return s;
}
```

To get a proper trace, you must locate *each* function exit point. Place a trace message before every return statement and at the end of the function.

You aren't restricted to "enter/exit" messages. You can report on progress inside a function:

```
string int_name(int n)
{
    . . .
    cout << "Inside int_name. Thousands\n";
    . . .
    cout << "Inside int_name. Hundreds\n";
    . . .
    cout << "Inside int_name. Tens\n";
    . . .
    cout << "Inside int_name. Ones\n");
    . . .
}
```

Here is a trace of a call to int_name and all the functions that it calls. The input is n = 12305.

```
Inside int_name. Thousands
Entering int_name. n = 12
Inside int_name. Teens
Entering teen_name. n = 12
Exiting teen_name. Return value = twelve
Exiting int_name. Return value = twelve
Inside int_name. Hundreds
Entering digit_name. n = 3
Exiting digit_name. Return value = three
Inside int_name. Ones
Entering digit_name. n = 5
Exiting digit_name. Return value = five
Exiting int_name. Return value = twelve thousand three hundred five
```

Program traces can be useful to analyze the behavior of a program, but they have several definite disadvantages. It can be quite time-consuming to find out which trace messages to insert. If you insert too many messages, you produce a flurry of output that is hard to analyze; if you insert too few, you may not have enough information to spot the cause of the error. When you are done with the program, you need to remove all trace messages. If you find another error, however, you need to stick the print statements back in. If you find that a hassle, you are not alone. Most professional programmers use a *debugger*, not trace messages, to locate errors in their code. The debugger is the topic of the remainder of this chapter.

8.6	**The Debugger**

As you have undoubtedly realized by now, computer programs rarely run perfectly the first time. At times, it can be quite frustrating to find the errors, or *bugs* as they are called by programmers. Of course, you can insert trace messages to show the program flow as well as the values of key variables, run the program, and try to analyze the printout. If the printout does not clearly point to the problem, you may need to add and remove print commands and run the program again; this can be a time-consuming process.

Modern development environments contain special programs, so-called *debuggers*, that help you locate bugs by letting you follow the execution of a program. You can stop and restart your program and see the contents of variables whenever your program is temporarily stopped. At each stop, you have the choice of what variables to inspect and how many program steps to run until the next stop.

Some people feel that debuggers are just a tool to make programmers lazy. Admittedly some people write sloppy programs and then fix them up with the debugger, but the majority of programmers make an honest effort to write the best program they can before trying to run it through the debugger. These programmers realize that the debugger, while more convenient than print statements, is not cost-free. It does take time to set up and carry out an effective debugging session.

In actual practice, you cannot avoid using the debugger. The larger your programs get, the harder it is to debug them simply by inserting print statements. You will find that the time invested in learning about the debugger is amply repaid in your programming career.

▶ 💬 Random Fact   8.1

The First Bug

According to legend, the first bug was found in the Mark II, a huge electromechanical computer at Harvard University. It really was caused by a bug—a moth was trapped in a relay switch.

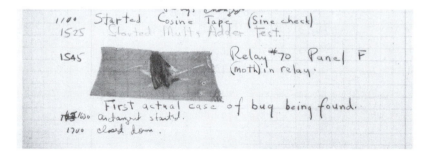

Figure 1

The First Bug

▼ Actually, from the note that the operator left in the log book next to the moth (see Figure 1), it appears as if the term "bug" had already been in active use at the time.

▼ The pioneering computer scientist Maurice Wilkes wrote: "Somehow, at the Moore School and afterwards, one had always assumed there would be no particular difficulty in getting programs right. I can remember the exact instant in time at which it dawned on me that a great part of my future life would be spent finding mistakes in my own programs."

8.6.1 — Using a Debugger

Like compilers, debuggers vary widely from one system to another. On some systems they are quite primitive and require you to memorize a small set of arcane commands; on others they have an intuitive window interface.

You will have to find out how to prepare a program for debugging and how to start the debugger on your system. If you use an integrated development environment, which contains an editor, compiler, and debugger, this step is usually very easy. You just build the program in the usual way and pick a menu command to start debugging. On many UNIX systems, you must manually build a debug version of your program and invoke the debugger.

Once you have started the debugger, you can go a long way with just three debugging commands: "run until this line", "step to next line", and "inspect variable". The names and keystrokes or mouse clicks for these commands differ widely between debuggers, but all debuggers support these basic commands. You can find out how either from the documentation or a lab manual, or by asking someone who has used the debugger before.

The "run until this line" command is the most important. Many debuggers show you the source code of the current program in a window. Select a line with the mouse or cursor keys. Then hit a key or select a menu command to run the program to the selected line. On other debuggers, you have to type in a command or a line number. In either

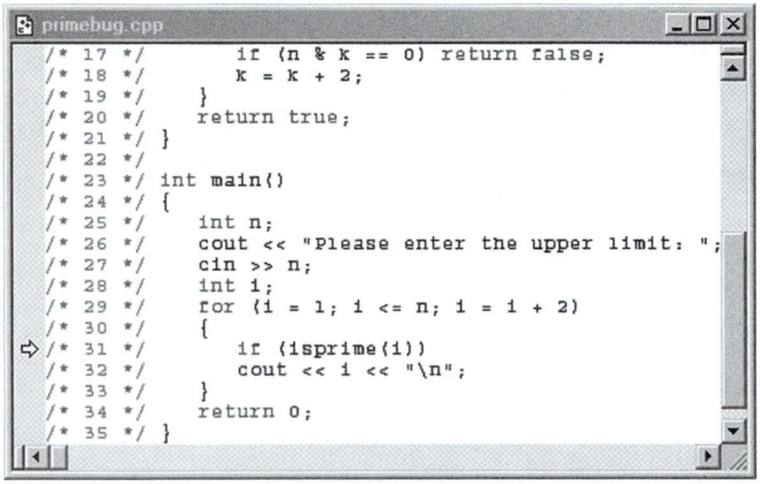

```
/* 17 */          if (n % k == 0) return false;
/* 18 */          k = k + 2;
/* 19 */       }
/* 20 */       return true;
/* 21 */ }
/* 22 */
/* 23 */ int main()
/* 24 */ {
/* 25 */    int n;
/* 26 */    cout << "Please enter the upper limit: ";
/* 27 */    cin >> n;
/* 28 */    int i;
/* 29 */    for (i = 1; i <= n; i = i + 2)
/* 30 */    {
/* 31 */       if (isprime(i))
/* 32 */          cout << i << "\n";
/* 33 */    }
/* 34 */    return 0;
/* 35 */ }
```

Figure 2

Debugger Stopped at Selected Line

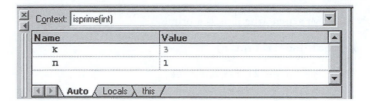

Figure 3

Inspecting Variables in the Debugger

case, the program starts execution and stops as soon as it reaches the line you selected (see Figure 2). Of course, you may have selected a line that will not be reached at all during a particular program run. Then the program terminates in the normal way. The very fact that the program has or has not reached a particular line can be valuable information.

The "step to next line" command executes the current line and stops at the next program line.

Once the program has stopped, you can look at the current values of variables. Again, the method for selecting the variables differs among debuggers. On some debuggers you select the variable name with the mouse or cursor keys and then issue a menu command such as "inspect variable". In other debuggers you must type the name of the variable into a dialog box. Some debuggers automatically show the values of all local variables of a function.

The debugger displays the name and contents of the inspected variable (Figure 3). If all variables contain what you expected, you can run the program until the next point where you want to stop.

The program also stops to read data, just as it does when you run it without the debugger. Just enter the inputs in the normal way, and the program will continue running.

Finally, when the program has completed running, the debug session is also finished. You can no longer inspect variables. To run the program again, you may be able to reset the debugger, or you may need to exit the debugging program and start over. Details depend on the particular debugger.

8.6.2 — A Sample Debugging Session

Consider the following program, whose purpose is to compute all prime numbers up to a number n. An integer is defined to be prime if it is not evenly divisible by any number except by 1 and itself. Also, mathematicians find it convenient not to call 1 a prime. Thus, the first few prime numbers are 2, 3, 5, 7, 11, 13, 17, 19.

File primebug.cpp

```
1  #include <iostream>
2
3  using namespace std;
4
5  /**
6     Tests if an integer is a prime.
```

```
7     @param n  any positive integer
8     @return true if n is a prime
9  */
10  bool isprime(int n)
11  {
12     if (n == 2) return true;
13     if (n % 2 == 0) return false;
14     int k = 3;
15     while (k * k < n)
16     {
17        if (n % k == 0) return false;
18           k = k + 2;
19     }
20     return true;
21  }
22
23  int main()
24  {
25     int n;
26     cout << "Please enter the upper limit: ";
27     cin >> n;
28     int i;
29     for (i = 1; i <= n; i = i + 2)
30     {
31        if (isprime(i))
32        cout << i << "\n";
33     }
34     return 0;
35  }
```

When you run this program with an input of 10, then the output is

```
1
3
5
7
9
```

This is not very promising; it looks as if the program just prints all odd numbers. Let us find out what it does wrong by using the debugger. Actually, for such a simple program, it is easy to correct mistakes simply by looking at the faulty output and the program code. However, we want to learn to use the debugger.

Let us first go to line 31. On the way, the program will stop to read the input into n. Supply the input value 10.

```
23  int main()
24  {
25     int n;
26     cout << "Please enter the upper limit: ";
27     cin >> n;
28     int i;
29     for (i = 1; i <= n; i = i + 2)
30     {
31        if (isprime(i))
32           cout << i << "\n";
33     }
```

```
34     return 0;
35 }
```

Start by investigating why the program treats 1 as a prime. Go to line 12.

```
10 bool isprime(int n)
11 {
12     if (n == 2) return true;
13     if (n % 2 == 0) return false;
14     int k = 3;
15     while (k * k < n)
16     {
17         if (n % k == 0) return false;
18         k = k + 2;
19     }
20     return true;
21 }
```

Convince yourself that the argument of isprime is currently 1 by inspecting n. Then execute the "run to next line" command. You will notice that the program goes to lines 13, 14, and 15, and then directly to line 20.

Inspect the value of k. It is 3, and therefore the while loop was never entered. It looks like the isprime function needs to be rewritten to treat 1 as a special case.

Next, we would like to know why the program doesn't print 2 as a prime even though the isprime function does recognize that 2 is a prime, whereas all other even numbers are not. Go again to line 10, the next call of isprime. Inspect n; you will note that n is 3. Now it becomes clear: The for loop in main tests only odd numbers. The main should either test both odd and even numbers or, better, just handle 2 as a special case.

Finally, we would like to find out why the program believes 9 is a prime. Go again to line 10 and inspect n; it should be 5. Repeat that step twice until n is 9. (With some debuggers, you may need to go from line 10 to line 11 before you can go back to line 10.) Now use the "run to next line" command repeatedly. You will notice that the program again skips past the while loop; inspect k to find out why. You will find that k is 3. Look at the condition in the while loop. It tests whether k * k < n. Now k * k is 9 and n is also 9, so the test fails. Actually, it does make sense to test divisors only up to $\sqrt{n}$; if n has any divisors except 1 and itself, at least one of them must be less than $\sqrt{n}$. However, that isn't quite true; if n is a perfect square of a prime, then its sole nontrivial divisor is *equal* to $\sqrt{n}$. That is exactly the case for $9 = 3^2$.

By running the debugger, we have now discovered three bugs in the program:

- isprime falsely claims 1 to be a prime.

- main doesn't handle 2.

- The test in isprime should be while (k * k <= n).

Here is the improved program:

File goodprim.cpp

```
1 #include <iostream>
2
3 using namespace std;
```

```
 4
 5  /**
 6      Tests if an integer is a prime.
 7      @param n  any positive integer
 8      @return true if n is a prime
 9  */
10  bool isprime(int n)
11  {
12      if (n == 1) return false;
13      if (n == 2) return true;
14      if (n % 2 == 0) return false;
15      int k = 3;
16      while (k * k <= n)
17      {
18          if (n % k == 0) return false;
19          k = k + 2;
20      }
21      return true;
22  }
23
24  int main()
25  {
26      int n;
27      cout << "Please enter the upper limit: ";
28      cin >> n;
29      int i;
30      if (n >= 2) cout << "2\n";
31      for (i = 3; i <= n; i = i + 2)
32      {
33          if (isprime(i))
34              cout << i << "\n";
35      }
36      return 0;
37  }
```

Is the program now free from bugs? That is not a question the debugger can answer. Remember: Testing can show only the presence of bugs, not their absence.

8.6.3 — Stepping through a Program

You have learned how to run a program until it reaches a particular line. Variations of this strategy are often useful.

There are two methods of running the program in the debugger. You can tell it to run to a particular line; then it gets speedily to that line, but you don't know how it got there. You can also *single-step* with the "run to next line" command. Then you know how the program flows, but it can take a long time to step through it.

Actually, there are two kinds of single-stepping commands, often called "step over" and "step into". The "step over" command always goes to the next program line. The "step into" command steps into function calls. For example, suppose the current line is

```
r = future_value(balance, p, n);
cout << setw(10) << r;
```

When you "step over" function calls, you get to the next line:

```
r = future_value(balance, p, n);
cout << setw(10) << r;
```

However, if you "step into" function calls, you enter the first line of the `future_value` function.

```
double future_value(double initial_balance,
    double p, int n)
{
    double b = initial_balance * pow(1 + p / 100), n);
    return b;
}
```

You should step into a function to check whether it carries out its job correctly. You should step over a function if you know it works correctly.

If you single-step past the last line of a function, either with the "step over" or the "step into" command, you return to the line in which the function was called.

You should not step into system functions like `setw`. It is easy to get lost in them, and there is no benefit in stepping through system code. If you do get lost, there are three ways out. You can just choose "step over" until you are finally again in familiar territory. Many debuggers have a command "run until function return" that executes to the end of the current function, and then you can select "step over" to get out of the function. Finally, most debuggers can show you a *call stack:* a listing of all currently pending function calls. On one end of the call stack is `main`, on the other the function that is currently executing (see Figure 4).

By selecting another function in the middle of the call stack, you can jump to the code line containing that function call. Then move the cursor to the next line and choose "run until this line". That way, you get out of any nested morass of function calls.

The techniques you've seen so far let you trace through the code in various increments. All debuggers support a second navigational approach: You can set so-called *breakpoints* in the code. Breakpoints are set at specific code lines, with a command "add breakpoint here"; again, the exact command depends on the debugger. You can set as many breakpoints as you like. When the program reaches any one of them, execution stops and the breakpoint that causes the stop is displayed.

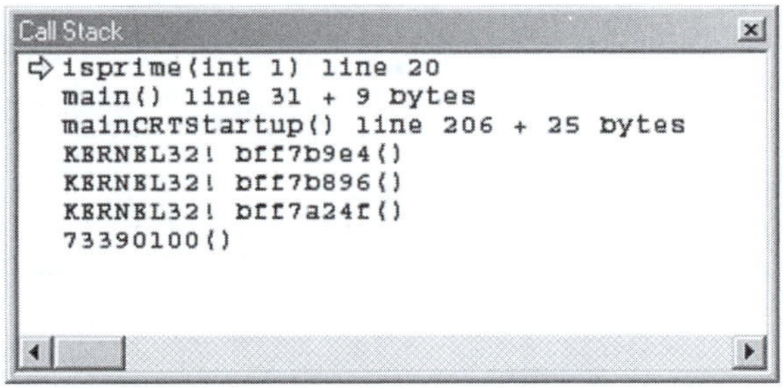

Figure 4

Call Stack Display

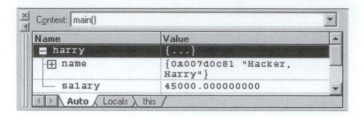

Figure 5

Inspecting an Object

Breakpoints are particularly useful when you know at which point your program starts doing the wrong thing. You can set a breakpoint, have the program run at full speed to the breakpoint, and then start tracing slowly to observe the program's behavior.

Some debuggers let you set *conditional breakpoints*. A conditional breakpoint stops the program only when a certain condition is met. You could stop at a particular line only if a variable n has reached 0, or if that line has been executed for the twentieth time. Conditional breakpoints are an advanced feature that can be indispensable in knotty debugging problems.

8.6.4 — Inspecting Objects

You have learned how to inspect variables in the debugger with the "inspect" command. The "inspect" command works well to show numeric values. When inspecting an object variable, all fields are displayed (see Figure 5). With some debuggers, you must "open up" the object, usually by clicking on a tree node.

To inspect a string object, you need to select the pointer variable that points to the actual character sequence in memory. That variable is called _Ptr or _str or a similar name, depending on the library implementation (see Figure 6). With some debuggers, you may need to select that variable to open it up. The debugger may also show other values, such as npos or allocator, which you should ignore.

Context: main()	
Name	**Value**
npos	4294967295
allocator	{...}
⊞ _Ptr	0x007d0c81 "Hacker, Harry"
_Len	13
Res	31
Auto ∧ Locals ∧ this	

Figure 6

Inspecting a String

Productivity Hint 8.2

Inspecting an Object in the Debugger

In C++ the expression *this denotes the implicit parameter of a member function. We have not discussed this notation, because you do not need it for programming and because it requires knowledge of pointers, which aren't covered until Chapter 10. However, inspecting *this in the debugger is a very handy trick.

When you trace inside a member function, tell the debugger you want to inspect *this. You will see all data fields of the implicit parameter (see Figure 7).

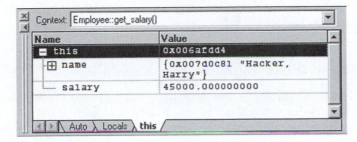

Figure 7

Implicit Parameter Display

8.7 Strategies

Now you know about the mechanics of debugging, but all that knowledge may still leave you helpless when you fire up the debugger to look at a sick program. There are a number of strategies that you can use to recognize bugs and their causes.

8.7.1 Reproduce the Error

As you test your program, you notice that your program sometimes does something wrong. It gives the wrong output, it seems to print something completely random, it runs in an infinite loop, or it crashes. Find out exactly how to *reproduce* that behavior. What numbers did you enter? Where did you click with the mouse?

Run the program again; type in exactly the same answers and click with the mouse on the same spots (or as close as you can get). Does the program exhibit the same behavior? If so, then you are ready to fire up the debugger to study this particular problem. Debuggers are good for analyzing particular failures. They aren't terribly useful for studying a program in general.

8.7.2 — Divide and Conquer

Now that you have a particular failure, you want to get as close to the failure as possible. Suppose your program dies with a division by 0. Since there are many division operations in a typical program, it is often not feasible to set breakpoints to all of them. Instead, use a technique of *divide and conquer*. Step over the procedures in main, but don't step inside them. Eventually, the failure will happen again. Now you know which procedure contains the bug: It is the last procedure that was called from main before the program died. Restart the debugger and go back to that line in main, then step inside that procedure. Repeat the process.

Eventually, you will have pinpointed the line that contains the bad division. Maybe it is completely obvious from the code why the denominator is not correct. If not, you need to find the location where it is computed. Unfortunately, you can't go *back* in the debugger. You need to restart the program and move to the point where the denominator computation happens.

8.7.3 — Know What Your Program Should Do

The debugger shows you what the program *does* do. You must know what the program *should* do, or you will not be able to find bugs. Before you trace through a loop, ask yourself how many iterations you *expect* the program to make. Before you inspect a variable, ask yourself what you expect to see. If you have no clue, set aside some time and think first. Have a calculator handy to make independent computations. When you know what the value should be, inspect the variable. This is the moment of truth. If the program is still on the right track, then that value is what you expected, and you must look further for the bug. If the value is different, you may be on to something. Double-check your computation. If you are sure your value is correct, find out why your program comes up with a different value.

In many cases, program bugs are the result of simple errors such as loop termination conditions that are off by one. Quite often, however, programs make computational errors. Maybe they are supposed to add two numbers, but by accident the code was written to subtract them. Unlike your calculus instructor, programs don't make a special effort to ensure that everything is a simple integer. You will need to make some calculations with large integers or nasty floating-point numbers. Sometimes these calculations can be avoided if you just ask yourself, "Should this quantity be positive? Should it be larger than that value?" Then inspect variables to verify those theories.

8.7.4 — Look at All Details

When you debug a program, you often have a theory about what the problem is. Nevertheless, keep an open mind and look around at all details. What strange messages are displayed? Why does the program take another unexpected action? These details count. When you run a debugging session, you really are a detective who needs to look at every clue available.

If you notice another failure on the way to the problem that you are about to pin down, don't just say, "I'll come back to it later". That very failure may be the original cause for your current problem. It is better to make a note of the current problem, fix what you just found, and then return to the original mission.

8.7.5 — Understand Each Error Before You Fix It

Once you find that a loop makes too many iterations, it is very tempting to apply a "Band-Aid" solution and subtract 1 from a variable so that the particular problem doesn't appear again. Such a quick fix has an overwhelming probability of creating trouble elsewhere. You really need to have a thorough understanding of how the program should be written before you apply a fix.

It does occasionally happen that you find bug after bug and apply fix after fix, and the problem just moves around. That usually is a symptom of a larger problem with the program logic. There is little you can do with the debugger. You must rethink the program design and reorganize it.

8.8 Debugger Limitations

A debugger is a tool, and like every tool, you can't expect it to be good at everything. Here are some problems that you will encounter in your use of the debugger.

8.8.1 — Recursive Functions

When you set a breakpoint into a function that calls itself, then the program stops as soon as that program line is encountered in *any* call to the function. Suppose you want to debug the `int_name` function.

```
68  string int_name(int n)
69  {
70     int c = n;
71     string r;
72
73     if (c >= 1000)
74     {
75        r = int_name(c / 1000) + "thousand";
76        c = c % 1000;
77     }
78
79     if (c >= 100)
80     {
81        r = r + " " + digit_name(c / 100)
82           + "hundred";
83        c = c % 100;
84     }
85     ...
```

Suppose you inspect c in line 73 and it is 23405. Tell the debugger to run until line 79; inspect c again, its value is 23! That makes no sense. The instruction c = c % 1000 should have set c to 405! Is that a bug?

Figure 8

Call Stack Display during
Recursive Call

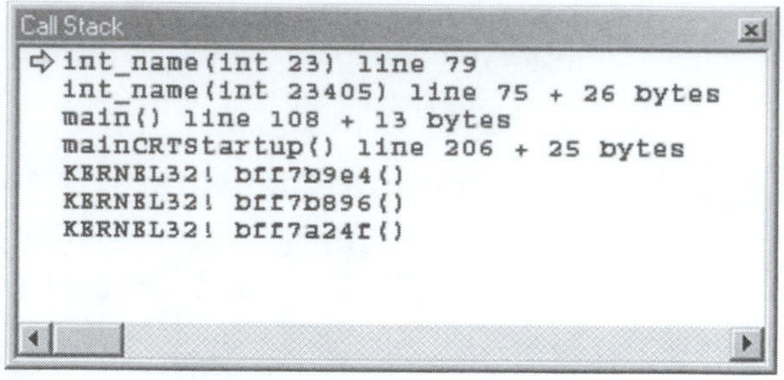

No. The program stopped in the first invocation of int_name that reached line 79. You can see from the call stack that two calls to int_name were pending (see Figure 8).

You can debug recursive functions with the debugger. You just need to be particularly careful, and watch the call stack frequently.

8.8.2 — Register Variables

Sometimes, the compiler realizes that it can generate faster code by keeping a variable in a processor register rather than reserving a memory location for it. This is common for loop counters and other short-lived integer variables, but it is hard on the debugger. It may happen that the debugger cannot find that variable, or that it displays the wrong value for it.

There is not much you can do. You can try to turn off all compiler optimizations and recompile. You can open a special register window that shows the status of all processor registers, but that is definitely an advanced technique.

8.8.3 — Errors That Go Away under the Debugger

Sometimes your program shows an error when you run it normally, but the error goes away when you run the program under the debugger. This is, of course, extremely annoying.

The cause for such flaky behavior is usually an uninitialized variable. Suppose you forgot to initialize a loop counter i and you use it.

```
int main()
{
   string s;
   . . .
   int i; /* Bug: forgot to initialize */
   while (i < s.length())
   {
      string ch = s.substr(i, 1);
      . . .
   }
   . . .
}
```

If i happens to be zero, then the code will run correctly, but if i is negative, then the call to s.substr(i, 1) will crash the program. There is a chance that the variable i happens to contain a negative value when the program is run by itself, but that it is zero when the debugger launches it. (In fact, there is at least one debugger that goes through the trouble of zeroing out all program memory areas before launching the debugging session, thereby making many bugs go away.) In that case, you cannot use the debugger to solve your problem. Inspect all variables manually and check that they are initialized, or go back to inserting print statements if you are desperate.

Random Fact   8.2

The Therac-25 Incidents

The Therac-25 is a computerized device that delivers radiation treatment to cancer patients (see Figure 9). Between June 1985 and January 1987, several of these machines delivered serious overdoses to at least six patients, killing some of them and seriously maiming the others.

The machines were controlled by a computer program. Bugs in the program were directly responsible for the overdoses. According to [1], the program was written by a single programmer, who had since left the manufacturing company producing the device and could not be located. None of the company employees interviewed could say anything about the educational level or qualifications of the programmer.

The investigation by the federal Food and Drug Administration (FDA) found that the program was poorly documented and that there was neither a specification document nor a formal test plan. (This should make you think. Do you have a formal test plan for your programs?)

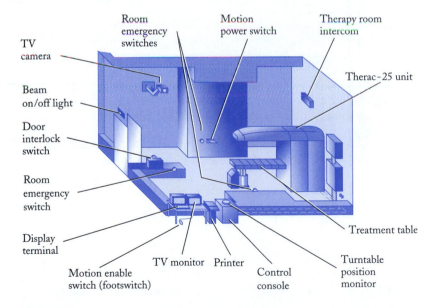

Figure 9

Typical Therac-25 Facility

The overdoses were caused by an amateurish design of the software that controlled different devices concurrently, namely the keyboard, the display, the printer, and the radiation device itself. Synchronization and data sharing between the tasks were done in an ad hoc way, even though safe multitasking techniques were known at the time. Had the programmer enjoyed a formal education that involved these techniques or taken the effort to study the literature, a safer machine could have been built. Such a machine would have probably involved a commercial multitasking system, which might have required a more expensive computer.

The same flaws were present in the software controlling the predecessor model, the Therac-20, but that machine had hardware interlocks that mechanically prevented overdoses. The hardware safety devices were removed in the Therac-25 and replaced by checks in the software, presumably to save cost.

Frank Houston of the FDA wrote in 1985 [1]: "A significant amount of software for life-critical systems comes from small firms, especially in the medical device industry; firms that fit the profile of those resistant to or uninformed of the principles of either system safety or software engineering".

Who is to blame? The programmer? The manager who not only failed to ensure that the programmer was up to the task but also didn't insist on comprehensive testing? The hospitals that installed the device, or the FDA, for not reviewing the design process? Unfortunately, even today there are no firm standards of what constitutes a safe software design process.

CHAPTER SUMMARY

1. Use *unit tests* to test each key function in isolation. Write a *test harness* to feed test data to the function being tested. Select test cases that cover each branch of the function.

2. You can debug a program by inserting trace printouts, but that gets quite tedious for even moderately complex debugging situations. You should learn to use the debugger.

3. You can make effective use of the debugger by mastering just three commands: "run until this line", "step to next line", and "inspect variable". The names and keystrokes or mouse clicks for these commands differ between debuggers.

4. Use the "divide-and-conquer" technique to locate the point of failure of a program. Inspect variables and compare their actual contents against the values that you know they should have.

5. The debugger can be used only to analyze the presence of bugs, not to show that a program is bug-free.

FURTHER READING

[1] Nancy G. Leveson and Clark S. Turner, "An Investigation of the Therac-25 Accidents", *IEEE Computer*, July 1993, pp. 18-41.

REVIEW EXERCISES

Exercise R8.1. Define the terms *unit test* and *test harness*.

Exercise R8.2. If you want to test a program that is made up of four different procedures, one of which is `main`, how many test harnesses do you need?

Exercise R8.3. What is an oracle?

Exercise R8.4. Define the terms *regression testing* and *test suite*.

Exercise R8.5. What is the debugging phenomenon known as "cycling"? What can you do to avoid it?

Exercise R8.6. The arc sine function is the inverse of the sine function. That is, $y = \arcsin x$ if $x = \sin y$. It is only defined if $-1 \le x \le 1$. Suppose you need to write a C++ function to compute the arc sine. List five positive test cases with their expected return values and two negative test cases with their expected outcomes.

Exercise R8.7. What is a program trace? When does it make sense to use a program trace, and when does it make more sense to use a debugger?

Exercise R8.8. Explain the differences between these debugger operations:
- Stepping into a function
- Stepping over a function

Exercise R8.9. Explain the differences between these debugger operations:
- Running until the current line
- Setting a breakpoint to the current line

Exercise R8.10. Explain the differences between these debugger operations:
- Inspecting a variable
- Watching a variable

Exercise R8.11. What is a call stack display in the debugger? Give two debugging scenarios in which the call stack display is useful.

Exercise R8.12. Explain in detail how to inspect the information stored in a `Point` object in your debugger.

Exercise R8.13. Explain in detail how to inspect the string stored in a `string` object in your debugger.

Exercise R8.14. Explain in detail how to inspect a string stored in an `Employee` object in your debugger.

Exercise R8.15. Explain the "divide-and-conquer" strategy to get close to a bug in the debugger.

Exercise R8.16. True or false:

(a) If a program has passed all tests in the test suite, it has no more bugs.

(b) If a program has a bug, that bug always shows up when running the program through the debugger.

(c) If all functions in a program were proven correct, then the program has no *bugs*.

PROGRAMMING EXERCISES

Exercise P8.1. The arc sine function is the inverse of the sine function. That is,

$$y = \arcsin x$$

if

$$x = \sin y$$

For example,

$$\arcsin(0) = 0$$
$$\arcsin(0.5) = \pi/6$$
$$\arcsin(\sqrt{2}/2) = \pi/4$$
$$\arcsin(\sqrt{3}/2) = \pi/3$$
$$\arcsin(1) = \pi/2$$
$$\arcsin(-1) = \pi/2$$

The arc sine is defined only for values between −1 and 1. This function is also often called $\sin^{-1}x$. Note, however, that it is not at all the same as $1/\sin x$. There is no C++ standard library function to compute the arc sine. For this exercise, write a C++ function that computes the arc sine from its Taylor series expansion

$$\arcsin x = x + x^3/3! + x^5 \cdot 3^2/5! + x^7 \cdot 3^2 \cdot 5^2/7! + x^9 \cdot 3^2 \cdot 5^2 \cdot 7^2/9! + \cdots$$

You should compute the sum until a new term is $< 10^{-6}$. This function will be used in subsequent exercises.

Exercise P8.2. Write a simple test harness for the `arcsin` function that reads floating-point numbers from `cin` and computes their arc sines, until the end of the input is reached. Then run that program and verify its outputs against the arc sine function of a scientific calculator.

Exercise P8.3. Write a test harness that automatically generates test cases for the `arcsin` function, namely numbers between −1 and 1 in a step size of 0.1.

Exercise P8.4. Write a test harness that generates 10 random floating-point numbers between −1 and 1 and feeds them to `arcsin`.

Exercise P8.5. Write a test harness that automatically tests the validity of the `arcsin` function by verifying that `sin(arcsin(x))` is approximately equal to `x`. Test with 100 random inputs.

Exercise P8.6. The arc sine function can be computed from the arc tangent function, according to the formula

$$\arcsin x = \arctan\left(x\Big/\sqrt{1-x^2}\right)$$

Use that expression as an *oracle* to test that your arc sine function works correctly. Test both functions with 100 random inputs.

Exercise P8.7. The domain of the arc sine function is $-1 \le x \le 1$. Supply an assertion to your `arcsin` function that checks that the input is valid. Test your function by computing `arcsin(1.1)`. What happens?

Exercise P8.8. Place trace messages into the loop of the arc sine function that computes the power series. Print the value of `n`, of the current term, and the current approximation to the result. What trace output do you get when you compute `arcsin(0.5)`?

Exercise P8.9. Add trace messages to the beginning and end of all functions in the program that computes the English names of integers. What trace output do you get when converting the number 12,345?

Exercise P8.10. Add trace messages to the beginning and end of the `isprime` function in the buggy prime program. Also put a trace message as the first statement of the `while` loop in the `isprime` function. Print relevant values such as function parameters, return values, and loop counters. What trace do you get when you compute all primes up to 20? Are the messages informative enough to spot the bug?

Exercise P8.11. Run a test harness of the `arcsin` function through the debugger. Step inside the computation of `arcsin(0.5)`. Step through the computation until the x^7 term has been computed and added to the sum. What is the value of the current term and of the sum at this point?

Exercise P8.12. Run a test harness of the `arcsin` function through the debugger. Step inside the computation of `arcsin(0.5)`. Step through the computation until the x^n term has become smaller than 10^{-6}. Then inspect `n`. How large is it?

Exercise P8.13. Consider the following buggy function:

```
Employee read_employee()
{
   cout << "Please enter the name: ";
   string name;
   getline(cin, name);
   cout << "Please enter the salary: ";
   double salary;
   cin >> salary;
   Employee r(name, salary);
   return r;
}
```

When you call this function once, it works fine. When you call it again in the same program, it won't return the second employee record correctly. Write a test harness that verifies the problem. Then step through the function. Inspect the contents of the string name and the Employee object r after the second call. What values do you get?

Vectors and Arrays

▶ To become familiar with using vectors to collect objects

▶ To be able to access vector elements and resize vectors

▶ To be able to pass vectors to functions

▶ To learn about common array algorithms

▶ To learn how to use one-dimensional and two-dimensional arrays

In many programs, you need to collect multiple objects of the same type. In standard C++, the vector construct allows you to conveniently manage collections that automatically grow to any desired size. In this chapter, you will learn about vectors and common vector algorithms.

The standard vectors are built on top of the lower-level array construct. The last part of this chapter shows you how to work with arrays. Two-dimensional arrays are useful for representing tabular arrangements of data.

9.1   Using Vectors to Collect Data Items

Suppose you write a program that reads a list of salary figures and prints out the list, marking the highest value, like this:

```
32000
54000
67500
29000
35000
80000
highest value => 115000
44500
100000
65000
```

In order to know which value to mark as the highest, the program must first read all of them. After all, the last value might be the highest one.

If you know that there are ten inputs, then you can store the data in ten variables salary1, salary2, salary3, . . ., salary10. Such a sequence of variables is not very prac-

---

Syntax 9.1 : Vector Variable Definition

vector<*type_name*> *variable_name*;
vector<*type_name*> *variable_name*(*initial_size*) ;

Example: vector<int> scores;
          vector<Employee> staff(20);

Purpose: Define a new variable of vector type, and optionally supply an initial size.

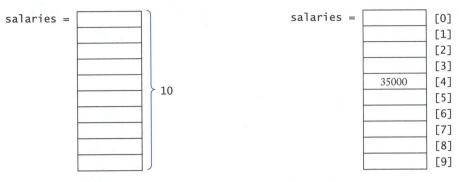

Figure 1

Vector of salaries

Figure 2

Vector Slot Filled with double Value

tical to use. You would have to write quite a bit of code ten times, once for each of the variables. There might also be a hundred employees on the staff.

In C++ there is a better way of implementing a sequence of data items: the vector construct.

A *vector* is a collection of data items of the same type. Every element of the collection can be accessed separately. Here we define a vector of ten employee salaries:

```
vector<double> salaries(10);
```

This is the definition of a variable salaries whose type is vector<double>. That is, salaries stores a sequence of double values. The (10) indicates that the vector holds ten values. (See Figure 1.) In general, vector variables are defined as in Syntax 9.1.

To get some data into salaries, you must specify which slot in the vector you want to use. That is done with the [] operator:

```
salaries[4] = 35000;
```

Now the slot with index 4 of salaries is filled with 35000. (See Figure 2).

Because salaries is a vector of double values, a slot such as salaries[4] can be used just like any variable of type double:

```
cout << salaries[4] << "\n";
```

Before continuing you must take care of one unpleasant detail of C++ vectors. If you look carefully at Figure 2, you will find that the *fifth* slot was filled with data when we changed salaries[4]. Unfortunately, in C++, the slots of vectors are numbered *starting at 0*. That is, the legal slots for the salaries vector are

salaries[0], the first slot
salaries[1], the second slot
salaries[2], the third slot
salaries[3], the fourth slot
salaries[4], the fifth slot

. . .

salaries[9], the tenth slot

Syntax 9.2 : Vector Subscript

vector_expression[*integer_expression*]

Example: `salaries[i + 1]`

Purpose: Access an element in a vector.

In "ancient" times there was a technical reason why this setup was a good idea. Because so many programmers got used to it, the `vector` construction imitates it. It is, however, a major source of grief for the newcomer.

The name *vector* is also somewhat unconventional. Most other programming languages call a sequence of values an *array*. However, in C++ an array is a lower-level construct that is addressed in Section 9.5. The name *vector* comes from mathematics. You can have a vector in a plane with (x, y) coordinates; a vector in space with (x, y, z) coordinates; or a vector in a space with more than three dimensions, in which case the coordinates are no longer given separate letters x, y, z, but a single letter with subscripts $(x_1, x_2, x_3, \ldots, x_{10})$. In C++ this would be implemented by a

```
vector<double> x(10);
```

Of course, in C++ the subscripts go from 0 to 9, not from 1 to 10.

There is no easy way of writing a subscript x_4 on the computer screen, so the bracket operator `x[4]` is used instead. A vector of floating-point numbers really has the same meaning as the mathematical construct. A vector of employees, on the other hand, has no mathematical meaning; it is just a sequence of individual employee data, each of which can be accessed with the `[]` operator. In mathematics the subscript i selecting a vector element x_i is often called an *index*. In C++ the value `i` of the expression `x[i]` is also called an index.

You now know how to fill a vector with values: by filling each slot. Now find the highest salary.

```
double highest = salaries[0];
for (i = 1; i < 10; i++)
   if (salaries[i] > highest)
      highest = salaries[i];
```

The key observation is that we can use a variable index `salaries[i]` to analyze the contents of the vector one element at a time (see Syntax 9.2).

9.2   Vector Subscripts

A C++ program accesses slots of a vector with the `[]` operator. Recall that the value of `i` in the expression `v[i]` is called an index or subscript. This subscript has an important restriction: trying to access a slot that does not exist in the vector is an error.

For example, if `salaries` holds ten values then the statement

```
int i = 20;
cout << salaries[i];
```

is an error. There is no `salaries[20]`. The compiler does not catch this error. Generally, it is too difficult for the compiler to follow the current contents of `salaries` and `i`. Even the running program generates *no* error message. If you make an index error, you silently read or overwrite another memory location.

The most common bounds error is the following:

```
vector<double> salaries(10);
cout << salaries[10];
```

There is no `salaries[10]` in a vector with ten elements—the legal subscripts are `salaries[0]` through `salaries[9]`.

Another common error is to forget to size the vector.

```
vector<double> salaries; /* no size given */
salaries[0] = 35000;
```

When a vector is defined without a size parameter, it is empty and can hold *no* elements.

You can find out the size of a vector by calling the `size` function. For example, the loop of the preceding section,

```
for (i = 1; i < 10; i++)
   if (salaries[i] > highest)
      highest = salaries[i];
```

can be written as

```
for (i = 1; i < salaries.size(); i++)
   if (salaries[i] > highest)
      highest = salaries[i];
```

Using `size` is actually a better idea than using the number 10. If the program changes, such as by allocating space for 20 employees in the `salaries` vector, the first loop is no longer correct, but the second loop automatically stays valid. This principle is another way to avoid magic numbers, as discussed in Quality Tip 2.3.

Note that `i` is a legal index for the vector `v` if $0 \le i$ and `i < v.size()`. Therefore the `for` loop

```
for (i = 0; i < v.size(); i++)
   do something with v[i];
```

is extremely common to visit all elements in a vector. By the way, do not write it as

```
for (i = 0; i <= v.size() - 1; i++)
```

The condition `i <= v.size() - 1` means the same thing as `i < v.size()`, but it is harder to read.

It is often difficult to know initially how many elements you need to store. For example, you may want to store all salaries that are entered in the salary chart program. You have no idea how many values the program user will enter. The function push_back allows you to start out with an empty vector and grow the vector whenever another employee is added:

```
vector<double> salaries;
. . .
double s;
cin >> s;
. . .
salaries.push_back(s);
```

The push_back command resizes the vector salary by adding one element to its end; then it sets that element to s. The strange name push_back indicates that s is *pushed* onto the *back* end of the vector.

Although it is undeniably convenient to grow a vector on demand with push_back, it is also inefficient. More memory must be found to hold the longer vector, and all elements must be copied into the larger space. If you already know how many elements you need in a vector, you should specify that size when you define it, and then fill it.

Another member function, pop_back, removes the last element of a vector, shrinking its size by one.

```
vector<double> salaries(10);
. . .
salaries.pop_back(); /* Now salaries has size 9 */
```

Note that the pop_back function does not return the element that is being removed. If you want to know what that element is, you need to capture it first.

```
double last = salaries[salaries.size() - 1];
salaries.pop_back(); /* removes last from the vector */
```

This is not very intuitive if you are familiar with the so-called *stack* data structure, whose pop operation returns the top value of the stack. Intuitive or not, the names push_back and pop_back are part of the standard for C++. The standard defines many more useful functions for vectors; in this book, we only use push_back and pop_back.

Now you have all the pieces to implement the program outlined at the beginning of the chapter. This program reads employee salaries and displays them, marking the highest salary.

File salvect.cpp

```
1  #include <iostream>
2  #include <vector>
3
4  using namespace std;
5
6  int main()
7  {
8     vector<double> salaries;
9     bool more = true;
10    while (more)
11    {
12       double s;
13       cout << "Please enter a salary, 0 to quit: ";
```

```
14        cin >> s;
15        if (s == 0)
16           , more = false;
17        else
18           salaries.push_back(s);
19     }
20
21     double highest = salaries[0];
22     int i;
23     for (i = 1; i < salaries.size(); i++)
24        if (salaries[i] > highest)
25           highest = salaries[i];
26
27     for (i = 0; i < salaries.size(); i++)
28     {
29        if (salaries[i] == highest)
30           cout << "highest value => ";
31        cout << salaries[i] << "\n";
32     }
33
34     return 0;
35 }
```

For simplicity, this program stores the salary values in a vector<double>. However, it is just as easy to use vectors of objects. For example, you create a vector of employees with a definition such as this one:

```
vector<Employee> staff(10);
```

You add elements by copying objects into the slots of the vector:

```
staff[0] = Employee("Hacker, Harry", 35000.0);
```

You can access any Employee object in the vector as staff[i]. Since the array entry is an object, you can apply a member function to it:

```
if (staff[i].get_salary() > 50000.0) ...
```

9.1

▼ **Common Error**

Bounds Errors

The most common vector error is accessing a nonexistent slot.

```
vector<double> data(10);
data[10] = 5.4;
    /* Error—data has 10 elements with subscripts 0 to 9 */
```

If your program accesses a vector through an out-of-bounds subscript, there is no error message. Instead, the program will quietly (or not so quietly) corrupt some memory. Except for very short programs, in which the problem may go unnoticed, that corruption will make the program act flaky or cause a horrible death many instructions later. These are serious errors that can be difficult to detect.

Productivity Hint 9.1

Inspecting Vectors in the Debugger

Vectors are more difficult to inspect in the debugger than numbers or objects. Suppose you are running a program and want to inspect the contents of

```
vector<double> salaries;
```

First, you tell the debugger to inspect the vector variable salaries. It shows you the inner details of an object. You need to find the data field that points to the vector elements (usually called start or _First or a similar name). That variable is a pointer—you will learn more about pointers in Chapter 10.

Try inspecting that variable. Depending on your debugger, you may need to click on it or select it and hit Enter. That shows you the *first* element in the vector. Then you must expand the range to show you as many elements as you would like to see. The commands to do so

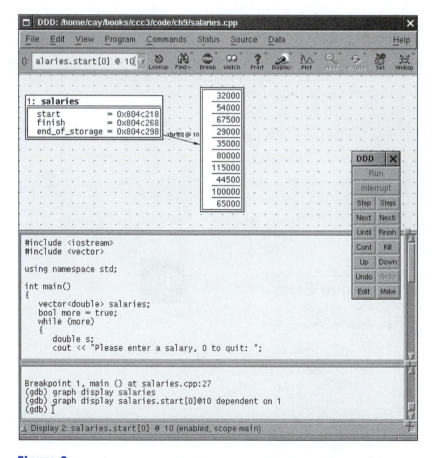

Figure 3

Display of Vector Elements

differ widely among debuggers. On one popular debugger, you must click on the field with the *right* mouse button and select "Range" from the menu. In another debugger, you need to type in an expression such as start[0]@10 to see ten elements. You will then get a display of all elements that you specified (see Figure 3).

Inspecting vectors is an important debugging skill. Read the debugger documentation, or ask someone who knows, such as your lab assistant or instructor, for details.

Quality Tip 9.1

Don't Combine Vector Access and Index Increment

It is possible to increment a variable that is used as an index, for example

```
x = v[i++];
```

That is a shortcut for

```
x = v[i];
i++;
```

Many years ago, when compilers were not very powerful, the v[i++] shortcut was useful, because it made the compiler generate faster code. Nowadays, the compiler generates the same efficient code for both versions. You should therefore use the second version, because it is clearer and less confusing.

Advanced Topic 9.1

Strings Are Vectors of Characters

A string variable is essentially a vector of characters. C++ has a basic data type char to denote individual characters. For example, the string greeting defined by

```
string greeting = "Hello";
```

can be considered a vector of five characters 'H', 'e', 'l', 'l', 'o'. Note that values of type char are enclosed in single quotes. 'H' denotes the individual character, "H" a string containing one character. An individual character can be stored in one byte. A string, even if it has length 1, needs to store both the contents and the length, which requires several bytes.

You can modify the characters in a string:

```
greeting[3] = 'p';
greeting[4] = '!';
```

Now the string is "Help!". Of course, the same effect can be achieved using string operations rather than direct character manipulation.

```
greeting = greeting.substr(0, 3) + "p!";
```

Manipulating the characters directly is more efficient than extracting substrings and concatenating strings. The [] operator is more convenient than the substr function if you want to visit a string one character at a time. For example, the following function makes a copy of a string and changes all characters to uppercase:

```
string uppercase(string s)
{
   string r = s;
   int i;
   for (i = 0; i < r.length(); i++)
      r[i] = toupper(r[i]);
   return r;
}
```

For example, `uppercase("Hello")` returns the string `"HELLO"`. The `toupper` function is defined in the `cctype` header. It converts lowercase characters to uppercase.

Random Fact   9.1

The Internet Worm

In November 1988, a college student from Cornell University launched a so-called virus program that infected about 6,000 computers connected to the Internet across the United States. Tens of thousands of computer users were unable to read their e-mail or otherwise use their computers. All major universities and many high-tech companies were affected. (The Internet was much smaller then than it is now.)

The particular kind of virus used in this attack is called a *worm*. The virus program crawled from one computer on the Internet to the next. The entire program is quite complex; its major parts are explained in [1]. However, one of the methods used in the attack is of interest here. The worm would attempt to connect to the `finger` program of its remote victim. Some versions of that program are known to contain sloppy C code that places characters into an array without checking that the array overflows. The worm program purposefully filled the 512-character array with 536 bytes, replacing the return address of the function reading the string. When that function was finished, it didn't return to its caller but to code supplied by the worm. That code ran under the same super-user privileges as `finger`, allowing the worm to gain entry into the remote system.

Had the programmer who wrote `finger` been more conscientious, this particular attack would not be possible. In C++, as in C, all programmers must be very careful not to overrun array boundaries.

One may well speculate what would possess a skilled programmer to spend many weeks or months to plan the antisocial act of breaking into thousands of computers and disabling them. It appears that the break-in was fully intended by the author, but the disabling of the computers was a side effect of continuous reinfection and efforts by the worm to avoid being killed. It is not clear whether the author was aware that these moves would cripple the attacked machines.

In recent years, the novelty of vandalizing other people's computers has worn off, and there are fewer jerks with programming skills who write new viruses. Other attacks by individuals with more criminal energy, whose intent has been to steal information or money, have surfaced. Reference [2] gives a very readable account of the discovery and apprehension of one such person.

Vector Parameters and Return Values

Functions and procedures often have vector parameters. This function computes the average of a vector of floating-point numbers:

File average.cpp

```
1  #include <iostream>
2  #include <vector>
3
4  using namespace std;
5
6  /**
7     Computes the average of a vector of floating-point values.
8     @param v a vector of floating-point values
9     @return the average of the values in v
10 */
11 double average(vector<double> v)
12 {
13    if (v.size() == 0) return 0;
14    double sum = 0;
15    for (int i = 0; i < v.size(); i++)
16       sum = sum + v[i];
17    return sum / v.size();
18 }
19
20 int main()
21 {
22    vector<double> salaries(5);
23    salaries[0] = 35000.0;
24    salaries[1] = 63000.0;
25    salaries[2] = 48000.0;
26    salaries[3] = 78000.0;
27    salaries[4] = 51500.0;
28
29    double avgsal = average(salaries);
30    cout << "The average salary is " << avgsal << "\n";
31    return 0;
32 }
```

To visit each element of the vector v, the function needs to determine the size of v. It inspects all elements, with index starting at 0 and going up to, but not including, v.size().

A function can modify a vector. Two kinds of modifications are common. The elements in a vector can be rearranged; for example, a vector can be sorted:

```
void sort(vector<double>& v)
```

(You will study algorithms for sorting a vector in Chapter 15.)

The individual elements of a vector can also be modified. The following program contains a function

```
void raise_by_percent(vector<double>& v, double p)
```

that raises all values in the vector by the given percentage.

File raisesal.cpp

```cpp
1  #include <iostream>
2  #include <vector>
3
4  using namespace std;
5
6  /**
7     Raises all values in a vector by a given percentage.
8     @param v vector of values
9     @param p percentage to raise values by
10 */
11 void raise_by_percent(vector<double>& v, double p)
12 {
13    for (int i = 0; i < v.size(); i++)
14       v[i] = v[i] * (1 + p / 100);
15 }
16
17 int main()
18 {
19    vector<double> salaries(5);
20    salaries[0] = 35000.0;
21    salaries[1] = 63000.0;
22    salaries[2] = 48000.0;
23    salaries[3] = 78000.0;
24    salaries[4] = 51500.0;
25
26    raise_by_percent(salaries, 4.5);
27
28    for (int i = 0; i < salaries.size(); i++)
29       cout << salaries[i] << "\n";
30
31    return 0;
32 }
```

In both cases of modification, the vector must be passed by reference (`vector <double>&`). If a vector is passed by value, and a function modifies the vector, the modification affects the local copy of that value only, not the call parameter. That either is a programming error, or, if done intentionally, is considered bad style.

A function can return a vector. This is useful if a function computes a result that consists of a collection of values of the same type. Here is a function that collects all values that fall within a certain range:

File between.cpp

```cpp
1  #include <iostream>
2  #include <vector>
3
4  using namespace std;
5
6  /**
7     Returns all values within a range.
8     @param v a vector of floating-point numbers
9     @param low the low end of the range
10    @param high the high end of the range
```

```
11     @return a vector of values from v in the given range
12 */
13 vector<double> between(vector<double> v,
14     double low, double high)
15 {
16     vector<double> result;
17     for (int i = 0; i < v.size(); i++)
18         if (low <= v[i] && v[i] <= high)
19             result.push_back(v[i]);
20     return result;
21 }
22
23 int main()
24 {
25     vector<double> salaries(5);
26     salaries[0] = 35000.0;
27     salaries[1] = 63000.0;
28     salaries[2] = 48000.0;
29     salaries[3] = 78000.0;
30     salaries[4] = 51500.0;
31
32     vector<double> midrange_salaries
33         = between(salaries, 45000.0, 65000.0);
34
35     for (int i = 0; i < midrange_salaries.size(); i++)
36         cout << midrange_salaries[i] << "\n";
37
38     return 0;
39 }
```

Now suppose you want to know *where* these values occur in the vector. Rather than returning the matching values, collect the positions of all matching values in a vector of integers. For example, if salaries[1], salaries[2], and salaries[4] are values matching your criterion, you would end up with a vector containing the integers 1, 2, and 4. Once you know where all matches occur, you can print just those:

File matches.cpp

```
1 #include <iostream>
2 #include <vector>
3
4 using namespace std;
5
6 /**
7     Returns the positions of all values within a range.
8     @param v a vector of floating-point numbers
9     @param low the low end of the range
10    @param high the high end of the range
11    @return a vector of positions of values in the given range
12 */
13 vector<int> find_all_between(vector<double> v,
14     double low, double high)
15 {
16     vector<int> pos;
17     for (int i = 0; i < v.size(); i++)
```

```
18    {
19        if (low <= v[i] && v[i] <= high)
20            pos.push_back(i);
21    }
22    return pos;
23 }
24
25 int main()
26 {
27    vector<double> salaries(5);
28    salaries[0] = 35000.0;
29    salaries[1] = 63000.0;
30    salaries[2] = 48000.0;
31    salaries[3] = 78000.0;
32    salaries[4] = 51500.0;
33
34    vector<int> matches
35        = find_all_between(salaries, 45000.0, 65000.0);
36
37    for (int j = 0; j < matches.size(); j++)
38        cout << salaries[matches[j]] << "\n";
39    return 0;
40 }
```

Note the nested subscripts, `salaries[matches[j]]`. Here `matches[j]` is the subscript of the jth match. In our example, `matches[0]` is 1, `matches[1]` is 2, and `matches[2]` is 4. Thus, `salaries[1]`, `salaries[2]`, and `salaries[4]` are printed.

Advanced Topic   9.2

Passing Vectors by Constant Reference

Passing a vector into a function by value is unfortunately somewhat inefficient, because the function must make a copy of all elements. As explained in Advanced Topic 5.2, the cost of a copy can be avoided by using a constant reference.

```
double average(const vector<double>& v)
```

instead of

```
double average(vector<double> v)
```

This is a useful optimization that greatly increases performance.

9.3.1 — Removing and Inserting Elements

Suppose you want to *remove* an element from a vector. If the elements in the vector are not in any particular order, that task is easy to accomplish. Simply overwrite the element to be removed with the *last* element of the vector, then shrink the size of the vector. (See Figure 4.)

Figure 4

Removing an Element in an
Unordered Vector

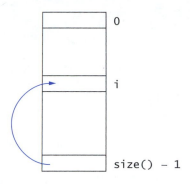

File erase1.cpp

```cpp
1  #include <iostream>
2  #include <string>
3  #include <vector>
4
5  using namespace std;
6
7  /**
8      Removes an element from an unordered vector.
9      @param v a vector
10     @param pos the position of the element to erase
11  */
12  void erase(vector<string>& v, int pos)
13  {
14     int last_pos = v.size() - 1;
15     v[pos] = v[last_pos];
16     v.pop_back();
17  }
18
19  /**
20     Prints all elements in a vector.
21     @param v the vector to print
22  */
23  void print(vector<string> v)
24  {
25     for (int i = 0; i < v.size(); i++)
26        cout << "[" << i << "] " << v[i] << "\n";
27  }
28
29  int main()
30  {
31     vector<string> staff(5);
32     staff[0] = "Hacker, Harry";
33     staff[1] = "Reindeer, Rudolf";
34     staff[2] = "Cracker, Carl";
35     staff[3] = "Lam, Larry";
36     staff[4] = "Sandman, Susan";
37     print(staff);
38
```

```
39      int pos;
40      cout << "Remove which element? ";
41      cin >> pos;
42
43      erase(staff, pos);
44      print(staff);
45      return 0;
46 }
```

The situation is more complex if the order of the elements matters. Then you must move all elements above the element to be removed down by one slot, and then shrink the size of the vector. (See Figure 5.)

File erase2.cpp

```
1  #include <iostream>
2  #include <string>
3  #include <vector>
4
5  using namespace std;
6
7  /**
8      Removes an element from an ordered vector.
9      @param v a vector
10     @param pos the position of the element to erase
11 */
12 void erase(vector<string>& v, int pos)
13 {
14     for (int i = pos; i < v.size() - 1; i++)
15         v[i] = v[i + 1];
16     v.pop_back();
17 }
18
19 /**
20     Prints all elements in a vector.
21     @param v the vector to print
22 */
23 void print(vector<string> v)
24 {
25     for (int i = 0; i < v.size(); i++)
26         cout << "[" << i << "] " << v[i] << "\n";
27 }
28
29 int main()
30 {
31     vector<string> staff(5);
32     staff[0] = "Cracker, Carl";
33     staff[1] = "Hacker, Harry";
34     staff[2] = "Lam, Larry";
35     staff[3] = "Reindeer, Rudolf";
36     staff[4] = "Sandman, Susan";
37     print(staff);
38
```

```
39      int pos;
40      cout << "Remove which element? ";
41      cin >> pos;
42
43      erase(staff, pos);
44      print(staff);
45      return 0;
46  }
```

Conversely, suppose you want to insert an element in the middle of a vector. Then you must add a new element at the end of the vector and move all elements above the insertion location up by one slot. Note that the order of the movement is different: When you remove an element, you first move the next element down, then the one after that, until you finally get to the end of the vector. When you insert an element, you start at the end of the vector, move that element up, then go to the one before that, until you finally get to the insertion location (see Figure 6).

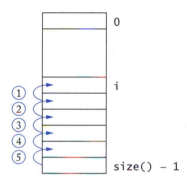

Figure 5

Removing an Element in an Ordered Vector

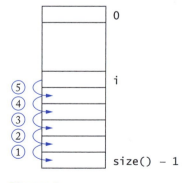

Figure 6

Inserting an Element in an Ordered Vector

File insert.cpp

```cpp
1  #include <iostream>
2  #include <string>
3  #include <vector>
4
5  using namespace std;
6
7  /**
8     Inserts an element into a vector.
9     @param v a vector
10    @param pos the position before which to insert the element
11    @param s the element to insert
12 */
13 void insert(vector<string>& v, int pos, string s)
14 {
15    int last = v.size() - 1;
16    v.push_back(v[last]);
17    for (int i = last; i > pos; i--)
18       v[i] = v[i - 1];
19    v[pos] = s;
20 }
21
22 /**
23    Prints all elements in a vector.
24    @param v the vector to print
25 */
26 void print(vector<string> v)
27 {
28    for (int i = 0; i < v.size(); i++)
29       cout << "[" << i << "] " << v[i] << "\n";
30 }
31
32 int main()
33 {
34    vector<string> staff(5);
35    staff[0] = "Cracker, Carl";
36    staff[1] = "Hacker, Harry";
37    staff[2] = "Lam, Larry";
38    staff[3] = "Reindeer, Rudolf";
39    staff[4] = "Sandman, Susan";
40    print(staff);
41
42    int pos;
43    cout << "Insert before which element? ";
44    cin >> pos;
45
46    insert(staff, pos, "New, Nina");
47    print(staff);
48    return 0;
49 }
```

9.4 Parallel Vectors

Suppose you want to process a series of product data, and then display the product information, marking the best value (with the best score/price ratio). For example,

```
ACMA P600 Price: 995 Score: 75
Alaris Nx686 Price: 798 Score: 57
AMAX Powerstation 600 Price: 999 Score: 75
AMS Infogold P600 Price: 795 Score: 69
AST Premmia Price: 2080 Score: 80
Austin 600 Price: 1499 Score: 95
best value => Blackship NX-600 Price: 598 Score: 60
Kompac 690 Price: 695 Score: 60
```

Here is a simple program that reads the data and displays the list, marking the best value.

File bestval1.cpp

```cpp
 1  #include <iostream>
 2  #include <string>
 3  #include <vector>
 4
 5  using namespace std;
 6
 7  int main()
 8  {
 9     vector<string> names;
10     vector<double> prices;
11     vector<int> scores;
12
13     double best_price = 1;
14     int best_score = 0;
15     int best_index = -1;
16
17     bool more = true;
18     while (more)
19     {
20        string next_name;
21        cout << "Please enter the model name: ";
22        getline(cin, next_name);
23        names.push_back(next_name);
24        double next_price;
25        cout << "Please enter the price: ";
26        cin >> next_price;
27        prices.push_back(next_price);
28        int next_score;
29        cout << "Please enter the score: ";
30        cin >> next_score;
31        scores.push_back(next_score);
32        string remainder; /* read remainder of line */
33        getline(cin, remainder);
34
35        if (next_score / next_price > best_score / best_price)
36        {
```

```
37            best_index = names.size() - 1;
38            best_score = next_score;
39            best_price = next_price;
40         }
41
42      cout << "More data? (y/n) ";
43      string answer;
44      getline(cin, answer);
45      if (answer != "y") more = false;
46   }
47
48   for (int i = 0; i < names.size(); i++)
49   {
50      if (i == best_index) cout << "best value => ";
51      cout << names[i]
52         << " Price: " << prices[i]
53         << " Score: " << scores[i] << "\n";
54   }
55
56   return 0;
57 }
```

The problem with this program is that it contains three vectors (`names`, `prices`, `scores`) of the same length, where the `i`th *slice* `names[i]`, `prices[i]`, `scores[i]`, contains data that needs to be processed together. These vectors are called *parallel vectors* (Figure 7).

Parallel vectors become a headache in larger programs. The programmer must ensure that the vectors always have the same length and that each slice is filled with values that actually belong together. Most importantly, any function that operates on a slice must get all vectors as parameters, which is tedious to program.

The remedy is simple. Look at the slice and find the *concept* that it represents. Then make the concept into a class. In the example each slice contains a name, a price, and a score, describing a *product;* turn this into a class.

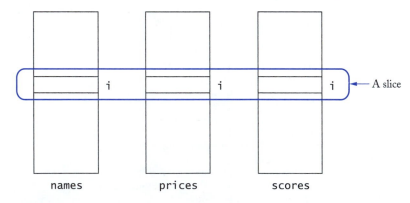

Figure 7

Parallel Vectors

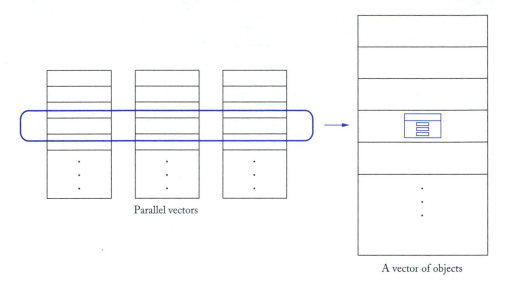

Parallel vectors

A vector of objects

Figure 8

Eliminating Parallel Vectors

```
class Product
{
public:
   . . .
private:
   string name;
   double price;
   int score;
};
```

This is, of course, precisely the Product class that we discovered in Chapter 6. You can now eliminate the parallel vectors and replace them with a single vector. Each slot in the resulting vector corresponds to a slice in the set of parallel vectors (see Figure 8).

Here is the main function of the revised program that uses a single vector of products.

File bestval2.cpp

```
73  ...
74  int main()
75  {
76     vector<Product> products;
77
78     Product best_product;
79     int best_index = -1;
80
81     bool more = true;
82     while (more)
83     {
```

```
84        Product next_product;
85        next_product.read();
86        products.push_back(next_product);
87
88        if (next_product.is_better_than(best_product))
89        {
90           best_index = products.size() - 1;
91           best_product = next_product;
92        }
93
94        cout << "More data? (y/n) ";
95        string answer;
96        getline(cin, answer);
97        if (answer != "y") more = false;
98     }
99
100    for (int i = 0; i < products.size(); i++)
101    {
102       if (i == best_index) cout << "best value => ";
103       products[i].print();
104    }
105
106    return 0;
107 }
```

Quality Tip   9.2

Make Parallel Vectors into Vectors of Objects

If you find yourself using two vectors that have the same length, ask yourself whether you couldn't replace them with a single vector of a class type. For example,

```
vector<string> name;
vector<double> salary;
```

could become

```
vector<Employee> staff;
```

Parallel vectors are evil because they lead to a greater evil: namely, global variables. It is tedious to write functions that work on a set of parallel vectors. Each of those functions would need all parallel vectors as parameters. Programmers using parallel vectors are therefore tempted to make the parallel vectors into global variables.

9.5   Arrays

Vectors are a convenient mechanism for collecting elements of the same type. At any time you can add elements to the collection and find out what elements are currently stored in the collection. C++ has a second mechanism for collecting elements of the same type, namely *arrays*. There are many similarities between arrays and vectors, but there are also some significant differences. Arrays are a lower-level abstraction than vectors, so they are less convenient. As you will soon see, an array cannot be resized—you usually create some extra space in each array, and then you must remember how much of it you actually used. These limits make arrays more cumbersome to use than vectors, so you may well wonder why you should learn about them. The reason is that vectors were a recent addition to C++, and many older programs use arrays instead. To understand those programs, you need a working knowledge of arrays. Arrays are also faster and more efficient than vectors. This can be important in some applications.

9.5.1 — Defining and Using Arrays

Here is the definition of an array of ten floating-point numbers (see Syntax 9.3):

```
double salaries[10];
```

This is very similar to a vector

```
vector<double> salaries(10);
```

Both the array and the vector have ten elements, `salaries[0]` . . . `salaries[9]`.

Unlike a vector, an array can never change size. That is, the `salaries` array will always have exactly ten elements. You cannot use `push_back` to add more elements to it. Furthermore, the size of the array has to be known *when the program is compiled*. That is, you can't ask the user how many elements are needed and then allocate a sufficient number, as you could with a vector.

```
int n;
cin >> n;
double salaries[n]; /* NO! */
vector<double> salaries(n); /* OK */
```

When defining an array, you must come up with a good guess on the maximum number of elements that you need to store, and be prepared to ignore any more than the maximum. Of course, it may well happen that one wants to store more than ten salaries, so we use a larger size:

```
const int SALARIES_CAPACITY = 100;
double salaries[SALARIES_CAPACITY];
```

In a typical program run, less than the maximum size will be occupied by actual elements. The constant `SALARIES_CAPACITY` gives you only the *capacity* of the array; it doesn't tell you how much of the array is actually *used*. You must keep a *companion variable* that counts how many elements are actually used. Here we call the companion variable `salaries_size`. The following loop collects data and fills up the `salaries` array.

Syntax 9.3 : Array Variable Definition

type_name variable_name[*size*];

Example: `int scores[20];`

Purpose: Define a new variable of an array type.

```
int salaries_size = 0;
while (more && salaries_size < SALARIES_CAPACITY)
{
   cout << "Enter salary or 0 to quit: ";
   double x;
   cin >> x;
   if (cin.fail())
      more = false;
   else
   {
      salaries[salaries_size] = x;
      salaries_size++;
   }
}
```

At the end of this loop, `salaries_size` contains the actual number of elements in the array. Note that you have to stop accepting inputs if the size of the array reaches the maximum size. The name `salaries_size` was chosen to remind you of the member function call `salaries.size()` which you would have used if `salaries` had been a vector. The difference between arrays and vectors is that you must manually update the `salaries_size` companion variable, whereas a vector automatically remembers how many elements it contains.

Here is a loop that computes the highest salary in the array. We can inspect only the elements with index less than `salaries_size`, since the remaining elements have never been set and their contents are undefined.

```
double highest = 0;
if (salaries_size > 0)
{
   highest = salaries[0];
   int i;
   for (i = 1; i < salaries_size; i++)
      if (salaries[i] > highest)
         highest = salaries[i];
}
```

9.5.2 — Array Parameters

When writing a function with an array parameter, you place an empty `[]` behind the parameter name:

```
double maximum(double a[], int a_size);
```

You also need to pass the size of the array to the function, because the function has no other way of querying the size of the array—there is no `size()` member function:

```
double maximum(double a[], int a_size)
{
   if (a_size == 0) return 0;
   double highest = a[0];
   int i;
   for (i = 1; i < a_size; i++)
      if (a[i] > highest)
         highest = a[i];
   return highest;
}
```

Unlike all other parameters, array parameters are *always passed by reference*. Functions can modify array parameters, and those modifications affect the array that was passed into the function. You never use an & when defining an array parameter. For example, the following function updates all elements in the array s:

```
void raise_by_percent(double s[], double s_size, double p)
{
   int i;
   for (i = 0; i < s_size; i++)
      s[i] = s[i] * (1 + p / 100);
}
```

It is considered good style to add the const keyword whenever a function does not actually modify an array:

```
double maximum(const double a[], int a_size)
```

If a function adds elements to an array, you need to pass three parameters to the function: the array, the maximum size, and the current size. The current size must be passed *as a reference parameter* so that the function can update it. Here is an example. The following function reads inputs into the array a (which has a capacity of a_capacity) and updates the variable a_size so that it contains the final size of the array when the end of input has been reached. Note that the function stops reading either at the end of input or when the array has been filled completely.

```
void read_data(double a[], int a_capacity, int& a_size)
{
   a_size = 0;
   while (a_size < a_capacity)
   {
      double x;
      cin >> x;
      if (cin.fail()) return;
      a[a_size] = x;
      a_size++;
   }
}
```

Although arrays can be function parameters, they cannot be function return types. If a function computes multiple values (such as the between function in Section 9.3), the caller of the function must provide an array parameter to hold the result.

The following program reads salary values from standard input, then prints the maximum salary.

File salarray.cpp

```
1  #include <iostream>
2
3  using namespace std;
4
5  /**
6     Reads data into an array.
7     @param a  the array to fill
8     @param a_capacity the maximum size of a
9     @param a_size filled with the size of a after reading
```

```
10  */
11  void read_data(double a[], int a_capacity, int& a_size)
12  {
13     a_size = 0;
14     double x;
15     while (a_size < a_capacity && (cin >> x))
16     {
17        a[a_size] = x;
18        a_size++;
19     }
20  }
21
22  /**
23     Computes the maximum value in an array.
24     @param a the array
25     @param a_size the number of values in a
26  */
27  double maximum(const double a[], int a_size)
28  {
29     if (a_size == 0) return 0;
30     double highest = a[0];
31     for (int i = 1; i < a_size; i++)
32        if (a[i] > highest)
33           highest = a[i];
34     return highest;
35  }
36
37  int main()
38  {
39     const int SALARIES_CAPACITY = 100;
40     double salaries[SALARIES_CAPACITY];
41     int salaries_size = 0;
42
43     cout << "Please enter all salary data: ";
44     read_data(salaries, SALARIES_CAPACITY, salaries_size);
45
46     if (salaries_size == SALARIES_CAPACITY && !cin.fail())
47        cout << "Sorry--extra data ignored\n";
48
49     double maxsal = maximum(salaries, salaries_size);
50     cout << "The maximum salary is " << maxsal << "\n";
51     return 0;
52  }
```

9.5.3 — Character Arrays

Just as arrays predate vectors, there was a time when C++ had no string class. All string processing was carried out by manipulating arrays of the type char.

The char type denotes an individual character. Individual character constants are delimited by single quotes; for example,

```
char input = 'y';
```

Note that 'y' is a single character, which is quite different from "y", a string containing a single character. Each character is actually encoded as an integer value. For example, in the ASCII encoding scheme, which is used on the majority of computers today, the character 'y' is encoded as the number 121. (You should never use these actual numeric codes in your programs, of course.)

Here is a definition of a character array that holds the string "Hello":

```
char greeting[6] = "Hello";
```

The array occupies six characters, namely 'H', 'e', 'l', 'l', 'o' and a *zero terminator* '\0'. (See Figure 9.) The terminator is a character that is encoded as the number zero—this is different from the character '0', the character denoting the zero digit. (Under the ASCII encoding scheme, the character denoting the zero digit is encoded as the number 48.)

If you initialize a character array variable with a character array constant (such as "Hello"), then you need not specify the size of the character array variable:

```
char greeting[] = "Hello";
   /* same as char greeting[6] */
```

The compiler counts the characters of the initializer (including the zero terminator) and uses that count as the size for the array variable.

A character array constant (such as "Hello") always has a zero terminator. When you create your own character arrays, it is very important that you add the zero terminator—the string functions in the standard library depend on it:

```
char mystring[5];
for (i = 0; i < 4; i++)
   mystring[i] = greeting[i];
mystring[4] = '\0'; /* add zero terminator*/
```

It is an extremely common error to forget the space for this character. You can make this added space requirement more explicit if you always make character arrays MAXLENGTH + 1 characters long:

```
const int MYSTRING_MAXLENGTH = 4;
char mystring[MYSTRING_MAXLENGTH + 1];
```

Here is an implementation of the standard library function strlen that computes the length of a character array. The function keeps counting characters until it encounters a zero terminator.

```
int strlen(const char s[])
{
   int i = 0;
   while (s[i] != '\0')
      i++;
   return i;
}
```

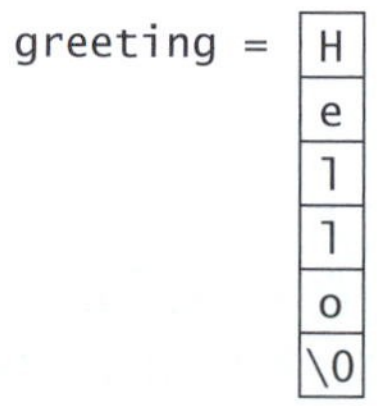

greeting =

H
e
l
l
o
\0

Figure 9

A Character Array

As you can imagine, this function will misbehave if the zero terminator is not present. It will keep on looking past the end of the array until it happens to encounter a zero byte.

Because the end of a character array is marked by a zero terminator, a function that reads from a character array (such as the `strlen` function above) does not need the size of the array as an additional parameter. However, any function that writes into a character array must know the maximum length. For example, here is a function that appends one character array to another. The function reads from the second array and can determine its length by the zero terminator. However, the capacity of the first array, to which more characters are added, must be specified as an extra parameter. The `s_maxlength` value specifies the maximum length of the string stored in the array. It is expected that the array has one more byte to hold the zero terminator.

File append.cpp

```
1  #include <iostream>
2
3  using namespace std;
4
5  /**
6     Appends as much as possible from a string to another string.
7     @param s the string to which t is appended
8     @param s_maxlength the maximum length of s (not counting '\0')
9     @param t the string to append
10 */
11 void append(char s[], int s_maxlength, const char t[])
12 {
13    int i = strlen(s);
14    int j = 0;
15    /* append t to s */
16    while (t[j] != '\0' && i < s_maxlength)
17    {
18       s[i] = t[j];
19       i++;
20       j++;
21    }
22    /* add zero terminator */
23    s[i] = '\0';
24 }
25
26 int main()
27 {
28    const int GREETING_MAXLENGTH = 10;
29    char greeting[GREETING_MAXLENGTH + 1] = "Hello";
30    char t[] = ", World!";
31    append(greeting, GREETING_MAXLENGTH, t);
32    cout << greeting << "\n";
33    return 0;
34 }
```

If you run this program, you will find that it prints `Hello, Wor`—the maximum possible, because the `greeting` character array can hold at most ten characters. With the `string` class you never have this problem, because the class finds enough storage space to hold all characters that are added to a string.

Unfortunately, some of the standard library functions do not check whether they write past the end of a character array. For example, the standard function strcat works just like the append function given above, except that it does not check for space in the array to which the characters are appended. Thus, the following call will lead to disaster:

```
const int GREETING_MAXLENGTH = 10;
char greeting[GREETING_MAXLENGTH + 1] = "Hello";
char t[] = ", World!";
strcat(greeting, t); /* NO! */
```

Four more characters ('l', 'd', '!', and the zero terminator '\0') will be written past the end of the array greeting, overwriting whatever may be stored there. This is an exceedingly common and dangerous programming error.

The standard library has a second function, strncat, that is designed to avoid this problem. You specify the maximum number of characters to copy. Sadly, it doesn't work too well. If the maximum number has been reached, no zero terminator is supplied, so you must manually set it:

```
const int GREETING_MAXLENGTH = 10;
char greeting[GREETING_MAXLENGTH + 1] = "Hello";
char t[] = ", World!";
strncat(greeting, t, GREETING_MAXLENGTH - strlen(greeting));
greeting[GREETING_MAXLENGTH] = '\0';
```

Generally, it is best to avoid the use of character arrays—the string class is safer and far more convenient. For example, appending a string object to another is trivial:

```
string greeting = "Hello";
string t = ", World!";
greeting = greeting + t;
```

However, occasionally you need to convert a string into a character array because you need to call a function that was written before the string class was invented. In that case, use the c_str member function of the string class. For example, the cstdlib header declares a useful function

```
int atoi(const char s[])
```

that converts a character array containing digits into its integer value:

```
char year[] = "1999";
int y = atoi(year); /* now y is the integer 1999 */
```

This functionality is inexplicably missing from the string class, and the c_str member function offers an "escape hatch":

```
string year = "1999";
int y = atoi(year.c_str());
```

(In Chapter 12, you will see another method for converting strings to numbers.)

9.5.4 — Two-Dimensional Arrays

Vectors and arrays can store linear sequences of numbers. It often happens that we want to store collections of numbers that have a two-dimensional layout. For example, in Section 6.7 you saw a program that produces a table of account balances, with varying interest rates over multiple years, as shown below.

12762.82	16288.95	20789.28	26532.98	33863.55	43219.42
13069.60	17081.44	22324.76	29177.57	38133.92	49839.51
13382.26	17908.48	23965.58	32071.35	42918.71	57434.91
13700.87	18771.37	25718.41	35236.45	48276.99	66143.66
14025.52	19671.51	27590.32	38696.84	54274.33	76122.55
14356.29	20610.32	29588.77	42478.51	60983.40	87549.55
14693.28	21589.25	31721.69	46609.57	68484.75	100626.57
15036.57	22609.83	33997.43	51120.46	76867.62	115582.52
15386.24	23673.64	36424.82	56044.11	86230.81	132676.78
15742.39	24782.28	39013.22	61416.12	96683.64	152203.13
16105.10	25937.42	41772.48	67275.00	108347.06	174494.02

Such an arrangement, consisting of rows and columns of values, is called a *two-dimensional array*, or a *matrix*. C++ uses an array with two subscripts to store a two-dimensional array:

```
const int BALANCES_ROWS = 11;
const int BALANCES_COLS = 6;
double balances[BALANCES_ROWS][BALANCES_COLS];
```

Just as you specify the size of arrays when you define them, you must specify how many rows and columns you need. In this case, you ask for 11 rows and 6 columns.

To set a particular element in the two-dimensional array, you need to specify two subscripts in separate brackets to select the row and column, respectively (see Syntax 9.4 and Figure 10):

```
balances[3][4] = future_value(10000, 6.5, 20);
```

Syntax 9.4 : Two-Dimensional Array Definition

type_name variable_name[*size*$_1$][*size*$_2$];

Example: `double monthly_sales[NREGIONS][12];`

Purpose: Define a new variable that is a two-dimensional array.

Figure 10

Accessing an Element in a
Two-Dimensional Array

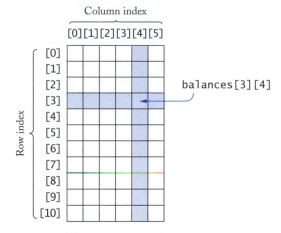

balances[3][4]

Just as with one-dimensional arrays, you cannot change the size of a two-dimensional array once it has been defined.

Although these arrays appear to be two-dimensional, they are still stored as a sequence of elements in memory. Figure 11 shows how the balances array is stored, row by row. For example, to reach

```
balances[3][4]
```

the program must first skip past rows 0, 1, and 2 and then locate offset 4 in row 3. The offset from the start of the array is

```
3 * BALANCES_COLS + 4
```

When passing a two-dimensional array to a function, you must specify the number of columns *as a constant* with the parameter type. The number of rows can be variable. For example,

```cpp
void print_table(const double table[][BALANCES_COLS], int table_rows)
{
   const int WIDTH = 10;
   cout << fixed << setprecision(2);
   for (int i = 0; i < table_rows; i++)
   {
      for (int j = 0; j < BALANCES_COLS; j++)
         cout << setw(WIDTH) << table[i][j];
      cout << "\n";
   }
}
```

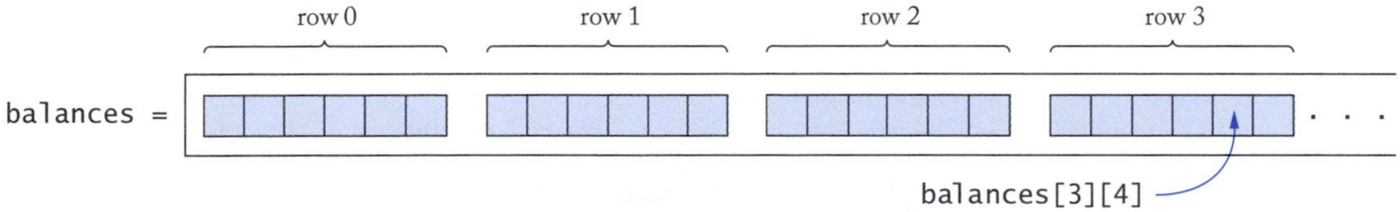

```
           row 0              row 1              row 2              row 3

balances =  ┌────────────┬────────────┬────────────┬────────────┐ . . .
            └────────────┴────────────┴────────────┴────────────┘

                                              balances[3][4]
```

Figure 11

A Two-Dimensional Array Is Stored as a Sequence of Rows

This function can print two-dimensional arrays with arbitrary numbers of rows, but the rows must have 6 columns. You have to write a different function if you want to print a two-dimensional array with 7 columns. The reason is that the compiler must be able to find the element

```
table[i][j]
```

by computing the offset

```
i * BALANCES_COLS + j
```

The compiler knows to use BALANCES_COLS as the number of columns in the computation of table[i][j] because it was specified in the definition of the table parameter as

```
double table[][BALANCES_COLS]
```

If you like, you can specify the number of rows as well:

```
void print_table(double table[BALANCES_ROWS][BALANCES_COLS])
```

However, the compiler completely ignores the first index. When you access table[i][j], it does not check whether i is less than BALANCES_ROWS. It does not check whether j is valid either. It merely computes the offset i * BALANCE_COLS + j and locates that element.

Here is a complete program that fills a two-dimensional array with data and then displays the contents.

File matrix.cpp

```
 1  #include <iostream>
 2  #include <iomanip>
 3  #include <cmath>
 4
 5  using namespace std;
 6
 7  const int BALANCES_ROWS = 11;
 8  const int BALANCES_COLS = 6;
 9
10  const double RATE_MIN = 5;
11  const double RATE_MAX = 10;
12  const double RATE_INCR =
13     (RATE_MAX - RATE_MIN) / (BALANCES_ROWS - 1);
14  const int YEAR_MIN = 5;
15  const int YEAR_MAX = 30;
16  const int YEAR_INCR =
17     (YEAR_MAX - YEAR_MIN) / (BALANCES_COLS - 1);
18
19
20  /**
21     Prints a table of account balances.
22     @param the table to print
23     @param table_rows the number of rows in the table.
24  */
25  void print_table(const double table[][BALANCES_COLS],
26     int table_rows)
27  {
28     const int WIDTH = 10;
29     cout << fixed << setprecision(2);
```

```
30     for (int i = 0; i < table_rows; i++)
31     {
32         for (int j = 0; j < BALANCES_COLS; j++)
33             cout << setw(WIDTH) << table[i][j];
34         cout << "\n";
35     }
36 }
37
38 /**
39     Computes the value of an investment with compound interest.
40     @param initial_balance  the initial value of the investment
41     @param p  the interest rate per period in percent
42     @param n  the number of periods the investment is held
43     @return  the balance after n  periods
44 */
45 double future_value(double initial_balance, double p, int n)
46 {
47     double b = initial_balance * pow(1 + p / 100, n);
48     return b;
49 }
50
51 int main()
52 {
53     double balances[BALANCES_ROWS][BALANCES_COLS];
54     for (int i = 0; i < BALANCES_ROWS; i++)
55         for (int j = 0; j < BALANCES_COLS; j++)
56             balances[i][j] = future_value(10000,
57                 RATE_MIN + i * RATE_INCR,
58                 YEAR_MIN + j * YEAR_INCR);
59
60     print_table(balances, BALANCES_ROWS);
61
62     return 0;
63 }
```

Quality Tip   9.3

Name the Array Size and Capacity Consistently

It is a good idea to have a consistent naming scheme for array size and capacity. In this section, you always appended _size and _CAPACITY to the array name to denote the size and capacity for an array:

```
const int A_CAPACITY = 20;
int a[A_CAPACITY];
int a_size = 0;
. . .
int x;
cin >> x;
a[a_size] = x;
a_size++;
```

If you follow this naming convention or one similar to it, you always know how to inquire about the size and capacity of an array. Remember that you need to pass the size to all functions that read the array, and both the size and capacity to all functions that add values to the array.

Common Error   9.2

Character Pointers

The most dangerous character array error is to copy a string into random memory. If you stick to the character arrays described in this section, that will not happen to you. However, if you listen to your friends who tell you that you can just use a `char*` whenever you want to store a character array, you are setting yourself up for trouble. The following code will compile, but the resulting program will mostly likely crash immediately:

```
char* greeting;
strcat(greeting, "Hello"); /* NO! */
```

The type `char*` denotes a *pointer* to a character, that is, the location of a character in memory. (You will learn more about pointers in Chapter 10.) Because `greeting` has never been initialized, it points to a random location. In C++, arrays and pointers are closely related, and in many cases there is no distinction between an array and a pointer to the starting element of that array. For that reason, the `strcat` function is willing to take a pointer as its first parameter. Of course, the function assumes that the location to which the pointer points is available for storing characters. When the function starts placing characters into a random location, there is a good chance that the operating system notices that the random memory location doesn't belong to the program. In that case, the operating system terminates the program with extreme prejudice. However, it is also possible that the random memory location happens to be accessible by the program. In that case some other, presumably useful, data will be overwritten.

To avoid these errors, do not use `char*` pointers. They are not required for basic character array handling. Sometime in the future you may need to work on a project that requires knowledge of character pointers. At that time, you will need to learn about the relationship between arrays and pointers in C and C++. See, for example, [3] for more information.

Common Error   9.3

Omitting the Column Size of a Two-Dimensional Array Parameter

When passing a one-dimensional array to a function, you specify the size of the array as a separate parameter:

```
double maximum(const double a[], int a_size)
```

This function can compute the maximum of arrays of any size. However, for two-dimensional arrays you cannot simply pass the numbers of rows and columns as parameters:

```
void print(const double table[][], int table_rows,
    int table_cols) /* NO! */
```

You must know how many columns the two-dimensional array has, and specify the number of columns in the array parameter. This number must be a constant:

```
const int TABLE_COLS = 6;
void print(const double table[][TABLE_COLS],
    int table_rows) /* OK */
```

Random Fact 9.2

International Alphabets

The English alphabet is pretty simple: upper- and lowercase *a* to *z*. Other European languages have accent marks and special characters. For example, German has three so-called *umlaut* characters, ä, ö, ü, and a *double-s* character ß. These are not optional frills; you couldn't write a page of German text without using these characters a few times. German computer keyboards have keys for these characters (see Figure 12).

This poses a problem for computer users and designers. The American standard character encoding (called ASCII, for American Standard Code for Information Interchange) specifies 128 codes: 52 upper- and lowercase characters, 10 digits, 32 typographical symbols, and 34 control characters (such as space, newline, and 32 others for controlling printers and other devices). The umlaut and double-s are not among them. Some German data processing systems replace seldom-used ASCII characters with German letters: [\]{|}~ are replaced with Ä Ö Ü ä ö ü ß. While most people can live without these characters, C++ programmers definitely cannot. Other encoding schemes take advantage of the fact that one byte can encode 256 different characters, of which only 128 are standardized by ASCII. Unfortunately, there are multiple incompatible standards for such encodings, resulting in a certain amount of aggravation among European computer users.

Many countries don't use the Roman script at all. Russian, Greek, Hebrew, Arabic, and Thai letters, to name just a few, have completely different shapes (see Figure 13). To complicate matters, Hebrew and Arabic are typed from right to left. Each of these alphabets has between 30 and 100 letters, and the countries using them have established encoding standards for them.

Figure 12

The German Keyboard

Figure 13

The Thai Script

ฐ	ก	ะ	เ	๐	๒
ก	ท	ม	◌ั	แ	๑	๒๐
ข	ฒ	ย	า	โ	๒	โ
ช	ณ	ร	◌ำ	ใ	๓	ใ
ค	ด	ฤ	◌ิ	ไ	๔	ไ
ฅ	ต	ล	◌ี	ๅ	๕	
ฆ	ถ	ฦ	◌ึ	◌ๅ	๖	
ง	ท	ว	◌ื	◌ื	๗	
จ	ธ	ศ	◌ุ	◌่	๘	
ฉ	น	ษ	◌ู	◌้	๙	
ช	บ	ส	◌.	◌๊	ๆ	
ซ	ป	ห		◌๋	ฯ	
ฌ	ผ	ฬ	◌์			
ญ	ฝ	อ	◌ํ			
ฎ	พ	ฮ	◌ะ			
ฏ	ฟ	ๆ				

The situation is much more dramatic in languages that use the Chinese script: the Chinese dialects, Japanese, and Korean. The Chinese script is not alphabetic but *ideographic* (see Figure 14). A character represents an idea or thing. Most words are made up of one, two, or

CLASSIC SOUPS

			Sm.	Lg.
清燉雞湯	57.	House Chicken Soup (Chicken, Celery, Potato, Onion, Carrot)	1.50	2.75
雞　飯　湯	58.	Chicken Rice Soup	1.85	3.25
雞　麵　湯	59.	Chicken Noodle Soup	1.85	3.25
廣東雲吞	60.	Cantonese Wonton Soup	1.50	2.75
蕃茄蛋湯	61.	Tomato Clear Egg Drop Soup	1.65	2.95
雲　吞　湯	62.	Regular Wonton Soup	1.10	2.10
酸　辣　湯	63. 🦐	Hot & Sour Soup	1.10	2.10
蛋　花　湯	64.	Egg Drop Soup	1.10	2.10
雲　蛋　湯	65.	Egg Drop Wonton Mix	1.10	2.10
豆腐菜湯	66.	Tofu Vegetable Soup	NA	3.50
雞玉米湯	67.	Chicken Corn Cream Soup	NA	3.50
蟹肉玉米湯	68.	Crab Meat Corn Cream Soup	NA	3.50
海　鮮　湯	69.	Seafood Soup	NA	3.50

Figure 14

The Chinese Script

▼

▼

▼

▼

three of these ideographic characters. Over 50,000 ideographs are known, of which about 20,000 are in active use. Therefore, two bytes are needed to encode them. China, Taiwan, Japan, and Korea have incompatible encoding standards for them. (Japanese and Korean writing uses a mixture of native syllabic and Chinese ideographic characters.)

The inconsistencies among character encodings have been a major nuisance for international electronic communication and for software manufacturers vying for a global market. Between 1988 and 1991 a consortium of hardware and software manufacturers developed a uniform 16-bit encoding scheme called *unicode* that is capable of encoding text in essentially all written languages of the world [4]. About 28,000 characters are given codes, including 21,000 Chinese ideographs. Since a 16-bit code can incorporate 65,000 codes, there is ample space for expansion. There are plans to add codes for American Indian languages and Egyptian hieroglyphs.

CHAPTER SUMMARY

1. Use a vector to collect multiple values of the same type. Individual values are accessed by an integer index or subscript: `v[i]`. Valid values for the index range from 0 to one less than the size of the array. Supplying an invalid index is a common programming error that has serious consequences.

2. When creating a vector, you can set it to a certain size, or you can start out with an empty vector. Use the `push_back` procedure to add more elements to a vector. Use `pop_back` to reduce the size. Use the `size` function to obtain the current size.

3. Vectors can occur as the parameters and return values of functions and procedures.

4. When inserting or removing elements in the middle of a vector, pay attention to the order in which you move the elements beyond the point of insertion or removal.

5. Avoid parallel vectors by changing them into vectors of objects.

6. Arrays are a more primitive construct for collecting elements than vectors. Once the size of an array has been set, it cannot be changed.

7. Character arrays are arrays of values of the character type `char`.

8. Vectors form a linear, one-dimensional sequence of values. Matrices form a tabular, two-dimensional arrangement. Individual elements are accessed by double subscripts `m[i][j]`.

FURTHER READING

[1] Peter J. Denning, *Computers under Attack*, Addison-Wesley, 1990.
[2] Cliff Stoll, *The Cuckoo's Egg*, Doubleday, 1989.
[3] Cay Horstmann, *Mastering C++*, 2nd ed., John Wiley & Sons, 1995.
[4] The Unicode Consortium, *The Unicode Standard Worldwide Character Encoding*, Version 1.0, Addison-Wesley, 1991.

REVIEW EXERCISES

Exercise R9.1. Write code that fills a vector v with each set of values below

(a) 1 2 3 4 5 6 7 8 9 10
(b) 0 2 4 6 8 10 12 14 16 18 20
(c) 1 4 9 16 25 36 49 64 81 100
(d) 0 0 0 0 0 0 0 0 0 0
(e) 1 4 9 16 9 7 4 9 11

Exercise R9.2. Write a loop that fills a vector v with ten random numbers between 1 and 100. Write code for two nested loops that fill v with ten *different* random numbers between 1 and 100.

Exercise R9.3. Write C++ code for a loop that simultaneously computes both the maximum and minimum of a vector.

Exercise R9.4. What is wrong with the following loop?

```
vector<int> v(10);
int i;
for (i = 1; i <= 10; i++) v[i] = i * i;
```

Explain two ways of fixing the error.

Exercise R9.5. What is an array index? What are the bounds of an array? What is a bounds error?

Exercise R9.6. Write a program that contains a bounds error. Run the program. What happens on your computer?

Exercise R9.7. Write a program that fills a vector with the numbers 1, 4, 9, . . ., 100. Compile it and launch the debugger. After the vector has been filled with three numbers, inspect it. Take a screen snapshot of the display that shows the ten slots of the vector.

Exercise R9.8. Write a loop that reads ten numbers and a second loop that displays them in the opposite order from which they were entered.

Exercise R9.9. Give an example of

(a) A useful function that has a vector of integers as a value parameter
(b) A useful function that has a vector of integers as a reference parameter
(c) A useful function that has a vector of integers as a return value

Describe each function; do not implement them.

Exercise R9.10. A function that has a vector as a reference parameter can change the vector in two ways. It can change the contents of individual vector elements, or it can rearrange the elements. Describe two useful functions with vector<Product>& parameters that change a vector of products in each of the two ways just described.

Exercise R9.11. What are parallel vectors? Why are parallel vectors indications of poor programming? How can they be avoided?

Exercise R9.12. Design a class `Staff` that stores a collection of employees. What public member functions should you support? What advantages and disadvantages does a `Staff` class have over a `vector<Employee>`?

Exercise R9.13. Suppose v is a *sorted* vector of employees. Give pseudocode that describes how a new employee can be inserted in its proper position so that the resulting vector stays sorted.

Exercise R9.14. In many programming languages it is not possible to grow a vector. That is, there is no analog to `push_back` in those languages. Write code that reads a sequence of numbers into a vector without using `push_back`. First create a vector of a reasonable size (say 20). Also, use an integer variable `length` that tests how *full* the vector currently is. Whenever a new element is read in, increase `length`. When `length` reaches the *size* of the vector (20 at the outset), create a new vector of twice the size and copy all existing elements into the new vector. Write C++ code that performs this task.

Exercise R9.15. How do you perform the following tasks with vectors in C++?

(a) Test that two vectors contain the same elements in the same order.
(b) Copy one vector to another. (*Hint:* You may copy more than one element at a time.)
(c) Fill a vector with zeroes, overwriting all elements in it.
(d) Remove all elements from a vector. (*Hint:* You need not remove them one by one.)

Exercise R9.16. True or false?

(a) All elements of a vector are of the same type.
(b) Vector subscripts must be integers.
(c) Vectors cannot contain strings as elements.
(d) Vectors cannot use strings as subscripts.
(e) Parallel vectors must have equal length.
(f) Matrices always have the same numbers of rows and columns.
(g) Two parallel arrays can be replaced by a matrix.
(h) Elements of different columns in a matrix can have different types.

Exercise R9.17. True or false?

(a) All vector parameters are reference parameters.
(b) A function cannot return a matrix.
(c) A procedure cannot change the dimensions of a matrix that is passed by value.
(d) A procedure cannot change the length of a vector that is passed by reference.
(e) A procedure can only reorder the elements of a vector, not change the elements.

CHAPTER 9

PROGRAMMING EXERCISES

Exercise P9.1. Write a function

```
double scalar_product(vector<double> a, vector<double> b)
```

that computes the scalar product of two vectors. The scalar product is

$$a_0 b_0 + a_1 b_1 + \cdots + a_{n-1} b_{n-1}$$

Exercise P9.2. Write a function that computes the *alternating sum* of all elements in a vector. For example, if alternating_sum is called with a vector containing

1   4   9   16   9   7   4   9   11

then it computes

$$1 - 4 + 9 - 16 + 9 - 7 + 4 - 9 + 11 = -2$$

Exercise P9.3. Write a procedure reverse that reverses the sequence of elements in a vector. For example, if reverse is called with a vector containing

1   4   9   16   9   7   4   9   11

then the vector is changed to

11   9   4   7   9   16   9   4   1

Exercise P9.4. Write a function

```
vector<int> append(vector<int> a, vector<int> b)
```

that appends one vector after another. For example, if a is

1   4   9   16

and b is

9   7   4   9   11

then append returns the vector

1   4   9   16   9   7   4   9   11

Exercise P9.5. Write a function

```
vector<int> merge(vector<int> a, vector<int> b)
```

that merges two arrays, alternating elements from both arrays. If one array is shorter than the other, then alternate as long as you can and then append the remaining elements from the longer array. For example, if a is

$$1 \quad 4 \quad 9 \quad 16$$

and b is

$$9 \quad 7 \quad 4 \quad 9 \quad 11$$

then merge returns the array

$$1 \quad 9 \quad 4 \quad 7 \quad 9 \quad 4 \quad 16 \quad 9 \quad 11$$

Exercise P9.6. Write a function

```
vector<int> merge_sorted(vector<int> a, vector<int> b)
```

that merges two *sorted* arrays, producing a new sorted array. Keep an index into each array, indicating how much of it has been processed already. Each time, append the smallest unprocessed element from either array, then advance the index. For example, if a is

$$1 \quad 4 \quad 9 \quad 16$$

and b is

$$4 \quad 7 \quad 9 \quad 9 \quad 11$$

then merge_sorted returns the array

$$1 \quad 4 \quad 4 \quad 7 \quad 9 \quad 9 \quad 9 \quad 11 \quad 16$$

Exercise P9.7. Write a predicate function

```
bool equals(vector<int> a, vector<int> b)
```

that checks whether two vectors have the same elements in the same order.

Exercise P9.8. Write a predicate function

```
bool same_set(vector<int> a, vector<int> b)
```

that checks whether two vectors have the same elements in some order, ignoring multiplicities. For example, the two vectors

$$1 \quad 4 \quad 9 \quad 16 \quad 9 \quad 7 \quad 4 \quad 9 \quad 11$$

and

$$11 \quad 11 \quad 7 \quad 9 \quad 16 \quad 4 \quad 1$$

would be considered identical. You will probably need one or more helper functions.

Exercise P9.9. Write a predicate function

```
bool same_elements(vector<int> a, vector<int> b)
```

that checks whether two vectors have the same elements in some order, with the same multiplicities. For example,

1   4   9   16   9   7   4   9   11

and

11   1   4   9   16   9   7   4   9

would be considered identical, but

1   4   9   16   9   7   4   9   11

and

11   11   7   9   16   4   1

would not. You will probably need one or more helper functions.

Exercise P9.10. Write a function that removes duplicates from a vector. For example, if `remove_duplicates` is called with a vector containing

1   4   9   16   9   7   4   9   11

then the vector is changed to

1   4   9   16   7   11

Exercise P9.11. A *polygon* is a closed sequence of lines. To describe a polygon, store the sequence of its corner points. Because the number of points is variable, use a vector.

```
class Polygon
{
public:
   Polygon();
   void add_point(Point p);
   void plot() const;
private:
   vector<Point> corners;
};
```

Implement this class and supply a test harness that plots a polygon such as the following:

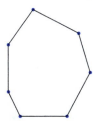

Exercise P9.12. Enhance the `Polygon` class of Exercise P9.11 by adding member functions

```
double Polygon::perimeter() const
```

and

```
double Polygon::area() const
```

that compute the perimeter and the area of a polygon. To compute the perimeter, compute the distance between adjacent points, and total up the distances.

The area of a polygon with corners $(x_0, y_0), \ldots, (x_{n-1}, y_{n-1})$ is

$$\frac{1}{2} \left| x_0 y_1 + x_1 y_2 + \cdots + x_{n-1} y_0 - y_0 x_1 - y_1 x_2 - \cdots - y_{n-1} x_0 \right|$$

As test cases, compute the perimeter and area of a rectangle and of a regular hexagon.

Exercise P9.13. Enhance the `Polygon` class of Exercise P9.11 by adding member functions

```
void Polygon::move(double dx, double dy);
void Polygon::scale(double factor);
```

The first procedure moves all points of a polygon by the specified amounts in the x- and y-directions. The second procedure performs a scaling with the given scale factor and updates the coordinates of the points of the polygon accordingly. *Hint:* Use the `move` member function of the `Point` class. To scale a point, multiply both the x- and y-coordinate with the scale factor.

Exercise P9.14. Write a program that asks the user to input a number n and prints all permutations of the sequence of numbers 1, 2, 3, . . ., n. For example, if n is 3, the program should print

1	2	3
1	3	2
2	1	3
2	3	1
3	1	2
3	2	1

Hint: Write a function

```
permutation_helper(vector<int> prefix, vector<int> to_permute)
```

that computes all the permutations in the array `to_permute` and prints each permutation, prefixed by all numbers in the array `prefix`. For example, if `prefix` contains the number 2 and `to_permute` the numbers 1 and 3, then `permutation_helper` prints

2	1	3
2	3	1

The `permutation_helper` function does the following: If `to_permute` has no elements, print the elements in `prefix`. Otherwise, for each element e in `to_permute`, make an array `to_permute2` that is equal to `permute` except for e and an array `prefixx2` consisting of `prefix` and e. Then call `permutation_helper` with `prefixx2` and `to_permute2`.

Exercise P9.15. Write a program that produces ten random permutations of the numbers 1 to 10. To generate a random permutation, you need to fill a vector with the numbers 1 to 10 so that no two entries of the vector have the same contents. You could do it by brute force, by calling `rand_int` until it produces a value that is not yet in the vector. Instead, you should implement a smart method. Make a second array and fill it with the numbers 1 to 10. Then pick one of those at random, remove it, and append it to the permutation vector. Repeat ten times.

Exercise P9.16. Write a procedure

```
void bar_chart(vector<double> data)
```

that displays a bar chart of the values in `data`. You may assume that all values in `data` are positive. *Hint:* You must figure out the maximum of the values in `data`. Set the coordinate system so that the *x*-range equals the number of bars and the *y*-range goes from 0 to the maximum.

Exercise P9.17. Improve the `bar_chart` procedure of the preceding exercise to work correctly when `data` contains negative values.

Exercise P9.18. Write a procedure

```
void pie_chart(vector<double> data)
```

that displays a pie chart of the values in `data`. You may assume that all values in `data` are positive.

Exercise P9.19. Write a program that prints out a bank statement. The program input is a sequence of transactions. Each transaction has the form

day amount description

For example,

```
15 -224 Check 2140
16 1200 ATM deposit
```

Your program should read in the descriptions and then print out a statement listing all deposits, withdrawals, and the daily balance for each day. You should then compute the interest earned by the account. Use both the *minimum daily balance* and the *average daily balance* methods for computing interest, and print out both values. Use an interest rate of 0.5 percent per month, and assume the month has 30 days. You may assume that the input data are sorted by the date. You may also assume that the first entry is of the form

```
1 1143.24 Initial balance
```

Exercise P9.20. Define a class

```
class Staff
{
public:
   . . .
private:
   vector<Employee> members;
};
```

and implement the `find` and `raise_salary` procedures for the `Staff` data type.

Exercise P9.21. Design a class `Student`, or use one from a previous exercise. A student has a name and a birthday. Make a vector

```
vector<Student> friends;
```

Read a set of names and birthdays in from a file or type them in, thus populating the `friends` vector. Then print out all friends whose birthday falls in the current month.

Exercise P9.22. Write a program that plays tic-tac-toe. The tic-tac-toe game is played on a 3×3 grid as in

The game is played by two players, who take turns. The first player marks moves with a circle, the second with a cross. The player who has formed a horizontal, vertical, or diagonal sequence of three marks wins. Your program should draw the game board, accept mouse clicks into empty squares, change the players after every successful move, and pronounce the winner.

Exercise P9.23. *Magic squares.* An $n \times n$ matrix that is filled with the numbers 1, 2, 3, ..., n^2 is a magic square if the sum of the elements in each row, in each column, and in the two diagonals is the same value. For example,

$$
\begin{array}{cccc}
16 & 3 & 2 & 13 \\
5 & 10 & 11 & 8 \\
9 & 6 & 7 & 12 \\
4 & 15 & 14 & 1
\end{array}
$$

Write a program that reads in n^2 values from the keyboard and tests whether they form a magic square when put into array form. You need to test three features:

1. Did the user enter n^2 numbers for some n?
2. Does each of the numbers 1, 2, ..., n^2 occur exactly once in the user input?
3. When the numbers are put into a square, are the sums of the rows, columns, and diagonals equal to each other?

Hint: First read the numbers into a vector. If the size of that vector is a square, test whether all numbers between 1 and n are present. Then fill the numbers into a matrix and compute the row, column, and diagonal sums.

Exercise P9.24. Implement the following algorithm to construct magic $n \times n$ squares; it works only if n is odd. Place a 1 in the middle of the bottom row. After k has been placed in the (i, j) square, place $k + 1$ into the square to the right and down, wrapping around the borders. However, if you reach a square that has already been filled, or if you reach the lower right corner, then you must move one square up instead. Here is the 5×5 square that you get if you follow this method:

$$
\begin{array}{ccccc}
11 & 18 & 25 & 2 & 9 \\
10 & 12 & 19 & 21 & 3 \\
4 & 6 & 13 & 20 & 22 \\
23 & 5 & 7 & 14 & 16 \\
17 & 24 & 1 & 8 & 15
\end{array}
$$

Write a program whose input is the number n and whose output is the magic square of order n if n is odd.

Exercise P9.25. The following table can be found in the "West Suburban Boston, Area Code 617, 1990–1991" telephone book.

	M	T	W	T	F	S	S
8 am – 5 pm	■	■	■	■	■	▫	▫
5 pm – 11 pm	▪	▪	▪	▪	▫	▫	▪
11 pm – 8 am	▫	▫	▫	▫	▫	▫	▫

Dial direct

Sample rates from city of **Waltham** to:	Mileage bands Airline miles	Weekday full rate First minute	Each additional minute	Evening 35% discount First minute	Each additional minute	Night & Weekend 60% discount First minute	Each additional minute
Sudbury	0–10	.19	.09	.12	.05	.07	.03
Framingham	11–14	.26	.12	.16	.07	.10	.04
Lowell	15–19	.32	.14	.20	.09	.12	.05
Brockton	20–25	.38	.15	.24	.09	.15	.06
Worcester	26–33	.43	.17	.27	.11	.17	.06
Rockport	34–43	.48	.19	.31	.12	.19	.07
Fall River	44–55	.51	.20	.33	.13	.20	.08
Falmouth	56–70	.53	.21	.34	.13	.21	.08
Hyannis	71–85	.54	.22	.35	.14	.21	.08

Write a program that asks the user:

- The destination of the call
- The starting time
- The length of the call
- The weekday

The program should compute and display the charge. Note that the rate may vary. If the call starts at 4:50 P.M. and ends at 5:10 P.M., then half of it falls into the day rate and half of it into the evening rate.

Pointers

► To learn how to declare, initialize, and use pointers

► To become familiar with dynamic memory allocation and deallocation

► To use pointers in common programming situations that involve optional and shared objects

► To avoid the common errors of dangling pointers and memory leaks

► To understand the relationship between arrays and pointers

► To be able to convert between string objects and character pointers

An object variable *contains* an object, but a pointer specifies *where* an object is located. In C++, pointers are important for several reasons. Pointers can refer to objects that are *dynamically* allocated whenever they are needed. Pointers can be used for *shared access* to objects. Furthermore, as you will see in Chapter 11, pointers are necessary for implementing *polymorphism*, an important concept in object-oriented programming.

In C++, there is a deep relationship between pointers and arrays. You will see in this chapter how this relationship explains a number of special properties and limitations of arrays. Finally, you will see how to convert between string objects and char* pointers, which is necessary when interfacing with legacy code.

10.1 Pointers and Memory Allocation

The C++ run-time system can create new objects for us. When we ask for a

```
new Employee
```

then a *memory allocator* finds a storage location for a new employee object. The memory allocator keeps a large storage area, called the *heap*, for that purpose. The heap is a very flexible pool for memory. It can hold values of any type. You can equally ask for

```
new Time
new Product
```

See Syntax 10.1.

When you allocate a new heap object, the memory allocator tells you where the object is located, by giving you the object's *memory address*. To manipulate memory

---

Syntax 10.1 : new **Expression**

new *type_name*
new *type_name*(*expression*$_1$, *expression*$_2$, ..., *expression*$_n$)

Example: new Time
       new Employee("Lin, Lisa", 68000)

Purpose: Allocate and construct a value on the heap and return a pointer to the value.

Syntax 10.2 : Pointer Variable Definition

type_name ∗ *variable_name*;
type_name ∗ *variable_name* = *expression*;

Example: `Employee* boss;`
`          Product* p = new Product;`

Purpose: Define a new pointer variable, and optionally supply an initial value.

---

addresses, you need to learn about a new C++ data type: the *pointer*. A pointer to an employee record,

```
Employee* boss;
```

contains the location or memory address for an employee object. A pointer to a time object,

```
Time* deadline;
```

stores the memory address for a time object. See Syntax 10.2.

The types `Employee*` and `Time*` denote pointers to employee and time objects. The boss and deadline variables of type `Employee*` and `Time*` store the locations or memory addresses of employee and time objects. They cannot store actual employee objects or time objects, however (see Figure 1).

When you create a new object on the heap, you usually want to initialize it. You can supply construction parameters, using the familiar syntax.

```
Employee* boss = new Employee("Lin, Lisa", 68000);
```

When you have a pointer to a value, you often want to access the value to which it points. That action—to go from the pointer to the value—is called *dereferencing*. In C++,

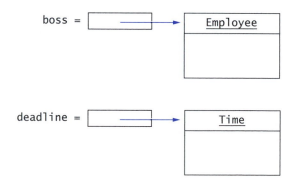

Figure 1

Pointers and the Objects to Which They Point

the * operator is used to indicate the value associated with a pointer. For example, if boss is an Employee*, then *boss is an Employee value:

```
Employee* boss = . . . .;
raise_salary(*boss, 10);
```

Suppose you want to find out the name of the employee to which boss points:

```
Employee* boss =  . . . .;
string name = *boss.get_name(); // Error
```

Unfortunately, that is a syntax error. The dot operator has a higher precedence than the * operator. That is, the compiler thinks that you mean

```
string name = *(boss.get_name()); // Error
```

However, boss is a pointer, not an object. You can't apply the dot (.) operator to a pointer, and the compiler reports an error. Instead, you must make it clear that you first want to apply the * operator, then the dot:

```
string name = (*boss).get_name(); // OK
```

Because this is such a common situation, the designers of C++ supply an operator to abbreviate the "dereference and access member" operation. That operator is written -> and usually pronounced as "arrow".

```
string name = boss->get_name(); // OK
```

Dereferencing of pointers and accessing members through pointers are summarized in Syntax 10.3.

There is one special value, NULL, that can be used to indicate a pointer that doesn't point anywhere. Instead of leaving pointer variables uninitialized, you should always set pointer variables to NULL when you define them.

```
Employee* boss = NULL; // will set later
. . .
if (boss != NULL) name = boss->get_name(); // OK
```

You cannot dereference the NULL pointer. That is, calling *boss or boss->get_name() is an error as long as boss is NULL.

```
Employee* boss = NULL;
string name = boss->get_name();  // NO!! Program will crash
```

The purpose of a NULL pointer is to test that it doesn't point to any valid object.

Syntax 10.3 : Pointer Dereferencing

pointer_expression
pointer_expression->class_member

Example: *boss
         boss->set_salary(70000)

Purpose: Access the object to which a pointer points.

Common Error   10.1

Confusing Pointers with the Data to Which They Point

A pointer is a memory address—a number that tells where a value is located in memory. You can only carry out a small number of operations on a pointer:

- assign it to a pointer variable
- compare it with another pointer or the special value NULL
- dereference it to access the value to which it points

However, it is a common error to confuse the pointer with the value to which it points:

```
Employee* boss = . . .;
raise_salary(boss, 10); // ERROR
```

Remember that the pointer boss only describes *where* the employee object is. To actually refer to the employee object, use *boss:

```
raise_salary(*boss, 10); // OK
```

Common Error   10.2

Declaring Two Pointers on the Same Line

It is legal in C++ to define multiple variables together, like this:

```
int i = 0, j = 1;
```

This style does *not* work with pointers:

```
Employee* p, q;
```

For historical reasons, the * associates only with the first variable. That is, p is a Employee* pointer, and q is an Employee object. The remedy is to define each pointer variable separately:

```
Employee* p;
Employee* q;
```

You will see some programmers group the * with the variable:

```
Employee *p, *q;
```

While it is a legal declaration, don't use that style. It makes it harder to tell that p and q are variables of type Employee*.

▽

Advanced Topic 10.1

The this Pointer

Each member function has a special parameter variable, called `this`, which is a pointer to the implicit parameter. For example, consider the `Product::is_better_than` function of Chapter 6. If you call

```
next.is_better_than(best)
```

then the `this` pointer has type `Product*` and points to the `next` object.

You can use the `this` pointer inside the definition of a method. For example,

```
bool Product::is_better_than(Product b)
{
   if (b.price == 0) return false;
   if (this->price == 0) return true;
   return this->score / this->price > b.score / b.price;
}
```

Here, the expression `this->price` refers to the `price` member of the object to which `this` points, that is, the `price` member of the implicit parameter, or `next.price`. The `this` pointer is not necessary, however, since by convention the expression `price` also refers to the field of the implicit parameter. Nevertheless, some programmers like to use the `this` pointer to make it explicit that `price` is a member and not a variable.

Note that `this` is a pointer whereas `b` is an object. Therefore, we access the `price` member of the implicit parameter as `this->price`, but for the explicit parameter we use `b.price`.

Very occasionally, a member function needs to pass the implicit parameter in its entirety to another function. Since `this` is a pointer to the implicit parameter, `*this` is the actual implicit parameter. For example, suppose someone defined a function

```
void debug_print(string message, Product p)
```

Then the code for the `is_better_than` function might start out with these statements:

```
debug_print("Implicit parameter:", *this);
debug_print("Explicit parameter:", b);
```

10.2 Deallocating Dynamic Memory

When you make a variable of type `Employee`, the memory for the employee object is allocated on the *run-time stack*. This memory automatically goes away when the program leaves the block in which the variable is allocated:

```
void f()
{
   Employee harry; // memory for employee allocated on the stack
   . . .
} // memory for employee automatically reclaimed
```

Values that are allocated on the heap do not follow this automatic allocation mechanism.

You allocate values on the heap with new, and you must reclaim them using the delete operator:

```
void g()
{
    Employee* boss;
    boss = new Employee(. . .);
        // memory for employee allocated on the heap
    . . .
    delete boss; // memory for employee manually reclaimed
}
```

Actually, the foregoing example is a little more complex than that. There are two allocations: one on the stack and one on the heap. The variable boss is allocated on the stack. It is of type Employee*; that is, boss can hold the address of an employee object. Defining the pointer variable does not yet create an Employee object. The next line of code allocates an Employee object on the heap and stores its address in the pointer variable.

At the end of the block, the storage space for the variable boss on the stack is automatically reclaimed. Reclaiming the pointer variable does not automatically reclaim the object to which it points. The memory address is merely forgotten. (That can be a problem—see Common Error 10.4). Therefore, you must manually delete the memory block holding the object.

Note that the pointer variable on the stack has a *name*, namely boss. But the employee object, allocated on the heap with new Employee, has no name! It can be reached only through the boss pointer. Values on the stack always have names; heap values do not.

When a pointer variable is first defined, it contains a random address. Using that random address is an error. In practice, your program will likely crash or mysteriously misbehave if you use an uninitialized pointer:

```
Employee* boss;
string name = boss->get_name(); // NO!! boss contains a random address
```

You must always initialize a pointer so that it points to an actual value before you can use it:

```
Employee* boss = new Employee("Lin, Lisa", 68000);
string name = boss->get_name(); // OK
```

After you delete the value attached to a pointer, you can no longer use that address! The storage space may already be reassigned to another value.

```
delete boss;
string name = boss->get_name(); // NO!! boss points to a deleted element
```

Syntax 10.4 : delete Expression

delete *pointer_expression*;

Example: delete boss;

Purpose: Deallocate a value that is stored on the heap and allow the memory to be reallocated.

⊗ Common Error   **10.3**

Dangling Pointers

The most common pointer error is to use a pointer that has not been initialized, or that has already been deleted. Such a pointer is called a *dangling* pointer, because it does point somewhere, just not to a valid object. You can create real damage by writing to the location to which it points. Even reading from the location can crash your program.

An uninitialized pointer has a good chance of pointing to an address that your program doesn't own. On most operating systems, attempting to access such a location causes a processor error, and the operating system shuts down the program. You may have seen that happen to other programs—a dialog with a bomb icon or a message such as "general protection fault" or "segmentation fault" comes up, and the program is terminated.

If a dangling pointer points to a valid address inside your program, then writing to it will damage some part of your program. You will change the value of one of your variables, or perhaps damage the control structures of the heap so that after several calls to new something crazy happens.

When your program crashes and you restart it, the problem may not reappear, or it may manifest itself in different ways because the random pointer is now initialized with a different random address. Programming with pointers requires iron discipline, because you can create true damage with dangling pointers.

Always initialize pointer variables. If you can't initialize them with the return value of new, then set them to NULL.

Never use a pointer that has been deleted. Some people immediately set every pointer to NULL after deleting it. That is certainly helpful:

```
delete first;
first = NULL;
```

However, it is not a complete solution.

```
second = first;
. . .
delete first;
first = NULL;
```

You must still remember that second is now dangling. As you can see, you must carefully keep track of all pointers and the corresponding heap objects to avoid dangling pointers.

⊗ Common Error   **10.4**

Memory Leaks

The second most common pointer error is to allocate memory on the heap and never deallocate it. A memory block that is never deallocated is called a *memory leak*.

If you allocate a few small blocks of memory and forget to deallocate them, this is not a huge problem. When the program exits, all allocated memory is returned to the operating system.

▼ But if your program runs for a long time, or if it allocates lots of memory (perhaps in a loop), then it can run out of memory. Memory exhaustion will cause your program to crash. In extreme cases, the computer may freeze up if your program exhausted all available mem-

▼ ory. Avoiding memory leaks is particularly important in programs that need to run for months or years, without restarting.

Even if you write short-lived programs, you should make it a habit to avoid memory

▼ leaks. Make sure that every call to the new operator has a corresponding call to the delete operator.

▼ ## Advanced Topic   10.2

The Address Operator

▼ The new operator returns the memory address of a value that is allocated on the heap. You can also obtain the address of a local or global variable, by applying the address (&) operator. For

▼ example,

```
Employee harry;
Employee* p = &harry;
```

▼ See Figure 2. However, you should never delete an address that you obtained from the & operator. Doing so would corrupt the heap, leading to errors in subsequent calls to new.

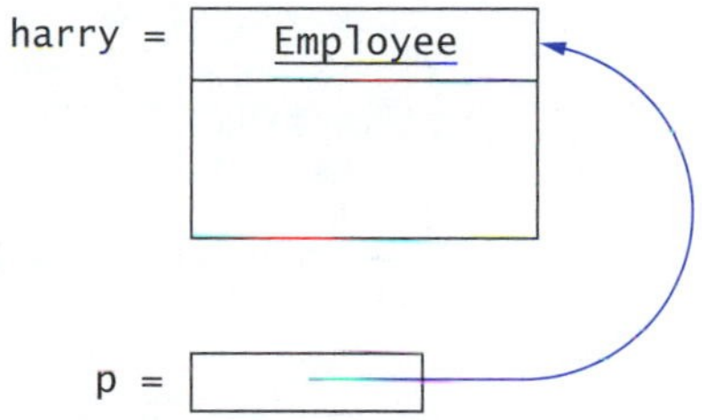

▼

▼

Figure 2

▼ The Address Operator

harry =

Employee

p =

10.3 # Common Uses for Pointers

In the preceding sections, you have seen how to define pointer variables, and how to make them point to dynamically allocated values. In this section, you will learn how pointers can be useful for solving common programming problems.

In our first example, we will model a Department class that describes a department in a company or university, such as the Shipping Department or the Computer Science Department. In our model, a department has

- a name of type string (such as "Shipping")

- an *optional* receptionist of type Employee

We will use a pointer to model the fact that the receptionist is optional:

```
class Department
{
   . . .
private:
   string name;
   Employee* receptionist;
};
```

If a particular department has a receptionist, then the pointer will be set to the address of an employee object. Otherwise, the pointer will be the special value NULL. In the constructor, we set the value to NULL:

```
Department::Department(String n)
{
   name = n;
   receptionist = NULL;
}
```

The set_receptionist function sets the pointer to the address of an employee object:

```
void Department::set_receptionist(Employee* r)
{
   receptionist = r;
}
```

The print function prints either the name of the receptionist or the string "None".

```
void Department::print() const
{
   cout << "Name: " << name
      << "\nReceptionist: ";
   if (receptionist == NULL)
      cout << "None";
   else
       cout << receptionist->get_name();
   cout << "\n";
}
```

Note the use of the -> operator when calling the get_name function. Since receptionist is a pointer, and not an object, it would be an error to use the dot operator.

Here we take advantage of pointers to model a relationship in which one object may refer to 0 or 1 occurrences of another object. Without pointers, it would have been more difficult and less efficient to express the optional nature of the employee object. You might use a Boolean variable and an object, like this:

```
class Department // modeled without pointers
{
   . . .
private:
   string name;
   boolean has_receptionist;
   Employee receptionist;
};
```

Now those department objects that don't have a receptionist still use up storage space for an unused employee object. Clearly, pointers offer a better solution.

Another common use of pointers is *sharing*. Some departments may have a receptionist and a secretary; in others, one person does double duty. Rather than duplicating objects, we can use pointers to share the object (see Figure 3).

```
class Department
{
    ...
private:
    string name;
    Employee* receptionist;
    Employee* secretary;
};
```

Sharing is particularly important when changes to the object need to be observed by all users of the object. Consider, for example, the following code sequence:

```
Employee* tina = new Employee("Tester, Tina", 50000);
Department qc("Quality Control");
qc.set_receptionist(tina);
qc.set_secretary(tina);
tina->set_salary(55000);
```

Now there are three pointers to the employee object: `tina` and the `receptionist` and `secretary` pointers in the `qc` object. When raising the salary, the new salary is set in the shared object, and the changed salary is visible from all three pointers.

In contrast, we might have modeled the department with two employee objects, like this:

```
class Department // modeled without pointers
{
    . . .
private:
    string name;
    Employee receptionist;
    Employee secretary;
};
```

Now consider the equivalent code:

```
Employee tina("Tester, Tina", 50000);
Department qc("Quality Control");
qc.set_receptionist(tina);
qc.set_secretary(tina);
tina.set_salary(55000);
```

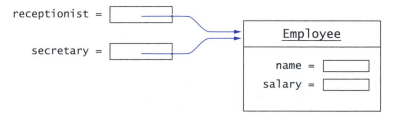

Figure 3

Two Pointers Share an
Employee Object

Figure 4

Three Separate Employee Objects

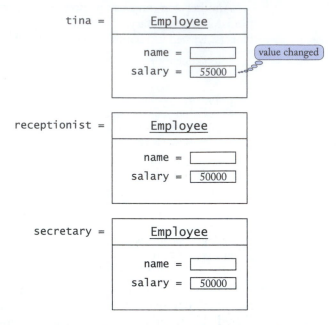

The department object contains two copies of the tina object. When raising the salary, the copies are not affected (see Figure 4).

This example shows that pointers are very useful to model a "*n* : 1" relationship, in which a number of different variables share the same object.

In Chapter 11, you will see another use of pointers, in which a pointer can refer to objects of varying types. That phenomenon, called *polymorphism*, is an important part of object-oriented programming.

The following program gives a complete implementation of the Department class. Note how the pointers are used to express optional and shared objects.

File department.cpp

```
 1 #include <string>
 2 #include <iostream>
 3
 4 using namespace std;
 5
 6 #include "ccc_empl.h"
 7
 8 /**
 9     A department in an organization.
10 */
11 class Department
12 {
13 public:
14    Department(string n);
15    void set_receptionist(Employee* e);
16    void set_secretary(Employee* e);
17    void print() const;
18 private:
```

```
19      string name;
20      Employee* receptionist;
21      Employee* secretary;
22  };
23
24  /**
25      Constructs a department with a given name.
26      @param n  the department name
27  */
28  Department::Department(string n)
29  {
30      name = n;
31      receptionist = NULL;
32      secretary = NULL;
33  }
34
35  /**
36      Sets the receptionist for this department.
37      @param e  the receptionist
38  */
39  void Department::set_receptionist(Employee* e)
40  {
41      receptionist = e;
42  }
43
44  /**
45      Sets the secretary for this department.
46      @param e  the secretary
47  */
48  void Department::set_secretary(Employee* e)
49  {
50      secretary = e;
51  }
52
53  /**
54      Prints a description of this department.
55  */
56  void Department::print() const
57  {
58      cout << "Name: " << name
59          << "\nReceptionist: ";
60      if (receptionist == NULL)
61         cout << "None";
62      else
63         cout << receptionist->get_name() << " "
64             << receptionist->get_salary();
65      cout << "\nSecretary: ";
66      if (secretary == NULL)
67         cout << "None";
68      else if (secretary == receptionist)
69         cout << "Same";
70      else
71         cout << secretary->get_name() << " "
72             << secretary->get_salary();
73      cout << "\n";
74  }
```

```
75
76  int main()
77  {
78      Department shipping("Shipping");
79      Department qc("Quality Control");
80      Employee* harry = new Employee("Hacker, Harry", 45000);
81      shipping.set_secretary(harry);
82      Employee* tina = new Employee("Tester, Tina", 50000);
83      qc.set_receptionist(tina);
84      qc.set_secretary(tina);
85      tina->set_salary(55000);
86      shipping.print();
87      qc.print();
88
89      return 0;
90  }
```

Advanced Topic   10.3

References

In Section 5.8, you saw how to use *reference parameters* in functions that modify variables. For example, consider the function

```
void raise_salary(Employee& e, double by)
{
    double new_salary = e.get_salary() * (1 + by / 100);
    e.set_salary(new_salary);
}
```

This function modifies the first parameter but not the second. That is, if you call the function as

```
raise_salary(harry, percent);
```

then the value of harry may change, but the value of percent is unaffected.

A reference is a pointer in disguise. The function receives two parameters: the address of an Employee object and a copy of a double value. The function is logically equivalent to

```
void raise_salary(Employee* pe, double by)
{
    double new_salary = pe->get_salary() * (1 + by / 100);
    pe->set_salary(new_salary);
}
```

The function call is equivalent to the call

```
raise_salary(&harry, percent);
```

This is an example of sharing: the pointer variable in the function modifies the original object, and not a copy.

When you use references, the compiler automatically passes parameter addresses and dereferences the pointer parameters in the function body. For that reason, references are more convenient for the programmer than explicit pointers.

10.4   Arrays and Pointers

There is an intimate connection between arrays and pointers in C++. Consider this declaration of an array:

```
int a[10];
```

The value of a is a pointer to the starting element (see Figure 5).

```
int* p = a; // now p points to a[0]
```

You can dereference a by using the * operator: The statement

```
*a = 12;
```

has the same effect as the statement

```
a[0] = 12;
```

Moreover, pointers into arrays support *pointer arithmetic*. You can add an integer offset to the pointer to point at another array location. For example,

```
a + 3
```

is a pointer to the array element with index 3. Dereferencing that pointer yields the element a[3]. In fact, for any integer n, it is true that

```
a[n] == *(a + n)
```

This relationship is called the *array/pointer duality law*.

This law explains why all C++ arrays start with an index of zero. The pointer a (or a + 0) points to the starting element of the array. That element must therefore be a[0].

The connection between arrays and pointers becomes even more important when considering array parameters of functions. Consider the maximum function from Section 9.5.2.

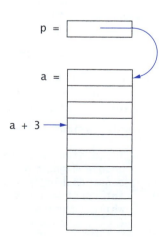

Figure 5

Pointers into an Array

```
double maximum(const double a[], int a_size)
{
   if (a_size == 0) return 0;
   double highest = a[0];
   int i;
   for (i = 0; i < a_size; i++)
      if (a[i] > highest)
         highest = a[i];
   return highest;
}
```

Call this function with a particular array:

```
double data[10];
. . . // initialize data
double m = maximum(data, 10);
```

Note the value data that is passed to the maximum function. It is actually a pointer to the starting element of the array. In other words, the maximum function could have equally well been declared as

```
double maximum(const double* a, int a_size)
{
   . . .
}
```

The const modifier indicates that the pointer a can only be used for reading, not for writing.

The parameter declaration of the first example

```
const double a[]
```

is merely another way of declaring a pointer parameter. The declaration gives the illusion that an entire array is passed to the function, but in fact the function receives only the starting address for the array.

It is essential that the function also knows where the array ends. The second parameter a_size indicates the size of the array that starts at a.

▼ **Advanced Topic**   **10.4**

▼

Using a Pointer to Step through an Array

▼

Now that you know that the first parameter of the maximum function is a pointer, you can implement the function in a slightly different way. Rather than incrementing an integer index, you can increment a pointer variable to visit all array elements in turn:

▼

```
double maximum(const double* a, int a_size)
{
   if (a_size == 0) return 0;
   double highest = *a;
   const double* p = a + 1;
   int count = a_size - 1;
   while (count > 0)
   {
```

▼

```
        if (*p > highest)
            highest = *p;
        p++;
        count--;
    }
    return highest;
}
```

Initially, the pointer p points to the element a[1]. The increment

```
p++;
```

moves it to point to the next element (see Figure 6).

It is a tiny bit more efficient to dereference and increment a pointer than to access an array element as a[i]. For this reason, some programmers routinely use pointers instead of indexes to access array elements. However, the efficiency gain is quite insignificant, and the resulting code is harder to understand, so it is not recommended. (See also Quality Tip 10.1.)

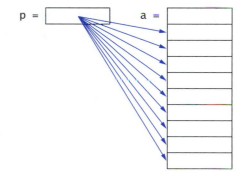

Figure 6

A Pointer Variable Traversing the
Elements of an Array

Quality Tip   10.1

Program Clearly, not Cleverly

Some programmers take great pride in minimizing the number of instructions, even if the resulting code is hard to understand. For example, here is a legal implementation of the maximum function:

```
double maximum(const double* a, int a_size)
{
    if (a_size == 0) return 0;
    double highest = *a;
    while (--a_size > 0)
        if (*++a > highest)
            highest = *a;
    return highest;
}
```

This implementation uses two tricks. First, the function parameters a and a_size are variables, and it is legal to modify them. Moreover, the expressions

```
--a_size
```

and

```
++a
```

mean "decrement or increment the variable and return the new value". Therefore, *++a is the location to which a points after it has been incremented.

Please do not use this programming style. Your job as a programmer is not to dazzle other programmers with your cleverness, but to write code that is easy to understand and maintain.

⊗ Common Error   10.5

Confusing Array and Pointer Declarations

It can be confusing to tell whether a particular variable declaration yields a pointer variable or an array variable. There are four cases:

```
int* p; // p is a pointer
int a[10]; // a is an array
int a[] = { 2, 3, 5, 7, 11, 13 }; // a is an array
void f(int a[]); // a is a pointer
```

In the first case, you must initialize p to point somewhere before you use it.

⊗ Common Error   10.6

Returning a Pointer to a Local Array

Consider this function that tries to return a pointer to an array containing two elements, the minimum and the maximum value of an array.

```
double* minmax(const double a[], int a_size)
{
   assert(a_size > 0);
   double result[2];
   result[0] = a[0]; /* result[0] is the minimum */
   result[1] = a[0]; /* result[1] is the maximum */

   for (int i = 0; i < a_size; i++)
   {
      if (a[i] < result[0]) result[0] = a[i];
      if (a[i] > result[1]) result[1] = a[i];
   }
   return result; // ERROR!
}
```

The function returns a pointer to the starting element of the `result` array. However, that array is a local variable of the `minmax` function. The local variable is no longer valid when the function exits, and the values will soon be overwritten by other functions calls.

Unfortunately, it depends on various factors when the values are overwritten. Consider this test of the flawed `minmax` function:

```
double a[] = { 3, 5, 10, 2 };
double* mm = minmax(a, 4);
cout << mm[0] << " " << mm[1] << "\n";
```

One compiler yields the expected result:

```
2 10
```

However, another compiler yields:

```
1.78747e-307 10
```

It just happens that the other compiler chose a different implementation of the `iostream` library that involved more function calls, thereby clobbering the `result[0]` value sooner.

It is possible to work around this limitation, by returning a pointer to an array that is allocated on the heap. But the best solution is to avoid arrays and pointers altogether and to use vectors instead. As you have seen in Chapter 9, a function can easily and safely receive and return `vector<double>` objects:

```
vector<double> minmax(const vector<double>& a)
{
    assert (a.size() > 0);
    vector<double> result(2);
    result[0] = a[0]; /* result[0] is the minimum */
    result[1] = a[0]; /* result[1] is the maximum */

    for (int i = 0; i < a.size(); i++)
    {
        if (a[i] < result[0]) result[0] = a[i];
        if (a[i] > result[1]) result[1] = a[i];
    }
    return result; // OK!
}
```

Advanced Topic 10.5

Dynamically Allocated Arrays

You can allocate arrays of values from the heap. For example,

```
int staff_capacity = . . . .;
Employee* staff = new Employee[staff_capacity];
```

The `new` operator allocates an array of n objects of type `Employee`, each of which is constructed with the default constructor. It returns a pointer to the starting element of the array. Because of array/pointer duality, you can access elements of the array with the `[]` operator: `staff[i]` is the `Employee` element with offset i.

▼ To deallocate the array, you use the `delete[]` operator.

```
delete[] staff;
```

▼ It is an error to deallocate an array with the `delete` operator (without the `[]`). However, the compiler can't detect this error—it doesn't remember whether a pointer variable points to a single object or to an array of objects. Therefore, you must be careful and remember which pointer variables point to individual objects and which pointer variables point to arrays.

▼ Heap arrays have one big advantage over array variables. If you declare an array variable, you must specify a fixed array size when you compile the program. But when you allocate an array on the heap, you can choose a different size for each program run.

▼ If you later need more elements, you can allocate a bigger heap array, copy the elements from the smaller array into the bigger array, and delete the smaller array:

```
int bigger_capacity = 2 * staff_capacity;
Employee* bigger = new Employee[bigger_capacity];
for (int i = 0; i < staff_capacity; i++)
   bigger[i] = staff[i];
delete[] staff;
staff = bigger;
staff_capacity = bigger_capacity;
```

▼ As you can see, heap arrays are more flexible than array variables. However, you should not actually use them in your programs. Use `vector` objects instead. A `vector` contains a pointer to a dynamic array, and it automatically manages it for you.

10.5 Pointers to Character Strings

C++ has two mechanisms for manipulating strings. The `string` class stores an arbitrary sequence of characters and supports many convenient operations such as concatenation and string comparison. However, C++ also inherits a more primitive level of string handling from the C language, in which strings are represented as arrays of `char` values.

While we don't recommend that you use character pointers or arrays in your programs, you occasionally need to interface with functions that receive or return `char*` values. Then you need to know how to convert between `char*` pointers and `string` objects.

In particular, literal strings such as `"Harry"` are actually stored inside `char` arrays, not `string` objects. When you use the literal string `"Harry"` in an expression, the compiler allocates an array of 6 characters (including a `'\0'` terminator—see Section 9.5.3). The value of the string expression is a `char*` pointer to the starting letter. For example, the code

```
string name = "Harry";
```

is equivalent to

```
char* p = "Harry"; // p points to the letter 'H'
name = p;
```

The `string` class has a constructor `string(char*)` that you can use to convert any character pointer or array to a safe and convenient `string` object. That constructor is called whenever you initialize a `string` variable with a `char*` object, as in the preceding example.

Here is another typical scenario. The `tmpnam` function of the standard library yields a unique string that you can use as the name of a temporary file. It returns a `char*` pointer:

```
char* p = tmpnam(NULL);
```

Simply turn the `char*` return value into a `string` object:

```
string name = p;
```

or

```
string name(p);
```

Conversely, some functions require a parameter of type `char*`. Then use the `c_str` member function of the `string` class to obtain a `char*` pointer that points to the first character in the string object.

For example, the `tempnam` function in the standard library, which also yields a name for a temporary file, lets the caller specify a directory. (Note that the `tmpnam` and `tempnam` function names are confusingly similar.) The `tempnam` function expects a `char*` parameter for the directory name. You can therefore call it as follows:

```
string dir = . . .;
char* p = tempnam(dir.c_str(), NULL);
```

As you can see, you don't have to use character arrays to interface with functions that use `char*` pointers. Simply use `string` objects and convert between `string` and `char*` types when necessary.

⊗ Common Error   10.7

Confusing Character Pointers and Arrays

Consider the pointer declaration

```
char* p = "Harry";
```

Note that this declaration is entirely different from the array declaration

```
char s[] = "Harry";
```

The second declaration is just a shorthand for

```
char s[6] = { 'H', 'a', 'r', 'r', 'y', '\0' };
```

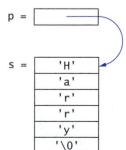

Figure 7

Character Pointers and Arrays

The variable p is a pointer that points to the starting character of the string. The characters of the string are stored elsewhere, not in p. In contrast, the variable s is an array of six characters. Perhaps confusingly, when used inside an expression, s denotes a pointer to the starting character in the array. But there is an important difference: p is a pointer *variable* that you can set to another character location. But the value s is *constant*—it always points to the same location. See Figure 7.

Common Error   10.8

Copying Character Pointers

There is an important difference between copying string objects and pointers of type char*. Consider this example:

```
string s = "Harry";
string t = s;
t[0] = 'L'; // now s is "Harry" and t is "Larry"
```

After copying s into t, the string object t contains a copy of the characters of s. Modifying t has no effect on s. However, copying character pointers has a completely different effect:

```
char* p = "Harry";
char* q = p;
q[0] = 'L'; // now both p and q point to "Larry"
```

After copying p into q, the pointer variable q contains the same memory address as p. The assignment to q[0] overwrites the starting letter in the string to which both p and q point (see Figure 8).

Note that you cannot assign one character array to another. The following assignment is illegal:

```
char a[] = "Harry";
char b[6];
b = a; // ERROR
```

The standard library provides the strcpy function to copy a character array to a new location:

```
strcpy(b, a);
```

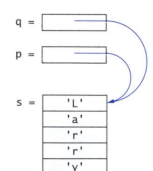

Figure 8

Two Character Pointers into the Same Character Array

▼ The target pointer b must point to an array with sufficient space in it. It is a common beginner's error to try to copy a string into a character array with insufficient space. There is a safer
▼ function, strncpy, with a third parameter that specifies the maximum number of characters to copy:

```
strncpy(b, a, 5);
```

An even worse error is to use an uninitialized pointer variable for the target of the copy:

```
char* p;
strcpy(p, "Harry");
```

This is not a syntax error. The strcpy function expects two character pointers. However, where is the string copied to? The target address p is an uninitialized pointer, pointing to a random location. The characters in the string "Harry" are now copied into that random location, either overwriting whatever was there before or triggering a processor exception that terminates the program.

There is an easy way to avoid this bug. Ask yourself, "Where does the storage for the target string come from?" Character arrays don't magically appear; you have to allocate them. The target of the string copy must be a character array of sufficient size to accommodate the characters.

```
char buffer[100];
strcpy(buffer, "Harry"); // OK
```

As you can see, string handling with character arrays and pointers is tedious and error-prone. The string class was designed to be a safe and convenient alternative. For that reason, we strongly recommend that you use the string class in your own code.

CHAPTER SUMMARY

1. A pointer denotes the location of a value in memory.

2. The * operator locates the value to which a pointer points.

3. Finding the value to which a pointer points is called dereferencing.

4. Use the -> operator to access a data member or a member function through an object pointer.

5. The NULL pointer does not point to any object.

6. It is an error to dereference an uninitialized pointer or the NULL pointer.

7. You can obtain values of any type from the heap with the new operator. You must recycle them with the delete operator.

8. Pointers can be used to model optional values (by using a NULL pointer when the value is not present).

9. Pointers can be used to provide shared access to a common value.

10. The value of an array variable is a pointer to the starting element of the array.

11. Pointer arithmetic means to add an integer offset to an array pointer. The result is a pointer that skips past the given number of elements.

12. The array-pointer duality law states that a[n] is identical to *(a + n), where a is a pointer into an array and n is an integer offset.

13. When passing an array to a function, only the starting address is passed. The parameter declaration *type_name* a[] is equivalent to *type_name** a.

14. Low-level string manipulation functions use pointers of type char*. You can construct string variables from char* pointers, and you can use the c_str member function to obtain a char* pointer from a string object.

REVIEW EXERCISES

Exercise R10.1. Find the mistakes in the following code. Not all lines contain mistakes. Each line depends on the lines preceding it. Watch out for uninitialized pointers, null pointers, pointers to deleted objects, and confusing pointers with objects.

```
1  int* p = new int;
2  p = 5;
3  *p = *p + 5;
4  Employee e1 = new Employee("Hacker, Harry", 34000);
5  Employee e2;
6  e2->set_salary(38000);
7  delete e2;
8  Time* pnow = new Time();
9  Time* t1 = new Time(2, 0, 0);
10 cout << t1->seconds_from(pnow);
11 delete *t1;
12 cout << t1->get_seconds();
13 Employee* e3 = new Employee("Lin, Lisa", 68000);
14 cout << c.get_salary();
15 Time* t2 = new Time(1, 25, 0);
16 cout << *t2.get_minutes();
17 delete t2;
```

Exercise R10.2. A pointer variable can contain a pointer to a valid object, a pointer to a deleted object, NULL, or a random value. Write code that creates and sets four pointer variables a, b, c, and d to show each of these possibilities.

Exercise R10.3. What happens when you dereference each of the four pointers that you created in the preceding assignment? Write a test program if you are not sure.

Exercise R10.4. What happens if you forget to delete an object that you obtained from the heap? What happens if you delete it twice?

Exercise R10.5. What does the following code print?

```
Employee harry = Employee("Hacker, Harry", 35000);
Employee boss = harry;
Employee* pharry = new Employee("Hacker, Harry", 35000);
Employee* pboss = pharry;
boss.set_salary(45000);
(*pboss).set_salary(45000);
cout << harry.get_salary() << "\n";
cout << boss.get_salary() << "\n";
cout << pharry->get_salary() << "\n";
cout << pboss->get_salary() << "\n";
```

Exercise R10.6. Pointers are addresses and have a numerical value. You can print out the value of a pointer as cout << (unsigned long)(p). Write a program to compare p, p + 1, q, and q + 1, where p is an int* and q is a double*. Explain the results.

Exercise R10.7. In Chapter 2, you saw that you can use a cast (int) to convert a double value to an integer. Explain why casting a double* pointer to an int* pointer doesn't make sense. For example,

```
double values[] = { 2, 3, 5, 7, 11, 13 };
int* p = (int*)values; // why won't this work?
```

Exercise R10.8. Which of the following assignments are legal in C++?

```
void f(int p[])
{
   int* q;
   const int* r;
   int s[10];
   p = q; // 1
   p = r; // 2
   p = s; // 3
   q = p; // 4
   q = r; // 5
   q = s; // 6
   r = p; // 7
   r = q; // 8
   r = s; // 9
   s = p; // 10
   s = q; // 11
   s = r; // 12
}
```

Exercise R10.9. Given the definitions

```
double values[] = { 2, 3, 5, 7, 11, 13 };
double* p = values + 3;
```

explain the meanings of the following expressions:

(a) values[1]

(b) values + 1

(c) *(values + 1)

(d) `p[1]`

(e) `p + 1`

(f) `p - values`

Exercise R10.10. Explain the meanings of the following expressions:

(a) `"Harry" + 1`

(b) `*("Harry" + 2)`

(c) `"Harry"[3]`

(d) `[4]"Harry"`

Exercise R10.11. How can you implement a function `minmax` that computes both the minimum and the maximum of the values in an array of integers and stores the result in an `int[2]` array?

Exercise R10.12. What is the difference between the following two variable definitions?

(a) `char a[] = "Hello";`

(b) `char* b = "Hello";`

Exercise R10.13. What is the difference between the following three variable definitions?

(a) `char* p = NULL;`

(b) `char* q = "";`

(c) `char r[] = { '\0' };`

Exercise R10.14. Consider this program segment:

```
char a[] = "Mary had a little lamb";
char* p = a;
int count = 0;
while (*p != '\0')
{
    count++;
    while (*p != ' ' && *p != '\0') p++;
    while (*p == ' ') p++;
}
```

What is the value of `count` at the end of the outer `while` loop?

Exercise R10.15. What are the limitations of the `strcat` and `strncat` functions when compared to the + operator for concatenating `string` objects?

PROGRAMMING EXERCISES

Exercise P10.1. Implement a class `Person` with the following fields:

- the name
- a pointer to the person's best friend (a `Person*`)
- a popularity counter that indicates how many other people have this person as their best friend

Write a program that reads in a list of names, allocates a new Person for each of them, and stores them in a vector<Person*>. Then ask the name of the best friend for each of the Person objects. Locate the object matching the friend's name and call a set_best_friend method to update the pointer and counter. Finally, print out all Person objects, listing the name, best friend, and popularity counter for each.

Exercise P10.2. Implement a class Person with two fields name and age, and a class Car with three fields:

- the model
- a pointer to the owner (a Person*)
- a pointer to the driver (also a Person*)

Write a program that prompts the user to specify people and cars. Store them in a vector<Person*> and a vector<Car*>. Traverse the vector of Person objects and increment their ages by one year. Finally, traverse the vector of cars and print out the car model, owner's name and age, and driver's name and age.

Exercise P10.3. Enhance the Employee class to include a pointer to a BankAccount. Read in employees and their salaries. Store them in a vector<Employee>. For each employee, allocate a new bank account on the heap, except that two consecutive employees with the same last name should share the same account. Then traverse the vector of employees and, for each employee, deposit 1/12th of their annual salary into their bank account. Afterwards, print all employee names and account balances.

Exercise P10.4. Enhance the preceding exercise to delete all bank account objects. Make sure that no object gets deleted twice.

Exercise P10.5. Write a function that computes the average value of an array of floating-point data:

```
double average(double* a, int a_size)
```

In the function, use a pointer variable, and not an integer index, to traverse the array elements.

Exercise P10.6. Write a function that returns a pointer to the maximum value of an array of floating-point data:

```
double* maximum(double a[], int a_size)
```

If a_size is 0, return NULL.

Exercise P10.7. Write a function that reverses the values of an array of floating-point data:

```
void reverse(double a[], int a_size)
```

In the function, use two pointer variables, and not integer indexes, to traverse the array elements.

Exercise P10.8. Implement the strncpy function of the standard library.

Exercise P10.9. Implement the standard library function

```
int strspn(const char s[], const char t[])
```

that returns the length of the prefix of s consisting of characters in t (in any order).

Exercise P10.10. Write a function

```
void reverse(char s[])
```

that reverses a character string. For example, "Harry" becomes "yrraH".

Exercise P10.11. Using the `strncpy` and `strncat` functions, implement a function

```
void concat(const char a[], const char b[], char result[],
    int result_maxlength)
```

that concatenates the strings a and b to the buffer `result`. Be sure not to overrun the result. It can hold `result_maxlength` characters, not counting the '\0' terminator. (That is, the buffer has `result_maxlength` + 1 bytes available.) Be sure to provide a '\0' terminator.

Exercise P10.12. Add a method

```
void Employee::format(char buffer[], int buffer_maxlength)
```

to the `Employee` class. The method should fill the `buffer` with the name and salary of the employee. Be sure not to overrun the buffer. It can hold `buffer_maxlength` characters, not counting the '\0' terminator. (That is, the buffer has `buffer_maxlength` + 1 bytes available.) Be sure to provide a '\0' terminator.

Exercise P10.13. Write a program that reads lines of text and appends them to a `char buffer[1000]`. Stop after reading 1,000 characters. As you read in the text, replace all newline characters '\n' with '\0' terminators. Establish an array `char* lines[100]`, so that the pointers in that array point to the beginnings of the lines in the text. Only consider 100 input lines if the input has more lines. Then display the lines in reverse order, starting with the last input line.

Exercise P10.14. The preceding program is limited by the fact that it can only handle inputs of 1,000 characters or 100 lines. Remove this limitation as follows. Concatenate the input in one long `string` object. Use the `c_str` method to obtain a `char*` into the string's character buffer. Establish the pointers to the offsets of the beginnings of the lines as a `vector<int>`.

Exercise P10.15. The preceding problem demonstrated how to use the `string` and `vector` classes to implement resizable arrays. In this exercise, you should implement that capability manually. Allocate a buffer of 1,000 characters from the heap (`new char[1000]`). Whenever the buffer fills up, allocate a buffer of twice the size, copy the buffer contents, and delete the old buffer. Do the same for the array of `char*` pointers—start with a `new char*[100]` and keep doubling the size.

Inheritance

In this chapter you will learn two of the most important concepts in object-oriented programming: inheritance and polymorphism. Through inheritance, you will be able to define new classes that are extensions of existing classes.

Polymorphism allows you to take advantage of the commonality between related classes, while still giving each class the flexibility to implement specific behavior. Using polymorphism, it is possible to build very flexible and extensible systems.

CHAPTER CONTENTS

11.1   Derived Classes

Inheritance is a mechanism for enhancing existing, working classes. If a new class needs to be implemented and a class representing a more general concept is already available, then the new class can *inherit* from the existing class. For example, suppose we need to define a class `Manager`. We already have a class `Employee`, and a manager is a special case of an employee. In this case, it makes sense to use the language construct of inheritance. Here is the syntax for the class definition:

```
class Manager : public Employee
{
public:
    new member functions
private:
    new data members
};
```

The : symbol denotes inheritance. The keyword `public` is required for a technical reason (see Common Error 11.1).

In the `Manager` class definition you specify only new member functions and data members. All member functions and data members of the `Employee` class are automatically inherited by the `Manager` class. For example, the `set_salary` function automatically applies to managers:

```
Manager m;
m.set_salary(68000);
```

Some more terminology must be introduced here. The existing, more general class is called the *base class*. The more specialized class that inherits from the base class is called the *derived class*. In our example, `Employee` is the base class and `Manager` is the derived class. The general form of the definition of a derived class is shown in Syntax 11.1.

Figure 1 is a *class diagram* showing the relationship between these classes. In the preceding chapters, our diagrams focused on individual objects, which were drawn as rectangular forms that contained boxes for the class name and the data members. Since inheritance is a relationship between classes, not objects, we show two simple boxes joined by an arrow with a hollow head, which indicates inheritance.

Syntax 11.1 : Derived Class Definition

```
class Derived_class_name : public Base_class_name
{
   features
};
```

Example:
```
class Manager : public Employee
   {
   public:
      Manager(string name, double salary, string dept);
      string get_department() const;
   private:
      string department;
   };
```

Purpose: Define a class that inherits features from a base class.

To better understand the mechanics of programming with inheritance, consider a more interesting programming problem: modeling a set of clocks that display the times in different cities.

Start with a base class Clock that can tell the current local time. In the constructor, you can set the format to either "military format" (such as 21:05) or "am/pm" format (such as 9:05 pm). You then call the functions

```
int get_hours() const
int get_minutes() const
```

to get the hours and minutes. In military format, the hours range from 0 to 23. In "am/pm" format, the hours range from 1 to 12. You can use the function

```
bool is_military() const
```

to test whether the clock uses military time format. Finally, the function

```
string get_location() const
```

returns the fixed string "Local". We will later redefine it to return a string that indicates the location of the clock.

The following program demonstrates the Clock class. The program constructs two Clock objects that display the time in both formats. If you run the program and wait a

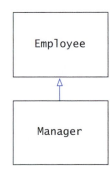

Figure 1

An Inheritance Diagram

minute before answering y to the prompt, you can see that the clock advances. Here is a typical program run:

```
Military time: 21:05
am/pm time: 9:05
Try again? (y/n) y
Military time: 21:06
am/pm time: 9:06
Try again? (y/n) n
```

File clocks1.cpp

```
1  #include <iostream>
2  #include <iomanip>
3  #include <string>
4
5  using namespace std;
6
7  #include "ccc_time.h"
8
9  class Clock
10 {
11 public:
12    /**
13       Constructs a clock that can tell the local time.
14       @param use_military true if the clock uses military format
15    */
16    Clock(bool use_military);
17
18    /**
19       Gets the location of this clock.
20       @return the location
21    */
22    string get_location() const;
23
24    /**
25       Gets the hours of this clock.
26       @return the hours, in military or am/pm format
27    */
28    int get_hours() const;
29
30    /**
31       Gets the minutes of this clock.
32       @return the minutes
33    */
34    int get_minutes() const;
35
36    /**
37       Checks whether this clock uses miltary format.
38       @return true if miltary format
39    */
40    bool is_military() const;
41 private:
42    bool military;
43 };
44
```

```
 45  Clock::Clock(bool use_military)
 46  {
 47     military = use_military;
 48  }
 49
 50  string Clock::get_location() const
 51  {
 52     return "Local";
 53  }
 54
 55  int Clock::get_hours() const
 56  {
 57     Time now;
 58     int hours = now.get_hours();
 59     if (military) return hours;
 60     if (hours == 0)
 61        return 12;
 62     else if (hours > 12)
 63        return hours - 12;
 64     else
 65        return hours;
 66  }
 67
 68  int Clock::get_minutes() const
 69  {
 70     Time now;
 71     return now.get_minutes();
 72  }
 73
 74  bool Clock::is_military() const
 75  {
 76     return military;
 77  }
 78
 79  int main()
 80  {
 81     Clock clock1(true);
 82     Clock clock2(false);
 83
 84     bool more = true;
 85     while (more)
 86     {
 87        cout << "Military time: "
 88           << clock1.get_hours() << ":"
 89           << setw(2) << setfill('0')
 90           << clock1.get_minutes()
 91           << setfill(' ') << "\n";
 92        cout << "am/pm time: "
 93           << clock2.get_hours() << ":"
 94           << setw(2) << setfill('0')
 95           << clock2.get_minutes()
 96           << setfill(' ') << "\n";
 97
 98        cout << "Try again? (y/n) ";
 99        string input;
100        getline(cin, input);
```

```
101        if (input != "y") more = false;
102     }
103     return 0;
104 }
```

Now form a derived class `TravelClock` that can show the time in another location. Consider how travel clocks are different from basic `Clock` objects. Travel clocks store city names, and they show the time in those cities. The time is computed by taking the local time and adding the time difference between the local time and the time at the other location. For example, suppose the local time is Pacific Standard Time. Then you can make a clock for traveling to New York as follows:

```
TravelClock clock(true, "New York", 3);
cout << "The time in " << clock.get_location() << " is "
    << clock.get_hours() << ":" << clock.get_minutes();
```

The value 3 in the constructor denotes the fact that the time in New York is 3 hours ahead of Pacific Standard Time.

A `TravelClock` object differs from a `Clock` object in three ways:

- Its objects store the location and time difference.

- The `get_hours` function of the `TravelClock` adds the time difference to the current time.

- The `get_location` function returns the actual location, not the string `"Local"`.

When the `TravelClock` class inherits from the `Clock` class, it needs only to spell out these three differences:

```
class TravelClock : public Clock
{
public:
    TravelClock(bool mil, string loc, int diff);
    int get_hours() const;
    string get_location() const;
private:
    string location;
    int time_difference;
};
```

Figure 2 shows the inheritance diagram.

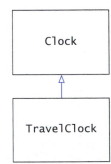

Figure 2

Inheritance Diagram for Clocks

Figure 3

Data Layout of
Derived Object

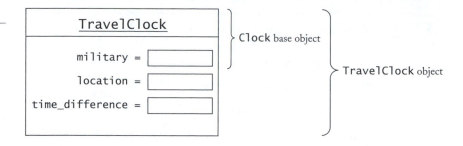

Figure 3 shows the layout of a `TravelClock` object. It inherits the `military` data field from the `Clock` base object, and it gains two additional data fields: `location` and `time_difference`.

It is important to note that the data members of the base class (such as the `military` field in our example) are present in each derived-class object, but they are not *accessible* by the member functions of the derived class. Since these fields are private data of the base class, only the base class has access to them. The derived class has no more access rights than any other class. In particular, none of the `TravelClock` member functions can access the `military` field.

Common Error   11.1

Private Inheritance

It is a common error to forget the keyword `public` that must follow the colon after the derived-class name.

```
class Manager : Employee /* Error */
{
    ...
};
```

The class definition will compile. The `Manager` still inherits from `Employee`, but it inherits *privately.* That is, only the member functions of `Manager` get to call member functions of `Employee`. Whenever you invoke an `Employee` member function on a `Manager` object elsewhere, the compiler will flag this as an error:

```
int main()
{
    Manager m;
    ...
    m.set_salary(65000); /* Error */
}
```

This private inheritance is rarely useful. In fact, it violates the spirit of using inheritance in the first place—namely, to create objects that are usable just like the base-class objects. You should always use public inheritance and remember to supply the `public` keyword in the definition of the derived class.

11.2 Calling the Base-Class Constructor

The constructor of a derived class has two tasks:

- Initialize the base object

- Initialize all data members

The second task is fairly straightforward. In order to avoid negative values in the remainder computation of the get_hours function, add 24 to negative time differences until they become positive.

```
TravelClock::TravelClock(bool mil, string loc, int diff)
/* not complete */
{
   location = loc;
   time_difference = diff;
   while (time_difference < 0)
      time_difference = time_difference + 24;
}
```

The first task is not as simple. You must construct the base object and tell it whether to use military time. However, the base class has no member function to set the clock format. The only way to set this value is through the Clock constructor. That is, you must somehow set the base object to

```
Clock(mil)
```

This is a common situation. Frequently, a derived-class constructor must invoke the base-class constructor before initializing the derived-class data. There is a special syntactical construct to denote the base construction:

```
TravelClock::TravelClock(bool mil, string loc, int diff)
   : Clock(mil)
{
   ...
}
```

The line

```
   : Clock(mil)
```

means: Call the Clock constructor with parameter mil before executing the code inside the { }. The colon is supposed to remind you of inheritance.

In general, the syntax for a derived-class constructor is shown in Syntax 11.2. (Actually, as explained in Advanced Topic 6.1, the same syntax can be used to invoke data field constructors as well, but then you place the name of the data field, not the name of the base class, after the colon. In this book, we choose not to use that syntax to initialize data fields.)

If you omit the base-class constructor, then the base object is constructed with the default constructor of the base class. However, if the base class has no default constructor (such as the Clock class), then you have to explicitly call the base-class constructor in the derived-class constructor.

> **Syntax 11.2 : Constructor with Base-Class Initializer**
>
> *Derived_class_name*::*Derived_class_name*(*expressions*)
>   : *Base_class_name*(*expressions*)
> {
>   *statements*
> }
>
> **Example:** `Manager::Manager(string name, double salary, string dept)`
>   `: Employee(name, salary)`
>   `{`
>   `department = dept;`
>   `}`
>
> **Purpose:** Supply the implementation of a constructor, initializing the base class before the body of the derived-class constructor.

11.3   Calling Base-Class Member Functions

Implement the `get_hours` function of the `TravelClock` class. To get the hour value, you need to

- Get the hour value of the local time
- Adjust it by the time difference

Here is the pseudocode for the function.

```
int TravelClock::get_hours() const
{
   int h = local hour value;
   if (clock uses military time)
      return (h + time_difference) % 24;
   else
   {
      h = (h + time_difference) % 12;
      if (h == 0) return 12;
      else return h;
   }
}
```

First determine how to find out whether the clock uses military time. You can't just access the `military` field in the base class. While it is true that each object of type `TravelClock` inherits the `military` data field from the `Clock` base class, accessing this data field is not allowed. It is private to `Clock` and only accessible through the `Clock` member functions.

Fortunately, the `Clock` class has a member function, `is_military`, that reports the value of the `military` flag. You can call that member function. On which object? The clock that you are currently querying—that is, the implicit parameter of the `TravelClock::get_hours` function. As you saw in Chapter 6, if you invoke another member function on the implicit parameter, you don't specify the parameter but just write the member function name:

```
if (is_military()) ...
```

The compiler interprets

```
is_military()
```

as

```
implicit parameter.is_military();
```

Note that the is_military function is inherited from the base class, so you can call it through the *implicit parameter* object of the derived class.

But how do you get the local hour value? You can ask the get_hours function of the base class. Thus, you have to invoke get_hours:

```
int TravelClock::get_hours() const
{
    int h = get_hours(); /* not complete */
    ...
}
```

But this won't quite work. Because the implicit parameter of TravelClock::get_hours is of type TravelClock, and there is a function named get_hours in the TravelClock class, that function will be called—but that is just the function you are currently writing! The function would call itself over and over, and the program would die in an infinite recursion.

Instead, you must be more specific which function named get_hours you want to call. You want Clock::get_hours:

```
int TravelClock::get_hours() const
{
    int h = Clock::get_hours();
    ...
}
```

This version of the get_hours member function is correct. To get the hours of a travel clock, first get the hours of its underlying Clock, then add the time difference.

In general, suppose $B::f$ is a function in a base class. Then the derived class D can take three kinds of actions:

- The derived class can *extend* $B::f$ by supplying a new implementation $D::f$ that calls $B::f$. For example, the TravelClock::get_hours function is an extension of Clock::get_hours.

- The derived class can *replace* $B::f$ by supplying a new implementation $D::f$ that is unrelated to $B::f$. For example, the TravelClock::get_location function (which returns the location field) is a replacement for Clock::get_location (which only returns the string "Local").

- The derived class can *inherit* $B::f$, simply by not supplying an implementation for f. For example, the TravelClock class inherits Clock::get_minutes and Clock::is_military.

Here is the complete program that displays a plain `Clock` object and two `TravelClock` objects. As you can see, the `TravelClock` code is quite short. This example shows how you can use inheritance to adapt existing code to a new purpose.

File clocks2.cpp

```
 1 #include <iostream>
 2 #include <iomanip>
 3 #include <string>
 4
 5 using namespace std;
 6
 7 #include "ccc_time.h"
 8
 9 class Clock
10 {
11 public:
12    /**
13        Constructs a clock that can tell the local time.
14        @param use_military true if the clock uses military format
15    */
16    Clock(bool use_military);
17
18    /**
19        Gets the location of this clock.
20        @return the location
21    */
22    string get_location() const;
23
24    /**
25        Gets the hours of this clock.
26        @return the hours, in military or am/pm format
27    */
28    int get_hours() const;
29
30    /**
31        Gets the minutes of this clock.
32        @return the minutes
33    */
34    int get_minutes() const;
35
36    /**
37        Checks whether this clock uses miltary format.
38        @return true if miltary format
39    */
40    bool is_military() const;
41 private:
42    bool military;
43 };
44
45 Clock::Clock(bool use_military)
46 {
47    military = use_military;
48 }
49
50 string Clock::get_location() const
```

```
51  {
52     return "Local";
53  }
54
55  int Clock::get_hours() const
56  {
57     Time now;
58     int hours = now.get_hours();
59     if (military) return hours;
60     if (hours == 0)
61        return 12;
62     else if (hours > 12)
63        return hours - 12;
64     else
65        return hours;
66  }
67
68  int Clock::get_minutes() const
69  {
70     Time now;
71     return now.get_minutes();
72  }
73
74  bool Clock::is_military() const
75  {
76     return military;
77  }
78
79  class TravelClock : public Clock
80  {
81  public:
82     /**
83         Constructs a travel clock that can tell the time
84         at a specified location.
85         @param mil true if the clock uses military format
86         @param loc the location
87         @param diff the time difference from the local time
88     */
89     TravelClock(bool mil, string loc, int diff);
90     string get_location() const;
91     int get_hours() const;
92  private:
93     string location;
94     int time_difference;
95  };
96
97  TravelClock::TravelClock(bool mil, string loc, int diff)
98     : Clock(mil)
99  {
100    location = loc;
101    time_difference = diff;
102    while (time_difference < 0)
103       time_difference = time_difference + 24;
104 }
105
106 string TravelClock::get_location() const
```

```
107  {
108     return location;
109  }
110
111  int TravelClock::get_hours() const
112  {
113     int h = Clock::get_hours();
114     if (is_military())
115        return (h + time_difference) % 24;
116     else
117     {
118        h = (h + time_difference) % 12;
119        if (h == 0) return 12;
120        else return h;
121     }
122  }
123
124  int main()
125  {
126     Clock clock1(true);
127     TravelClock clock2(true, "Rome", 9);
128     TravelClock clock3(false, "Tokyo", -7);
129
130     cout << clock1.get_location() << " time: "
131        << clock1.get_hours() << ":"
132        << setw(2) << setfill('0')
133        << clock1.get_minutes()
134        << setfill(' ') << "\n";
135     cout << clock2.get_location() << " time: "
136        << clock2.get_hours() << ":"
137        << setw(2) << setfill('0')
138        << clock2.get_minutes()
139        << setfill(' ') << "\n";
140     cout << clock3.get_location() << " time: "
141        << clock3.get_hours() << ":"
142        << setw(2) << setfill('0')
143        << clock3.get_minutes()
144        << setfill(' ') << "\n";
145     return 0;
146  }
```

11.2 Common Error

Attempting to Access Private Base-Class Fields

A derived class inherits all fields from the base class. However, if the fields are private, the derived-class functions have no rights to access them. For example, suppose the salary of a manager is computed by adding a bonus to the annual salary:

```
double Manager::get_salary() const
{
   return salary + bonus;
      /* Error—salary is private to Employee */
}
```

The `Manager::get_salary` function has no more rights to access the private `Employee` fields than any other function. The remedy is to use the public interface of the base class:

```
double Manager::get_salary() const
{
    return Employee::get_salary() + bonus;
}
```

⊗ Common Error   11.3

Forgetting the Base-Class Name

A common error in extending the functionality of a base-class function is to forget the base-class name. For example, to compute the salary of a manager, get the salary of the underlying `Employee` object and add a bonus:

```
double Manager::get_salary() const
{
    double base_salary = get_salary();
        /* Error—should be Employee::get_salary() */
    return base_salary + bonus;
}
```

Here `get_salary()` refers to the `get_salary` function applied to the implicit parameter of the member function. The implicit parameter is of type `Manager`, and there is a `Manager::get_salary` function, so that function is called. Of course, that is a recursive call to the function that we are writing. Instead, you must be precise which `get_salary` function you want to call. In this case, you need to call `Employee::get_salary` explicitly.

Whenever you call a base-class function from a derived-class function with the same name, be sure to give the full name of the function, including the base-class name.

🎓 Advanced Topic   11.1

Protected Access

You ran into some degree of grief when trying to implement the `get_hours` member function of the `TravelClock` class. That member function needed access to the `military` data field of the base class. Your remedy was to have the base class provide the appropriate accessor function.

C++ offers another solution. The base class can declare the data field as protected:

```
class Clock
{
public:
    ...
protected:
    bool military
};
```

▼ Protected data can be accessed by the member functions of a class and all its derived classes. For example, `TravelClock` inherits from `Clock`, so its member functions can access the protected data fields of the `Clock` class.

▼ Some programmers like the `protected` access feature because it seems to strike a balance between absolute protection (making all data members private) and no protection at all (making all data members public). However, experience has shown that protected data members are subject to the same kind of problems as public data members. The designer of the base class has no control over the authors of derived classes. Any of the derived-class member functions can corrupt the base-class data. Furthermore, classes with protected data members are hard to modify. Even if the author of the base class would like to change the data implementation, the protected data members cannot be changed, because someone might have written a derived class whose code depends on them.

▼ It is best to leave all data private. If you want to grant access to the data only to derived-class member functions, consider making the *accessor* function protected.

11.4 Polymorphism

In the preceding sections you saw one important use of inheritance: to reuse existing code in a new problem. In this section you will see an even more powerful application of inheritance: to model variation in object behavior.

If you look into the `main` program of the preceding program, you will find that there was quite a bit of repetitive code. It would be nicer if all three clocks were collected in an array and one could use a loop to print the clock values:

```
vector<Clock> clocks;
clocks[0] = Clock(true);
clocks[1] = TravelClock(true, "Rome", 9);
clocks[2] = TravelClock(false, "Tokyo", -7);

for (int i = 0; i < clocks.size(); i++)
{
   cout << clocks[i].get_location() << " time: "
      << clocks[i].get_hours() << ":"
      << setw(2) << setfill('0')
      << clocks[i].get_minutes()
      << setfill(' ') << "\n";
}
```

Unfortunately, that does not work. The vector `clocks` holds objects of type `Clock`. The compiler realizes that a `TravelClock` is a special case of a `Clock`. Thus it permits the assignment from a travel clock to a clock:

```
clocks[1] = TravelClock(true, "Rome", 9);
```

However, a `TravelClock` object has three data fields, whereas a `Clock` object has just one field, the `military` flag. There is no room to store the derived-class data. That data simply gets *sliced away* when you assign a derived-class object to a base-class variable (see Figure 4).

If you run the resulting program, the output is:

```
Local time is 21:15
Local time is 21:15
Local time is 9:15
```

This problem is very typical of code that needs to manipulate objects from a mixture of data types. Derived-class objects are usually bigger than base-class objects, and objects of different derived classes have different sizes. A vector of objects cannot deal with this variation in sizes.

Instead, you need to store the actual objects elsewhere and collect their locations in a vector by storing pointers. (If you have skipped Chapter 10, you will now need to turn to Section 10.1 to learn about pointers. You can read that section independently of the remainder of Chapter 10.)

Figure 5 shows the array of pointers. The reason for using pointers is simple: Pointers to the various clock objects all have the same size—namely, the size of a memory address—even though the objects themselves may have different sizes.

Here is the code to set up the array of pointers:

```
vector<Clock*> clocks;
/* populate clocks */
clocks[0] = new Clock(true);
clocks[1] = new TravelClock(true, "Rome", 9);
clocks[2] = new TravelClock(false, "Tokyo", -7);
```

As the highlighted code shows, you simply declare the array to hold pointers, and allocate all objects by calling new.

Note that the last two assignments assign a derived-class pointer of type TravelClock* to a base-class pointer of type Clock*. This is perfectly legal. A pointer is the starting address of an object. Since every TravelClock is a special case of a Clock, the starting address of a TravelClock object is, in particular, the starting address of a Clock object. The reverse assignment—from a base-class pointer to a derived-class pointer—is an error.

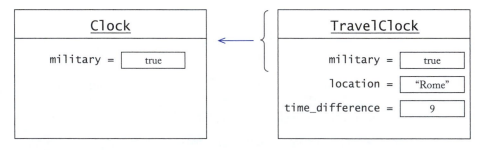

Figure 4

Slicing Away Derived-Class Data

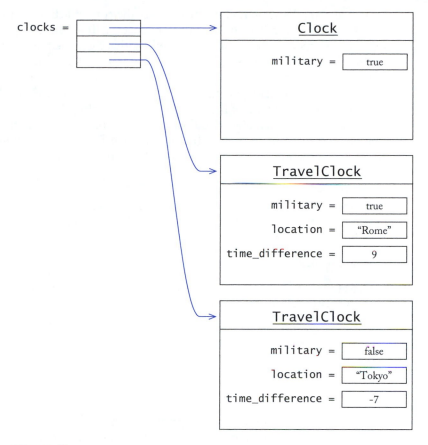

Figure 5

A Polymorphic Array

Of course, `clocks[i]` is a pointer to the `i`th object, not the `i`th object itself. Thus, the code to print all clocks is

```
cout << clocks[i]->get_location() << " time: "
    << clocks[i]->get_hours() << ":"
    << setw(2) << setfill('0')
    << clocks[i]->get_minutes()
    << setfill(' ') << "\n";
```

Note the use of the `->` operators since `clocks[i]` is a pointer.
   Unfortunately, there remains a problem. The output is still

```
Local time is 21:15
Local time is 21:15
Local time is 9:15
```

As you can see, none of the travel clock code was executed. The compiler generated code only to call the `Clock` functions, not the functions that are appropriate for each object.

In the compiler's defense, it actually took the correct action. A member function call is compiled into a call to one particular function. It is the compiler's job to find the appropriate function that should be called. In this case, the pointer `clocks[i]` points to the implicit parameter; it is a pointer of type `Clock*`. Therefore, the compiler calls `Clock` member functions.

However, in this case you really do not want a simple function call. You want first to determine the actual type of the object to which `clocks[i]` points, which can be either a `Clock` or a `TravelClock` object, and then call the appropriate functions. This too can be arranged in C++. You must alert the compiler that the function call needs to be preceded by the appropriate function selection, which can be a different one for every iteration in the loop.

Such a selection/call combination is called *dynamic binding*. In contrast, the traditional call, which always invokes the same function, is called *static binding*. To tell the C++ compiler that a particular function needs to be bound dynamically, the function must be tagged as `virtual`:

```
class Clock
{
public:
   Clock(bool use_military);
   virtual string get_location() const;
   virtual int get_hours() const;
   int get_minutes() const;
   bool is_military() const;
private:
   ...
};
```

The `virtual` keyword must be used in the *base class*. All functions with the same name and parameter types in derived classes are then automatically virtual. However, it is considered good taste to supply the `virtual` keyword for the derived-class functions as well.

Syntax 11.3 : Virtual Function Definition

```
class Class_name
{
   virtual return_type function_name(parameter₁, parameter₂, ..., parameterₙ);
   ...
};
```

Example:
```
class Employee
{
public:
   virtual double get_salary();
   ...
};
```

Purpose: Define a dynamically bound function that can be redefined in derived classes. When the function is called, the actual type of the implicit parameter determines which version of the function executes.

```
class TravelClock : public Clock
{
public:
    TravelClock(bool mil, string loc, int diff);
    virtual string get_location() const;
    virtual int get_hours() const;
private:
    ...
};
```

You do not supply the keyword virtual in the function definition:

```
string Clock::get_location() const /* no virtual keyword */
{
    return "Local";
}
```

Whenever a virtual function is called, the compiler determines the type of the implicit parameter in the particular call at run time. The appropriate function for that object is then called. For example, when the get_location function is declared virtual, the call

```
clocks[i]->get_location();
```

always calls the function belonging to the actual type of the object to which clocks[i] points—either Clock::get_location or TravelClock::get_location.

Only member functions can be virtual. A member function that is not tagged as virtual is statically bound. That is, the type of the implicit parameter, as it is known at compile time, is used to select one function, and that function is always called. Because static binding is less complex, it is the default in C++. You should use virtual functions only when you need the flexibility of dynamic binding at run time.

The clocks vector collects a mixture of both kinds of clock. Such a collection is called *polymorphic* (literally, "of multiple shapes"). Objects in a polymorphic collection have some commonality but are not necessarily of the same type. Inheritance is used to express this commonality, and virtual functions enable variations in behavior.

Virtual functions give programs a great deal of flexibility. The printing loop describes only the general mechanism: "Print the location, hours, and minutes of each clock". Each object knows on its own how to carry out the specific tasks: "Get your location" and "Get your hours".

Using virtual functions makes programs *easily extensible*. Suppose we want to have a new kind of clock for space travel. All we need to do is to define a new class SpaceTravelClock, with its own get_location and get_hours functions. Then we can populate the clocks array with a mixture of plain clocks, travel clocks, and space travel clocks. The code that prints all clocks need not be changed at all! The calls to the virtual get_location and get_hours functions automatically select the correct member functions of the newly defined classes.

Here is the complete clock program, using virtual functions. When you run the program, you will find that the three Clock* pointers call the appropriate versions of the virtual functions. A typical printout is:

```
Local time is 21:15
Rome time is 6:15
Tokyo time is 2:15
```

File clocks3.cpp

```
 1  #include <iostream>
 2  #include <iomanip>
 3  #include <string>
 4  #include <vector>
 5
 6  using namespace std;
 7
 8  #include "ccc_time.h"
 9
10  class Clock
11  {
12  public:
13     /**
14         Constructs a clock that can tell the local time.
15         @param use_military true if the clock uses military format
16     */
17     Clock(bool use_military);
18
19     /**
20         Gets the location of this clock.
21         @return  the location
22     */
23     virtual string get_location() const;
24
25     /**
26         Gets the hours of this clock.
27         @return  the hours, in military or am/pm format
28     */
29     virtual int get_hours() const;
30
31     /**
32         Gets the minutes of this clock.
33         @return  the minutes
34     */
35     int get_minutes() const;
36
37     /**
38         Checks whether this clock uses miltary format.
39         @return  true if miltary format
40     */
41     bool is_military() const;
42  private:
43     bool military;
44  };
45
46  Clock::Clock(bool use_military)
47  {
48     military = use_military;
49  }
50
51  string Clock::get_location() const
52  {
53     return "Local";
54  }
```

```
55
56  int Clock::get_hours() const
57  {
58     Time now;
59     int hours = now.get_hours();
60     if (military) return hours;
61     if (hours == 0)
62        return 12;
63     else if (hours > 12)
64        return hours - 12;
65     else
66        return hours;
67  }
68
69  int Clock::get_minutes() const
70  {
71     Time now;
72     return now.get_minutes();
73  }
74
75  bool Clock::is_military() const
76  {
77     return military;
78  }
79
80  class TravelClock : public Clock
81  {
82  public:
83     /**
84        Constructs a travel clock that can tell the time
85        at a specified location.
86        @param mil  true if the clock uses military format
87        @param loc  the location
88        @param diff  the time difference from the local time
89     */
90     TravelClock(bool mil, string loc, int diff);
91     string get_location() const;
92     int get_hours() const;
93  private:
94     string location;
95     int time_difference;
96  };
97
98  TravelClock::TravelClock(bool mil, string loc, int diff)
99     : Clock(mil)
100 {
101    location = loc;
102    time_difference = diff;
103    while (time_difference < 0)
104       time_difference = time_difference + 24;
105 }
106
107 string TravelClock::get_location() const
108 {
109    return location;
110 }
```

```
111
112  int TravelClock::get_hours() const
113  {
114     int h = Clock::get_hours();
115     if (is_military())
116        return (h + time_difference) % 24;
117     else
118     {
119        h = (h + time_difference) % 12;
120        if (h == 0) return 12;
121        else return h;
122     }
123  }
124
125  int main()
126  {
127     vector<Clock*> clocks(3);
128     clocks[0] = new Clock(true);
129     clocks[1] = new TravelClock(true, "Rome", 9);
130     clocks[2] = new TravelClock(false, "Tokyo", -7);
131
132     for (int i = 0; i < clocks.size(); i++)
133     {
134        cout << clocks[i]->get_location() << " time: "
135           << clocks[i]->get_hours() << ":"
136           << setw(2) << setfill('0')
137           << clocks[i]->get_minutes()
138           << setfill(' ') << "\n";
139     }
140     return 0;
141  }
```

⊗ Common Error   11.4

Slicing an Object

In C++ it is legal to copy a derived-class object into a base-class variable. However, any derived-class information is lost in the process. For example, when a Manager object is assigned to a variable of type Employee, the result is only the employee portion of the manager data:

```
Manager m;
...
Employee e = m; /* holds only the Employee base data of m */
```

Any information that is particular to managers is sliced off, because it would not fit into a variable of type Employee. This slicing may indeed be what you want. The code using the variable e may not care about the Manager part of the object and just needs to consider it as an employee.

Note that the reverse assignment is not legal. That is, you cannot copy a base-class object into a derived-class variable.

```
Employee e;
...
Manager m = e; /* Error */
```

Advanced Topic 11.2

Virtual Self-Calls

Add the following `print` function to the `Clock` class:

```
void Clock::print() const
{
    cout << get_location() << " time: "
        << get_hours() << ":"
        << setw(2) << setfill('0')
        << get_minutes()
        << setfill(' ') << "\n";
}
```

Do *not* redefine the `print` function in the `TravelClock` class. Now consider the call

```
TravelClock rome_clock(true, "Rome", 9);
rome_clock.print();
```

Which `get_location` and `get_hours` function will the `print` function call? If you look inside the code of the `Clock::print` function, you can see that these functions are executed on the implicit object.

```
void Clock::print() const
{
    cout << implicit parameter.get_location() << " time: "
        << implicit parameter.get_hours() << ":"
        << setw(2) << setfill('0')
        << implicit parameter.get_minutes()
        << setfill(' ') << "\n";
}
```

The implicit parameter in our call is `rome_clock`, an object of type `TravelClock`. Because the `get_location` and `get_hours` functions are virtual, the `TravelClock` versions of the function are called automatically. This happens even though the `print` function is defined in the `Clock` class, which has no knowledge of the `TravelClock` class.

As you can see, virtual functions are a very powerful mechanism. The `Clock` class supplies a `print` function that specifies the common nature of printing, namely to print the location and time. How the location and time are determined is left to the derived classes.

Random Fact 11.1

Operating Systems

Without an operating system, a computer would not be useful. Minimally, you need an operating system to locate files and to start programs. The programs that you run need services from the operating system to access devices and to interact with other programs. Operating systems on large computers need to provide more services than those on personal computers.

Here are some typical services:

- *Program loading.* Every operating system provides some way of launching application programs. The user indicates what program should be run, usually by typing in the name of the program or by clicking on an icon. The operating system locates the program code, loads it in memory, and starts it.

- *Managing files.* A storage device such as a hard disk is, electronically, simply a device capable of storing a huge sequence of zeroes and ones. It is up to the operating system to bring some structure to the storage layout and organize it into files, folders, and so on. The operating system also needs to impose some amount of security and redundancy into the file system so that a power outage does not jeopardize the contents of an entire hard disk. Some operating systems do a better job in this regard than others.

- *Virtual memory.* Memory is expensive, and few computers have enough RAM to hold all programs and their data that a user would like to run simultaneously. Most operating systems extend the available memory by storing some data on the hard disk. The application programs do not realize what is happening. When a program accesses a data item that is currently not in memory, the processor senses this and notifies the operating system. The operating system swaps the needed data from the hard disk into RAM, simultaneously swapping out a memory block of equal size that has not been accessed for some time.

- *Handling multiple users.* The operating systems of large and powerful computers allow simultaneous access by multiple users. Each user is connected to the computer through a separate terminal. The operating system authenticates users by checking that they have a valid account and password. It gives each user a small *slice* of processor time, then serves the next user.

- *Multitasking.* Even if you are the sole user of a computer, you may want to run multiple applications—for example, to read your e-mail in one window and run the C++ compiler in another. The operating system is responsible for dividing processor time between the applications you are running, so that each can make progress.

- *Printing.* The operating system queues up the print requests that are sent by multiple applications. This is necessary to make sure that the printed pages do not contain a mixture of words sent simultaneously from separate programs.

- *Windows.* Many operating systems present their users with a desktop made up of multiple windows. The operating system manages the location and appearance of the window frames; the applications are responsible for the interior.

- *Fonts.* To render text on the screen and the printer, the shapes of characters must be defined. This is especially important for programs that can display multiple type styles and sizes. Modern operating systems contain a central font repository.

- *Communicating between programs.* The operating system can facilitate the transfer of information between programs. That transfer can happen through *cut and paste* or *interprocess communication.* Cut and paste is a user-initiated data transfer in which the user copies data from one application into a transfer buffer (often called a "clipboard") managed by the operating system and inserts the buffer's contents into another application. Interprocess communication is initiated by applications that transfer data without direct user involvement.

▼   • *Networking.* The operating system provides protocols and services for enabling applications to reach information on other computers attached to the network.

▼ Today, the most popular operating systems are Microsoft Windows, UNIX and its variants
(such as Linux), and the Macintosh OS.

CHAPTER SUMMARY

1. Inheritance is a mechanism for extending classes. When a derived class inherits
   from a base class, the derived class defines only the data fields and functions that are
   specific to it.

2. The derived class inherits from the base class all data fields and all functions that it
   does not redefine.

3. The constructor of a derived class can pass parameters to the constructor of the base
   class. If no parameters are passed explicitly, the default constructor of the base class
   is invoked.

4. The derived class can choose to replace functions from the base class, either by completely redefining them or by extending them. When extending a function in a
   derived class, you explicitly call the base-class function.

5. Virtual functions are bound dynamically. When a virtual function is called, the
   actual type of the implicit parameter object determines which implementation of the
   virtual function is invoked.

6. In contrast, all other function calls are statically bound. The compiler determines
   which function is called, by looking only at the type of the implicit parameter
   variable.

7. Polymorphism (literally, "having multiple shapes") describes a set of objects of different classes with similar behavior. Inheritance is used to express the commonality
   between the classes, and virtual functions enable variations in behavior.

REVIEW EXERCISES

Exercise R11.1. An object-oriented traffic simulation system has the following classes:

```
Vehicle     PickupTruck
Car         SportUtilityVehicle
Truck       Minivan
Sedan       Bicycle
Coupe       Motorcycle
```

Draw an inheritance diagram that shows the relationships between these classes.

Exercise R11.2. What inheritance relationships would you establish among the following classes?

```
Student
Professor
TeachingAssistant
Employee
Secretary
DepartmentChair
Janitor
SeminarSpeaker
Person
Course
Seminar
Lecture
ComputerLab
```

Exercise R11.3. Consider the following classes B and D:

```
class B
{
public:
   B();
   B(int n);
};

B::B()
{
   cout << "B::B()\n";
}
B::B(int n)
{
   cout << "B::B(" << n << ")\n";
}

class D : public B
{
public:
   D();
   D(int n);
private:
   B b;
};

D::D()
{
   cout << "D::D()\n";
}
D::D(int n) : B(n)
{
```

```
   b = B(-n); cout << "D::D("<< n <<")\n";
}
```

What does the following program print?

```
int main()
{
   D d(3);
   return 0;
}
```

Determine the answer by hand, not by compiling and running the program.

Exercise R11.4. What does the following program print?

```
class B
{
public:
   void print(int n) const;
};

void B::print(int n) const
{
   cout << n << "\n";
}

class D : public B
{
public:
   void print(int n) const;
};

void D::print(int n) const
{
   if (n <= 1) B::print(n);
   else if (n % 2 == 0) print(n / 2);
   else print(3 * n + 1);
}

int main()
{
   D d;
   d.print(3);
   return 0;
}
```

Determine the answer by hand, not by compiling and running the program.

Exercise R11.5. What is wrong with the following code?

```
class B
{
public:
   B();
   B(int n);
   void print() const;
private:
   int b;
```

```
};

B::B()
{
    b = 0;
}
B::B(int n)
{
    b = n;
}
void B::print() const
{
    cout << "B: " << b << "\n";
}

class D : public B
{
public:
    D();
    D(int n);
    void print() const;
};

D::D()
{
}
D::D(int n)
{
    b = n;
}
void D::print() const
{
    cout << "D: " << b << "\n";
}
```

How can you fix the errors?

Exercise R11.6. Suppose the class D inherits from B. Which of the following assignments are legal?

```
B  b;
D  d;
B* pb;
D* pd;
```

(a)   b = d;

(b)   d = b;

(c)   pd = pb;

(d)   pb = pd;

(e)   d = pd;

(f)   b = *pd;

(g)   *pd = *pb;

Exercise R11.7. Which of the following calls are statically bound, and which are dynamically bound? What does the program print?

```cpp
class B
{
public:
    B();
    virtual void p() const;
    void q() const;
};

B::B()
void B::p() const
{
    cout << "B::p\n";
}
void B::q() const
{
    cout << "B::q\n";
}

class D : public B
{
public:
    D();
    virtual void p() const;
    void q() const;
};

D::D()
{
}
void D::p() const
{
    cout << "D::p\n";
}
void D::q() const
{
    cout << "D::q\n";
}

int main()
{
    B b;
    D d;
    B* pb = new B;
    B* pd = new D;
    D* pd2 = new D;

    b.p(); b.q();
    d.p(); d.q();
    pb->p(); pb->q();
    pd->p(); pd->q();
    pd2->p(); pd2->q();
    return 0;
}
```

Determine the answer by hand, not by compiling and running the program.

Exercise R11.8. True or false?

(a) When a member function is invoked through a pointer, it is always statically bound.

(b) When a member function is invoked through an object, it is always statically bound.

(c) Only member functions can be dynamically bound.

(d) Only nonmember functions can be statically bound.

(e) When a function is virtual in the base class, it cannot be made nonvirtual in a derived class.

(f) Calling a virtual function is slower than calling a nonvirtual function.

(g) Constructors can be virtual.

(h) It is good programming practice to make all member functions virtual.

PROGRAMMING EXERCISES

Exercise P11.1. Derive a class `Programmer` from `Employee`. Supply a constructor `Programmer(string name, double salary)` that calls the base-class constructor. Supply a function `get_name` that returns the name in the format `"Hacker, Harry (Programmer)"`.

Exercise P11.2. Implement a base class `Person`. Derive classes `Student` and `Instructor` from `Person`. A person has a name and a birthday. A student has a major, and an instructor has a salary. Write the class definitions, the constructors, and the member functions `print()` for all classes.

Exercise P11.3. Derive a class `Manager` from `Employee`. Add a data field, named `department`, of type `string`. Supply a function `print` that prints the manager's name, department, and salary. Derive a class `Executive` from `Manager`. Supply a function `print` that prints the string `Executive`, followed by the information stored in the `Manager` base object.

Exercise P11.4. Implement a base class `Account` and derived classes `Savings` and `Checking`. In the base class, supply member functions `deposit` and `withdraw`. Provide a function `daily_interest` that computes and adds the daily interest. For calculations, assume that every month has 30 days. Checking accounts yield interest of 3 percent monthly on balances over $1,000. Savings accounts yield interest of 6 percent on the entire balance. Write a driver program that makes a month's worth of deposits and withdrawals and calculates the interest every day.

Exercise P11.5. Measure the speed difference between a statically bound call and a dynamically bound call. Use the `Time` class to measure the time spent in one loop of virtual function calls and another loop of regular function calls.

Exercise P11.6. Write a base class `Worker` and derived classes `HourlyWorker` and `SalariedWorker`. Every worker has a name and a salary rate. Write a virtual function `compute_pay(int hours)` that computes the weekly pay for every worker. An hourly worker gets paid the hourly wage for the actual number of hours worked, if `hours` is at most 40. If the hourly worker worked more than 40 hours, the excess is paid at time and a half. The salaried worker gets paid the hourly wage for 40 hours, no matter what the actual number of hours is.

Exercise P11.7. Implement a base class `Vehicle` and derived classes `Car` and `Truck`. A vehicle has a position on the screen. Write virtual functions `draw` that draw cars and trucks as follows:

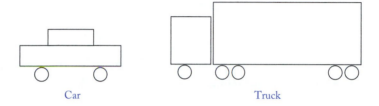

Car   Truck

Then populate a vector of `Vehicle*` pointers with a mixture of cars and trucks, and draw all of them.

Exercise P11.8. Implement a base class `Appointment` and derived classes `Onetime`, `Daily`, `Weekly`, and `Monthly`. An appointment has a description (for example, "see the dentist") and a date and time. Write a virtual function `occurs_on(int year, int month, int day)` that checks whether the appointment occurs on that date. For example, for a monthly appointment, you must check whether the day of the month matches. Then fill a vector of `Appointment*` with a mixture of appointments. Have the user enter a date and print out all appointments that happen on that date.

Exercise P11.9. Improve the appointment book program of the preceding exercise. Give the user the option to add new appointments. The user must specify the type of the appointment, the description, and the date and time.

Exercise P11.10. Improve the appointment book program of the preceding exercises by letting the user save the appointment data to a file and reload the data from a file. The saving part is straightforward: Make a virtual function `save`. Save out the type, description, date, and time. The loading part is not so easy. You must first determine the type of the appointment to be loaded, create an object of that type with its default constructor, and then call a virtual `load` function to load the remainder.

Exercise P11.11. Implement a base class `Shape` and derived classes `Rectangle`, `Triangle`, and `Square`. Derive `Square` from `Rectangle`. Supply virtual functions `double area()` and `void plot()`. Fill a vector of `Shape*` pointers with a mixture of the shapes, plot them all, and compute the total area.

Exercise P11.12. Use the preceding exercise as the basis for a drawing program. Users can place various shapes onto the screen by first clicking on a shape icon and then clicking on the desired screen location:

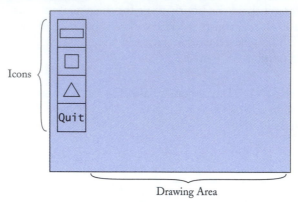

Drawing Area

Hint: Supply virtual functions make_shape(Point p) that return a new shape of default size anchored at the point p.

Exercise P11.13. Extend the program of the preceding exercise by adding another shape type: CircleShape. (You cannot call it Circle, because there already is a Circle class in the graphics library.) Explain what changes you needed to make in the program to implement this extension. How do virtual functions help in making the program easily extensible?

Exercise P11.14. Write a base class Chart that stores a vector of floating-point values. Implement derived classes, PieChart and BarChart, with a virtual plot function that can plot the data as a pie chart and as a bar chart.

Chapter 12

Streams

CHAPTER GOALS

▶ To be able to read and write files

▶ To convert between strings and numbers using string streams

▶ To learn how to process the command line

▶ To understand the concepts of sequential and random access

▶ To be able to build simple random-access database files

▶ To learn about encryption

All of the programs that you have written until now have read their input from the keyboard and displayed their output on the screen. However, many practical programs need to be able to use disk files for reading input and writing output. In this chapter, you will learn how to access files from C++ programs.

The C++ input/output library is organized in an object-oriented fashion, based on the concept of *streams*. An *input stream* is a source of characters, and an *output stream* is a destination for characters. File streams are just one subclass of streams. In this chapter you will learn how to use string streams for parsing and formatting character strings.

12.1 Reading and Writing Text Files

To access a disk file, you need to open a file variable. File variables are variables of type ifstream (for input), ofstream (for output), or fstream (for both input and output). For example,

```
ifstream input_data;
```

You must include the header file fstream to use file variables.

To read anything from a file, you need to *open* it. When you open a file, you give the name of the disk file. Suppose you want to read data from a file named input.dat, located in the same directory as the program. Then you use the following command to open the file:

```
input_data.open("input.dat");
```

This procedure call associates the file variable input_data with the disk file named input.dat. Reading from the file is now completely straightforward: You simply use the same functions that you have always used.

```
int n;
double x;
input_data >> n >> x;
```

You read strings in the same way:

```
string s;
input_data >> s; /* read a word */
getline(input_data, s); /* read a line */
```

You read a single character with the get method:

```
char ch;
input_data.get(ch);
```

If you read a character and you regretted it, you can *unget* it, so that the next input operation can read it again. However, you can unget only one character at a time. This is called *one-character lookahead:* At the next character in the input stream you can make a decision what you want to read in next, but not more than one character.

```
char ch;
input_data.get(ch);
if ('0' <= ch && ch <= '9') /* it was a digit */
{
    input_data.unget(); /* oops—didn't want to read it */
    int n;
    input_data >> n; /* read integer starting with ch */
}
```

Older implementations of the stream library do not have the `unget` member function. In that case you need to remember the last input character and call `input_data.put_back(ch)`.

The `fail` function tells you whether input has failed. Just as for standard input, the file can be in a failed state because you reached the end of file or because of a formatting error. There can be yet another reason for a failed state: If you open a file and the name is invalid, or if there is no file of that name, then the file is also in a failed state. It is a good idea to test for failure whenever you open a file.

When you are done reading from a file, you should *close* it:

```
input_data.close();
```

Writing to a file is just as simple. You open the file for writing:

```
ofstream output_data;
output_data.open("output.dat");
```

Now you send information to the output file in the usual way.

```
output_data << n << " " << x << "\n";
```

To write a single character, use

```
output_data.put(ch);
```

When you are finished with the output, remember to *close* the file.

```
output_data.close();
```

To open the same file for both reading and writing, you use an `fstream` variable:

```
fstream datafile;
datafile.open("employee.dat");
```

With older implementations of the stream library, you may need to supply a second construction parameter to open the file both for input and output:

```
datafile.open("employee.dat", ios::in | ios::out);
```

The file name that you give to the `open` command may be a string constant:

```
ifstream input_data;
input_data.open("input.dat");
```

It may also be a string variable that contains a file name supplied by the program user:

```
string input_name =
    cwin.get_string("Please enter the file name:");
ifstream input_data;
input_data.open(input_name);
```

Actually, many compilers don't yet support `string` parameters for the `open` function. If yours does not support it, use the `c_str` function to convert the `string` parameter to a character array.

```
input_data.open(input_name.c_str());
   /* use if open doesn't work with string parameter */
```

File names can contain directory path information, as in

```
~/homework/input.dat /* UNIX */
c:\homework\input.dat /* Windows */
```

When you specify the file name as a constant string, and the name contains backslash characters (as in a Windows filename), you must supply each backslash *twice:*

```
input_data.open("c:\\homework\\input.dat");
```

Recall that a single backslash inside quoted strings is an *escape character* that is combined with another character to form a special meaning, such as \n for a newline character. The \\ combination denotes a single backslash. When the file name is entered into a string variable by the user, the user should not type the backslash twice.

Have a look at the maxtemp.cpp program in Section 4.6, which reads in temperature data and then displays the highest value. That program prompts the user to enter all data values. Of course, if the user makes a single mistake in a data value, then there is no going back. The user must then restart the program and reenter all data values. It makes more sense for the user to place the data values into a file using a text editor and then to specify the name of that file when the data values are to be used.

Here is the modified program that incorporates this improvement. The program queries the user for an input file name, opens a file variable, and passes that variable to the read_data function. Inside the function, we use the familiar >> operator to read the data values from the input file.

Note that the ifstream parameter of the read_data function is passed by *reference.* Reading from a file modifies the file variable. The file variable monitors how many characters have been read or written so far. Any read or write operation changes that data. For that reason, you must always pass file variables by reference.

File maxval1.cpp

```
1  #include <string>
2  #include <iostream>
3  #include <fstream>
4
5  using namespace std;
6
7  /**
8     Reads numbers from a file and finds the maximum value.
9     @param in the input stream to read from
10    @return the maximum value or 0 if the file has no numbers
11 */
12 double read_data(ifstream& in)
13 {
14    double highest;
15    double next;
16    if (in >> next)
17       highest = next;
18    else
19       return 0;
```

```
20
21     while (in >> next)
22     {
23         if (next > highest)
24             highest = next;
25     }
26
27     return highest;
28  }
29
30  int main()
31  {
32     string filename;
33     cout << "Please enter the data file name: ";
34     cin >> filename;
35
36     ifstream infile;
37     infile.open(filename.c_str());
38
39     if (infile.fail())
40     {
41         cout << "Error opening " << filename << "\n";
42         return 1;
43     }
44
45     double max = read_data(infile);
46     cout << "The maximum value is " << max << "\n";
47
48     infile.close();
49     return 0;
50  }
```

12.2 The Inheritance Hierarchy of Stream Classes

The C++ input/output library consists of several classes that are related by inheritance. The most fundamental classes are the istream and ostream classes. An istream is a source of bytes. The get, getline, and >> operations are defined for istream objects. The ifstream class derives from the istream class. Therefore, it automatically inherits all istream operations. In Section 12.3, you will encounter another class, istringstream, that also derives from the istream class. It too inherits the istream operations. However, the open function is a member function of the ifstream class, not the istream class. You can only open file streams, not general input streams or string streams.

Similarly, an ostream is a destination for bytes. Several forms of the << operator are defined for ostream objects, to print out numbers, strings, and other types. The ofstream class derives from the ostream class and inherits the << operators.

An iostream combines the capabilities of an istream and ostream, by deriving from both classes (see Figure 1). The fstream class derives from iostream. (Note that, for technical reasons, fstream does *not* derive from ifstream or ofstream, even if it would make sense for it to do so.)

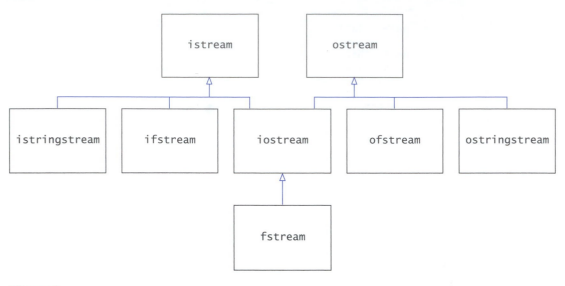

Figure 1

The Inheritance Hierarchy of Stream Classes

Finally, the standard `cin` and `cout` objects belong to specialized system-dependent classes with nonstandard names (such as `istream_with_assign` and `ostream_with_assign`, or something similar). Even though you don't know the exact classes, you can be assured that `cin` belongs to a class that is derived from `istream` and `cout` belongs to a class that is derived from `ostream`.

You should take advantage of the inheritance relationships between the stream classes whenever you write functions with stream parameters. Consider the `read_data` function in the preceding example program. It is declared as

```
double read_data(ifstream& in)
```

However, if you look inside the code of the function, you will see that the function never requires that the `in` parameter be a file stream. The function can equally well read data from any `istream` object. For that reason, you should declare such a function with a parameter of type `istream`, not `ifstream`:

```
double read_data(istream& in)
```

Now you can pass parameters of types other than `ifstream`, such as the `cin` object (which belongs to a derived class of `istream` but not to `ifstream`).

The following example program illustrates this concept. Note that the `read_data` function takes an `istream` parameter. In the `main` function, the program user can choose to supply the data in a file, or to type them in manually. The `main` function then calls the `read_data` function in one of two ways, either as

```
max = read_data(infile);
```

or

```
max = read_data(cin);
```

The `infile` and `cin` objects belong to different classes, but both classes inherit from `istream`.

As you already saw in the preceding section, the stream parameter must be passed by reference since the stream data structure is modified when you read from a stream. Now there is a second reason why you must use call by reference. If you used call by value,

```
double read_data(istream in) /* Error! Missing & */
```

then the parameter object would be *sliced* when copied into the parameter object `in` (see Common Error 11.4). Therefore, you must always use call by reference with stream parameters.

File maxval2.cpp

```
 1  #include <string>
 2  #include <iostream>
 3  #include <fstream>
 4
 5  using namespace std;
 6
 7  /**
 8      Reads numbers from a file and finds the maximum value.
 9      @param in the input stream to read from
10      @return the maximum value or 0 if the file has no numbers
11  */
12  double read_data(istream& in)
13  {
14     double highest;
15     double next;
16     if (in >> next)
17        highest = next;
18     else
19        return 0;
20
21     while (in >> next)
22     {
23        if (next > highest)
24           highest = next;
25     }
26
27     return highest;
28  }
29
30  int main()
31  {
32     double max;
33
34     string input;
35     cout << "Do you want to read from a file? (y/n) ";
36     cin >> input;
37
38     if (input == "y")
39     {
40        string filename;
41        cout << "Please enter the data file name: ";
```

```
42        cin >> filename;
43
44        ifstream infile;
45        infile.open(filename.c_str());
46
47        if (infile.fail())
48        {
49           cout << "Error opening " << filename << "\n";
50           return 1;
51        }
52
53        max = read_data(infile);
54        infile.close();
55     }
56     else
57        max = read_data(cin);
58
59     cout << "The maximum value is " << max << "\n";
60
61     return 0;
62  }
```

12.3   String Streams

In the preceding section, you saw how the `ifstream` and `ofstream` classes can be used to read characters from a file and write characters to a file. In other words, you use a file stream if the source or the destination of the characters is a file. You can use other stream classes to read characters from a different source or to send them to a different destination.

The `istringstream` class reads characters from a string, and the `ostringstream` class writes characters to a string. That doesn't sound so exciting—we already know how to access and change the characters of a string. However, the string stream classes have the same *interface* as the other stream classes. In other words, using an `istringstream` you can read numbers that are stored in a string, simply by using the familiar `>>` operator. The string stream classes are defined in the `sstream` header.

Here is an example. The string `input` contains a date, and we want to separate it into month, day, and year. First, construct an `istringstream` object. The construction parameter is the string containing the characters that we want to read:

```
string input = "January 23, 1955";
istringstream instr(input);
```

Next, simply use the `>>` operator to read off the month name, the day, the comma separator, and the year:

```
string month;
int day;
string comma;
int year;
instr >> month >> day >> comma >> year;
```

Now `month` is `"January"`, `day` is 23, and `year` is 1955. Note that this input statement yields `day` and `year` as *integers*. Had we taken the string apart with `substr`, we would have obtained only strings, not numbers.

In fact, converting strings that contain digits to their integer values is such a common operation that it is useful to write a helper function for this purpose:

```
int string_to_int(string s)
{
    istringstream instr(s);
    int n;
    instr >> n;
    return n;
}
```

For example, `string_to_int("1999")` is the *integer* 1999.

By writing to a string stream, you can convert numbers to strings. First construct an `ostringstream` object:

```
ostringstream outstr;
```

Next, use the << operator to add a number to the stream. The number is converted into a sequence of characters:

```
outstr << setprecision(5) << sqrt(2);
```

Now the stream contains the string `"1.41421"`. To obtain that string from the stream, call the `str` member function:

```
string output = outstr.str();
```

You can build up more complex strings in the same way. Here we build a data string of the month, day, and year:

```
string month = "January";
int day = 23;
int year = 1955;
ostringstream outstr;
outstr << month << " " << day << "," << year;
string output = outstr.str();
```

Now `output` is the string `"January 23, 1955"`. Note that we converted the integers `day` and `year` into a string. Again, converting an integer into a string is such a common operation that is useful to have a helper function for it:

```
string int_to_string(int n)
{
    ostringstream outstr;
    outstr << n;
    return outstr.str();
}
```

For example, `int_to_string(1955)` is the string `"1955"`.

A very common use of string streams is to accept input one line at a time and then to analyze it further. This avoids the complications that arise from mixing >> and `getline` that were discussed in Common Error 6.1. Simply call `getline` to read the input one line at a time, and then read items from the input lines by using string streams.

Here is an example. You prompt the user for a time, and want to accept inputs such as

```
21:30
9:30 pm
9 am
```

That is, the input line consists of a number, maybe followed by a colon and another number, maybe followed by am or pm. In the read_time procedure of the following program, you first read in the entire input line, then analyze what the user typed. The result is a pair of integers, hours and minutes, adjusted to military (24-hour) time if the user entered "pm".

In the time_to_string function, the integer values for hours and minutes are converted back to a string. Using the aforementioned int_to_string function, the integer values are converted to strings. A : separator is added between them. If the military parameter is false, an "am" or "pm" string is appended.

File readtime.cpp

```
 1  #include <string>
 2  #include <iostream>
 3  #include <sstream>
 4
 5  using namespace std;
 6
 7  /**
 8      Converts an integer value to a string, e.g., 3 -> "3".
 9      @param s an integer value
10      @return the equivalent string
11  */
12  string int_to_string(int n)
13  {
14      ostringstream outstr;
15      outstr << n;
16      return outstr.str();
17  }
18
19  /**
20      Reads a time from standard input in the format hh:mm or
21      hh:mm am or hh:mm pm.
22      @param hours filled with the hours
23      @param minutes filled with the minutes
24  */
25  void read_time(int& hours, int& minutes)
26  {
27      string line;
28      getline(cin, line);
29      istringstream instr(line);
30
31      instr >> hours;
32
33      minutes = 0;
34
35      char ch;
36      instr.get(ch);
37
38      if (ch == ':')
39          instr >> minutes;
40      else
41          instr.unget();
42      /*
43          use
```

```
44          instr.putback(ch);
45       if your compiler doesn't support the ANSI unget function
46    */
47
48    string suffix;
49    instr >> suffix;
50
51    if (suffix == "pm")
52       hours = hours + 12;
53 }
54
55 /**
56    Computes a string representing a time.
57    @param hours the hours (0 . . . 23)
58    @param minutes the minutes (0 . . . 59)
59    @param military true for military format,
60    false for am/pm format
61 */
62 string time_to_string(int hours, int minutes, bool military)
63 {
64    string suffix;
65    if (!military)
66    {
67       if (hours < 12)
68          suffix = "am";
69       else
70       {
71          suffix = "pm";
72          hours = hours - 12;
73       }
74       if (hours == 0) hours = 12;
75    }
76    string result = int_to_string(hours) + ":";
77    if (minutes < 10) result = result + "0";
78    result = result + int_to_string(minutes);
79    if (!military)
80       result = result + " " + suffix;
81    return result;
82 }
83
84 int main()
85 {
86    cout << "Please enter the time: ";
87
88    int hours;
89    int minutes;
90
91    read_time(hours, minutes);
92
93    cout << "Military time: "
94       << time_to_string(hours, minutes, true) << "\n";
95    cout << "Using am/pm: "
96       << time_to_string(hours, minutes, false) << "\n";
97
98    return 0;
99 }
```

12.4   Command Line Arguments

Depending on the operating system and C++ development system used, there are different methods of starting a program—for example, by selecting "Run" in the compilation environment, by clicking on an icon, or by typing the name of the program at a prompt in a terminal or shell window. The latter method is called "invoking the program from the command line". When you use this method, you must of course type the name of the program, but you can also type in additional information that the program can use. These additional strings are called *command line arguments*. For example, if you start a program with the command line

```
prog -v input.dat
```

then the program receives two command line arguments: the strings "-v" and "input.dat". It is entirely up to the program what to do with these strings. It is customary to interpret strings starting with a - as options and other strings as file names.

Only text mode programs receive command line arguments; the graphics library that comes with this book does not collect them.

To receive command line arguments, you need to define the main function in a different way. You define two parameters: one integer and one with a type called char*[], which denotes an array of pointers to C character arrays.

```
int main(int argc, char* argv[])
{
   ...
}
```

Here argc is the count of arguments, and argv contains the values of the arguments. Because they are character arrays, you should convert them to C++ strings. string(argv[i]) is the ith command line argument, ready to use in C++.

In our example, argc is 3, and argv contains the three strings

```
string(argv[0]):   "prog"
string(argv[1]):   "-v"
string(argv[2]):   "input.dat"
```

Note that string(argv[0]) is always the name of the program and that argc is always at least 1.

Let us write a program that *encrypts* a file—that is, scrambles it so that it is unreadable except to those who know the decryption method and the secret keyword. Ignoring 2000 years of progress in the field of encryption, we will use a method familiar to Julius Caesar. The person performing any encryption chooses an *encryption key*; here the key is a number between 1 and 25 that indicates the shift to be used in encrypting each letter. For example, if the key is 3, replace A with a D, B with an E, and so on (see Figure 2).

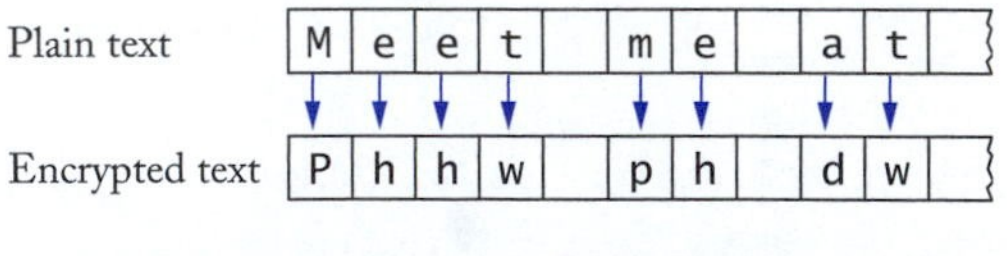

Figure 2

Caesar Cipher

The program takes the following command line arguments:

> An optional -d flag to indicate decryption instead of encryption
>
> An optional encryption key, specified with a -k flag
>
> The input file name
>
> The output file name

If no key is specified, then 3 is used. For example,

```
caesar input.txt encrypt.txt
```

encrypts the file input.txt with a key of 3 and places the result into encrypt.txt.

```
caesar -d -k11 encrypt.txt output.txt
```

decrypts the file encrypt.txt with a key of 11 and places the result into output.txt.
Here is the program. (See Section 9.5.3 to review character integer values.)

File caesar.cpp

```cpp
 1  #include <iostream>
 2  #include <fstream>
 3  #include <string>
 4  #include <sstream>
 5
 6  using namespace std;
 7
 8  /**
 9      Prints usage instructions.
10      @param program_name  the name of this program
11  */
12  void usage(string program_name)
13  {
14     cout << "Usage: " << program_name
15        << " [-d] [-kn] infile outfile\n";
16     exit(1);
17  }
18
19  /**
20      Prints file opening error message.
21      @param filename  the name of the file that could not be opened
22  */
23  void open_file_error(string filename)
24  {
25     cout << "Error opening file " << filename << "\n";
26     exit(1);
27  }
28
29  /**
30      Computes correct remainder for negative dividend.
31      @param a  an integer
32      @param n  an integer > 0
33      @return  the mathematically correct remainder r such that
34         a - r is divisible by n and 0 <= r and r < n
35  */
36  int remainder(int a, int n)
```

```
37 {
38     if (a >= 0)
39         return a % n;
40     else
41         return n - 1 - (-a - 1) % n;
42 }
43
44 /**
45     Encrypts a character using the Caesar cipher.
46     @param ch  the character to encrypt
47     @param k the encryption key
48     @return the encrypted character
49 */
50 char encrypt(char ch, int k)
51 {
52     const int NLETTER = 'Z' - 'A' + 1;
53     if ('A' <= ch && ch <= 'Z')
54         return static_cast<char>(
55             'A' + remainder(ch - 'A' + k, NLETTER));
56     if ('a' <= ch && ch <= 'z')
57         return static_cast<char>(
58             'a' + remainder(ch - 'a' + k, NLETTER));
59     return ch;
60 }
61
62 /**
63     Encrypts a stream using the Caesar cipher.
64     @param in  the stream to read from
65     @param out  the stream to write to
66     @param k  the encryption key
67 */
68 void encrypt_file(istream& in, ostream& out, int k)
69 {
70     char ch;
71     while (in.get(ch))
72         out.put(encrypt(ch, k));
73 }
74
75 /**
76     Converts a string to an integer, e.g., "3" -> 3.
77     @param s  a string representing an integer
78     @return the equivalent integer
79 */
80 int string_to_int(string s)
81 {
82     istringstream instr(s);
83     int n;
84     instr >> n;
85     return n;
86 }
87
88 int main(int argc, char* argv[])
89 {
90     bool decrypt = false;
91     int key = 3;
92     int nfile = 0; /* the number of files specified */
```

```
93      ifstream infile;
94      ofstream outfile;
95
96      if (argc < 3 || argc > 5) usage(string(argv[0]));
97
98      int i;
99      for (i = 1; i < argc; i++)
100     {
101        string arg = string(argv[i]);
102        if (arg.length() >= 2 && arg[0] == '-')
103        /* it is a command line option */
104        {
105           char option = arg[1];
106           if (option == 'd')
107           decrypt = true;
108           else if (option == 'k')
109           key = string_to_int(arg.substr(2, arg.length() - 2));
110        }
111        else
112        {
113           nfile++;
114           if (nfile == 1)
115           {
116              infile.open(arg.c_str());
117              if (infile.fail()) open_file_error(arg);
118           }
119           else if (nfile == 2)
120           {
121              outfile.open(arg.c_str());
122              if (outfile.fail()) open_file_error(arg);
123           }
124        }
125     }
126
127     if(nfile != 2) usage(string(argv[0]));
128
129     if (decrypt) key = -key;
130
131     encrypt_file(infile, outfile, key);
132     infile.close();
133     outfile.close();
134     return 0;
135  }
```

 Random Fact   `12.1`

Encryption Algorithms

The exercises at the end of this chapter give a few algorithms to encrypt text. Don't actually use any of those methods to send secret messages to your lover. Any skilled cryptographer can *break* these schemes in a very short time—that is, reconstruct the original text without knowing the secret keyword.

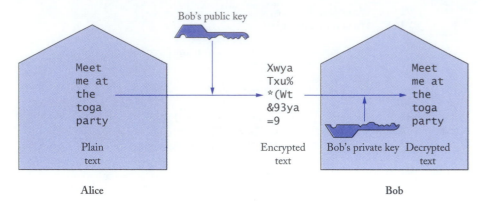

Figure 3

Public-Key Encryption

In 1978 Ron Rivest, Adi Shamir, and Leonard Adleman introduced an encryption method that is much more powerful. The method is called *RSA encryption,* after the last names of its inventors. The exact scheme is too complicated to present here, but it is not actually difficult to follow. You can find the details in [1].

RSA is a remarkable encryption method. There are two keys: a public key and a private key. (See Figure 3.) You can print the public key on your business card (or in your e-mail signature block) and give it to anyone. Then anyone can send you messages that only you can decrypt. Even though everyone else knows the public key, and even if they intercept all the messages coming to you, they cannot break the scheme and actually read the messages. In 1994, hundreds of researchers, collaborating over the Internet, cracked an RSA message encrypted with a 129-digit key. Messages encrypted with a key of 230 digits or more are expected to be secure.

The inventors of the algorithm obtained a *patent* for it. That means that anyone using it must seek a license from the inventors. They have given permission for most noncommercial usage, but if you implement RSA in a product that you sell, you must get their permission and probably pay them some amount of money.

A patent is a deal that society makes with an inventor. For a period of 17 years after the patent is awarded (or 20 years after the filing date), the inventor has an exclusive right for its commercialization, may collect royalties from others wishing to manufacture the invention, and may even stop competitors from marketing it altogether. In return, the inventor must publish the invention, so that others may learn from it, and must relinquish all claim to it after the protection period ends. The presumption is that in the absence of patent law, inventors would be reluctant to go through the trouble of inventing, or they would try to cloak their techniques to prevent others from copying their devices. The RSA patent expired on September 20, 2000.

What do you think? Are patents a fair deal? Unquestionably, some companies have chosen not to implement RSA, and instead chose a less capable method, because they could not or would not pay the royalties. Thus, it seems that the patent may have hindered, rather than advanced, commerce. Had there not been patent protection, would the inventors have published the method anyway, thereby giving the benefit to society without the cost of the 17-year monopoly? In this case, the answer is probably yes; the inventors were academic researchers, who live on salaries rather than sales receipts and are usually rewarded for their discoveries by a boost in their reputation and careers. Would their followers have been as active in discovering (and patenting) improvements? There is no way of knowing, of course. Is an algorithm even patentable, or is it a mathematical fact that belongs to nobody? The patent office did take the latter attitude for a long time. The RSA inventors and many others described their inventions in terms of imaginary electronic devices, rather than algorithms, to circumvent that restriction. Nowadays, the patent office will award software patents.

There is another fascinating aspect to the RSA story. A programmer, Phil Zimmermann, developed a program called PGP (for *Pretty Good Privacy*) [2]. PGP implements RSA. That is, you can have it generate a pair of public and private keys, publish the public key, receive encrypted messages from others who use their copy of PGP and your public key, and decrypt them with your private key. Even though the encryption can be performed on any personal computer, decryption is not feasible even with the most powerful computers. You can get a copy of PGP on the Web from `http://web.mit.edu/network/pgp.html`. As long as it is for personal use, there is no charge, courtesy of Phil Zimmermann and the folks at RSA.

The existence of PGP bothers the government to no end. They worry that criminals use the package to correspond by e-mail and that the police cannot tap those "conversations". Foreign governments can send communications that the National Security Agency (the premier electronic spy organization of the United States) cannot decipher. At the time of this writing, the government is attempting to standardize on a different encryption scheme, called *Skipjack*, to which government organizations hold a decryption key that—of course—they promise not to use without a court order. There have been serious proposals to make it illegal to use any other encryption method in the United States. At one time, the government considered charging Mr. Zimmermann with breaching another law that forbids the unauthorized export of munitions as a crime and defines cryptographic technology as "munitions". They made the argument that, even though Mr. Zimmermann never exported the program, he should have known that it would immediately spread through the Internet when he released it in the United States.

What do you think? Will criminals and terrorists be harder to detect and convict once encryption of e-mail and phone conversations is widely available? Should the government therefore have a backdoor key to any legal encryption method? Or is this a gross violation of our civil liberties? Is it even possible to put the genie back into the bottle at this time?

12.5   Random Access

Consider a file that contains a set of employee data. You want to give some of the employees a raise. Of course, you can read all data into an array, update the information that has changed, and save the data out again. If the data set in the file is very large, you may end up doing a lot of reading and writing just to update a handful of records. It would be better if you could locate the changed information in the file and just replace it.

This is quite different from the file access that you programmed up to now. So far, you've read from a file an item at a time and written to a file an item at a time. That access pattern is called *sequential access*. Now we would like to access specific locations in a file and only change those locations. This access pattern is called *random access* (see Figure 4). There is nothing "random" about random access—the term means that you can read and modify any character stored at any location in the file.

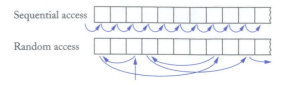

Sequential access

Random access

Get position

5 4 9 0 3 . 2 5

Put position

Figure 4

Sequential and Random Access

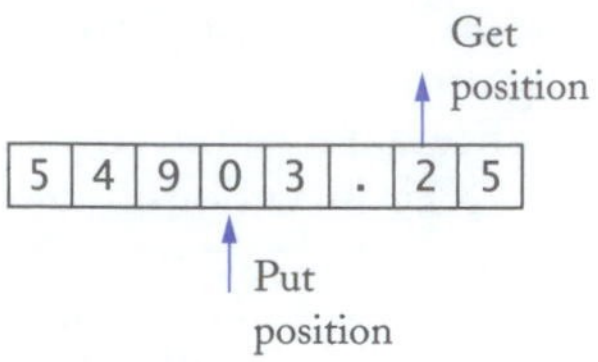

Figure 5

Get and Put Positions

Only disk files support random access; the cin and cout streams, which are attached to the keyboard and the terminal, do not. Each disk file has two special positions: the *get* position and the *put* position (see Figure 5). Normally, the put position is at the end of the file, and any output is appended to the end. However, if you move the put position to the middle of the file and write to the file, the output overwrites what is already there. Normally, the get position starts at the beginning of the file and is moved toward the end as you read from the file. However, if you move the get position to another location, the next read command starts reading input at that location. Of course, you cannot move the get or put position beyond the last character currently in the file.

The following procedure calls move the get and put positions to character n counted from the beginning of the file fs.

```
fs.seekg(n, ios::beg);
fs.seekp(n, ios::beg);
```

To move to the position n characters away from the end of the file or the current position, use ios::end or ios::cur, respectively, instead of ios::beg. To determine the current position of the get and put positions (counted from the beginning of the file), use

```
n = fs.tellg();
n = fs.tellp();
```

Because files can be very large, the file positions are long integers. To find out the number of characters in a file, move the get position to the end and then find out the distance from the beginning of the file:

```
fs.seekg(0, ios::end);
long file_length = fs.tellg();
```

If you want to manipulate a data set in a file, you have to pay special attention to the formatting of the data. Suppose you just store the data as text:

| H | a | c | k | e | r | , | | H | a | r | r | y | | 3 | 4 | 5 | 0 | 0 | \n | C | r | a | c | k | e | r | |

If Harry's salary is increased by 5.5 percent, the new salary is $36,397.50. If one places the put position to the first character of the old value and simply writes out the new value, the result is

| H | a | c | k | e | r | , | | H | a | r | r | y | | 3 | 6 | 3 | 9 | 7 | . | 5 | r | a | c | k | e | r | |

This does not work too well. The update overwrites some characters in the next field.

In order to be able to update a file, you must give each field a *fixed* size that is sufficiently large. As a result, every record in the file has the same size. This has another

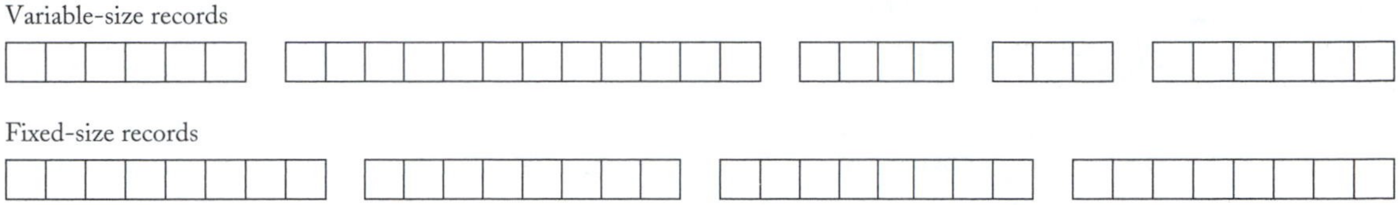

Variable-size records

Fixed-size records

Figure 6

Variable-Size and Fixed-Size Records

advantage: It is then easy to skip quickly to, say, the 50th record, without having to read in the first 49 records. Because records can be accessed at random when they all have the same size, a file with that structure is called a *random-access file*. (See Figure 6.)

To structure the data file in our example for random access, set the field lengths to the following dimensions:

Name: 30 characters

Salary: 10 characters

The file then looks as follows:

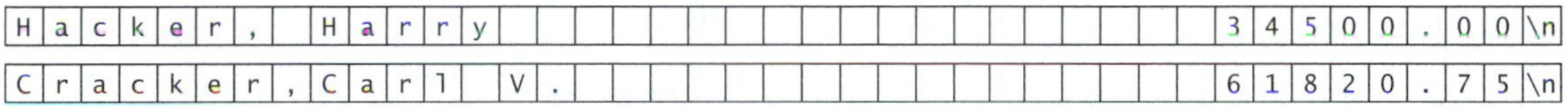

How large is each record? It would appear to be 30 + 10 = 40 characters long. However, you must also count the newline character at the end of each line. Unfortunately, some operating systems—in particular Windows—store a newline as two separate characters (a so-called *carriage return* and a so-called *line feed*). Our programs never see that, because the input and output functions automatically convert between the '\n' character in strings and the carriage return/line feed combination in files. When counting file positions, though, you must take both characters into account. An alternative is not to separate lines at all but simply to store the entire data set as one huge line, but then it is hard to look at the data file with a text editor.

The fact that the newline character may occupy one or two characters on disk, depending on the operating system, is an annoyance. To write programs that work on either platform, you define a constant NEWLINE_LENGTH and set it to the appropriate value for the operating system:

```
const int NEWLINE_LENGTH = 1; /* or 2 on Windows */
```

Now that you have determined the file layout, you can implement your random-access file functions. The following program asks the user to enter the position of the record that should be updated, and the price increase.

File database.cpp

```
1  #include <iostream>
2  #include <iomanip>
3  #include <fstream>
4  #include <sstream>
5
```

```
6  using namespace std;
7
8  #include "ccc_empl.h"
9
10 const int NEWLINE_LENGTH = 2; /* or 1 on Unix */
11 const int RECORD_SIZE = 30 + 10 + NEWLINE_LENGTH;
12
13 /**
14    Converts a string to a floating-point value, e.g.,
15    "3.14" -> 3.14.
16    @param s a string representing a floating-point value
17    @return the equivalent floating-point value
18 */
19 double string_to_double(string s)
20 {
21    istringstream instr(s);
22    double x;
23    instr >> x;
24    return x;
25 }
26
27 /**
28    Raises an employee salary.
29    @param e employee receiving raise
30    @param percent the percentage of the raise
31 */
32 void raise_salary(Employee& e, double percent)
33 {
34    double new_salary = e.get_salary() * (1 + percent / 100);
35    e.set_salary(new_salary);
36 }
37
38 /**
39    Reads an employee record from a file.
40    @param e filled with the employee
41    @param in the stream to read from
42 */
43 void read_employee(Employee& e, istream& in)
44 {
45    string line;
46    getline(in, line);
47    if (in.fail()) return;
48    string name = line.substr(0, 30);
49    double salary = string_to_double(line.substr(30, 10));
50    e = Employee(name, salary);
51 }
52
53 /**
54    Writes an employee record to a stream.
55    @param e the employee record to write
56    @param out the stream to write to
57 */
58 void write_employee(Employee e, ostream& out)
59 {
60    out << e.get_name()
61        << setw(10 + (30 - e.get_name().length()))
```

```
62          << fixed << setprecision(2)
63          << e.get_salary()
64          << "\n";
65 }
66
67 int main()
68 {
69    cout << "Please enter the data file name: ";
70    string filename;
71    cin >> filename;
72    fstream fs;
73    fs.open(filename.c_str());
74    fs.seekg(0, ios::end); /* go to end of file */
75    int nrecord = fs.tellg() / RECORD_SIZE;
76
77    cout << "Please enter the record to update: (0 - "
78       << nrecord - 1 << ") ";
79    int pos;
80    cin >> pos;
81
82    const double SALARY_CHANGE = 5.0;
83
84    Employee e;
85    fs.seekg(pos * RECORD_SIZE, ios::beg);
86    read_employee(e, fs);
87    raise_salary(e, SALARY_CHANGE);
88    fs.seekp(pos * RECORD_SIZE, ios::beg);
89    write_employee(e, fs);
90
91    fs.close();
92    return 0;
93 }
```

Advanced Topic   12.1

Binary Files

When a program saves numeric data to disk with the << operation, the data is saved in text format. For example, the floating-point number 314.7 is saved as 314.7 or perhaps 3.147E2. Actually, it is more efficient to save the number in the same format in which it is represented in the computer: as a set of four bytes. That has the added advantage that the number automatically occupies a fixed size in the file, making random access easier.

When saving large data sets, it makes a lot of sense to use a binary format. We have not done that in this book, because it requires a little more technical overhead in C++.

Another disadvantage of binary format is that it makes debugging *much* harder. When you look into a text file with a text editor, you can see exactly what is inside. To look inside a binary file, or to make a minor modification, you need special tools. We recommend using text files for saving data until an application is fully debugged. If the added efficiency of binary files is crucial, then rewrite just the input/output procedures to switch to binary format.

Random Fact 12.2

Databases and Privacy

Most companies use computers to keep huge data files of customer records and other business information. Special C++ database programs are used to search and update that information rapidly. This sounds like a straightforward extension of the techniques we learned in this chapter, but it does take special skills to handle truly massive amounts of data. You will likely take a course in database programming as part of your computer science education.

Databases not only lower the cost of doing business; they improve the quality of service that companies can offer. Nowadays it is almost unimaginable how time-consuming it used to be to withdraw money from a bank branch or to make travel reservations.

Today most databases are organized according to the *relational model*. Suppose a company stores your orders and payments. They will probably not repeat your name and address on every order; that would take unnecessary space. Instead, they will keep one file of all their customer names and identify each customer by a unique customer number. Only that customer number, not the entire customer information, is kept with an order record. (See Figure 7.)

To print an invoice, the database program must issue a *query* against both the customer and order files and pull the necessary information (name, address, articles ordered) from both.

Frequently, queries involve more than two files. For example, the company may have a file of addresses of car owners and a file of people with good payment history and may want to

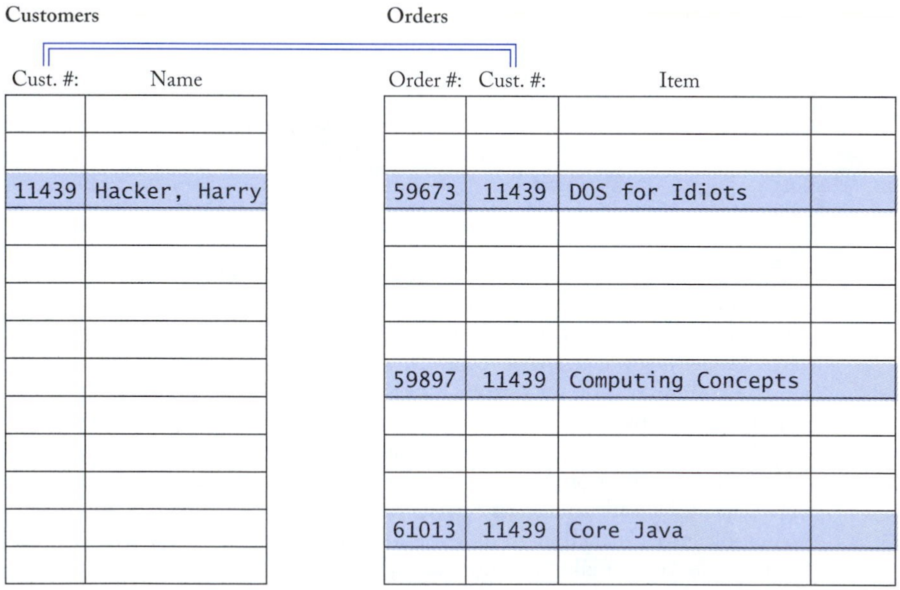

Customers

Cust. #:	Name
11439	Hacker, Harry

Orders

Order #:	Cust. #:	Item	
59673	11439	DOS for Idiots	
59897	11439	Computing Concepts	
61013	11439	Core Java	

Figure 7

Relational Database Files

▼

▼   **Figure 8**

▼   Social Security Card

▼

▼

▼

find all of its customers who placed an order in the last month, drive an expensive car, and pay
their bills, to send them another catalog. This kind of query is, of course, much faster if all
customer files use the *same* key, which is why so many organizations in the United States try
to collect the Social Security numbers of their customers.

The Social Security Act of 1935 provided that each contributor be assigned a Social
Security number to track contributions into the Social Security Fund. These numbers have a
distinctive format, such as 078-05-1120. (This particular number is not actually a Social
Security number belonging to any person. It was printed on sample cards that were inserted
in wallets in the 1940s and 1950s.) Figure 8 shows a Social Security card.

Although they had not originally been intended for use as a universal identification number, Social Security numbers have become just that in the last 60 years. The tax authorities
and many other government agencies are required to collect the numbers, as are banks (for
the reporting of interest income) and, of course, employers. Many other organizations find it
convenient to use the number as well.

From a technical standpoint, Social Security numbers are a lousy method for indexing a
database. There is a risk of having two records with the same number, because many illegal
immigrants use fake numbers. Not everyone has a number—in particular, foreign customers.
Because there is no checksum, a clerical error (such as transposing two digits) cannot be
detected. (Credit card numbers have a checksum.) For the same reason, it is easy for anyone
to make up a number.

Some people are very concerned about the fact that just about every organization wants to
store their Social Security number. Unless there is a legal requirement, such as for banks, one
can usually fight it or take one's business elsewhere. Even when an organization is required to
collect the number, such as an employer, one can insist that the number be used only on tax
and Social Security paperwork, not on the face of an ID card. Unfortunately, it usually takes
near-superhuman effort to climb the organizational ladder to find someone with the author-
ity to process paperwork with no Social Security number or to assign another identification
number.

The discomfort that many people have about the computerization of their personal information is understandable. There is the possibility that companies and the government can
merge multiple databases and derive information about us that we may wish they did not
have or that simply may be untrue. An insurance company may deny coverage, or charge a
higher premium, if it finds that you have too many relatives with a certain disease. You may
be denied a job because of an inaccurate credit or medical report, and you may not even know
the reason. These are very disturbing developments that have had a very negative impact for a
small but growing number of people. See [3] for more information.

Chapter Summary

1. To read or write disk files, you need to use objects of type `fstream`, `ifstream`, or `ofstream`. When opening the file object, you supply the name of the disk file. When you are done using the file, you should close the file object.

2. To read and write data, use the operations `<<`, `>>`, `getline`, and `fail` in the same way they are used with `cin` and `cout`.

3. Use string streams to read numbers that are contained in strings, or to convert numbers to strings.

4. Programs that start from the command line can retrieve the name of the program and the command line arguments in the `main` procedure.

5. You can access any position in a random access file by moving the *file pointer* prior to a read or write operation. That is particularly useful if all records in a file have the same size.

Further Reading

[1] Bruce Schneier, *Applied Cryptography*, John Wiley & Sons, 1994.
[2] Philip R. Zimmermann, *The Official PGP User's Guide*, MIT Press, 1995.
[3] David F. Linowes, *Privacy in America*, University of Illinois Press, 1989.
[4] Abraham Sinkov, *Elementary Cryptanalysis*, Mathematical Association of America, 1966.
[5] Don Libes, *Obfuscated C and Other Mysteries*, John Wiley & Sons, 1993.

Review Exercises

Exercise R12.1. Write C++ code to open a file with the name `Hello.txt`, store the message "Hello, World!" in the file, and close the file. Then open the same file again and read the message into a string variable. Close the file again.

Exercise R12.2. When do you open a file as an `ifstream`, as an `ofstream`, or as an `fstream`? Could you simply open all files as an `fstream`?

Exercise R12.3. What happens if you write to a file that you only opened for reading? Try it out if you don't know.

Exercise R12.4. What happens if you try to open a file for reading that doesn't exist? What happens if you try to open a file for writing that doesn't exist?

Exercise R12.5. What happens if you try to open a file for writing, but the file or device is write-protected (sometimes called read-only)? Try it out with a short test program.

Exercise R12.6. How do you open a file whose name contains a backslash, like `temp\output.dat` or `c:\temp\output.dat`?

Exercise R12.7. Why is the `ifstream` parameter of the `read_data` procedure in Section 12.2 a reference parameter and not a value parameter?

Exercise R12.8. How can you convert the string `"3.14"` into the floating-point number 3.14? How can you convert the floating-point number 3.14 into the string `"3.14"`?

Exercise R12.9. What is a command line? How can a program read its command line?

Exercise R12.10. If a program `woozle` is started with the command

```
woozle -DNAME=Piglet -I\eeyore -v heff.cpp a.cpp lump.cpp
```

what is the value of `argc`, and what are the values of `string(argv[0])`, `string (argv[1])`, and so on?

Exercise R12.11. How can you break the Caesar cipher? That is, how can you read a letter that was encrypted with the Caesar cipher, even though you don't know the key?

Exercise R12.12. What is the difference between sequential access and random access?

Exercise R12.13. What is the difference between a text file and a binary file?

Exercise R12.14. Some operating systems, in particular Windows, convert a `'\n'` character into a two-character sequence (carriage return/line feed) whenever writing a text file and convert the two-character sequence back into a newline when reading the text file back in. This is normally transparent to the C++ programmer. Why do we need to consider this issue in the database program of Section 12.5?

Exercise R12.15. What are the get and put positions in a file? How do you move them? How do you tell their current positions? Why are they `long` integers?

Exercise R12.16. How do you move the get position to the first byte of a file? To the last byte? To the exact middle of the file?

Exercise R12.17. What happens if you try to move the get or put position past the end of a file? What happens if you try to move the get or put position of `cin` or `cout`? Try it out and report your results.

PROGRAMMING EXERCISES

Exercise P12.1. Write a program that asks the user for a file name and displays the number of characters, words, and lines in that file. Then have the program ask for the name of the next file. When the user enters a file that doesn't exist (such as the empty string), the program should exit.

Exercise P12.2. *Random monoalphabet cipher.* The Caesar cipher, to shift all letters by a fixed amount, is ridiculously easy to crack—just try out all 25 keys. Here is a better idea. As the key, don't use numbers but words. Suppose the key word is FEATHER. Then you first remove duplicate letters, yielding FEATHR, and append the other letters of the alphabet in reverse order:

F	E	A	T	H	R	Z	Y	X	W	V	U	S	Q	P	O	N	M	L	K	J	I	G	D	C	B

Now encrypt the letters as follows:

A	B	C	D	E	F	G	H	I	J	K	L	M	N	O	P	Q	R	S	T	U	V	W	X	Y	Z
F	E	A	T	H	R	Z	Y	X	W	V	U	S	Q	P	O	N	M	L	K	J	I	G	D	C	B

Write a program that encrypts or decrypts a file using this cipher. For example,

```
crypt -d -kFEATHER encrypt.txt output.txt
```

decrypts a file using the keyword FEATHER. It is an error not to supply a keyword.

Exercise P12.3. *Letter frequencies.* If you encrypt a file using the cipher of the preceding exercise, it will have all of its letters jumbled up, and it doesn't look as if there was any hope of decrypting it without knowing the keyword. Guessing the keyword seems hopeless too. There are just too many possible keywords. However, someone who is trained in decryption will be able to break this cipher in no time at all. The average letter frequencies of English letters are well known. The most common letter is E, which occurs about 13 percent of the time. Here are the average frequencies of the letters (see [4]).

A	8%	H	4%	O	7%	U	3%
B	<1%	I	7%	P	3%	V	<1%
C	3%	J	<1%	Q	<1%	W	2%
D	4%	K	<1%	R	8%	X	<1%
E	13%	L	4%	S	6%	Y	2%
F	3%	M	3%	T	9%	Z	<1%
G	2%	N	8%				

Write a program that reads an input file and displays the letter frequencies in that file. Such a tool will help a code breaker. If the most frequent letters in an encrypted file are H and K, then there is an excellent chance that they are the encryptions of E and T.

Exercise P12.4. *Vigenère cipher.* The trouble with a monoalphabetic cipher is that it can be easily broken by frequency analysis. The so-called Vigenère cipher overcomes this problem by encoding a letter into one of several cipher letters, depending on its position in the input document. Choose a keyword, for example TIGER. Then encode the first letter of the input text like this:

A	B	C	D	E	F	G	H	I	J	K	L	M	N	O	P	Q	R	S	T	U	V	W	X	Y	Z
T	U	V	W	X	Y	Z	A	B	C	D	E	F	G	H	I	J	K	L	M	N	O	P	Q	R	S

The encoded alphabet is just the regular alphabet shifted to start at T, the first letter of the keyword TIGER. The second letter is encrypted according to the following map.

A	B	C	D	E	F	G	H	I	J	K	L	M	N	O	P	Q	R	S	T	U	V	W	X	Y	Z
I	J	K	L	M	N	O	P	Q	R	S	T	U	V	W	X	Y	Z	A	B	C	D	E	F	G	H

The third, fourth, and fifth letters in the input text are encrypted using the alphabet sequences beginning with characters G, E, and R, and so on. Because the key is only five letters long, the sixth letter of the input text is encrypted in the same way as the first.

Write a program that encrypts or decrypts an input text according to this cipher.

Exercise P12.5. *Playfair cipher.* Another way of thwarting a simple letter frequency analysis of an encrypted text is to encrypt *pairs* of letters together. A simple scheme to do this is the Playfair cipher. You pick a keyword and remove duplicate letters from it. Then you fill the keyword, and the remaining letters of the alphabet, into a 5 x 5 square. (Since there are only 25 squares, I and J are considered the same letter.)

Here is such an arrangement with the keyword PLAYFAIR.

```
P L A Y F
I R C D E
G H K M N
O Q R S T
U V W X Z
```

To encrypt a letter pair, say AM, look at the rectangle with corners A and M:

```
P L A Y F
I R C D E
G H K M N
O Q R S T
U V W X Z
```

The encoding of this pair is formed by looking at the other two corners of the rectangle, in this case, YK. If both letters happen to be in the same row or column, such as GO, simply swap the two letters. Decryption is done in the same way.

Write a program that encrypts or decrypts an input text according to this cipher.

Exercise P12.6. *Junk mail.* Write a program that reads in two files: a *template* and a *database*. The template file contains text and tags. The tags have the form |1| |2| |3| . . . and need to be replaced with the first, second, third, . . . field in the current database record.

A typical database looks like this:

```
Mr.|Harry|Hacker|1105 Torre Ave.|Cupertino|CA|95014
Dr.|John|Lee|702 Ninth Street Apt. 4|San Jose|CA|95109
Miss|Evelyn|Garcia|1101 S. University Place|Ann Arbor|MI|48105
```

And here is a typical form letter:

```
To:
|1| |2| |3|
|4|
|5|, |6| |7|

Dear |1| |3|:

You and the |3| family may be the lucky winners of $10,000,000 in the C++
compiler clearinghouse sweepstakes! ...
```

Exercise P12.7. The program in Section 12.5 only locates one record and updates the price. Write a program that raises or lowers the salaries of all employees by a given percentage.

Exercise P12.8. The program in Section 12.5 asks the user to specify the record number. More likely than not, a user has no way of knowing the record number. Write a program that asks the user for the name of an employee, finds the record with that name, and displays the record. Then the program should give the following options to the user:

- Change the salary of this record
- View the next record
- Find another employee
- Quit

Exercise P12.9. To find a particular employee in a database file, the program needs to search one record at a time. If the records are *sorted*, there is a faster way. Count the number of records in the file, by dividing the length of the file by the length of each record. Set a variable `first` to 1, `last` to `nrecords`. Compute `mid = (first + last)/2`. Read the record at `mid`. Maybe you are lucky, and you actually found the record you wanted. If so, print it and exit. Is its name before or after the name that you are searching? Adjust either `last` to `mid - 1` or `first` to `mid + 1` and repeat the search. This searching method is called a *binary search*, and it is much faster than a sequential search through all records. Implement this searching method.

Exercise P12.10. It is unpleasant to have to use the constant `NEWLINE_LENGTH`. One must remember to change the constant when porting the database program from UNIX to DOS. Implement the following strategy that avoids the problem. Write a function

```
int newline_length(fstream& fs)
```

Remember the current get position. Reset it to the beginning of the file. Keep calling `tellg` and reading characters. When the character is a `"\n"`, check whether the get position jumps by 1 or 2. Return that value. If you don't find a newline in the entire file, then report 0. Before exiting, restore the get position to its original value.

Write this function and put it inside the database program.

Exercise P12.11. Write a program that keeps an employee database in a random-access file. Implement functions for adding and removing employees. You need not keep employees in sorted order. To remove an employee, just fill the entire record with spaces. When adding an employee, try to add it into one of those empty spots first before appending it to the end of the file.

Exercise P12.12. Write a program that manipulates three database files. The first file contains the names and telephone numbers of a group of people. The second file contains the names and Social Security numbers of a group of people. The third file contains the Social Security numbers and annual salaries of a group of people. The groups of people should overlap but need not be completely identical. Your program should ask the user for a telephone number and then print the name, Social Security number, and annual income, if it can determine that information.

Exercise P12.13. Write a program that prints out a student grade report. There is a file, `classes.txt`, that contains the names of all classes taught at a college, such as

File classes.txt

```
1  CSC1
2  CSC2
3  CSC46
4  CSC151
5  MTH121
6  ...
```

For each class, there is a file with student numbers and grades:

File csc2.txt

```
1  11234 A-
2  12547 B
3  16753 B+
4  21886 C
5  ...
```

Write a program that asks for a student ID and prints out a grade report for that student, by searching all class files. Here is a sample report

```
Student ID 16753
CSC2 B+
MTH121 C+
CHN1 A
PHY50 A-
```

Exercise P12.14. A bank keeps all bank accounts in a random access file in which each line has the format

account_number balance

Write a program that simulates an automatic teller machine. A user can deposit money to an account by specifying the account number and amount, withdraw money, query the account balance, or transfer money from one account to another.

Exercise P12.15. Write a program `copyfile` that copies one file to another. The file names are specified on the command line. For example,

```
copyfile report.txt report.sav
```

Exercise P12.16. Write a program that *concatenates* the contents of several files into one file. For example,

```
catfiles chapter1.txt chapter2.txt chapter3.txt book.txt
```

makes a long file `book.txt` that contains the contents of the files `chapter1.txt`, `chapter2.txt`, and `chapter3.txt`. The target file is always the last file specified on the command line.

Exercise P12.17. Write a program `find` that searches all files specified on the command line and prints out all lines containing a keyword. For example, if you call

```
find Tim report.txt address.txt homework.cpp
```

then the program might print

```
report.txt: discussed the results of my meeting with Tim T
address.txt: Torrey, Tim|11801 Trenton Court|Dallas|TX
address.txt: Walters, Winnie|59 Timothy Circle|Detroit|MI
homework.cpp: Time now;
```

The keyword is always the first command line argument.

Exercise P12.18. Write a program that checks the spelling of all words in a file. It should read each word of a file and check whether it is contained in a word list. A word list is available on most UNIX systems in the file `/usr/dict/words`. (If you don't have access to a UNIX system, your instructor should be able to get you a copy.) The program should print out all words that it cannot find in the word list.

Exercise P12.19. Write a program that opens a file for reading and writing, and replaces each line with its reverse. For example, if you run

```
reverse hello.cpp
```

then the contents of `hello.cpp` is changed to

```
>maertsoi< edulcni#
;dts ecapseman gnisu
()niam tni
{
;"n\!dlrow, olleH" << tuoc
;0 nruter
}
```

Of course, if you run `reverse` twice on the same file, then the original file is displayed.

Exercise P12.20. The preceding exercise shows a limitation of the `hello.cpp` program. If you reverse every line, it no longer is a legal C++ program. You may not think that this is much to worry about, but there are people who try hard to write programs that can be scrambled in various ways. For example, a winner of the 1989 Obfuscated C Contest wrote a program that can be reversed and still does something useful. The grand prize winner of the 1990 contest wrote a C program that can be sorted! The unsorted version solves a differential equation, whereas the version in which the lines are sorted in alphabetical order prints Fibonacci numbers. Look at [5] for a highly entertaining account of these contests.

Your task is to write a C++ program that turns into another legal C++ program when you reverse each line.

Object-Oriented Design

To implement a software system successfully, be it as simple as your next homework project or as complex as the next air traffic monitoring system, some amount of planning, design, and testing is required. In fact, for larger projects, the amount of time spent on planning is much higher than the amount of time spent on programming and testing.

If you find that most of your homework time is spent in front of the computer, keying in code and fixing bugs, you are probably spending more time on your homework than you should. You could cut down your total time by spending more on the planning and design phase. This chapter tells you how to approach these tasks in a systematic manner.

13.1 The Software Life Cycle

In this section we will discuss the *software life cycle:* the activities that take place between the time a software program is first conceived and the time it is finally retired.

Many software engineers break the development process down into the following five phases:

- analysis

- design

- implementation

- testing

- deployment

In the *analysis* phase, you decide *what* the project is supposed to accomplish; you do not think about *how* the program will accomplish its tasks. The output of the analysis phase is a *requirements document,* which describes in complete detail what the program will be able to do once it is completed. Part of this requirements document can be a user manual that tells how the user will operate the program to derive the promised benefits. Another part sets performance criteria—how many inputs the program must be able to handle in what time, or what its maximum memory and disk storage requirements are.

In the *design* phase, you develop a plan for how you will implement the system. You discover the structures that underlie the problem to be solved. When you use object-oriented design, you decide what classes you need and what their most important member functions are. The output of this phase is a description of the classes and member functions, with diagrams that show the relationships among the classes.

In the *implementation* phase, you write and compile program code to implement the classes and member functions that were discovered in the design phase. The output of this phase is the completed program.

In the *testing* phase, you run tests to verify that the program works correctly. The output of this phase is a report describing the tests that you carried out and their results.

In the *deployment* phase, the users of the program install it and use it for its intended purpose.

When managing a large software project, it is not obvious how to organize these phases. A manager needs to know when to stop analyzing and start designing, when to stop coding and start testing, and so on. *Formal processes* have been established to help in the management of software projects. A formal process identifies the activities and deliverables of different phases and gives guidelines how to carry out the phases and when to move from one phase to the next.

When formal development processes were first established in the early 1970s, software engineers had a very simple visual model of these phases. They postulated that one phase would run to completion, its output would spill over to the next phase, and the next phase would begin. This model is called the *waterfall model* of software development (see Figure 1).

In an ideal world the waterfall model has a lot of appeal: You figure out what to do; then you figure out how to do it; then you do it; then you verify that you did it right; then you hand the product to the customer. When rigidly applied, though, the waterfall

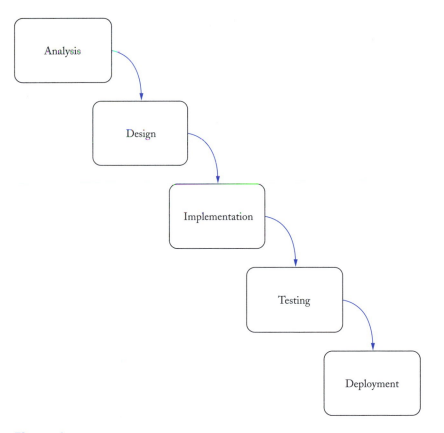

Figure 1

The Waterfall Model

model simply did not work. It was very difficult to come up with a perfect requirements specification. It was quite common to discover in the design phase that the requirements were not consistent or that a small change in the requirements would lead to a system that was both easier to design and more useful for the customer, but the analysis phase was over, so the designers had no choice—they had to take the existing requirements, errors and all. This problem would repeat itself during implementation. The designers may have thought they knew how to solve the problem as efficiently as possible, but when the design was actually implemented, it turned out that the resulting program was not as fast as the designers had thought. The next transition is one with which you are surely familiar. When the program was handed to the quality assurance department for testing, many bugs were found that would best be fixed by reimplementing, or maybe even redesigning, the program, but the waterfall model did not allow for this. Finally, when the customers received the finished product, they were often not at all happy with it. Even though the customers typically were very involved in the analysis phase, often they themselves were not sure exactly what they needed. After all, it can be very difficult to describe how you want to use a product that you have never seen before. But when the customers started using the program, they began to realize what they would have liked. Of course, then it was too late, and they had to live with what they got.

Having some level of iteration is clearly necessary. There simply must be a mechanism to deal with errors from the preceding phase. The spiral model, proposed by Barry Boehm in 1988, breaks down the development process into multiple phases (see Figure 2). Early phases focus on the construction of *prototypes*. A prototype is a small system

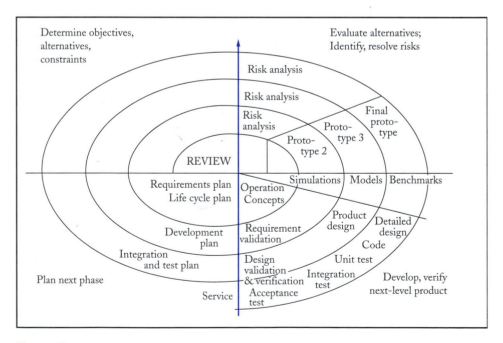

Figure 2

The Spiral Model

that shows some aspects of the final system. Because prototypes model only a part of a system and do not need to withstand customer abuse, they can be implemented quickly. It is common to build a *user interface prototype* that shows the user interface in action. This gives customers an early chance to become more familiar with the system and to suggest improvements before the analysis is complete. Other prototypes can be built to validate interfaces with external systems, to test performance, and so on. Lessons learned from the development of one prototype can be applied to the next iteration of the spiral.

By building in repeated trials and feedback, a development process that follows the spiral model has a greater chance of delivering a satisfactory system. However, there is also a danger. If engineers believe that they don't have to do a good job because they can always do another iteration, then there will be many iterations, and the process will take a very long time to complete.

Figure 3 (from [1]) shows activity levels in the "Rational Unified Process", a commonly used development process methodology by the inventors of the UML notation that you saw in Chapter 12. You can see that this is a complex process involving multiple iterations.

In your first programming course, you will not develop systems that are so complex that you need a full-fledged methodology to solve your homework problems. This introduction to the development process should, however, show you that successful software development involves more than just coding. In the remainder of this chapter, we will have a closer look at the design phase of the software development process.

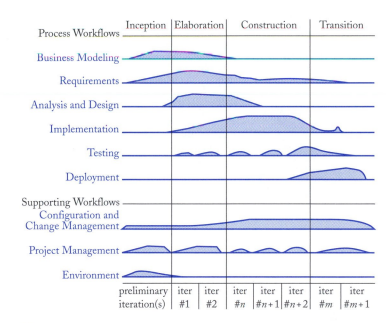

Figure 3

Activity Levels in the Rational Unified Process
Methodology

Random Fact 13.1

Extreme Programming

Even complex development processes with many iterations have not always met with success. In fact, there have been many reports of spectacular failures. Unsuccessful project teams followed the guidelines of their chosen methodology. They produced reams of analysis and design documentation. Unfortunately, it is very difficult for development managers to distinguish between good and bad designs. When a naive design turns out to be unimplementable, much time is wasted, often greatly surprising the managers who put their faith in the formal process.

In 1999, Kent Beck published an influential book [2] on *extreme programming*, a development methodology that strives for simplicity by cutting out most of the formal trappings of a traditional development methodology and instead focusing on a set of *practices:*

- *Pair programming:* Put programmers together in pairs, and require each pair to write code on a single computer. (You may want to try this out—many programmers have found that it is surprisingly effective to have one pair of hands and two pairs of eyes on the computer.)

- *Realistic planning:* Customers are to make business decisions, programmers are to make technical decisions. Update the plan when it conflicts with reality.

- *Small releases:* Release a useful system quickly, then release updates on a very short cycle.

- *Metaphor:* All programmers should have a simple shared story that explains the system under development.

- *Simplicity:* Design everything to be as simple as possible instead of preparing for future complexity.

- *Testing:* Both programmers and customers are to write test cases. The system is continuously tested.

- *Refactoring:* Programmers are to restructure the system continuously to improve the code and eliminate duplication.

- *Collective ownership:* All programmers are to have permission to change all code as it becomes necessary.

- *Continuous integration:* Whenever a task is completed, build the entire system and test it.

- *40-hour week:* Don't cover up unrealistic schedules with bursts of heroic effort.

- *On-site customer:* An actual customer of the system is to be accessible to team members at all times.

- *Coding standards:* Programmers are to follow standards that emphasize self-documenting code.

Many of these practices are common sense. Beck claims that the value of the extreme programming approach lies in the synergy of these practices—the sum is bigger than the parts.

▼

▼

Extreme programming is controversial—it is not at all proven that this set of practices by itself will consistently produce good results. For many projects, the best management policy may be to combine good practices with a development process that does not overwhelm developers with unnecessary activities.

13.2   CRC Cards

In the design phase of software development, your task is to discover structures that make it possible to implement a set of tasks on a computer. When you use the object-oriented design process, you carry out the following tasks:

1. Discover classes.
2. Determine the responsibilities of each class.
3. Describe the relationships between the classes.

A class represents some useful concept. You have seen classes for concrete entities such as products, circles, and clocks. Other classes represent abstract concepts such as streams and strings. A simple rule for finding classes is to look for nouns in the task description. For example, suppose your job is to print an invoice such as the one in Figure 4. Obvious classes that come to mind are Invoice, Item, and Customer. It is a good idea to keep a list of candidate classes on a whiteboard or a sheet of paper. As you brainstorm, simply put all ideas for classes on the list. You can always cross out the ones that weren't useful.

Once a set of classes has been identified, you need to define the behavior for each class. That is, you need to determine what member functions each object needs to carry out to solve the programming problem. A simple rule for finding these methods is to

INVOICE

Sam's Small Appliances
100 Main Street
Anytown, CA 98765

Item	Qty	Price	Total
Toaster	3	$29.95	$89.85
Hair Dryer	1	$24.95	$24.95
Car Vacuum	2	$19.99	$39.98

AMOUNT DUE: $154.78

Figure 4

An Invoice

look for verbs in the task description, and then match the verbs to the appropriate objects. For example, in the invoice program, some class needs to compute the amount due. Now you need to figure out which class is responsible for this method. Do customers compute what they owe? Do invoices total up the amount due? Do the items total themselves up? The best choice is to make "compute amount due" the responsibility of the Invoice class.

An excellent way to carry out this task is the so-called CRC card method. "CRC" stands for "classes", "responsibilities", "collaborators". In its simplest form, the method works as follows. Use an index card for each class (see Figure 5). As you think about verbs in the task description that indicate member functions, you pick the card of the class that you think should be responsible, and write that responsibility on the card. For each responsibility, you record which other classes are needed to fulfill it. Those classes are the collaborators.

For example, suppose you decide that an invoice should compute the amount due. Then you write "compute amount due" on the left-hand side of an index card with the title Invoice.

If a class can carry out that responsibility all by itself, you do nothing further. But if the class needs the help of other classes, you write the names of those collaborators on the right-hand side of the card.

To compute the total, the invoice needs to ask each item about its total price. Therefore, the Item class is a collaborator.

This is a good time to look up the index card for the Item class. Does it have a "get total price" member function? If not, add one.

How do you know that you are on the right track? For each responsibility, ask yourself how it can actually be done, using just the responsibilities written on the various cards. Many people find it helpful to group the cards on a table so that the collaborators are close to each other, and to simulate tasks by moving a token (such as a coin) from one card to the next to indicate which object is currently active.

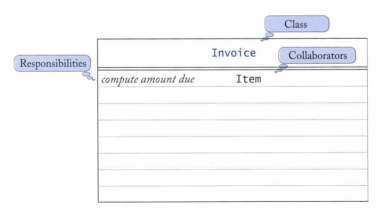

Figure 5

A CRC Card

Keep in mind that the responsibilities that you list on the CRC card are on a high level. Sometimes a single responsibility may need two or more member functions for carrying it out. Some researchers say that a CRC card should have no more than three distinct responsibilities.

The CRC card method is informal on purpose, so that you can be creative and discover classes and their properties. Don't be afraid to cross out, move, split, or merge responsibilities. Rip up cards if they become too messy. This is an informal process.

You are done when you have walked through all major tasks and satisfied yourself that they can all be solved with the classes and responsibilities that you discovered.

13.3   Cohesion

You have used a good number of classes in the preceding chapters and probably designed a few classes yourself as part of your programming assignments. Designing a class can be a challenge—it is not always easy to tell how to start or whether the result is of good quality.

Students who have prior experience with programming in a non-object-oriented style are used to programming *functions*. A function carries out an action. In object-oriented programming, however, each function belongs to a class. Classes are collections of objects, and objects are not actions—they are entities. So you have to start the programming activity by identifying objects and the classes to which they belong.

Remember the rule of thumb from Section 13.2: Class names should be nouns, and member function names should be verbs.

What makes a good class? Most importantly, a class should *represent a single concept*. Some of the classes that you have seen represent concepts from mathematics or physics:

- `Point`

- `Circle`

- `Time`

Other classes are abstractions of real-life entities.

- `Product`

- `Employee`

For these classes, the properties of a typical object are easy to understand. A `Circle` object has a center and radius. Given an `Employee` object, you can raise the salary. Generally, concepts from the part of the universe that our program concerns, such as science, business, or a game, make good classes. The name for such a class should be a noun that describes the concept.

What might not be a good class? If you can't tell from the class name what an object of the class is supposed to do, then you are probably not on the right track. For example, your homework assignment might ask you to write a program that prints paychecks. Suppose you start by trying to design a class `PaycheckProgram`. What would an object of this class do? An object of this class would have to do everything that the homework needs to do. That doesn't simplify anything. A better class would be `Paycheck`. Then your program can manipulate one or more `Paycheck` objects.

Another common mistake, particularly by students who are used to writing programs that consist of functions, is to turn an action into a class. For example, if your homework assignment is to compute a paycheck, you may consider writing a class `ComputePaycheck`. But can you visualize a "ComputePaycheck" object? The fact that "ComputePaycheck" isn't a noun tips you off that you are on the wrong track. On the other hand, a `Paycheck` class makes intuitive sense. The word "paycheck" is a noun. You can visualize a paycheck object. You can then think about useful member functions of the `Paycheck` class, such as `compute_net_pay`, that help you solve the assignment.

Let's return to the observation that a class should represent a single concept. The member functions and constants that the public interface exposes should be *cohesive*. That is, all interface features should be closely related to the single concept that the class represents.

If you find that the public interface of a class refers to multiple concepts, then that is a good sign that it may be time to use separate classes instead. Consider, for example, the public interface of a `Purse` class:

```cpp
class Purse
{
public:
   Purse();
   void add_nickels(int count);
   void add_dimes(int count);
   void add_quarters(int count);
   double get_total() const;
private:
   ...
};
```

There are really two concepts here: a purse that holds coins and computes their total, and the individual coins, each with their own names and values. It would make more sense to have a separate `Coin` class. Each coin should be responsible for knowing its name and value.

```cpp
class Coin
{
public:
   Coin(double v, string n);
   double get_value() const;
private:
   ...
};
```

Then the `Purse` class can be simplified:

```cpp
class Purse
{
```

```
public:
    Purse();
    void add(Coin c);
    double get_total() const;
private:
    ...
};
```

This is clearly a better solution, because it separates the concepts of the purse and the coins. Each of the resulting classes is more cohesive than the original Purse class was.

13.4 Coupling

Many classes need other classes to do their job. For example, the restructured Purse class of the preceding section *depends on* the Coin class. In general, a class depends on another if one of its member functions uses an object of the other class in some way.

In particular, the "collaborators" column of the CRC cards tell you which classes depend on another.

In Chapter 11, you saw the UML notation for inheritance. In a UML class diagram, you denote dependency in a similar way, by a dashed line with an open arrow tip that points to the dependent class. Figure 6 shows a class diagram that indicates that the Purse class depends on the Coin class.

Note that the Coin class does *not* depend on the Purse class. Coins have no idea that they are being collected in purses, and they can carry out their work without ever calling any member function in the Purse class.

If many classes of a program depend on each other, then we say that the *coupling* between classes is high. Conversely, if there are few dependencies between classes, then we say that the coupling is low (see Figure 7).

Why does coupling matter? If the Coin class changes in the next release of the program, all the classes that depend on it may be affected. If the change is drastic, the coupled classes must all be updated. Furthermore, if you would like to use the class in another program, you have to take with it all the classes on which it depends. Thus, in general, you want to remove unnecessary coupling between classes.

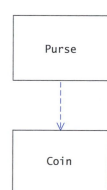

Figure 6

Dependency Relationship between the Purse and Coin Classes

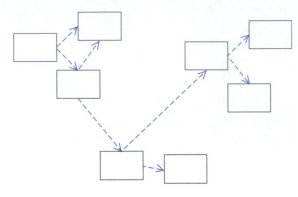

Low coupling

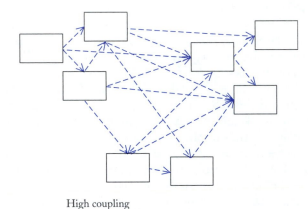

High coupling

Figure 7

High and Low Coupling between Classes

13.1

▼ **Quality Tip**

▼

Consistency

▼

In the preceding sections, you learned two criteria that are used to analyze the quality of the public interface of a class. You should maximize cohesion and remove unnecessary coupling. There is another criterion that you should pay attention to—consistency. When you have a set of member functions, follow a consistent scheme for their names and parameters. This is simply a sign of good craftsmanship.

▼

Sadly, you can find any number of inconsistencies in the standard library. Here is an example. To set the precision of an output stream, you use the `setprecision` manipulator:

```
cout << setprecision(2);
```

▼

To set the field width, you call

```
cout << setw(8);
```

▼

Why not `setwidth`? And why does the setting for precision persist until you change it, while the width keeps reverting to 0? Why the inconsistency? It would have been an easy matter to supply a `setwidth` manipulator that exactly mirrors `setprecision`. There is probably no good reason why the designers of the C++ library made these decisions. They just happened, and then nobody bothered to clean them up.

▼

Inconsistencies such as these are not a fatal flaw, but they are an annoyance, particularly because they can be so easily avoided. When designing your own classes, you should make an effort to periodically inspect them for consistency.

▼

13.5   Relationships between Classes

When designing a program, it is useful to document the relationships between classes. This helps you in a number of ways. For example, if you find classes with common behavior, you can save effort by placing the common behavior into a base class. If you know that some classes are *not* related to each other, you can assign different programmers to implement each of them, without worrying that one of them has to wait for the other.

You have seen the inheritance relationship between classes in Chapter 11. Inheritance is a very important relationship between classes, but, as it turns out, it is not the only useful relationship, and it can be overused.

Inheritance is a relationship between a more general class (the base class) and a more specialized class (the derived class). This relationship is often described as the *is-a* relationship. Every truck is a vehicle. Every savings account is a bank account. Every square is a rectangle (with equal width and height).

Inheritance is sometimes abused, however. For example, consider a `Tire` class that describes a car tire. Should the class `Tire` be a derived class of a class `Circle`? It sounds convenient. There are probably quite a few useful member functions in the `Circle` class—for example, the `Tire` class may inherit member functions that compute the radius, perimeter, and center point. All that should come in handy when drawing tire shapes. Yet, though it may be convenient for the programmer, this arrangement makes no sense conceptually. It isn't true that every tire is a circle. Tires are car parts, whereas circles are geometric objects.

There is a relationship between tires and circles, though. A tire *has* a circle as its boundary. C++ lets us model that relationship, too. Use a data field:

```
class Tire
{
   ...
private:
   string rating;
   Circle boundary;
};
```

The technical term for this relationship is *association*. Each `Tire` object is associated with a `Circle` object.

Here is another example. Suppose you are designing a program that produces a graphical simulation of freeway traffic. Your program models cars, trucks, and other vehicles.

Every car *is a* vehicle. Every car *has a* tire (in fact, it has four or, if you count the spare, five). Thus, you would use inheritance from Vehicle and use association of Tire objects:

```
class Car : public Vehicle
{
   ...
private:
   vector<Tire> tires;
};
```

In the UML notation, association is denoted by a solid line with an open arrow tip. Figure 8 shows a class diagram with an inheritance and an association relationship.

A class is associated with another if you can *navigate* from objects of one class to objects of the other class. For example, given a Car object, you can navigate to the Tire objects, simply by accessing the tires data field. When a class has a data field whose type is another class, then the two classes are associated.

The association relationship is related to the *dependency* relationship, which you saw in the preceding section. Recall that a class depends on another if one of its member functions uses an object of the other class in some way. Association is a stronger form of dependency. If a class is associated with another, it also depends on the other class.

However, the converse is not true. If a class is associated with another, objects of the class can locate objects of the associated class, usually because they store data fields of the associated type. If a class depends on another, it comes in contact with objects of the other class in some way, not necessarily through navigation. For example, the Purse class depends on the Coin class, but it is not necessarily associated with it. Given a Purse object, you can't necessarily navigate to the Coin objects. It is entirely possible that the

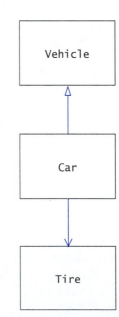

Figure 8

UML Notation for Inheritance and Association

add member function simply adds the coin value to the total without storing any actual coin objects.

As you saw in the preceding section, the UML notation for dependency is a dashed line with an open arrow that points to the dependent class.

The arrows in the UML notation can get confusing. The table below shows the three UML relationship symbols that we use in this book.

Relationship	Symbol	Line style	Arrow tip
Inheritance	⟶▷	Solid	Closed
Association	⟶	Solid	Open
Dependency	-------->	Dotted	Open

Advanced Topic   13.1

Attributes and Member Functions in UML Diagrams

Sometimes it is useful to indicate class attributes and member functions in a class diagram. An attribute is an externally observable property that objects of a class have. For example, name and price would be attributes of the Product class. Usually, attributes correspond to data fields. But they don't have to—a class may have a different way of organizing its data. Consider the Time class from the library for this book. Conceptually, it has attributes seconds, minutes, and hours, but it doesn't actually store the minutes and hours in separate data members. Instead, it stores the number of seconds since midnight and computes the minutes and hours from it.

You can indicate attributes and member functions in a class diagram by dividing a class rectangle into three compartments, with the class name in the top, attributes in the middle, and member functions in the bottom (see Figure 9). You need not list *all* attributes and member functions in a particular diagram. Just list the ones that are helpful to understand whatever point you are making with a particular diagram.

Also, don't list as an attribute what you also draw as an association. If you denote by association the fact that a Vehicle has Tire objects, don't add an attribute tires.

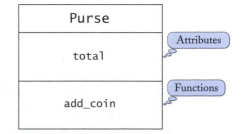

Figure 9

Attributes and Member Functions in a Class Diagram

Advanced Topic   13.2

Association, Aggregation, and Composition

The association relationship is the most complex relationship in the UML notation. It is also the least standardized. As you read other books and see class diagrams produced by fellow programmers, you may encounter quite a few different flavors of the association relationship.

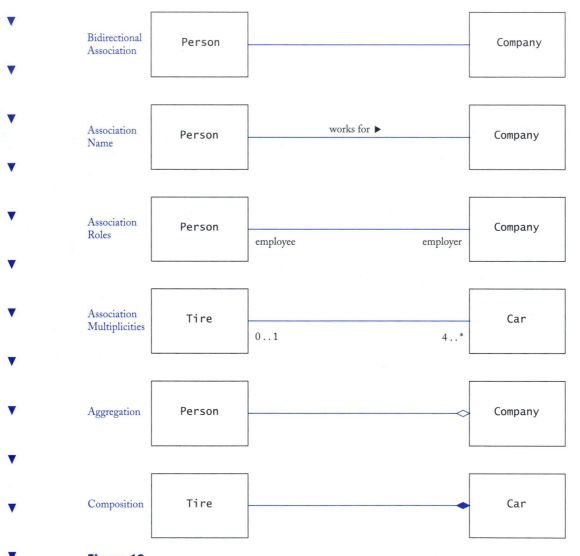

Figure 10

Variations of the Association Notation

The association relationship that we use in this book is called a directed association. It implies that you can navigate from one class to another, but not the other way around. For example, given a `Vehicle` object, you can navigate to `Tire` objects. But if you have a `Tire` object, then there is no indication to which vehicle it belongs.

Of course, a `Tire` object may contain a pointer back to the `Vehicle` object so that you can navigate from the tire back to the vehicle to which it belongs. Then the association is *bidirectional*. For vehicles and tires, this is an unlikely implementation. But consider the example of `Employee` and `Company` objects. The company may keep a list of employees working for it, and each employee object may keep a pointer to the current employer.

According to the UML standard, a bidirectional association is drawn as a solid line with *no* arrow tips. (See Figure 10 for this and other variations of the association notation.) But some designers interpret an association without arrow tips as an "undecided" association, where it is not yet known in which direction the navigation can happen.

Some designers like to add *adornments* to the association relationships. An association can have a name, roles, or multiplicities. A name describes the nature of the relationship. Role adornments express specific roles that the associated classes have toward each other. Multiplicities state how many objects can be reached when navigating the association relationship. The example in Figure 10 expresses the fact that every tire is associated with 0 or 1 vehicle, whereas every vehicle must have 4 or more tires.

Aggregation is a stronger form of association. A class aggregates another if there is a "whole-part" relationship between the classes. For example, the `Company` class may aggregate the `Employee` class because a company (the "whole") is made up from people (the "parts"), namely its employees and contractors. But a `BankAccount` class does not aggregate a `Person` class, even though it may be possible to navigate from a bank customer object to a person object—the owner of the account. Conceptually, a person is not a part of the bank account.

Composition is an even stronger form of aggregation that denotes that a "part" can belong to only one "whole" at a given point in time. Furthermore, if the "whole" goes away, then the "part" goes away as well. For example, a tire can be in only one vehicle at a time, but an employee can work for two separate companies at the same time.

Frankly, the differences between association, aggregation, and composition are subtle and can be confusing, even to experienced designers. If you find the distinctions helpful, by all means use them. But don't lose sleep pondering the differences between these concepts.

13.6 Implementing Associations

Associations between classes are usually implemented as data fields. For example, if the `Company` class is associated with the `Employee` class, the company needs to store one or more `Employee` objects or pointers.

When implementing the association, you need to make two important choices. Should you store a single `Employee` or a vector of `Employee` objects? Should you store objects or pointers?

To answer these questions, ask yourself two questions. First, what is the *multiplicity* of the association. The three most common choices are

- 1 : many (for example, every company has many employees)

- 1 : 1 (for example, every bank account has one owner)

- 1 : 0 or 1 (for example, every department has 0 or 1 receptionist)

For a "1 : many" relationship, you need to use a vector (or some other data structure—see Chapter 16).

Next, you need to ask whether you store objects or pointers. You must use pointers in three circumstances:

- For a "1 : 0 or 1" relationship (see Chapter 10)

- For object sharing (see Chapter 10)

- For polymorphism, to refer to an object that may belong to a base class or a derived class (see Chapter 11)

Consider a few examples. A `BankAccount` object is associated with a `Person` object, the owner of the account. Suppose that in our application, an account has a single owner. (In real life, there are accounts with multiple owners, but we will ignore that complexity for now.) Should you store a `Person` object, or a pointer of type `Person*`? Since multiple bank accounts can share the same owner, it makes sense to use a pointer:

```
class BankAccount
{
    ...
private:
    Person* owner;
};
```

On the other hand, consider a `Vehicle` class that is associated with the `Tire` class. A vehicle has multiple tires, so you would use a vector to store them. Should you store objects or pointers? A particular tire can only be a part of a single vehicle, so you can store objects.

```
class Vehicle
{
    ...
private:
    vector<Tire> tires;
};
```

13.7   Example: Printing an Invoice

In this chapter, we discuss a five-part development process that is recommended for you to follow:

1. Gather requirements.
2. Use CRC cards to find classes, responsibilities, and collaborators.
3. Use UML diagrams to record class relationships.
4. Document classes and member functions.
5. Implement your program.

This process is particularly well suited for beginning programmers. There isn't a lot of notation to learn. The class diagrams are simple to draw. The deliverables of the design phase are immediately useful for the implementation phase. Of course, as your projects get more complex, you will want to learn more about formal design methods. There are many techniques to describe object scenarios, call sequencing, the large-scale structure of programs, and so on, that are very beneficial even for relatively simple projects. The book [1] gives a good overview of these techniques.

In this section, we will walk through the object-oriented design technique with a very simple example. In this case, the methodology will certainly feel overblown, but it is a good introduction to the mechanics of each step. You will then be better prepared for the more complex example that follows.

As you read how the solution to the programming problem unfolds in the following sections, please be aware that this solution is only one of many reasonable approaches. It is a good idea to develop an alternate solution to each of the steps and to compare your version with the results that are presented here.

13.7.1 — Requirements

The task of this program is to print out an invoice. An invoice describes the charges for a set of products in certain quantities. (Complexities such as dates, taxes, and invoice and customer numbers are omitted.) The program simply prints the billing address, all line items, and the amount due. Each line item contains the description and unit price of a product, the quantity ordered, and the total price.

```
              I N V O I C E

      Sam's Small Appliances
      100 Main Street
      Anytown, CA 98765

      Description            Price  Qty  Total
      Toaster                29.95   3   89.85
      Hair dryer             24.95   1   24.95
      Car vacuum             19.99   2   39.98

      AMOUNT DUE: $154.78
```

Also, in the interest of simplicity, no user interface is required. Simply use a test harness that adds items to the invoice and then prints it.

13.7.2 — CRC Cards

First, you need to discover classes. Classes correspond to nouns in the problem description. In this problem, it is pretty obvious what the nouns are:

```
Invoice
Address
Item
Product
Description
Price
Quantity
Total
Amount Due
```

(Of course, Toaster doesn't count—it is the description of an Item object and therefore a data value, not the name of a class.)

The product description and price are fields of the Product class. What about the quantity? The quantity is not an attribute of a Product. Just as in the printed invoice, let's have a class Item that records the product and the quantity (such as "3 toasters").

The total and amount due are computed—not stored anywhere. Thus, they don't lead to classes.

After this process of elimination, four candidates for classes are left:

```
Invoice
Address
Item
Product
```

Each of them represents a useful concept, so make them all into classes.

The purpose of the program is to print an invoice. Record that responsibility in a CRC card:

Invoice
print the invoice

How does an invoice print itself? It must print the billing address, print all items, and then add the amount due. How can the invoice print an address? It can't—that really is the responsibility of the Address class. This leads to a second CRC card:

Address
print the address

Similarly, printing of an item is the responsibility of the Item class.

The print member function of the Invoice class calls the print member functions of the Address and Item classes. Whenever a member function uses another class, you list that other class as a collaborator. In other words, `Address` and `Item` are collaborators of `Invoice`:

Invoice	
print the invoice	Address
	Item

When formatting the invoice, the invoice also needs to compute the total amount due. To obtain that amount, it must ask each item about the total price of the item.

How does an item obtain that total? It must ask the product for the unit price, and then multiply it by the quantity. That is, the `Product` class must reveal the unit price, and it is a collaborator of the `Item` class.

Product	
get description	
get unit price	

Item	
print the item	Product
get total price	

Finally, the invoice must be populated with products and quantities, so that it makes sense to print the result. This too is a responsibility of the `Invoice` class.

Invoice	
print the invoice	Address
add a product and quantity	Item
	Product

You now have a set of CRC cards that completes the CRC card process.

13.7.3 — UML Diagrams

You get the dependency relationships from the collaboration column in the CRC cards. Each class depends on the classes with which it collaborates. In our example, the Invoice class collaborates with the Address, Item, and Product classes. The Item class collaborates with the Product class.

Now ask yourself which of these dependencies are actually associations. How does an invoice know about the address, item, and product objects with which it collaborates? An invoice object must hold the address and the items when it prints the invoice. But an invoice object need not hold a product object when adding a product. The product is turned into an item, and then it is the item's responsibility to hold it.

Therefore, the Invoice class is associated with the Address class and the Item class, but not the Product class. You cannot directly navigate from an invoice to a product. An invoice doesn't store products directly—they are stored in the Item objects. The Item class is associated with the Product class.

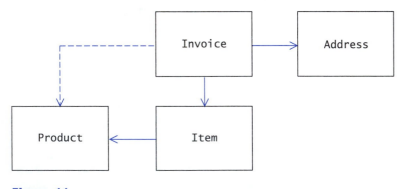

Figure 11

The Relationships between the Invoice Classes

There is no inheritance in the example that is developed in this section. Figure 11 shows the class relationships between the invoice classes.

13.7.4 — Class and Function Comments

The final step of the design phase is to write the documentation of the discovered classes and member functions. Simply write the comments for the classes that you discovered. For the member functions, you'll have to work a little harder. The CRC cards only contain the member functions in a high-level description. You need to come up with reasonable parameters and return types.

Here is the documentation for the invoice classes.

```cpp
/**
    Describes an invoice for a set of purchased products.
*/
class Invoice
{
public:
    /**
        Adds a charge for a product to this invoice.
        @param p the product that the customer ordered
        @param quantity the quantity of the product
    */
    void add(Product p, int quantity);
    /**
        Prints the invoice.
    */
    void print() const;
};

/**
    Describes a quantity of an article to purchase and its price.
*/
class Item
{
public:
    /**
        Computes the total cost of this item.
        @return the total price
    */
    double get_total_price() const;

    /**
        Prints this item.
    */
    void print() const;
};

/**
    Describes a product with a description and a price.
*/
class Product
{
```

```
public:
   /**
       Gets the product description.
       @return the description
   */
   string get_description() const;

   /**
       Gets the product price.
       @return the unit price
   */
   double get_price() const;
};

/**
    Describes a mailing address.
*/
class Address
{
public:
   /**
       Prints the address.
   */
   void print() const;
};
```

You can then run a comment extraction program to obtain a prettily formatted version of your documentation in HTML format (see Figure 12). One such program is doxygen; see this book's companion Web site for more information.

This approach for documenting your classes has a number of advantages. You can share the documentation with others if you work in a team. You use a format that is

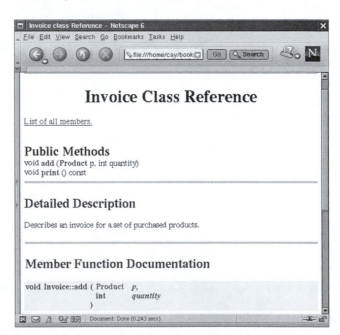

Figure 12

The Class Documentation in the HTML Format

immediately useful—C++ files that you can carry into the implementation phase. And, most importantly, you supply the comments for the key member functions—a task that less prepared programmers leave for later, and then often neglect for lack of time.

13.7.5 — Implementation

Finally, you are ready to implement the classes.

You already have the member function signatures and comments from the previous step. Now look at the associated classes in the UML diagram to add data fields. Start with the `Invoice` class. An invoice is associated with `Address` and `Item`. Every invoice has one billing address, but it can have many items. To store multiple `Item` objects, you use a vector. Now you have the data fields of the `Invoice` class:

```
class Invoice
{
   ...
private:
   Address billing_address;
   vector<Item> items;
};
```

As you can see from the UML diagram, the `Item` class is associated with a product. Also, you need to store the product quantity, which leads to the following data fields:

```
class Item
{
   ...
private:
   Product prod;
   int quantity;
};
```

The member functions themselves are now very easy. Here is a typical example. You already know what the `get_total_price` member function of the `Item` class needs to do—get the unit price of the product and multiply it with the quantity.

```
double Item::getTotalPrice()
{
   return prod.get_price() * quantity;
}
```

The other member functions are equally straightforward and won't be discussed in detail.

Finally, you need to supply constructors, another routine task. Here is the entire program. It is a good practice to go through it in detail and match up the classes and member functions against the CRC cards and UML diagram.

File invoice.cpp

```
1  #include <iostream>
2  #include <string>
3  #include <vector>
4
5  using namespace std;
6
7  /**
```

```
8       Describes a product with a description and a price.
9  */
10 class Product
11 {
12 public:
13     Product();
14     Product(string d, double p);
15     /**
16         Gets the product description.
17         @return the description
18     */
19     string get_description() const;
20
21     /**
22         Gets the product price.
23         @return the unit price
24     */
25     double get_price() const;
26
27 private:
28     string description;
29     double price;
30 };
31
32 Product::Product()
33 {
34     price = 0;
35 }
36
37 Product::Product(string d, double p)
38 {
39     description = d;
40     price = p;
41 }
42
43 string Product::get_description() const
44 {
45     return description;
46 }
47
48 double Product::get_price() const
49 {
50     return price;
51 }
52
53 /**
54     Describes a quantity of an article to purchase and its price.
55 */
56 class Item
57 {
58 public:
59     Item();
60     Item(Product p, int q);
61     /**
62         Computes the total cost of this item.
63         @return the total price
```

```
64      */
65      double get_total_price() const;
66
67      /**
68          Prints this item.
69      */
70      void print() const;
71   private:
72      Product prod;
73      int quantity;
74   };
75
76
77   Item::Item()
78   {
79      quantity = 0;
80   }
81
82   Item::Item(Product p, int q)
83   {
84      prod = p;
85      quantity = q;
86   }
87
88   double Item::get_total_price() const
89   {
90      return prod.get_price() * quantity;
91   }
92
93   void Item::print() const
94   {
95      const int COLUMN_WIDTH = 30;
96      string description = prod.get_description();
97
98      cout << description;
99
100     // pad with spaces to fill column
101
102     int pad = COLUMN_WIDTH - description.length();
103     for (int i = 1; i <= pad; i++)
104        cout << " ";
105
106     cout << prod.get_price()
107        << "    " << quantity
108        << "    " << get_total_price() << "\n";
109  }
110
111  /**
112     Describes a mailing address.
113  */
114  class Address
115  {
116  public:
117     Address();
118     Address(string n, string s,
119        string c, string st, string z);
```

```
120    /**
121        Prints the address.
122    */
123    void print() const;
124 private:
125    string name;
126    string street;
127    string city;
128    string state;
129    string zip;
130 };
131
132 Address::Address() {}
133
134 Address::Address(string n, string s,
135    string c, string st, string z)
136 {
137    name = n;
138    street = s;
139    city = c;
140    state = st;
141    zip = z;
142 }
143
144 void Address::print() const
145 {
146    cout << name << "\n" << street << "\n"
147        << city << ", " << state << " " << zip << "\n";
148 }
149
150 /**
151    Describes an invoice for a set of purchased products.
152 */
153 class Invoice
154 {
155 public:
156    Invoice(Address a);
157    /**
158        Adds a charge for a product to this invoice.
159        @param p the product that the customer ordered
160        @param quantity the quantity of the product
161    */
162    void add(Product p, int quantity);
163    /**
164        Prints the invoice.
165    */
166    void print() const;
167 private:
168    Address billing_address;
169    vector<Item> items;
170 };
171
172 Invoice::Invoice(Address a)
173 {
174    billing_address = a;
175 }
```

```
176
177  void Invoice::add(Product p, int q)
178  {
179     Item it(p, q);
180     items.push_back(it);
181  }
182
183  void Invoice::print() const
184  {
185     cout << "                        I N V O I C E\n\n";
186     billing_address.print();
187     cout <<
188        "\n\nDescription                     Price   Qty   Total\n";
189     for (int i = 0; i < items.size(); i++)
190        items[i].print();
191
192     double amount_due = 0;
193     for (int i = 0; i < items.size(); i++)
194        amount_due = amount_due + items[i].get_total_price();
195
196     cout << "\nAMOUNT DUE: $" << amount_due;
197  }
198
199  int main()
200  {
201     Address sams_address("Sam's Small Appliances",
202           "100 Main Street", "Anytown", "CA", "98765");
203
204     Invoice sams_invoice(sams_address);
205     sams_invoice.add(Product("Toaster", 29.95), 3);
206     sams_invoice.add(Product("Hair dryer", 24.95), 1);
207     sams_invoice.add(Product("Car vacuum", 19.99), 2);
208
209     sams_invoice.print();
210     return 0;
211  }
```

Common Error

13.1

Ordering Class Definitions

When you write a program that contains multiple classes, you must be careful about the order in which the compiler sees their definitions.

Consider the classes of the invoice example.

- Invoice has fields of type Address and vector<Item>. Therefore, Address and Item must be defined before Invoice.

- Item has a field of type Product. Therefore, Product must be defined before Item.

Here are two possible ways in which you can order the classes:

```
Product
Item
Address
Invoice
```

or

```
Address
Product
Item
Invoice
```

Either ordering is fine.

This simple ordering mechanism can break down if one class declares a pointer to another class. Consider this example:

```
class Person
{
   ...
private:
   BankAccount retirement_account; // ERROR
};

class BankAccount
{
   ...
private:
   Person* owner;
};
```

This definition order is not correct. Since Person objects contain BankAccount objects, the compiler needs to know the data layout of the BankAccount class in order to make sense of the Person class.

On the other hand, a BankAccount object merely contains a pointer to a Person class. As long as the compiler knows that Person is a class, it can allocate space for the pointer. (Pointers to objects of any class have a fixed size.) To tell the compiler that Person is a class that will be defined later, you use the class *declaration*

```
class Person;
```

Therefore, the correct ordering is:

```
class Person; // declaration
class BankAccount { ... }; // definition
class Person { ... }; // definition
```

In general, follow these two rules:

- If a class declares a field of another class, then the compiler must have seen its *definition*.

- If a class declares a pointer to another class, then the compiler must have seen its *declaration* or *definition*.

13.8   Example: An Educational Game

This example uses the optional graphics library that is described in Chapter 3.

13.8.1 — Requirements

Your task is to write a game program that teaches your baby sister how to read the clock (see Figure 13). The game should do the following: randomly generate a time, draw a clock face with that time, and ask the player to type in the time. The player gets two tries before the game displays the correct time. Whenever the player gets the right answer, the score increases by one point. There are four levels of difficulty. Level 1 teaches full hours, level 2 teaches 15-minute intervals, level 3 teaches 5-minute intervals, and level 4 displays all times. When the player has reached a score of five points on one level, the game advances to the next level.

At the beginning, the game asks for the player's name and the desired starting level. After every round, the player is asked whether he or she wants to play more. The game ends when the player decides to quit.

13.8.2 — CRC Cards

What classes can you find? You need to look at nouns in the problem description; here are several:

```
Player
Clock
Time
Level
Game
Round
```

Not all nouns that you find make useful objects. For example, the Level is just an integer between 1 and 4; it doesn't really do anything. At this time, the best course of action is to

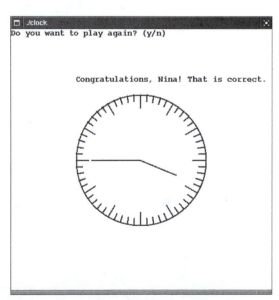

Figure 13

The Screen Display of the
Clock Program

leave it in the list of possible classes and to abandon it later if it turns out not to have any useful actions.

Start with a simple class: the Clock class. The clock object has one important responsibility: to draw the clock face.

Clock
draw

When a clock draws itself, it must draw the hour and minute hands to show the current times. To get the hours and minutes of the current time, it must collaborate with the Time class.

How does the clock know what time it is? You need to tell it:

Clock	
draw	Time
set time	

Next, take up the Time class. You need to get the hours and minutes of a given time, and be able to tell when two times are the same.

Time
get hours and minutes
check if equal to another   Time *object*

Now look at the player. A player has a name, a level, and a score. Every time the player gets a correct answer, the score must be incremented.

Player
increment score

After every five score increments, the level is incremented as well. Let the *increment score* function take care of that. Of course, then you must find out what the current level is.

Player
increment score
get level

Now you are in a fairly typical situation. You have a mess of classes, each of which seems to do interesting things, but you don't know how they will all work together.

A good plan is to introduce a class that represents the entire program—in our case, the game:

Game
play

Unlike the previously discovered functions, it is not at all obvious how this function works. You must use the process of stepwise refinement, which we discussed in Chapter 5.

What does it mean to play the game? The game starts by asking the player's name and level. Then the player plays a round, the game asks whether the player wants to play again, and so on.

Play the game:

> *read player information*
> do
> {
>   *play a round*
>   *ask whether player wants to play again*
> }
> while (*player wants to play again*) ;

A couple of new actions are required: to get player information and to play a round. Add *read player information* to the Game class:

Game
play
read player information

Now, how about *play a round?* Should the Game class or the Player class implement this function? What is involved in playing a round? You must make a time, depending on the selected level. You must draw the clock, ask for input, check whether the input is correct, play again if it is not, and increment the player's score if it is.

The responsibility can be assigned either way. In this discussion, let the Game class take care of playing the round. It informs the player about the game progress, which makes the Player class a collaborator. Note that the game must draw a clock face when playing a round, so Clock is a collaborator. Furthermore, the game generates Time objects, which makes Time another collaborator.

Game	
play	Player
read player information	Clock
play round	Time

So far there is no need for the classes Round and Level that were tentatively noted in the class discovery step, so do not implement them.

13.8.3 — UML Diagrams

From the collaborator columns of the CRC cards, you can determine that the Game class uses the Player, Clock, and Time classes, and the Clock class uses the Time class.

Next, ask yourself whether any of these dependencies are actually associations. Can you navigate from a Game object to a Player object? Or do the Game member functions only use local or parameter variables of type Player? Since the same player object must be manipulated during several rounds, one can't just construct local player objects in each round. That is, there must be a Player object that persists during the lifetime of the game. Conceivably, that Player object might be passed as a parameter to the *play round* function, but that seems far-fetched. It makes much more sense for the Game object to have a data field of type Player, to initialize that object in the "read player information" function, and to have the *play round* function modify its state. Thus, you may conclude that the Player class is associated with the Game class.

On the other hand, there is no pressing need for the Clock and Time classes to be associated with the Game class. The *play round* function can construct local Clock and Time objects.

Since the Clock CRC card shows a *set time* function, you can conclude that the Time class is associated with the Clock class.

Figure 14 shows the UML diagram for the clock game classes.

13.8.4 — Class and Function Comments

Translating the responsibilities from the CRC cards to member functions is straightforward. Following are the commented Clock, Player, and Game classes.

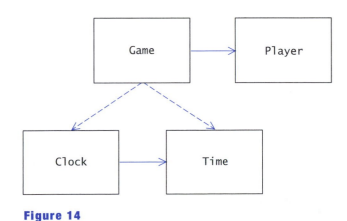

Figure 14

The Relationships between the Clock Game Classes

```cpp
/**
    A clock that can draw its face.
*/
class Clock
{
public:
    /**
        Sets the current time.
        @param t the time to set
    */
    void set_time(Time t);

    /**
        Draws the clock face, with tick marks and hands.
    */
    void draw() const;
};

/**
    The player of the clock game.
*/
class Player
{
public:
    /**
        Increments the score. Moves to next level if current
        level complete.
    */
    void increment_score();

    /**
        Gets the current level.
        @return the level
    */
    int get_level() const;
};

/**
    The clock game.
*/
class Game
{
public:
    /**
        Plays the game while the player wants to continue.
    */
    void play();

    /**
        Reads player name and level.
    */
    void read_player_information();

    /**
        Plays a round, with up to two guesses.
    */
    void play_round();
};
```

Now turn to the `Time` class. You will need the following functionality:

- Get the hours and minutes of a `Time` object.
- Check whether two `Time` objects are identical.

This class seems to be similar to the `Time` class that is a part of the library of this book (see Chapter 3). Rather than reinventing the wheel, determine whether you can use this class.

If you want to use the existing `Time` class, you must also specify seconds, but you can set the seconds to zero. To see whether two times are identical, check whether there are zero seconds from the first to the second time, that is, test whether `time1.seconds_from(time2)` is 0. Thus, to everyone's relief, you can use the library class and don't need to write a new one.

Now you have a set of classes, with reasonably complete interfaces. Is the design complete? In practice, that is not always an easy question to answer. It is quite common to find during the implementation phase that a particular task cannot be carried out with the interface functions. Then one needs to go back and revise the classes and interfaces.

13.8.5 — Implementation

Start with the `Clock` class. The clock must remember the time that is set with `set_time` so that it can draw the clock face. It must also remember where to draw the clock. Store the current time, the center point, and the radius of the clock face.

```
class Clock
{
    ...
private:
    Time current_time;
    Point center;
    double radius;
};
```

The `set_time` function is straightforward:

```
void Clock::set_time(Time t)
{
    current_time = t;
}
```

The `draw` function is more complex. Use the process of stepwise refinement to simplify it.

Draw the clock:

draw a circle
draw the hour "ticks"
draw the minute "ticks"
draw the hour hand
draw the minute hand

You need a function to draw a tick and a function to draw a hand. Each of these functions takes two parameters: the angle of the line segment to draw and its length. For convenience, the angle is measured clockwise, in multiples of six degrees (the angle between two adjacent minute ticks), starting from the 12 o'clock position.

```
void Clock::draw_tick(double angle, double length) const
{
   double alpha = PI / 2 - 6 * angle * PI / 180;
   Point from(
      center.get_x() + cos(alpha) * radius * (1 - length),
      center.get_y() + sin(alpha) * radius * (1 - length));
   Point to(center.get_x() + cos(alpha) * radius,
      center.get_y() + sin(alpha) * radius);
   cwin << Line(from, to);
}

void Clock::draw_hand(double angle, double length) const
{
   double alpha = PI / 2 - 6 * angle * PI / 180;
   Point from = center;
   Point to(center.get_x() + cos(alpha) * radius * length,
      center.get_y() + sin(alpha) * radius * length);
   cwin << Line(from, to);
}
```

Then the function to draw the clock face is relatively simple:

```
void Clock::draw() const
{
   cwin << Circle(center, radius);
   const double HOUR_TICK_LENGTH = 0.2;
   const double MINUTE_TICK_LENGTH = 0.1;
   const double HOUR_HAND_LENGTH = 0.6;
   const double MINUTE_HAND_LENGTH = 0.75;
   for (int i = 0; i < 12; i++)
   {
      draw_tick(i * 5, HOUR_TICK_LENGTH);
      for (int j = 1; j <= 4; j++)
         draw_tick(i * 5 + j, MINUTE_TICK_LENGTH);
   }

   draw_hand(current_time.get_minutes(), MINUTE_HAND_LENGTH);
   draw_hand((current_time.get_hours() +
      current_time.get_minutes() / 60.0) * 5,
      HOUR_HAND_LENGTH);
}
```

The `draw` function illustrates an important point. Object-oriented design does not replace the process of stepwise refinement. It is quite common to have member functions that are complex and need to be refined further. Because the helper functions `draw_tick` and `draw_hand` are only meant to be called by `draw`, they should be placed in the private section of the class.

The `Clock` constructor constructs a clock from a given center and radius:

```
Clock::Clock(Point c, double r)
{
   center = c;
   radius = r;
}
```

Now we turn to the `Player` class. A player needs to store the current level and score:

```
class Player
{
    ...
private:
    int level;
    int score;
};
```

The constructor and the `get_level` function are straightforward—see the code at the end of this section.

The `increment_score` function is more interesting. Of course, it increments the score. When the score becomes a multiple of five, and the level is less than four, the level is also incremented:

```
void Player::increment_score()
{
    score++;
    if (score % 5 == 0 and level < 4)
        level++;
}
```

The last class to consider is the `Game` class. What data fields does the game need? It needs a player. How about the clock and the time? Each round generates a new random time, and the time is not needed in the other functions. Therefore, do not make the clock and time data fields of the `Game` class. They will just be local variables of the `play_round` function.

You already saw the pseudocode for the `play` procedure. Here is the full C++ code:

```
void Game::play()
{
    rand_seed();
    read_player_information();
    string response;
    do
    {
        play_round();
        response = cwin.get_string(
            "Do you want to play again? (y/n)");
    }
    while (response == "y");
}
```

The `read_player_information` function is straightforward:

```
void Game::read_player_information()
{
    string name = cwin.get_string("What is your name?");
    int initial_level;
    do
    {
        initial_level = cwin.get_int(
            "At what level do you want to start? (1-4)");
    }
    while (initial_level < 1 || initial_level > 4);
    player = Player(name, initial_level);
}
```

Not unexpectedly, the `play_round` function is the hardest. Here is a refinement:

Play a round:

> *make a random time*
> *show the time*
> *get a guess*
> `if` (*guess is not correct*)
>   *get a guess*
> `if` (*guess is correct*)
> `{`
>   *congratulate player*
>   *increment score*
> `}`
> `else`
>   *give correct answer*

The *random time* depends on the level. If the level is 1, then the time must be a full hour—that is, a multiple of 60. If the level is 2, then the number of minutes is a multiple of 15. If the level is 3, then the number of minutes is a multiple of 5. Otherwise, it can be any number.

```
Time Game::random_time()
{
   int level = player.get_level();

   int minutes;
   if (level == 1) minutes = 0;
   else if (level == 2) minutes = 15 * rand_int(0, 3);
   else if (level == 3) minutes = 5 * rand_int(0, 11);
   else minutes = rand_int(0, 59);
   int hours = rand_int(1, 12);
   return Time(hours, minutes, 0);
}
```

Since *get a guess* occurs twice, make that into a separate function:

```
Time Game::get_guess()
{
   int hours;
   do
   {
      hours = cwin.get_int("Please enter hours: (1-12)");
   }
   while (hours < 1 || hours > 12);
   int minutes;
   do
   {
      minutes = cwin.get_int("Please enter minutes: (0-59)");
   }
   while (minutes < 0 || minutes > 59);

   return Time(hours, minutes, 0);
}
```

You are now ready to implement the `play_round` function.

```
void Game::play_round()
{
   cwin.clear();
   Time t = random_time();
   const double CLOCK_RADIUS = 5;
   Clock clock(Point(0, 0), CLOCK_RADIUS);
   clock.set_time(t);
   clock.draw();

   Time guess = get_guess();
   if (t.seconds_from(guess) != 0)
      guess = get_guess();

   string text;
   if (t.seconds_from(guess) == 0)
   {
      text = "Congratulations, " + player.get_name()
         + "! That is correct.";
      player.increment_score();
   }
   else
      text = "Sorry, " + player.get_name()
         + "! That is not correct.";

   cwin <<
      Message(Point(-CLOCK_RADIUS, CLOCK_RADIUS + 1), text);
}
```

There is, however, a slight problem. We want to be friendly and congratulate the player by name:

```
Congratulations, Susan! That is correct.
```

However, if you look at the Player class, you won't find a get_name function. This was an oversight; it is easy to remedy:

```
class Player
{
public:
   ...
   /**
      Gets the player's name.
      @return the name
   */
   string get_name() const;
   ...
};

string Player::get_name() const
{
   return name;
}
```

When designing a collection of collaborating classes, as you are doing to implement this game, it is quite common to discover imperfections in some of the classes. This is not a problem. Revisiting a class to add more member functions is perfectly acceptable.

The `main` program is now quite short. You need to make a `Game` object and call `play`:

```
int ccc_win_main()
{
   Game clock_game;
   clock_game.play();

   return 0;
}
```

This is actually quite anticlimactic after the complicated development of the classes and member functions. As a consistency check, write down a call tree that shows how the program unfolds. Do not list constructors or very simple accessor functions such as `get_minutes`.

```
main
     ├── Game::play
     ├── Game::get_player_information
     └── Game::play_round
          ┌── Game::random_time
          ├── Clock::set_time
          ├── Clock::draw
          ├── Game::get_guess
          └── Player::increment_score
```

This example shows the power of the methods of finding objects and stepwise refinement. It also shows that designing and implementing even a moderately complex program is a lot of work.

Here is the entire program—the longest program we have developed in this book:

File clock.cpp

```
 1  #include <cstdlib>
 2  #include <cmath>
 3  #include <ctime>
 4
 5  using namespace std;
 6
 7  #include "ccc_win.h"
 8  #include "ccc_time.h"
 9
10  const double PI = 3.141592653589793;
11
12  /**
13      A clock that can draw its face.
14  */
15  class Clock
16  {
17  public:
18     /**
19         Constructs a clock with a given center and radius.
20         @param c the center of the clock
21         @param r the radius of the clock
22     */
23     Clock(Point c, double r);
```

```
24
25      /**
26          Sets the current time.
27          @param t the time to set
28      */
29      void set_time(Time t);
30
31      /**
32          Draws the clock face, with tick marks and hands.
33      */
34      void draw() const;
35  private:
36      /**
37          Draw a tick mark (hour or minute mark).
38          @param angle the angle in minutes (0...59, 0 = top)
39          @param length the length of the tick mark
40      */
41      void draw_tick(double angle, double length) const;
42
43      /**
44          Draw a hand, starting from the center.
45          @param angle the angle in minutes (0...59, 0 = top)
46          @param length the length of the hand
47      */
48      void draw_hand(double angle, double length) const;
49
50      Time current_time;
51      Point center;
52      double radius;
53  };
54
55  /**
56      The player of the clock game.
57  */
58  class Player
59  {
60  public:
61      /**
62          Constructs a player with no name, level 1, and score 0.
63      */
64      Player();
65
66      /**
67          Constructs a player with given name and level.
68          @param player_name the player name
69          @param initial_level the player's level (1...4)
70      */
71      Player(string player_name, int initial_level);
72
73      /**
74          Increments the score. Moves to next level if current
75          level complete.
76      */
77      void increment_score();
78
79      /**
```

```
80          Gets the current level.
81          @return the level
82      */
83      int get_level() const;
84
85      /**
86          Gets the player's name.
87          @return the name
88      */
89      string get_name() const;
90   private:
91      string name;
92      int score;
93      int level;
94   };
95
96   /**
97       The clock game.
98   */
99   class Game
100  {
101  public:
102      /**
103          Constructs the game with a default player.
104      */
105      Game();
106
107      /**
108          Plays the game while the player wants to continue.
109      */
110      void play();
111
112      /**
113          Reads player name and level.
114      */
115      void read_player_information();
116
117      /**
118          Plays a round, with up to two guesses.
119      */
120      void play_round();
121  private:
122      /**
123          Makes a random time, depending on the level.
124          @return the random time
125      */
126      Time random_time();
127
128      /**
129          Gets a time input from the user.
130          @return the time guessed by the user
131      */
132      Time get_guess();
133
134      Player player;
135  };
```

```cpp
136
137 /**
138     Sets the seed of the random number generator.
139 */
140 void rand_seed()
141 {
142    int seed = static_cast<int>(time(0));
143    srand(seed);
144 }
145
146 /**
147     Returns a random integer in a range.
148     @param a  the bottom of the range
149     @param b  the top of the range
150     @return a random number x, a <= x and x <= b
151 */
152 int rand_int(int a, int b)
153 {
154    return a + rand() % (b - a + 1);
155 }
156
157 Clock::Clock(Point c, double r)
158 {
159    center = c;
160    radius = r;
161 }
162
163 void Clock::set_time(Time t)
164 {
165    current_time = t;
166 }
167
168 void Clock::draw_tick(double angle, double length) const
169 {
170    double alpha = PI / 2 - 6 * angle * PI / 180;
171    Point from(
172       center.get_x() + cos(alpha) * radius * (1 - length),
173       center.get_y() + sin(alpha) * radius * (1 - length));
174    Point to(center.get_x() + cos(alpha) * radius,
175       center.get_y() + sin(alpha) * radius);
176    cwin << Line(from, to);
177 }
178
179 void Clock::draw_hand(double angle, double length) const
180 {
181    double alpha = PI / 2 - 6 * angle * PI / 180;
182    Point from = center;
183    Point to(center.get_x() + cos(alpha) * radius * length,
184       center.get_y() + sin(alpha) * radius * length);
185    cwin << Line(from, to);
186 }
187
188 void Clock::draw() const
189 {
190    cwin << Circle(center, radius);
191    const double HOUR_TICK_LENGTH = 0.2;
```

```
192     const double MINUTE_TICK_LENGTH = 0.1;
193     const double HOUR_HAND_LENGTH = 0.6;
194     const double MINUTE_HAND_LENGTH = 0.75;
195     for (int i = 0; i < 12; i++)
196     {
197         draw_tick(i * 5, HOUR_TICK_LENGTH);
198         int j;
199         for (j = 1; j <= 4; j++)
200             draw_tick(i * 5 + j, MINUTE_TICK_LENGTH);
201     }
202     draw_hand(current_time.get_minutes(), MINUTE_HAND_LENGTH);
203     draw_hand((current_time.get_hours() +
204         current_time.get_minutes() / 60.0) * 5, HOUR_HAND_LENGTH);
205 }
206
207 Player::Player()
208 {
209     level = 1;
210     score = 0;
211 }
212
213 Player::Player(string player_name, int initial_level)
214 {
215     name = player_name;
216     level = initial_level;
217     score = 0;
218 }
219
220 int Player::get_level() const
221 {
222     return level;
223 }
224
225 string Player::get_name() const
226 {
227     return name;
228 }
229
230 void Player::increment_score()
231 {
232     score++;
233     if (score % 5 == 0 && level < 4)
234         level++;
235 }
236
237 Game::Game()
238 {
239 }
240
241 void Game::play()
242 {
243     rand_seed();
244     read_player_information();
245     string response;
246     do
247     {
```

```
248        play_round();
249        response = cwin.get_string(
250            "Do you want to play again? (y/n)");
251    }
252    while (response == "y");
253 }
254
255 void Game::read_player_information()
256 {
257    string name = cwin.get_string("What is your name?");
258    int initial_level;
259    do
260    {
261        initial_level = cwin.get_int(
262            "At what level do you want to start? (1-4)");
263    }
264    while (initial_level < 1 || initial_level > 4);
265    player = Player(name, initial_level);
266 }
267
268 Time Game::random_time()
269 {
270    int level = player.get_level();
271    int minutes;
272    if (level == 1) minutes = 0;
273    else if (level == 2) minutes = 15 * rand_int(0, 3);
274    else if (level == 3) minutes = 5 * rand_int(0, 11);
275    else minutes = rand_int(0, 59);
276    int hours = rand_int(1, 12);
277    return Time(hours, minutes, 0);
278 }
279
280 Time Game::get_guess()
281 {
282    int hours;
283    do
284    {
285        hours = cwin.get_int("Please enter hours: (1-12)");
286    }
287    while (hours < 1 || hours > 12);
288    int minutes;
289    do
290    {
291        minutes = cwin.get_int("Please enter minutes: (0-59)");
292    }
293    while (minutes < 0 || minutes > 59);
294
295    return Time(hours, minutes, 0);
296 }
297
298 void Game::play_round()
299 {
300    cwin.clear();
301    Time t = random_time();
302    const double CLOCK_RADIUS = 5;
303    Clock clock(Point(0, 0), CLOCK_RADIUS);
```

```
304        clock.set_time(t);
305        clock.draw();
306
307        Time guess = get_guess();
308        if (t.seconds_from(guess) != 0)
309           guess = get_guess();
310
311        string text;
312        if (t.seconds_from(guess) == 0)
313        {
314           text = "Congratulations, " + player.get_name()
315               + "! That is correct.";
316           player.increment_score();
317        }
318        else
319           text = "Sorry, " + player.get_name()
320               + "! That is not correct.";
321        cwin << Message(Point(-CLOCK_RADIUS, CLOCK_RADIUS + 1), text);
322     }
323
324     int ccc_win_main()
325     {
326        Game clock_game;
327        clock_game.play();
328
329        return 0;
330     }
```

CHAPTER SUMMARY

1. The life cycle of software encompasses all activities from initial analysis until obsolescence.

2. A formal process for software development describes phases of the development process and gives guidelines for how to carry out the phases.

3. The waterfall model of software development describes a sequential process of analysis, design, implementation, testing, and deployment.

4. The spiral model of software development describes an iterative process in which design and implementation are repeated.

5. Extreme programming is a development methodology that strives for simplicity by removing formal structure and focusing on best practices.

6. In object-oriented design, you discover classes, determine the responsibilities of classes, and describe the relationships between classes.

7. A CRC card describes a class, its responsibilities, and its collaborating classes.

8. A class should represent a single concept from the problem domain, such as business, science, or mathematics.

9. The public interface of a class is cohesive if all of its features are related to the concept that the class represents.

10. A class depends on another class if it uses objects of that other class.

11. It is a good practice to minimize the coupling (i.e., dependency) between classes

12. Inheritance (the "is-a" relationship) is sometimes inappropriately used when the "has-a" relationship would be more appropriate.

13. A class is associated with another class if you can navigate from its objects to objects of the other class, usually by following data fields.

14. You need to be able to distinguish the UML notations for inheritance, association, and dependency.

15. You can use documentation comments (with the bodies of the functions left blank) to formally record the behavior of the classes and member functions that you discovered.

FURTHER READING

[1] Grady Booch, James Rumbaugh, and Ivar Jacobson, *The Unified Modeling Language User Guide*, Addison-Wesley, 1999.
[2] Kent Beck, *Extreme Programming Explained*, Addison-Wesley, 1999.

REVIEW EXERCISES

Exercise R13.1. What is the software life cycle?

Exercise R13.2. Explain the process of object-oriented design.

Exercise R13.3. Give a rule of thumb for how to find classes when designing a program.

Exercise R13.4. Give a rule of thumb for how to find member functions when designing a program.

Exercise R13.5. After discovering a function, why is it important to identify the object that is *responsible* for carrying out the action?

Exercise R13.6. Consider the following problem description:

Users place coins in a vending machine and select a product by pushing a button. If the inserted coins are sufficient to cover the purchase price of the product, the product is dispensed and change is given. Otherwise, the inserted coins are returned to the user.

What classes should you use to implement it?

Exercise R13.7. Consider the following problem description:

Employees receive their biweekly paycheck. They are paid their hourly wage for each hour worked; however, if they worked more than 40 hours per week, they are paid overtime at 150 percent of their regular wage.

What classes should you use to implement it?

Exercise R13.8. Consider the following problem description:

> Customers order products from a store. Invoices are generated to list the items and quantities ordered, payments received, and amounts still due. Products are shipped to the shipping address of the customer, and invoices are sent to the billing address.

What classes should you use to implement the problem?

Exercise R13.9. Suppose a vending machine contains products, and users insert coins into the vending machine to purchase products. Draw a UML diagram showing the dependencies between the classes VendingMachine, Coin, and Product.

Exercise R13.10. What relationship is appropriate between the following classes: association, inheritance, or neither?

(a) University–Student

(b) Student–TeachingAssistant

(c) Student–Freshman

(d) Student–Professor

(e) Car–Door

(f) Truck–Vehicle

(g) Traffic–TrafficSign

(h) TrafficSign–Color

Exercise R13.11. Every BMW is a car. Should a class BMW inherit from the class Car? BMW is a car manufacturer. Does that mean that the class BMW should inherit from the class CarManufacturer?

Exercise R13.12. Some books on object-oriented programming recommend deriving the class Circle from the class Point. Then the Circle class inherits the set_location function from the Point base class. Explain why the set_location function need not be redefined in the derived class. Why is it nevertheless not a good idea to have Circle inherit from Point? Conversely, would deriving Point from Circle fulfill the "is-a" rule? Would it be a good idea?

Programming Exercises

Exercise P13.1. Write a program that implements a different game, to teach arithmetic to your baby brother. The program tests addition and subtraction. In level 1 it tests only addition of numbers less than 10 whose sum is less than 10. In level 2 it tests addition of arbitrary one-digit numbers. In level 3 it tests subtraction of one-digit numbers with a nonnegative difference. Generate random problems and get the player input. The player gets up to two tries per problem. As in the clock game, advance from one level to the next when the player has achieved a score of five points.

Exercise P13.2. Write a bumper car game with the following rules. Bumper cars are located in grid points (x, y), where x and y are integers between –10 and 10. A bumper car starts moving in a random direction, either left, right, up, or down. If it reaches the boundary of its track (that is, x or y is 10 or −10), then it reverses direction. If it is about to bump into another bumper car, it reverses direction. Model a track with two bumper cars. Make each of them move 100 times, alternating between the two cars. Display the movement on the graphics screen. Use at least two classes in your program. There should be no global variables.

Exercise P13.3. In the clock game program, we assigned the `play_round` function to the `Game` class. That choice was somewhat arbitrary. Modify the clock program so that the `Player` class is responsible for `play_round`.

Exercise P13.4. Write a program that can be used to design a suburban scene, with houses, streets, and cars. Users can add houses and cars of various sizes to a street. Design a user interface that firms up the requirements, use CRC cards to discover classes and methods, provide UML diagrams, and implement your program.

Exercise P13.5. Design a simple e-mail messaging system. A message has a recipient, a sender, and a message text. A mailbox can store messages. Supply a number of mailboxes for different users and a user interface for users to log in, send messages to other users, read their own messages, and log out. Follow the design process described in this chapter.

Exercise P13.6. Write a program that allows an instructor to keep a grade book. Each student has scores for exams, homework assignments, and quizzes. Grading scales convert the total scores in each category into letter grades (e.g., 100–94 = A, 93–91 = A−, 90–88 = B+, etc.) To determine the final grade, the category grades are converted to numeric values (A = 4.0, A− = 3.7, B+ = 3.3, etc.). Those scores are weighted according to a set of weights (e.g., exams 40%, homework 35%, quizzes 25%), and the resulting numeric value is again converted into a letter grade. Design a user interface that firms up the requirements, use CRC cards to discover classes and methods, provide UML diagrams, and implement your program.

Exercise P13.7. Write a program that simulates a vending machine. Products can be purchased by inserting the correct number of coins into the machine. A user selects a product from a list of available products, adds coins, and either gets the product or gets the coins returned if insufficient money was supplied or if the product is sold out. Products can be restocked and money removed by an operator. Follow the design process that was described in this chapter.

Exercise P13.8. Write a program to design an appointment calendar. An appointment includes the appointment day, starting time, ending time, and a description; for example,

```
2003/10/1 17:30 18:30 Dentist
2003/10/2 08:30 10:00 CS1 class
```

Supply a user interface to add appointments, remove canceled appointments, and print out a list of appointments for a particular day. Follow the design process that was described in this chapter.

Exercise P13.9. *Airline seating.* Write a program that assigns seats on an airplane. Assume the airplane has 20 seats in first class (5 rows of 4 seats each, separated by an aisle) and 180 seats in economy class (30 rows of 6 seats each, separated by an aisle). Your program should take three commands: add passengers, show seating, and quit. When passengers are added, ask for the class (first or economy), the number of passengers traveling together (1 or 2 in first class; 1 to 3 in economy), and the seating preference (aisle or window in first class; aisle, center, or window in economy). Then try to find a match and assign the seats. If no match exists, print a message. Your user interface can be text-based or graphical. Follow the design process that was described in this chapter.

Exercise P13.10. Write a tic-tac-toe game that lets a human player play against the computer. Your program will play many turns against a human opponent, and it will learn. When it is the computer's turn, the computer randomly selects an empty field, except that it won't ever choose a losing combination. For that purpose, your program must keep an array of losing combinations. Whenever the human wins, the immediately preceding combination is stored as losing. For example, suppose that x = computer and o = human. Suppose the current combination is

```
 o | x | x
---+---+---
   | o |
---+---+---
   |   |
```

Now it is the human's turn, who will of course choose

```
 o | x | x
---+---+---
   | o |
---+---+---
   |   | o
```

The computer should then remember the preceding combination

```
 o | x | x
---+---+---
   | o |
---+---+---
   |   |
```

as a losing combination. As a result, the computer will never again choose that combination from

```
 o | x |
---+---+---
   | o |
---+---+---
   |   |
```

or

```
 o |   | x
---+---+---
   | o |
---+---+---
   |   |
```

Discover classes and supply a UML diagram before you begin to program.

Recursion

► To learn about the method of recursion

► To understand the relationship between recursion and iteration

► To analyze problems that are much easier to solve by recursion than by iteration

► To learn to "think recursively"

► To be able to use recursive helper functions

► To understand when the use of recursion affects the efficiency of an algorithm

The method of recursion is a powerful technique to break up complex computational problems into simpler ones. The term "recursion" refers to the fact that the same computation recurs, or occurs repeatedly, as the problem is solved. Recursion is often the most natural way of thinking about a problem, and there are some computations that are very difficult to perform without recursion. This chapter shows you both simple and complex examples of recursion and teaches you how to "think recursively".

14.1   Triangle Numbers

In this example, we will look at triangle shapes such as the one shown here:

```
[]
[][]
[][][]
```

Suppose you'd like to compute the area of a triangle of width n, assuming that each [] square has area 1. This value is sometimes called the *nth triangle number*. For example, as you can tell from looking at the above triangle, the third triangle number is 6.

You may know that there is a very simple formula to compute these numbers, but you should pretend for now that you don't know about it. The ultimate purpose of this section is not to compute triangle numbers, but to learn about the concept of recursion in a simple situation.

Here is the outline of the class that we will develop:

```
class Triangle
{
public:
   Triangle(int w);
   int get_area() const;
private:
   int width;
};
Triangle::Triangle(int w)
{
   width = w;
}
```

If the width of the triangle is 1, then the triangle consists of a single square, and its area is 1. Take care of this case first.

```
int Triangle::get_area()
{
   if (width == 1) return 1;
   ...
}
```

To deal with the general case, consider this picture.

```
[]
[][]
[][][]
[][][][]
```

Suppose you knew the area of the smaller, colored triangle. Then you could easily compute the area of the larger triangle as

```
smaller_area + width
```

How can you get the smaller area? Make a smaller triangle and ask it!

```
Triangle smaller_triangle(width - 1);
int smaller_area = smaller_triangle.get_area();
```

Now we can complete the get_area function:

```
int Triangle::get_area() const
{
   if (width == 1) return 1;
   Triangle smaller_triangle(width - 1);
   int smaller_area = smaller_triangle.get_area();
   return smaller_area + width;
}
```

Here is an illustration of what happens when we compute the area of a triangle of width 4.

- The get_area function makes a smaller triangle of width 3.
  - It calls get_area on that triangle.
    - That function makes a smaller triangle of width 2.
      - It calls get_area on that triangle.
        - That function makes a smaller triangle of width 1.
          - It calls get_area on that triangle.
        - That function returns 1.
      - The function returns smaller_area + width $= 1 + 2 = 3$.
    - The function returns smaller_area + width $= 3 + 3 = 6$.
  - The function returns smaller_area + width $= 6 + 4 = 10$.

This solution has one remarkable aspect. To solve the area problem for a triangle of a given width, we use the fact that we can solve the same problem for a lesser width. This is called a *recursive* solution.

The call pattern of a recursive function looks complicated, and the key to the successful design of a recursive function is *not to think about it*. Instead, look at the get_area function one more time and notice how utterly reasonable it is. If the width is 1, then of course the area is 1. The next part is just as reasonable. Compute the area of the smaller triangle *and don't think about why that works*. Then the area of the larger triangle is clearly the sum of the smaller area and the width.

There are two key requirements to make sure that the recursion is successful:

- Every recursive call must simplify the computation in some way.

- There must be special cases to handle the simplest computations directly.

The get_area function calls itself again with smaller and smaller width values. Eventually the width must reach 1, and there is a special case for computing the area of a triangle with width 1. Thus, the get_area function always succeeds.

Actually, you have to be careful. What happens when you call the area of a triangle with width –1? It computes the area of a triangle with width –2, which computes the area of a triangle with width –3, and so on. To avoid this, the get_area function should return 0 if the width is ≤ 0.

Recursion is not really necessary to compute the triangle numbers. The area of a triangle equals the sum

```
1 + 2 + 3 + ... + width
```

Of course, we can program a simple loop:

```
double area = 0;
for (int i = 1; i <= width; i++)
   area = area + i;
```

Many simple recursions can be computed as loops. However, loop equivalents for more complex recursions—such as the one in our next example—can be complex.

Actually, in this case, you don't even need a loop to compute the answer. The sum of the first n integers can be computed as

$$1 + 2 + \cdots + n = n \times (n + 1)/2$$

Thus, the area equals

```
width * (width + 1) / 2
```

Therefore, neither recursion nor a loop are required to solve this problem. The recursive solution is intended as a "warm-up" for the next section.

File triangle.cpp

```
1  #include <iostream>
2
3  using namespace std;
4
5  /**
6     A class that describes triangle shapes like this:
7     []
8     [][]
9     [][][]
10    ...
11 */
12 class Triangle
13 {
14 public:
15    Triangle(int w);
16    int get_area() const;
17 private:
18    int width;
19 };
20
```

```
21 /**
22     Constructs a triangle with a given width.
23     @param w the width of the triangle base
24 */
25 Triangle::Triangle(int w)
26 {
27     width = w;
28 }
29
30 /**
31     Computes the area of the triangle shape.
32     @return the area
33 */
34 int Triangle::get_area() const
35 {
36     if (width <= 0) return 0;
37     if (width == 1) return 1;
38     Triangle smaller_triangle(width - 1);
39     int smaller_area = smaller_triangle.get_area();
40     return smaller_area + width;
41 }
42
43 int main()
44 {
45     Triangle t(4);
46     cout << "Area: " << t.get_area() << "\n";
47     return 0;
48 }
```

▼   ⊗   **Common Error**   14.1 ▶

Infinite Recursion

▼

A common programming error is an infinite recursion: a function calling itself over and over with no end in sight. The computer needs some amount of memory for bookkeeping for each call. After some number of calls, all memory that is available for this purpose is exhausted.
▼ Your program shuts down and reports a "stack fault".

Infinite recursion happens either because the parameter values don't get simpler or because a special terminating case is missing. For example, suppose the get_area function computes the area of a triangle with width 0. If it wasn't for the special test, the function
▼ would have constructed triangles with width -1, -2, -3, and so on.

14.2   ## Permutations

Now consider a more complex example of recursion that would be difficult to program with a simple loop. We will design a function that lists all *permutations* of a string. A permutation is simply a rearrangement of the letters. For example, the string "eat" has six permutations (including the original string itself):

```
"eat"
"eta"
"aet"
"ate"
"tea"
"tae"
```

If the string has n letters, then the *number* of permutations is given by the factorial function:

$$n! = 1 \times 2 \times 3 \times \ldots \times n$$

For example, $3! = 1 \times 2 \times 3 = 6$, and there are six permutations of the three-character string "eat".

In Chapter 7, you saw a program that uses a for loop to compute the factorial function. Now develop a recursive solution.

Look at the table of factorials in Section 7.5. The last entry is

$$8! = 1 \times 2 \times 3 \times 4 \times 5 \times 6 \times 7 \times 8 = 40,320$$

Now suppose you need to compute 9! with a calculator. Of course, you don't have to compute

$$1 \times 2 \times 3 \times 4 \times 5 \times 6 \times 7 \times 8 \times 9$$

Instead, just take the last known value and multiply it by 9:

$$9! = 40,320 \times 9 = 362,880$$

In other words, it is an easy matter to compute $n!$ if you already know $(n - 1)!$ since

$$n! = (n - 1)! \times n$$

As always, when you solve a problem by reducing it to a simpler problem, you need to separately take care of the most fundamental cases. Of course,

$$2! = 1 \times 2 = 2$$

Can you go even further? When considering 1! or even 0!, you run into somewhat metaphysical questions. What is the product of a single number? No number at all? Rather than philosophizing, mathematicians tend to take a very mercenary approach. It is customary to define

$$1! = 1$$

because it makes the equation

$$2! = 1! \times 2$$

work. Also, it makes sense that there is just one permutation of a single-character string such as "a", since we always include the "do-nothing" permutation in our count. For the same reason, mathematicians define

$$0! = 1$$

In C++, you can therefore implement a recursive `factorial` function as follows.

```
int factorial(int n)
{
   if (n == 0) return 1;
   int smaller_factorial = factorial(n - 1);
   int result = smaller_factorial * n;
   return result;
}
```

Of course, this function only counts how many permutations there are. Now consider a more challenging problem, to actually list the permutations. We will develop a function

```
vector<string> generate_permutations(string word)
```

that generates all permutations of a word.

Here is how you would use the function. The following code displays all permutations of the string "eat":

```
vector<string> v = generate_permutations("eat");
for (int i = 0; i < v.size(); i++)
   cout << v[i] << "\n";
```

Now you need a way to generate the permutations recursively. Consider the string "eat" and simplify the problem. First, generate all permutations that start with the letter 'e', then those that start with 'a', and finally those that start with 't'. How do you generate the permutations that start with 'e'? You need to know the permutations of the substring "at". But that's the same problem—to generate all permutations—with a simpler input, namely the shorter string "at". Using recursion generates the permutations of the substring "at". You will get the strings

```
"at"
"ta"
```

For each result of the simpler problem, add the letter 'e' in front. Now you have all permutations of "eat" that start with 'e', namely

```
"eat"
"eta"
```

Next, turn your attention to the permutations of "eat" that start with 'a'. You must create the permutations of the remaining letters, "et", namely:

```
"et"
"te"
```

Add the letter 'a' to the front of the strings and obtain

```
"aet"
"ate"
```

Generate the permutations that start with 't' in the same way.

That's the idea. To carry it out, you must implement a loop that iterates through the character positions of the word. Each loop iteration creates a shorter word that omits the current position:

```
vector<string> generate_permutations(string word)
{
   vector<string> result;
   ...
   for (int i = 0; i < word.length(); i++)
   {
      string shorter_word = word.substr(0, i)
         + word.substr(i + 1, word.length() - i - 1);
      ...
   }
   return result;
}
```

The next step is to compute the permutations of the shorter word.

```
vector<string> shorter_permutations
   = generate_permutations(shorter_word);
```

For each of the shorter permutations, add the omitted letter:

```
for (int j = 0; j < shorter_permutations.size(); j++)
{
   string longer_word = word[i] + shorter_permutations[j];
   result.push_back(longer_word);
}
```

The permutation generation algorithm is recursive—it uses the fact that we can generate the permutations of shorter words. When does the recursion stop? You must build in a stopping point, as a special case to handle words of length 1. A word of length 1 has a single permutation, namely itself. Here is the added code to handle a word of length 1.

```
vector<string> generate_permutations(string word)
{
   vector<string> result;
   if (word.length() == 1)
   {
      result.push_back(word);
      return result;
   }
   ...
}
```

Here is the complete program.

File permute.cpp

```
1 #include <iostream>
2 #include <string>
3 #include <vector>
4
5 using namespace std;
6
7 /**
8    Computes n!
```

```
 9      @param n a nonnegative integer
10      @return n! = 1 * 2 * 3 * ... * n
11   */
12   int factorial(int n)
13   {
14      if (n == 0) return 1;
15      int smaller_factorial = factorial(n - 1);
16      int result = smaller_factorial * n;
17      return result;
18   }
19
20   /**
21      Generates all permutations of the characters in a string.
22      @param word a string
23      @return a vector that is filled with all permutations
24      of the word
25   */
26   vector<string> generate_permutations(string word)
27   {
28      vector<string> result;
29      if (word.length() == 1)
30      {
31         result.push_back(word);
32         return result;
33      }
34
35      for (int i = 0; i < word.length(); i++)
36      {
37         string shorter_word = word.substr(0, i)
38            + word.substr(i + 1, word.length() - i - 1);
39         vector<string> shorter_permutations
40            = generate_permutations(shorter_word);
41         for (int j = 0; j < shorter_permutations.size(); j++)
42         {
43            string longer_word = word[i] + shorter_permutations[j];
44            result.push_back(longer_word);
45         }
46      }
47      return result;
48   }
49
50   int main()
51   {
52      cout << "Enter a string: ";
53      string input;
54      getline(cin, input);
55      cout << "There are " << factorial(input.length())
56         << "permutations.\n";
57      vector<string> v = generate_permutations(input);
58      for (int i = 0; i < v.size(); i++)
59         cout << v[i] << "\n";
60      return 0;
61   }
```

Compare the algorithms for computing the triangle area, the factorial function, and the word permutations. All of them work on the same principle. When they work on a more complex input, they first solve the problem with a simpler input. Then they turn the simpler result into the result for the more complex input. There really is no particular complexity behind that process as long as you think about the solution on that level only. However, behind the scenes, the function that computes the simpler input calls yet another function that works on even simpler input, which calls yet another, and so on, until one function's input is so simple that it can compute the results without further help. It is interesting to think about that process, but it can also be confusing. What's important is that you can focus on the one level that matters—putting a solution together from the slightly simpler problem, ignoring the fact that it also uses recursion to get its results.

Common Error   14.2

Tracing through Recursive Functions

Debugging a recursive function can be somewhat challenging. When you set a breakpoint in a recursive function, the program stops as soon as that program line is encountered in *any call*

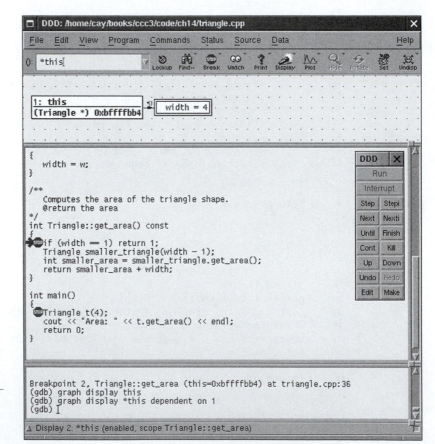

Figure 1

Debugging
a Recursive
Function

to the recursive function. Suppose you want to debug the recursive `get_area` function of the `Triangle` class. Debug the program with an input of 4. Run until the beginning of the `get_area` function (Figure 1). Inspect the `width` instance variable. It is 4.

Remove the breakpoint and now run until the statement

```
return smaller_area + width;
```

When you inspect `width` again, its value is 2! That makes no sense. There was no instruction that changed the value of `width`! Is that a bug with the debugger?

No. The program stopped in the first *recursive* call to get_area that reached the `return` statement. If you are confused, look at the *call stack* (Figure 2). You will see that three calls to `get_area` are pending.

You can debug recursive functions with the debugger. You just need to be particularly careful, and watch the call stack to understand which nested call you currently are in.

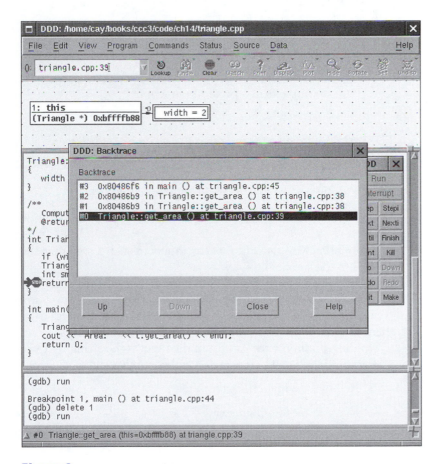

Figure 2

Call Stack Display

14.3   Thinking Recursively

To solve a problem recursively requires a different mindset than to solve it by programming loops. In fact, it helps if you are, or pretend to be, a bit lazy and let others do most of the work for you. If you need to solve a complex problem, pretend that "someone else" will do most of the heavy lifting and solve the problem for all simpler inputs. Then you only need to figure out how you can turn the solutions with simpler inputs into a solution for the whole problem.

This section gives you a step-by-step guide to the method of recursion. To illustrate the steps, use the following problem to test whether a sentence is a *palindrome*—a string that is equal to itself when you reverse all characters. Typical examples of palindromes are

- rotor

- A man, a plan, a canal—Panama!

- Go hang a salami, I'm a lasagna hog

and, of course, the oldest palindrome of all:

- Madam, I'm Adam

Our goal is to implement a predicate function

```
bool is_palindrome(string s)
```

For simplicity, assume for now that the string has only lowercase letters and no punctuation marks. Exercise P14.12 asks you to generalize the function to arbitrary strings.

Step 1   Consider various ways for simplifying inputs.

In your mind, fix a particular input or set of inputs for the problem that you want to solve.

Think how you can simplify the inputs in such a way that the same problem can be applied to the simpler input.

When you consider simpler inputs, you may want to remove just a little bit from the original input—maybe remove one or two characters from a string, or remove a small portion of a geometric shape. But sometimes it is more useful to cut the input in half and then see what it means to solve the problem for both halves.

In the palindrome test problem, the input is the string that we need to test. How can you simplify the input? Here are several possibilities:

- Remove the first character.

- Remove the last character.

- Remove both the first and the last character.

- Remove a character from the middle.

- Cut the string into two halves.

These simpler inputs are all potential inputs for the palindrome test.

Step 2   Combine solutions with simpler inputs to a solution of the original problem.

In your mind, consider the solutions of your problem for the simpler inputs that you have discovered in Step 1. Don't worry *how* those solutions are obtained. Simply have faith that the solutions are readily available. Just say to yourself: These are simpler inputs, so someone else will solve the problem for me.

Now think how you can turn the solution for the simpler inputs into a solution for the input that you are currently thinking about. Maybe you need to add a small quantity, related to the quantity that you lopped off to arrive at the simpler input. Maybe you cut the original input in two halves and have solutions for both halves. Then you may need to add both solutions to arrive at a solution for the whole.

Consider the methods for simplifying the inputs for the palindrome test. Cutting the string in half doesn't seem a good idea. If you cut

```
"rotor"
```

in half, you get two strings:

```
"rot"
```

and

```
"or"
```

Neither of them is a palindrome. Cutting the input in half and testing whether the halves are palindromes seems a dead end.

The most promising simplification is to remove the first *and* last characters.

Removing the r at the front and back of "rotor" yields

```
"oto"
```

Suppose you can verify that the shorter string is a palindrome. Then *of course* the original string is a palindrome—we put the same letter in the front and the back. That's extremely promising. A word is a palindrome if

- The first and last letters match

and

- The word obtained by removing the first and last letters is a palindrome.

Again, don't worry how the test works for the shorter string. It just works.

Step 3   Find solutions to the simplest inputs.

A recursive computation keeps simplifying its inputs. Eventually it arrives at very simple inputs. To make sure that the recursion comes to a stop, you must deal with the simplest inputs separately. Come up with special solutions for them. That is usually very easy.

However, sometimes you get into philosophical questions dealing with *degenerate* inputs: empty strings, shapes with no area, and so on. Then you may want to investigate a slightly larger input that gets reduced to such a trivial input and see what value you should attach to the degenerate inputs so that the simpler value, when used according to the rules you discovered in Step 2, yields the correct answer.

Look at the simplest strings for the palindrome test:

- Strings with two characters
- Strings with a single character
- The empty string

You don't have to come up with a special solution for strings with two characters. Step 2 still applies to those strings—either or both of the characters are removed. But you do need to worry about strings of length 0 and 1. In those cases, Step 2 can't apply. There aren't two characters to remove.

A string with a single character, such as "I", is a palindrome.

The empty string is a palindrome—it's the same string when you read it backwards. If you find that too artificial, consider a string "oo". According to the rule discovered in Step 2, this string is a palindrome if the first and last character of that string match and the remainder—that is, the empty string—is also a palindrome. Therefore, it makes sense to consider the empty string a palindrome.

Thus, all strings of length 0 or 1 are palindromes.

Step 4 Implement the solution by combining the simple cases and the reduction step.

Now you are ready to implement the solution. Make separate cases for the simple inputs that you considered in Step 3. If the input isn't one of the simplest cases, then implement the logic you discovered in Step 2.

The following program shows the complete `is_palindrome` function.

File palindrome.cpp

```
 1  #include <iostream>
 2  #include <string>
 3  #include <vector>
 4
 5  using namespace std;
 6
 7  /**
 8      Tests whether a string is a palindrome. A palindrome
 9      is equal to its reverse, for example "rotor" or "racecar".
10      @param s a string
11      @return true if s is a palindrome
12  */
13  bool is_palindrome(string s)
14  {
15      // separate case for shortest strings
16      if (s.length() <= 1) return true;
17
18      // get first and last character, converted to lowercase
19      char first = s[0];
20      char last = s[s.length() - 1];
21
22      if (first == last)
23      {
24          string shorter = s.substr(1, s.length() - 2);
```

```
25          return is_palindrome(shorter);
26      }
27      else
28          return false;
29  }
30
31  int main()
32  {
33      cout << "Enter a string: ";
34      string input;
35      getline(cin, input);
36      cout << input << " is ";
37      if (!is_palindrome(input)) cout << "not ";
38      cout << "a palindrome\n";
39      return 0;
40  }
```

14.4   Recursive Helper Functions

Sometimes it is easier to find a recursive solution if you change the original problem slightly. Then the original problem can be solved by calling a recursive helper function.

Here is a typical example. Consider the palindrome test of the preceding section. It is a bit inefficient to construct new string objects in every step. Now consider the following change in the problem. Rather than testing whether the entire sentence is a palindrome, check whether a substring is a palindrome:

```
/*
    Tests whether a substring of a string is a palindrome.
    @param s the string to test
    @param start the index of the first character of the substring
    @param end the index of the last character of the substring
    @return true if the substring is a palindrome
*/
bool substring_is_palindrome(string s, int start, int end)
```

This function turns out to be even easier to implement than the original test. In the recursive calls, simply adjust the start and end parameters to skip over matching letter pairs. There is no need to construct new string objects to represent the shorter strings.

```
bool substring_is_palindrome(string s, int start, int end)
{
    // separate case for substrings of length 0 and 1
    if (start >= end) return true;

    if (s[start] == s[end])
        // test substring that doesn't contain the first and last letters
        return substring_is_palindrome(s, start + 1, end - 1);
    else
        return false;
}
```

You should supply a function to solve the whole problem—the user of your function shouldn't have to know about the trick with the substring positions. Simply call the helper function with positions that test the entire string:

```
bool is_palindrome(string s)
{
    return substring_is_palindrome(s, 0, s.length() - 1);
}
```

Note that the `is_palindrome` function is *not* recursive. It just calls a recursive helper function.

Use the technique of recursive helper functions whenever it is easier to solve a recursive problem that is slightly different from the original problem.

14.5   Mutual Recursion

In the preceding examples, a function called itself to solve a simpler problem. Sometimes, a set of cooperating functions calls each other in a recursive fashion. In this section, we will explore a typical situation of such a mutual recursion.

We will develop a program that can compute the values of arithmetic expressions such as

```
3 + 4 * 5
(3 + 4) * 5
1 - (2 - (3 - (4 - 5)))
```

Computing such an expression is complicated by the fact that * and / bind more strongly than + and -, and that parentheses can be used to group subexpressions.

Figure 3 shows a set of *syntax diagrams* that describes the syntax of these expressions. An expression is either a term, or a sum or difference of terms. A term is either a factor,

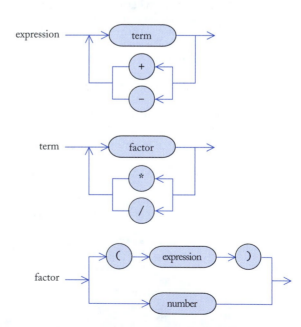

Figure 3

Syntax Diagrams for Evaluating an Expression

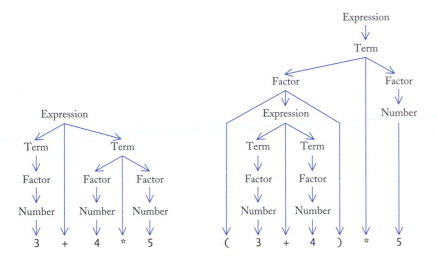

Figure 4

Syntax Trees for Two Expressions

or a product or quotient of factors. Finally, a factor is either a number or an expression enclosed in parentheses.

Figure 4 shows how the expressions 3 + 4 * 5 and (3 + 4) * 5 are derived from the syntax diagram.

Why do the syntax diagrams help us compute the value of the tree? If you look at the syntax trees, you will see that they accurately represent which operations should be carried out first. In the first tree, 4 and 5 should be multiplied, and then the result should be added to 3. In the second tree, 3 and 4 should be added, and the result should be multiplied by 5.

To compute the value of an expression, we implement three functions: `expression_value`, `term_value`, and `factor_value`. The `expression_value` function first calls `term_value` to get the value of the first term of the expression. Then it checks whether the next input character is one of + or -. If so, it calls `term_value` again and adds or subtracts it.

```cpp
int expression_value()
{
   int result = term_value();
   bool more = true;
   while (more)
   {
      char op = cin.peek();
      if (op == '+' || op == '-')
      {
         cin.get();
         int value = term_value();
         if (op == '+') result = result + value;
         else result = result - value;
```

```
        }
        else more = false;
    }
    return result;
}
```

The `term_value` function calls `factor_value` in the same way, multiplying or dividing the factor values.

Finally, the `factor_value` function checks whether the next input character is a `'('` or a digit. In the latter case, the value is simply the value of the number. However, if the function sees a parenthesis, the `factor_value` function makes a recursive call to `expression_value`. Thus, the three functions are mutually recursive.

```
int factor_value()
{
    int result = 0;
    char c = cin.peek();
    if (c == '(')
    {
        cin.get();
        result = expression_value();
        cin.get(); // read ")"
    }
    else // assemble number value from digits
    {
        while (isdigit(c))
        {
            result = 10 * result + c - '0';
            cin.get();
            c = cin.peek();
        }
    }
    return result;
}
```

As always with a recursive solution, you need to ensure that the recursion terminates. In this situation, that is easy to see. If `expression_value` calls itself, the second call works on a shorter subexpression than the original expression. At each recursive call, at least some of the characters of the input are consumed, so eventually the recursion must come to an end.

File eval.cpp

```
1  #include <iostream>
2  #include <cctype>
3
4  using namespace std;
5
6  int term_value();
7  int factor_value();
8
9  /**
10     Evaluates the next expression found in cin.
11     @return the value of the expression
12  */
13  int expression_value()
14  {
```

```
15      int result = term_value();
16      bool more = true;
17      while (more)
18      {
19         char op = cin.peek();
20         if (op == '+' || op == '-')
21         {
22            cin.get();
23            int value = term_value();
24            if (op == '+') result = result + value;
25            else result = result - value;
26         }
27         else more = false;
28      }
29      return result;
30   }
31
32   /**
33      Evaluates the next term found in cin.
34      @return the value of the term.
35   */
36   int term_value()
37   {
38      int result = factor_value();
39      bool more = true;
40      while (more)
41      {
42         char op = cin.peek();
43         if (op == '*' || op == '/')
44         {
45            cin.get();
46            int value = factor_value();
47            if (op == '*') result = result * value;
48            else result = result / value;
49         }
50         else more = false;
51      }
52      return result;
53   }
54
55   /**
56      Evaluates the next factor found in cin.
57      @return the value of the factor.
58   */
59   int factor_value()
60   {
61      int result = 0;
62      char c = cin.peek();
63      if (c == '(')
64      {
65         cin.get();
66         result = expression_value();
67         cin.get(); // read ")"
68      }
69      else // assemble number value from digits
70      {
```

```
71         while (isdigit(c))
72         {
73            result = 10 * result + c - '0';
74            cin.get();
75            c = cin.peek();
76         }
77      }
78      return result;
79   }
80
81   int main()
82   {
83      cout << "Enter an expression: ";
84      cout << expression_value() << "\n";
85      return 0;
86   }
```

14.6   The Efficiency of Recursion

As you have seen in this chapter, recursion can be a powerful tool to implement complex algorithms. On the other hand, recursion can lead to algorithms that perform poorly. In this section, we will analyze the question of when recursion is beneficial and when it is inefficient.

The Fibonacci sequence is a sequence of numbers defined by the equation

$$f_1 = 1$$
$$f_2 = 1$$
$$f_n = f_{n-1} + f_{n-2}$$

That is, each value of the sequence is the sum of the two preceding values. The first ten terms of the sequence are

1, 1, 2, 3, 5, 8, 13, 21, 34, 55

It is easy to extend this sequence indefinitely. Just keep appending the sum of the last two values of the sequence. For example, the next entry is $34 + 55 = 89$.

We would like to write a function that computes f_n for any value of n. Suppose we translate the definition directly into a recursive function:

File fibtest.cpp

```
1   #include <iostream>
2
3   using namespace std;
4
5   /**
6      Computes a Fibonacci number.
7      @param n an integer
8      @return the nth Fibonacci number
9   */
10  int fib(int n)
```

```
11  {
12     if (n <= 2) return 1;
13     else return fib(n - 1) + fib(n - 2);
14  }
15
16  int main()
17  {
18     cout << "Enter n: ";
19     int n;
20     cin >> n;
21     int f = fib(n);
22     cout << "fib(" << n << ") = " << f << "\n";
23     return 0;
24  }
```

That is certainly simple, and the function will work correctly. But watch the output closely as you run the test program. For small input values, the program is quite fast. Even for moderately large values, though, the program pauses an amazingly long time between outputs. Try out some numbers between 30 and 50 to see this effect.

That makes no sense. Armed with pencil, paper, and a pocket calculator you could calculate these numbers pretty quickly, so it shouldn't take the computer long.

To determine the problem, insert trace messages into the function:

File fibtrace.cpp

```
1  #include <iostream>
2
3  using namespace std;
4
5  /**
6     Computes a Fibonacci number.
7     @param n  an integer
8     @return the nth Fibonacci number
9  */
10  int fib(int n)
11  {
12     cout << "Entering fib: n = " << n << "\n";
13     int f;
14     if (n <= 2) f = 1;
15     else f = fib(n - 1) + fib(n - 2);
16     cout << "Exiting fib: n = " << n
17        << " return value = " << f << "\n";
18     return f;
19  }
20
21  int main()
22  {
23     cout << "Enter n: ";
24     int n;
25     cin >> n;
26     int f = fib(n);
27     cout << "fib(" << n << ") = " << f << "\n";
28     return 0;
29  }
```

Following is the trace for computing `fib(6)`. Figure 5 shows the call tree.

```
Entering fib: n = 6
Entering fib: n = 5
Entering fib: n = 4
Entering fib: n = 3
Entering fib: n = 2
Exiting fib: n = 2 return value = 1
Entering fib: n = 1
Exiting fib: n = 1 return value = 1
Exiting fib: n = 3 return value = 2
Entering fib: n = 2
Exiting fib: n = 2 return value = 1
Exiting fib: n = 4 return value = 3
Entering fib: n = 3
Entering fib: n = 2
Exiting fib: n = 2 return value = 1
Entering fib: n = 1
Exiting fib: n = 1 return value = 1
Exiting fib: n = 3 return value = 2
Exiting fib: n = 5 return value = 5
Entering fib: n = 4
Entering fib: n = 3
Entering fib: n = 2
Exiting fib: n = 2 return value = 1
Entering fib: n = 1
Exiting fib: n = 1 return value = 1
Exiting fib: n = 3 return value = 2
Entering fib: n = 2
Exiting fib: n = 2 return value = 1
Exiting fib: n = 4 return value = 3
Exiting fib: n = 6 return value = 8
```

Now it is becoming apparent why the function takes so long. It is computing the same values over and over. For example, the computation of `fib(6)` calls `fib(4)` twice and

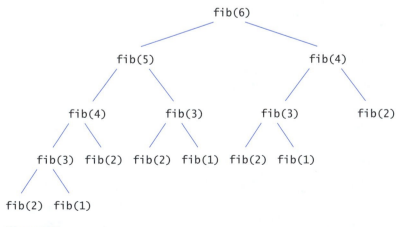

Figure 5

Call Pattern of the Recursive `fib` Function

fib(3) three times. That is very different from the computation you would do with pencil and paper. There you would just write down the values as they were computed and add up the last two to get the next one until you reached the desired entry; no sequence value would ever be computed twice.

If you imitate the pencil-and-paper process, then you get the following program.

File fibloop.cpp

```
 1  #include <iostream>
 2
 3  using namespace std;
 4
 5  /**
 6      Computes a Fibonacci number.
 7      @param n  an integer
 8      @return  the nth Fibonacci number
 9  */
10  int fib(int n)
11  {
12      if (n <= 2) return 1;
13      int fold = 1;
14      int fold2 = 1;
15      int fnew;
16      for (int i = 3; i <= n; i++)
17      {
18         fnew = fold + fold2;
19         fold2 = fold;
20         fold = fnew;
21      }
22      return fnew;
23  }
24
25  int main()
26  {
27      cout << "Enter n: ";
28      int n;
29      cin >> n;
30      int f = fib(n);
31      cout << "fib(" << n << ") = " << f << "\n";
32      return 0;
33  }
```

This function runs *much* faster than the recursive version.

In this example of the fib function, the recursive solution was easy to program because it exactly followed the mathematical definition, but it ran far more slowly than the iterative solution, because it computed many intermediate results multiple times.

Can you always speed up a recursive solution by changing it into a loop? Frequently, the iterative and recursive solution have essentially the same performance. For example, here is an iterative solution for the palindrome test.

```
public bool is_palindrome(string s)
{
```

```
    int start = 0;
    int end = text.length() - 1;
    while (start < end)
    {
        if (s[start] != s[end]) return false;
        start++;
        end--;
    }
    return true;
}
```

This solution keeps two index variables: start and end. The first index starts at the beginning of the string and is advanced whenever a letter has been matched or a non-letter has been ignored. The second index starts at the end of the string and moves toward the beginning. When the two index variables meet, then the iteration stops.

Both the iteration and the recursion run at about the same speed. If a palindrome has n characters, the iteration executes the loop $n/2$ times. Similarly, the recursive solution calls itself $n/2$ times, because two characters are removed in each step.

In such a situation, the iterative solution tends to be a bit faster, because each recursive function call takes a certain amount of processor time. In principle, it is possible for a smart compiler to avoid recursive function calls if they follow simple patterns, but most compilers don't do that. From that point of view, an iterative solution is preferable.

There are quite a few problems that are dramatically easier to solve recursively than iteratively. For example, it is not at all obvious how you can come up with a nonrecursive solution for generating all permutations of a string. As Exercise P14.11 shows, it is possible to avoid the recursion, but the resulting solution is quite complex (and no faster).

Often, recursive solutions are easier to understand and implement correctly than their iterative counterparts. There is a certain elegance and economy of thought to recursive solutions that makes them more appealing. As the computer scientist (and creator of the GhostScript interpreter for the PostScript graphics description language) L. Peter Deutsch put it: "To iterate is human, to recurse divine."

Random Fact   14.1

The Limits of Computation

Have you ever wondered how your instructor or grader makes sure your programming homework is correct? In all likelihood, they look at your solution and perhaps run it with some test inputs. But usually they have a correct solution available. That suggests that there might be an easier way. Perhaps they could feed your program and their correct program into a program comparator, a computer program that analyzes both programs and determines whether they both compute the same results. Of course, your solution and the program that is known to be correct need not be identical—what matters is that they produce the same output when given the same input.

How could such a program comparator work? Well, the C++ compiler knows how to read a program and make sense of the classes, functions, and statements. So it seems plausible that someone could, with some effort, write a program that reads two C++ programs, analyzes what they do, and determines whether they solve the same task. Of course, such a program would be very attractive to instructors, because it could automate the grading process. Thus, even though no such program exists today, it might be tempting to try to develop one and sell it to universities around the world.

However, before you start raising venture capital for such an effort, you should know that theoretical computer scientists have proven that it is impossible to develop such a program, *no matter how hard you try.*

There are quite a few of these unsolvable problems. The first one, called the *halting problem,* was discovered by the British researcher Alan Turing in 1936 (see Figure 6). Because his research occurred before the first actual computer was constructed, Turing had to devise a theoretical device, the *Turing machine,* to explain how computers could work. The Turing machine consists of a long magnetic tape, a read/write head, and a program that has numbered instructions of the form: "If the current symbol under the head is x, then replace it with y, move the head one unit left or right, and continue with instruction n" (see Figure 7). Interestingly enough, with just these instructions, you can program just as much as with C++, even though it is incredibly tedious to do so. Theoretical computer scientists like Turing machines because they can be described using nothing more than the laws of mathematics.

Expressed in terms of C++, the halting problem states: "It is impossible to write a program with two inputs, namely the source code of an arbitrary C++ program P and a string I, that decides whether the program P, when executed with the input I, will halt without getting into an infinite loop". Of course, for some kinds of programs and inputs, it is possible to decide whether the programs halt with the given input. The halting problem asserts that it is impossible to come up with a single decision-making algorithm that works with all programs and inputs. Note that you can't simply run the program P on the input I to settle this question. If the program runs for 1,000 days, you don't know that the program is in an infinite loop. Maybe you just have to wait another day for it to stop.

Such a "halt checker", if it could be written, might also be useful for grading homework. An instructor could use it to screen student submissions to see if they get into an infinite loop

Figure 6

Alan Turing

Program

Instruction number	If tape symbol is	Replace with	Then move head	Then go to instruction
1	0	2	right	2
1	1	1	left	4
2	0	0	right	2
2	1	1	right	2
2	B	0	left	3
3	0	0	left	3
3	1	1	left	3
3	2	2	right	1
4	1	1	right	5
4	2	0	left	4

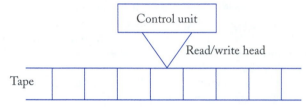

Figure 7

A Turing Machine

with a particular input, and then not check them any further. However, as Turing demonstrated, such a program cannot be written. His argument is ingenious and quite simple.

Suppose a "halt checker" program existed. Let's call it *H*. From *H*, we will develop another program, the "killer" program *K*. *K* does the following computation. Its input is a string containing the source code for a program *R*. It then applies the halting checker on the input program *R* and the input string *R*. That is, it checks whether the program *R* halts if its input is its own source code. It sounds bizarre to feed a program to itself, but it isn't impossible. For example, the C++ compiler is written in C++, and you can use it to compile itself. Or, as a simpler example, you can use the word count program from Chapter 7 to count the words in its own source code.

When *K* gets the answer from *H* that *R* halts when applied to itself, it is programmed to enter an infinite loop. Otherwise *K* exits. In C++, the program might look like this:

```
int main
{
    string r = read program input;
    HaltChecker checker;
    if (checker.check(r, r))
        while (true) { } // infinite loop
    else
        return 0;
}
```

Now ask yourself: What does the halt checker answer when asked if *K* halts when given *K* as the input? Maybe it finds out that *K* gets into an infinite loop with such an input. But wait,

▼ that can't be right. That would mean that `checker.check(r, r)` returns `false` when r is the
program code of *K*. As you can plainly see, in that case, the `main` function returns, so *K* didn't
▼ get into an infinite loop. That shows that *K* must halt when analyzing itself, so
`checker.check(r, r)` should return `true`. But then the `main` function doesn't terminate—it
goes into an infinite loop. That shows that it is logically impossible to implement a program
that can check whether *every* program halts on a particular input.

▼ It is sobering to know that there are *limits* to computing. There are problems that no
computer program, no matter how ingenious, can answer.

Theoretical computer scientists are working on other research involving the nature of
computation. One important question that remains unsettled to this day deals with problems
▼ that in practice are very time-consuming to solve. It may be that these problems are intrinsi-
cally hard, in which case it would be pointless to try to look for better algorithms. Such theoretical research can have important practical applications. For example, right now, nobody
▼ knows whether the most common encryption schemes used today could be broken by discovering a new algorithm (see Random Fact 12.1 for more information on encryption algorithms). Knowing that no fast algorithms exist for breaking a particular code could make us
▼ feel more comfortable about the security of encryption.

Chapter Summary

1. A recursive computation solves a problem by using the solution of the same problem
   with simpler inputs.

2. For a recursion to terminate, there must be special cases for the simplest inputs.

3. Sometimes it is easier to find a recursive solution if you make a slight change to the
   original problem.

4. In a mutual recursion, a set of cooperating functions calls each other repeatedly.

5. Occasionally, a recursive solution runs much slower than its iterative counterpart.
   However, in most cases, the recursive solution is only slightly slower.

6. In many cases, a recursive solution is easier to understand and implement correctly
   than an iterative solution.

Review Exercises

Exercise R14.1. Define the terms

   (a)   recursion

   (b)   iteration

   (c)   infinite recursion

   (d)   indirect recursion

Exercise R14.2. Outline, but do not implement, a recursive solution for finding the
smallest value in an array.

Exercise R14.3. Outline, but do not implement, a recursive solution for sorting an array of numbers. *Hint:* First find the smallest value in the array.

Exercise R14.4. Outline, but do not implement, a recursive solution for generating all subsets of the set $\{1, 2, \ldots, n\}$.

Exercise R14.5. Exercise P14.11 shows an iterative way of generating all permutations of the sequence $(0, 1, \ldots, n-1)$. Explain why the algorithm produces the right result.

Exercise R14.6. Write a recursive definition of x^n, where $x \geq 0$, similar to the recursive definition of the Fibonacci numbers. *Hint:* How do you compute x^n from x^{n-1}? How does the recursion terminate?

Exercise R14.7. Write a recursive definition of $n! = 1 \times 2 \times \ldots \times n$, similar to the recursive definition of the Fibonacci numbers.

Exercise R14.8. Find out how often the recursive version of `fib` calls itself. Keep a global variable `fib_count` and increment it once in every call of `fib`. What is the relationship between `fib(n)` and `fib_count`?

Exercise R14.9. How many moves are required to move n disks in the "Towers of Hanoi" problem of Exercise P14.13? *Hint:* As explained in the exercise,

$$\text{moves}(1) = 1$$
$$\text{moves}(n) = 2 \cdot \text{moves}(n-1) + 1$$

Programming Exercises

Exercise P14.1. Write a recursive function `void reverse()` that reverses a sentence. For example:

```
Sentence greeting = new Sentence("Hello!");
greeting.reverse();
cout << greeting.get_text() << "\n";
```

prints the string `"!olleH"`. Implement a recursive solution by removing the first character, reversing a sentence consisting of the remaining text, and combining the two.

Exercise P14.2. Redo Exercise P14.1 with a recursive helper function that reverses a substring of the message text.

Exercise P14.3. Implement the `reverse` function of Exercise P14.1 as an iteration.

Exercise P14.4. Use recursion to implement a function `bool find(string s, string t)` that tests whether a string t is contained in a string s:

```
bool b = s.find("Mississippi!", "sip"); // returns true
```

Hint: If the text starts with the string you want to match, then you are done. If not, consider the sentence that you obtain by removing the first character.

Exercise P14.5. Use recursion to implement a function `int index_of(string s, string t)` that returns the starting position of the first substring of the string s that matches t. Return −1 if t is not a substring of s. For example,

```
int n = s.index_of("Mississippi!", "sip"); // returns 6
```

Hint: This is a bit trickier than the preceding problem, because you need to keep track of how far the match is from the beginning of the sentence. Make that value a parameter of a helper function.

Exercise P14.6. Using recursion, find the largest element in an array.

```
int maximum(vector<int> values)
```

Hint: Find the largest element in the subset containing all but the last element. Then compare that maximum to the value of the last element.

Exercise P14.7. Using recursion, compute the sum of all values in an array.

Exercise P14.8. Using recursion, compute the area of a polygon. Cut off a triangle and use the fact that a triangle with corners (x_1, y_1), (x_2, y_2), (x_3, y_3) has area $(x_1 y_2 + x_2 y_3 + x_3 y_1 - y_1 x_2 - y_2 x_3 - y_3 x_1)/2$.

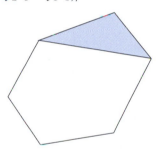

Exercise P14.9. Implement a function

```
vector<string> generate_substrings(string s)
```

that generates all substrings of a string. For example, the substrings of the string `"rum"` are the seven strings

```
"r", "ru", "rum", "u", "um", "m", ""
```

Hint: First enumerate all substrings that start with the first character. There are *n* of them if the string has length *n*. Then enumerate the substrings of the string that you obtain by removing the first character.

Exercise P14.10. Implement a function

```
vector<string> generate_subsets(string s)
```

that generates all subsets of characters of a string. For example, the subsets of characters of the string `"rum"` are the eight strings

```
"rum", "ru", "rm", "r", "um", "u", "m", ""
```

Note that the subsets don't have to be substrings—for example, `"rm"` isn't a substring of `"rum"`.

Exercise P14.11. The following program generates all permutations of the numbers 0, 1, 2, . . . , $n - 1$, without using recursion.

```
using namespace std;

void swap(int& x, int& y)
{
   int temp = x;
   x = y;
   y = temp;
}

void reverse(vector<int>& a, int i, int j)
{
   while (i < j)
   {
      swap(a[i], a[j]); i++; j--;
   }
}

bool next_permutation(vector<int>& a)
{
   for (int i = a.size() - 1; i > 0; i--)
   {
      if (a[i - 1] < a[i])
      {
         int j = a.size() - 1;
         while (a[i - 1] > a[j]) j--;
         swap(a[i - 1], a[j]);
         reverse(a, i, a.size() - 1);
         return true;
      }
   }
   return false;
}

void print(const vector<int>& a)
{
   for (int i = 0; i < a.size(); i++)
      cout << a[i] << " ";
   cout << "\n";
}

int main()
{
   const int n = 4;
   vector<int> a(n);
   for (int i = 0; i < a.size(); i++) a[i] = i;
   print(a);
   while (next_permutation(a))
      print(a);
   return 0;
}
```

The algorithm uses the fact that the set to be permuted consists of distinct numbers. Thus, you cannot use the same algorithm to compute the permutations of the characters in a string. You can, however, use this technique to get all permutations of the character positions and then compute a string whose ith character is s[a[i]]. Use this approach to reimplement the generate_permutations function without recursion.

Exercise P14.12. Refine the is_palindrome function to work with arbitrary strings, by ignoring non-letter characters and the distinction between upper- and lowercase letters. For example, if the input string is

    "Madam, I'm Adam!"

then you'd first strip off the last character because it isn't a letter, and recursively check whether the shorter string

    "Madam, I'm Adam"

is a palindrome.

Exercise P14.13. *Towers of Hanoi.* This is a well-known puzzle. A stack of disks of decreasing size is to be transported from the left-most peg to the right-most peg. The middle peg can be used as a temporary storage. (See Figure 8.) One disk can be moved at one time, from any peg to any other peg. You can place smaller disks only on top of larger ones, not the other way around.

Write a program that prints the moves necessary to solve the puzzle for *n* disks. (Ask the user for *n* at the beginning of the program.) Print moves in the form

    Move disk from peg 1 to peg 3

Hint: Write a helper function

    void hanoi(int from, int to, int n)

that moves the top n disks from the peg from to the peg to. Then figure out how you can achieve that by first moving the pile of the top n - 1 disks to the third peg, moving the nth disk to the destination, and then moving the pile from the third peg to the destination peg, this time using the original peg as the temporary storage. Extra credit if you write the program to actually draw the moves on the graphics screen!

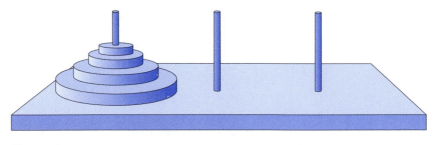

Figure 8

Towers of Hanoi

Sorting and Searching

One of the most common tasks in data processing is sorting. For example, a collection of employees needs to be printed out in alphabetical order or sorted by salary. You will learn several sorting methods in this chapter and compare their performance. This is by no means an exhaustive treatment on the subject of sorting. You will revisit this topic at a later time in your computer science studies. Reference [1] gives a good overview of the many sorting methods available.

Once a sequence of records is sorted, one can rapidly locate individual records. You will study the *binary search* algorithm that carries out this fast lookup.

CHAPTER CONTENTS

15.1   Selection Sort

To keep the examples simple, you will first learn how to sort a vector of integers before going on to sorting strings or employee data. Consider the following vector a:

| 11 | 9 | 17 | 5 | 12 |

An obvious first step is to find the smallest element. In this case the smallest element is 5, stored in a[3]. You should move the 5 to the beginning of the vector. Of course, there is already an element stored in a[0], namely 11. Therefore you cannot simply move a[3] into a[0] without moving the 11 somewhere else. You don't yet know where the 11 should end up, but you know for certain that it should not be in a[0]. Simply get it out of the way by *swapping it* with a[3].

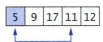

Now the first element is in the correct place. In the foregoing figure, the color indicates the portion of the vector that is already sorted from the unsorted remainder.

Next take the minimum of the remaining entries a[1]...a[4]. That minimum value, 9, is already in the correct place. You don't need to do anything in this case, simply extend the sorted area by one to the right:

| 5 | 9 | 17 | 11 | 12 |

Repeat the process. The minimum value of the unsorted region is 11, which needs to be swapped with the first value of the unsorted region, 17.

| 5 | 9 | 11 | 17 | 12 |

Now the unsorted region is only two elements long; keep to the same successful strategy. The minimum element is 12. Swap it with the first value, 17.

That leaves you with an unprocessed region of length 1, but of course a region of length 1 is always sorted. You are done.

Now program this algorithm.

File selsort.cpp

```
1  #include <iostream>
2  #include <vector>
3  #include <cstdlib>
4  #include <ctime>
5
6  using namespace std;
7
8  /**
9     Swaps two integers.
10    @param x  the first integer to swap
11    @param y  the second integer to swap
12 */
13 void swap(int& x, int& y)
14 {
15    int temp = x;
16    x = y;
17    y = temp;
18 }
19
20 /**
21    Gets the position of the smallest element in a vector range.
22    @param a  the vector
23    @param from  the beginning of the range
24    @param to  the end of the range
25    @return  the position of the smallest element in
26    the range a[from]...a[to]
27 */
28 int min_position(vector<int>& a, int from, int to)
29 {
30    int min_pos = from;
31    int i;
32    for (i = from + 1; i <= to; i++)
33       if (a[i] < a[min_pos]) min_pos = i;
34    return min_pos;
35 }
36
37 /**
38    Sorts a vector using the selection sort algorithm.
39    @param a  the vector to sort
40 */
41 void selection_sort(vector<int>& a)
42 {
43    int next; /* the next position to be set to the minimum */
44
45    for (next = 0; next < a.size() - 1; next++)
46    {
47       /* find the position of the minimum */
48       int min_pos = min_position(a, next, a.size() - 1);
49       if (min_pos != next)
```

```
50              swap(a[min_pos], a[next]);
51      }
52  }
53
54  /**
55      Prints all elements in a vector.
56      @param a  the vector to print
57  */
58  void print(vector<int> a)
59  {
60      for (int i = 0; i < a.size(); i++)
61          cout << a[i] << " ";
62      cout << "\n";
63  }
64
65  /**
66      Sets the seed of the random number generator.
67  */
68  void rand_seed()
69  {
70      int seed = static_cast<int>(time(0));
71      srand(seed);
72  }
73
74  /**
75      Computes a random integer in a range.
76      @param a  the bottom of the range
77      @param b  the top of the range
78      @return a random integer x, a <= x and x <= b
79  */
80  int rand_int(int a, int b)
81  {
82      return a + rand() % (b - a + 1);
83  }
84
85  int main()
86  {
87      rand_seed();
88      vector<int> v(20);
89      for (int i = 0; i < v.size(); i++)
90          v[i] = rand_int(1, 100);
91      print(v);
92      selection_sort(v);
93      print(v);
94      return 0;
95  }
```

The algorithm will sort any array of integers. If speed were not an issue for us, or if there simply were no better sorting method available, we could stop the discussion of sorting right here. As the next section shows, however, this algorithm, while entirely correct, shows disappointing performance when run on a large data set.

Profiling the Selection Sort Algorithm

To measure the performance of a program, one could simply run it and measure how long it takes by using a stopwatch. However, most of our programs run very quickly, and it is not easy to time them accurately in this way. Furthermore, when a program does take a noticeable time to run, a certain amount of that time may simply be used for loading the program from disk into memory (for which it should not be penalized) or for screen output (whose speed depends on the computer model, even for computers with identical CPUs). Instead use the Time class. Recall that

```
Time now;
```

sets now to the current time.

Here is how to use the timer to measure the performance of the sorting algorithm.

```
int main()
{
   rand_seed();
   cout << "Enter vector size: ";
   int n;
   cin >> n;
   vector<int> v(n);
   for (int i = 0; i < v.size(); i++)
      v[i] = rand_int(1, 100);
   Time before;
   selection_sort(v);
   Time after;

   cout << "Elapsed time = " << after.seconds_from(before)
      << " seconds\n";
   return 0;
}
```

By measuring the time just before the sorting and stopping it just afterwards, you don't count the time it takes to initialize the vector or the time during which the program waits for the user to type in n.

Here are the results of some sample runs.

n	Seconds
10,000	4
20,000	14
30,000	30
40,000	54
50,000	86
60,000	124

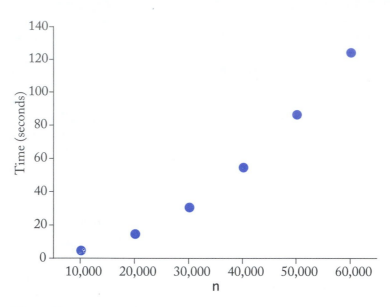

Figure 1

Time Taken by Selection Sort

These measurements were obtained on a Pentium III processor with a clock speed of 750 MHz running Linux. On another computer, the actual numbers will differ, but the relationship between the numbers will be the same. Figure 1 shows a plot of the measurements.

As you can see, doubling the size of the data set more than doubles the time needed to sort it.

15.3 Analyzing the Performance of the Selection Sort Algorithm

Let us count the number of operations that the program must carry out to sort an array by the selection sort algorithm. Actually, we don't know how many machine operations are generated for each C++ instruction or which of those instructions are more time-consuming than others, but we can make a simplification. Simply count how often an array element is *visited*. Each visit requires about the same amount of work by other operations, such as incrementing subscripts and comparing values.

Let n be the size of the array. First, you must find the smallest of n numbers. To achieve this, you must visit n array elements. Then swap the elements, which takes two visits. (You may argue that there is a certain probability that you don't need to swap the values. That is true, and one can refine the computation to reflect that observation. As we will soon see, doing so would not affect the overall conclusion.) In the next step, you need to visit only $n - 1$ elements to find the minimum and then visit two of them to swap them. In the following step, $n - 2$ elements are visited to find the minimum. The last run visits two elements to find the minimum and requires two visits to swap the elements. Therefore, the total number of visits is

$$n + 2 + (n - 1) + 2 + \cdots + 2 + 2 = n + (n - 1) + \cdots + 2 + (n - 1) \cdot 2$$
$$= 2 + \cdots + (n - 1) + n + (n - 1) \cdot 2$$
$$= \frac{n(n + 1)}{2} - 1 + (n - 1) \cdot 2$$

because

$$1 + 2 + \cdots + (n - 1) + n = \frac{n(n + 1)}{2}$$

After multiplying out and collecting terms of n, you find that the number of visits is

$$\tfrac{1}{2}n^2 + \tfrac{5}{2}n - 3$$

This is a quadratic equation in n. That explains why the graph of Figure 1 looks approximately like a parabola.

Now simplify the analysis further. When you plug in a large value for n (for example, 1,000 or 2,000), then $\tfrac{1}{2}n^2$ is 500,000 or 2,000,000. The lower term, $\tfrac{5}{2}n - 3$, doesn't contribute much at all; it is just 2,497 or 4,997, a drop in the bucket compared to the hundreds of thousands or even millions of comparisons specified by the $\tfrac{1}{2}n^2$ term. Just ignore these lower-level terms. Next, ignore the constant factor $\tfrac{1}{2}$. You need not be interested in the actual count of visits for a single n. You need to compare the ratios of counts for different values of n^2. For example, you can say that sorting an array of 2,000 numbers requires four times as many visits as sorting an array of 1,000 numbers:

$$\left(\tfrac{1}{2} \times 2000^2\right) / \left(\tfrac{1}{2} \times 1000^2\right) = 4$$

The factor $\tfrac{1}{2}$ cancels out in comparisons of this kind. We will simply say, "The number of visits is of order n^2". That way, we can easily see that the number of comparisons increases fourfold when the size of the vector doubles: $(2n)^2 = 4n^2$.

To indicate that the number of visits is of order n^2, computer scientists often use *big-Oh notation:* The number of visits is $O(n^2)$. This is a convenient shorthand.

To turn an exact expression like

$$\tfrac{1}{2}n^2 + \tfrac{5}{2}n - 3$$

into big-Oh notation, simply locate the fastest-growing term, n^2, and ignore the constant coefficient $\tfrac{1}{2}$.

You observed before that the actual number of machine operations, and the actual number of microseconds that the computer spends on them, is approximately proportional to the number of element visits. Maybe there are about 10 machine operations (increments, comparisons, memory loads, and stores) for every element visit. The number of machine operations is then approximately $10 \times \tfrac{1}{2}n^2$. Again, we aren't interested in the coefficient and can say that the number of machine operations, and hence the time spent on the sorting, is of the order of n^2 or $O(n^2)$. The sad fact remains that doubling the size of the vector causes a fourfold increase in the time required for sorting it. To sort a vector of 100,000 entries, for example to create a telephone directory, takes 10,000 times as long as sorting 1,000 entries. If 1,000 entries can be sorted in 11 seconds (as in the example), then 100,000 entries require over 30 hours. This is a problem. You will see in the next section how one can dramatically improve the performance of the sorting process by choosing a more sophisticated algorithm.

15.4   Merge Sort

Suppose you have a vector of 10 integers. Engage in a bit of wishful thinking and hope that the first half of the vector is already perfectly sorted, and the second half is too, like this:

5	9	11	12	17	1	8	11	20	32

Now it is an easy matter to *merge* the two sorted arrays into a sorted array, simply by taking a new element from either the first or the second subvector and choosing the smaller of the elements each time:

5	9	10	12	17	1̶	8	11	20	32		1									
5̶	9	10	12	17	1̶	8	11	20	32		1	5								
5̶	9	10	12	17	1̶	8̶	11	20	32		1	5	8							
5̶	9̶	10	12	17	1̶	8̶	11	20	32		1	5	8	9						
5̶	9̶	10̶	12	17	1̶	8̶	11	20	32		1	5	8	9	10					
5̶	9̶	10̶	12	17	1̶	8̶	11̶	20	32		1	5	8	9	10	11				
5̶	9̶	10̶	12̶	17	1̶	8̶	11̶	20	32		1	5	8	9	10	11	12			
5̶	9̶	10̶	12̶	17̶	1̶	8̶	11̶	20	32		1	5	8	9	10	11	12	17		
5̶	9̶	10̶	12̶	17̶	1̶	8̶	11̶	20	32		1	5	8	9	10	11	12	17	20	
5̶	9̶	10̶	12̶	17̶	1̶	8̶	11̶	20̶	32		1	5	8	9	10	11	12	17	20	32

In fact, you probably performed this merging before when you and a friend had to sort a pile of papers. You and the friend split up the pile in the middle, each of you sorted your half, and then you merged the results together.

This is all well and good, but it doesn't seem to solve the problem for the computer. It still has to sort the first and the second half of the array, because it can't very well ask a few buddies to pitch in. As it turns out, though, if the computer keeps dividing the vector into smaller and smaller subvectors, sorting each half and merging them back together, it carries out dramatically fewer steps than the selection sort requires.

Write a program that implements this idea. Because you will call the sort procedure multiple times to sort portions of the array, you will supply the range of elements that you would like to have sorted.

```cpp
void merge_sort(vector<int>& a, int from, int to)
{
    if (from == to) return;
    int mid = (from + to) / 2;

    /* sort the first and the second half */
    merge_sort(a, from, mid);
    merge_sort(a, mid + 1, to);
    merge(a, from, mid, to);
}
```

The `merge` procedure is somewhat long but quite straightforward—see the following code listing for details.

File mergsort.cpp

```cpp
1  #include <iostream>
2  #include <vector>
3  #include <cstdlib>
4  #include <ctime>
5
6  using namespace std;
7
8  /**
9      Merges two adjacent ranges in a vector.
10     @param a  the vector with the elements to merge
11     @param from  the start of the first range
12     @param mid  the end of the first range
13     @param to  the end of the second range
14  */
15  void merge(vector<int>& a, int from, int mid, int to)
16  {
17     int n = to - from + 1; /* size of the range to be merged */
18     /* merge both halves into a temporary vector b */
19     vector<int> b(n);
20
21     int i1 = from;
22         /* next element to consider in the first half */
23     int i2 = mid + 1;
24         /* next element to consider in the second half */
25     int j = 0; /* next open position in b */
26
27     /*
28         As long as neither i1 nor i2 is past the end, move the smaller
29         element into b
30     */
31     while (i1 <= mid && i2 <= to)
```

```
32      {
33          if (a[i1] < a[i2])
34          {
35              b[j] = a[i1];
36              i1++;
37          }
38          else
39          {
40              b[j] = a[i2];
41              i2++;
42          }
43          j++;
44      }
45
46      /*
47          Note that only one of the two while loops below is executed.
48      */
49
50      /* Copy any remaining entries of the first half */
51      while (i1 <= mid)
52      {
53          b[j] = a[i1];
54          i1++;
55          j++;
56      }
57      /* Copy any remaining entries of the second half */
58      while (i2 <= to)
59      {
60          b[j] = a[i2];
61          i2++;
62          j++;
63      }
64
65      /* Copy back from the temporary vector */
66      for (j = 0; j < n; j++)
67          a[from + j] = b[j];
68  }
69
70  /**
71      Sorts the elements in a range of a vector.
72      @param a  the vector with the elements to sort
73      @param from  start of the range to sort
74      @param to  end of the range to sort
75  */
76  void merge_sort(vector<int>& a, int from, int to)
77  {
78      if (from == to) return;
79      int mid = (from + to) / 2;
80      /* sort the first and the second half */
81      merge_sort(a, from, mid);
82      merge_sort(a, mid + 1, to);
83      merge(a, from, mid, to);
84  }
85
86  /**
87      Prints all elements in a vector.
```

```
88        @param a the vector to print
89    */
90    void print(vector<int> a)
91    {
92        for (int i = 0; i < a.size(); i++)
93            cout << a[i] << " ";
94        cout << "\n";
95    }
96
97    /**
98        Sets the seed of the random number generator.
99    */
100   void rand_seed()
101   {
102       int seed = static_cast<int>(time(0));
103       srand(seed);
104   }
105
106   /**
107       Computes a random integer in a range.
108       @param a the bottom of the range
109       @param b the top of the range
110       @return a random integer x, a <= x and x <= b
111   */
112   int rand_int(int a, int b)
113   {
114       return a + rand() % (b - a + 1);
115   }
116
117   int main()
118   {
119       rand_seed();
120       vector<int> v(20);
121       for (int i = 0; i < v.size(); i++)
122           v[i] = rand_int(1, 100);
123       print(v);
124       merge_sort(v, 0, v.size() - 1);
125       print(v);
126       return 0;
127   }
```

15.5   Analyzing the Merge Sort Algorithm

This algorithm looks much more complicated than the selection sort algorithm, and it appears that it may well take much longer to carry out these repeated subdivisions. However, the timing results for merge sort look much better than those for selection sort. Sorting an array with 100,000 elements takes less than one second on our test machine, whereas the selection sort takes 394 seconds.

To study the relationship between the input size and the running time, you have to analyze much larger data sets. Here is a table with measurements.

n	Merge sort (seconds)
1,000,000	6
2,000,000	12
3,000,000	18
4,000,000	24
5,000,000	31
6,000,000	38

Figure 2 shows a graph plotting the relationship. Note that the graph does not have a parabolic shape. Instead, it appears as if the running time grows approximately linearly with the size of the array.

To understand why the merge sort algorithm is such a tremendous improvement, estimate the number of array element visits. First, tackle the merge process that happens after the first and second half have been sorted.

Each step in the merge process adds one more element to b. There are n elements in b. That element may come from the first or second half, and in most cases the elements from the two halves must be compared to see which one to take. Count that as 3 visits

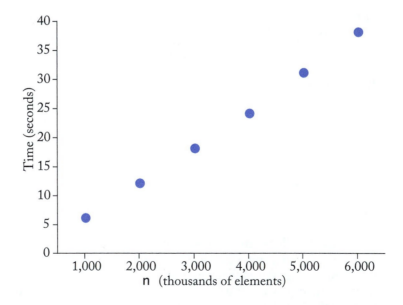

Figure 2

Merge Sort Timing

(one for b and one each for the two halves of a) per element, or 3n visits total. Then you must copy back from b to a, yielding another 2n visits, for a total of 5n.

If you let $T(n)$ denote the number of visits required to sort a range of n elements through the merge sort process, then you obtain

$$T(n) = T\left(\frac{n}{2}\right) + T\left(\frac{n}{2}\right) + 5n$$

because sorting each half takes $T(n/2)$ visits. (Actually, if n is not even, then you have one subarray of size $(n-1)/2$ and one of size $(n+1)/2$. While it turns out that this detail does not affect the outcome of the computation, you can assume for now that n is a power of 2, say $n = 2^m$. This way, all subarrays can be evenly divided into two parts.)

Unfortunately, the formula

$$T(n) = 2T\left(\frac{n}{2}\right) + 5n$$

does not clearly tell you the relationship between n and $T(n)$. To understand the relationship, evaluate $T(n/2)$, using the same formula:

$$T\left(\frac{n}{2}\right) = 2T\left(\frac{n}{4}\right) + 5\frac{n}{2}$$

Therefore

$$T(n) = 2 \times 2T\left(\frac{n}{4}\right) + 5n + 5n$$

Do this again:

$$T\left(\frac{n}{4}\right) = 2T\left(\frac{n}{8}\right) + 5\frac{n}{4}$$

hence

$$T(n) = 2 \times 2 \times 2T\left(\frac{n}{8}\right) + 5n + 5n + 5n$$

This generalizes from 2, 4, 8, to arbitrary powers of 2:

$$T(n) = 2^k T\left(\frac{n}{2^k}\right) + 5nk$$

Recall that you assume that $n = 2^m$; hence, for $k = m$,

$$T(n) = 2^m T\left(\frac{n}{2^m}\right) + 5nm$$
$$= nT(1) + 5nm$$
$$= n + 5n\log_2 n$$

(Because $n = 2^m$, you have $m = \log_2 n$.) To establish the growth order, you drop the lower order term n and are left with $5n\log_2 n$. Drop the constant factor 5. It is also customary to drop the base of the logarithm because all logarithms are related by a constant factor. For example,

$$\log_2 x = \log_{10} x / \log_{10} 2 \approx \log_{10} x \times 3.32193$$

Hence we say that merge sort is an $O(n\log n)$ algorithm.

Is the $O(n\log n)$ merge sort algorithm better than an $O(n^2)$ selection sort algorithm? You bet it is. Recall that it took $100^2 = 10,000$ times longer to sort 1,000,000 records than it took to sort 10,000 records with the $O(n^2)$ algorithm. With the $O(n\log n)$ algorithm, the ratio is

$$\frac{1,000,000 \log 1,000,000}{10,000 \log 10,000} = 100\left(\frac{6}{4}\right) = 150$$

Suppose for the moment that merge sort takes the same time as selection sort to sort an array of 10,000 integers, that is, 4 seconds on the test machine. (Actually, it is much faster than that.) Then it would take about 4×150 seconds, or 10 minutes, to sort 1,000,000 integers. Contrast that with selection sort, which would take over 11 hours for the same task. As you can see, even if it takes you 11 hours to learn about a better algorithm, that can be time well spent.

In this chapter you have barely begun to scratch the surface of this interesting topic. There are many sort algorithms, some with even better performance than the merge sort algorithm, and the analysis of these algorithms can be quite challenging. You will revisit these important issues in a later computer science class.

Random Fact 15.1

Ada

In the early 1970s, the U.S. Department of Defense (DoD) was seriously concerned about the high cost of the software components of its weapons equipment. It was estimated that more than half of the total DoD budget was spent on the development of this *embedded-systems software*—that is, the software that is embedded in some machinery, such as an airplane or missile, to control it. One of the perceived problems was the great diversity of programming languages that were used to produce the software. Many of these languages, such as TACPOL, CMS-2, SPL/1, and JOVIAL, were virtually unknown outside the defense sector.

In 1976 a committee of computer scientists and defense industry representatives was asked to evaluate existing programming languages. The committee was to determine whether any of them could be made the DoD standard for all future military programming. To nobody's surprise, the committee decided that a new language would need to be created. Contractors were then invited to submit designs for such a new language. Of 17 initial proposals, 4 were chosen to develop their languages. To ensure an unbiased evaluation, the languages received code names: Red (by Intermetrics), Green (by CII Honeywell Bull), Blue (by Softech), and Yellow (by SRI International). All four languages were based on Pascal.

The Green language emerged as the winner in 1979. It was named Ada, after Ada Augusta, Countess of Lovelace (1815–1852), a sponsor of Charles Babbage, the 19th-century pioneer who built several enormous programmable mechanical calculators (see Figure 3). Ada Lovelace was one of the first people to realize the potential of such a machine, not just for computing mathematical tables but for nonnumerical data processing. She is considered by many to be the world's first programmer.

In 1983 the Ada standard was finalized. Besides the usual unreadable reference manual that is *de rigueur* for most language standards, the Ada standard had one major innovation: a huge *validation suite* of test cases that a compiler had to pass in order to be labeled conformant. Because of this validation suite, Ada compilers from different vendors are highly compatible with one another. In 1995, a second generation of Ada was standardized that supports object-oriented programming and an improved definition of parallel execution of functions.

Ada was not an immediate success. It was a complex language, laden with every feature imaginable that was perceived to be useful for embedded-systems programming. Initial versions of compilers and development systems were slow, unreliable, and expensive. The

Figure 3

Babbage's Difference Engine

▼

language was roundly derided by academics as a typical bloated Defense Department product. Military contractors routinely sought, and obtained, exemptions from the requirement that they had to use Ada on their projects. Outside the defense industry, few companies used

▼

Ada.

This has slowly changed. Ada is now established as the principal language for military software, and it has found application in other large projects.

▼

In hindsight, many of the criticisms leveled against Ada are unfair. C++ has become a language that is every bit as complex and difficult to compile as Ada, but Ada has a more strictly defined standard and a cleaner interaction between language constructs. Ada was ahead of its time in realizing that a modern programming language requires a large number of built-in

▼

features to free programmers from having to reinvent these mechanisms.

15.6   Searching

Suppose you need to find the telephone number of your friend. You look up his name in the telephone book, and naturally you can find it quickly, because the telephone book is sorted alphabetically. Quite possibly, you may never have thought how important it is that the telephone book is sorted. To see that, think of the following problem: Suppose you have a telephone number and you must know to what party it belongs. You could of course call that number, but suppose nobody picks up on the other end, or you just get a recording. You could look through the telephone book, one number at a time, until you find the number. This would obviously be a tremendous amount of work, and you would have to be desperate to attempt that.

This thought experiment shows the difference between a search through an unsorted data set and a search through a sorted data set. The following two sections will analyze the difference formally.

If you want to find a number in a sequence of values that occur in arbitrary order, there is nothing you can do to speed up the search. You must simply look through all elements until you have found a match or until you reach the end. This is called a *linear* or *sequential search*.

Here is a procedure that performs a linear search through a vector v of integers for the value a. The procedure then returns the index of the match, or −1 if a does not occur in v.

File lsearch.cpp

```
 1  #include <iostream>
 2  #include <vector>
 3  #include <cstdlib>
 4  #include <ctime>
 5
 6  using namespace std;
 7
 8  /**
 9      Finds an element in a vector.
10      @param v the vector with the elements to search
11      @param a the value to search for
12      @return the index of the first match, or -1 if not found
```

```
13  */
14  int linear_search(vector<int> v, int a)
15  {
16     for (int i = 0; i < v.size(); i++)
17     {
18        if (v[i] == a)
19           return i;
20     }
21     return -1;
22  }
23
24  /**
25     Prints all elements in a vector.
26     @param a  the vector to print
27  */
28  void print(vector<int> a)
29  {
30     for (int i = 0; i < a.size(); i++)
31        cout << a[i] << " ";
32     cout << "\n";
33  }
34
35  /**
36     Sets the seed of the random number generator.
37  */
38  void rand_seed()
39  {
40     int seed = static_cast<int>(time(0));
41     srand(seed);
42  }
43
44  /**
45     Computes a random integer in a range.
46     @param a  the bottom of the range
47     @param b  the top of the range
48     @return a random integer x, a <= x and x <= b
49  */
50  int rand_int(int a, int b)
51  {
52     return a + rand() % (b - a + 1);
53  }
54
55  int main()
56  {
57     rand_seed();
58     vector<int> v(20);
59     for (int i = 0; i < v.size(); i++)
60        v[i] = rand_int(1, 100);
61     print(v);
62     cout << "Enter number to search for: ";
63     int n;
64     cin >> n;
65     int j = linear_search(v, n);
66     cout << "Found in position " << j << "\n";
67     return 0;
68  }
```

How long does a linear search take? If you assume that the element a is present in the vector v, then the average search visits $n/2$ elements. If it is not present, then all n elements must be inspected to verify the absence. Either way, a linear search is an $O(n)$ algorithm.

15.7   Binary Search

Now search an item in a data sequence that has been previously sorted. Of course, you could still do a linear search, but it turns out you can do much better than that.

Consider the following example: The data set is

v[0]	v[1]	v[2]	v[3]	v[4]	v[5]	v[6]	v[7]
14	43	76	100	115	290	400	511

and you want to see whether the value 123 is in the data set. The last point in the first half of the data set, v[3], is 100. It is smaller than the value you are looking for; hence, you should look in the second half of the data set for a match, that is, in the sequence

v[4]	v[5]	v[6]	v[7]
115	290	400	411

Now the last value of the first half of this sequence is 290; hence, the value must be located in the sequence

v[4]	v[5]
115	290

The last value of the first half of this very short sequence is 115, which is smaller than the value that you are searching, so you must look in the second half:

v[5]
290

It is trivial to see that you don't have a match, because $123 \neq 290$. If you wanted to insert 123 into the sequence, you would need to insert it just before v[5].

This search process is called a *binary search*, because the size of the search is cut in half in each step. That cutting in half works only because you know that the sequence of values is sorted.

The following function implements a binary search in a sorted array of integers. It returns the position of the match if the search succeeds, or −1 if a is not found in v:

```
int binary_search(vector<int> v, int from, int to, int a)
{
   if (from > to)
      return -1;
   int mid = (from + to) / 2;
   if (v[mid] == a)
      return mid;
   else if (v[mid] < a)
      return binary_search(v, mid + 1, to, a);
   else
      return binary_search(v, from, mid - 1, a);
}
```

Now determine the number of visits of array elements required to carry out a search. Use the same technique as in the analysis of merge sort and observe that

$$T(n) = T\left(\frac{n}{2}\right) + 1$$

since you look at the middle element, which counts as one comparison, and then search either the left or the right subarray. Using the same equation,

$$T\left(\frac{n}{2}\right) = T\left(\frac{n}{4}\right) + 1$$

and, by plugging it into the original equation, you get

$$T(n) = T\left(\frac{n}{4}\right) + 2$$

This generalizes to

$$T(n) = T\left(\frac{n}{2^k}\right) + k$$

As in the analysis of merge sort, you make the simplifying assumption that n is a power of 2, $n = 2^m$, where $m = \log_2 n$. Then you obtain

$$T(n) = 1 + \log_2 n$$

Therefore, binary search is an $O(\log n)$ algorithm.

This result makes intuitive sense. Suppose that n is 100. Then after each search, the size of the search range is cut in half, to 50, 25, 12, 6, 3, and 1. After seven comparisons we are done. This agrees with our formula since $\log_2 100 \approx 6.64386$, and indeed the next larger power of 2 is $2^7 = 128$.

Since a binary search is so much faster than a linear search, is it worthwhile to sort an array first and then use a binary search? It depends. If you only search the array once, then it is more efficient to pay for an $O(n)$ linear search than for an $O(n \log n)$ sort and $O(\log n)$ binary search. But if one makes a number of searches in the same array, then sorting it is definitely worthwhile.

Here is a complete program that demonstrates the binary search algorithm.

File bsearch.cpp

```
1  #include <iostream>
2  #include <vector>
3  #include <cstdlib>
4  #include <ctime>
5
6  using namespace std;
7
8  /**
9      Finds an element in a sorted vector.
10     @param v the sorted vector with the elements to search
11     @param from the start of the range to search
12     @param to the end of the range to search
13     @param a the value to search for
14     @return the index of the first match, or -1 if not found
15  */
16  int binary_search(vector<int> v, int from, int to, int a)
17  {
18     if (from > to)
19        return -1;
20     int mid = (from + to) / 2;
21     if (v[mid] == a)
22        return mid;
23     else if (v[mid] < a)
24        return binary_search(v, mid + 1, to, a);
25     else
26        return binary_search(v, from, mid - 1, a);
27  }
28
29  /**
30      Prints all elements in a vector.
31      @param a the vector to print
32  */
33  void print(vector<int> a)
34  {
35     for (int i = 0; i < a.size(); i++)
36        cout << a[i] << " ";
37     cout << "\n";
38  }
39
40  /**
41      Sets the seed of the random number generator.
42  */
43  void rand_seed()
44  {
45     int seed = static_cast<int>(time(0));
46     srand(seed);
47  }
48
49  /**
50      Computes a random integer in a range.
51      @param a the bottom of the range
52      @param b the top of the range
```

```
53     @return a random integer x, a <= x and x <= b
54 */
55 int rand_int(int a, int b)
56 {
57     return a + rand() % (b - a + 1);
58 }
59
60 int main()
61 {
62     rand_seed();
63     vector<int> v(20);
64     v[0] = 1;
65     for (int i = 1; i < v.size(); i++)
66         v[i] = v[i - 1] + rand_int(1, 10);
67
68     print(v);
69     cout << "Enter number to search for: ";
70     int n;
71     cin >> n;
72     int j = binary_search(v, 0, v.size() - 1, n);
73     cout << "Found in position " << j << "\n";
74     return 0;
75 }
```

15.8   Searching and Sorting Real Data

In this chapter, you have seen how to search and sort vectors of integers. Of course, in real programming there is rarely a need to search through a collection of integers.

However, the procedures can be modified easily to search through real data. Here is a procedure that applies the binary search algorithm to find an employee by name. Of course, we must assume that the vector is currently sorted on the name field!

File esearch.cpp

```
1 #include <iostream>
2 #include <vector>
3
4 using namespace std;
5
6 #include "ccc_empl.h"
7
8 /**
9     Finds an employee in a sorted vector.
10    @param v the sorted vector with the employees to search
11    @param from the start of the range to search
12    @param to the end of the range to search
13    @param n the employee name to search for
14    @return the index of the first match, or -1 if not found
15 */
16 int binary_search(vector<Employee> v, int from, int to, string n)
17 {
18     if (from > to)
19         return -1;
```

```
20      int mid = (from + to) / 2;
21      if (v[mid].get_name() == n)
22          return mid;
23      else if (v[mid].get_name() < n)
24          return binary_search(v, mid + 1, to, n);
25      else
26          return binary_search(v, from, mid - 1, n);
27  }
28
29  int main()
30  {
31      vector<Employee> staff(5);
32      staff[0] = Employee("Cracker, Carl", 48000.0);
33      staff[1] = Employee("Hacker, Harry", 35000.0);
34      staff[2] = Employee("Lam, Larry", 78000.0);
35      staff[3] = Employee("Reindeer, Rudolf", 63000.0);
36      staff[4] = Employee("Sandman, Susan", 51500.0);
37
38      cout << "Enter name of employee to search for: ";
39      string name;
40      getline(cin, name);
41
42      int i = binary_search(staff, 0, staff.size() - 1, name);
43
44      if (i >= 0)
45          cout << staff[i].get_name() << " "
46              << staff[i].get_salary() << "\n";
47      else
48          cout << "Not found.\n";
49
50      return 0;
51  }
```

Random Fact   15.2

Cataloging Your Necktie Collection

People and companies use computers to organize just about every aspect of their lives. On the whole, computers are tremendously good for collecting and analyzing data. In fact, the power offered by computers and their software makes them seductive solutions for just about any organizational problem. It is easy to lose sight of the fact that using a computer is not always the best solution to a problem.

John Bear [2] describes a home computer user who wrote him to describe how he uses a personal computer. That user catalogs his necktie collection, putting descriptions of the ties into a database and generating reports that list them by color, price, or style. Hopefully that person had another use to justify the purchase of a piece of equipment worth several thousand dollars, but that application was so dear to his heart that he wanted to share it. Perhaps not surprisingly, few other users share that excitement, and you don't find the shelves of your local software store lined with necktie-cataloging software.

▼

▼

▼

▼

▼

▼

▼

▼

▼

▼

▼

The phenomenon of using technology for its own sake is quite widespread. In the 1990s, several large corporations showed great enthusiasm for using computer networks to deliver movies to home viewers on demand. With the technology available at that time, this was an expensive way of getting a movie to a person's home. Fast network connections and new receiving equipment are required. It sounds like a lot of trouble just to eliminate the trip to the video rental store. Indeed, initial field experiments were sobering. In these experiments, the network lines and computers were simulated by employees putting tapes into remote video tape players. Few customers were willing to pay a sufficient premium for this service to warrant the huge investments needed. At some point in the future, it may well be economical to send movies over computer networks, but today the inexpensive video players and rental movies do an adequate job at an acceptable cost.

In the "Internet bubble" of 2000, hundreds of companies were founded on the premise that the Internet made it technologically possible to order items such as groceries and pet food from a home computer, and therefore the traditional stores would be replaced by Web stores. Again, technological feasibility did not ensure economic success. Trucking groceries and pet foods to households wasn't cost-effective, and few customers were willing to pay for the added convenience.

At the time of this writing, many elementary schools are spending tremendous resources to bring computers and the Internet into the classroom. Indeed, it is easy to understand why teachers, school administrators, parents, and politicians are in favor of computers in the classroom. Isn't computer literacy absolutely essential for youngsters in the new millennium? Isn't it particularly important to give low-income students, whose parents may not be able to afford a home computer, the opportunity to master computer skills? However, schools have found that computers are enormously expensive. The initial cost of purchasing the equipment, while substantial when compared to the cost of books and other teaching materials, is not beyond the budget of most schools. However, the *total cost of ownership*—that is, the initial cost plus the cost of keeping the computers in working order and of upgrading them when they become outdated—is staggering. Schools were confronted with hard choices—should they lay off librarians and art instructors to hire more computer technicians, or should they let the expensive equipment become useless? Interestingly, many schools were so caught up in the hype that they never evaluated the cost/benefit tradeoffs until after the computers arrived.

As computer programmers, it is our desire to program everything. As computer professionals, though, we owe it to our employers and clients to understand their work process and to deploy computers and software only where they add more value than cost.

Chapter Summary

1. Algorithms that perform the same task can have significant differences in performance. You analyzed two sorting algorithms: selection sort and merge sort. Both rearrange an array in sorted order, but merge sort is much faster on large data sets.

2. Computer scientists use big-Oh notation to give approximate descriptions of the efficiency of algorithms. In big-Oh notation only the fastest-growing term is important; constant factors are ignored. Selection sort is an $O(n^2)$ algorithm; merge sort is an $O(n \log n)$ algorithm.

3. Searching a value in an unsorted data set requires $O(n)$ steps. If the data set is sorted, binary search can find it in $O(\log n)$ steps.

FURTHER READING

[1] Robert Sedgewick, *Algorithms in C++*, 3rd ed., Addison-Wesley, 1999.
[2] John Bear, *Computer Wimp*, Ten Speed Press, 1983.
[3] Donald E. Knuth, *The Art of Computer Programming, Vol. 1: Fundamental Algorithms*, Addison-Wesley, 1973.

REVIEW EXERCISES

Exercise R15.1. *Checking against off-by-one errors.* When writing the selection sort algorithm of Section 15.1, a programmer must make the usual choices of < against <=, a.size() against a.size() - 1, and next against next + 1. This is fertile ground for off-by-one errors. Make code walkthroughs of the algorithm with arrays of length 0, 1, 2, and 3 and check carefully that all index values are correct.

Exercise R15.2. What is the difference between searching and sorting?

Exercise R15.3. For the following expressions, what is the order of the growth of each?

(a) $n^2 + 2n + 1$

(b) $n^{10} + 9n^9 + 20n^8 + 145n^7$

(c) $(n + 1)^4$

(d) $\left(n^2 + n\right)^2$

(e) $n + 0.001n^3$

(f) $n^3 - 1000n^2 + 10^9$

(g) $n + \log n$

(h) $n^2 + n\log n$

(i) $2^n + n^2$

(j) $\left(n^3 + 2n\right)/\left(n^2 + 0.75\right)$

Exercise R15.4. You determined that the actual number of visits in the selection sort algorithm is

$$T(n) = \tfrac{1}{2}n^2 + \tfrac{5}{2}n - 3$$

You then characterized this function as having $O(n^2)$ growth. Compute the actual ratios

$$T(2{,}000)/T(1{,}000)$$
$$T(5{,}000)/T(1{,}000)$$
$$T(10{,}000)/T(1{,}000)$$

and compare them with

$$f(2{,}000)/f(1{,}000)$$
$$f(5{,}000)/f(1{,}000)$$
$$f(10{,}000)/f(1{,}000)$$

where $f(n) = n^2$.

Exercise R15.5. Suppose algorithm A takes five seconds to handle a data set of 1,000 records. If the algorithm A is an $O(n)$ algorithm, how long will it take to handle a data set of 2,000 records? Of 10,000 records?

Exercise R15.6. Suppose an algorithm takes five seconds to handle a data set of 1,000 records. Fill in the following table, which shows the approximate growth of the execution times depending on the complexity of the algorithm.

	$O(n)$	$O(n^2)$	$O(n^3)$	$O(n \log n)$	$O(2^n)$
1,000	5	5	5	5	5
2,000					
3,000		45			
10,000					

For example, since $3000^2/1000^2 = 9$, the $O(n^2)$ algorithm would take nine times as long, or 45 seconds, to handle a data set of 3,000 records.

Exercise R15.7. Sort the following growth rates from slowest growth to fastest growth.

$$O(n)$$
$$O(n^3)$$
$$O(n^n)$$
$$O(\log n)$$
$$O(n^2 \log n)$$
$$O(n \log n)$$
$$O(2^n)$$
$$O(\sqrt{n})$$
$$O(n\sqrt{n})$$
$$O(n^{\log n})$$

Exercise R15.8. What is the order of complexity of the standard algorithm to find the minimum value of an array? Of finding both the minimum and the maximum?

Exercise R15.9. What is the order of complexity of the following function?

```
int count(vector<int> a, int c)
{
   int i;
   int count = 0;

   for (i = 0; i < a.size(); i++)
   {
      if (a[i] == c) count++;
   }
   return count;
}
```

Exercise R15.10. Your task is to remove all duplicates from an array. For example, if the array has the values

4   7   11   4   9   5   11   7   3   5

then the array should be changed to

4   7   11   9   5   3

Here is a simple algorithm. Look at a[i]. Count how many times it occurs in a. If the count is larger than 1, remove it. What is the order of complexity of this algorithm?

Exercise R15.11. Consider the following algorithm to remove all duplicates from an array. Sort the array. For each element in the array, look at its two neighbors to decide whether it is present more than once. If so, remove it. Is this a faster algorithm than the one in the preceding exercise?

Exercise R15.12. Develop a fast algorithm for removing duplicates from an array if the resulting array must have the same ordering as the original array.

Exercise R15.13. Consider the following sorting algorithm. To sort a, make a second array b of the same size. Then insert elements from a into b, keeping b in sorted order. For each element, call the binary search function of Exercise P15.7 to determine where it needs to be inserted. To insert an element into the middle of an array, you need to move all elements above the insert location up.

Is this an efficient algorithm? Estimate the number of array element visits in the sorting process. Assume that on average half of the elements of b need to be moved to insert a new element.

Exercise R15.14. Make a walkthrough of selection sort with the following data sets.

(a)   4   7   11   4   9   5   11   7   3   5
(b)   -7   6   8   7   5   9   0   11   10   5   8

Exercise R15.15. Make a walkthrough of merge sort with the following data sets.

(a) 5 11   7   3   5   4   7   11   4   9
(b) 9 0   11   10   5   8   -7   6   8   7   5

Exercise R15.16. Make a walkthrough of the following:

(a) Linear search for 7 in   -7   1   3   3   4   7   11   13
(b) Binary search for 8 in   -7   2   2   3   4   7   8   11   13
(c) Binary search for 8 in   -7   1   2   3   5   7   10   13

PROGRAMMING EXERCISES

Exercise P15.1. Modify the selection sort algorithm to sort a vector of integers in descending order.

Exercise P15.2. Modify the selection sort algorithm to sort a vector of employees by salary.

Exercise P15.3. Write a program that generates the table of sample runs of the selection sort times automatically. The program should ask for the smallest and largest value of n and the number of measurements and then make all sample runs.

Exercise P15.4. Modify the merge sort algorithm to sort a vector of employees by salary.

Exercise P15.5. Write a telephone lookup program. Read a data set of 1,000 names and telephone numbers from a file that contains the numbers in random order. Handle lookups by name and also reverse lookups by phone number. Use a binary search for both lookups.

Exercise P15.6. Modify the binary search algorithm so that you can search the records stored in a *database file* without actually reading them into a vector. Use the employee database of Section 12.5, sort it by product name, and make lookups for products.

Exercise P15.7. Consider the binary search function in Section 15.7. If no match is found, the function returns -1. Modify the function so that it returns a bool value indicating whether a match was found. Add a reference parameter m, which is set to the location of the match if the search was successful. If a was not found, set m to the index of the next larger value instead, or to a.size() if a is larger than all the elements of the vector.

Exercise P15.8. Use the modification of the binary search function of the preceding exercise to sort an array. Make a second array of the same size as the array to be sorted. For each element in the first array, call binary search on the second array to find out where the new element should be inserted. Then move all elements above the insertion point up by one slot and insert the new element. Thus, the second array is always kept sorted. Implement this algorithm and measure its performance.

Exercise P15.9. Implement the merge_sort procedure without recursion, where the size of the vector is a power of 2. First merge adjacent regions of size 1, then adjacent regions of size 2, then adjacent regions of size 4, and so on.

Exercise P15.10. Implement the merge_sort procedure without recursion, where the size of the vector is an arbitrary number. *Hint:* Keep merging adjacent areas whose size is a power of 2, and pay special attention to the last area in the array.

Exercise P15.11. Give a *graphical animation* of selection sort as follows: Fill an array with a set of random numbers between 1 and 100. Set the window coordinate system to a.size() by 100. Draw each array element as a stick, as in Figure 4. Whenever you change the array, clear the screen and redraw.

Exercise P15.12. Write a graphical animation of merge sort.

Exercise P15.13. Write a graphical animation of binary search. Highlight the currently inspected element.

Exercise P15.14. Write a program that keeps an appointment book. Make a class Appointment that stores a description of the appointment, the appointment day, the starting time, and the ending time. Your program should keep the appointments in a sorted vector. Users can add appointments and print out all appointments for a given day. When a new appointment is added, use binary search to find where it should be inserted in the vector. Do not add it if it conflicts with another appointment.

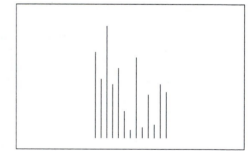

Figure 4

Graphical Animation

Chapter 16

An Introduction to Data Structures

- ▶ To be able to write programs with standard lists and iterators
- ▶ To understand the advantages and disadvantages of the list data structure
- ▶ To be able to implement linked lists
- ▶ To learn about stacks and queues
- ▶ To become familiar with common containers and algorithms from the Standard Template Library

U p to this point, we have used the vector construct as a one-size-fits-all mechanism for collecting values. However, computer scientists have developed many different data structures that have varying performance tradeoffs. In this chapter, you will learn about the linked list, a data structure that allows you to add and remove values efficiently, without moving any existing values. You will also learn about data structures and algorithms in the Standard Template Library (STL) that is an important part of the C++ standard.

16.1   Linked Lists

Imagine a program that maintains a vector of employee records, sorted by the last name of the employees. When a new employee is hired, a record needs to be inserted into the vector. Unless the name of the new employee begins with Z, it needs to be inserted into the middle of the vector; then many other employee records must be moved downwards (see Figure 6 in Chapter 9). Conversely, if an employee leaves the company, the hole in the sequence needs to be closed up by moving all employee records that came after it (see Figure 5 in Chapter 9).

In a realistic application, employee records contain the employee's name, salary, address, telephone extension, and other information. These can be fairly substantial data sets. When an employee record is moved, all those data need to be copied from the old location to the new location. Moving a large number of employee records can involve a substantial amount of computer time.

Vectors and arrays store a sequence of values in one long block of memory. Another container structure, a *linked list*, uses a different strategy. Each value is stored in its own memory block, together with the locations of the neighboring blocks in the sequence (see Figure 1). It is now an easy matter to add another value into the sequence, or to remove a value from the sequence, without moving the others (see Figures 2 and 3).

The standard C++ library has an implementation of the linked list container structure. In this section, you will learn how to use the standard linked list structure. Later you will look "under the hood" and find out how to implement linked lists. (The linked list of the standard C++ library has links going in both directions. Such a list is often called a *doubly-linked* list. A *singly-linked* list lacks the links to the predecessor elements.)

Building a list is very similar to building a vector. Just like vector, the standard list is a *template:* You can declare lists for different types. For example, to make a list of strings, define an object of type list<string>. Then you can use the push_back function

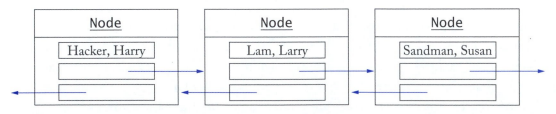

Figure 1

A Linked List

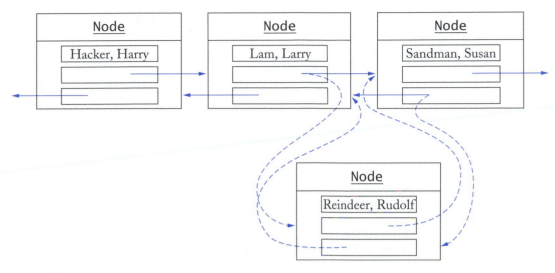

Figure 2

Adding a Node to a Linked List

to add strings to the list. The following code segment defines a list of strings, `staff`, and adds four strings to it:

```
list<string> staff;

staff.push_back("Cracker, Carl");
staff.push_back("Hacker, Harry");
staff.push_back("Lam, Larry");
staff.push_back("Sandman, Susan");
```

This code looks exactly like the code that you would use to build a vector of strings. There is, however, one major difference. Suppose you want to access the fourth element in the list. You cannot directly refer to `staff[3]`. Since the values are not stored in one contiguous block in memory, there is no fast way to access the fourth element. Instead,

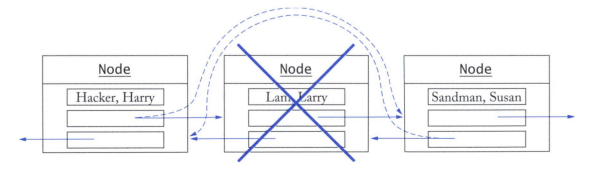

Figure 3

Removing a Node from a Linked List

you must visit each element in turn, starting at the beginning of the list and then proceeding to the next element.

To visit an element, you use a *list iterator*. An iterator marks a *position* in the list. To get an iterator that marks the beginning position in the list, you define an iterator variable, then call the `begin` function of the `list` class to get the beginning position:

```
list<string>::iterator pos;
pos = staff.begin();
```

To move the iterator to the next position, use the `++` operator:

```
pos++;
```

To move it to the fourth position, increment it two more times. You can also move the iterator backwards with the `--` operator:

```
pos--;
```

You can find the value that is stored in the position with the `*` operator:

```
string value = *pos;
```

You have to be careful to distinguish between the iterator `pos`, which represents a position in the list, and the value `*pos`, which represents the value that is stored in the list. For example, if you change `*pos`, then you update the contents in the list:

```
*pos = "Van Dyck, Vicki";
   /* the list value at the position is changed */
```

If you change `pos`, then you merely change the current position.

```
pos = staff.begin();
   /* the position is again at the beginning of the list */
```

To insert another string before the iterator position, use the `insert` function:

```
staff.insert(pos, "Reindeer, Rudolph");
```

The `insert` function inserts the new element *before* the iterator position, rather than after it. This convention makes it easy to insert a new element before the first value of the list:

```
pos = staff.begin();
staff.insert(pos, "Bourbon, Bruce");
```

That raises the question of how you insert a value after the end of the list. Each list has an *end position* that does not correspond to any value in the list but that points past the list's end. The `end` function returns that position:

```
pos = staff.end(); /* points past the end of the list */
staff.insert(pos, "Yaglov, Yvonne");
   /* insert past the end of the list */
```

It is an error to compute

```
string value = *staff.end(); /* ERROR */
```

The end position does not point to any value, so you cannot look up the value at that position. This error is equivalent to the error of accessing `s[10]` in a vector with 10 elements.

The end position has another useful purpose: it is the stopping point for traversing the list. The following code iterates over all elements of the list and prints them out:

```
pos = staff.begin();
while (pos != staff.end())
{
   cout << *pos << "\n";
   pos++;
}
```

The traversal can be described more concisely with a for loop:

```
for (pos = staff.begin(); pos != staff.end(); pos++)
   cout << *pos << "\n";
```

Of course, this looks very similar to the typical for loop for traversing a vector:

```
for (i = 0; i < s.size(); i++)
   cout << s[i] << "\n";
```

Finally, to remove an element from a list, you move an iterator to the position that you want to remove, then call the erase function. The following code erases the second element of the list:

```
pos = staff.begin();
pos++;
staff.erase(pos);
```

Here is a short example program that adds elements to a list, inserts and erases list elements, and finally traverses the resulting list.

File list1.cpp

```
1  #include <string>
2  #include <list>
3  #include <iostream>
4
5  using namespace std;
6
7  int main()
8  {
9     list<string> staff;
10
11    staff.push_back("Cracker, Carl");
12    staff.push_back("Hacker, Harry");
13    staff.push_back("Lam, Larry");
14    staff.push_back("Sandman, Susan");
15
16    /* add a value in fourth place */
17
18    list<string>::iterator pos;
19    pos = staff.begin();
20    pos++;
21    pos++;
22    pos++;
23
24    staff.insert(pos, "Reindeer, Rudolf");
```

```
25
26    /* remove the value in second place */
27
28    pos = staff.begin();
29    pos++;
30
31    staff.erase(pos);
32
33    /* print all values */
34
35    for (pos = staff.begin(); pos != staff.end(); pos++)
36       cout << *pos << "\n";
37
38    return 0;
39 }
```

You now know how to put linked lists to use. However, since the implementation of the list class template is hidden from you, you had to take it on faith that the list values are really stored in separate memory blocks, and that the insert and erase operations are faster than the equivalent vector operations. In the next section, you will learn how the list and iterator classes can be implemented, and you will understand how the list operations can update a list without moving the stored values around.

16.2   Implementing Linked Lists

Let us now turn to the implementation of a linked list. In this section, we will start with a linked list of strings. In Chapter 17, you will see how to use templates to implement linked lists that can hold values of arbitrary types, and how to use nested classes and overloaded operators to implement iterators that behave exactly like the ones in the standard C++ library.

16.2.1   The Classes for Lists, Nodes, and Iterators

The list class of the standard library defines many useful member functions. For simplicity, we will only study the implementation of the most useful ones: push_back, insert, erase, and the iterator operations. We call our class List, with an uppercase L, to differentiate it from the standard list class template.

A linked list stores each value in a separate object, called a *node*. A node object holds a value, together with pointers to the previous and next nodes:

```
class Node
{
public:
   Node(string s);
private:
   string data;
   Node* previous;
   Node* next;
friend class List;
friend class Iterator;
};
```

Note the `friend` declarations. They indicate that the `List` and `Iterator` member functions are allowed to inspect and modify the data members of the `Node` class, which we will write presently.

A class should not grant friendship to another class lightly, because it breaks the privacy protection. In this case, it makes sense, though, since the list and iterator functions do all the necessary work and the node class is just an artifact of the implementation that is invisible to the users of the list class. Note that no code other than the member functions of the list and iterator classes can access the node fields, so the data integrity is still guaranteed.

A list object holds the locations of the first and last nodes in the list:

```
class List
{
public:
   List();
   void push_back(string s);
   void insert(Iterator pos, string s);
   Iterator erase(Iterator pos);
   Iterator begin();
   Iterator end();
private:
   Node* first;
   Node* last;
};
```

If the list is empty, then the `first` and `last` pointers are `NULL`. Note that a list object stores no data; it just knows where to find the node objects that store the list contents.

Finally, an *iterator* denotes a position in the list. It holds a pointer to the list into which it points, and a pointer to the node that denotes its current position. For now, we use member functions get, next, and equals instead of operators `*`, `++`, and `==`. For example, we will call `pos.next()` instead of `pos++`. You will see in Chapter 17 how to enable the use of operators.

```
class Iterator
{
public:
   Iterator();
   string get() const;
   void next();
   void previous();
   bool equals(Iterator b) const;
private:
   Node* position;
   Node* last;
friend class List;
};
```

If the iterator points past the end of the list, then the `position` pointer is `NULL`. The iterator object also stores a pointer to the last element of the list, so that the `previous` method can move the iterator back from the past-the-end position to the last element of the list. (This is only one possible choice for implementing the past-the-end position. Another choice would be to store an actual dummy node at the end of the list. Some implementations of the standard `list` class do just that.)

16.2.2 Implementing Iterators

Iterators are created by the begin and end member functions of the List class. The begin function creates an iterator whose position pointer points to the first node in the list. The end function creates an iterator whose position pointer is NULL.

```
Iterator List::begin()
{
   Iterator iter;
   iter.position = first;
   iter.last = last;
   return iter;
}

Iterator List::end()
{
   Iterator iter;
   iter.position = NULL;
   iter.last = last;
   return iter;
}
```

The next function (which is the equivalent of the ++ operator) advances the iterator to the next position. This is a very typical operation in a linked list; let us study it in detail.

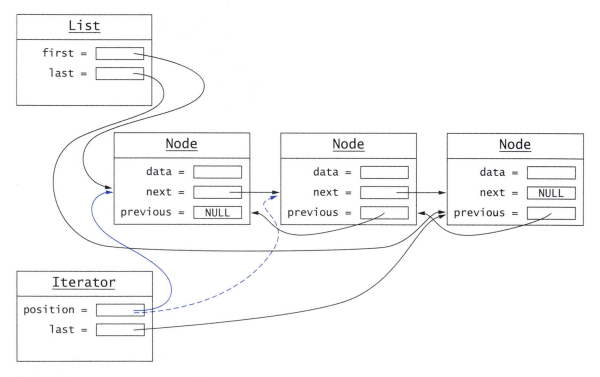

Figure 4

Advancing an Iterator

The `position` pointer points to the current node in the list. That node has a field `next`. Because `position` is a node pointer, the `next` field in the node to which `position` points is referred to as

```
position->next
```

That `next` field is itself a pointer, pointing to the next node in the linked list (see Figure 4). To make `position` point to that next node, write

```
position = position->next;
```

However, you can evaluate `position->next` only if `position` is not `NULL`, because it is an error to dereference a `NULL` pointer. That is, it is illegal to advance the iterator once it is in the past-the-end position.

Here is the complete code for the `next` function:

```
void Iterator::next()
{
    assert(position != NULL);
    position = position->next;
}
```

The `previous` function (which is the equivalent of the `--` operator) is a bit more complex. In the ordinary case, you move the position backwards with the instruction

```
position = position->previous;
```

However, if the iterator is currently past the end, then you must make it point to the last element in the list. Also, when the iterator points to the first element in the list, it is illegal to move it further backward. The first element in the list can be recognized by the fact that its `previous` pointer is `NULL`:

```
void Iterator::previous()
{
  if (position == NULL)
      position = last;
    else
      position = position->previous;
    assert(position != NULL);
}
```

The `get` function (which is the equivalent of the `*` operator) simply returns the `data` value of the node to which `position` points—that is, `position->data`. It is illegal to call `get` if the iterator points past the end of the list:

```
string Iterator::get() const
{
    assert(position != NULL);
    return position->data;
}
```

Finally, the `equals` function (which is the equivalent of the `==` operator) compares two `position` pointers:

```
bool Iterator::equals(Iterator b) const
{
  return position == b.position;
}
```

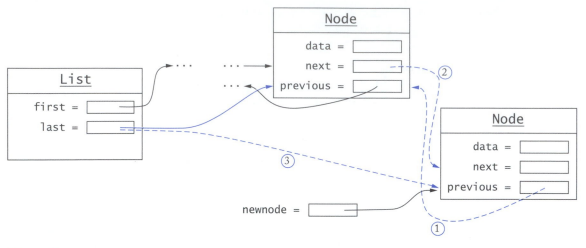

Figure 5

Appending a Node to the End of a Linked List

16.2.3 — Implementing Insertion and Removal

In the last section you saw how to implement the iterators that traverse an existing list. Now you will see how to build up lists by adding and removing elements, one step at a time.

First, study the push_back function. It appends an element to the end of the list (see Figure 5). Make a new node:

```
Node* newnode = new Node(s);
```

This new node must be integrated into the list after the node to which the last pointer points. That is, the next field of the last node (which is currently NULL) must be updated to newnode. Also, the previous field of the new node must point to what used to be the last node:

```
newnode->previous = last; ①
last->next = newnode; ②
```

Finally, you must update the last pointer to reflect that the new node is now the last node in the list:

```
last = newnode; ③
```

However, there is a special case when last is NULL, which can happen only when the list is empty. After the call to push_back, the list has a single node—namely, newnode. In that case, both first and last must be set to newnode:

```
void List::push_back(string s)
{
    Node* newnode = new Node(s);
    if (last == NULL) /* list is empty */
    {
        first = newnode;
        last = newnode;
```

```
        }
        else
        {
            newnode->previous = last;
            last->next = newnode;
            last = newnode;
        }
    }
```

Inserting an element in the middle of a linked list is a little more difficult, because the node pointers in the *two* nodes surrounding the new node need to be updated. The function declaration is

```
    void List::insert(Iterator iter, string s)
```

That is, a new node containing s is inserted before iter.position (see Figure 6).

Give names to the surrounding nodes. Let before be the node before the insertion location, and let after be the node after that. That is,

```
    Node* after = iter.position;
    Node* before = after->previous;
```

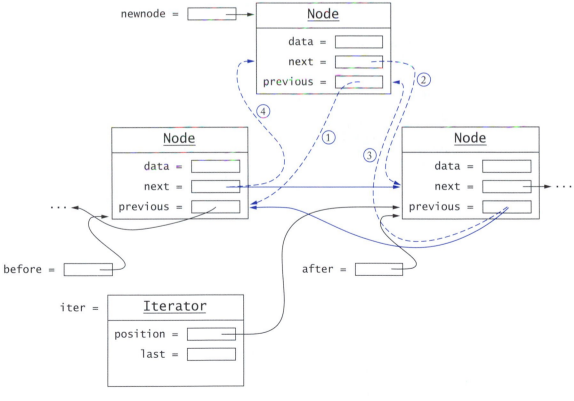

Figure 6

Inserting a Node into a Linked List

What happens if after is NULL? After all, it is illegal to apply -> to a NULL pointer. In this situation, you are inserting past the end of the list. Simply call push_back to handle that case separately. Otherwise, you need to insert newnode between before and after:

```
newnode->previous = before; ①
newnode->next = after; ②
```

You must also update the nodes from before and after to point to the new node:

```
after->previous = newnode; ③
before->next = newnode; /* if before != NULL */ ④
```

However, you must be careful. You know that after is not NULL, but it is possible that before is NULL. In that case, you are inserting at the beginning of the list and need to adjust first:

```
if (before = NULL) /* insert at beginning */
   first = newnode;
else
   before->next = newnode;
```

Here is the complete code for the insert function:

```
void List::insert(Iterator iter, string s)
{
   if (iter.position == NULL)
   {
      push_back(s);
      return;
   }

   Node* after = iter.position;
   Node* before = after->previous;
   Node* newnode = new Node(s);
   newnode->previous = before;
   newnode->next = after;
   after->previous = newnode;
   if (before == NULL) /* insert at beginning */
      first = newnode;
   else
      before->next = newnode;
}
```

Finally, look at the implementation of the erase function:

```
Iterator List::erase(Iterator iter)
```

You want to remove the node to which iter.position points. It is illegal to erase the past-the-end position, so assert that iter.position points to an actual list element:

```
assert(iter.position != NULL);
```

As before, give names to the node to be removed, the node before it, and the node after it:

```
Node* remove = iter.position;
Node* before = remove->previous;
Node* after = remove->next;
```

You need to update the next and previous pointers of the before and after nodes to bypass the node that is to be removed (see Figure 7).

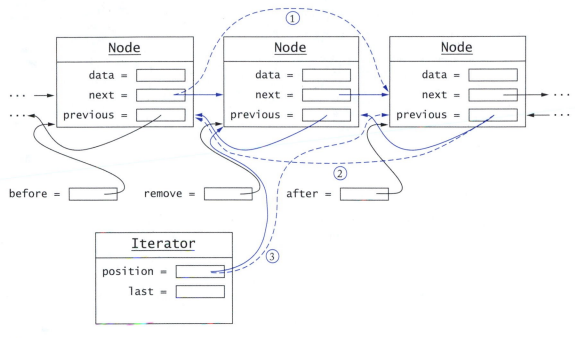

Figure 7

Removing a Node from a Linked List

```
before->next = after; /* if before != NULL */ ①
after->previous = before; /* if after != NULL */ ②
```

However, as before, you need to cope with the possibility that before, after, or both are NULL. If before is NULL, you are erasing the first element in the list. It has no predecessor to update, but you must change the first pointer of the list. Conversely, if after is NULL, you are erasing the last element of the list and must update the last pointer of the list:

```
if (remove == first)
   first = after;
else
   before->next = after;
if (remove == last)
   last = before;
else
   after->previous = before;
```

You must adjust the iterator position so that it no longer points to the removed element.

```
iter.position = after; ③
```

Finally, you must remember to recycle the removed node:

```
delete remove;
```

Here is the complete `erase` function.

```
Iterator List::erase(Iterator i)
{
   Iterator iter = i;
   assert(iter.position != NULL);
   Node* remove = iter.position;
   Node* before = remove->previous;
   Node* after = remove->next;
   if (remove == first)
      first = after;
   else
      before->next = after;
   if (remove == last)
      last = before;
   else
      after->previous = before;
   iter.position = after;
   delete remove;
   return iter;
}
```

Implementing these linked list operations is somewhat complex. It is also error-prone. If you make a mistake and misroute some of the pointers, you can get subtle errors. For example, if you make a mistake with a `previous` pointer, you may never notice it until you traverse the list backwards. If a node has been deleted, then that same storage area may later be reallocated for a different purpose, and if you have kept a pointer to it, following that invalid node pointer will lead to disaster. You must exercise special care when implementing any operations that manipulate the node pointers directly.

Here is a program that puts our linked list to use and demonstrates the `insert` and `erase` operations.

File list2.cpp

```
 1  #include <string>
 2  #include <iostream>
 3  #include <cassert>
 4
 5  using namespace std;
 6
 7  class List;
 8  class Iterator;
 9
10  class Node
11  {
12  public:
13     /*
14         Constructs a node with a given data value.
15         @param s the data to store in this node
16     */
17     Node(string s);
18  private:
19     string data;
20     Node* previous;
21     Node* next;
```

```
22  friend class List;
23  friend class Iterator;
24  };
25
26  class List
27  {
28  public:
29      /**
30          Constructs an empty list.
31      */
32      List();
33      /**
34          Appends an element to the list.
35          @param s  the value to append
36      */
37      void push_back(string s);
38      /**
39          Inserts an element into the list.
40          @param iter  the position before which to insert
41          @param s  the value to append
42      */
43      void insert(Iterator iter, string s);
44      /**
45          Removes an element from the list.
46          @param i  the position to remove
47          @return  an iterator pointing to the element after the
48          erased element
49      */
50      Iterator erase(Iterator i);
51      /**
52          Gets the beginning position of the list.
53          @return  an iterator pointing to the beginning of the list
54      */
55      Iterator begin();
56      /**
57          Gets the past-the-end position of the list.
58          @return  an iterator pointing past the end of the list
59      */
60      Iterator end();
61  private:
62      Node* first;
63      Node* last;
64  };
65
66  class Iterator
67  {
68  public:
69      /**
70          Constructs an iterator that does not point into any list.
71      */
72      Iterator();
73      /**
74          Looks up the value at a position.
75          @return  the value of the node to which the iterator points
76      */
77      string get() const;
```

```
78     /**
79         Advances the iterator to the next node.
80     */
81     void next();
82     /**
83         Moves the iterator to the previous node.
84     */
85     void previous();
86     /**
87         Compares two iterators.
88         @param b the iterator to compare with this iterator
89         @return true if this iterator and b are equal
90     */
91     bool equals(Iterator b) const;
92  private:
93     Node* position;
94     Node* last;
95  friend class List;
96  };
97
98  Node::Node(string s)
99  {
100    data = s;
101    previous = NULL;
102    next = NULL;
103 }
104
105 List::List()
106 {
107    first = NULL;
108    last = NULL;
109 }
110
111 void List::push_back(string s)
112 {
113    Node* newnode = new Node(s);
114    if (last == NULL) /* list is empty */
115    {
116       first = newnode;
117       last = newnode;
118    }
119    else
120    {
121       newnode->previous = last;
122       last->next = newnode;
123       last = newnode;
124    }
125 }
126
127 void List::insert(Iterator iter, string s)
128 {
129    if (iter.position == NULL)
130    {
131       push_back(s);
132       return;
133    }
```

```
134
135     Node* after = iter.position;
136     Node* before = after->previous;
137     Node* newnode = new Node(s);
138     newnode->previous = before;
139     newnode->next = after;
140     after->previous = newnode;
141     if (before == NULL) /* insert at beginning */
142        first = newnode;
143     else
144        before->next = newnode;
145  }
146
147  Iterator List::erase(Iterator i)
148  {
149     Iterator iter = i;
150     assert(iter.position != NULL);
151     Node* remove = iter.position;
152     Node* before = remove->previous;
153     Node* after = remove->next;
154     if (remove == first)
155        first = after;
156     else
157        before->next = after;
158     if (remove == last)
159        last = before;
160     else
161        after->previous = before;
162     iter.position = after;
163     delete remove;
164     return iter;
165  }
166
167  Iterator List::begin()
168  {
169     Iterator iter;
170     iter.position = first;
171     iter.last = last;
172     return iter;
173  }
174
175  Iterator List::end()
176  {
177     Iterator iter;
178     iter.position = NULL;
179     iter.last = last;
180     return iter;
181  }
182
183  Iterator::Iterator()
184  {
185     position = NULL;
186     last = NULL;
187  }
188
189  string Iterator::get() const
```

```
190  {
191      assert(position != NULL);
192      return position->data;
193  }
194
195  void Iterator::next()
196  {
197      assert(position != NULL);
198      position = position->next;
199  }
200
201  void Iterator::previous()
202  {
203      if (position == NULL)
204          position = last;
205      else
206          position = position->previous;
207      assert(position != NULL);
208  }
209
210  bool Iterator::equals(Iterator b) const
211  {
212      return position == b.position;
213  }
214
215  int main()
216  {
217      List staff;
218
219      staff.push_back("Cracker, Carl");
220      staff.push_back("Hacker, Harry");
221      staff.push_back("Lam, Larry");
222      staff.push_back("Sandman, Susan");
223
224      /* add a value in fourth place */
225
226      Iterator pos;
227      pos = staff.begin();
228      pos.next();
229      pos.next();
230      pos.next();
231
232      staff.insert(pos, "Reindeer, Rudolf");
233
234      /* remove the value in second place */
235
236      pos = staff.begin();
237      pos.next();
238
239      staff.erase(pos);
240
241      /* print all values */
242
243      for (pos = staff.begin(); !pos.equals(staff.end()); pos.next())
244          cout << pos.get() << "\n";
245
```

```
246    return 0;
247 }
```

▼ **Random Fact** 16.1 ▶

Garbage Collection

▼

Managing heap memory is a tedious and error-prone activity. You have to allocate memory (for example for the nodes of a list) when you need it. This is usually not a problem. The problem is that you must remember to get rid of it again when you don't need it any more. If you don't ever delete heap memory and your program runs for a long time, it will exhaust all available memory. If you delete it too early and continue using it, your program will crash or act flaky.

▼

Heap allocation bugs are among the most insidious bugs in C++ programs. They are quite common but extremely difficult and time-consuming to track down. Many modern languages, but unfortunately not C++, offer a better way: *garbage collection*. A garbage collector periodically identifies which heap objects are still pointed at by some pointer, and reclaims those that are no longer in use. There is a problem with garbage collection: It is slow. It takes time to track all pointers and the locations to which they point. However, garbage collection algorithms have improved in recent years, and the cost is now tolerable for many applications.

▼

16.3 Stacks and Queues

In this section, you will consider two common data types that allow insertion and removal of items at the ends only, not in the middle. A *stack* lets you insert and remove elements at one end only, traditionally called the *top* of the stack. To visualize a stack, think of a stack of books (see Figure 8).

New items can be added to the top of the stack. Items are removed from the top of the stack as well. Therefore, they are removed in the order that is opposite from the order in which they have been added, also called *last in, first out* or *LIFO* order. For example, if you insert strings "Tom", "Dick", and "Harry" into a stack, and then remove them, then you will first see "Harry", then "Dick", and finally "Tom".

Figure 8

A Stack of Books

Traditionally, the addition and removal operations are called push and pop. To obtain a stack in the standard C++ library, you use the stack template:

```
stack<string> s;
s.push("Tom");
s.push("Dick");
s.push("Harry");
while (s.size() > 0)
{
   cout << s.top() << "\n";
   s.pop();
}
```

A *queue* is similar to a stack, except that you add items to one end of the queue (the *back*) and remove them from the other end of the queue (the *front*). To visualize a queue, simply think of people lining up (see Figure 9). People join the back of the queue and wait until they have reached the front of the queue. Queues store items in a *first in, first out* or *FIFO* fashion. Items are removed in the same order in which they have been added.

There are many uses of queues in computer science. For example, consider a printer that receives requests to print documents from multiple sources, either several computers or just several applications that print at the same time on one computer. If each of the applications sends printing data to the printer at the same time, then the printouts will be garbled. Instead, each application places all data that need to be sent to the printer into a file and inserts that file into the *print queue*. When the printer is done printing one

Figure 9

A Queue

file, it retrieves the next one from the queue. Therefore, print jobs are printed using the first in, first out rule, which is a fair arrangement for users of the shared printer.

The standard queue template implements a queue in C++. For example,

```
queue<string> q;
q.push("Tom");
q.push("Dick");
q.push("Harry");
while (q.size() > 0)
{
    cout << q.front() << "\n";
    q.pop();
}
```

The following program demonstrates the FIFO and LIFO behaviors of queues and stacks.

File fifolifo.cpp

```
 1 #include <iostream>
 2 #include <string>
 3 #include <queue>
 4 #include <stack>
 5
 6 using namespace std;
 7
 8 int main()
 9 {
10     cout << "FIFO order:\n";
11
12     queue<string> q;
13     q.push("Tom");
14     q.push("Dick");
15     q.push("Harry");
16
17     stack<string> s;
18     while (q.size() > 0)
19     {
20         string name = q.front();
21         q.pop();
22         cout << name << "\n";
23         s.push(name);
24     }
25
26     cout << "LIFO order:\n";
27
28     while (s.size() > 0)
29     {
30         cout << s.top() << "\n";
31         s.pop();
32     }
33
34     return 0;
35 }
```

16.4 Other Standard Containers

You have now seen the standard `vector`, `list`, `stack`, and `queue` classes. The standard library contains several other useful containers. The C++ `set` always keeps its elements in sorted order, no matter in which order you insert them.

For example, consider the following code, which inserts strings in random order. When traversing the set, the elements are automatically sorted!

```
set<string> s;

s.insert("Tom");
s.insert("Dick");
s.insert("Harry");

set<string>::iterator p;
for (p = s.begin(); p != s.end(); p++)
   cout << *p << "\n";
```

This code displays the strings in sorted order: Dick, Harry, and Tom.

The `set` data structure achieves this effect by keeping the values in a special tree-shaped data structure. Each time an element is inserted, the tree is reorganized. This turns out to be much faster than keeping the values in a vector or a linked list. You will learn more about these very useful data structures in a more advanced course on data structures.

Like a mathematical set, the C++ `set` ignores duplicates. If you insert an element into the set that is already present, then the second insertion has no effect. If you want to be able to keep track of multiple occurrences of identical values, use a `multiset` instead. The `count` function returns the number of times that an element is contained in a set or multiset. For example,

```
set<string> s;

s.insert("Tom");
s.insert("Tom");
cout << s.count() << "\n"; /* displays 1 */

multiset<string> m;

m.insert("Tom");
m.insert("Tom");
cout << m.count() << "\n"; /* displays 2 */
```

Another useful data structure is the *map* (sometimes called an associative array). A map is similar to a vector, but you can use another data type for the indexes! Here is an example:

```
map<string, double> scores;

scores["Tom"] = 90;
scores["Dick"] = 86;
scores["Harry"] = 100;
```

Advanced Topic 16.1

Defining an Ordering for Set Elements

When you use a set, the elements that you put into the set must be capable of being *ordered*. Suppose that you want to build a set<Employee>. The compiler will complain that it does not know how to compare two employees.

To solve this problem you can overload the < operator for Employee objects:

```
bool operator<(Employee a, Employee b)
{
    return a.get_name() < b.get_name();
}
```

This < operator compares employees by name. You will learn more about overloading operators in Chapter 17.

16.5   Standard Algorithms

You have seen how to iterate through a linked list by using an iterator. You can use the same technique to traverse a vector:

```
vector<double> data;
. . .
double sum = 0;
vector<double>::iterator p;
for (p = data.begin(); p != data.end(); p++)
    sum = sum + *p;
```

This does not sound too exciting by itself, since it offers no advantage over using an index variable:

```
for (i = 0; i < data.size(); i++)
    sum = sum + data[i];
```

However, having the same programming style for different kinds of containers has one significant advantage; it is possible to supply *generic functions* that can carry out a task with the elements in *any* container that uses iterators. For example, the standard C++ library has a function accumulate that can compute the sum of a vector or a list.

```
vector<double> data;
double vsum = 0;
accumulate(data.begin(), data.end(), vsum);
/* now vsum contains the sum of the elements in the vector */
list<double> salaries;
double lsum = 0;
accumulate(data.begin(), data.end(), lsum);
/* now lsum contains the sum of the elements in the list */
```

Here is another example. Suppose you want to find a particular name in a linked list. Of course, you can code the search by hand:

```
list<string>::iterator it = staff.begin();
while (it != staff.end() && *it != name)
    it++;
```

But the standard library gives you an easier way, using the `find` algorithm:

```
list<string>::iterator it =
    find(staff.begin(), staff.end(), name);
```

The `find` algorithm returns the second iterator (that is, past the end of the search interval), if the search failed.

There are dozens of other functions in the standard library that work in a similar way. Here is a list of the most useful ones. All but the last three work with all data structures; the last three require a `vector`.

- `for_each` applies a function to each element
- `find` locates the first element matching a given object, `find_if` locates the first element fulfilling a condition
- `count` counts the elements matching a given object, `count_if` counts the number of elements fulfilling a condition
- `equal` tests if containers have the same elements in the same order
- `copy` copies elements from one container to another (possibly of a different type)
- `replace`/`replace_if` replace all matching elements with a new one
- `fill` overwrites a range with a new value
- `remove`/`remove_if` removes all matching values
- `unique` removes adjacent identical values
- `min_element`, `max_element` find the smallest and largest element
- `next_permutation` rearranges the elements; calling it $n!$ times iterates through all permutations
- `sort` sorts the elements; `stable_sort` performs better if the container is already almost sorted.
- `random_shuffle` randomly rearranges the elements
- `nth_element` finds the nth element, on average in linear time, without sorting the container. This is most useful to get the median or the second smallest/largest element.

As you can see, the standard library offers a wealth of ready-to-use and fully debugged data structures and algorithms. Before writing a lot of code from scratch, it is a good idea to check whether the standard library already has what you need. See [1, part III], for a comprehensive description of the standard library.

CHAPTER SUMMARY

1. Linked lists permit faster insertion and removal in the middle of a data set than vectors do.

2. You can inspect and edit a linked list with an iterator. An iterator points to a node in a linked list.

3. The nodes of a linked list are obtained from the heap. They are allocated with the `new` operator and recycled with the `delete` operator.

4. The nodes of a linked list are connected by pointers. Each node contains a pointer that either is `NULL` or specifies the location of the successor node.

5. A stack is a container with "last in, first out" retrieval.

6. A queue is a container of items with "first in, first out" retrieval.

7. The standard C++ `set` template stores values in sorted order.

8. The standard C++ `map` template is similar to a vector. It stores values for given index values. However, the index values are not restricted to integers.

9. The standard library contains a wealth of algorithms that can perform both simple and complex operations on multiple data structures.

FURTHER READING

[1] Bjarne Stroustrup, *The C++ Programming Language, 3rd ed.*, Addison-Wesley, 1997.

REVIEW EXERCISES

Exercise R16.1. If a list has *n* elements, how many legal positions are there for inserting a new element? For erasing an element?

Exercise R16.2. What happens if you keep advancing an iterator past the end of the list? Before the beginning of the list? What happens if you look up the value at an iterator that is past the end? Erase the past-the-end position? All these are illegal operations, of course. What does the list implementation of your compiler do in these cases?

Exercise R16.3. Write a function that prints all values in a linked list, starting from the end of the list.

Exercise R16.4. The following code edits a linked list consisting of three nodes.

Draw a diagram showing how they are linked together after the following code is executed.

```
Node* p1 = first->next;
Node* p2 = first;
while (p2->next != NULL) p2 = p2->next;
first->next = p2;
p2->next = p1;
p1->next = NULL;
p2->previous = first;
p1->previous = p2;
last = p1;
```

Exercise R16.5. Explain what the following code prints.

```
list<string> staff;
list<string>::iterator p = staff.begin();
staff.insert(p, "Hacker, Harry");
p = staff.begin();
staff.insert(p, "Lam, Larry");
p++;
staff.insert(p, "Cracker, Carl");
for (p = staff.begin(); p != staff.end(); p++)
    cout << *p << "\n";
```

Exercise R16.6. The insert procedure of Section 16.2 inserts a new element before the iterator position. To understand the updating of the nodes, draw before/after node diagrams for the following four scenarios.

(a) The list is completely empty.

(b) The list is not empty, and the iterator is at the beginning of the list.

(c) The list is not empty, and the iterator is at the end of the list.

(d) The list is not empty, and the iterator is in the middle of the list.

Exercise R16.7. What advantages do lists have over vectors? What disadvantages do they have?

Exercise R16.8. Suppose you needed to organize a collection of telephone numbers for a company division. There are currently about 6,000 employees, and you know that the phone switch can handle at most 10,000 phone numbers. You expect several hundred lookups against the collection every day. Would you use a vector or a linked list to store the information?

Exercise R16.9. Suppose you needed to keep a collection of appointments. Would you use a linked list or a vector of Appointment objects?

Exercise R16.10. Suppose you write a program that models a card deck. Cards are taken from the top of the deck and given out to players. As cards are returned to the deck, they are placed on the bottom of the deck. Would you store the cards in a stack or a queue?

Exercise R16.11. Suppose the strings "A" through "Z" are pushed onto a stack. Then they are popped off the stack and pushed onto a second stack. Finally, they are popped off the second stack and printed. In which order are the strings printed?

PROGRAMMING EXERCISES

Exercise P16.1. Write a linked list of integers by modifying the `Node`, `List`, and `Iterator` classes of Section 16.2 to hold integers instead of strings.

Exercise P16.2. Write a member function `List::reverse()` that reverses the nodes in a list.

Exercise P16.3. Write a function

```
void downsize(list<string>& staff)
```

that removes every second value from a linked list.

Exercise P16.4. Write a function `maximum` that computes the largest element in a list.

Exercise P16.5. Repeat the preceding exercise by using an algorithm from the C++ standard library.

Exercise P16.6. Write a function `print` to display a linked list on the graphics screen. Draw each element of the list as a box, and indicate the links with arrows.

Exercise P16.7. Write a member function `List::push_front()` that adds a value to the beginning of a list.

Exercise P16.8. Write a member function `List::get_size()` that computes the number of elements in the list, by counting the elements until the end of the list is reached.

Exercise P16.9. Add a `size` field to the `List` class. Modify the `insert` and `erase` functions to update the `size` field so that it always contains the correct size. Change the `get_size()` function of the preceding exercise to take advantage of this data field.

Exercise P16.10. Write a function `sort` that sorts the elements of a linked list (without copying them into a vector).

Exercise P16.11. Write a class `Polynomial` that stores a polynomial such as

$$p(x) = 5x^{10} + 9x^7 - x - 10$$

Store it as a linked list of terms. A term contains the coefficient and the power of x. For example, you would store $p(x)$ as

$$(5,10),(9,7),(-1,1),(-10,0)$$

Supply member functions to add, multiply, and print polynomials. Supply a constructor that makes a polynomial from a single term. For example, the polynomial p can be constructed as

```
Polynomial p(Term(-10, 0));
p.add(Polynomial(Term(-1, 1)));
p.add(Polynomial(Term(9, 7)));
p.add(Polynomial(Term(5, 10)));
```

Then compute $p(x) \times p(x)$.

```
Polynomial q = p.multiply(p);
q.print();
```

Exercise P16.12. Reimplement the `Polynomial` class of the preceding exercise by using a `map<int, double>` to store the coefficients.

Exercise P16.13. Design a structure `Set` that can hold a set of integers. Hide the private implementation: a linked list of integers. Provide the following member functions:

A constructor making an empty set

`is_element(int x)` returns `true` if x is present

`insert(int x)` to insert x if it is not present

`erase(int x)` to erase x if it is present

Iterators to traverse the set

Exercise P16.14. Enhance the `Set` class from the previous example. Write functions

```
Set set_union(Set a, Set b)
Set intersection(Set a, Set b)
```

that compute the set union and intersection of the sets a and b. (Don't name the first function `union`—that is a reserved word in C++.) Of course, you should use only the public interface of the `Set` class.

Exercise P16.15. Implement the *sieve of Eratosthenes:* a method for computing prime numbers, known to the ancient Greeks. Choose an integer n. This method will compute all prime numbers up to n. First insert all numbers from 1 to n into a set. Then erase all multiples of 2 (except 2): that is, 4, 6, 8, 10, 12, ... Erase all multiples of 3, that is, 6, 9, 12, 15, ... Go up to $\sqrt{n}$. The remaining numbers are all primes. Use the `Set` class of Exercise P16.13. Of course, you should use only the public interface of the class.

Exercise P16.16. Reimplement the preceding exercise by using `set<int>` from the standard C++ library.

Exercise P16.17. Implement a `Stack` class, using a linked list of strings. Supply operations `push`, `pop`, and `top`, just like in the standard `stack` template.

Exercise P16.18. Demonstrate the `next_permutation` algorithm from the standard library. Fill a vector v with the numbers 1, 2, 3, and 4, call

```
next_permutation(v.begin(), v.end())
```

and print the contents of the vector. Repeat until all permutations have been displayed.

Exercise P16.19. Demonstrate the `random_shuffle` algorithm from the standard library. Fill a vector v with the numbers 1, 2, 3, and 4, call

```
random_shuffle(v.begin(), v.end())
```

and print the contents of the vector. Repeat 10 times.

Advanced C++ Topics

CHAPTER GOALS

▶ To learn about operator overloading

▶ To learn how to automatically manage dynamic memory

▶ To understand nested classes

▶ To define and use name spaces

▶ To be able to implement templates

▶ To become familiar with exception handling

T his chapter introduces several advanced C++ topics that are particularly useful for programmers who provide libraries that are used by other programmers. You will learn how to define the meaning of operators (such as ++ or <) when they are applied to objects and how to build class templates that can be instantiated with type parameters. More technical topics include the automatic management of memory and exception handling. Finally, you will see how to avoid naming conflicts by the use of nested classes and name spaces.

Using these techniques, you will understand how standard C++ templates such as vector<T> actually work, and you will be able to turn the List class of the preceding chapter into a template that is very similar to the standard list<T> template.

CHAPTER CONTENTS

17.1   Operator Overloading

The iterators of the standard `list` class use operators ++, *, and ==. In Chapter 16, you did not yet know how to define the meaning of operators that are applied to objects, so you implemented them as member functions `next`, `get`, and `equals`. Giving a new meaning to an operator is called *operator overloading*. For example, the ++ operator is always defined for numbers, but not for objects. To define it for objects of the `Iterator` class, you need to overload it.

17.1.1   Operator Functions

In C++, you overload an operator by defining a function whose name is `operator` followed by the operator symbol, as shown in Syntax 17.1. For example, suppose you want

---

Syntax 17.1 : Overloaded Operator Definition

return_type operator*operator_symbol*(*parameters*)
{
    statements
}

Example: `int operator-(Time a, Time b)`
               `{`
                   `return a.seconds_from(b);`
               `}`

Purpose: Supply the implementation of an overloaded operator.

to define the *difference* between two Time objects as the number of seconds between them. The following operator- function lets you do that:

```
int operator-(Time a, Time b)
{
    return a.seconds_from(b);
}
```

Then you can simply use the - operator instead of calling seconds_from:

```
Time now;
Time morning(9, 0, 0);
int seconds_elapsed = now - morning;
```

Note that the operator- function is not a member function. It is a nonmember function with two parameters. Alternatively, you can implement the operator function as a member function with one explicit parameter; see Section 17.1.5.

Can you use the + operator to *add* two times? Of course you can, simply by defining an operator+(Time a, Time b). But that doesn't mean you should. A Time object represents a *point in time*, not a duration. For example, 3 P.M. means "a particular time in the afternoon", which is quite different from "3 hours" or "15 hours". It does not make any sense to add two points in time. (For example, what should 3 P.M. + 1 P.M. be? 4 P.M.? How about 3 P.M. + 1 A.M.?)

However, it does make sense to add a number of seconds to a Time object, resulting in a new Time object. Here is an overloaded + operator for that task.

```
Time operator+(Time a, int sec)
{
    Time r = a;
    r.add_seconds(sec);
    return r;
}
```

For example:

```
Time now;
Time later = now + 60; /* 60 seconds later */
```

17.1.2 — Overloading Comparison Operators

A commonly overloaded operator is the == operator, to compare two values. Two Time values are equal if the number of seconds between them is zero. Therefore, you can define

```
bool operator==(Time a, Time b)
{
    return a.seconds_from(b) == 0;
}
```

For completeness, it is a good idea to also define a != operator:

```
bool operator!=(Time a, Time b)
{
    return a.seconds_from(b) != 0;
}
```

If you want to insert `Time` objects into a standard C++ `set` or `map` container, you need to define the `<` operator:

```
bool operator<(Time a, Time b)
{
    return a.seconds_from(b) < 0;
}
```

17.1.3 — Input and Output

You may want to print a `Time` object with the familiar `<<` notation. That operator takes a parameter of type `ostream&` (because printing modifies the stream) and, of course, the time to be printed.

```
ostream& operator<<(ostream& out, Time a)
{
    out << a.get_hours() << ":"
        << setw(2) << setfill('0')
        << a.get_minutes() << ":"
        << setw(2) << a.get_seconds() << setfill(' ');
    return out;
}
```

The `<<` operator returns the `out` stream. This is what enables *chaining* of the `<<` operator. For example,

```
cout << now << "\n";
```

really means

```
(cout << now) << "\n";
```

that is

```
operator<<(cout, now) << "\n"
```

The call to `operator<<(cout, now)` prints the time `now` and then returns `cout`. Then `cout << "\n"` prints a newline.

You can also define an `operator>>` to read a `Time` object from an input stream. For simplicity, assume that the `Time` value is entered as three separate integers, such as

```
9 15 00
```

Here is the definition of the `>>` operator:

```
istream& operator>>(istream& in, Time& a)
{
    int hours;
    int minutes;
    int seconds;
    in >> hours >> minutes >> seconds;
    a = Time(hours, minutes, seconds);
    return in;
}
```

You can use the technique described in Section 12.2 to read in other input formats.

Note that the `>>` operator returns the input stream, just like the `<<` operator. However, unlike the `<<` operator, the `>>` operator must have a parameter of type `Time&`. The parameter is modified when it is filled with the input.

Basic operator overloading is relatively easy and many people find it fun. However, do not go overboard. Using inappropriate operators can make programs more difficult to read. Here is a sample program that defines several overloaded operators for the `Time` class.

File overload.cpp

```cpp
1  #include <iostream>
2  #include <iomanip>
3
4  using namespace std;
5
6  #include "ccc_time.h"
7
8  /**
9      Computes the number of seconds between two points in time.
10     @param a a point in time
11     @param b another point in time
12     @return the number of seconds that a is away from b
13  */
14  int operator-(Time a, Time b)
15  {
16     return a.seconds_from(b);
17  }
18
19  /**
20     Computes a point in time that is some number of seconds away.
21     @param a a point in time
22     @param sec the seconds to add
23     @return a point in time that is sec seconds away from a
24  */
25  Time operator+(Time a, int sec)
26  {
27     Time r = a;
28     r.add_seconds(sec);
29     return r;
30  }
31
32  /**
33     Compares two points in time.
34     @param a a point in time
35     @param b another point in time
36     @return true if they are the same
37  */
38  bool operator==(Time a, Time b)
39  {
40     return a.seconds_from(b) == 0;
41  }
42
43  /**
44     Compares two points in time.
45     @param a a point in time
46     @param b another point in time
47     @return true if they are different
48  */
49  bool operator!=(Time a, Time b)
```

```
50 {
51    return a.seconds_from(b) != 0;
52 }
53
54 /**
55    Prints a Time object.
56    @param out an output stream
57    @param a a point in time
58    @return out
59 */
60 ostream& operator<<(ostream& out, Time a)
61 {
62    out << a.get_hours() << ":"
63       << setw(2) << setfill('0')
64       << a.get_minutes() << ":"
65       << setw(2) << a.get_seconds() << setfill(' ');
66    return out;
67 }
68
69 int main()
70 {
71    Time now;
72    cout << "Now it is " << now << "\n";
73    Time later = now + 1000;
74    cout << "A thousand seconds later it is " << later << "\n";
75    Time now2;
76    if (now == now2)
77       cout << "It still is " << now2 << "\n";
78    if (now != now2)
79       cout << "It is already " << now2 << "\n";
80    cout << "Another " << later - now2
81       << " seconds until " << later << "\n";
82    return 0;
83 }
```

17.1.4 — Overloading Increment and Decrement Operators

Now that you have seen the basics of overloading, it is time to delve into a couple of technical areas. There is a problem with overloading the ++ and -- operators. There are actually two forms of these operators: a *prefix* form

```
++x;
```

and a *postfix* form

```
x++;
```

For numbers, both of these two forms have the same effect: they increment x. However, they return different values: ++x evaluates to x after the increment, but x++ evaluates to x before the increment. You notice the difference only if you combine the increment expression with another expression. For example,

```
int i = 0;
int j = 0;
vector<double> s(10);
double a = s[i++]; /* a is s[0], i is 1 */
double b = s[++j]; /* b is s[1], j is 1 */
```

We recommend against this style (see Quality Tip 9.1)—it is confusing and a common source of programming errors. Use ++ only to increment a variable and never use the return value. Then it doesn't make any difference whether you use x++ or ++x.

Nevertheless, there are two separate ++ operators—the prefix form and the postfix form—and the compiler must distinguish between them when they are overloaded. To overload the prefix form for Time objects, to increment the object by one second, you define

```
void operator++(Time& a)
```

To overload the postfix form, you define

```
void operator++(Time& a, int dummy)
```

The int dummy parameter is not used inside the function; it merely serves to differentiate the two operator++ functions.

17.1.5 — Operator Members

For our linked list, we want to overload operators of the Iterator class. These functions must access the internals of the Iterator class; that is, they must be member functions. Operator functions can be member functions. For example, instead of a function

```
bool operator==(Iterator a, Iterator b)
```

we will supply a member function

```
bool Iterator::operator==(Iterator b) const
```

Notice that the member function form has the left operand of the operator as the implicit parameter, the right operand as the explicit parameter. If the operator is unary, then the member function has no explicit parameter:

```
string Iterator::operator*() const
```

The exception is the postfix form of the ++ operator, which still has an integer dummy parameter:

```
void Iterator::operator++(int dummy)
```

After all this preparation, the actual implementation of the ++, *, ==, and != operators for iterators is somewhat anticlimactic. You simply change next, get, and equals to operator++, operator*, and operator==, and you are done. Well, almost. Define operator!= to be the opposite of operator==. Remember to supply int dummy to operator++:

```
void Iterator::operator++(int dummy)
{
   assert(position != NULL);
   position = position->next;
}

string Iterator::operator*() const
{
   assert(position != NULL);
   return position->data;
}

bool Iterator::operator==(Iterator b) const
{
   return position == b.position;
```

```
}

bool Iterator::operator!=(Iterator b) const
{
    return !(*this == b); // calls operator==
}
```

Now the list iterators of Chapter 16 can be used just like the standard list iterators, with ++, *, == and != operators. This improvement is a part of the list implementation in Section 17.3.

Quality Tip

17.1

Overload Operators Only to Make Programs Easier to Read

Some programmers are so enamored with operator overloading that they use it in ways that make programs hard to read. For example, some programmers might want to overload the push_back operation of a list so that you can append an element to a list by calling

```
List staff;
staff += "Harry";
```

Maybe that's clever, but it can also be bewildering. It is best to overload operators to mimic existing use in mathematics or computer science. For example, it is reasonable to overload + and * for complex or matrix arithmetic, or to overload ++ and * to make iterators look like pointers.

17.2   Automatic Memory Management

In this section, you will consider a modification of the Department class that was originally introduced in Chapter 10. For simplicity, only the department's receptionist will be modeled in this example. However, we will take the point of view that the Department object *owns* the Employee object that denotes the receptionist. When constructing a Department object with a given employee, the constructor makes a copy of the object.

```
class Department
{
    ...
private:
    string name;
    Employee* receptionist;
};

Department::Department(string n, Employee e)
{
    name = n;
    receptionist = new Employee(e.get_name(), e.get_salary());
}
```

There is also a second constructor that constructs a department without a receptionist.

```
Department::Department(string n)
{
    name = n;
    receptionist = NULL;
}
```

Use a pointer for the `receptionist` field to model the "0 or 1" multiplicity of the relationship between the `Department` and `Employee` classes.

17.2.1 — Destructors

When a `Department` object is no longer needed, its memory is reused. However, that poses a problem. The object contains a pointer to an `Employee` object (see Figure 1).

If the `Employee` object is not deleted, a memory leak occurs. When the `Department` object is no longer available, it is no longer possible to locate the private pointer to the `Employee`, and the memory for the `Employee` object cannot be recycled.

The C++ language has a special mechanism to overcome this potential problem. You can define a *destructor*, a function that is always called when an object is about to go out of scope. The destructor for the `Department` class should delete the `receptionist` pointer.

Here is the code for the destructor (see Syntax 17.2). Note that the name of the destructor is the name of the class, prefixed by the ~ symbol.

```
Department::~Department()
{
    delete receptionist;
}
```

What should happen in the case that `receptionist` is a `NULL` pointer? Calling `delete` on a `NULL` pointer is safe—it simply does nothing. Therefore, you don't need a special case for that situation.

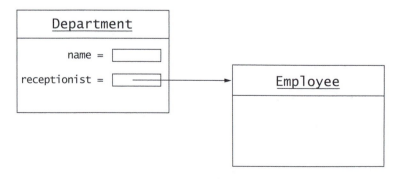

Figure 1

A Department Object

Syntax 17.2 : Destructor Definition

Class_name::~*Class_name*()
{
    statements
}

Example:
```
Department::~Department()
{
    delete receptionist;
}
```

Purpose: Supply the implementation of a destructor that is invoked whenever an object goes out of scope.

The destructor is automatically invoked whenever an object goes out of scope:

```
{
    Department dept;
    ...
} // dept.~Department() automatically invoked here
```

Destructors are also invoked when a heap object is deleted.

```
Department* p = new Department(...);
...
delete p; // p->~Department() automatically invoked here
```

A class can have many overloaded constructors, but it can have at most one destructor, with no explicit parameters. After all, programmers don't explicitly invoke a destructor.

You should always supply a destructor when some amount of cleanup is required when an object goes out of scope. Very commonly, that cleanup involves recycling dynamic memory. But in some situations, a destructor might close a file or relinquish some other resource.

The standard containers (vector, list, and so on) supply destructors that automatically recycle the dynamic memory that these classes use.

17.2.2 — Overloading the Assignment Operator

Introducing a destructor solves an important problem. Objects that are no longer used do not cause memory leaks. However, the solution is not perfect. Consider the following situation:

```
Department qc("Quality Control", Employee("Tester, Tina", 50000));
Department dept("Shipping", Employee("Hacker, Harry", 35000));
```

The first part of Figure 2 shows the memory layout. Now suppose that we assign one Department object to another:

```
dept = qc;
```

Assigning an object to another assigns each of the data fields. That means:

```
dept.name = qc.name
dept.receptionist = qc.receptionist
```

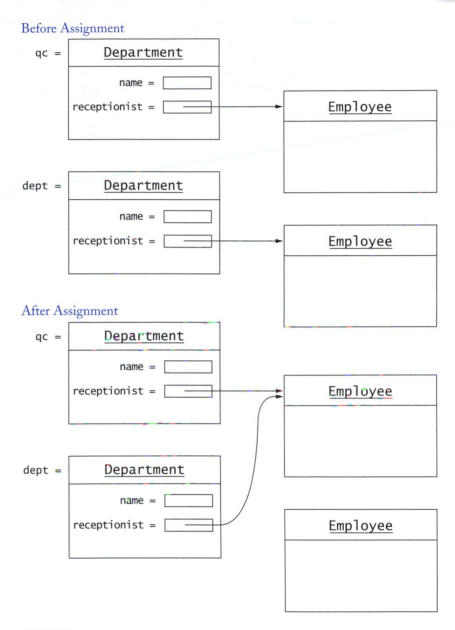

Figure 2

Assignment without an Overloaded Assignment Operator

The second part of Figure 2 shows the situation after the assignment. You will immediately see a problem. The old receptionist of the dept object is now orphaned—another memory leak has occurred.

Furthermore, there is a more subtle problem. Eventually, the dept and qc objects will go out of scope. Their destructors will be invoked. Objects are destroyed in the opposite order of constructions. That is, dept gets destroyed first. The first part of Figure 3 shows what happens in the destructor. The Employee object is deleted.

Note that the receptionist pointer in the dept object points to the deleted Employee object. When the qc object is destroyed, the Employee object is deleted twice. That is a fatal error that will compromise the internal structure of the heap.

The remedy is to overload the = operator to make the assignment safe by making a copy of the Employee object.

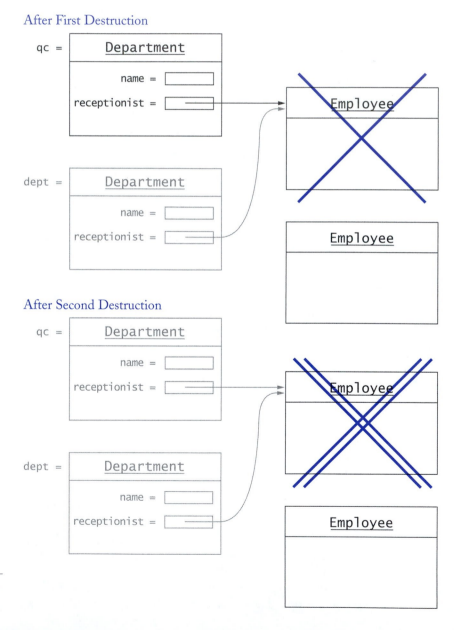

Figure 3

Double Deletion of a
Shared Object

```
Department& Department::operator=(const Department& b)
{
    ...
    name = b.name;
    delete receptionist;
    if (b.receptionist == NULL)
        receptionist = NULL;
    else
        receptionist = new Employee(b.receptionist->get_name(),
            b.receptionist->get_salary());
    ...
}
```

The basic concept behind the assignment operator is straightforward. The assignment first deletes the old receptionist, and then copies the receptionist of the assigned object.

In the remainder of this section, we discuss several technical points that you have to know when overloading the = operator.

Unlike most other overloaded operators, operator= must be a member function. It is a syntax error to define a nonmember operator=.

The operator= function must take care not to carry out a destructive "self-assignment". It can happen that a programmer assigns an object to itself, for example in a context such as

```
v[0] = v[i];
```

where v is a vector of objects and i is allowed to have the value 0.

However, the operator= function first deletes the receptionist. If both departments are the same object, then the receptionist is deleted and no longer available for copying. The test

```
if (this != &b)
```

tests whether the implicit and explicit argument have different addresses and are therefore different list objects. Thus, an operator= function should include the test against self-assignment:

```
Department& Department::operator=(const Department& b)
{
    if (this != &b)
    {
        ...
    }
    ...
}
```

Sometimes, programmers chain the = operator like this:

```
z = y = x;
```

To make this chaining work, an operator= function should always return *this, a reference to the left-hand side of the assignment:

```
Department& Department::operator=(const Department& b)
{
    ...
    return *this;
}
```

Because the = operator is right associative, the expression

```
z = y = x;
```

is equivalent to

```
z = (y = x);
```

The parenthesized expression is executed first. It becomes a function call

```
y.operator=(x);
```

That function call returns a reference to y. The second assignment is therefore the call

```
z.operator=(y);
```

The overall effect is that the contents of x is first copied to y and then to z.

Putting everything together yields the following code for the assignment operator:

```
Department& Department::operator=(const Department& b)
{
   if (this != &b)
   {
      name = b.name;
      delete receptionist;
      if (b.receptionist == NULL)
         receptionist = NULL;
      else
         receptionist = new Employee(b.receptionist->get_name(),
            b.receptionist->get_salary());
   }
   return *this;
}
```

You should always overload the = operator if your class has data fields that are pointers, and a simple copy of objects leads to dangerous shared pointers.

17.2.3 — Copy Constructors

Consider the following definition of a Department variable:

```
Department dept = qc;
```

Even though this definition looks like an assignment, operator= is not invoked. The purpose of operator= is to set an *existing* object equal to another object. However, the object dept has not yet been constructed. That is, the pointer dept.receptionist is set to a random value. If you review the code for the operator= function, you will note that the first part deletes the old receptionist. It would be fatal if operator= were to be executed with an uninitialized object since it would then delete an uninitialized pointer, causing a program crash or heap corruption.

Instead, the compiler invokes another memory management function, the *copy constructor*. The copy constructor defines how to construct an object of a class as a copy of another object of the same class.

If you don't define a copy constructor, then the compiler provides a version that simply constructs the data fields of the new object as copies of the corresponding data fields of the existing object. For the Department class, the action of the default copy constructor would be

```
dept.name = qc.name;
dept.receptionist = qc.receptionist;
```

However, this version of the copy constructor is inappropriate. It can lead to the same kind of errors as the default version of the assignment operator. You must define the copy constructor to make a copy of the receptionist.

Here is a valid copy constructor for the `Department` class:

```
Department::Department(const Department& b)
{
   name = b.name;
   if (b.receptionist == NULL)
      receptionist = NULL;
   else
      receptionist = new Employee(b.receptionist->get_name(),
         b.receptionist->get_salary());
}
```

The assignment operator, copy constructor, and destructor are collectively called the "big three". You must implement them for any class that manages heap memory. As Marshall Cline [1] says, "it's not just a good idea, it's the law". While this law may be about as pleasant as the tax laws, it is not actually that hard to comply with. Define the three functions with the following logic.

Destructor

Free all dynamic memory that the object manages.

Copy Constructor

Initialize the object as a copy of the explicit parameter object.

Assignment Operator

Check whether `this` == &b. If so, do nothing.
Free the dynamic memory of the object that is no longer needed.
Set the object as a copy of the explicit parameter object.
Return `*this`

Note that you only need to worry about the "big three" if your class manages heap memory. If you use the library classes, such as `vector` or `list`, there is nothing to worry about. These classes already implement the "big three" for you.

Following is a program that tests the `Department` class with the "big three" memory management functions. For testing purposes, the memory management functions display trace messages. The program prints

```
Constructor: [name=Shipping,receptionist=NULL]
Constructor: [name=Quality Control,receptionist=Tester, Tina]
Copy constructor: [name=Quality Control,receptionist=Tester, Tina]
Assignment: [name=Quality Control,receptionist=Tester, Tina]
   = [name=Shipping,receptionist=NULL]
Destructor: [name=Shipping,receptionist=NULL]
Destructor: [name=Quality Control,receptionist=Tester, Tina]
Destructor: [name=Shipping,receptionist=NULL]
```

As you can see, there are three constructor calls and three matching destructor calls.

File department.cpp

```cpp
1  #include <string>
2  #include <iostream>
3
4  using namespace std;
5
6  #include "ccc_empl.h"
7
8  /**
9      A department in an organization.
10 */
11 class Department
12 {
13 public:
14    Department(string n);
15    Department(string n, Employee e);
16    ~Department();
17    Department& operator=(const Department& b);
18    Department(const Department& b);
19    void print() const;
20 private:
21    string name;
22    Employee* receptionist;
23 };
24
25 /**
26     Constructs a department with a given name and no receptionist.
27     @param n the department name
28 */
29 Department::Department(string n)
30 {
31    name = n;
32    receptionist = NULL;
33
34    cout << "Constructor: ";
35    print();
36 }
37
38 /**
39     Constructs a department with a given name and receptionist.
40     @param n the department name
41     @param e the receptionist
42 */
43 Department::Department(string n, Employee e)
44 {
45    name = n;
46    receptionist = new Employee(e.get_name(), e.get_salary());
47
48    cout << "Constructor: ";
49    print();
50 }
51
52 /**
53     Deletes the Employee object that this Department
54     object manages.
55 */
56 Department::~Department()
```

```
57  {
58     cout << "Destructor: ";
59     print();
60
61     delete receptionist;
62  }
63
64  /**
65     Constructs a Department object as a copy of another
66     Department object.
67     @param b the object to copy
68  */
69  Department::Department(const Department& b)
70  {
71     cout << "Copy constructor: ";
72     b.print();
73
74     name = b.name;
75     if (b.receptionist == NULL)
76        receptionist = NULL;
77     else
78        receptionist = new Employee(b.receptionist->get_name(),
79           b.receptionist->get_salary());
80  }
81
82  /**
83     Sets this Department object to a copy of another
84     Department object.
85     @param b the object to copy
86  */
87  Department& Department::operator=(const Department& b)
88  {
89     cout << "Assignment: ";
90     print();
91     cout << "= ";
92     b.print();
93
94     if (this != & b)
95     {
96        name = b.name;
97        delete receptionist;
98        if (b.receptionist == NULL)
99           receptionist = NULL;
100       else
101          receptionist = new Employee(b.receptionist->get_name(),
102             b.receptionist->get_salary());
103    }
104    return *this;
105 }
106
107 /**
108    Prints a description of this department.
109 */
110 void Department::print() const
111 {
112    cout << "[name=" << name << ",receptionist=";
113    if (receptionist == NULL)
114       cout << "NULL";
```

```
115     else
116        cout << receptionist->get_name();
117     cout << "]\n";
118  }
119
120  int main()
121  {
122     Department shipping("Shipping");
123     Department qc("Quality Control",
124        Employee("Tester, Tina", 50000));
125     Department dept(qc);
126     dept = shipping;
127     return 0;
128  }
```

17.2.4 — Memory Management for Linked Lists

In Chapter 16, you saw how to implement a linked list class. When a linked list is no longer needed, the links should be deleted. To automate this task, you can define a destructor.

```
List::~List()
{
   free();
}

void List::free()
{
   while (begin() != end())
      erase(begin());
}
```

The destructor automatically invokes the free function when a list goes out of scope. The free function erases all nodes. You will need it again in the assignment operator.

```
List& List::operator=(const List& b)
{
   if (this != &b)
   {
      free();
      copy(b);
   }
   return *this;
}

void List::copy(const List& b)
{
   for (Iterator p = b.begin(); p != b.end(); p++)
      push_back(*p);
}
```

Finally, as the last part of the "big three", supply a copy constructor for the List class:

```
List::List(const List& b)
{
   first = NULL;
   last = NULL;
   copy(b);
}
```

These memory management functions will be included in the `List` implementation in Section 17.3.

⊗ Common Error   17.1

Defining a Destructor without the Other Two Functions of the "Big Three"

It is often intuitively obvious to programmers when a class needs a destructor. If a class contains a pointer to heap memory, or an open file, or some other resource that requires cleanup, then the destructor gets to do the cleanup.

But a user-defined destructor is usually incompatible with the system-defined assignment and copy operations. Consider this case:

```
Department qc;
Department dept = qc;
```

If no copy constructor is defined for the `Department` class, then `dept` just contains copies of pointers in `qc`. When `qc` and `dept` go out of scope, then the `Department` destructor calls follow the pointers *twice*, once to delete the receptionist of `dept` and again to delete the receptionist of `qc`. (Destructors are invoked in the opposite order from constructors.) The second destruction is fatal—deleting a memory block twice corrupts the heap.

To avoid this problem, always define an assignment operator and copy constructor when defining a destructor.

⊗ Common Error   17.2

Confusing Destruction and Deletion

Beginning programmers often confuse destruction and deletion. These concepts are closely related, but it is important that you separate them in your mind.

- Deletion means that a pointer is passed to the `delete` operator

- Destruction means that a destructor (`~ClassName()`) is called when an object goes out of scope

In other words, pointers are deleted and objects are destroyed.

Now run through a couple of examples. Here, the `dept` object goes out of scope:

```
{
    Department dept;
    ...
} // dept.~Department() automatically invoked here
```

The `dept` object is destroyed. That is, the destructor is executed. As a consequence, the pointer `dept.receptionist` is deleted.

▼

The next example is more complex. Consider this deletion of a pointer to a heap object.

```
Department* p = new Department(...);
...
```

▼

```
delete p; // p->~Department() automatically invoked here
```

The `delete` operator causes destruction of the object to which p points, which in turn causes the pointer p->receptionist to be deleted. In other words, two blocks of memory are recy-

▼

cled to the heap: the `Employee` object and the `Department` object.

17.3   Templates

Suppose you want to write a function that traverses a vector and simultaneously keeps track of the minimum and the maximum.

```
int min = v[0];
int max = v[0];
for (int i = 1; i < v.size(); i++)
{
   if (v[i] < min) min = v[i];
   if (v[i] > max) max = v[i];
}
```

To return both values, make a simple `Pair` class.

```
class Pair
{
public:
   Pair(int a, int b);
   int get_first() const;
   int get_second() const;
private:
   int first;
   int second;
};

Pair::Pair(int a, int b)
{
   first = a;
   second = b;
}

int Pair::get_first() const
{
   return first;
}

int Pair::get_second() const
{
   return second;
}
```

Now you can complete the function as follows:

```
Pair minmax(vector<int> v)
{
```

```
        ...
        return Pair(min, max);
    }
```

The caller of the function retrieves both values like this:

```
    Pair p = minmax(data);
    cout << p.get_first() << " " << p.get_second() << "\n";
```

However, the Pair class is not very flexible. Suppose you want to gather a pair of double or string values. Then you need to define another class. What is really needed is a mechanism to define pairs of arbitrary types. For this purpose, you can define a *class template*, which can produce pairs of particular types. The template can be *instantiated* to classes Pair<int>, Pair<string>, and so on. You can think of the Pair template as a factory for classes, and an instantiated class such as Pair<int> as a class produced by that factory.

To define the template, denote the arbitrary type with a *type parameter* T as shown in Syntax 17.3. Replace all int types by the type variable T. Finally, add a line template<typename T> before the class definition:

```
    template<typename T>
    class Pair
    {
    public:
        Pair(T a, T b);
        T get_first() const;
        T get_second() const;
    private:
        T first;
        T second;
    };
```

Syntax 17.3 : Template Class Definition

```
template<typename type_variable>
class Class_name
{
    features
};
```

Example:
```
template<typename T>
class Pair
{
public:
    Pair(T a, T b);
    T get_first() const;
    T get_second() const;
private:
    T first;
    T second;
};
```

Purpose: Define a class template with a type parameter.

With older compilers, you must use `template<class T>` instead of `template<typename T>`. The C++ standard allows either choice; `typename` is preferred because it makes it clear that `T` can be any type, not just a class. For example, you can form a `Pair<int>`, even though `int` is not a class type.

Finally, you must turn *each* member function definition into a template, as shown in Syntax 17.4:

```
template<typename T>
Pair<T>::Pair(T a, T b)
{
   first = a;
   second = b;
}

template<typename T>
T Pair<T>::get_first() const
{
   return first;
}

template<typename T>
T Pair<T>::get_second() const
{
   return second;
}
```

Note that each function is turned into a separate template. Each function name is prefixed by the "`Pair<T>::`" qualifier. And, of course, the type variable `T` is used in place of the `int` type.

The `Pair` template is a simple example that was introduced for demonstration purposes. (Actually, there is a `pair` template in the standard C++ library that is similar to this template.) The most common use of templates is in container classes. Of course, the standard `vector` and `list` constructs are templates.

Syntax 17.4 : Template Member Function Definition

```
template<typename type_variable>
return_type Class_name<type_variable>::function_name(parameters) const_opt
{
   statements
}
```

Example:
```
template<typename T>
T Pair<T>::get_first() const
{
   return first;
}
```

Purpose: Supply the implementation of a member function for a class template.

In Chapter 16, you saw how to implement your own linked list class. That class stored lists of strings. You now know how to store values of arbitrary types, by turning the class into a template.

Because the `List` class uses the `Node` and the `Iterator` classes, you need to make templates for these classes as well. Start with the `Node` class. The original `Node` class stored a string value:

```
class Node
{
public:
   Node(string s);
private:
   string data;
   Node* previous;
   Node* next;
};
```

The templatized version is

```
template<typename T>
class Node
{
public:
   Node(T s);
private:
   T data;
   Node<T>* previous;
   Node<T>* next;
};
```

You do the same with the `List` class:

```
template<typename T>
class List
{
public:
   List();
   void push_back(T s);
   void insert(Iterator<T> pos, T s);
   Iterator<T> erase(Iterator<T> pos);
   Iterator<T> begin();
   Iterator<T> end();
private:
   Node<T>* first;
   Node<T>* last;
};
```

Finally, turn *each* member function definition into a template, as shown in Syntax 17.4:

```
template<typename T>
Iterator<T> List<T>::begin()
{
   Iterator<T> iter;
   iter.position = first;
   iter.last = last;
   return iter;
}
```

The following program shows the end result of this process for the list class.

File list.cpp

```
 1 #include <string>
 2 #include <iostream>
 3 #include <cassert>
 4
 5 using namespace std;
 6
 7 /* forward declarations */
 8 template<typename T> class List;
 9 template<typename T> class Iterator;
10
11 /**
12     A class to hold the nodes of the linked list.
13 */
14 template<typename T>
15 class Node
16 {
17 public:
18     /**
19         Constructs a node for a given data value.
20         @param s the data to store in this node
21     */
22     Node(T s);
23 private:
24     T data;
25     Node<T>* previous;
26     Node<T>* next;
27 friend class List<T>;
28 friend class Iterator<T>;
29 };
30
31 /**
32     An iterator denotes a position in the list or
33     past the end of the list.
34 */
35 template<typename T>
36 class Iterator
37 {
38 public:
39     /**
40         Constructs an iterator that is not attached to any list.
41     */
42     Iterator();
43     /**
44         Looks up the value at a position.
45         @return the value of the Node to which the iterator
46         points
47     */
48     T operator*() const;
49     /**
50         Advances the iterator to the next position.
51     */
52     void operator++(int dummy);
```

```
53      /**
54          Moves the iterator to the previous position.
55      */
56      void operator--(int dummy);
57      /**
58          Compares two iterators.
59          @param b the iterator to compare with this iterator
60          @return true if this iterator and b are equal
61      */
62      bool operator==(Iterator<T> b) const;
63      /**
64          Compares two iterators.
65          @param b the iterator to compare with this iterator
66          @return true if this iterator and b are not equal
67      */
68      bool operator!=(Iterator<T> b) const;
69  private:
70      Node<T>* position;
71      Node<T>* last;
72  friend class List<T>;
73  };
74
75  /**
76      A linked list of values of a given type.
77      @param T the type of the list values
78  */
79  template<typename T>
80  class List
81  {
82  public:
83      /**
84          Constructs an empty list.
85      */
86      List();
87      /**
88          Constructs a list as a copy of another list.
89          @param b the list to copy
90      */
91      List(const List<T>& b);
92      /**
93          Deletes all nodes of this list.
94      */
95      ~List();
96      /**
97          Assigns another list to this list.
98          @param b the list to assign
99          @return a reference to this list
100     */
101     List<T>& operator=(const List<T>& b);
102
103     /**
104         Appends an element to the list.
105         @param s the value to append
106     */
107     void push_back(T s);
108     /**
```

```
109            Inserts an element into the list.
110            @param iter the position before which to insert
111            @param s the value to append
112     */
113     void insert(Iterator<T> iter, T s);
114     /**
115            Removes an element from the list.
116            @param i the position to remove
117            @return an iterator pointing to the element after the
118            erased element
119     */
120     Iterator<T> erase(Iterator<T> i);
121     /**
122            Gets the beginning position of the list.
123            @return an iterator pointing to the beginning of the list
124     */
125     Iterator<T> begin();
126     /**
127            Gets the past-the-end position of the list.
128            @return an iterator pointing past the end of the list
129     */
130     Iterator<T> end();
131
132 private:
133     /**
134            Copies another list to this list.
135            @param b the list to copy
136     */
137     void copy(const List<T>& b);
138     /**
139            Deletes all nodes of this list.
140     */
141     void free();
142
143     Node<T>* first;
144     Node<T>* last;
145 };
146
147 template<typename T>
148 List<T>::List()
149 {
150     first = NULL;
151     last = NULL;
152 }
153
154 template<typename T>
155 List<T>::~List()
156 {
157     free();
158 }
159
160 template<typename T>
161 List<T>::List(const List<T>& b)
162 {
163     first = NULL;
164     last = NULL;
```

```
165        copy(b);
166    }
167
168    template<typename T>
169    List<T>& List<T>::operator=(const List<T>& b)
170    {
171        if (this != &b)
172        {
173            free();
174            copy(b);
175        }
176        return *this;
177    }
178
179
180    template<typename T>
181    void List<T>::push_back(T s)
182    {
183        Node<T>* newnode = new Node<T>(s);
184        if (last == NULL) /* list is empty */
185        {
186            first = newnode;
187            last = newnode;
188        }
189        else
190        {
191            newnode->previous = last;
192            last->next = newnode;
193            last = newnode;
194        }
195    }
196
197    template<typename T>
198    void List<T>::insert(Iterator<T> iter, T s)
199    {
200        if (iter.position == NULL)
201        {
202            push_back(s);
203            return;
204        }
205
206        Node<T>* after = iter.position;
207        Node<T>* before = after->previous;
208        Node<T>* newnode = new Node<T>(s);
209        newnode->previous = before;
210        newnode->next = after;
211        after->previous = newnode;
212        if (before == NULL) /* insert at beginning */
213            first = newnode;
214        else
215            before->next = newnode;
216    }
217
218    template<typename T>
219    Iterator<T> List<T>::erase(Iterator<T> i)
220    {
```

```
221      Iterator<T> iter = i;
222      assert(iter.position != NULL);
223      Node<T>* remove = iter.position;
224      Node<T>* before = remove->previous;
225      Node<T>* after = remove->next;
226      if (remove == first)
227         first = after;
228      else
229         before->next = after;
230      if (remove == last)
231         last = before;
232      else
233         after->previous = before;
234      iter.position = after;
235      delete remove;
236      return iter;
237   }
238
239   template<typename T>
240   Iterator<T> List<T>::begin()
241   {
242      Iterator<T> iter;
243      iter.position = first;
244      iter.last = last;
245      return iter;
246   }
247
248   template<typename T>
249   Iterator<T> List<T>::end()
250   {
251      Iterator<T> iter;
252      iter.position = NULL;
253      iter.last = last;
254      return iter;
255   }
256
257   template<typename T>
258   Iterator<T>::Iterator()
259   {
260      position = NULL;
261      last = NULL;
262   }
263
264   template<typename T>
265   T Iterator<T>::operator*() const
266   {
267      assert(position != NULL);
268      return position->data;
269   }
270
271   template<typename T>
272   void Iterator<T>::operator++(int dummy)
273   {
274      assert(position != NULL);
275      position = position->next;
276   }
```

```
277
278  template<typename T>
279  void Iterator<T>::operator--(int dummy)
280  {
281     if (position == NULL)
282        position = last;
283     else
284        position = position->previous;
285     assert(position != NULL);
286  }
287
288  template<typename T>
289  bool Iterator<T>::operator==(Iterator<T> b) const
290  {
291     return position == b.position;
292  }
293
294  template<typename T>
295  bool Iterator<T>::operator!=(Iterator<T> b) const
296  {
297     return position != b.position;
298  }
299
300  template<typename T>
301  Node<T>::Node(T s)
302  {
303     data = s;
304     previous = NULL;
305     next = NULL;
306  }
307
308  template<typename T>
309  void List<T>::copy(const List<T>& b)
310  {
311     for (Iterator<T> p = b.begin(); p != b.end(); p++)
312        push_back(*p);
313  }
314
315  template<typename T>
316  void List<T>::free()
317  {
318     while (begin() != end())
319        erase(begin());
320  }
321
322  int main()
323  {
324     List<string> staff;
325
326     staff.push_back("Cracker, Carl");
327     staff.push_back("Hacker, Harry");
328     staff.push_back("Lam, Larry");
329     staff.push_back("Sandman, Susan");
330
331     /* add a value in fourth place */
332
```

```
333    Iterator<string> pos;
334    pos = staff.begin();
335    pos++;
336    pos++;
337    pos++;
338
339    staff.insert(pos, "Reindeer, Rudolf");
340
341    /* remove the value in second place */
342
343    pos = staff.begin();
344    pos++;
345
346    staff.erase(pos);
347
348    /* print all values */
349
350    for (pos = staff.begin(); pos != staff.end(); pos++)
351       cout << *pos << "\n";
352
353    return 0;
354 }
```

17.4   Nested Classes and Name Spaces

There is a slight difference between the List template you defined and the list template of standard C++. With your template, you define an iterator as

```
Iterator<string> pos = staff.begin();
```

However, with the standard list class, you use a slightly different syntax:

```
list<string>::iterator pos = staff.begin();
```

In the standard library, the iterator class is *nested* inside the list class (see Syntax 17.5). This allows other collection classes, such as vectors, maps, and sets, to define their own iterators. All of these iterators have different internal implementations. They just share the same name, iterator, because they represent the same concept. To avoid name conflicts, each of the container classes uses nesting to make sure it owns the name for its iterator. Nested names are expressed with a ::, as follows:

```
vector<double>::iterator p = a.begin();
list<string>::iterator q = b.begin();
```

Let's do the same for the List and Iterator classes. For simplicity, revert to the version without templates. You want to nest the Iterator class inside the List class and then use it as

```
List::Iterator pos = staff.begin();
```

Syntax 17.5 : Nested Class Declaration

```
class Outer_class_name
{
   . . .
   class Nested_class_name;
   . . .
};
```

Example:
```
class List
{
   . . .
   class Iterator;
};
```

Purpose: Declare a class whose scope is contained in the scope of another class.

To nest a class inside another involves two steps. First, declare the nested class inside the outer class:

```
class List
{
   . . .
   class Iterator;
   . . .
};
```

Then define the class and its member functions, always referring to it by its full name (such as `List::Iterator`).

```
class List::Iterator
{
public:
   Iterator();
   string get() const;
   . . .
};

List::Iterator::Iterator()
{
   . . .
}

string List::Iterator::get() const
{
   . . .
}
```

Note that the name of the class is `List::Iterator`, but the name of the constructor is still just `Iterator`.

With older compilers, you must include the *entire* definition of the nested class *inside* the definition of the outer class:

```
class List
{
   ...
   class Iterator
   {
   public:
      Iterator();
      string get() const;
      ...
   };
   ...
};
```

This looks quite confusing, and it makes it appear as if the List object contained an Iterator object inside it. That is not the case. The List class merely owns the Iterator class, or, in other words, the name Iterator is in the scope of the List class. The List member functions can simply refer to it as Iterator, all other functions must refer to it as List::Iterator.

In general, you use nested classes for just one reason: to place the name of a class inside the scope of another class.

Name spaces have a purpose that is similar to that of nested classes—to avoid naming conflicts. For example, in a large software project, it is quite possible that several programmers come up with names for functions or classes that conflict with another. Suppose another programmer comes up with a class called map, perhaps to denote a map in a computer game, unaware that there is already a map class in the standard library. By using name spaces, it becomes possible to use both classes in the same program. The standard library classes are in the std name space. You can unambiguously reference the standard map class as std::map. If the other map class is in a different name space, say acme, then you can specify it as acme::map.

To add classes, functions, or variables to a name space, surround their declarations with a namespace block (see Syntax 17.6):

```
namespace acme
{
   class map
   {
      ...
   };

   void draw(map m);
}
```

Unlike classes, name spaces are *open*. You can add as many items to a name space as you like, simply by starting another namespace block.

```
namespace acme
{
   class maze
   {
      ...
   };
}
```

Syntax 17.6 : Name Space Definition

```
namespace name_space_name
{
    feature₁
    feature₂
    ...
    featureₙ
}
```

Example:
```
namespace ACME_Software_San_Jose_CA_US
{
    class map
    {
        ...
    };
}
```

Purpose: Include a class, function, or variable in a name space.

Of course, it is tedious to prefix all standard classes with the `std::` qualifier if there are no name conflicts. Therefore, your programs start out with the declaration

```
using namespace std;
```

The purpose of that declaration is to specify that all names should be looked up in the `std` name space. For example, when the compiler sees `cout`, it will find the declaration of `std::cout` in the `<iostream>` header, and know that you really want to use that variable.

However, in one important aspect, the `std` name space is atypical. Since you use name spaces to avoid name clashes, you normally want to use name space names that are truly unambiguous and therefore long, such as `ACME_Software_San_Jose_CA_US`. At first glance, that looks very tedious—programmers would not be happy to type

```
ACME_Software_San_Jose_CA_US::map
```

To solve this problem, you can define a short alias for a long name space, for example

```
namespace acme = ACME_Software_San_Jose_CA_US;
```

(See Syntax 17.7.) Then you use the alias in your program, such as `acme::map`, and the compiler automatically translates the alias to the complete name of the name space. You can use different aliases for the same name space in different source files, in case you have a conflict of alias names.

Syntax 17.7 : Name Space Alias

```
namespace alias_name = name_space_name;
```

Example: `namespace acme = ACME_Software_San_Jose_CA_US;`

Purpose: Introduce a short alias for the long name of a name space.

In professional programs, it is an excellent idea to use name spaces, particularly if you build libraries for other programmers. Follow these rules:

- Come up with long and unique names for your name spaces.

- Use the alias feature to establish short aliases.

- Don't use the using declaration, except for the std name space.

Quality Tip   17.2

Use Unambiguous Names for Name Spaces

Some programmers use their initials or the initials of a product or company as names for name spaces. Searching on the Web, one can find C++ libraries with name spaces such as MRI and IPL. This is not a good practice—it is just a matter of time before Irene P. Lee uses her initials for her name space, and then needs to use the Image Processing Library that does the same.

Use a long name, such as

```
Image_Proc_Lib_ACME_Software_San_Jose_CA_US
```

for the library name space. Programmers using the library can easily use a convenient alias of their own choice.

17.5   Exception Handling

17.5.1   Signaling Error Conditions

Suppose a programmer makes an error when using a class, such as getting an element from the past-the-end iterator position. Then the author of the class can choose between these alternatives:

- Not checking the error condition and executing the code anyway, possibly causing severe problems

- Checking the error condition and doing nothing if it occurs

- Checking the error condition and alerting the caller if it occurs

Many programmers take the first approach. If you make a call that you should have known to be invalid, something mysterious or terrible may happen. For example, consider the future_value function of Chapter 5.

```
double future_value(double initial_balance, double p, int n)
{
   return initial_balance * pow(1 + p / 100, n);
}
```

Now suppose a programmer calls future_value(1000, -100, -1). Then the function computes pow(0, -1) or $1/0$, which is an error.

The `future_value` and `pow` functions don't check for error conditions. Instead, they rely on programmers to be competent enough to understand their preconditions. Generally, the reason for omitting checks is maximum performance. Checking for error conditions takes some time and it penalizes the programmers who call a function correctly. However, in many programming contexts, raw speed is not the only consideration, and it makes sense to focus on reliability and avoid errors.

You may have implemented functions that check for error conditions and safely do nothing if the method was called in error. For example,

```cpp
double future_value(double initial_balance, double p, int n)
{
    if (p < 0 || n < 0) return 0;
    return initial_balance * pow(1 + p / 100, n);
}
```

That approach looks good at first glance, but in practice, it can cause severe problems. When the function is called in error, it doesn't take the desired action and returns a fake value, but the caller doesn't know that there was an error. The caller will continue, and perhaps incorporate the fake value into its computations, which may cause problems later whose cause is hard to understand.

In Chapter 5, you saw how to use the `assert` mechanism to alert the programmer to error conditions:

```cpp
double future_value(double initial_balance, double p, int n)
{
    assert(p >= 0 && n >= 0);
    return initial_balance * pow(1 + p / 100, n);
}
```

Whenever someone calls this function with invalid parameters, the program exits with an error report that pinpoints the cause of the problem.

That's a good solution for student programs, but in real life, you don't want to terminate the program that controls a rocket or a medical device. Instead, you want to notify some other part of the program whose job it is to deal with error conditions.

C++ has such a notification mechanism, called *exception handling*. When a function detects an error, it can signal that condition to a handler by *throwing an exception* (see Syntax 17.8). For example,

```cpp
double future_value(double initial_balance, double p, int n)
{
    if (p < 0 || n < 0)
    {
        logic_error description("illegal future_value parameter");
        throw description;
    }
    return initial_balance * pow(1 + p / 100, n);
}
```

Here, `logic_error` is a standard exception class that is declared in the `<stdexcept>` header.

Many programmers don't bother to give the exception object a name and just throw an anonymous object, like this:

```cpp
if (p < 0 || n < 0)
    throw logic_error("illegal future_value parameter");
```

Syntax 17.8 : Throwing an Exception

throw *expression*;

Example: `throw logic_error("illegal future_value parameter");`

Purpose: Abandon this function and throw a value to an exception handler.

The keyword throw indicates that the function exits immediately. However, the function does not return to its caller. Instead, it searches the caller, the caller's caller, and so forth, for a *handler* that specifies how to handle a logic error.

17.5.2 — Catching Exceptions

You supply an exception handler with the try statement (see Syntax 17.9):

```
try
{
    code
}
catch (logic_error& e)
{
    handler
}
```

If any of the functions in the try clause throw a logic_error, or call another function that throws such an exception, then the code in the catch clause executes immediately.

For example, you can place a handler into the main function that tells the user that something has gone very wrong, and offers a chance to try again with different inputs.

```
int main()
{
    bool more = true;
    while (more)
    {
        try
        {
            code
        }
        catch (logic_error& e)
        {
            cout << "A logic error has occurred: "
                << e.what() << "\n"
                << "Retry? (y/n)";
            string input;
            getline(cin, input);
            if (input == "n") more = false;
        }
    }
}
```

This handler inspects the exception object that was thrown. Note that the catch clause looks somewhat like a function with a parameter variable e of type logic_error&. (You can give any name you like to the exception variable.) The catch clause then applies the what member function of the logic_error class to the exception object e. That function returns the string that was passed to the constructor of the error object in the throw statement.

It is a good idea to use inheritance to define your own exception types. For example,

```cpp
class FutureValueError : public logic_error
{
public:
    FutureValueError(const char reason[]);
};

FutureValueError::FutureValueError(const char reason[])
    : logic_error(reason) {}
```

Syntax 17.9 : Try Block

```cpp
try
{
    statements
}
catch (type_name₁ variable_name₁)
{
    statements
}
catch (type_name₂ variable_name₂)
{
    statements
}
...
catch (type_nameₙ variable_nameₙ)
{
    statements
}
```

Example:
```cpp
try
{
    List staff = read_list();
    process_list(staff);
}
catch (logic_error& e)
{
    cout << "Processing error " << e.what() << "\n";
}
```

Purpose: Provide one or more handlers for types of exceptions that may be thrown when executing a block of statements.

The `FutureValueError` class is a subclass of `logic_error`. The `FutureValueError` constructor passes the character string parameter to the base class constructor.

The `future_value` function can now throw a `FutureValueError` object:

```
if (p < 0 || n < 0)
   throw FutureValueError("illegal parameter");
```

Because a `FutureValueError` is a `logic_error`, you can still catch it with a

```
catch (logic_error& e)
```

clause—that is the reason for using inheritance. Alternatively, you can supply a

```
catch (FutureValueError& e)
```

clause that only catches `FutureValueError` objects and not other logic errors. You can even do both:

```
try
{
   code
}
catch (FutureValueError& e)
{
   handler₁
}
catch (logic_error& e)
{
   handler₂
}
catch (bad_alloc& e)
{
   handler₃
}
```

In this situation, the first handler catches all future value errors, the second handler catches the logic errors that are not future value errors, and the third handler catches the `bad_alloc` exception that is thrown when the `new` operator runs out of memory. The order of `catch` clauses is important. When an exception occurs, the exception handling mechanism matches the handlers top to bottom, and executes the first matching handler. If you reversed the handlers in the preceding code, then the `logic_error` handler would match a `FutureValueError`, and the handler for future value errors would never be executed.

17.5.3 — Stack Unwinding

One common use of exception handling is in functions that read input. Consider a function such as the `Product::read` function of Chapter 6. It expects the name, price, and score of a product. What should happen if no price or score is given? This may be an indication of a corrupted file. In such a case, it makes sense to throw an exception.

```
bool Product::read(fstream& fs)
{
```

```
        getline(fs, name);
        if (name == "") return false; // end of file
        fs >> price >> score;
        if (fs.fail())
           throw runtime_error("Error while reading product");
        string remainder;
        getline(fs, remainder);
        return true;
   }
```

Here, `runtime_error` is another standard exception type defined in the header `<stdexcept>`. The standard library distinguishes between "logic errors" and "runtime errors". When a logic error occurs, it never makes sense to retry the same operation, but a runtime error may have some chance of going away when the operation is attempted a second time. For example, the iron force of logic dictates that getting data from an empty list is doomed to failure. But reading from a file on a networked file system may fail, due to an intermittent network error, and then work when the network is up again.

Figure 4 shows the standard exception types in C++.

The `read` function shows another interesting distinction, between the *expected* end of file, and an unexpected problem. All files must come to an end, and the function returns `false` if the end has been reached in the normal way. But if an error has occurred in the middle of a product record, then the function throws an exception. Therefore, the caller

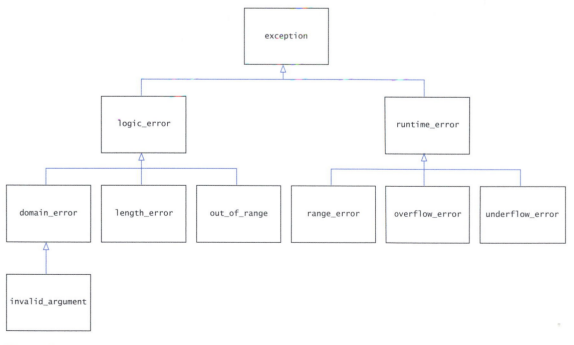

Figure 4

The Hierarchy of Standard Exception Types in C++

of the function only has to worry about the normal case and can leave the processing of the exceptional case to a specialized handler.

Consider this calling function:

```
void process_products(fstream& fs)
{
   list<Product> products;
   boolean more = true;
   while (more)
   {
      Product p;
      if (p.read(fs)) products.push_back(p);
      else more = false;
   }
   do something with products
}
```

Now suppose that the read function throws an exception. Then the exception handling mechanism abandons the process_products function and searches its callers for an appropriate handler.

But there is a problem. When the process_products function is abandoned, what happens to the memory in the products list? The list contains some number of links that were allocated on the heap and that need to be deleted.

The C++ exception handling mechanism is prepared for this situation. It invokes *all destructors of stack objects* before it abandons a function. In our example, the ~list destructor is called and all links are deleted. Thus, there is no memory leak.

Note that this automatic invocation of destructors only applies to *objects*. If you use a pointer in your own code, then no destructor is called. Pointers don't belong to classes, and only classes can have destructors. For example, consider this scenario.

```
Product* p = new Product();
if (p->read())
{
   . . .
}
delete p; // never executes if read throws an exception
```

If an exception occurs in the read function, then the calling function is abandoned. But p isn't an object, so it receives no special treatment from the exception handler. The memory to which it points is not deleted, causing a memory leak.

This is a serious problem. There are two remedies. The best remedy is to make sure that all allocated memory is deleted in a destructor. For example, that is the case for the nodes of a linked list.

However, if a local pointer variable is unavoidable, you can use the following construct:

```
Product* p = NULL;
try
{
   p = new Product();
   if (p->read())
   {
      . . .
```

```
            }
            delete p;
        }
        catch (...)
        {
            delete p;
            throw;
        }
```

The special clause `catch (...)` matches any exception. The handler contains the local cleanup, followed by the `throw` statement without an exception object. That special form of the `throw` statement *rethrows* the current exception. It is important to rethrow the exception so that a competent handler can process it. After all, the `catch` clause didn't properly handle the exception.

This local cleanup mechanism is clearly tedious. You therefore have an excellent incentive to arrange your code in an object-oriented way. Place the pointer variables inside classes, and put the destructor in charge of cleanup.

17.5.4 — Exception Specifications

If an exception is thrown and no `catch` clause exists to catch it, then the program terminates with an error message. Furthermore, as you have seen in the preceding section, if an exception occurs, then some important code may not be executed. Therefore, it is somewhat dangerous to throw exceptions, or to call methods that can throw exceptions. In C++, a function can declare that it throws only exceptions of a certain type, or no exceptions at all. You can use that knowledge to make sure that it is safe to call certain functions, or to know which kinds of exceptions your program needs to catch.

A function signature can optionally be followed by the keyword `throw` and a parenthesized, comma-separated list of exception types, for example:

```
void process_products(fstream& fs)
    throw (UnexpectedEndOfFile, bad_alloc)
```

To denote the fact that a function throws no exceptions, use an empty exception list.

```
void print_products(const list<Product>& products)
    throw ()
```

A function without a `throw` specification is allowed to throw any exceptions (see Syntax 17.10).

Syntax 17.10 : Exception Specification

return_type function_name(parameters)
    throw (*type_name*$_1$, *type_name*$_2$, ..., *type_name*$_n$)

Example: `void process_products(fstream& fs)`
            `throw (UnexpectedEndOfFile, bad_alloc)`

Purpose: List the types of all exceptions that a function can throw.

You must be careful when using exception specifications. The compiler does not enforce them. If a function with an exception specification throws an unexpected exception object whose type is not in the approved list, the exception handling mechanism terminates the program.

Quality Tip   17.3

Use Exceptions for Exceptional Cases

Consider the `read` function of the `Product` class. It returns `false` at the end of the stream. Why doesn't it throw an exception?

The designer of this function realized that every stream must come to an end. In other words, the end of input is a normal condition, not an exceptional one. Whenever you attempt to read a data record, you must be prepared to deal with the possibility that you reached the end. However, if the end of input occurs inside a data record that should be complete, then you can throw an exception to indicate that the input came to an *unexpected* end. This must have been caused by some exceptional event, perhaps a corrupted file.

In particular, you should *never* use exceptions as a "`break` statement on steroids". Don't throw an exception to exit a deeply nested loop or a set of recursive method calls. That is considered an abuse of the exception mechanism.

Quality Tip   17.4

Throwing an Exception Is Not a Sign of Shame

Some programmers prefer to patch up a problem locally rather than throw an exception, because they consider it irresponsible not to handle all problems.

For example, some programmers may implement the `Iterator::get` method to return an empty string when the iterator is in an invalid position.

However, that view is short-sighted. By supplying a false return value, a program may muddle through for a while, but it will likely produce unexpected and useless results. Furthermore, suppressing the error report deprives an exception handler of effectively dealing with the problem.

It is entirely honorable to throw exceptions to indicate failures that a function cannot competently handle. Of course, it is a good idea to document these exceptions.

Random Fact 17.1

The Ariane Rocket Incident

The European Space Agency, Europe's counterpart to NASA, had developed a rocket model called Ariane that it had successfully used several times to launch satellites and scientific experiments into space. However, when a new version, the Ariane 5, was launched on June 4, 1996, from ESA's launch site in Kourou, French Guiana, the rocket veered off course approximately 40 seconds after liftoff. Flying at an angle of more than 20 degrees, rather than straight up, exerted such an aerodynamic force that the boosters separated, which triggered the automatic self-destruction mechanism. The rocket blew itself up.

The ultimate cause of this accident was an unhandled exception! The rocket contained two identical devices (called inertial reference systems) that processed flight data from measuring devices and turned the data into information about the rocket position. The onboard computer used the position information for controlling the boosters. The same inertial reference systems and computer software had worked fine on the Ariane 4 predecessor.

However, due to design changes of the rocket, one of the sensors measured a larger acceleration force than had been encountered in the Ariane 4. That value, computed as a floating-point value, was stored in a 16-bit integer. Unlike C++, the Ada language, used for the device software, generates an exception if a floating-point number is too large to be converted to an integer. Unfortunately, the programmers of the device had decided that this situation would never happen and didn't provide an exception handler.

When the overflow did happen, the exception was triggered and, since there was no handler, the device shut itself off. The onboard computer sensed the failure and switched over to the backup device. However, that device had shut itself off for exactly the same reason, something that the designers of the rocket had not expected. They figured that the devices might fail for mechanical reasons, and the chances of two devices having the same mechanical failure was considered remote. At that point, the rocket was without reliable position information and went off course.

Perhaps it would have been better if the software hadn't been so thorough? If it had ignored the overflow, the device wouldn't have been shut off. It would have just computed bad data. But then the device would have reported wrong position data, which could have been equally fatal. Instead, a correct implementation should have caught overflow exceptions and come up with some strategy to recompute the flight data. Clearly, ignoring an exception was not a reasonable option in this context.

Figure 5

The Explosion of the Ariane Rocket

CHAPTER SUMMARY

1. You can define new meanings for C++ operators by defining functions whose name is operator followed by the operator symbol.

2. To implement classes that automatically manage dynamic memory, you need to define the "big three" functions: the assignment operator, copy constructor, and destructor.

3. Use templates to define classes and functions with type parameters. Templates are defined by prefixing the class and function definitions with the template keyword. Type parameters are enclosed in angle brackets.

4. Nested classes are defined inside other classes to make their names part of the outer class scope.

5. Name spaces are used to avoid name conflicts. In larger programming projects, you should place the names of all classes, global functions, and global variables in a name space with a unique (and therefore, long) name. Use name space aliases to conveniently refer to the long names of name spaces.

6. Use exceptions to transmit error conditions to special handlers. When you detect an error condition, you use the throw statement to signal the exception. One of the callers must supply a try block with a catch clause that matches the exception type.

FURTHER READING

[1] Marshall Cline and Greg A. Lomow, *C++ Frequently Asked Questions*, Addison-Wesley, 1995.

REVIEW EXERCISES

Exercise R17.1. When would you choose an overloaded operator for a particular operation, and when would you choose a function?

Exercise R17.2. Overload the + operator to raise an employee salary. For example, harry + 5 gives Harry a 5 percent raise. Is this a good use for operator overloading?

Exercise R17.3. When should an operator function be a member function?

Exercise R17.4. To print an object, access to the private data fields is often necessary. Can the operator<< function be defined as a member function to grant this access? If so, give an example. If not, explain why not.

Exercise R17.5. Why are there two versions of the ++ and -- operator functions? Are there any other operators with two versions?

Exercise R17.6. Which operators does the string class overload?

Exercise R17.7. What problems would a programmer encounter if you define a destructor for a class but no assignment operator?

Exercise R17.8. What problems would a programmer encounter if you define a destructor for a class but no copy constructor?

Exercise R17.9. The copy constructor for a class X has the form X(const X& b). Why is the construction parameter passed by reference? Explain why you can't define a constructor of the form X(X b).

Exercise R17.10. You can find the code for the vector template in the header file <vector>. Locate and copy the "big three" memory management functions in the class definition.

Exercise R17.11. Consider this code:

```
void f(int n)
{
   list<Employee*> e;
   for (int i = 1; i <= n; i++)
      e.push_back(new Employee());
}
```

At the end of the function, the list destructor deletes the nodes of e. Why does the function still have a memory leak?

Exercise R17.12. What is the difference between destruction and deletion of an object?

Exercise R17.13. Which objects are destroyed when the following function exits?

```
void f(List a)
{
   List b = a;
   List* c = new List();
   List* d = new List(b);
   List* e = d;
   delete e;
}
```

Exercise R17.14. Explain in which sense classes are closed while name spaces are open.

Exercise R17.15. When would you define a class as a nested class, and when would you define it in a name space?

Exercise R17.16. Suppose Harry J. Hacker develops a code library that he wants others to use. Why would it not be a good idea to place it into a name space hjh? What name space name might be appropriate?

Exercise R17.17. Why is it acceptable to use short aliases for name spaces, even though short names for name spaces are not appropriate?

Exercise R17.18. Give the statements to throw

(a)   a runtime_error with an explanation "Network failure"

(b)   a string "Network failure"

(c)   the unlucky number 13

Exercise R17.19. Give the statements to catch the exceptions of the preceding exercise.

Exercise R17.20. Give the statements to catch

(a) any `logic_error`

(b) any `ListError` or `runtime_error`

(c) any exception

Exercise R17.21. When do you use the `throw;` statement without argument?

Exercise R17.22. Consider the following code:

```
void f()
{
   List a;
   List* b = new List();
   throw runtime_error("");
}
```

Which objects are destroyed? Are there any memory leaks?

Exercise R17.23. What is the difference between

```
void f();
```

and

```
void f() throw ();
```

Exercise R17.24. How do you denote a function that throws only `bad_alloc` exceptions? A function that throws no exceptions at all? A function that can throw exceptions of any type?

Exercise R17.25. What happens in your programming environment if you throw an exception that is never caught? What happens if you throw an exception that violates an exception specification?

Programming Exercises

Exercise P17.1. Define a class `Fraction` with overloaded +, -, * and / operators. A `Fraction` object stores two integer data fields, the numerator and denominator. Use the familiar mathematical laws for fraction arithmetic, such as

$$n_1/d_1 + n_2/d_2 = (n_1d_2 + n_2d_1)/d_1d_2$$

and reduce to lowest terms afterwards. Overload the << operator to send the fraction to a stream. For example,

```
Fraction a(1, 2);
Fraction b(1, 3);
cout << a + b;
```

prints `5/6`.

Exercise P17.2. Define a class `BigInteger` that stores arbitrarily large integers, by keeping their digits in a `vector<int>`. Supply a constructor `BigInteger(string)` that reads a sequence of digits from a string. Overload the +, -, * and operators to add, subtract and multiply the digit sequences. Overload the << operator to send the big integer to a stream. For example,

```
BigInteger a("123456789");
BigInteger b("987654321");
cout << a * b;
```

prints 121932631112635269.

Exercise P17.3. Define a class `Set` that stores a finite set of integers. (In a set, the order of elements does not matter, and every element can occur at most once.) Supply `add` and `remove` member functions to add and remove set elements. Overload the | and & operators to compute the union and intersection of the set, and the << operator to send the set contents to a stream.

Exercise P17.4. Continue the preceding exercise and overload the ~ operator to compute the complement of a set. That is, ~a is the set of all integers that are not present in the set a. *Hint:* Add a `bool` field to the `Set` class to keep track whether a set is finite or has a finite complement.

Exercise P17.5. Consider this `String` class that stores the string contents in a dynamically allocated character array.

```
class String
{
public:
   String(const char s[]);
   ...
private:
   char* chars;
};

String::String(const char s[])
{
   chars = new char[strlen(s) + 1];
   strcpy(chars, s);
}
```

Implement the copy constructor, destructor, and assignment operator.

Exercise P17.6. Define a class `Set` that stores integers in a dynamically allocated array of integers.

```
class Set
{
public:
   void add(int n);
   bool contains(int n) const;
   int get_size() const;
   ...
private:
   int* elements;
   int size;
};
```

In a set, the order of elements does not matter, and every element can occur at most once.

Supply the add, contains, and get_size member functions and the "big three" memory management functions.

Exercise P17.7. Write a class Tracer in which the default constructor and the "big three" memory management functions are defined to print trace messages. Use this class to demonstrate

(a) the difference between initialization

```
Tracer t;
Tracer u = t;
```
and assignment
```
Tracer t;
Tracer u;
u = t;
```

(b) the fact that all constructed objects are automatically destroyed

(c) the fact that the copy constructor is invoked if an object is passed by value to a function

(d) the fact that the copy constructor is not invoked when a parameter is passed by reference

(e) the fact that the copy constructor is used to copy a return value to the caller

Exercise P17.8. Define two functions

```
void cout(string& s)
void cin(string& s)
```

The first one removes all consonants from the string s. The second removes all vowels from the string s. Place both functions into a name space whose name is your name and student ID number. Then write a program that prompts the user to enter a string and prints the result of applying both functions.

Exercise P17.9. Define two functions

```
bool endl(string s)
void setw(string& s, char c)
```

The first function returns true if s ends in a lowercase letter. The second function changes all whitespace in s to the character c. Place both functions into a name space whose name is your name and student ID number. Then write a program that prompts the user to enter a string and prints the result of applying both functions.

Exercise P17.10. Write a template Pair<T, U> that stores a pair of objects of an arbitrary type, with a constructor Pair(T a, U b) and member functions T get_first() and U get_second().

Exercise P17.11. Write a template `Optional<T>` that stores an optional element of type T. Here is a typical usage:

```
class Department
{
private:
   ...
   Optional<Employee> secretary;
};
```

Supply a member function

```
bool exists() const
```

that tests whether the optional element exists, a member function

```
void set(const T& t)
```

to set it, and

```
T get() const
```

to get it. As the internal representation, use a `boolean` field and a field of type T.

Exercise P17.12. Repeat the preceding exercise, but use as the internal representation a `T*` pointer. Provide the necessary memory management functions.

Exercise P17.13. Enhance the `List` class of Chapter 16 to throw an exception whenever an error condition occurs. Use exception specifications for all functions.

Exercise P17.14. Change the `Product` class of Chapter 6 so that the `read` member function reads a product record from a file and throws an `IOException` when there is an unexpected problem. Change the `main` function of the `product2.cpp` program to prompt the user for a file name, read the file, and print the best product. However, if an error occurs during reading, offer the user the choice of reading another file name. Test your program with a file that you purposely corrupted.

Exercise P17.15. Change the `database.cpp` program of Chapter 12 so that the `read_employee` function throws a `BadFileException` when there is an unexpected problem. If an error occurs during reading, offer the user the choice of reading another file name. Test your program with a file that you purposely corrupted.

Graphical User Interfaces

▶ To learn about event-driven programming

▶ To learn how to use an application framework

▶ To implement menus and buttons and their associated actions

▶ To understand the concept of layout management for graphical user interface components

▶ To understand window repainting

▶ To be able to implement simple applications with graphical user interfaces

Y ou know how to implement console programs that read input from cin and send output to cout. However, these programs are hardly typical of today's applications. Modern applications have a user interface with menus, buttons, scroll bars, and other elements. Those programs are often called graphical user interface (GUI) applications. Many programmers pronounce GUI as "gooey".

There is an essential difference between a console application and a GUI application. A console application is in complete control of the user input. The program asks the user a series of questions, in an order that is convenient for processing the input. The user must supply the responses in exactly the order in which the program requests them. In contrast, the user of a GUI application can click on buttons, pull down menus, and type text in any order. The user is in charge of providing input, and the program must adapt to the user. For that reason, GUI applications are much more difficult to program than the console applications you have seen so far. In this chapter, you will learn how to create programs with a graphical user interface.

CHAPTER CONTENTS

18.1 The wxWindows Toolkit

Modern operating systems provide libraries for GUI programming. However, those libraries are typically complex and hard to use. Most programmers use a toolkit that provides an object-oriented abstraction layer over the low-level graphical services. By far the most commonly used C++ GUI toolkit is MFC (Microsoft Foundation Classes). MFC is used to write Microsoft Windows programs, and it is a part of the Microsoft Visual C++ compiler.

However, in this chapter, we will use a different toolkit, called wxWindows. The wxWindows toolkit is conceptually very similar to MFC, but it has a number of advantages for our purposes.

- wxWindows is freely available.

- wxWindows runs on several platforms, not just Microsoft Windows. In particular, it runs on Linux and the Macintosh OS.

- wxWindows works with a large number of compilers.

- wxWindows is more transparent to the beginning programmer. MFC is tightly integrated with the Visual Studio environment, and it hides quite a bit of magic behind wizards and builder tools.

- wxWindows is structurally very similar to MFC. Thus, the skills that you learn in this chapter transfer immediately to MFC and other GUI toolkits.

You can download the wxWindows software from `www.wxwindows.org`. The companion Web site for this book contains detailed instructions on how to compile wxWindows programs on a number of platforms.

The following sections contain a step-by-step guide to user interface programming, beginning with a very simple program that displays an empty window and ending up with a GUI implementation of the clock game from Chapter 13. Here are the steps:

1. Create an empty frame window—your first GUI program.
2. Add a text control that can be used to display or enter text.
3. Add menus to the top of the frame window.
4. Add event handling code that is executed when the program user selects a menu item.
5. Lay out buttons and other user interface controls.
6. Paint geometric shapes inside a window.
7. Handle mouse input.
8. Use dialog boxes to obtain user input.
9. Put it all together with the clock game.

18.2   Frames

To get started with wxWindows, you will write a very simple program that simply puts up a *frame*, a window with the typical decorations that the windowing system provides. The decorations depend on the windowing system—Figures 1 through 3 show the same frame under Linux (with the WindowMaker window manager), Macintosh OS X, and Microsoft Windows 98. If you look carefully, you can see that the icons for common window operations, such as minimizing and closing the window, are different. These differences are not important for GUI programming, so you shouldn't worry if the figures shown here look slightly different from your programs.

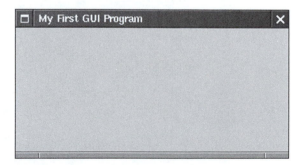

Figure 1

A Frame in Linux (with the WindowMaker Window Manager)

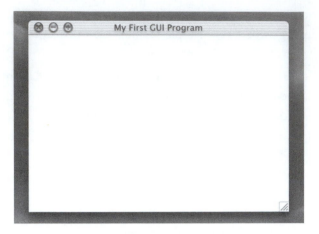

Figure 2

The Same Frame in Macintosh OS X

The program listing at the end of this section shows the program that displays a blank frame (see page 658). As you can see, the program is fairly simple. Let us walk through its features.

To use the wxWindows toolkit in your program, you need to include the header file wx/wx.h. You then define a class that contains details about the workings of your application. This class must be derived from the class wxApp that the wxWindows toolkit provides.

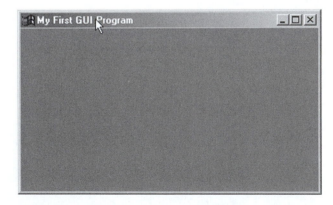

Figure 3

The Same Frame in Windows 98

```
class BasicApp : public wxApp
{
public:
    BasicApp();
    virtual bool OnInit();
private:
    wxFrame* frame;
};
```

Here you specify that your application is identical to the default application defined by wxApp, except that your application has a frame, and that you want to override the OnInit function.

The frame is initialized in the constructor.

```
BasicApp::BasicApp()
{
    frame = new wxFrame(NULL, -1, "My First GUI Program");
}
```

Note the window title "My First GUI Program" in the wxFrame constructor. The other constructor parameters specify that the window has no parent window and a default window ID.

In the OnInit function, you show the frame and return true to indicate that the initialization was successful.

```
bool BasicApp::OnInit()
{
    frame->Show(true);
    return true;
}
```

The names of the wxWindows framework functions (such as OnInit and Show) start with an uppercase letter. That differs from the convention in the standard C++ library, but it is the convention used in MFC. You need to be careful about capitalization when overriding or calling wxWindows functions.

Finally, note that the program listing contains the lines

```
DECLARE_APP(BasicApp)
IMPLEMENT_APP(BasicApp)
```

These are two preprocessor macros, defined in the wx/wx.h header file. These macros carry out some magic that the framework needs to make an application out of the BasicApp class. If you distribute the code for an application class into separate header and implementation files, then you need to place the DECLARE_APP macro into the header (.h) file and the IMPLEMENT_APP macro into the implementation (.cpp) file.

Our BasicApp class inherits a large number of functions from the wxApp class. One of those functions will, at the appropriate time, call the OnInit function. When the user closes the frame, another function of the wxApp class will be called to take care of necessary cleanup. All of this is entirely transparent to the programmer.

The wxWindows toolkit supplies several base classes (such as wxApp) from which programmers derive classes to specify the behavior of their application. Such a toolkit is called an *application framework*. An application framework contains classes that perform a fair amount of complex work, such as interfacing with the operating system and the window environment. However, application programmers need not know about these technical details. They must simply supply their derived classes, according to the rules of the framework.

One of the rules of the wxWindows framework is that you must initialize the top window of an application in the `OnInit` function. It is usually quite difficult for a programmer who learns a new framework to know what exactly is required to build an application. See Productivity Hint 18.1 for some tips.

Compiling a wxWindows program is not as simple as compiling a console program, and the instructions differ quite a bit, depending on your compiler and platform. The companion Web site for this book has quick-start instructions for several popular compilers and platforms. For more detailed information, turn to the wxWindows documentation. You should set aside some time to install the toolkit and compile this simple program—see Productivity Hint 18.2.

Of course, this program isn't terribly exciting—it just shows an empty frame. You will see in the following sections how to add menus, buttons, and text fields, and how to display graphical images in the frame.

File basic.cpp

```
 1  #include <wx/wx.h>
 2
 3  /**
 4      A basic application that shows an empty frame.
 5  */
 6  class BasicApp : public wxApp
 7  {
 8  public:
 9      /**
10          Constructs the frame.
11      */
12      BasicApp();
13      /**
14          Shows the frame.
15          @return true
16      */
17      virtual bool OnInit();
18  private:
19      wxFrame* frame;
20  };
21
22  DECLARE_APP(BasicApp)
23
24  IMPLEMENT_APP(BasicApp)
25
26  BasicApp::BasicApp()
27  {
28      frame = new wxFrame(NULL, -1, "My First GUI Program");
29  }
30
31  bool BasicApp::OnInit()
32  {
33      frame->Show(true);
34      return true;
35  }
```

Productivity Hint 18.1

Learning about a New Toolkit

When you are faced with learning a new framework, you want to look for the following information:

- A tutorial that gives you step-by-step instructions for building simple applications. This chapter is such a tutorial.

- Sample applications that show techniques used in more ambitious programs. The wxWindows distribution contains a number of sample applications.

- Documentation that describes the details of the various classes and functions. For example, you can look up the meaning of the parameters of the `wxFrame` constructor in the wxWindows documentation.

The rules for using a framework are necessarily somewhat arbitrary. It is not necessary or possible to completely understand the details of every function call in the routine code that is needed for initialization and other mundane tasks. Framework programmers engage in a fair amount of "copy and paste" from tutorials and samples. You should do the same when you work with wxWindows. Just start with an application that is similar to the one that you want to create, and modify it.

Productivity Hint 18.2

Becoming Familiar with a Complex Tool

When you first use a complex tool, such as the wxWindows framework, you will likely face quite a few difficulties when trying to compile your first program. Because you don't yet know the "rules of the game", you are likely to make lots of mistakes and it may appear as if success will never come. This is a particularly frustrating experience, and many beginners give up in disgust. Here are a few tips.

- *Set aside plenty of time.* This is the most important tip of all. Learning a new tool is time-consuming for beginners and professionals alike. Trying to do it in a hurry adds a tremendous amount of stress.

- *Expect mistakes.* You will make plenty of mistakes before you hit upon the right pathway. If you hope for instant success, it is very easy to become frustrated and demoralized.

- *Don't think you are stupid.* Even professional programmers find it difficult and frustrating to learn a new environment.

- *Start with an easy task.* Find an extremely simple program, preferably one that you are absolutely certain is correct. Get it to compile and run.

- *Read the error messages.* With a complex tool, lots of things can go wrong. Just saying "it didn't work" will get you nowhere. Of course, the error messages may be confusing. Be on the lookout for clues and for red herrings, just like a detective.

- *Keep a log.* You will likely try several approaches, spread out over hours or days, and observe more details than you can remember. Open your text editor, start a new file, and keep track of the commands that you tried. Paste in all error messages that you got. Include links to promising parts of the documentation.

- *Browse the documentation.* Most programs come with "readme" or installation instructions that contain tips for quick start and troubleshooting. Find them and look at them. It is usually pointless to try to understand everything, but knowing what's where can be very helpful when you get stuck.

- *Try something else.* It is extremely common for beginners to give up because they got stuck with their initial approach. You'll be amazed how often a breakthrough comes from trying some slight variation, no matter how improbable. Of course, the variation won't lead to instant success, but watching how the error messages change can give you invaluable clues.

- *Work with a friend.* It is much easier to tolerate errors and come up with creative approaches when working with someone else.

- *Ask someone who knows.* The Internet has lots of useful discussion groups where people help each other. However, nobody likes to spend time helping a lazy person, so you have to do your own research first. Read through other people's problems and solutions, and formulate your question so that it is clear that you tried your best.

18.3   Adding a Text Control to the Frame

The frame of the preceding example was completely empty. In this section, you will see how to make the frame more interesting. Since you want a more interesting frame than the basic wxFrame, you use inheritance and define your own frame class. As you can see from Figure 4, the frame of this sample program contains a text area into which users can type any text.

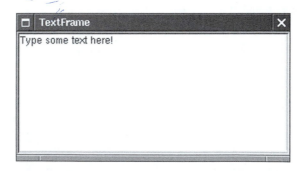

Figure 4

A Frame with a Text Control

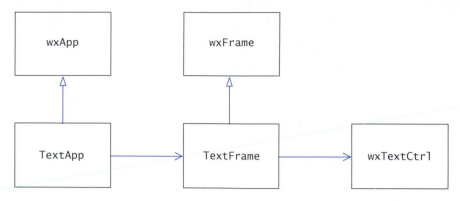

Figure 5

The Classes of the Text Program

Here is the definition of your derived frame class:

```
class TextFrame : public wxFrame
{
public:
   TextFrame();
private:
   wxTextCtrl* text;
};
```

The TextFrame constructor initializes the base class and the text control:

```
TextFrame::TextFrame()
   : wxFrame(NULL, -1, "TextFrame")
{
   text = new wxTextCtrl(this, -1, "Type some text here!",
      wxDefaultPosition, wxDefaultSize, wxTE_MULTILINE);
}
```

The first construction parameter of the wxTextCtrl class denotes that the parent of the text control is this frame. The text control moves wherever its parent moves. (Recall that the frame has no parent—it is a top-level window.) As with the wxFrame constructor, -1 denotes a default window ID. The third construction parameter is the initial contents of the text control. The next two parameters specify a default size and position, and the final parameter turns on the "multiline" style, which allows the text control to hold multiple lines of text.

Now you need to make a slight change to the application class. This time, you want it to show a TextFrame, not a wxFrame.

```
class TextApp : public wxApp
{
public:
   TextApp();
   virtual bool OnInit();
private:
   TextFrame* frame;
```

```
};

TextApp::TextApp()
{
    frame = new TextFrame();
}
```

This application uses inheritance in two places, to customize the application and to customize a frame (see Figure 5). Here is the complete program.

File text.cpp

```
 1  #include <wx/wx.h>
 2
 3  /**
 4      A frame that contains a text control.
 5  */
 6  class TextFrame : public wxFrame
 7  {
 8  public:
 9      /**
10          Constructs the text control.
11      */
12      TextFrame();
13  private:
14      wxTextCtrl* text;
15  };
16
17  /**
18      An application that shows a frame with a text control.
19  */
20  class TextApp : public wxApp
21  {
22  public:
23      /**
24          Constructs the frame.
25      */
26      TextApp();
27      /**
28          Shows the frame.
29          @return true
30      */
31      virtual bool OnInit();
32  private:
33      TextFrame* frame;
34  };
35
36  DECLARE_APP(TextApp)
37
38  IMPLEMENT_APP(TextApp)
39
40  TextFrame::TextFrame()
41      : wxFrame(NULL, -1, "TextFrame")
42  {
43      text = new wxTextCtrl(this, -1, "Type some text here!",
44          wxDefaultPosition, wxDefaultSize, wxTE_MULTILINE);
45  }
```

```
46
47  TextApp::TextApp()
48  {
49      frame = new TextFrame();
50  }
51
52  bool TextApp::OnInit()
53  {
54      frame->Show(true);
55      return true;
56  }
```

18.4   Menus

In this step, you will add a menu to your sample application (see Figure 6).

If you look carefully at Figure 6, you will see that the frame now has a *menu bar*. The menu bar contains the names of the top-level menus. In this case, there is a single top-level menu named "Say". That menu contains two *menu items*, "Hello" and "Goodbye".

Each menu item must have an integer ID number. The ID numbers are used to match up menu items with their actions—you will see the details in the next section. It doesn't matter what the numbers are, as long as the numbers for different actions are distinct. It is customary to give the constants names that start with ID_.

```
const int ID_SAY_HELLO = 1000;
const int ID_SAY_GOODBYE = 1001;
```

Now construct a menu and append the two menu items to it.

```
wxMenu* menu = new wxMenu();
menu->Append(ID_SAY_HELLO, "Hello");
menu->Append(ID_SAY_GOODBYE, "Goodbye");
```

Finally, construct a menu bar object, set it as the menu bar of the frame, and append the menu:

```
wxMenuBar* menu_bar = new wxMenuBar();
SetMenuBar(menu_bar);
menu_bar->Append(menu, "Say");
```

Figure 6

An Application with a Menu

No further changes to the program are required. Here is the complete program listing. Compile the program and verify that the menu works!

File menu.cpp

```
1  #include <wx/wx.h>
2
3  const int ID_SAY_HELLO = 1000;
4  const int ID_SAY_GOODBYE = 1001;
5
6  /**
7      A frame with a simple menu and a text control.
8  */
9  class MenuFrame : public wxFrame
10 {
11 public:
12     /**
13         Constructs the menu and text control.
14     */
15     MenuFrame();
16 private:
17     wxTextCtrl* text;
18 };
19
20 /**
21     An application with a frame that has a menu and text control.
22 */
23 class MenuApp : public wxApp
24 {
25 public:
26     /**
27         Constructs the frame.
28     */
29     MenuApp();
30     /**
31         Shows the frame.
32         @return true
33     */
34     virtual bool OnInit();
35 private:
36     MenuFrame* frame;
37 };
38
39 DECLARE_APP(MenuApp)
40
41 IMPLEMENT_APP(MenuApp)
42
43 MenuFrame::MenuFrame()
44     : wxFrame(NULL, -1, "MenuFrame")
45 {
46     text = new wxTextCtrl(this, -1, "",
47         wxDefaultPosition, wxDefaultSize, wxTE_MULTILINE);
48
49     // initialize menu
50     wxMenu* menu = new wxMenu();
```

```
51     menu->Append(ID_SAY_HELLO, "Hello");
52     menu->Append(ID_SAY_GOODBYE, "Goodbye");
53
54     // add menu to menu bar
55     wxMenuBar* menu_bar = new wxMenuBar();
56     SetMenuBar(menu_bar);
57     menu_bar->Append(menu, "Say");
58 }
59
60 MenuApp::MenuApp()
61 {
62     frame = new MenuFrame();
63 }
64
65 bool MenuApp::OnInit()
66 {
67     frame->Show(true);
68     return true;
69 }
```

18.5   Event Handling

In the preceding section, you saw how to attach a menu bar with menus to a frame. However, when you run the program and select a menu item, nothing happens. Now you will attach actions to the menu items.

Define a function for each action. It is customary to give these functions names that begin with On, such as OnSayHello. Here is the function for the "Hello" menu option. It appends a greeting to the text control.

```
void EventFrame::OnSayHello(wxCommandEvent& event)
{
    text->AppendText("Hello, World!\n");
}
```

Whenever the program user selects the menu option, you want this function to run. In order to do that, you need to build an *event table*. Here is an example of an event table. It routes menu events with an ID of ID_SAY_HELLO to the OnSayHello function.

```
BEGIN_EVENT_TABLE(EventFrame, wxFrame)
    EVT_MENU(ID_SAY_HELLO, EventFrame::OnSayHello)
END_EVENT_TABLE()
```

These entries are again macros, somewhat similar to the IMPLEMENT_APP macro that causes the application to start by constructing a particular application object. The details of capturing user interface events differ among platforms. These macros automatically produce the correct code to capture the events and call the designated functions when the events occur. An event table has the format

```
BEGIN_EVENT_TABLE(ClassName, BaseClassName)
    EVT_TYPE(parameters, function)
    . . .
END_EVENT_TABLE()
```

There are several different event types; you will encounter a couple of them in this chapter. The MENU event type requires a menu ID as a parameter. Other event types may require different information. The final parameter of the event macro is the name of the function that should be called when the event occurs.

The event handler functions have parameters that describe the triggering event. For example, as you have seen, the handler for the "Hello" menu item has a parameter of type wxCommandEvent. That particular handler function has no interest in the event description, but you must nevertheless declare the handler function with the appropriate event type. Otherwise, you will get a bewildering error message when the event macro generates code that doesn't match the rules of the framework.

You need to know which class handles a particular event. Menu events are handled by the frame that contains the menu bar. Later you will see that button events are handled by the window that contains the button.

Finally, you need to insert another macro into the definition of each class that has an event table. For example,

```
class EventFrame : public wxFrame
{
    . . .
private:
    wxTextCtrl* text;
    DECLARE_EVENT_TABLE()
};
```

That macro generates the necessary data fields and function declarations for the event table.

Here is the code for the complete program. Select the "Hello" and "Goodbye" menu items and observe how they append text to the text control.

File event.cpp

```
 1  #include <wx/wx.h>
 2
 3  const int ID_SAY_HELLO = 1000;
 4  const int ID_SAY_GOODBYE = 1001;
 5
 6  /**
 7      A frame with a simple menu that adds greetings to a
 8      text control.
 9  */
10  class EventFrame : public wxFrame
11  {
12  public:
13      /**
14          Constructs the menu and text control.
15      */
16      EventFrame();
17      /**
18          Adds a "Hello, World!" message to the text control.
19          @param event the event descriptor
20      */
21      void OnSayHello(wxCommandEvent& event);
22      /**
```

```
23              Adds a "Goodbye, World!" message to the text control.
24          @param event the event descriptor
25       */
26       void OnSayGoodbye(wxCommandEvent& event);
27    private:
28       wxTextCtrl* text;
29       DECLARE_EVENT_TABLE()
30    };
31
32    /**
33        An application to demonstrate the handling of menu events.
34    */
35    class EventApp : public wxApp
36    {
37    public:
38       /**
39           Constructs the frame.
40       */
41       EventApp();
42       /**
43           Shows the frame.
44           @return true
45       */
46       virtual bool OnInit();
47    private:
48       EventFrame* frame;
49    };
50
51    DECLARE_APP(EventApp)
52
53    IMPLEMENT_APP(EventApp)
54
55    BEGIN_EVENT_TABLE(EventFrame, wxFrame)
56       EVT_MENU(ID_SAY_HELLO, EventFrame::OnSayHello)
57       EVT_MENU(ID_SAY_GOODBYE, EventFrame::OnSayGoodbye)
58    END_EVENT_TABLE()
59
60    EventFrame::EventFrame()
61       : wxFrame(NULL, -1, "EventFrame")
62    {
63       text = new wxTextCtrl(this, -1, "",
64          wxDefaultPosition, wxDefaultSize, wxTE_MULTILINE);
65
66       // initialize menu
67       wxMenu* menu = new wxMenu();
68       menu->Append(ID_SAY_HELLO, "Hello");
69       menu->Append(ID_SAY_GOODBYE, "Goodbye");
70
71       // add menu to menu bar
72       wxMenuBar* menuBar = new wxMenuBar();
73       SetMenuBar(menuBar);
74       menuBar->Append(menu, "Say");
75    }
76
77    void EventFrame::OnSayHello(wxCommandEvent& event)
78    {
```

```
79      text->AppendText("Hello, World!\n");
80  }
81
82  void EventFrame::OnSayGoodbye(wxCommandEvent& event)
83  {
84      text->AppendText("Goodbye, World!\n");
85  }
86
87  EventApp::EventApp()
88  {
89      frame = new EventFrame();
90  }
91
92  bool EventApp::OnInit()
93  {
94      frame->Show(true);
95      return true;
96  }
```

18.6   Layout Management

The next sample program is similar to the preceding one, except that you use buttons instead of menus to add greetings to a text control (see Figure 7).

Conceptually, buttons are very similar to menu items. When the user presses a button, a function is called that carries out the button action. To associate the button with its action, you use an event table. Each button has an ID, and the event table matches the ID with a function.

When you construct a button, you specify the parent window, the button ID, and the button label:

```
wxButton* hello_button = new wxButton(this,
    ID_SAY_HELLO, "Say Hello");
```

Figure 7

An Application with Two Buttons

In the event table of the parent window, you use the EVT_BUTTON macro to specify the event handler function.

```
BEGIN_EVENT_TABLE(ButtonFrame, wxFrame)
    EVT_BUTTON(ID_SAY_HELLO, ButtonFrame::OnSayHello)
END_EVENT_TABLE()
```

The event handler has the same form as a menu event handler.

```
void ButtonFrame::OnSayHello(wxCommandEvent& event)
{
    text->AppendText("Hello, World!\n");
}
```

That's all you need to do to activate a button. There is just one additional problem—you need to make sure the buttons are placed correctly inside the frame. It turns out that placing buttons is more complex than arranging menus. Menus, after all, have a simple layout, on top of the frame. Buttons, on the other hand, can be located anywhere inside a frame.

Some user interface toolkits supply a graphical layout tool to define the placement of buttons, text controls, and other user interface elements in a frame. Such a tool makes it simple to design a user interface with a few "drag and drop" operations. However, the resulting design tends to be fragile. If the sizes of the components change, then the components no longer line up, and someone has to run the tool again to fix the layout. Why would the component sizes change? There are two common reasons. First, if an application is translated to another language, text strings can change dramatically in length and may no longer fit. For example, a button that holds "Goodbye" may be too small to hold the German equivalent "Auf Wiedersehen". Furthermore, if an application is ported to another windowing system, the sizes of buttons, scroll bars, and other elements is likely to change.

If you only write applications for a single language and a single platform, then a "drag and drop" tool is a good solution. But for more robust layouts, you want to describe the logic behind the placement of the user interface elements. Consider for example the layout of Figure 7. We have a text control that expands to fill the entire frame, except for a horizontal row of buttons on the bottom. Those buttons don't expand. The row of buttons is centered horizontally.

In wxWindows, you use objects of the wxSizer class or one of its derived classes to specify the layout of user interface elements. One subclass is wxBoxSizer. It defines a horizontal or vertical arrangement. For example, here is how you line up the buttons horizontally:

```
wxBoxSizer* button_sizer = new wxBoxSizer(wxHORIZONTAL);
button_sizer->Add(hello_button);
button_sizer->Add(goodbye_button);
```

You use a second sizer to place the text control on top of the button row.

```
wxBoxSizer* frame_sizer = new wxBoxSizer(wxVERTICAL);
frame_sizer->Add(text, 1, wxGROW);
frame_sizer->Add(button_sizer, 0, wxALIGN_CENTER);
```

The second parameter of the Add method is a value that tells the sizer by how much to grow the component vertically. A value of 0 does not grow the component—the button row stays at its natural size. You can use different non-zero weights to indicate which components should grow fastest. For example, if you specified a value of 2 for the text control and 1 for the button bar, then the text control would grow twice as fast. If you have only one expanding component, simply give it a weight of 1.

The third parameter of the Add method describes the horizontal growth behavior. We want the text control to grow to take up all horizontal space. But the button bar shouldn't grow—it is kept at its normal size and centered.

Finally, turn on auto layout and tell the frame which sizer to use. Then the frame consults the sizer when it is first shown, and whenever the user resizes it.

```
SetAutoLayout(true);
SetSizer(frame_sizer);
```

Here is the complete program. Run the program and resize the frame. Observe how the sizers grow the text control and keep the button bar centered.

File button.cpp

```
 1  #include <wx/wx.h>
 2
 3  const int ID_SAY_HELLO = 1000;
 4  const int ID_SAY_GOODBYE = 1001;
 5
 6  /**
 7      A frame with buttons that add greetings to a
 8      text control.
 9  */
10  class ButtonFrame : public wxFrame
11  {
12  public:
13      /**
14          Constructs and lays out the text control and buttons.
15      */
16      ButtonFrame();
17      /**
18          Adds a "Hello, World!" message to the text control.
19          @param event  the event descriptor
20      */
21      void OnSayHello(wxCommandEvent& event);
22      /**
23          Adds a "Goodbye, World!" message to the text control.
24          @param event  the event descriptor
25      */
26      void OnSayGoodbye(wxCommandEvent& event);
27  private:
28      wxTextCtrl* text;
29      DECLARE_EVENT_TABLE()
30  };
31
32  /**
33      An application to demonstrate button layout.
34  */
35  class ButtonApp : public wxApp
36  {
37  public:
```

```
38      /**
39          Constructs the frame.
40      */
41      ButtonApp();
42      /**
43          Shows the frame.
44          @return true
45      */
46      virtual bool OnInit();
47 private:
48      ButtonFrame* frame;
49 };
50
51 DECLARE_APP(ButtonApp)
52
53 IMPLEMENT_APP(ButtonApp)
54
55 BEGIN_EVENT_TABLE(ButtonFrame, wxFrame)
56      EVT_BUTTON(ID_SAY_HELLO, ButtonFrame::OnSayHello)
57      EVT_BUTTON(ID_SAY_GOODBYE, ButtonFrame::OnSayGoodbye)
58 END_EVENT_TABLE()
59
60 ButtonFrame::ButtonFrame()
61      : wxFrame(NULL, -1, "ButtonFrame")
62 {
63      text = new wxTextCtrl(this, -1, "",
64          wxDefaultPosition, wxDefaultSize, wxTE_MULTILINE);
65
66      wxButton* hello_button = new wxButton(this,
67          ID_SAY_HELLO, "Say Hello");
68
69      wxButton* goodbye_button = new wxButton(this,
70          ID_SAY_GOODBYE, "Say Goodbye");
71
72      wxBoxSizer* button_sizer = new wxBoxSizer(wxHORIZONTAL);
73      button_sizer->Add(hello_button);
74      button_sizer->Add(goodbye_button);
75
76      wxBoxSizer* frame_sizer = new wxBoxSizer(wxVERTICAL);
77      frame_sizer->Add(text, 1, wxGROW);
78      frame_sizer->Add(button_sizer, 0, wxALIGN_CENTER);
79
80      SetAutoLayout(true);
81      SetSizer(frame_sizer);
82 }
83
84 void ButtonFrame::OnSayHello(wxCommandEvent& event)
85 {
86      text->AppendText("Hello, World!\n");
87 }
88
89 void ButtonFrame::OnSayGoodbye(wxCommandEvent& event)
90 {
91      text->AppendText("Goodbye, World!\n");
92 }
93
```

```
 94  ButtonApp::ButtonApp()
 95  {
 96     frame = new ButtonFrame();
 97  }
 98
 99  bool ButtonApp::OnInit()
100  {
101     frame->Show(true);
102     return true;
103  }
```

18.7   Painting

In this section, you will see how to draw images in a GUI program. Drawing images in a windowing environment is not quite as straightforward as you may think. Consider the program in Figure 8. The program draws an ellipse that fills the entire window. When does the program need to draw the ellipse? Of course, the drawing must happen when the program's frame is first displayed. But that may not be enough. If the user resizes the frame, or minimizes and restores it, or if another frame pops up over it and then vanishes again, the program must redraw the image. The program has no idea when these events will happen. But the window manager knows when the contents of a window have been corrupted. Whenever that happens, the program receives a paint event. Thus, the program needs to draw the image not just once, but *every time a paint event occurs*.

Therefore, you need to place all drawing instructions into a function, and set that function as the target of paint events. Place an entry such as the following into the event table:

```
EVT_PAINT(EllipseWindow::OnPaint)
```

Here is the paint function. It obtains a *device context*, an object that represents the surface of the window. By default, the device context fills the inside of a geometric shape with a fill color. For compatibility with this book's drawing library, we turn that feature off by setting the brush to a transparent brush.

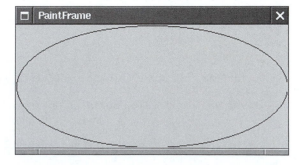

Figure 8

A Program That Draws a Graphical Shape

The device context class has drawing functions such as DrawLine, DrawEllipse, and DrawText. Use the DrawEllipse function to draw an ellipse that fills the entire window.

```
void EllipseWindow::OnPaint(wxPaintEvent& event)
{
   wxPaintDC dc(this);
   dc.SetBrush(*wxTRANSPARENT_BRUSH);
   wxSize size = GetSize();
   int x = 0;
   int y = 0;
   int width = size.GetWidth();
   int height = size.GetHeight();
   dc.DrawEllipse(x, y, width, height);
}
```

The DrawEllipse function is a bit odd. You don't specify the center of the ellipse but the top left corner of the bounding box (see Figure 9).

The device context coordinates are in pixels. The (0, 0) point is the top left corner, and the y-coordinates increase towards the bottom of the screen (see Figure 10). That is a common source of confusion, because it is the opposite of the convention in mathematics (and this book's graphics library).

The device context drawing operations are somewhat less object-oriented than those of this book's graphics library. There are no classes for lines, ellipses, and so on. Instead, you call functions whenever you want to draw a shape. On the other hand, the device context supports many advanced features. You can easily change brush colors, pen sizes, and text fonts. If you are interested in creating fancy drawings, check out the wxWindows documentation for more information.

Finally, note that the OnPaint function does not draw directly on the application's frame but on a separate window of type EllipseWindow, derived from wxWindow. We take the attitude that an "ellipse window" is a user interface element, just like a text control or button, and that it deserves its own class. In Section 18.10, you will see a more realistic

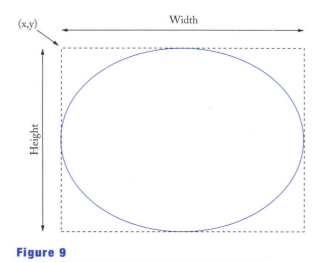

Figure 9

Specifying the Bounding Box of an Ellipse

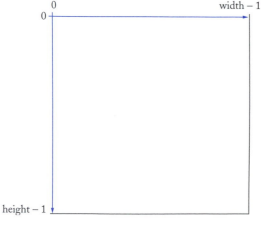

Figure 10

The Device Context Coordinate System

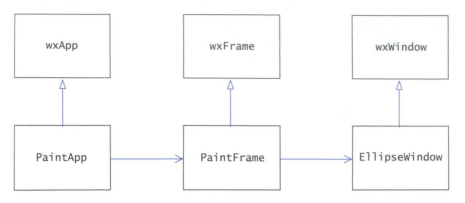

Figure 11

The Classes of the Paint Program

example where the paint function draws a clock in its own `ClockWindow`. That clock window is then placed inside a frame, along with text controls and buttons.

Figure 11 shows the classes of the sample program. Note that we have three derived classes—this program specializes the application, frame, and window classes from the application framework.

Here is the complete program. Run the program and resize the frame. Note how the ellipse is automatically repainted to fit the new frame size.

File paint.cpp

```
 1 #include <wx/wx.h>
 2
 3 /**
 4    A window onto which an ellipse is painted.
 5 */
 6 class EllipseWindow : public wxWindow
 7 {
 8 public:
 9    /**
10       Initializes the base class.
11       @param parent the parent window
12    */
13    EllipseWindow(wxWindow* parent);
14    /**
15       Draws an ellipse on the window.
16       @param event the event descriptor
17    */
18    void OnPaint(wxPaintEvent& event);
19 private:
20    DECLARE_EVENT_TABLE()
21 };
22
23 /**
24    A frame with a window that shows an ellipse.
25 */
26 class PaintFrame : public wxFrame
```

```
27  {
28  public:
29     /**
30         Constructs the window.
31     */
32     PaintFrame();
33  private:
34     EllipseWindow* window;
35  };
36
37  /**
38     An application to demonstrate painting.
39  */
40  class PaintApp : public wxApp
41  {
42  public:
43     /**
44         Constructs the frame.
45     */
46     PaintApp();
47     /**
48         Shows the frame.
49         @return true
50     */
51     virtual bool OnInit();
52  private:
53     PaintFrame* frame;
54  };
55
56  DECLARE_APP(PaintApp)
57
58  IMPLEMENT_APP(PaintApp)
59
60  BEGIN_EVENT_TABLE(EllipseWindow, wxWindow)
61     EVT_PAINT(EllipseWindow::OnPaint)
62  END_EVENT_TABLE()
63
64  EllipseWindow::EllipseWindow(wxWindow* parent)
65     : wxWindow(parent, -1)
66  {
67  }
68
69  void EllipseWindow::OnPaint(wxPaintEvent& event)
70  {
71     wxPaintDC dc(this);
72     dc.SetBrush(*wxTRANSPARENT_BRUSH);
73     wxSize size = GetSize();
74     int x = 0;
75     int y = 0;
76     int width = size.GetWidth();
77     int height = size.GetHeight();
78     dc.DrawEllipse(x, y, width, height);
79  }
80
81  PaintFrame::PaintFrame()
82     : wxFrame(NULL, -1, "PaintFrame")
```

```
83  {
84      window = new EllipseWindow(this);
85  }
86
87  PaintApp::PaintApp()
88  {
89      frame = new PaintFrame();
90  }
91
92  bool PaintApp::OnInit()
93  {
94      frame->Show(true);
95      return true;
96  }
```

18.8   Mouse Events

To handle mouse input in a graphical window, you install a function that is notified when mouse events occur. There are several kinds of mouse events:

- motion
- dragging (moving while depressing a mouse button)
- mouse button going down
- mouse button going up
- clicking (mouse button going down and up within a short period)
- double-clicking

You install the mouse handler with the EVT_MOUSE_EVENTS macro. In the notification function, you can query the wxMouseEvent parameter about the event type. For example, the function ButtonDown returns true for a "button down" event. You can also obtain the mouse position by calling the GetX/GetY functions of the wxMouseEvent class.

In our sample program, we allow a user to specify a triangle by clicking on the three corners. The principal difficulty in this program lies in the fact that the mouse handler is called separately for each mouse press. With each press, we record the mouse position. Then we need to carry out some drawing to give visual feedback to the user.

It is not a good idea to do the drawing in the mouse handler. All drawing should happen in the paint handler so that the logic for drawing is contained in a single location. Depending on the number of corners that have already been specified, the paint handler draws

- a small circle for the first mouse click
- a line after the first two mouse clicks
- a triangle after three mouse clicks

See Figure 12.

Figure 12

The Three Phases of the Mouse Program

The mouse handler stores the corner points and then calls the Refresh function. That function generates a paint event, which eventually causes the paint function to be called. You should never call the paint function directly but always call Refresh to request repainting.

```
void TriangleWindow::OnMouseEvent(wxMouseEvent& event)
{
    if (event.ButtonDown() && corners < 3)
    {
        x[corners] = event.GetX();
        y[corners] = event.GetY();
        corners++;
        Refresh();
    }
}
```

Here is the paint function:

```
void TriangleWindow::OnPaint(wxPaintEvent& event)
{
    const int RADIUS = 2;
    wxPaintDC dc(this);
    if (corners == 1)
        dc.DrawEllipse(x[0] - RADIUS, y[0] - RADIUS,
            2 * RADIUS, 2 * RADIUS);
    if (corners >= 2)
        dc.DrawLine(x[0], y[0], x[1], y[1]);
    if (corners >= 3)
    {
        dc.DrawLine(x[1], y[1], x[2], y[2]);
        dc.DrawLine(x[2], y[2], x[0], y[0]);
    }
}
```

This program is very typical for event-driven programming. Each mouse event causes a small change in the program state, increasing the corners counter and adding values to the x and y arrays. Whenever a paint event occurs, then the paint function consults that state to carry out the drawing operations. It is immaterial whether the paint event is the consequence of a mouse event or some other event.

Whenever you design such a program, it is a good idea to "work backwards" from the paint handler. What are the various kinds of drawings that the paint handler needs to create? What values does it need to have available to create these drawings? Those values need to be a part of the window state. Then ask yourself which events update those values. The code for updating the values needs to be placed into mouse handlers, button handlers, or other event handlers.

File mouse.cpp

```
1  #include <wx/wx.h>
2
3  /**
4      A window on which the program user can draw
5      a triangle by clicking on the three corners.
6  */
7  class TriangleWindow : public wxWindow
8  {
9  public:
10     /**
11         Initializes the base class.
12         @param parent the parent window
13     */
14     TriangleWindow(wxWindow* parent);
15     /**
16         Paints the corners and lines that have already been
17         entered.
18         @param event the event descriptor
19     */
20     void OnPaint(wxPaintEvent& event);
21     /**
22         Adds another corner to the triangle.
23         @param event the event descriptor
24     */
25     void OnMouseEvent(wxMouseEvent& event);
26  private:
27     int x[3];
28     int y[3];
29     int corners;
30     DECLARE_EVENT_TABLE()
31  };
32
33  /**
34      A frame with a window that shows a triangle.
35  */
36  class MouseFrame : public wxFrame
37  {
38  public:
39     /**
40         Constructs the window.
41     */
42     MouseFrame();
43  private:
44     TriangleWindow* window;
45  };
46
47  /**
48      An application to demonstrate mouse event handling.
49  */
```

```
50  class MouseApp : public wxApp
51  {
52  public:
53      /**
54          Constructs the frame.
55      */
56      MouseApp();
57      /**
58          Shows the frame.
59          @return true
60      */
61      virtual bool OnInit();
62  private:
63      MouseFrame* frame;
64  };
65
66  DECLARE_APP(MouseApp)
67
68  IMPLEMENT_APP(MouseApp)
69
70  BEGIN_EVENT_TABLE(TriangleWindow, wxWindow)
71      EVT_MOUSE_EVENTS(TriangleWindow::OnMouseEvent)
72      EVT_PAINT(TriangleWindow::OnPaint)
73  END_EVENT_TABLE()
74
75  TriangleWindow::TriangleWindow(wxWindow* parent)
76      : wxWindow(parent, -1)
77  {
78      corners = 0;
79  }
80
81  void TriangleWindow::OnMouseEvent(wxMouseEvent& event)
82  {
83      if (event.ButtonDown() && corners < 3)
84      {
85          x[corners] = event.GetX();
86          y[corners] = event.GetY();
87          corners++;
88          Refresh();
89      }
90  }
91
92  void TriangleWindow::OnPaint(wxPaintEvent& event)
93  {
94      const int RADIUS = 2;
95      wxPaintDC dc(this);
96      dc.SetBrush(*wxTRANSPARENT_BRUSH);
97      if (corners == 1)
98          dc.DrawEllipse(x[0] - RADIUS, y[0] - RADIUS,
99              2 * RADIUS, 2 * RADIUS);
100     if (corners >= 2)
101         dc.DrawLine(x[0], y[0], x[1], y[1]);
102     if (corners >= 3)
103     {
104         dc.DrawLine(x[1], y[1], x[2], y[2]);
105         dc.DrawLine(x[2], y[2], x[0], y[0]);
```

```
106     }
107 }
108
109 MouseFrame::MouseFrame()
110     : wxFrame(NULL, -1, "MouseFrame")
111 {
112     window = new TriangleWindow(this);
113 }
114
115 MouseApp::MouseApp()
116 {
117     frame = new MouseFrame();
118 }
119
120 bool MouseApp::OnInit()
121 {
122     frame->Show(true);
123     return true;
124 }
```

18.9 Dialogs

When designing a user interface, it is generally preferred to minimize *modes*. A mode restricts what a user can do at any given time, or interprets a user input in a way that depends on the mode. One example of a mode is the overtype mode in a word processor. In overtype mode, the typed characters replace existing characters instead of inserting themselves before the cursor. However, experience has shown that modes burden program users. To anticipate the behavior of the program, the user must expend some mental effort and keep track of the current mode. Mode errors are common. For example, if you accidentally activate overtype mode in a word processor, you delete text and must spend time to correct your error.

Another example of a special program mode is a dialog box that requires immediate input from the user. The user can do nothing else except fill in or cancel the dialog. This too can be burdensome for the user. Perhaps the user doesn't want to fill in all the information right now. Suppose you fill out a dialog box in the word processor, and then you remember that you need to make a change to the document. You can abandon the dialog, losing the information that you already typed. Or you can complete the dialog, and hopefully you then still remember what changes you wanted to make. Issues such as these can subject users to a certain amount of stress, and good user interface designers will want to minimize stressful situations. One alternative is to make a dialog modeless, allowing users to switch back and forth between dialog windows and other windows.

Nevertheless, modal dialog boxes are necessary whenever a program simply cannot proceed without user intervention. They are also very easy to program, so you see them quite often in many applications, perhaps more often than good user interface design would suggest.

The wxWindows toolkit makes it very easy to program several kinds of common dialogs. You can display a message for the user as follows:

```
wxMessageDialog* dialog = new wxMessageDialog(parent, message);
dialog->ShowModal();
dialog->Destroy();
```

Then a dialog pops up (see Figure 13). The dialog is displayed until the user clicks the "OK" button. No other program window receives input until the user dismisses the dialog.

The parent parameter is a pointer to the parent window. The dialog box is placed over its parent window. Often, the code that pops up the dialog is a member function of a class derived from wxFrame or wxWindow. Then you pass this as the parent window pointer.

The message parameter is of type wxString, a class that is similar to the standard string type. You occasionally encounter such library classes that replicate standard library classes, usually because the library was older than the C++ standard. The wxString class has a constructor that accepts a C style (char*) string. We recommend that you use the standard string class for all string computations, then use the c_str function to convert to a C string, which is then automatically converted to a wxString. For example,

```
string message = "Hello, " + name;
dialog = new wxMessageDialog(this, message.c_str());
```

When you are done with a dialog, you should destroy it. That function carries out a "delayed delete". It waits until all user interface messages to the dialog have been processed, and then deletes the memory. (You don't delete or destroy frames, windows, buttons, and menus that are a permanent part of the program.)

Another convenient dialog is the text entry dialog that asks the user to supply a single line of text (see Figure 14). For example,

```
wxTextEntryDialog* dialog = new wxTextEntryDialog(this,
    "What is your name?");
dialog->ShowModal();
string name = dialog->GetValue().c_str();
dialog->Destroy();
```

The GetValue function returns a wxString. That class has a c_str function to convert to a C string, which you can immediately convert to a standard string object.

Figure 13

A Message Dialog

Figure 14

A Text Entry Dialog

Advanced Topic **18.1**

Custom Dialogs

If you want to show a custom dialog, such as the one in Figure 15, you need to derive a class from the wxDialog class. Supply OK and Cancel buttons with the standard IDs wxID_OK and wxID_CANCEL. If the dialog is made up of labeled text fields, you can use a wxFlexGridSizer to lay them out in two columns. Finally, call the Fit function of the dialog sizer to give the dialog the exact size needed to lay out the component.

```cpp
class PlayerInfoDialog : public wxDialog
{
public:
   PlayerInfoDialog(wxWindow* parent);
   string get_name() const;
   int get_level() const;
private:
   wxTextCtrl* name_text;
   wxTextCtrl* level_text;
};

PlayerInfoDialog::PlayerInfoDialog(wxWindow* parent)
   : wxDialog(parent, -1, wxString("Player information"))
{
   name_text = new wxTextCtrl(this, -1);
   level_text = new wxTextCtrl(this, -1);

   wxFlexGridSizer* text_sizer = new wxFlexGridSizer(2);
   text_sizer->Add(new wxStaticText(this, -1, "Name:"));
   text_sizer->Add(name_text);
   text_sizer->Add(new wxStaticText(this, -1, "Level:"));
   text_sizer->Add(level_text);

   wxBoxSizer* button_sizer = new wxBoxSizer(wxHORIZONTAL);
   button_sizer->Add(new wxButton(this, wxID_OK, "OK"));
   button_sizer->Add(new wxButton(this, wxID_CANCEL, "Cancel"));
   wxBoxSizer* dialog_sizer = new wxBoxSizer(wxVERTICAL);
   dialog_sizer->Add(text_sizer, 1, wxGROW);
   dialog_sizer->Add(button_sizer, 0, wxALIGN_CENTER);

   SetAutoLayout(true);
   SetSizer(dialog_sizer);
   dialog_sizer->Fit(this);
}
```

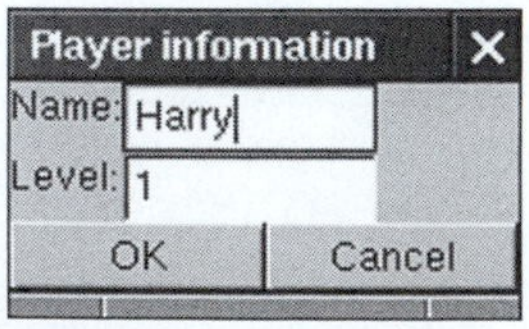

Figure 15

A Custom Dialog

▼

Then you call the ShowModal function in the usual way. That function returns wxID_OK if the user clicked on OK or wxID_CANCEL if the user cancels the dialog.

▼

```
PlayerInfoDialog* dialog = new PlayerInfoDialog(this);
if (dialog->ShowModal() == wxID_OK)
{
        player.set_name(dialog->get_name());
        player.set_level(dialog->get_level());
}
dialog->Destroy();
```

▼

18.10   A Complete Example

In the final example of this chapter, we will put together a longer program, namely a wxWindows version of the clock game of Chapter 13 (see Figure 16). The program has menus, buttons, text fields, dialog boxes, and a paint function. It is a good exercise for you to go through the program code and identify the various event handlers and their purposes. Figure 17 shows a diagram of all classes in the program.

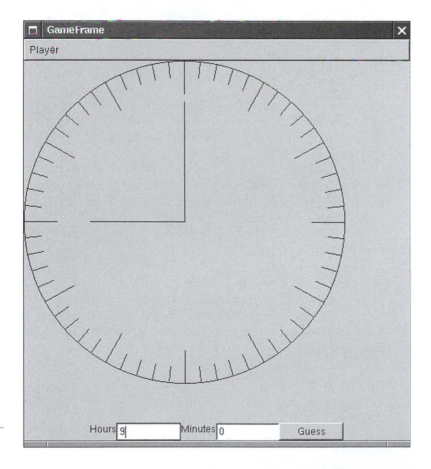

Figure 16

The Clock Game

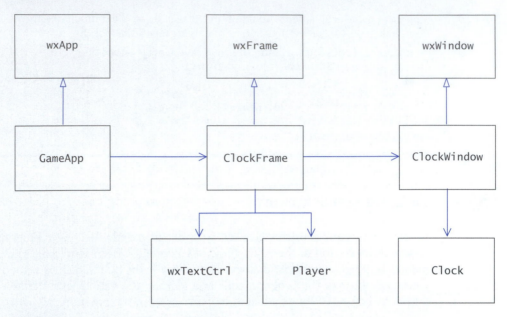

Figure 17

The Classes of the Clock Game

Because of the event-driven nature of GUI programming, several modifications had to be made to the program logic. For example, the original program asks the user for a guess, then asks again if the guess was not correct. In this program, each guess is communicated to the program in the handler of the "Guess" button. The program must keep track whether the guess is the first or second guess. A data field `tries` has been added for that purpose.

The original program queried the user name and level upon startup. The GUI version uses a different mechanism. The user selects menu options that lead to dialog boxes for entering this information. That is actually a better solution—a user can now change the level at any time during the game.

To simplify compilation, the nonstandard `Point` and `Time` classes have been eliminated from this program.

Here is the complete program. As you can see, the GUI programming strategies in this chapter allow you to produce professional looking applications with a relatively modest amount of programming. That is a tribute to the power of C++, classes, inheritance, and application frameworks. By using the wxWindows framework, you inherit a tremendous amount of general purpose functionality, which leaves you to focus on the tasks that are specific to your application.

File game.cpp

```
1  #include <wx/wx.h>
2  #include <string>
3  #include <cstdlib>
4
```

```
5  const double PI = 3.141592653589793;
6
7  const int ID_GUESS = 1000;
8  const int ID_PLAYER_NAME = 1001;
9  const int ID_PLAYER_LEVEL = 1002;
10
11 /**
12    A clock that can draw its face.
13 */
14 class Clock
15 {
16 public:
17    /**
18       Constructs a clock with a given center and radius.
19       @param x  the x-coordinate of the center
20       @param y  the y-coordinate of the center
21       @param r  the radius of the clock
22    */
23    Clock(int x, int y, int r);
24
25    /**
26       Sets the current time.
27       @param h  the hours to set
28       @param m  the minutes to set
29    */
30    void set_time(int h, int m);
31
32    /**
33       Draws the clock face, with tick marks and hands.
34       @param dc  the device context to draw on
35    */
36    void draw(wxDC& dc) const;
37 private:
38    /**
39       Draws a tick mark (hour or minute mark).
40       @param dc  the device context to draw on
41       @param angle  the angle in minutes (0...59, 0 = top)
42       @param length  the length of the tick mark, as a fraction
43       of the radius (between 0.0 and 1.0)
44    */
45    void draw_tick(wxDC& dc, double angle, double length) const;
46
47    /**
48       Draws a hand, starting from the center.
49       @param dc  the device context to draw on
50       @param angle  the angle in minutes (0...59, 0 = top)
51       @param length  the length of the hand, as a fraction
52       of the radius (between 0.0 and 1.0)
53    */
54    void draw_hand(wxDC& dc, double angle, double length) const;
55
56    int hours;
57    int minutes;
58    int centerx;
59    int centery;
60    int radius;
```

```
61  };
62
63  /**
64      The player of the clock game.
65  */
66  class Player
67  {
68  public:
69      /**
70          Constructs a player with name "Player",
71          level 1, and score 0.
72      */
73      Player();
74
75      /**
76          Increments the score. Moves to next level if current
77          level complete.
78      */
79      void increment_score();
80
81      /**
82          Gets the current level.
83          @return the level
84      */
85      int get_level() const;
86
87      /**
88          Gets the player's name.
89          @return the name
90      */
91      string get_name() const;
92
93      /**
94          Sets the player's level.
95          @param l the level
96      */
97      void set_level(int l);
98
99      /**
100         Sets the player's name.
101         @param n the name
102     */
103     void set_name(string n);
104 private:
105     string name;
106     int score;
107     int level;
108 };
109
110 /**
111     The window that shows the clock.
112 */
113 class ClockWindow : public wxWindow
114 {
115 public:
116     /**
```

```
117          Constructs a clock window.
118          @param parent  the parent window
119      */
120      ClockWindow(wxWindow* parent);
121      /**
122          Sets the time of the clock and repaints it.
123          @param h  the hours
124          @param m  the minutes
125      */
126      void set_time(int h, int m);
127      /**
128          Paints the clock.
129          @param event  the event descriptor
130      */
131      void OnPaint(wxPaintEvent& event);
132   private:
133      Clock clock;
134      DECLARE_EVENT_TABLE()
135   };
136
137   /**
138       The frame that contains the clock window and the
139       fields for entering a guess.
140   */
141   class GameFrame : public wxFrame
142   {
143   public:
144      /**
145          Constructs the game frame.
146      */
147      GameFrame();
148
149      /**
150          Starts a new round, with a new clock time.
151      */
152      void new_round();
153      /**
154          Processes the player's guess.
155          @param event  the event descriptor
156      */
157      void OnGuess(wxCommandEvent& event);
158      /**
159          Prompts the player to enter a name.
160          @param event  the event descriptor
161      */
162      void OnPlayerName(wxCommandEvent& event);
163      /**
164          Prompts the player to enter a level.
165          @param event  the event descriptor
166      */
167      void OnPlayerLevel(wxCommandEvent& event);
168   private:
169      ClockWindow* window;
170      wxTextCtrl* hour_text;
171      wxTextCtrl* minute_text;
172      Player player;
```

```
173     int current_hours;
174     int current_minutes;
175     int tries;
176     DECLARE_EVENT_TABLE()
177 };
178
179 /**
180     The clock game application.
181 */
182 class GameApp : public wxApp
183 {
184 public:
185     /**
186         Constructs the application.
187     */
188     GameApp();
189     virtual bool OnInit();
190 private:
191     GameFrame* frame;
192 };
193
194 DECLARE_APP(GameApp)
195
196 IMPLEMENT_APP(GameApp)
197
198 BEGIN_EVENT_TABLE(ClockWindow, wxWindow)
199     EVT_PAINT(ClockWindow::OnPaint)
200 END_EVENT_TABLE()
201
202 BEGIN_EVENT_TABLE(GameFrame, wxFrame)
203     EVT_BUTTON(ID_GUESS, GameFrame::OnGuess)
204     EVT_MENU(ID_PLAYER_NAME, GameFrame::OnPlayerName)
205     EVT_MENU(ID_PLAYER_LEVEL, GameFrame::OnPlayerLevel)
206 END_EVENT_TABLE()
207
208 /**
209     Sets the seed of the random number generator.
210 */
211 void rand_seed()
212 {
213     int seed = static_cast<int>(time(0));
214     srand(seed);
215 }
216
217 /**
218     Returns a random integer in a range.
219     @param a the bottom of the range
220     @param b the top of the range
221     @return a random number x, a <= x and x <= b
222 */
223 int rand_int(int a, int b)
224 {
225     return a + rand() % (b - a + 1);
226 }
227
228 Clock::Clock(int x, int y, int r)
```

```
229  {
230     centerx = x;
231     centery = y;
232     radius = r;
233  }
234
235  void Clock::set_time(int h, int m)
236  {
237     hours = h;
238     minutes = m;
239  }
240
241  void Clock::draw_tick(wxDC& dc, double angle,
242     double length) const
243  {
244     double alpha = -PI / 2 + 6 * angle * PI / 180;
245     dc.DrawLine(
246        centerx + static_cast<int>(
247           cos(alpha) * radius * (1 - length)),
248        centery + static_cast<int>(
249           sin(alpha) * radius * (1 - length)),
250        centerx + static_cast<int>(cos(alpha) * radius),
251        centery + static_cast<int>(sin(alpha) * radius));
252  }
253
254  void Clock::draw_hand(wxDC& dc, double angle,
255     double length) const
256  {
257     double alpha = -PI / 2 + 6 * angle * PI / 180;
258     dc.DrawLine(centerx, centery,
259        centerx + static_cast<int>(cos(alpha) * radius * length),
260        centery + static_cast<int>(sin(alpha) * radius * length));
261  }
262
263  void Clock::draw(wxDC& dc) const
264  {
265     dc.DrawEllipse(centerx - radius, centery - radius,
266        2 * radius, 2 * radius);
267     const double HOUR_TICK_LENGTH = 0.2;
268     const double MINUTE_TICK_LENGTH = 0.1;
269     const double HOUR_HAND_LENGTH = 0.6;
270     const double MINUTE_HAND_LENGTH = 0.75;
271     for (int i = 0; i < 12; i++)
272     {
273        draw_tick(dc, i * 5, HOUR_TICK_LENGTH);
274        int j;
275        for (j = 1; j <= 4; j++)
276           draw_tick(dc, i * 5 + j, MINUTE_TICK_LENGTH);
277     }
278     draw_hand(dc, minutes, MINUTE_HAND_LENGTH);
279     draw_hand(dc, (hours + minutes / 60.0) * 5, HOUR_HAND_LENGTH);
280  }
281
282  Player::Player()
283  {
284     name = "Player";
```

```
285        level = 1;
286        score = 0;
287    }
288
289    void Player::set_level(int l)
290    {
291        level = l;
292    }
293
294    void Player::set_name(string n)
295    {
296        name = n;
297    }
298
299    int Player::get_level() const
300    {
301        return level;
302    }
303
304    string Player::get_name() const
305    {
306        return name;
307    }
308
309    void Player::increment_score()
310    {
311        score++;
312        if (score % 5 == 0 && level < 4)
313            level++;
314    }
315
316    ClockWindow::ClockWindow(wxWindow* parent)
317        : wxWindow(parent, -1),
318        clock(200, 200, 200)
319    {
320    }
321
322    void ClockWindow::OnPaint(wxPaintEvent& event)
323    {
324        wxPaintDC dc(this);
325        dc.SetBrush(*wxTRANSPARENT_BRUSH);
326        clock.draw(dc);
327    }
328
329    void ClockWindow::set_time(int h, int m)
330    {
331        clock.set_time(h, m);
332        Refresh();
333    }
334
335    GameFrame::GameFrame()
336        : wxFrame(NULL, -1, "GameFrame")
337    {
338        // initialize menu
339        wxMenu* menu = new wxMenu();
340        menu->Append(ID_PLAYER_NAME, "Name");
```

```
341      menu->Append(ID_PLAYER_LEVEL, "Level");
342
343      // add menu to menu bar
344      wxMenuBar* menu_bar = new wxMenuBar();
345      SetMenuBar(menu_bar);
346      menu_bar->Append(menu, "Player");
347
348      window = new ClockWindow(this);
349
350      hour_text = new wxTextCtrl(this, -1);
351      minute_text = new wxTextCtrl(this, -1);
352
353      wxButton* guess_button = new wxButton(this,
354         ID_GUESS, "Guess");
355
356      wxBoxSizer* bottom_sizer = new wxBoxSizer(wxHORIZONTAL);
357      bottom_sizer->Add(new wxStaticText(this, -1, "Hours"));
358      bottom_sizer->Add(hour_text);
359      bottom_sizer->Add(new wxStaticText(this, -1, "Minutes"));
360      bottom_sizer->Add(minute_text);
361      bottom_sizer->Add(guess_button);
362
363      wxBoxSizer* frame_sizer = new wxBoxSizer(wxVERTICAL);
364      frame_sizer->Add(window, 1, wxGROW);
365      frame_sizer->Add(bottom_sizer, 0, wxALIGN_CENTER);
366
367      SetAutoLayout(true);
368      SetSizer(frame_sizer);
369
370      new_round();
371   }
372
373   void GameFrame::OnGuess(wxCommandEvent& event)
374   {
375      tries++;
376      int hours = atoi(hour_text->GetValue().c_str());
377      int minutes = atoi(minute_text->GetValue().c_str());
378      if (hours < 1 || hours > 12)
379      {
380         wxMessageDialog* dialog = new wxMessageDialog(this,
381            "Hours must be between 1 and 12");
382         dialog->ShowModal();
383         dialog->Destroy();
384         return;
385      }
386      if (minutes < 0 || minutes > 59)
387      {
388         wxMessageDialog* dialog = new wxMessageDialog(this,
389            "Hours must be between 1 and 12");
390         dialog->ShowModal();
391         dialog->Destroy();
392         return;
393      }
394      if (current_hours == hours && current_minutes == minutes)
395      {
396         string text = "Congratulations, " + player.get_name()
```

```
397                + "! That is correct.";
398            wxMessageDialog* dialog = new wxMessageDialog(this,
399                text.c_str());
400            dialog->ShowModal();
401            dialog->Destroy();
402            player.increment_score();
403            new_round();
404        }
405        else
406        {
407            string text = "Sorry, " + player.get_name()
408                + "! That is not correct.";
409            wxMessageDialog* dialog = new wxMessageDialog(this,
410                text.c_str());
411            dialog->ShowModal();
412            dialog->Destroy();
413            if (tries == 2) new_round();
414        }
415    }
416
417    void GameFrame::new_round()
418    {
419        tries = 0;
420        int level = player.get_level();
421        if (level == 1) current_minutes = 0;
422        else if (level == 2) current_minutes = 15 * rand_int(0, 3);
423        else if (level == 3) current_minutes = 5 * rand_int(0, 11);
424        else current_minutes = rand_int(0, 59);
425        current_hours = rand_int(1, 12);
426        window->set_time(current_hours, current_minutes);
427    }
428
429    void GameFrame::OnPlayerName(wxCommandEvent& event)
430    {
431        wxTextEntryDialog* dialog = new wxTextEntryDialog(this,
432            "What is your name?");
433        dialog->ShowModal();
434        player.set_name(dialog->GetValue().c_str());
435        dialog->Destroy();
436    }
437
438    void GameFrame::OnPlayerLevel(wxCommandEvent& event)
439    {
440        wxTextEntryDialog* dialog = new wxTextEntryDialog(this,
441            "At what level do you want to play? (1-4)");
442        dialog->ShowModal();
443        int level = atoi(dialog->GetValue().c_str());
444        dialog->Destroy();
445        if (level < 1 || level > 4)
446        {
447            wxMessageDialog* dialog = new wxMessageDialog(this,
448                "The level must be between 1 and 4");
449            dialog->ShowModal();
450            dialog->Destroy();
451            return;
452        }
```

```
453        player.set_level(level);
454  }
455
456  GameApp::GameApp()
457  {
458        rand_seed();
459        frame = new GameFrame();
460  }
461
462  bool GameApp::OnInit()
463  {
464        frame->Show(true);
465        return true;
466  }
```

Random Fact   18.1

Visual Programming

Programming as you know it involves typing code into a text editor and then running it. A programmer must be familiar with a programming language to write even the simplest of programs. When programming menus or buttons, one must write code to direct the layout of these user interface elements.

A new *visual* style of programming makes this much easier. When you use a visual programming environment, such as Visual Basic, you use your mouse to specify where buttons, text fields, and other fields should appear on the screen (see Figure 18). You still need to do some programming. You need to write code for every event. For example, you can drag a button to its desired location, but you still need to specify what should happen when the user clicks on that button.

Visual programming offers several benefits. It is much easier to lay out a screen by dragging buttons and menu items with the mouse than it is to write the layout code. Most visual programming environments are also very extensible. You can add user interface elements from third parties, many with sophisticated behavior. For example, a calendar element can show the current month's calendar, with buttons to move to the next or previous month. All of that has been preprogrammed by someone (usually the hard way, using a traditional programming language), but you can add a fully working calendar to your program simply by dragging it off a toolbar and dropping it into your program.

A prebuilt component, such as a calendar chooser, usually has a large number of *properties* that you can simply choose from a table. For example, you can simply check whether you want the calendar to be weekly or monthly. The provider of the calendar component had to work hard to include code for both cases, but the developer using the component can customize the component without any programming.

You should select visual GUI builders with care. Some environments force you to use mouse clicks even when editing a text file would be much faster. For example, it is nice for a beginner to drag and drop menu trees, but experienced programmers find it much easier to modify a text file. A good environment should offer both options. Some environments only remember your mouse clicks, and not the intentions behind them. Then it can be tedious to adapt your visual design to other languages or platforms.

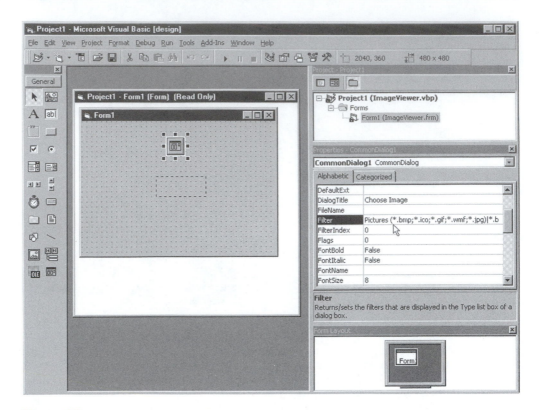

Figure 18

A Visual Programming Environment

A good GUI builder can make building an effective GUI *much* easier than writing the equivalent code in C++. These systems are highly recommended for professional user interface programming.

CHAPTER SUMMARY

1. Graphical user interfaces can be programmed through low-level libraries that are closely related to a particular operating system and window manager, or through higher-level application frameworks.

2. In an application framework, you use inheritance to describe the difference between the generic application classes of the framework and the functionality required by your application.

3. The wxWindows framework is suitable for GUI programming with various platforms and compilers. It is conceptually very similar to the MFC framework for Microsoft Windows programming.

4. The control flow of a GUI program differs greatly from a console program. In a GUI application, the user, and not the program, controls the order in which commands are issued. The program must be able to receive commands independent of a particular order.

5. GUI programs are event-driven. The window manager sends events to the program, and the program provides event handlers—functions that are called when particular events occur.

6. In wxWindows (and MFC), event tables map events to functions. You use different table entries for each event type (such as menu, button, or mouse events).

7. When placing user interface elements in a window, you need to specify the layout of the components. The wxWindows framework uses sizers to specify the sizing rules so that programs can be ported to different languages and windowing environments.

8. A GUI program receives paint events whenever the contents of a window need to be painted. That is the case when the window is first shown, when the contents are overwritten by another window, or when the program requests repainting.

9. Modal dialog boxes interrupt the event flow of a GUI program. The user must fill in the dialog before being able to interact with other windows. The wxWindows toolkit has convenience classes for simple dialogs.

REVIEW EXERCISES

Exercise R18.1. What is the essential difference in control flow between graphical user interface applications and console applications?

Exercise R18.2. List at least eight user interface elements that you have encountered in commonly used GUI programs.

Exercise R18.3. What is an application framework?

Exercise R18.4. What is the essential difference between a frame and a window?

Exercise R18.5. When do you form derived classes of wxFrame and when do you form derived classes of wxWindow?

Exercise R18.6. Into which class do you place the event table of a menu? Of a button? Of paint events? Of mouse events?

Exercise R18.7. What happens if you forget to place the DECLARE_APP or IMPLEMENT_APP macro into your application? Try it out and explain the error message that you get.

Exercise R18.8. What happens if your event table maps an event to a function with the wrong signature? Try it out and explain the error message that you get.

Exercise R18.9. What is the difference between a single-line and a multi-line text control? How do you construct each kind?

Exercise R18.10. Explain why you need sizers to lay out buttons but you don't need them to lay out menus.

Exercise R18.11. Explain under which circumstances paint events are generated. You may want to place a print statement into the paint function of a sample program and find out when it is called.

Exercise R18.12. List the different kinds of mouse events. Find out from the documentation of the wxMouseEvent class how you can tell them apart.

Exercise R18.13. What is a mode in a program? Give three examples of modes in commonly used applications.

Exercise R18.14. What is the difference between a modal and a modeless dialog?

Exercise R18.15. Which wxWindows objects do you allocate on the stack? Which do you allocate with new? Which of them do you destroy?

Exercise R18.16. How do you convert between standard strings and wxString objects? Why are there two separate classes?

PROGRAMMING EXERCISES

Exercise P18.1. Implement a program that shows the growth of a $10,000 investment that earns interest at 5 percent per year. Supply a menu called "Bank" and a menu item called "Add Interest". When the user selects that menu item, add the interest to the current balance and append a message showing the current balance to a text control.

Exercise P18.2. Add menu options to change the current balance and interest rate to the preceding exercise.

Exercise P18.3. Write a wxWindows program that displays a square. Initially, the square is displayed in the center of the window. Supply a menu called "Move" and four menu items called "Left", "Right", "Up", and "Down" that move the square by 10 pixels in the indicated direction. *Hint:* In the event handlers, change the position of the square, then call Refresh.

Exercise P18.4. Implement the same functionality as in the preceding exercise, except supply a row of four buttons to move the square.

Exercise P18.5. Write a wxWindows program that displays the temperature chart of Section 3.6. Since you can't change the coordinate system of the window, you must manually transform logical units to pixel units.

Exercise P18.6. Add a menu option to the program in the preceding exercise that changes the temperature value of a given month.

Exercise P18.7. *Implement a TicTacToe board.* Draw the grid lines and process mouse events. When the user clicks on a field, draw an "x" mark for all even moves and an "o" mark for all odd moves. You don't have to check for illegal moves.

Exercise P18.8. Refine the program of the preceding exercise so that it checks for illegal moves, pronounces winners and ties, and resets the game after a win or tie.

Exercise P18.9. Write a program that paints a clock face at the current time. That is, in the paint handler, get the current time and draw the clock's hands accordingly.

Exercise P18.10. Consult the wxWindows documentation to find out about timer events. Add a timer event handler to the preceding program that refreshes the clock window once a second, so that it always shows the correct time.

Exercise P18.11. Change the clock game by showing the current level in a text control. Place a button "Set level" next to the text control so that the user can change the level at any time.

Exercise P18.12. Write a wxWindows program that implements a different game, to teach arithmetic to your younger brother. The program tests addition and subtraction. In level 1 it tests only addition of numbers less than 10 whose sum is less than 10. In level 2 it tests addition of arbitrary one-digit numbers. In level 3 it tests subtraction of one-digit numbers with a nonnegative difference. Generate random problems and get the player input. The player gets up to two tries per problem. Advance from one level to the next when the player has achieved a score of five points.

C++ Language Coding Guidelines

Introduction

This coding style guide is a simplified version of one that has been used with good success both in industrial practice and for college courses. It lays down rules that you must follow for your programming assignments.

A style guide is a set of mandatory requirements for layout and formatting. Uniform style makes it easier for you to read code from your instructor and classmates. You will really appreciate the consistency if you do a team project. It is also easier for your instructor and your grader to grasp the essence of your programs quickly.

A style guide makes you a more productive programmer because it *reduces gratuitous choice*. If you don't have to make choices about trivial matters, you can spend your energy on the solution of real problems.

In these guidelines a number of constructs are plainly outlawed. That doesn't mean that programmers using them are evil or incompetent. It does mean that the constructs are of marginal utility and can be expressed just as well or even better with other language constructs.

If you have already programmed in C or C++, you may be initially uncomfortable about giving up some fond habits. However, it is a sign of professionalism to set aside personal preferences in minor matters and to compromise for the benefit of your group.

These guidelines are necessarily somewhat long and dull. They also mention features that you may not yet have seen in the class. Here are the most important highlights:

1. Tabs are set every three spaces.
2. Variable and function names are lowercase.
3. Constant names are uppercase. Class names start with an uppercase letter.
4. There are spaces after keywords and between binary operators.
5. Braces must line up.
6. No magic numbers may be used.
7. Every function must have a comment.
8. At most 30 lines of code may be used per function.
9. No `goto`, `continue`, or `break` is allowed.
10. At most two global variables may be used per file.

A note to the instructor: Of course, many programmers and organizations have strong feelings about coding style. If this style guide is incompatible with your own preferences or with local custom, please feel free to modify it. For that purpose, this coding style guide is available in electronic form on the companion Web site for this book.

Source Files

Each program is a collection of one or more files or modules. The executable program is obtained by compiling and linking these files. Organize the material in each file as follows:

- Header comments
- `#include` statements
- Constants
- Classes
- Global variables
- Functions

It is common to start each file with a comment block. Here is a typical format:

```
/**
   @file invoice.cpp
   @author Jenny Koo
   @date 2003-01-24
   @version 3.14
*/
```

You may also want to include a copyright notice, such as

```
/* Copyright 2002 Jenny Koo */
```

A valid copyright notice consists of

- the copyright symbol © or the word "Copyright" or the abbreviation "Copr."

- the year of first publication of the work

- the name of the owner of the copyright

(Note: To save space, this header comment has been omitted from the programs in this book as well as the programs on disk so that the actual line numbers match those that are printed in the book.)

Next, list all included header files.

```
#include <iostream>
#include "ccc_empl.h"
```

Do not embed absolute path names, such as

```
#include "c:\me\my_homework\widgets.h"   /* Don't !!! */
```

After the header files, list constants that are needed throughout the program file.

```
const int GRID_SIZE = 20;
const double CLOCK_RADIUS = 5;
```

Then supply the definitions of all classes.

```
class Product
{
   ...
};
```

Order the class definitions so that a class is defined before it is used in another class. Very occasionally, you may have mutually dependent classes. To break cycles, you can declare a class, then use it in another class, then define it:

```
class Link; /* class declaration */

class List
{
   ...
   Link* first;
};

class Link /* class definition */
{
   ...
};
```

Continue with the definitions of global variables.

```
ofstream out; /* the stream for the program output */
```

Every global variable must have a comment explaining its purpose. Avoid global variables whenever possible. You may use at most two global variables in any one file.

Finally, list all functions of the modules, including member functions of classes and nonmember functions. Order the nonmember functions so that a function is defined before it is called. As a consequence, the `main` function will be the last function in your file.

Functions

Supply a comment of the following form for every function.

```
/**
    Explanation.
    @param argument₁ explanation
    @param argument₂ explanation
    ...
    @return explanation
*/
```

The introductory explanation is required for all functions except `main`. It should start with an uppercase letter and end with a period. Some documentation tools extract the first sentence of the explanation into a summary table. Thus, if you provide an explanation that consists of multiple sentences, formulate the explanation such that the first sentence is a concise explanation of the function's purpose.

Omit the `@param` comment if the function takes no parameters. Omit the `@return` comment for procedures (`void` functions). Here is a typical example.

```
/**
    Converts calendar date into Julian day. This algorithm is from Press
    et al., Numerical Recipes in C, 2nd ed., Cambridge University Press, 1992.
    @param year  the year of the date to be converted
    @param month  the month of the date to be converted
    @param day  the day of the date to be converted
    @return  the Julian day number that begins at noon of the given
    calendar date
*/

long dat2jul(int year, int month, int day)
{
    ...
}
```

Parameter names must be explicit, especially if they are integers or Boolean.

```
Employee remove(int d, double s); /* Huh? */
Employee remove(int department, double severance_pay); /* OK */
```

Of course, for very generic functions, short names may be very appropriate.

Do not write procedures (`void` functions) that return exactly one answer through a reference. Instead, make the result into a return value.

```
void find(vector<Employee> c, bool& found); /* Don't!*/
bool find(vector<Employee> c); /* OK */
```

Of course, if the function computes more than one value, some or all results can be returned through reference parameters.

Functions must have at most 30 lines of code. (Comments, blank lines, and lines containing only braces are not included in this count.) Functions that consist of one long `if/else if/else` statement sequence may be longer, provided each branch is 10 lines or less. This rule forces you to break up complex computations into separate functions.

Local Variables

Do not define all local variables at the beginning of a block. Define each variable just before it is used for the first time.

Every variable must be either explicitly initialized when defined or set in the immediately following statement (for example, through a >> instruction).

```
int pennies = 0;
```

or

```
int pennies;
cin >> pennies;
```

Move variables to the innermost block in which they are needed.

```
while (...)
{
    double xnew = (xold + a / xold) / 2;
    ...
}
```

Do not define two variables in one statement:

```
int dimes = 0, nickels = 0; /* Don't */
```

When defining a pointer variable, place the * with the type, not the variable:

```
Link* p; /* OK */
```

not

```
Link *p; /* Don't */
```

Constants

In C++, do not use #define to define constants:

```
#define CLOCK_RADIUS 5 /* Don't */
```

Use const instead:

```
const double CLOCK_RADIUS = 5; /* the radius of the clock face */
```

You may not use magic numbers in your code. (A magic number is an integer constant embedded in code without a constant definition.) Any number except 0, 1, or 2 is considered magic:

```
if (p.get_x() < 10) /* Don't */
```

Use a const variable instead:

```
const double WINDOW_XMAX = 10;
if (p.get_x() < WINDOW_XMAX) /* OK */
```

Even the most reasonable cosmic constant is going to change one day. You think there are 365 days per year? Your customers on Mars are going to be pretty unhappy about your silly prejudice. Make a constant

```
const int DAYS_PER_YEAR = 365;
```

so that you can easily cut a Martian version without trying to find all the 365's, 364's, 366's, 367's, and so on in your code.

Classes

Lay out the items of a class as follows:

```
class Class_name
{
public:
    constructors
    mutators
    accessors
private:
    data
};
```

All data fields of classes must be private. Do not use `friend`, except for classes that have no public member functions.

Supply a default constructor for every class.

Control Flow

The `if` Statement

Avoid the "`if...if...else`" trap. The code

```
if (...)
    if (...) ...;
else
{
    ...;
    ...;
}
```

will not do what the indentation level suggests, and it can take hours to find such a bug. Always use an extra pair of {...} when dealing with "`if...if...else`":

```
if (...)
{
    if (...) ...;
    else (...) ...;
}   /* {...} not necessary, but they keep you out of trouble */

if (...)
{
    if (...) ...;
}   /* {...} are necessary */
else ...;
```

The `for` Statement

Use `for` loops only when a variable runs from somewhere to somewhere else with some constant increment/decrement.

```
for (i = 0; i < a.size(); i++)
    print(a[i]);
```

Do not use the `for` loop for weird constructs such as

```
for (xnew = a / 2; count < ITERATIONS; cout << xnew) /* Don't */
{
    xold = xnew;
    xnew = xold + a / xold;
    count++;
}
```

Make such a loop into a `while` loop, so the sequence of instructions is much clearer.

```
xnew = a / 2;
while (count < ITERATIONS) /* OK */
{
    xold = xnew;
    xnew = xold + a / xold;
    count++;
    cout << xnew;
}
```

A `for` loop traversing a linked list can be neat and intuitive:

```
for (p = a.begin(); p != a.end(); p++)
    cout << *p << "\n";
```

Nonlinear Control Flow

Don't use the `switch` statement. Use `if/else` instead.

Do not use the `break`, `continue`, or `goto` statement. Use a `bool` variable to control the execution flow.

Lexical Issues

Naming Conventions

The following rules specify when to use upper- and lowercase letters in identifier names.

1. All variable and function names and all data fields of classes are in lowercase, sometimes with an underscore in the middle. For example, `first_player`.

2. All constants are in uppercase, with an occasional underscore. For example, `CLOCK_RADIUS`.

3. All class names start with uppercase and are followed by lowercase letters, with an occasional uppercase letter in the middle. For example, `BankTeller`.

Names must be reasonably long and descriptive. Use `first_player` instead of `fp`. No drppng f vwls. Local variables that are fairly routine can be short (`ch`, `i`) as long as they are really just boring holders for an input character, a loop counter, and so on. Also, do not use `ctr`, `c`, `cntr`, `cnt`, `c2` for five counter variables in your function. Surely each of these variables has a specific purpose and can be named to remind the reader of it (for example, `ccurrent`, `cnext`, `cprevious`, `cnew`, `cresult`).

Indentation and White Space

Use tab stops every three columns. Save your file so that it contains no tabs at all. That means you will need to change the tab stop setting in your editor! In the editor, make sure to select "3 spaces per tab stop" and "save all tabs as spaces". Every programming editor has these settings. If yours doesn't, don't use tabs at all but type the correct number of spaces to achieve indentation.

Use blank lines freely to separate logically distinct parts of a function.

Use a blank space around every binary operator:

```
x1 = (-b - sqrt(b * b - 4 * a * c)) / (2 * a); /* Good */
x1=(-b-sqrt(b*b-4*a*c))/(2*a); /*Bad*/
```

Leave a blank space after (and not before) each comma, semicolon, and keyword, but not after a function name.

```
if (x == 0) ...
f(a, b[i]);
```

Every line must fit on 80 columns. If you must break a statement, add an indentation level for the continuation:

```
a[n] = ...............................................
     + ................;
```

Start the indented line with an operator (if possible).

If a line break happens in an `if` or `while` condition, be sure to put a brace in the next statement, *even if there is only one:*

```
if (...............................................
   && ................
   || ..........)
{
   ...
}
```

If it weren't for the braces, it would be hard to distinguish the continuation of the condition visually from the statement to be executed.

Braces

Opening and closing braces must line up, either horizontally or vertically.

```
while (i < n) { print(a[i]); i++; } /* OK */
while (i < n)
{
   print(a[i]);
   i++;
} /* OK */
```

Some programmers don't line up vertical braces but place the { *behind* the `while`:

```
while (i < n) { /* Don't */
   print(a[i]);
   i++;
}
```

This style saves a line, but it is difficult to match the braces.

Unstable Layout

Some programmers take great pride in lining up the names of structure fields:

```
class Employee
{
    ...
private:
  string   name;
     int   age;
  double   hourly_wage;
    Time   start_time;
};
```

This is undeniably neat, and we recommend it if your editor does it for you, but *don't* do it manually. The layout is not *stable* under change. A data type that is longer than the preallotted number of columns requires that you move *all* entries around.

Some programmers like to format multiline comments so that every line starts with **:

```
/* This is a comment
** that extends over
** three source lines
*/
```

Again, this is neat if your editor has a command to add and remove the asterisks, and if you know that all programmers who will maintain your code also have such an editor. Otherwise, it can be a powerful method of *discouraging* programmers from editing the comment. If you have to choose between pretty comments and comments that reflect the current facts of the program, facts win over beauty.

C++ Language and Library Summary

CONTENTS

- ▶ Keyword Summary
- ▶ Operator Summary
- ▶ Character Escape Sequences
- ▶ ASCII Code Table
- ▶ Standard Code Libraries
- ▶ Containers
- ▶ Algorithms and Exceptions
- ▶ Book Library
- ▶ wxWindows Library

Keyword Summary

Keyword	Description	Reference Location
asm	Insert assembly instructions	Not covered
auto	Define a local variable (optional)	Not covered
bool	The Boolean type	Section 4.7
break	Break out of a loop or switch	Advanced Topic 4.2
case	A label in a switch statement	Advanced Topic 7.1
catch	A handler of an exception	Section 17.5
char	The character type	Section 7.8, Section 9.5
class	Definition of a class	Section 6.2
const	Definition of a constant value, reference, member function, or pointer	Section 2.4, Advanced Topic 5.2, Section 6.2, Section 9.5, Section 10.4
const_cast	Cast away const-ness	Not covered
continue	Jump to the next iteration of a loop	Not covered
default	The default case of a switch statement	Advanced Topic 7.1
delete	Return a memory block to the heap	Section 10.2
do	A loop that is executed at least once	Section 7.6
double	The double-precision floating-point type	Section 2.1
dynamic_cast	A cast to a derived class that is checked at runtime	Not covered
else	The alternative condition in an if statement	Section 4.2
enum	Definition of an enumerated type	Advanced Topic 2.5
explicit	A constructor that is not a type converter	Not covered
export	Export a template to other modules	Not covered
extern	A global variable or function defined in another module	Section 6.9

false	The false Boolean value	Section 4.7
float	The single-precision floating-point type	Advanced Topic 2.1
for	A loop that is intended to initialize, test, and update a variable	Section 7.5
friend	Allows another class or function to access the private features of this class	Section 16.2
goto	Jump to another location in a function	Not covered
if	The conditional branch statement	Section 4.1
inline	A function whose body is inserted into the calling code	Not covered
int	The integer type	Section 2.1
long	A modifier for the int and double types that indicates that the type may have more bytes	Advanced Topic 2.1
mutable	A data field that may be modified by a constant member function	Not covered
namespace	A name space for disambiguating names, or a declaration of an alias	Section 17.4
new	Allocate a memory block from the heap	Section 10.1
operator	An overloaded operator	Section 17.1
private	Features of a class that can only be accessed by this class and its friends	Section 6.2
protected	Features that can only be accessed by this class and its friends and subclasses	Advanced Topic 11.1
public	Features of a class that can be accessed by all functions	Section 6.2
register	A recommendation to place a local variable in a processor register	Not covered
reinterpret_cast	A cast that reinterprets a value in a non-portable way	Not covered
return	Returns a value from a function	Section 5.4

short	A modifier for the `int` type that indicates that the type may have fewer bytes	Not covered
signed	A modifier for the `int` and `char` types that indicates that values of the type can be negative	Not covered
sizeof	The size of a value or type, in bytes	Not covered
static	A global variable that is private to a module, or a local variable that persists between function calls, or a class feature that does not vary among instances	Not covered
static_cast	Convert from one type to another	Advanced Topic 2.3
struct	Defines a class type whose features are public by default	Not covered
switch	A statement that selects among multiple branches, depending upon the value of an expression	Advanced Topic 7.1
template	Defines a parameterized type or function	Section 17.3
this	The pointer to the implicit parameter of a member function	Advanced Topic 10.1
throw	Throw an exception	Section 17.5
true	The true value of the Boolean type	Section 4.7
try	Execute a block and catch exceptions	Section 17.5
typedef	Defines a type synonym	Not covered
typeid	Gets the `type_info` object of a value or type	Not covered
typename	A type parameter in a template	Section 17.3
union	Multiple fields that share the same memory region	Not covered
unsigned	A modifier for the `int` and `char` types that indicates that values of the type cannot be negative	Not covered
using	Importing a name space into a module	Section 17.4

virtual	A member function with dynamic dispatch	Section 11.4
void	The empty type of a function or pointer	Section 5.7
volatile	A variable whose value can change through actions that are not defined in a function	Not covered
wchar_t	The 16-bit wide character type	Not covered
while	A loop statement that is controlled by a condition	Section 4.5

Operator Summary

The operators are listed in groups of decreasing precedence. The horizontal lines in the table below indicate a change in operator precedence. For example,

```
z = x - y;
```

means

```
z = (x - y);
```

because = has a lower precedence than - .

The prefix unary operators and the assignment operators associate right-to-left. All other operators associate left-to-right. For example,

```
x - y - z
```

means

```
(x - y) - z
```

because - associates left-to-right, but

```
x = y = z
```

means

```
x = (y = z)
```

because = associates right-to-left.

Operator	Description	Reference Location
::	Scope resolution	Section 6.4
.	Access member	Section 2.6
->	Dereference and access member	Section 10.1
[]	Vector or array subscript	Section 9.1
()	Function call	Section 2.5

++	Increment	Section 2.3
--	Decrement	Section 2.3
!	Boolean NOT	Section 7.3
~	Bitwise NOT	Not covered
+ (unary)	Positive	Not covered
- (unary)	Negative	Section 2.5
* (unary)	Pointer dereferencing	Section 10.1
& (unary)	Address of variable	Advanced Topic 10.2
new	Heap allocation	Section 10.1
delete	Heap recycling	Section 10.2
sizeof	Size of variable or type	Not covered
(type)	Cast	Advanced Topic 2.3
.*	Access pointer to member	Not covered
->*	Dereference and access pointer to member	Not covered
*	Multiplication	Section 2.5
/	Division or integer division	Section 2.5
%	Integer remainder	Section 2.5
+	Addition	Section 2.5
-	Subtraction	Section 2.5
<<	Output (or bitwise shift)	Section 2.5
>>	Input (or bitwise shift)	Section 2.3
<	Less than	Section 4.3
<=	Less than or equal	Section 4.3
>	Greater than	Section 4.3
>=	Greater than or equal	Section 4.3
==	Equal	Section 4.3
!=	Not equal	Section 4.3
&	Bitwise AND	Not covered
^	Bitwise XOR	Not covered

|	Bitwise OR	Not covered
&&	Boolean AND	Section 7.3
||	Boolean OR	Section 7.3
? :	Selection	Advanced Topic 4.1
=	Assignment	Section 2.3
+= -= *= /= %= &= |= ^= >>= <<=	Combined operator and assignment	Advanced Topic 2.4
,	Sequencing of expressions	Not covered

Character Escape Sequences

These escape sequences can occur in strings (for example, "\n") and characters (for example, '\'') .

Escape Sequence	Description
\n	Newline
\r	Carriage return
\t	Tab
\v	Vertical tab
\b	Backspace
\f	Form feed
\a	Alert
\\	Backslash
\"	Double quote
\'	Single quote
\?	Question mark
\x$h_1h_2$	Code specified in hexadecimal
\$o_1o_2o_3$	Code specified in octal

ASCII Code Table

Decimal Code	Hex Code	Character	Decimal Code	Hex Code	Character	Decimal Code	Hex Code	Character	Decimal Code	Hex Code	Character
0	00		32	20	Space	64	40	@	96	60	'
1	01		33	21	!	65	41	A	97	61	a
2	02		34	22	"	66	42	B	98	62	b
3	03		35	23	#	67	43	C	99	63	c
4	04		36	24	$	68	44	D	100	64	d
5	05		37	25	%	69	45	E	101	65	e
6	06		38	26	&	70	46	F	102	66	f
7	07	\a	39	27	'	71	47	G	103	67	g
8	08	\b	40	28	(	72	48	H	104	68	h
9	09	\t	41	29	)	73	49	I	105	69	i
10	0A	\n	42	2A	*	74	4A	J	106	6A	j
11	0B	\v	43	2B	+	75	4B	K	107	6B	k
12	0C	\f	44	2C	,	76	4C	L	108	6C	l
13	0D	\r	45	2D	-	77	4D	M	109	6D	m
14	0E		46	2E	.	78	4E	N	110	6E	n
15	0F		47	2F	/	79	4F	O	111	6F	o
16	10		48	30	0	80	50	P	112	70	p
17	11		49	31	1	81	51	Q	113	71	q
18	12		50	32	2	82	52	R	114	72	r
19	13		51	33	3	83	53	S	115	73	s
20	14		52	34	4	84	54	T	116	74	t
21	15		53	35	5	85	55	U	117	75	u
22	16		54	36	6	86	56	V	118	76	v
23	17		55	37	7	87	57	W	119	77	w
24	18		56	38	8	88	58	X	120	78	x
25	19		57	39	9	89	59	Y	121	79	y
26	1A		58	3A	:	90	5A	Z	122	7A	z
27	1B		59	3B	;	91	5B	[	123	7B	{
28	1C		60	3C	<	92	5C	\	124	7C		
29	1D		61	3D	=	93	5D	]	125	7D	}
30	1E		62	3E	>	94	5E	^	126	7E	~
31	1F		63	3F	?	95	5F	_	127	7F	

Standard Code Libraries

<cmath>	
Function	**Description**
`double sqrt(double x)`	Square root, $\sqrt{x}$
`double pow(double x, double y)`	Power, x^y. If $x > 0$, y can be any value. If x is 0, y must be > 0. If $x < 0$, y must be an integer.
`double sin(double x)`	Sine, $\sin x$ (x in radians)
`double cos(double x)`	Cosine, $\cos x$ (x in radians)
`double tan(double x)`	Tangent, $\tan x$ (x in radians)
`double asin(double x)`	Arc sine, $\sin^{-1} x \in \left[-\pi/2, \ \pi/2\right]$, $x \in [-1,1]$
`double acos(double x)`	Arc cosine, $\cos^{-1} x \in [0, \ \pi]$, $x \in [-1,1]$
`double atan(double x)`	Arc tangent, $\tan^{-1} x \in \left(-\pi/2, \ \pi/2\right)$
`double atan2(double y, double x)`	Arc tangent, $\tan^{-1}\left(y/x\right) \in \left[-\pi/2, \ \pi/2\right]$, x may be 0
`double exp(double x)`	Exponential, e^x
`double log(double x)`	Natural log, $\ln(x)$, $x > 0$
`double log10(double x)`	Decimal log, $\log_{10}(x)$, $x > 0$
`double sinh(double x)`	Hyperbolic sine, $\sinh x$
`double cosh(double x)`	Hyperbolic cosine, $\cosh x$
`double tanh(double x)`	Hyperbolic tangent, $\tanh x$
`double ceil(double x)`	Smallest integer $\geq x$
`double floor(double x)`	Largest integer $\leq x$
`double fabs(double x)`	Absolute value, $|x|$

<cstdlib>	
Function	**Description**
`int abs(int x)`	Absolute value, $|x|$
`int rand()`	Random integer
`void srand(int n)`	Sets the seed of the random number generator to n.
`void exit(int n)`	Exits the program with status code n.

`<cctype>`

Function	Description
`bool isspace(char c)`	Tests whether c is white space.
`bool isdigit(char c)`	Tests whether c is a digit.
`bool isalpha(char c)`	Tests whether c is a letter.
`char toupper(char c)`	Returns the uppercase of c.
`char tolower(char c)`	Returns the lowercase of c.

`<ctime>`

Function	Description
`time_t time(time_t* p)`	Returns the number of seconds since January 1, 1970, 00:00:00 GMT. If p is not NULL, the return value is also stored in the location to which p points.

`<string>`

Function	Description
`istream& getline(istream& in, string s)`	Gets the next input line from the input stream in into the string s.

class `string`

Member Function	Description
`int string::length() const`	The length of the string.
`string string::substr(int i, int n) const`	The substring of length n starting at index i.
`const char* string::c_str() const`	A char array with the characters in this string.

`<iostream>`

class `istream`

Member Function	Description
`bool istream::fail() const`	True if input has failed.
`istream& istream::get(char& c)`	Gets the next character and places it into c.
`istream& istream::unget()`	Puts the last character read back onto the stream, to be read again in the next input operation; only one character can be put back at a time.

`<iostream>` (continued)

class `istream` (continued)

Member Function	Description
`istream& istream::seekg(long p)`	Moves the get position to position p.
`istream& istream::seekg(` `    long n, int f)`	Moves the get position by n. f is one of `ios::beg`, `ios::cur`, `ios::end`.
`long istream::tellg()`	Returns the get position.

class `ostream`

Member Function	Description
`ostream& ostream::seekp(long p)`	Moves the put position to position p.
`ostream& ostream::seekp(` `    long n, int f)`	Moves the put position by n. f is one of `ios::beg`, `ios::cur`, `ios::end`.
`long ostream::tellp()`	Returns the put position.

class `ios`

Flag	Description
`ios::left`	Left alignment.
`ios::right`	Right alignment.
`ios::internal`	Sign left, remainder right.
`ios::dec`	Decimal base.
`ios::hex`	Hexadecimal base.
`ios::oct`	Octal base.
`ios::showbase`	Show base (as `0x` or `0` prefix).
`ios::uppercase`	Uppercase E, X, and hex digits A...F.
`ios::fixed`	Fixed floating-point format.
`ios::scientific`	Scientific floating-point format.
`ios::showpoint`	Show trailing decimal point and zeroes.
`ios::beg`	Seek relative to the beginning of the file.

`<iostream>` (continued)

class `ios` (continued)

Flag	Description
`ios::cur`	Seek relative to the current position.
`ios::end`	Seek relative to the end of the file.

Notes:
- Older versions of the C++ library don't support the `fixed` and `scientific` manipulators. Use `setiosflags(ios::fixed)` and `setiosflags(ios::scientific)` instead.
- Use `setfill('0')` in combination with `setw` to show leading zeroes.

`<iomanip>`

Manipulator	Description
`setw(int n)`	Sets the width of the next field.
`setprecision(int n)`	Sets the precision of floating-point values to n digits after the decimal point.
`fixed`	Selects fixed floating-point format, with trailing zeroes.
`scientific`	Selects scientific floating-point format, with exponential notation.
`setiosflags(int flags)`	Sets one or more flags. Flags are listed below.
`resetiosflags(int flags)`	Resets one or more flags. Flags are listed below.
`setfill(char c)`	Sets the fill character to the character c.
`setbase(int n)`	Sets the number base for integers to base n.
`hex`	Sets hexadecimal integer format.
`oct`	Sets octal integer format.
`dec`	Sets decimal integer format.

`<fstream>`

class `ifstream`

Member Function	Description
`void ifstream::open(string n)`	Opens a file with name n for reading.

`<fstream>` (continued)

class ofstream

Member Function	Description
`void ofstream::open(string n)`	Opens a file with name n for writing.

class fstream

Member Function	Description
`void fstream::open(string n)`	Opens a file with name n for reading and writing.

class fstreambase

Member Function	Description
`void fstreambase::close()`	Closes the file stream.

Notes:
- `fstreambase` is the common base class of `ifstream`, `ofstream`, and `fstream`.
- At the time of this writing, not all compilers support a `string` parameter for the open function. Use `s.open(n.c_str())` instead.
- With older implementations of the stream library, you may need to supply a second construction parameter to open a file both for input and output:
  `f.open(n, ios::in | ios::out)`

`<strstream>`

class istringstream

Member Function	Description
`istringstream::istringstream(string s)`	Constructs a string stream that reads from the string s.

class ostringstream

Member Function	Description
`string ostringstream::str() const`	Returns the string that was collected by the string stream.

Notes:
- At the time of this writing, not all compilers support the `istringstream` and `ostringstream` class. You can use the `istrstream` and `ostrstream` classes in the `<strstream>` header instead.
- Call `istrstream(s.c_str())` to construct an `istrstream`.
- Call `s = string(out.str())` to get a string object that contains the characters collected by the `ostrstream` out.

Containers

All STL Containers	
Member Function	**Description**
`int C::size() const`	The number of elements in the container.
`C::iterator C::begin()`	Gets an iterator that points to the first element in the container.
`C::iterator C::end()`	Gets an iterator that points past the last element in the container.

Notes:
- *C* is any STL container such as `vector<T>`, `list<T>`, `set<T>`, `multiset<T>`, or `map<T>`.

`<vector>`

class `vector<T>`

Member Function	**Description**
`vector<T>::vector(int n)`	Constructs a vector with n elements.
`void vector<T>::push_back(const T& x)`	Inserts x after the last element.
`void vector<T>::pop_back()`	Removes (but does not return) the last element.
`T& vector<T>::operator[](int n)`	Accesses the element at index n.
`vector<T>::iterator vector<T>::insert(vector<T>::iterator p, const T& x)`	Inserts x before p. Returns an iterator that points to the inserted value.
`vector<T>::iterator vector<T>::erase(vector<T>::iterator p)`	Erases the element to which p points. Returns an iterator that points to the next element.

`<list>`

class `list<T>`

Member Function	**Description**
`void list<T>::push_back(     const T& x)`	Inserts x after the last element.
`void list<T>::pop_back()`	Removes (but does not return) the last element.
`void list<T>::push_front(     const T& x)`	Inserts x before the first element.
`void list<T>::pop_front()`	Removes (but does not return) the first element.
`T& list<T>::front()`	The first element of the container.

<list> (continued)

class list<T> (continued)

Member Function	Description
T& list<T>::back()	The last element of the container.

list<T>::iterator
list<T>::insert(
   list<T>::iterator p,
   const T& x)
	Inserts x before p. Returns an iterator that points to the inserted value.

list<T>::iterator list<T>::erase(list<T>::iterator p)	Erases the element to which p points. Returns an iterator that points to the next element.

<set>

class set<T>

Member Function	Description
pair< set<T>::iterator, bool > set<T>::insert(const T& x)	If x is not present in the list, inserts it and returns an iterator that points to the newly inserted element and the Boolean value true. If x is present, returns an iterator pointing to the existing set element and the Boolean value false.
int set<T>::erase(const T& x)	Removes x and returns 1 if it occurs in the set, returns 0 otherwise.
void set<T>::erase(set<T>::iterator p)	Erases the element at the given position.
int set<T>::count(const T& x) const	Returns 1 if x occurs in the set, returns 0 otherwise.
set<T>::iterator set<T>::find(const T& x)	Returns an iterator to the element equal to x in the set, or end() if no such element exists.

Notes: • The type T must be totally ordered by a < comparison operator.

`<multiset>`

class `multiset<T>`

Member Function	Description
`multiset<T>::iterator multiset<T>::insert(` `    const T& x)`	Inserts x into the container. Returns an iterator that points to the inserted value.
`int multiset<T>::erase(const T& x)`	Removes all occurrences of x . Returns the number of removed elements.
`void multiset<T>::erase(` `    multiset<T>::iterator p)`	Erases the element at the given position.
`int multiset<T>::count(const T& x) const`	Counts the elements equal to x.
`multiset<T>::iterator multiset<T>::find(` `    const T& x)`	Returns an iterator to an element equal to x, or `end()` if no such element exists.

Notes: • The type T must be totally ordered by a `<` comparison operator.

`<map>`

class `map<K, V>`

Member Function	Description
`V& map<K, V>::operator[](const K& k)`	Accesses the value with key k.
`int map<K, V>::erase(const K& k)`	Removes all occurrences of elements with key k. Returns the number of removed elements.
`void map<K, V>::` `    erase(map<K, V>::iterator p)`	Erases the element at the given position.
`int map<K, V>::count(const K& k) const`	Counts the elements with key k.
`map<K, V>::` `    iterator map<K, V>::find(const K& k)`	Returns an iterator to an element with key k, or `end()` if no such element exists.

Notes: • The key type K must be totally ordered by a `<` comparison operator.

•   A map iterator points to `pair<K, V>` entries.

<stack>

class stack<T>

Member Function	Description
T& stack<T>::top()	The value at the top of the stack.
void stack<T>::push(const T& x)	Adds x to the top of the stack.
void stack<T>::pop()	Removes (but does not return) the top value of the stack.

<queue>

class queue<T>

Member Function	Description
T& queue<T>::front()	The value at the front of the queue.
T& queue<T>::back()	The value at the back of the queue.
void queue<T>::push(const T& x)	Adds x to the back of the queue.
void queue<T>::pop()	Removes (but does not return) the front value of the queue.

<utility>

class pair

Member Function	Description
pair<F, S>::pair(const F& f, const F& s)	Constructs a pair from a first and second value.
F pair<F, S>::first	The public field holding the first value of the pair.
S pair<F, S>::second	The public field holding the second value of the pair.

Algorithms and Exceptions

`<algorithm>`	
Function	**Description**
`T min(T x, T y)`	The minimum of x and y.
`T max(T x, T y)`	The maximum of x and y.
`I min_element(I begin, I end)`	Returns an iterator pointing to the minimum element in the iterator range [begin, end).
`I max_element(I begin, I end)`	Returns an iterator pointing to the maximum element in the iterator range [begin, end).
`F for_each(I begin, I end, F f)`	Applies the function f to all elements in the iterator range [begin, end). Returns f.
`I find(I begin, I end, T x)`	Returns the iterator pointing to the first occurrence of x in the iterator range [begin, end), or end if there is no match.
`I find_if(I begin, I end, F f)`	Returns the iterator pointing to the first element x in the iterator range [begin, end) for which f(x) is true, or end if there is no match.
`int count(I begin, I end, T x)`	Counts how many values in the iterator range [begin, end) are equal to x.
`int count_if(I begin, I end, F f)`	Counts for how many values x in the iterator range [begin, end) f(x) is true.
`bool equal(` `    I1 begin1, I1 end1, I2 begin2)`	Tests whether the range [begin1, end1) equals the range of the same size starting at begin2.
`I2 copy(` `    I1 begin1, I1 end1, I2 begin2)`	Copies the range [begin1, end1) to the range of the same size starting at begin2. Returns the iterator past the end of the destination of the copy.
`void replace(` `    I begin, I end, T xold, T xnew)`	Replaces all occurrences of xold in the range [begin, end) with xnew.
`void replace_if(` `    I begin, I end, F f, T xnew)`	Replaces all values x in the range [begin, end) for which f(x) is true with xnew.
`void fill(I begin, I end, T x)`	Fills the range [begin, end) with x.
`void fill(I begin, int n, T x)`	Fills n copies of x into the range that starts at begin.
`I remove(I begin, I end, T x)`	Removes all occurrences of x in the range [begin, end). Returns the end of the resulting range.

<algorithm> (continued)	
Function	**Description**
`I remove_if(I begin, I end, F f)`	Removes all values x in the range `[begin, end)` for which `f(x)` is true. Returns the end of the resulting range.
`I unique(I begin, I end)`	Removes adjacent identical values from the range `[begin, end)`. Returns the end of the resulting range.
`void random_shuffle(I begin, I end)`	Randomly rearranges the elements in the range `[begin, end)`.
`void next_permutation(I begin, I end)`	Rearranges the elements in the range `[begin, end)`. Calling it $n!$ times iterates through all permutations.
`void sort(I begin, I end)`	Sorts the elements in the range `[begin, end)`.
`I nth_element(I begin, I end, int n)`	Returns an iterator that points to the value that would be the nth element if the range `[begin, end)` was sorted.
`bool binary_search(` `    I begin, I end, T x)`	Checks whether the value x is contained in the sorted range `[begin, end)`.

`<stdexcept>`	
Exception Class	**Description**
`exception`	Base class for all standard exceptions.
`logic_error`	An error that logically results from conditions in the program.
`domain_error`	A value is not in the domain of a function.
`invalid_argument`	A parameter value is invalid.
`out_of_range`	A value is outside the valid range.
`length_error`	A value exceeds the maximum length.
`runtime_error`	An error that occurs as a consequence of conditions beyond the control of the program.
`range_error`	An operation computes a value that is outside the range of a function.
`overflow_error`	An operation yields an arithmetic overflow.
`underflow_error`	An operation yields an arithmetic underflow.

Notes:
- All standard exception classes have a constructor:
  Exception_class::*Exception_class*(`string` *reason*)

- The `exception` class has a member function `const char* exception::what() const` to retrieve the reason for the exception.

Book Library

class Time

Member Function	Description
`Time::Time()`	Constructs the current time.
`Time::Time(int h, int m, int s)`	Constructs the time with hours h, minutes m, seconds s.
`int Time::get_seconds() const`	Returns the seconds value of this time.
`int Time::get_minutes() const`	Returns the minutes value of this time.
`int Time::get_hours() const`	Returns the hours value of this time.
`void Time::add_seconds(int n)`	Changes this time to move by n seconds.
`int Time::seconds_from(t) const`	Computes the number of seconds between this time and t.

class Employee

Member Function	Description
`Employee::Employee(string n, double s)`	Constructs an employee with name n and salary s.
`string Employee::get_name() const`	Returns the name of this employee.
`double Employee::get_salary() const`	Returns the salary of this employee.
`void Employee::set_salary(double s)`	Sets salary of this employee to s.

"ccc_win.h"

class GraphicWindow

Member Function	Description

void GraphicWindow::coord(
    double x1, double y1, double x2,
    double y2)
	Sets the coordinate system for subsequent drawing; (x1, y1) is the top left corner, (x2, y2) is the bottom right corner.

void GraphicWindow::clear()	Clears the window (that is, erases its contents).
string GraphicWindow::get_string(string p)	Displays prompt p and returns the entered string.
int GraphicWindow::get_int(string p)	Displays prompt p and returns the entered integer.
double GraphicWindow::get_double(string p)	Displays prompt p and returns the entered value.
Point GraphicWindow::get_mouse(string p)	Displays prompt p and returns the mouse click point.

class Point

Member Function	Description
Point::Point(double x, double y)	Constructs a point at location (x, y).
double Point::get_x() const	Returns the x-coordinate of the point.
double Point::get_y() const	Returns the y-coordinate of the point.
void Point::move(double dx, double dy)	Moves the point by (dx, dy).

class Circle

Member Function	Description
Circle::Circle(Point p, double r)	Constructs a circle with center p and radius r.
Point Circle::get_center() const	Returns the center point of the circle.
double Circle::get_radius() const	Returns the radius of the circle.
void Circle::move(double dx, double dy)	Moves the circle by (dx, dy).

"ccc_win.h" (continued)

class Line

Member Function	Description
`Line::Line(Point p, Point q)`	Constructs a line joining the points p and q.
`Point Line::get_start() const`	Returns the starting point of the line.
`Point Line::get_end() const`	Returns the ending point of the line.
`void Line::move(double dx, double dy)`	Moves the line by (dx, dy).

class Message

Member Function	Description
`Message::Message(Point p, string s)`	Constructs a message with starting point p and text string s.
`Message::Message(Point p, double x)`	Constructs a message with starting point p and label equal to the number x.
`Point Message::get_start() const`	Returns the starting point of the message.
`string Message::get_text() const`	Gets the text string of the message.
`void Message::move(double dx, double dy)`	Moves the message by (dx, dy).

wxWindows Library

<wx/wx.h>

class wxApp

Member Function	Description
`bool wxApp::OnInit()`	Overrides this function to initialize the application. Returns true to continue, false to terminate.

class wxFrame

Member Function	Description
`wxFrame::wxFrame(wxWindow* parent, wxWindowID id, const wxString& title)`	Constructs a frame. Use NULL if the frame has no parent and -1 for a default ID.
`void SetMenuBar(wxMenuBar* menu_bar)`	Sets the menu bar.

`<wx/wx.h>` (continued)

class `wxWindow`

Member Function	Description
`void wxWindow::show(bool b)`	If b is true, shows the window. Otherwise, hides the window.
`wxSize wxWindow::getSize() const`	Gets the size of the window in pixels.
`void Refresh()`	Causes the window to be repainted.
`void wxWindow::SetAutoLayout(bool b)`	If b is true, the window is automatically laid out whenever it is resized.
`void wxWindow::setSizer( wxSizer* sizer)`	Sets a sizer to lay out the controls in this window.
`bool wxWindow::Destroy()`	Deletes this window and its children. Returns true if the window is destroyed immediately, false if the window will be destroyed later.

Notes: • `wxWindow` is the common base class of `wxFrame`, `wxPanel`, and `wxDialog`.

class `wxTextCtrl`

Member Function	Description
`wxTextCtrl::wxTextCtrl(wxWindow* parent, int id)`	Constructs a single-line text control with the given parent and ID. Use -1 for a default ID.
`wxTextCtrl::wxTextCtrl(wxWindow* parent, int id, const wxString& value, const wxPoint& pos, const wxSize& size, long style)`	Constructs a text control. Use -1 for a default ID, `wxDefaultPosition` and `wxDefaultSize` for default position and size, and a style of `wxTE_MULTILINE` to display multiple lines of text.
`void wxTextCtrl::AppendText( const wxString& text)`	Appends text to this text control.

class `wxStaticText`

Member Function	Description
`wxStaticText::wxStaticText(wxWindow* parent, int id, const wxString& text)`	Constructs a static text control. Use -1 for a default ID.

`<wx/wx.h>` (continued)

class `wxMenu`

Member Function	Description
`wxMenu::wxMenu()`	Constructs an empty menu.
`void wxMenu::Append(int id, const` 　`wxString& item)`	Appends a menu item with the given ID.
`void wxMenu::Append(int id, const` 　`wxString& name, wxMenu* sub_menu)`	Appends a submenu with the given name. You can use -1 for the ID.

class `wxMenuBar`

Member Function	Description
`wxMenuBar::wxMenuBar()`	Constructs an empty menu bar.
`void wxMenu::Append(wxMenu* menu,` 　`const wxString& name)`	Appends a menu with the given name.

class `wxButton`

Member Function	Description
`wxButton::wxButton(wxWindow* parent,` 　`int id, const wxString& name)`	Constructs a button.

class `wxBoxSizer`

Member Function	Description
`wxBoxSizer::wxBoxSizer(` 　`int orientation)`	Constructs a box sizer that lays out components in one direction. `orientation` is `wxHORIZONTAL` or `wxVERTICAL`.

class `wxFlexGridSizer`

Member Function	Description
`wxFlexGridSizer::wxFlexGridSizer(` 　`int columns)`	A sizer that arranges its children into rows and columns.

<wx/wx.h> (continued)

class wxSizer

Member Function	Description
`void wxSizer::Add(wxWindow* window)`	Adds the given window to this sizer.
`void wxSizer::Add(wxSizer* item, int option, int flag)`	Adds a control or child sizer to a sizer. The `option` parameter is relevant for `wxBoxSizer` only; it is a weight that indicates the growth relative to the other item weights. The `flag` should be `wxGROW`, `wxALIGN_CENTER`, `wxALIGN_LEFT`, `wxALIGN_TOP`, `wxALIGN_RIGHT`, or `wxALIGN_BOTTOM`.
`void wxSizer::Fit(wxWindow* window)`	Fits the window to match the sizer's minimum size.

class wxPaintDC

Member Function	Description
`wxPaintDC::wxPaintDC(wxWindow* window)`	Constructs a paint device context for the given window.

class wxDC

Member Function	Description
`void wxDC::SetBrush(const wxBrush& brush)`	Sets the brush that is used for filling areas. Use `*wxTRANSPARENT_BRUSH` to turn off filling.
`void wxDC::DrawLine(int x1, int x2, int y1, int y2)`	Draws a line from (x1, y1) to (x2, y2).
`void wxDC::DrawEllipse(int x, int y, int width, int height)`	Draws an ellipse whose bounding box has top left corner (x, y) and the given width and height.
`void wxDC::DrawText(int x, int y, const wxString& text)`	Draws text whose top-left corner is at (x, y).

<wx/wx.h> (continued)

class wxMouseEvent

Member Function	Description
`wxPoint wxMouseEvent::GetPosition() const`	Gets the mouse position of this event.
`bool wxMouseEvent::ButtonDown()`	Returns true if this is a button down event.
`bool wxMouseEvent::ButtonUp()`	Returns true if this is a button up event.
`bool wxMouseEvent::Moving()`	Returns true if this is a motion event (no button down).
`bool wxMouseEvent::Dragging()`	Returns true if this is a drag event (moving with button down).

class wxMessageDialog

Member Function	Description
`wxMessageDialog::wxMessageDialog(wxWindow* parent, const wxString& message)`	Constructs a dialog that displays a message.

class wxTextEntryDialog

Member Function	Description
`wxTextEntryDialog::wxTextEntryDialog( wxWindow* parent, const wxString& prompt)`	Constructs a dialog that prompts the user to enter a text string.
`wxString wxTextEntryDialog::GetValue() const`	Gets the value that the user supplied.

class wxDialog

Member Function	Description
`wxDialog::wxDialog(wxWindow* parent, int id, const wxString& title)`	Constructs a dialog. Use –1 for a default ID.
`bool wxDialog::ShowModal()`	Shows the dialog and waits until the user accepts or cancels it. Returns true if the user accepts the dialog.

class wxString

Member Function	Description
`wxString::wxString(const char* s)`	Constructs a wxString from a character array.
`const char* wxString::c_str() const`	Returns the character array contained in this wxString.

<wx/wx.h> (continued)

class wxSize

Member Function	Description
int wxSize::GetWidth() const	Gets the width of this size.
int wxSize::GetHeight() const	Gets the height of this size.

class wxPoint

Data Field	Description
int wxPoint::x	The public field containing the x-value.
int wxPoint::y	The public field containing the y-value.

Macro	Description
DECLARE_APP(AppClass)	Place in header file of AppClass. The class must inherit from wxApp.
IMPLEMENT_APP(AppClass)	Place in source file of AppClass.
DECLARE_EVENT_TABLE()	Place in class that contains event handler functions.
BEGIN_EVENT_TABLE(Class, BaseClass)	Begins defining event handlers.
END_EVENT_TABLE()	Ends defining event handlers.
EVT_MENU(id, Class::function)	Declares a menu event handler. The function must have the form void Class::function(wxCommandEvent& event).
EVT_BUTTON(id, Class::function)	Declares a button event handler. The function must have the form void Class::function(wxCommandEvent& event).
EVT_PAINT(Class::function)	Declares a paint event handler. The function must have the form void Class::function(wxPaintEvent& event).
EVT_MOUSE_EVENTS(Class:: function)	Declares a mouse event handler. The function must have the form void Class::function(wxMouseEvent& event).

Glossary

Accessor function A function that accesses an object but does not change it.

Address A value that specifies the location of a variable in memory.

Aggregation relationship The "has-a" relationship between classes.

Algorithm An unambiguous, executable, and terminating specification to solve a problem.

ANSI/ISO C++ Standard The standard for the C++ language that was developed by the American National Standards Institute and the International Standards Organization.

Argument A parameter value in a function call, or one of the values combined by an operator.

Array A collection of values of the same type, each of which can be accessed by an integer index.

Arrow operator The -> operator. p->m is the same as (*p).m.

ASCII code The American Standard Code for Information Interchange, which associates code values between 0 and 127 to letters, digits, punctuation marks, and control characters.

Assertion A claim that a certain condition holds in a particular program location; often tested with the assert macro.

Assignment Placing a new value into a variable.

Association A relationship between classes in which one can navigate from objects of one class to objects of the other class, usually by following object references.

Base class A class from which another class is derived.

Big-Oh notation The notation $g(n) = O(f(n))$, which denotes that the function g grows at a rate that is bounded by the growth rate of the function f with respect to n. For example, $10n^2 + 100n - 1000 = O(n^2)$.

"Big three" management functions The three management functions that are essential for classes that manage heap memory or other resources: copy constructor, destructor, and assignment operator.

Binary file A file in which values are stored in their binary representation and cannot be read as text.

Binary operator An operator that takes two arguments, for example in $x + y$.

Binary search A fast algorithm to find a value in a sorted array. It narrows the search down to half of the array in every step.

Binary tree A tree in which each node has at most two child nodes.

Bit Binary digit; the smallest unit of information, having two possible values, 0 and 1. A data element consisting of n bits has 2^n possible values.

Black-box testing Testing functions without knowing their implementation.

Block A group of statements bracketed by { }.

Boolean operator A logical operator

Boolean type A type with two values, `true` and `false`.

Boundary test case A test case involving values that are at the outer boundary of the set of legal values. For example, if a function is expected to work for all nonnegative integers, then 0 is a boundary test case.

Bounds error Trying to access an array element that is outside the legal range.

break statement A statement that terminates a loop or `switch` statement.

Breakpoint A point in a program, specified in a debugger, at which the debugger stops executing the program and lets the user inspect the program state.

Buffered input Input that is gathered in batches, for example, one line at a time.

Byte A number between 0 and 255 (eight bits). Essentially all currently manufactured computers use a byte as the smallest unit of storage in memory.

Call stack The set of all functions that currently have been called but not terminated, starting with the current function and ending with `main`.

Case-sensitive Distinguishing upper- and lowercase characters.

Cast Converting a value from one type to a different type. For example, the cast from a floating-point number x to an integer is expressed in C++ by the cast notation, `static_cast<int>(x)`.

Class A programmer-defined data type.

Command line The line you type when you start a program in a command window in Windows or UNIX. It consists of the program name and the command line arguments.

Comment An explanation to make the human reader understand a section of a program; ignored by the compiler.

Compiler A program that translates code in a high-level language such as C++ to machine instructions.

Compile-time error See Syntax error.

Compound statement A statement such as `if` or `for` that is made up of several parts (condition, body).

Concatenation Placing one string after another.

Constant A value that cannot be changed by the program.

Construction Setting a newly allocated object to an initial value.

Constructor A function that initializes a newly allocated object.

Copy constructor A function that initializes an object as a copy of another.

Coupling The degree to which classes are related to each other by dependency.

CPU (Central Processing Unit) The part of a computer that executes the machine instructions.

Dangling pointer A pointer that does not point to a valid location.

Data field A variable that is present in every object of a class.

Debugger A program that lets a user run another program one or a few steps at a time, stop execution, and inspect the variables in order to analyze it for bugs.

Declaration A statement that announces the existence of a variable, function, or class but does not define it.

Default constructor A constructor that can be invoked with no parameters.

#define directive A directive that defines constant values and macros for the preprocessor. Values can be queried during the preprocessing phase with the #if and #ifdef directives. Macros are replaced by the preprocessor when they are encountered in the program file.

Definition A statement or series of statements that fully describes a variable, a function and its implementation, a type, or a class and its properties.

delete operator The operator that recycles memory to the heap.

Dereferencing Locating an object when a pointer to the object is given.

Derived class A class that modifies a base class by adding data fields or member functions or by redefining member functions.

Destructor A function that is executed whenever an object goes out of scope.

Dictionary ordering Lexicographic ordering.

Directory A structure on a disk that can hold files or other directories; also called a folder.

Dot notation The notation *object.function(parameters)* used to invoke a member function on an object.

Doubly linked list A linked list in which each list has a pointer to both its predecessor and successor nodes.

Dynamic binding Selecting a particular function to be called, depending on the exact type of the object invoking the function when the program executes.

Dynamic memory allocation Allocating memory as a program runs as required by the program's needs.

Encapsulation The hiding of implementation details.

End of file Condition that is true when all characters of a file have been read. Note that there is no special "end-of-file character". When composing a file on the keyboard, you may need to type a special character to tell the operating system to end the file, but that character is not part of the file.

Enumerated type A type with a finite number of values, each of which has its own symbolic name.

Escape character A character in text that is not taken literally but has a special meaning when combined with the character or characters that follow it. The \ character is an escape character in C++ strings.

Exception A class that signals a condition that prevents the program from continuing normally. When such a condition occurs, an exception object is thrown.

Exception handler A sequence of statements that is given control when an exception of a particular type has been thrown and caught.

Executable file The file that contains a program's machine instructions.

Explicit parameter A parameter of a member function other than the object invoking the function.

Expression A syntactical construct that is made up of constants, variables, function calls, and the operators combining them.

Extension The last part of a file name, which specifies the file type. For example, the extension .cpp denotes a C++ file.

Failed stream state The state of a stream after an invalid operation has been attempted, such as reading a number when the next stream position yielded a nondigit, or reading after the end of file was reached.

Fibonacci numbers The sequence of numbers 1, 1, 2, 3, 5, 8, 13, . . ., in which every term is the sum of its two predecessors.

Field accessor A member function that returns the value of a data field.

Field mutator A member function that sets a data field to a new value.

File A sequence of bytes that is stored on disk.

File pointer The position within a file of the next byte to be read or written. It can be moved so as to access any byte in the file.

Floating-point number A number with a fractional part.

Folder Directory.

Function A sequence of statements that can be invoked multiple times, with different values for its parameters.

Garbage collection Automatic reclamation of heap memory that is no longer needed; C++ does not have garbage collection.

Global variable A variable whose scope is not restricted to a single function.

goto statement A statement that transfers control to a different statement that is tagged with a label.

grep The "global regular expression print" search program, useful for finding all strings matching a pattern in a set of files.

Header file A file that informs the compiler of features that are available in another module or library.

Heap A reservoir of storage from which memory can be allocated when a program runs.

IDE (Integrated Development Environment) A programming environment that includes an editor, compiler, and debugger.

#if directive A directive to the preprocessor to include the code contained between the #if and the matching #endif if a condition is true.

Implicit parameter The object that calls a member function. For example, in the call x.f(y), the object x is the implicit parameter of f.

#include directive An instruction to the preprocessor to include a header file.

Inheritance The "is-a" relationship between a general base class and a specialized derived class.

Initialization Setting a variable to a well-defined value when it is created.

Instantiation of a class Constructing an object of that class.

Integer A number without a fractional part.

Integer division Taking the quotient of two integers, discarding the remainder. In C++, the / symbol denotes integer division if both arguments are integers. For example, 11 / 4 is 2, not 2.75.

Interface The set of functions that can be applied to objects of a given type.

Iterator An object that can inspect all elements in a container such as a linked list.

javadoc The documentation generator in the Java SDK. It extracts documentation comments from Java source files and produces a set of linked HTML files.

Lexicographic ordering Ordering strings in the same order as in a dictionary, by skipping all matching characters and comparing the first nonmatching characters of both strings. For example, "orbit" comes before "orchid" in the lexicographic ordering. Note that in C++, unlike a dictionary, the ordering is case-sensitive: z comes before a.

Library A set of precompiled functions that can be included in programs.

Linear search Searching a container (such as an array, list, or vector) for an object by inspecting each element in turn.

Linked list A data structure that can hold an arbitrary number of objects, each of which is stored in a node object, which contains a pointer to the next node.

Linker The program that combines object and library files into an executable file.

Local variable A variable whose scope is a single block.

Logic error An error in a syntactically correct program that causes it to act differently from its specification.

Logical operator An operator that can be applied to Boolean values. C++ has three logical operators: &&, ||, and !.

Loop A sequence of instructions that is executed repeatedly.

Loop and a half A loop whose termination decision is neither at the beginning nor at the end.

Loop invariant A statement about the program state that is preserved when the statements in the loop are executed once.

Machine code Instructions that can be executed directly by the CPU.

Macro A mechanism to replace a command with a predefined sequence of other commands.

Magic number A number that appears in a program without explanation.

main function The function that is first called when a program executes.

make file A file that contains directives for how to build a program by compiling and linking the constituent files. When the make program is run, only those source files that are newer than their corresponding object files are rebuilt.

Member function A function that is defined by a class and operates on objects of that class.

Merge sort A sorting algorithm that first sorts two halves of an array and then merges the sorted subarrays together.

Module A program unit that contains related classes and functions. C++ has no explicit support for modules. By convention, each module is stored in a separate source file.

Mutator function A member function that changes the state of an object.

Name clash Accidentally using the same name to denote two program features in a way that cannot be resolved by the compiler.

Negative test case A test case that is expected to fail. For example, when testing a root-finding program, an attempt to compute the fourth root of 1 is a negative test case.

Nested block A block that is contained inside another block.

new operator The operator that allocates new memory from the heap.

Newline The '\n' character, which indicates the end of a line.

Null pointer The value that indicates that a pointer does not point to any object.

Object A value of a user-defined type.

Object file A file that contains machine instructions from a module. Object files must be combined with library files by the linker to form an executable file.

Object-oriented design Designing a program by discovering objects, their properties, and their relationships.

Off-by-one error A common programming error in which a value is one larger or smaller than it should be.

Opening a file Preparing a file for reading or writing.

Operating system The software that launches application programs and provides services (such as a file system) for those programs.

Operator A symbol denoting a mathematical or logical operation, such as + or and.

Operator associativity The rule that governs in which order operators of the same precedence are executed. For example, in C++ the - operator is left-associative, since a - b - c is interpreted as (a - b) - c, and = is right-associative, since a = b = c is interpreted as a = (b = c).

Operator precedence The rule that governs which operator is evaluated first. For example, in C++ the && operator has a higher precedence than the || operator. Hence a || b && c is interpreted as a || (b && c).

Oracle A program that predicts how another program should behave.

Overloading Giving more than one meaning to a function name or operator.

Parallel vectors Vectors of the same length, in which corresponding elements are logically related.

Parameter The values in the execution of a function that can be set when the function is called. For example, in the function `double root(int n, float x)`, n and x are parameters.

Parameter passing Using expressions to initialize the parameter variables of a function when it is called.

Parameter value The expression supplied for a parameter by the caller of a function.

Parameter variable A variable in a function that is initialized with the parameter value when the function is called.

Pointer A value that denotes the memory location of an object.

Polymorphism Selecting a function among several functions with the same name, by comparing the actual types of the parameters.

Popping a value Removing a value from the top of a stack.

Positive test case A test case that a function is expected to handle correctly.

Postfix operator A unary operator that is written behind its argument.

Precondition A condition that must be true when a function is called.

Predicate function A function that returns a Boolean value.

Prefix operator A unary operator that is written before its argument.

Preprocessor A program that processes a source file before the compiler. The preprocessor includes files, conditionally includes code sections, and performs macro replacement.

Private inheritance Inheritance in which only the member functions can use the base-class functions.

Procedure A function that does not return a value.

Project A collection of source files and their dependencies.

Prompt A string that prompts the program user to provide input.

Prototype See Declaration.

Pseudocode A mixture of English and C++ that is used when developing the code for a program.

Pushing a value Adding a value to the top of a stack.

RAM (random-access memory) The computer memory that stores code and data of running programs.

Random access The ability to access any value directly without having to read the values preceding it.

Recursive function A function that can call itself with simpler values. It must handle the simplest values without calling itself.

Redirection Linking input or output of a program to a file instead of the keyboard or display.

Reference parameter A parameter that is bound to a variable supplied in the call. Changes made to the parameter within the function affect the variable outside the function.

Regression testing Keeping old test cases and testing every revision of a program against them.

Regular expression An expression denoting a set of strings. A regular expression can consist of individual characters, sets of characters such as abc; ranges such as a-z; sets of all characters outside a range, such as 94 0-9; repetitions of other expressions, such as 0-9*; alternative choices such as +-; and concatenations of other expressions.

Reserved word A word that has a special meaning in a programming language and therefore cannot be used as a name by the programmer.

Return value The value returned by a function through a return statement.

Roundoff error An error introduced by the fact that the computer can store only a finite number of digits of a floating-point number.

Run-time error See Logic error.

Run-time stack The data structure that stores the local variables and return addresses of functions when a program runs.

Scope The part of a program in which a variable is defined.

Selection sort A sorting algorithm in which the smallest element is repeatedly found and removed until no elements remain.

Sentinel A value in input that is not to be used as an actual input value but to signal the end of input.

Separate compilation Compiling each source file separately and combining the object files later into an executable program.

Sequential access Accessing values one after another without skipping over any of them.

Shadowing Hiding a variable by defining another one with the same name in a nested block.

Shell A part of an operating system in which the user types commands to execute programs and manipulate files.

Shell script A file that contains commands for running programs and manipulating files. Typing the name of the shell script file on the command line causes those commands to be executed.

Side effect An effect of a function other than returning a value.

Simple statement A statement consisting only of an expression.

Single-stepping Executing a program in the debugger one statement at a time.

Slicing objects Copying an object of a derived class into a variable of the base class, thereby losing the derived-class data.

Source file A file containing instructions in a programming language.

Stack A data structure in which elements can only be added and removed at one location, called the top of the stack.

Statement A syntactical unit in a program. In C++ a statement is either a simple statement, a compound statement, or a block.

Static binding Selecting a particular function to be called, depending on the type of the object invoking the function, which is known when the program is compiled.

static keyword A C++ keyword with several unrelated meanings: It denotes local variables that are not allocated on the stack; global variables or functions that are private to a module; class variables that are shared among all objects of a class; or member functions that do not have an implicit parameter.

Stepwise refinement Solving a problem by breaking it into smaller problems and then further decomposing those smaller problems.

Stream An abstraction for a sequence of bytes from which data can be read or to which data can be written.

String A sequence of characters.

Stub A function with no or minimal functionality.

Syntax Rules that define how to form instructions in a particular programming language.

Syntax error An instruction that does not follow the programming language rules and is rejected by the compiler.

Tab character The '\t' character, which advances the next character on the line to the next one of a set of fixed screen positions known as tab stops.

Template A definition for a set of classes. For example, the vector template defines a class vector<T> (a vector of T objects) for any type T.

Ternary operator An operator with three arguments. C++ has one ternary operator, a ? b : c.

Test coverage The instructions of a program that are executed in a set of test cases.

Test harness A program that calls a function that needs to be tested, supplying parameters and analyzing the function's return value.

Test suite A set of test cases for a program.

Text file A file in which values are stored in their text representation.

Trace message A message that is printed during a program run for debugging purposes.

Turing machine A very simple model of computation that is used in theoretical computer science to explore computability of problems.

Unary operator An operator with one argument.

Unicode A standard code that assigns code values consisting of two bytes to characters used in scripts around the world.

Uninitialized variable A variable that has not been set to a particular value. It is filled with whatever "random" bytes happen to be present in the memory location that the variable occupies.

Unit test A test of a function by itself, isolated from the remainder of the program.

Value parameter A function parameter whose value is copied into a parameter variable of a function. If a variable is passed as a value parameter, changes made to the parameter inside the function do not affect the original variable outside the program.

Variable A storage location that can hold different values.

Vector The standard C++ template for a dynamically growing array.

Virtual function A function that can be redefined in a derived class. The actual function being called depends on the type of the object invoking it at run time.

Visual programming Programming by arranging graphical elements on a form, setting program behavior by selecting properties for these elements, and writing only a small amount of "glue" code linking them.

void keyword A keyword indicating no type or an unknown type. A procedure is a function returning `void`.

Walkthrough Simulating a program or a part of a program by hand to test for correct behavior.

Watch window A window in a debugger that shows the current values of selected variables.

White-box testing Testing functions taking their implementation into account; for example, by selecting boundary test cases and ensuring that all branches of the code are covered by some test case.

White space A sequence of space, tab, and newline characters.

Index

Specific classes, functions, operators, and statements are lowercase.

Illustration Credits